EFFECTIVE REPORT WRITING

EFFECTIVE REPORT WRITING

For BUSINESS, INDUSTRY, and GOVERNMENT

NORMAN B. SIGBAND, Ph.D.

Professor
DePAUL UNIVERSITY
and
Industrial Consultant

HARPER & BROTHERS, PUBLISHERS
New York

To My Wife
Joanie

Contents

Points to remember in making up the outline · Form of
the outline · A final word · Questions for discussion

Considerations in graphic presentation · Use of tables ·
Graphic presentation of data · Types of Charts · Central tendencies or averages · Frequency distributions ·
Sketches and pictograph charts · Choice of illustration
· Readability and analysis · Truthfulness · Number
and use of illustrations · Illustrations should be meaningful · Questions for discussion

Words · Sentence sense · Questions for discussion

Tone · Style · Writing the first draft · Revision and
correction of the first draft · Steps in the editing process
· Questions for discussion

Letter reports · Memorandum reports · Periodic reports · Progress reports · Questions for discussion

Credit reports · Examination reports · Recommendation reports · Questions for discussion

Components of the long report · Text of the report ·
Supplementary sections of the formal report · Questions for discussion

Accounting reports · Reports in management and
marketing · Questions for discussion

PART II BUSINESS LETTER WRITING

PART III A BIBLIOGRAPHY OF BIBLIOGRAPHIES AND
          REFERENCE GUIDE

Preface

The tremendously important role which communication plays in industry, government, and education has been recognized in the past few years as never before. The more complex our government bureaus and industrial organizations become, the greater is the need for written records of transactions. It is the exchange of reports, letters, and memoranda that permit us to reach decisions, issue policies, recommend action, and record information. Communication is a vital and necessary tool of the teacher, engineer, student, businessman, doctor, public administrator—in fact every interested, intelligent person.

This book is designed to assist that individual to fashion the best tools possible so that he may transmit his ideas in all activities, as well as in his specialized area, with the greatest effectiveness and profit.

Whether the reader is a student, a teacher, or an employee in an industrial organization, a business firm, or a government bureau, he will find this book to be practical. For many years I have taught in the university as well as in industry in this area of communication. This experience plus my work as a consultant to many large and small corporations has permitted me to bring to this book the opinions, examples, and problems taken from actual business situations. There is little "ivory tower" reflection included; the material has been drawn almost completely from practical business problems.

This text has been designed to serve effectively in the classroom and on the job. The teacher in the college of commerce or in the school of engineering will find that the book may be used in courses in report writing, business letters, technical writing, business writing, or a combination report and letter writing course.

Students who have not had a great deal of writing experience will find the early chapters on primary and secondary research, writing style, and the reference guide, to be of value. More advanced students, or those who are only concerned with reports, will find the sections on various types of reports and those in special fields to be of primary interest.

In addition to the thorough treatment offered in the areas of reports and business letters, the specialized sections on employer-employee communications, tabular and graphic presentation, speech and conference leadership, technical writing, the reference guide in grammar, rhetoric, and diction, and the bibliography of bibliographies should all prove to be valuable aids to the serious communicator.

For those readers who are in government or industry, the book is especially adaptable to training programs, seminars, or conferences.

Readers will find that the many examples of reports, technical writing, and business letters which are presented in and at the end of each chapter are helpful for classroom analysis and discussion. Another teaching aid may be found in the many end-of-chapter problems and questions which provide a generous source for class and home assignments.

To summarize, then, this book may well serve as a course text in a wide variety of communication areas, as well as a guide for professional personnel now employed in business, industry, and government. Both groups will find that this text is also a useful source of reference.

The author has received assistance in the preparation of this book from so many sources that an attempt to acknowledge this aid is fraught with the danger of overlooking various persons and companies. Specific references are made in footnotes to many corporations and authors who have been most generous in permitting the utilization of their materials. The Western Electric Company, Incorporated, has been especially helpful in allowing me to use a great many illustrations, drawings, and excerpts from its bulletins, journals, and booklets. The coöperation received from Mr. John H. Bolt, Director, and Mr. Otis H. Detrick, College Coördinator, of the Graduate Engineering Training Center of Western Electric in Chicago, is especially appreciated.

Through the years, I have been constantly encouraged in this endeavor by the President of DePaul University, the Very Reverend C. J. O'Malley, and the Reverend E. J. Kammer, Executive Vice-

President. Mrs. W. E. Baum of the Chicago Public Library staff has contributed a great deal of help in the area of research. Miss Frances Plass, now Sister Anton, and Miss Judy Francois transformed the almost illegible handwritten manuscript into neatly typed pages. Mr. M. Meshboum drew many of the illustrations in Chapters 6 and 17. Assistance in the writing of Chapter 12 was received from Professors T. Hilliard, R. Bannon, and A. Farber of the Accounting Department of DePaul University.

Assistance was also received from the American Business Writing Association and many of its members, such as Professors F. Weeks, and C. R. Anderson, of the University of Illinois; J. Harold Janis of New York University; E. Hedgcock of the Agricultural and Mechanical College of Texas; and D. Lang of Northwestern University. Dr. E. C. Estabrooke of American School and others have provided helpful suggestions.

To my children, Robin, Shelley, and Betsy, a word of thanks for their interest and love. And finally, a special and deeply grateful acknowledgment to my wife, Joan, for her encouragement, contributions, work, and assistance in a dozen different ways from the beginning to the end of this task.

NORMAN BRUCE SIGBAND

March, 1960

Part I

Report Writing

Chapter 1

Background to Report Writing

INTRODUCTION TO REPORT WRITING

In this increasingly complex world of ours, the process of communication is all-important. There are letters, reports, books, magazines, and newspapers; there are movies, radio, and television; and there are conferences, speeches, and addresses. These are only some of the communication devices which inform us, entertain us, teach us, and sometimes irritate us. But we would find it difficult to exist without them.

Among these media of communication the report stands high in importance. Surely every scientist will first examine the reports on and in a specific area of research before he proceeds further with his own investigations. Every business executive will read the reports submitted by his department heads before he renders decisions on future planning and operation. No surgeon will lift a scalpel without carefully analyzing the laboratory, x-ray, and diagnostician's reports. And we hope that every government official will investigate and study reports on an issue before taking a stand or casting a vote.

And so it goes in every phase of today's society: political, industrial, medical, governmental, scientific, financial, social, and cultural—we "look at the record" before we act. That record is usually contained in a report. Were these reports not available, there would be tremendous duplications of effort.

What Is a Report?

Because the word *report* may be interpreted so differently by so many people, it is probably hazardous for us to attempt to define

3

the word. If you ask a sales manager to list the major appliances sold today, he may submit a memo stating:

2 Acme Model 212 Washers
4 Seewell Model 114 TV Sets
2 Polar Model 116 Refrigerators

That is a report on merchandise sold. On the other hand, if the President of the United States requests a report from the Department of Health, Education, and Welfare on the national polio inoculation program, he will be given quite a hefty tome. Long or short, they are both explanations of activities carried through. Note that the report is written by a competent person or department for a specific reader who may take some action on the basis of the facts presented.

If we were seeking a rather formal definition, we might say that a report is a written record of activities based on authoritative sources. It should be written by a person well qualified in the specific field which the report covers and directed to a predetermined reading group. It may be a thorough analysis of a problem under investigation and contain such recommendations and suggestions as are indicated by the findings.

Use of Reports

In a text of this nature we are primarily concerned with the use of reports in the modern world of business, science, engineering, and government. There is the report submitted by department heads in sales, production, advertising, personnel, research, engineering, or construction. Then there are the special reports on sales in a specific area, on labor turnover in a designated market, or on troublesome problems in various phases of management or science. There is the report that is designed strictly for purposes of information: for the stockholder, for the employee, for government agencies. There is the report that must be filled out each evening before one goes home and the report that is completed after weary hours of research in a laboratory. And there is the report that is written to evaluate progress on specific assignments. But this is only the beginning. Everyone who has worked in any phase of the modern world knows of the need and demand for reports. The types are endless and to the report writer (and sometimes to the reader), it seems as though the numbers are also endless. The point is, they *are* demanded today, and we must write the best possible reports we can. The former Chairman of the Board of Montgomery Ward and Company, Mr. Sewell Avery, had this to say:

Internal corporate reports are a necessary tool for effective and successful executive management of any large business enterprise. Such reports are the means by which pertinent information about the various phases of a company's operations are communicated to the appropriate managers and executives for their use in judging the effectiveness of personnel and policies. If reports are to contribute to smooth corporate functioning they must be accurate, timely, and reduced to simplicity even though comprehensive in their coverage. Management, in turn, must be competent in order to effectively use the reports in grasping the full significance of all the situations which they portray, and in correcting the unsatisfactory situations. It is axiomatic that one of the many components of a successful large enterprise is a thoroughly integrated system of internal reports tailored specifically to its own needs.[1]

Some years ago a committee of The American Business Writing Association surveyed 150 nationally known companies on specific areas concerned with reports. Here are excerpts from the comments received from a few of the companies regarding the importance of reports:

First National Bank of Boston. The importance of the ability to write worthwhile reports cannot be overemphasized. We have many employees who know their work thoroughly and yet are not reaching top-level jobs, principally because they cannot write brief, well-constructed, and understandable reports.

Glenn L. Martin Company. We are in full accord with your objective of developing, by means of actual examples and otherwise, an ability . . . to write good intra-company reports. In our opinion, it cannot be impressed too strongly upon potential administrative personnel that their value to their employers, and hence their possibility of advancement, are contingent to a most important extent upon the effectiveness with which they can convey their thoughts in writing. This is true whether they intend to be engaged in the sales, financial, public relations, engineering, production, or virtually any other function of the business, and this facility tends to increase in importance with the size of the firm.

[1] Letter from Sewell Avery, former Chairman of the Board, Montgomery Ward and Company, to the author.

North America Companies. Why are reports prepared? So far as I can see, a report is prepared to give to someone else the experiences undergone by the report-makers. . . . The person to whom the report is made has not had the opportunity as a rule to attend the meeting or the convention or to investigate the problem personally. Instead he wants a report made to him by someone . . . for that specific purpose.

Peoples Gas Light and Coke Company. Your subject is indeed one that needs attention; the only opportunity many young executives have of presenting their views and becoming known to their superior officers is through their reports; therefore, they must be good.

In business and industry, internal communication moves in three different directions. In moving *down,* policies, directives, decisions, and information are brought to the action level. When communications move *up,* management is informed of problems, ideas, and activities. This knowledge from below permits management to be informed and to make intelligent decisions. And finally communications move *laterally* to bring about an interchange of ideas and information among departments. This improves coördination and lessens duplication of effort and activity.

Reports are the media which most frequently transfer these ideas. In large corporations, the top echelon receives periodic reports from department heads and then issues decisions. In accounting, the work of auditors and other specialists is presented in reports to clients and directors. The progress of engineering projects is detailed in the reports issued. In the complex web of government administration, reports are important so that bureau chiefs and citizens may weigh the value of work accomplished. In almost every field of activity, reports are written and presented so that individuals may be informed of the status of situations.

The Writer of the Report

You, as a report writer, should possess specific skills and attributes which are as necessary in your field as are the qualifications of the engineer, the chemist, and the physician in their fields.

The report writer should have a thorough and complete knowledge of the area in which he is working. Although it is not necessary that one be a so-called expert, the individual should be thoroughly conversant with the terminology, problems, and sources of information in his field. If the completion of the report requires capabilities that the investigator does not have (such as ability to work with statistics, knowledge of machine tools, finance, etc.), the report writer should recognize his limitations immediately and employ a technical expert who can solve the report writer's problems.

Although we recognize that many reports are written by individuals who are not as conscientious and interested in their jobs as is desirable, we would agree that the competent report writer does possess specific qualifications. He should be able to recognize a problem, clearly see the purpose of the investigation, know in what areas he must seek information, and employ the most expedient method by which he may arrive at a logical conclusion. He should have no patience with superficial investigations of the problem; rather, he should be a person who desires to examine every possible piece of material that is available to him within the limitations of time, money, and sources. And his objective conclusions and evaluations should be based on the careful examination of the data he has gathered.

Presentation of the Report

A report can be the product of careful and painstaking research; its objective conclusions can be drawn from adequate data, and its appearance can be attractive and impressive. Yet the reader may find it boring and dull. The fault lies in the writer's inability to express himself properly. Many days of research are wasted when the facts are not presented so that the reader can easily assimilate and understand them.

There is nothing mysterious about writing a report. It is similar to almost all other types of communication. The report must be written in clear, well-constructed sentences. Unity of subject matter is an important consideration; coherence between and among sentences and paragraphs should also be present; topics must be given emphasis where necessary; and the style of writing should be interesting. In other words, the basic concepts of diction, rhetoric, and grammar *must* be followed. Yet it is somewhat surprising how many reports fail simply because of the awkward and confused manner in which the ideas are presented. Certainly the accountant should be competent in his field of cost or auditing analysis; the marketing expert should know as much as possible about consumer preferences; the engineer should be efficient in determining the proper incline of a curve on a superhighway; and other specialists should be able to carry through their technical tasks competently. But each of these persons has need for communicating his ideas with clarity and facility. If the specialist does not possess this ability, he should attempt to develop it, for the most effective ideas may be lost when they are poorly communicated. Here is what the director of a large corporation had to say on this topic:

Modern executive management is a new phenomenon in society. The function of executive management is to coordinate and direct the activities of groups of varied specialists. The executive must have the ability not only to see the goal himself, but to be able to lead and direct others to that goal.

The executive does not deal with physical matter. He deals exclusively with ideas and with men. In his work he is not a scientist. He is a skilled and practical humanist.

The only tool that the executive uses is language. He is constantly using words for the conveyance of ideas and for the understanding and persuasion of other men. He uses language during every minute of his business day, in dictating letters, in conferring with other men individually or in groups, in issuing memoranda and directions to his staff, in reading and in writing reports, in conversing over the telephone.

Ideas are valueless if they cannot be conveyed. The executive must know how to convey ideas succinctly, and with absolute clarity, for the slightest obscurity in his directives will result in confusion. He must know the variations and nuances of expression, for he is dealing with human beings of different temperaments. He must know the power, and the weakness, of language.[2]

The Reader of the Report

Some of the questions which the report writer may well ask himself before he sets his pen to paper are these: Exactly who is the prospective reader of this report? What will he look for? What does he expect to find? What special considerations shall I make for him? And at what level shall I write?

We have already suggested answers to some of these questions. Of course information will be presented in a very different manner if it is directed to the board of directors rather than to the stock-

---

[2] Arthur A. Houghton, Jr., President, Steuben Glass, "College English and the Executive Career," *The American Business Writing Association Bulletin,* November, 1952, p. 13.

holders or the employees of the corporation. In the presentation of material it is not only the level of language that changes for different groups; it is also the complexity or simplicity of the data which go into the report, the make-up of the charts and graphs, the length and detail of the conclusions and recommendations, the financial information, and even the layout and pictures used.

General Procedure in Writing a Report

The presentation of the report will differ according to the field, the problem, and the reader. However, in every situation, there will be need for a *plan*. No good report can be written without a series of carefully organized steps.

Once the report writer has fixed his objective clearly in mind, his next goal is to secure the information which he will use in writing his material. These data may be gathered from many primary and secondary sources. In the gathering process, of course, a system should be employed in recording data in the most efficient manner possible. Immediately after, or during the process of gathering information, a tentative outline should be established. And once the data have been reduced to notes and statistics, they must be arranged in their most logical order. Categories should be set up, and the various pieces of information should be assigned to their logical niches. A careful analysis should follow, and reliable interpretations should be drawn. Now the report writer is ready to arrange a detailed outline of his report and to test that outline for its logic, its completeness, and its validity. Finally the last task is reached: the writing of the report. These individual steps will be examined in detail in the chapters that follow, but they are noted here as a bird's-eye view of report writing procedure.

Classification of Reports

The task of classifying reports is somewhat difficult for the student of report writing because he will often find similar types of reports designated with different names. A report whose primary purpose is to *analyze* a situation may be labeled an "examination report" by one writer, an "analytical report" by another, and an "investigative report" by a third. Here are methods that are sometimes used to classify reports.

1. *Classification by Purpose.* Reports will usually attempt to

accomplish one or more of the following purposes: (a) to analyze, (b) to inform, and (c) to persuade or recommend. The length and method of development will vary according to the problem.

2. *Classification by Type.* Frequently reports are expected to explain to the reader what progress has been made on a specific project, what activities have taken place during a specific block of time, or simply to indicate other specialized data. Some of these types are: (a) progress reports, (b) periodic reports, (c) credit reports, (d) letter reports, (e) memorandum reports, (f) examination reports, and (g) recommendation reports.

3. *Classification by Form.* The two usual *forms* for reports are usually designated as: (a) short form and (b) long form. It is obvious that such *types* as letters, memos, progress reports, and periodic reports may follow a *short form,* whereas the examination or recommendation report may be ten, twenty, or several hundred pages in length.

4. *Classification by Field.* Still another method of classification is to refer to reports as accounting, engineering, marketing, or medical reports. It is obvious that each field utilizes most of the *types* and *forms* of reports listed above.

5. *Special Reports.* Reports which have a highly specialized function are sometimes assigned to another group. The *annual report* which carries a specific type of message to shareholders, citizens, or employees is one of these. *Public reports* which are issued by local, state, or federal governmental agencies to the citizen are another. In addition, there is the *research report* that explains the results of pure laboratory investigation.

These are *some* of the ways reports are classified by the people who work with them. It is easy to see how an annual report may be called a periodic report, a special report, an examination report, or a long-form report by different persons. However, this should not disturb us; this discussion of classifications is presented to emphasize to the student the various existing points of view.

It is uniformly agreed that careful research, competent analysis of data, objective evaluation of the findings, and clear presentation of the facts are the standards for *all* reports regardless of *type, form, purpose, field,* or *length.* Because the tools for writing all reports are similar, the attention of this text will be directed toward the development of competence in the use of these tools.

STEPS PRECEDING RESEARCH

Choice of a Subject and Mental Attitude

The first step in writing a good report is the choice or assignment of a subject for investigation, research, and examination. The topic should be one of real interest to the researcher. Under some situations we are assigned a subject which we do not find completely intriguing, but we should do our best to interest ourselves in it. This interest is important because it influences our mental attitude toward the entire problem.

The attitude we have toward our subject will be a vital factor in the final quality of the paper. If our desire is to search deeply, investigate thoroughly, analyze objectively, and present clearly, our report will probably be good. But this mental attitude must be sincere. It must force us to carry through the best possible job we can, regardless of what sources we are led to, the amount of work involved, and the disappointments and frustrations which are encountered. All of these obstacles may be surmounted if our purpose is to produce a report which is no less than excellent.

With such an attitude, and the high caliber of work which must accompany it, the job will almost certainly be completed competently. And when the job is done, the dedicated report writer will honestly feel that he has examined all sources on his subject which are available to him in the area, that he has carried through all those questionnaire and interview studies which were necessary, and that he has searched widely and deeply within the limits of his time and energy. With the confidence which such self-analysis brings, he will also feel that he has done a thorough and efficient job.

This all comes from the mental attitude toward the job of writing a report and recognizing that it is not a chore to be completed as quickly and easily as possible, but a challenge which must be met and a job which must be accomplished at a level that will reflect high credit on the researcher.

Purpose of the Report

Very early in his analysis of the problem, the report writer must have a clear idea of the purpose the report is to serve. If he knows that the purpose is to present recommendations on whether or not a plant site should be purchased, or a new package designed, or a new product developed, he will be able to formulate the scope of his investigation and limit his area of research.

Let us say, for example, that we are requested to write a report on whether or not a surplus plant in Los Angeles should be purchased. The purpose then becomes obvious; it is to examine various aspects of the plant so that the one question may be answered: should it be purchased? The purpose is not to compare the purchase of the Los Angeles factory with the proposed purchase of another factory offered for sale or to compare the Los Angeles plant with the construction of a new one. The purpose has been established, and when that is done, the researcher may proceed toward his objective after he limits his subject area and establishes the scope of his investigation.

Limitation of Subject Area

The narrower and more specific the topic area is, the easier it is for the researcher to pursue it and produce something worth while. A subject that is wide and broad will result in a report that is superficial and general. Nothing new, vital, or important will be produced because the investigation is usually shallow due to the breadth of the subject matter. However if one is assigned a narrow, limited topic, he can "dig" deeply in an area which may not as yet have been thoroughly explored.

What can be done with the topic "Conditions in Latin America"? Certainly this cannot be handled effectively in less that 15 volumes. "Economic Conditions in Latin America" is still too broad. "Economic Conditions in the Copper Industry in Latin America" is an improvement but still unworkable. "Economic Conditions in the Copper Industry in Chile" is still better but not as precise a topic as "Economic Conditions in the Copper Industry in Chile in the Period 1956-1960."

Notice that a topic may be narrowed geographically, chronologically, by area of activity, of interest, and/or of historical, political, social, or cultural significance.

Let us again look at the factory that is for sale in Los Angeles. The report writer could examine at least the following areas in an attempt to answer the question of whether or not the plant should be purchased:

Labor Supply
Physical Condition of the Plant (interior)
Physical Condition of the Plant (exterior)
Financing
Tax Structure
Transportation (rail, truck, and air)
Utilities
Local Ordinances and Regulations
Raw Material Sources
Market

However, if information is already available or is not desired in the areas of Plant Facilities and Financing the report is thereby *limited* to the remaining topics.

This limitation of the subject is one of the first steps the report writer must carry through after the *purpose* of the investigation has been established.

The Scope of the Report

After the report writer has limited his topic, the remaining areas indicate the *scope* of the report. The individual segments which make up the scope of the report also serve as the major points in the tentative outline. Thus, in our examination of the "factory for sale" problem above, we have *limited* the areas of investigation to the following, which in turn give us the major points in our tentative outline.

    I. Labor Supply
   II. Tax Structure
 III. Transportation (rail, truck, and air)
 IV. Utilities
  V. Local Ordinances and Regulations
 VI. Raw Material Sources
VII. Market

From this brief explanation, it is easy to see how logical is the development of a report topic.

With the approval of the tentative outline by the interested parties, the investigator may go ahead and carry through research on each of the points listed. That process of examining primary and secondary sources for information will be discussed in the two chapters which follow.

QUESTIONS FOR DISCUSSION

I. Secure definitions of a formal report from an executive in your major field of concentration and from an executive in another field. Briefly note the similarities and differences in both.

II. Examine the report beginning on page 290. In what way may it be classified? Explain why you chose each of the various classification types.

III. Make a list of ten report topics which might serve as valuable and interesting areas of research in your major area of concentration.

IV. List those factors that would differ in a report (containing essentially the same information) sent out by the U.S. Automobile Corporation to: stockholders, employees, and the board of directors. Why would these factors differ?

V. As corporations become larger and more diversified in their activities, the need for reports also seems to increase. Explain this.

VI. "American industry travels on paper wheels," said a corporation executive recently. What do you think he meant by this statement?

VII. Why is it necessary in industry to have a precise system for reporting from one management echelon to another?

VIII. Examine three books on report writing; then, indicate each author's method of classifying reports.

IX. What common attributes are shared by a business executive and a writer of reports?

X. "Adapt your report to the reader," said an executive at a recent conference. What principle do you think he was attempting to emphasize?

XI. Limit the scope of each of the following so that they are sufficiently narrow to serve as a report topic. Make any reasonable changes in the title as given.

1. The Development of the Oil Industry
2. Advertising in the Modern World
3. Commercial Air Transportation
4. The Consulting Engineer
5. Communication in Industry
6. Management of Personnel
7. Employer-Employee Relations
8. The Benefits of Executive Training in Report Writing
9. Passenger Air Travel, 1958-1960
10. Economic Gains of Chicago as a Result of the St. Lawrence Seaway, 1959-1960

XII. Limit the scope of each of the following so that they are sufficiently narrow to serve as a report topic. Make any reasonable changes in the title as given.
1. The Technical Report
2. Steel Versus Nylon Bearings
3. Opportunities for Women in Industry
4. Depth Interviewing
5. Plant Layout
6. Machine Tool Design
7. The Newsletter as a Factor in Building Employer-Employee Relations
8. Factors Influencing the Change in the Price of Steel in 1960
9. The Executive Secretary
10. Motivation Research

Chapter 2

Working with Secondary
Sources of Information

Almost all the sources which the writer will utilize for his report will be either primary or secondary in nature. Primary information is information derived from experimentation or from observation, is secured from interviews or questionnaires, or is gathered from company records, memoirs, diaries, manuscripts, letters, or artifacts. These are all examples of information which have not been analyzed and interpreted by someone other than the author before being presented. Secondary sources, with which research usually begins, consist of such materials as textbooks, magazines, journals, bulletins, reports, newspapers, and related items. The author who records a battle action after he has observed it is using a primary source. If he does not see the action but reads about it in several newspapers and magazines and then writes his account, he has utilized secondary sources.

A wealth of information is available to the report writer who uses secondary sources. It is true that many reports are largely based on primary data, but much background material, statistics, and valuable facts may be secured from journals, books, magazines, typed and published company reports, pamphlets, booklets, newspapers, handbooks, bulletins, directories, and various collections of printed material.

The work, effort, and findings of thousands of persons have been recorded for each of us to use. Our research should be directed toward utilizing the data which have been recorded and building on top of them; we should avoid doing work which has already been completed. We must constantly strive to determine first what has been done on our problem and then go on from that point.

Because of the mountains of material which exist, it is understandable that sometimes difficulty is encountered in finding specific secondary materials. The inexperienced researcher may spend dozens of hours or days in fruitless and exasperating "digging" through card catalogs, magazine files, and shelves of books.

However, the report writer who is familiar with the techniques of research and the intelligent use of reference guides can find most of the material on his topic easily and quickly. Once he has secured his source material he need only examine it, analyze it, and then utilize it to his best advantage.

Now let us examine the many tools which are designed to assist us in our research so that we may save time and complete an excellent job.

THE LIBRARY AS A SOURCE OF INFORMATION

A good library houses a tremendous amount of secondary source material. All too often, however, individuals have never mastered the techniques necessary for accurate and profitable use of such library materials as the card catalog, reference works, indexes, microcards, and microfilm. If a particular assignment is concerned with a report that is an analysis of wage payments in a narrow branch of the steel industry, one can hardly expect to find a book on such a topic. However, there must certainly be—somewhere, someplace—a variety of magazine articles, booklets, and pamphlets on the subject. The question, of course, is, "How and where can I find such information?" The next few paragraphs are designed to illustrate some of the short cuts in library use.

Library Classification Systems

The two most commonly utilized methods of classification in libraries in the United States are the Dewey Decimal and Library of Congress Systems. There are several others, such as the Cutter Expansive Method or individual systems that some libraries have established to fit their specific needs.

THE DEWEY DECIMAL SYSTEM

This system divides knowledge into nine major groups. Each of these groups is split into nine subdivisions and further subdivided into smaller units. In addition to the nine primary groups, there is one labeled "O," which includes works of a broad nature which do not fit into any of the specific groups. This division classifies general publications, reference material, encyclopedias, and other

A

000-099	General Works
100-199	Philosophy
200-299	Religion
300-399	Social Sciences
400-499	Philology
500-599	Pure Science
600-699	Useful Arts
700-799	Fine Arts
800-899	Literature
900-999	History

B

PURE SCIENCE

500	Science in general
510	Mathematics
520	Astronomy
530	Physics
540	Chemistry
550	Geology
560	Paleontology
570	Biology—Archeology
580	Botany
590	Zoology

C

PHYSICS

531	Mechanics
532	Liquids—Hydrostatics—Hydraulics
533	Gases Pneumatics
534	Sound Acoustics
535	Light Optics
536	Heat
537	Electricity
538	Magnetism
539	Molecular physics

D

HEAT

536.1	Theory-nature
536.2	Communication
536.3	Action of bodies on heat
536.4	Effects—Action of heat on bodies
536.5	Temperature
536.6	Calorimetry
536.7	Thermodynamics—Mechanical Equivalent
536.8	Application
536.9	Tables—Problems Questions

The Library Dewey Decimal Classification System

ting of a similar nature. Biographies are usually designated
th a "B" and fiction with an "F." In the former, the books are
helved alphabetically according to the name of the person writ-
en about. In fiction, the books appear on the shelf alphabetically
according to the author's last name.

The Library of Congress System

This method was designed especially for our national library in
Washington, D.C. The system is very valuable for large collections
and is being utilized by a great many libraries today. This method
of classification is based on letters followed by Arabic figures and
in some cases, additional letters and figures. Libraries using this
method usually buy Library of Congress cards for their card
catalog. Title and subject entries are usually typed at the top of
the card.

A   General Works; Polygraphy
B   Philosophy; Religion
C   History; Auxiliary Sciences
D   History and Topography (except American)
E and F   American History
G   Geography; Anthropology
H   Social Science
J   Political Science
K   Law
L   Education
M   Music
N   Fine Arts
P   Language and Literature
Q   Science
R   Medicine
S   Agriculture
T   Technology
U   Military Science
V   Naval Science
Z   Bibliography and Library Science

Works in fiction and biography, because they may be said to
belong to no one field of knowledge, are usually classified under
"F" for fiction and "B" for biography. In the case of the former,
the books are shelved alphabetically under the names of the

authors. In biography, the list is also alphabetica
surname of the individual who is the subject of the woi

Library Catalog Cards

Most of the books, collections, and periodicals in the library
contained in the stackrooms. Because the average individual do
not have ready access to this storehouse of knowledge, he must
utilize the card catalog to find the name of the work he desires.
He then submits his order at the library desk and waits a few
minutes while the librarian secures his book.

This procedure sounds very simple and indicates that the
assembling of a large mass of material to work on is only a matter
of hasty routine. Basically that statement is true, as long as the
researcher knows *how* to use the card catalog. But the problem is
sometimes complicated when the name of the book or the author
has been forgotten. However, if the report writer possesses a good
working knowledge of the card catalog, he will have no difficulty
in collecting a sizable quantity of pertinent data.

Material is listed in the card catalog in three ways: under the
title, the author, and the subject of the book.

In addition to these three types of cards, most libraries also use
the *cross-reference cards* (sometimes referred to as "see" and "see
also" cards), the *analytical card,* and a *series card.*

Author and Title Cards

The catalog card is filed under the author's last name and indicates the reference information which leads to the book; remember
that the names are filed alphabetically. If the name of the author is
not known but the title is, the book may be found because the
titles of books are also listed alphabetically in the card catalog.

Subject Cards

If neither the author nor the title is known, the work, and others
in the same field, may still be located if the researcher looks under
the subject heading. Some libraries place the subject heading in
red type to distinguish it from author and title headings.

In looking for books under a subject designation, a narrow area

```
            Power of words
400         Chase, Stuart
C487p         Power of words, by Stuart Chase in
            collaboration with Marian Tyler Chase.
            New York, Harcourt, Brace
              1954
                308 p.
```

Title Card

should be chosen rather than a broad one. Of course, too narrow a designation is unwise (such as "Analytical Reports in the Plastic Tile Industry"), for cards may not have been made by the library for that specific field.

In this giant index, the card catalog, one may also find cross-reference cards. These do not lead directly to the books, but they

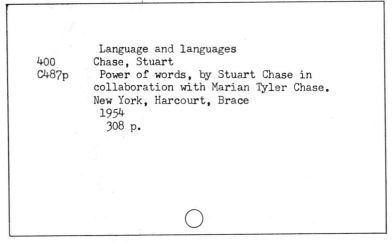

```
            Language and languages
400         Chase, Stuart
C487p         Power of words, by Stuart Chase in
            collaboration with Marian Tyler Chase.
            New York, Harcourt, Brace
              1954
                308 p.
```

Subject Card

will aid in locating the work. There are "see also" cards which suggest additional references in the same or related fields. The "see" card will direct the researcher from a specific topic heading that he used to one the library follows. Some libraries also use "analytical" cards which tell the individual in what book he may find a chapter or a selection dealing with a narrow and specific topic.

These are standard types of cards which are found in most card catalogs. In addition, libraries will frequently utilize cards which have been printed by the Library of Congress or the H. W. Wilson Company. These offer more information concerning the book than is normally found on the regular catalog cards.

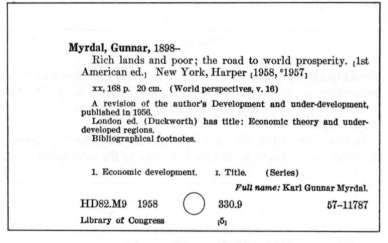

Library of Congress Card

The Use of Reference Works as an Aid in Securing Information

The utilization of the card catalog is only the beginning in the search for secondary sources of information; it will not usually lead to pertinent material which may be found in periodicals, government reports, bulletins, and newspapers. It is quite obvious that the report writer cannot thumb through hundreds of issues of magazines just looking for an article which he believes he saw "sometime." Nor can he examine files of newspapers looking for an article that someone *thinks* appeared about two or three months ago. Such haphazard looking and thumbing can be eliminated by using the available reference works intelligently. Not only will countless hours be saved, but also more information may be found easily.

In using reference works, it is important that the signs, symbols, and abbreviations are understood and utilized. The key to these various devices is normally found in the first few pages of the reference work, and an expenditure of a moment or two on those pages will prove profitable. Because there are so many excellent reference works available to the researcher, it is often wise to check one or two guides to reference books. One of the most complete is Constance M. Winchell, *Guide to Reference Works,* 7th ed. (formerly edited by I. G. Mudge); there are also L. Shores, *Basic Reference Books,* H. S. Hirshberg, *Subject Guide to Reference Books,* and R. W. Murphy, *How and Where to Look It Up, A Guide to Standard Sources of Information.*

The careful and intelligent use of reference works is a tremendous aid in gathering information for reports. Below is listed a variety of guides which may be used frequently in the course of research. However, these are works of a general nature; with a little investigation one may draw up an extended bibliography in his own narrow field of specialization.

DICTIONARIES

New English Dictionary on Historical Principles. Oxford: The Clarendon Press, 1933. 12 vols. and supplement.

This is usually referred to as the OED or Oxford English Dictionary. It is a most scholarly work which attempts to show the history of both current and obsolete words. It illustrates when and how each word came into the language and changes that have taken place in words in spelling, meaning, and usage. This authoritative work serves as an indispensable guide to word derivation, spelling of current and obsolete words, and changes in meaning and connotation.

New Century Dictionary of the English Language. New York: Appleton-Century-Crofts, 1948.

This two-volume work contains some 160,000 entries.

Webster's New International Dictionary. Springfield, Mass.: G. & C. Merriam Co., 1950.

This excellent work contains some 600,000 entries and is liberally supplemented by illustrations. Definitions of words are given with the oldest meaning first and the later definitions following. The

dictionary also contains obsolete words and valuable appendixes.
Funk and Wagnalls New Standard Dictionary. New York: Funk &
Wagnalls Co., 1947.

The number of entries in this work is slightly less than in the
Webster, with emphasis on American pronunciation and current
information.

The Shorter Oxford English Dictionary. Oxford: The Clarendon Press,
1936. 2 vols.

This is an abridged edition of the OED (above).

Craigie, Sir William A., and Hulbert, James R. (eds.). *Dictionary of
American English on Historical Principles.* Chicago: University of
Chicago Press, 1936-1944.

This dictionary contains words and phrases that are American in
their origin and may also be connected, or reflect, the history of
this country. Like the OED, it gives the history and definition of
words. It is a very valuable source for examining words originating
in this country.

Mathews, Mitford (ed.). *Dictionary of Americanisms.* Chicago: University of Chicago Press, 1951. 2 vols.

This work contains some 50,000 words which originated in the
United States or words which have been given new meanings. It
traces words used by Americans from the Colonial time to the
present.

As for the smaller or hand dictionaries, there are several that
can serve the college student admirably. Among these are the
Merriam Webster's New Collegiate Dictionary, Harper's *American
College Dictionary, Concise Oxford Dictionary,* Funk and Wagnalls *College Standard Dictionary,* and others.

There are also dictionaries of synonyms that prove valuable for
suggesting various phrases or words that might better express an
idea than those words which might immediately occur to the writer.
Frederick Sturges Allen's *Allen's Synonyms and Antonyms,* New
York: Harper & Brothers, 1938; J. C. Fernald's *English Synonyms
and Antonyms,* New York: Funk & Wagnalls Co., 1947; *Webster's
Dictionary of Synonyms;* and certainly an outstanding work,
Roget's International Thesaurus, New York: Thomas Y. Crowell
Company, 1957. There are also Henry Watson Fowler's *Dictionary
of Modern English Usage,* Oxford: The Clarendon Press, 1926;
Henry Louis Mencken's *The American Language,* New York: Al-
fred A. Knopf, Inc., 1936-1945; and Eric Partridge's *Dictionary of
Slang and Unconventional English,* 2nd ed., New York: The Mac-

millan Co., 1949. In addition there are dictionaries of basic English, abbreviations, idioms, slang, pronunciation, rhymes, punctuation, synonyms and antonyms, and others.

ENCYCLOPEDIAS

The report writer, who is usually engaged in detailed research, often finds encyclopedia articles unsatisfactory because of their rather superficial treatment of subjects. However, the experienced individual knows that not only will such articles give him good background material, but that they will also provide him with valuable bibliographies. These listings may lead him into further areas of research.

Encyclopaedia Britannica, 14th ed. Chicago: Encyclopaedia Britannica, Inc., 1959. 24 vols.

A very fine work containing excellent articles and illustrations. Attention has been focused on scientific topics especially. The *Britannica Book of the Year* does much to keep the entire set up to date. Earlier editions (9th and 11th) may also prove valuable. Some articles are initialed, and a key to authorship is provided.

Encyclopedia Americana. New York: Encyclopedia Americana Corporation, 1949. 30 vols.

A very good set of books with valuable illustrations, maps, and bibliographies. The arrangement is alphabetical word by word instead of letter by letter as in the case of the *Encyclopaedia Britannica.* Many of the more important articles are signed. Articles on American places, persons, organizations, and institutions are especially complete.

Munn, Glenn G. *Encyclopedia of Banking and Finance.* Cambridge, Mass.: The Banker's Publishing Company, 1949.

New International Encyclopedia, 2nd ed. New York: Dodd, Mead & Co., 1914-1916. 24 vols. (with supplementary volumes, 1925, 1930).

Many short articles of value with excellent bibliographies. Biographies of Americans are especially valuable.

Columbia Encyclopedia. New York: Columbia University Press, 1950.

This is an excellent one volume reference work that is invaluable for student use. The articles are short and the bibliographies good.

Encyclopedia of the Social Sciences. New York: The Macmillan Co., 1930-1935. 15 vols.

A scholarly work covering such fields as philosophy, education, economics, political science, ethics, government, sociology, and others.

The Catholic Encyclopedia. New York: Catholic Encyclopedia Press, 1907-1922. 17 vols.

This records the accomplishments of Catholics in a great many fields in addition to Catholic history, doctrine, and laws. May well be utilized for medieval history, literature, and philosophy.

Universal Jewish Encyclopedia. New York: Universal Jewish Encyclopedia, Inc., 1939-1944. 10 vols.

A wide coverage is attempted in this excellent work with emphasis on Jewish achievement. It supplements the work of the older *Jewish Encyclopedia,* New York: Funk, 1901-1906. 12 vols.

ATLASES AND GAZETTEERS

Shepherd, William Robert. *Historical Atlas,* 7th ed. New York: Henry Holt & Co., Inc., 1929.

A very good historical atlas covering the period about 2000 B.C. to 1929. It displays treaty lines, war campaigns, and commerce development.

Lippincott's New Gazetteer. Philadelphia: J. B. Lippincott Co., 1931.

This geographical dictionary lists in alphabetical order the names of mountains, lakes, rivers, islands, towns, cities, and countries. For each, the altitude, location, and pronunciation are given. For cities, towns, and nations, the population, brief history, and information on industry are given.

The New-World Atlas. New York: Garden City Publishing Company, 1947.

Originally published in loose-leaf form by C. S. Hammond & Co., Inc.

Seltzer, Leon E. (ed.). *The Columbia Lippincott Gazetteer of the World.* New York: Columbia University Press, 1952.

Rand McNally Commerical Atlas and Marketing Guide, 82nd ed. New York: 1959.

This very excellent atlas is revised annually and its maps are kept up to date. The individual interested in commerce finds this especially valuable.

ANNUALS

Statesman's Year-Book. London: Macmillan, 1864 to date.

The World Almanac and Book of Facts. New York: World-Telegram, 1868 to date.

A very thorough international annual containing much valuable information.

U.S. Bureau of Foreign and Domestic Commerce. *Statistical Abstract of the United States.* Washington, D.C.: Government Printing Office, 1879 to date.

A digest of facts on population, vital statistics, commerce, finance, immigration, and many other topics. Published yearly.

Whitaker's Almanack. London: Whitaker, 1869 to date.

Especially valuable for information relative to the British Empire.

BIOGRAPHICAL DICTIONARIES

Who's Who. London: Black, 1849 to date.

An annual publication that concentrates on outstanding Englishmen, but it includes famous personages of other nationalities also.

Who's Who in America. Chicago: Marquis, 1899 to date.

This work appears every other year and includes some 40,000 names of notable living Americans.

International Who's Who. London: Europa Publications, 1935 to date.

An attempt to bridge the above two works by listing outstanding persons throughout the world.

Biography Index: A Cumulative Index to Biographical Material in Books and Magazines. New York: H. W. Wilson Co., September 1946 to date.

This new quarterly guide indexes material published in English books anywhere and some 1300 periodicals.

Current Biography: Who's News and Why. New York: H. W. Wilson Co., 1940 to date.

This is issued monthly (except August) and cumulated annually. It contains biographies of persons outstanding as news value.

Stephen, L., and Lee, S. (eds.). *Dictionary of National Biography.* London: Oxford University Press, 1938. 22 vols.

This lists individuals of England and her colonies who were deceased at the date of publication of this work. It has over 31,000 excellent biographies. Commonly referred to as the "DNB."

Johnson, Allen, and Malone, Dumas (eds.). *Dictionary of American Biography.* New York: Charles Scribner's Sons, 1928-1944. 21 vols. and supplement.

This is the American counterpart to the "DNB." The articles are, for the most part, very carefully written and the bibliographies helpful. Frequently called the "DAB," this very scholarly work lists Americans no longer living who have made important contributions to American life.

American Women. Los Angeles: American Publications, Inc., 1935-1939.

The work contains some 13,000 articles written by well over 2000 well-qualified persons.

Kunitz, S. J. (ed.). *Twentieth Century Authors,* First Supplement. New
York: H. W. Wilson Co., 1955.

Cattell, Jacques (ed.). *Directory of American Scholars,* 3rd ed. New
York: R. R. Bowker, 1957.
     This is a listing of scholars in the humanities and social sciences.

Webster's Biographical Dictionary. Springfield, Mass.: G & C. Merriam
Co., 1943.

Joseph, Thomas. *Universal Pronouncing Dictionary of Biography and
Mythology,* 5th ed. Philadelphia: J. B. Lippincott Co., 1930.

Official Congressional Dictionary for the Use of the U.S. Congress.
1809 to date.

In addition to the above biographical references, there are *Who
Was Who in America; Who's Who in Canada; Who's Who in the
East; Who's Who in China; Who's Who in Commerce and Industry;
Who's Who in Journalism; Who's Who in Education; Who's Who
in American Sports; Who's Who in Law; Who's Who in Colored
America; Who's Who in American Jewry; Who's Who in New
York; Who's Who in Chicago and Illinois;* and many others which
may be found in specific professions and groups.

GUIDES TO BOOKS AND PERIODICALS IN PRINT

Burnham, Mary (ed.). *U.S. Catalog: Books in Print,* 4th ed. New
York: H. W. Wilson Co., 1933.
     This work, with its supplements, offers the scholar a very thorough
     list of American publications from 1900 to 1933. Because of the
     tremendous number of books that have appeared in recent years,
     it is doubtful if this work will be issued again.

*Cumulative Book Index: A World List of Books in the English Lan-
guage.* New York: H. W. Wilson Co., 1928 to date.
     This index supplements the *U.S. Catalog.* It lists all books pub-
     lished in the English language throughout the world. Like the
     card catalog, the *Cumulative Book Index* is arranged by author,
     title, and subject. It is issued monthly (except August) with
     frequent cumulations.

Union List of Serials in Libraries of the United States and Canada.
New York: H. W. Wilson Co., 1943. Supplement 1944-1949.
     This very comprehensive guide cites magazine lists and in what
     libraries the magazines may be found.

Ulrich, Carolyne (ed.). *Ulrich's Periodicals Directory.* New York:
R. R. Bowker Co., 1947.
     A guide to some 7500 domestic and foreign periodicals. Emphasis

is on periodicals published in North and South America and England. Periodicals classified by subject.

Directory of Newspapers and Periodicals. Philadelphia: N. W. Ayer, 1880 to date.

Contains comments on circulation statistics, rates, names of publisher, size of page, politics, and other facts of some 22,000 newspapers and periodicals published in the United States, Canada, Cuba, Bermuda, and islands belonging to the U.S. Information is listed relative to price, circulation, editor, political affiliation, etc.

Cumulative Book Index (vol. 62, no. 4)

American Newspapers, 1821-1936; A Union List. New York: H. W. Wilson Co., 1937.

This excellent work indicates where existing files of newspapers published in the United States from 1821 to date may be found. It is very valuable for the individual who wishes to determine where a specific file of newspapers may be found.

INDEXES TO PERIODICALS

In carrying through research, much material will be found in journals, magazines, and periodicals of various kinds. But how may one know which issue of *Fortune Magazine,* for example, contains an important article on a topic? Is there any way to avoid the time-consuming task of laboriously going through dozens of back numbers? There is. Periodical indexes will do the work, and their value is inestimable.

Poole's Index to Periodical Literature. Boston: Houghton Mifflin Co., 1888-1908. 5 vols. and supplements.

This index lists, under *subject* only, important magazine articles between 1802 and 1908. Poole's index is no longer printed, but its work has been carried on by the *Readers' Guide.*

Readers' Guide to Periodical Literature. New York: H. W. Wilson Co., 1900 to date.

Through the use of this invaluable reference work, students working in many fields can either trace or find the names of periodicals containing articles on their topics. If the library does not carry the set of magazines the *Readers' Guide* suggests, the name of the nearby library which does may be found by using the *Union List of Serials* (see above). *The Readers' Guide* appears twice a month (except for one issue each in July and August) and is cumulated frequently. It indexes about 120 current periodicals. It lists articles under author, subject, and titles.

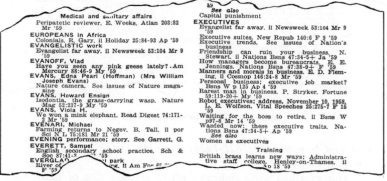

Readers' Guide to Periodical Literature (vol. 59, no. 6)

Industrial Arts Index. New York: H. W. Wilson Co., 1913 to 1958.

This index will be found extremely valuable by those persons engaged in commerce. It is a cumulative index to over 200 periodicals on business, finance, applied science, and technology. It was published monthly until January 1958 when it was discontinued and replaced by the *Business Periodicals Index* and *The Applied Science and Technology Index.*

Business Periodicals Index. New York: H. W. Wilson Co., 1958 to date.

This index indexes 120 periodicals in the fields of business, finance, labor relations, insurance, advertising, office management, etc. This is published monthly and cumulated annually. Approximately 140 additional periodicals are indexed in the two new indexes (*Applied Science and Technology Index* and *Business Periodical Index*) which have replaced the *Industrial Arts Index.*

Applied Science and Technology Index. New York: H. W. Wilson Co., 1958 to date.

This index, like the *Business Periodicals Index,* was begun in January, 1958 to replace the *Industrial Arts Index.* The *Applied Science and Technology Index* indexes nearly 200 periodicals in the fields of engineering, chemistry, physics, geology, metallurgy, aeronautics, automation, electronics, etc. This index is published monthly and cumulated into annual volumes.

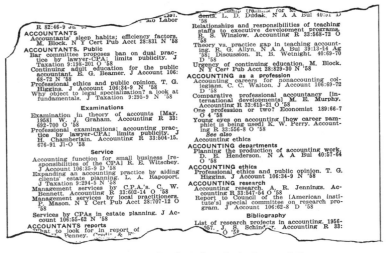

Business Periodicals Index (vol. 1, no. 15)

International Index to Periodicals. New York: H. W. Wilson Co., 1907 to date.

This is an author, subject, and title index of a selected group of about 175 periodicals. It is issued quarterly and cumulated annually.

Catholic Periodical Index. New York: The Catholic Library Association, 1930 to date.

This serves as an index to outstanding Catholic periodicals, newspapers, and bulletins. In addition, it notes many articles written from a Catholic viewpoint appearing elsewhere. It is published quarterly with cumulations.

Annual Magazine Subject Index. Boston: F. W. Faxon Co., Inc., 1908 to date.

Agricultural Index. New York: H. W. Wilson Co., 1916 to date.

The Art Index. New York: H. W. Wilson Co., 1929 to date.

Dramatic Index. Boston: F. W. Faxon Co., Inc., 1909 to date.

The Education Index. New York: H. W. Wilson Co., 1930 to date.

Engineering Index. New York: Engineering Magazine, 1892-1906. 4 vols.

Engineering Index. New York: Engineering Index Service.
Information concerning articles in engineering, chemistry, and physics journals is printed on 3″ x 5″ cards and sent to subscribers. In addition, data from technical magazines, government bureaus, and research laboratories are recorded as well as abstracts of reports and reviews of books and articles. Once each year the data are cumulated in a large volume.

Engineering Index Annual. New York: American Society of Mechanical Engineers, 1906 to date.

Index to Legal Periodicals. New York: H. W. Wilson Co., 1908 to date.

Index to Pamphlets

Vertical File Index. New York: H. W. Wilson Co., 1932 to date.
This is a monthly descriptive list of new pamphlets. These are grouped under subjects in the main part of the catalog with an alphabetical list of titles in the index. The pamphlets are described together with the price and name and address of the publisher.

Newspaper Guide

The student who is working on a subject of current interest or affairs will find newspaper sources as valuable as periodicals, especially to reflect views and opinions of individuals, parties, statesmen, and sections of the country. The *New York Times Index* will guide the scholar to articles not only in the *Times* but, by using the date as a clue, to articles in other newspapers of similar dates.

New York Times Index. New York: New York *Times,* 1913 to date.
It is now issued twice a month and annually. Entries are for narrow subjects appearing in the *Times* and are most valuable.

Book Reviews

Book Review Digest. New York: H. W. Wilson Co., 1905 to date.
This very valuable reference work lists books reviewed in about 80 periodicals containing book reviews. For each book, selections from the review are given, the number of words in the original review noted, and a plus or minus sign to indicate if the comments were favorable or unfavorable. This digest appears every

month (except July) and is cumulated each year. The arrangement is under author with subjects and titles listed in the index.

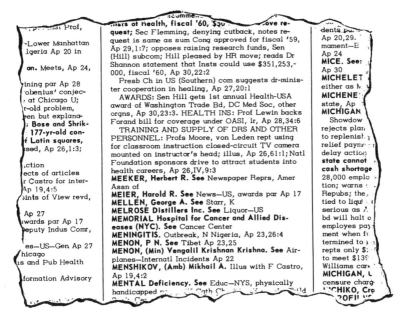

New York Times Index (Courtesy of the New York Times)

GOVERNMENT DOCUMENTS

A great deal of valuable data may be secured from government publications. These cover materials issued by national, state, and local government agencies. Almost every topic of information is treated in some government publication; however, the number issued is tremendous. Nevertheless, careful and competent use of reference works will quickly lead the researcher to the specific title of value.

Childs, James Bennett. *Government Document Bibliography in the U.S. and Elsewhere*. Washington, D.C.: Government Printing Office, 1942.

> This lists catalogs, guides, and indexes to the documents of the countries and states listed.

Greely, A. W. *Public Documents of the First Fourteen Congresses, 1789-1817*. Washington, D.C.: Government Printing Office, 1900. Supplement, 1904.

Poore, Benjamin P. *A Descriptive Catalog of the Government Publications of the United States, Sept. 1774-March 1881*. Washington, D.C.: Government Printing Office, 1885.

   Material is arranged chronologically, giving the full title, author, date, and a brief abstract of the contents of each document.

Ames, John Griffith. *Comprehensive Index to the Publications of the U.S. Government, 1881-1893*. Washington, D.C.: Government Printing Office, 1905. 2 vols.

   A valuable index to publications for the period noted.

U.S. Superintendent of Documents. *Checklist of U.S. Public Documents, 1789-1909*. Washington, D.C.: Government Printing Office, 1911.

U.S. Superintendent of Documents. *Catalog of the Public Documents of Congress and of All Departments of the U.S. for the Period March 4, 1893—December 31, 1940*. Washington, D.C.: Government Printing Office, 1896-1945. Vols. 1-25.

   This detailed work indexes all government publications, both congressional and departmental. Listings are made under author, subject, and title. This is a very detailed and worth-while guide.

U.S. Superintendent of Documents. *United States Government Publications, Monthly Catalog*. Washington, D.C.: Government Printing Office, 1895 to date.

   A bibliography of publications issued by all branches of the government together with instructions for ordering, prices, and full titles. This index appears monthly.

U.S. Library of Congress, Processing Department. *Monthly Checklist of State Publications*. Washington, D.C.: Government Printing Office, 1910 to date.

   A current bibliography, arranged by states' names, of the publications of the states, territories, and insular possessions of the United States. Published monthly.

Hirshberg, H. S., and Melinat, C. *Subject Guide to United States Government Publications*. Chicago: American Library Association, 1947.

Miscellaneous

Public Affairs Information Service. New York: Public Affairs Information Service, 1915 to date.

   This is a weekly subject index to current literature primarily in political science, government, economics, and legislation. Indexes books, documents, pamphlets, and selected articles in over 1000 periodicals.

Facts on File. New York: Facts on File, Inc., 1940 to date.

A weekly news digest of information on world, national affairs, Latin America, finance, economics, arts, science, education, religion, sports, obituaries, and miscellaneous. Cumulated.

DIRECTORIES

Directories are extremely valuable sources of information. Although there are various types, most of them offer information in one or more of the following areas:

Sources of supply
Names and addresses of manufacturers, suppliers, or dealers in a specific area of interest. This might be a directory of rug manufacturers, pet dealers, or electronic equipment suppliers, etc.
Service and product listings
Geographical listings of manufacturers and suppliers

The serious researcher will discover that there are usually several directories in each field. The wise course of action is to check all those available. Large libraries have collections of directories which may number several thousand; smaller libraries frequently subscribe to only those which have the widest use.

BUSINESS DIRECTORIES

Directories in business are often called "trade directories." Usually a business directory is limited to a specific manufacturing or distribution trade. A directory in a given field may offer information in an allied business area also. Normally the information includes the names of companies, their addresses, products, changes in personnel, and related statistical and factual data.

Davis, Marjorie V. *Guide to American Business Directories.* Washington, D.C.: Public Affairs Press, 1948.
This volume lists, under subject headings, a brief description of American business directories in some 77 different areas of activities. Among the 77 fields for which directories are listed, there are advertising, apparel, chemicals, banking, construction, food, hardware, insurance, real estate, and transportation. This book contains much of the information originally presented in a Department of Commerce pamphlet published in 1947.
Trade Directories of the World. Queens Village, N.Y.: Croner Publications, 1958.

This is a loose-leaf handbook which lists business and trade directories in the United States and Canada.
Guide to American Directories for Compiling Mailing Lists. New York: B. Klein, 1958.
Encyclopedia of American Associations; Guide to National Organizations of the United States. 2nd ed. Detroit: Gale Company, 1959.

FOREIGN DIRECTORIES

There are also a score of business and trade directories which list dealers and suppliers in Europe, the Scandinavian nations, the Far East, Latin America, and the British Empire. These may be found in any extensive business library. Perhaps a good source to begin with is *A Guide to Foreign Business Directories* published by the United States Department of Commerce in 1955.

DIRECTORIES OF CORPORATIONS

Directories which offer information on the structure of corporations are very valuable to investors, financing agencies, companies doing business with corporations, banks, and other institutions. The data given on large firms usually include company organization, history, financial structure, stock issued and level, names and positions of plants, offices, and subsidiaries. Some directories do not offer information in all the areas listed above; other directories offer more.

Moody's Investor Service
Moody's Service is divided into five areas: Transportation, Industrials, Public Utilities, Bank and Finance, and Municipal and Government. In addition, Moody's offers a *Stock Survey, Advisory Reports, Dividend Record, Bond Record,* and *Handbook of Common Stock.*
Poor's Register of Directors and Executives of the United States and Canada.
This directory has seven main sections:
1. It contains an index of products manufactured by the companies listed.
2. The Classified Index presents the names of corporations under 200 industrial categories.
3. The Corporation Directory alphabetically lists corporations. For each company, the names of all officers and directors are given as well as number of employees and products manufactured.
4. The Register of Directors cites facts on business leaders.

5. The Obituary Section lists deaths of executives during the preceding year.
6. The New Names Section lists those persons whose names appear for the first time in the Directory.
7. The New Individuals Section lists those persons whose names appeared for the first time in the Register of Directors division.

Standard and Poor's Corporation Services

This is a loose-leaf folder primarily designed for the investor. It, like Moody's to some extent, offers detailed background on the structure and financial background of corporations. Additional services offered are *The Bond Outlook, Industry Surveys, Railroad Securities, Daily Dividend Record, Called Bond Record, Stock Reports Over-the-Counter and Regional Exchanges, Listed Stock Reports, Facts and Forecasts Service,* and *Listed Bond Reports.*

Thomas' Register of American Manufacturers

This is an excellent list of sources of supply. Names and addresses of manufacturers, producers, importers, and other suppliers are listed. *Thomas' Register* is made up of five volumes. The first three list Product Classifications from A to Z; Volume IV lists manufacturers, trade names, trade papers, boards of trade and other commercial organizations; and Volume V is a Product Finding Guide.

Reference Guides and the Report

If the report writer will pause and review the previous pages of this chapter, he will recall that reference guides have been listed to help him secure data from the following sources:

Books
Journals, magazines, and periodicals
Bulletins, brochures, reports, and pamphlets
Newspapers
Miscellaneous sources such as government publications, commercial services, encyclopedias, and others

However, the "miscellaneous" category is the one almost without end and sometimes the most valuable. Dissertations, handbooks, directories, foreign references, and bibliographies are just a few of the published works which may fall into "miscellaneous" sources. But where, for example, do you find the name of a guide to dissertations? There may be several dissertations written on your topic. You should profit from the work of those who wrote these extensive papers. But again, where is a guide?

The answer to this question and others in this "miscellaneous" category may be found in the work mentioned earlier: Winchell, *Guide to Reference Works.* Here, in the section titled "Dissertations," one or more book titles appear which in turn list authors and titles of dissertations. Once this information is noted, the librarian may be requested to secure the specific dissertations through interlibrary loan. Thus you may build on the work of others.

But dissertations make up only one category; a guide to reference works will assist you in other areas as well.

Utilize all your tools effectively; they will save you time and help you write an excellent report.

MAKING UP A BIBLIOGRAPHY AND TAKING NOTES

Bibliographical Entries

Before recording data from his source material, the report writer should first make out a bibliography card. This card should indicate all the pertinent data which are used in footnote and bibliography entries. It is also helpful to list the library call number in the event it becomes necessary to secure the book again. Many researchers and scholars feel that a critical entry on a bibliography card is of immeasurable value. Such a brief comment may indicate an outstanding characteristic of the source or its excellence or faults.

651.78
K 39 R 2

F. Kerkes and R. Winfrey, *Report Preparation,* Ames, Iowa: Iowa State College Press, 1951.

A very good coverage of report writing with emphasis in the field of engineering. Also contains a section on business correspondence and technical writing.

Bibliography Card

The Technique of Taking Notes

Before taking notes, the researcher should be fairly well acquainted with the subject matter of the field which he is investigating. When one knows his field and his objectives in research, he may choose information for note taking more judiciously. The person who carries on research with only a vague idea of his goal and his topic may take a great many unnecessary notes or overlook data that will later prove of real importance. Thus there is merit in first examining the topic quite thoroughly, drawing up a tentative outline, and deciding what paths will and will not be necessary to cover.

As far as the mechanical aspect of taking notes is concerned, some suggestions may be offered. All information should be entered in ink on note cards. The card size most frequently suggested is 4″ x 6″. However, many persons feel that a larger size is superior. It is not wise to use quarter- or half-sheets of paper. Too often these slips of paper may be lost, and they are difficult to sort, examine, and use.

Note Card Content

Each note card should carry only one idea or thought. This rule should be followed whether the note is one line in length or fifty. As soon as more than one note appears on a card, that card becomes extremely difficult to handle in the filing and sorting process. Under which category shall a card with two or more ideas be filed? The only answer, if one wishes to avoid difficulty, is to place only one idea on a note card.

The topic heading for each card should appear in the upper left-hand corner. These headings should normally be taken from the tentative outline. If the note is of obvious importance, and there is no outline heading to match it, then a title should be made up and placed on the card; that heading would then be added, in its proper place, to the outline.

These card headings should not be composed and written haphazardly but should be chosen with thought. Then when the task of sorting the note cards is met, it should prove simple, for each card, already categorized, will fit into its proper slot. This is one reason why researchers often find that many of their outline entries also serve as note card headings.

In the upper right-hand portion of the card, reference to the source should be made. Many individuals find that the last name of the author and the page number are sufficient. However, care should be exercised if more than one volume in a series is used and if more than one book by the same author is covered. In either of these cases, it is a simple matter to add a few words for the book's title (as well as the author's name) and the proper volume number.

Some scholars prefer to place a number on each bibliography card that is made. This number (usually circled) is then placed in the right-hand corner of each note card made from that source. Care must be exercised so that the page number and source number are not confused.

In either case, footnote entries can be made (when the paper is being written) by extracting the necessary information from the proper note and bibliography cards.

Types of Notes

Several types of notes may be taken. For that reason one may find it advisable to use any one of several forms, depending on the importance of the source, the advisability of quoting or summarizing from the source, or the need for making a critical evaluation of the source.

1. *Précis or Summary Note.* This note is written in the researcher's own words but is completely and thoroughly true to the original source. This note is much shorter than the basic passage and normally 50 percent or less in length.

Follow-Up on Questionnaire   Anderson, Saunders
                                     and Weeks, p. 218

When replies to questionnaires are not returned as expected, it is suggested that follow-up letters to the persons on the mailing list be sent out requesting that the original inquiry be completed and returned.

Précis or Summary Note

2. *Paraphrase Note.* This type of note is used most frequently for important passages where it is desired to restate in the researcher's words all of the original author's points. This usually involves some slight reduction in the number of words used.

Principles in Sampling   Hansen & Hurwitz, p. 371

    Similar basic principles apply in sampling problems of business establishments, homes, farms, factories, and other groups; altho the importance of the different principles change according to the problem.

Paraphrase Note

3. *Quotation Note.* This note is probably used more often than it should be, probably because the researcher often attaches more importance to a passage than it deserves; or he simply finds it easier to write exactly what the author has noted instead of transposing the thoughts into his own words.

In any event, the quotation note is written in the *exact* form the author of the source used, and it is enclosed in quotation marks. This means that no change takes place: not a word, not a date, not a comma! If words are omitted within the quote, that omission is indicated by an ellipsis (. . .). If one desires to insert his own comments or remarks into the body of the quotation, his contribution must be enclosed in brackets [ ].

The Qualitative Interview   R. S. Blankenship (ed.) p. 425

    "The qualitative interview is a personal interview in which there is no set list of formal questions, but in which the interviewer uses a guide around which he attempts to get complete reaction from the respondent."

Quotation Note

The quotation note is certainly valuable when it is felt that the original author's words say exactly, emphatically, and most accurately what is desired. Then, too, an exact quotation from a recognized authority may lend credence to the report writer's argument.

4. *Critical Note.* This is a criticism or comment on a specific item of source material. A comment may be a critical evaluation of the work from the point of authenticity, writing, or obvious bias of the author. Or it may be a comparison with another work in the same field.

"Questionnaire Preparation   A. Blankenship
and Interview Technique"

This article on questionnaire preparation was presented as a committee report to the Amer. Mkting Ass'n. It is a most thorough analysis, and its authors are recognized authorities.

Critical Note

Summary Comments on Note-Taking Techniques

There are a few miscellaneous factors that might be wise to remember in connection with taking notes.

First, never attempt to economize on cards. Place only *one* complete idea on a card, even if that note is made up of only a few words. Adequate notes should be made, but the researcher should try to be reasonable so that he is not buried under an avalanche of note cards. When there is any question about the future possibility of using the card, the note should be taken; this is a much safer plan than trusting to memory.

The report writer should be sure that the note will be completely clear if read several weeks after it has been taken. Thus, he must be careful to get the author's exact meaning on the note card. If the writer has stated a point in an excellent manner, the researcher should quote him and make sure that such statements, taken verbatim from the text, are enclosed in quotation marks. If any portion of a direct quotation is omitted, an ellipsis should be used.

And if additions to an original quotation are made, such comments should be enclosed in brackets.

Page numbers on note cards should not be forgotten. Much time may be wasted in going back to the library for the magazine article or pamphlet and determining from what page a particular note was drawn.

The caliber of the note cards will determine, to a large extent, the caliber of the report. Notes should be taken carefully and judiciously.

DOCUMENTATION OF MATERIAL

As stated earlier, the content of a report is usually drawn from primary sources. However, when secondary areas of information are investigated and pertinent data extracted, those secondary sources must be given credit for the information that the report writer uses. It is sometimes difficult to draw a line of demarcation and indicate that in this case the secondary source *should* be given credit, but in this case it is not necessary. How may one decide what is common knowledge and what is not? It is a most difficult situation at times, and an involved discussion of what may or may not be considered plagiarism will not be attempted here. Suffice it to say that all ideas, principles, facts, and statistical data borrowed from someone else, whether in the author's words or in the researcher's, should be credited to the original source. That credit is in the form of documentation which is usually referred to as a footnote. Material that is said to be "common knowledge" in a field is not usually documented.

In addition to using footnotes to credit the source of a direct quotation, they may also be utilized for other cases:

1. To acknowledge indebtedness to a source for the idea which the original author has set down.
2. To present additional information such as statistics, graphs, or comments which will supplement what is in the text but is not of such primary importance as to warrant inclusion in the body of the paper.
3. To display other comments which may not be immediately relevant to the text material but sufficiently related to appear in the report.

4. To suggest additional sources of information, disagreement among authors on a specific point, or other miscellaneous comments.

Footnotes should be numbered with an arabic numeral, and a corresponding designation should appear in the body of the report at the proper point of reference. All numbering should be consecutive within the report. However, it is sometimes suggested that where the number of footnotes is large, the first footnote in each section should be designated "1."

Normally, footnotes are placed at the bottom of the appropriate page with a double space left between the text of the report and the first footnote. Usually a line is drawn between the text and the first footnote on the page. There are no spaces left between the footnotes which appear on the same page. Some researchers find it desirable to place footnotes at the end of the report rather than at the bottom of the page. The form used depends on the preference of the report writer.

The following sample entries should give every student a clear idea of how to document a paper. Almost every type of footnote is cited, the uses of *ibid.* and *op. cit.* are explained, a bibliography is presented, and a list of common abbreviations used in documentation is noted.

Suggested Footnote Form

1. *One Author*
   Robert R. Aurner, *Effective Communication in Business,* Cincinnati: South-Western Publishing Company, 1958, p. 87.
2. *Two Authors*
   Harold Koontz and Cyril O'Donnell, *Principles of Management,* New York: McGraw-Hill Book Company, Inc., 1955, p. 37.
3. *Several Authors*
   Hilton D. Shepherd *et al.* (*or* Hilton D. Shepherd and Others), *Introduction to Modern Business,* Englewood Cliffs, N.J.: Prentice-Hall, Inc., 1955, p. 16.
4. *No Author Cited*
   "Anon." may be used in place of the author's name, or the title may be moved directly to the left-hand margin.
5. *Editor of a Collection*
   Rufus Wixon (ed.), *Accountants' Handbook,* New York: The Ronald Press Company, 1956, pp. 1-19.

6. *Editors of a Collection*
   William G. Ireson and Eugene L. Grant (eds.), *Handbook of Industrial Engineering and Management*, Englewood Cliffs, N.J.: Prentice-Hall, Inc., 1955, p. 145.
7. *Translation of an Original Work*
   Rudolf Allers, *The Psychology of Character*, trans. E. B. Strauss, New York: The Macmillan Company, 1931, p. 43.
8. *Portion of a Book*
   T. S. Eliot, "Religion Without Humanism," *Humanism and America*, ed. Norman Foerster, New York: Farrar and Rinehart, 1930, p. 108.
9. *Journal Article*
   Norman B. Sigband, "The Cover Letter," *The Journal of Marketing*, XVII, no. 4 (April, 1953), 424-428.
   Norman B. Sigband, "School-Community Communications," *Junior College Journal*, March, 1955, pp. 395-397.
10. *Reports*
    Federal Trade Commission, *Report of the Federal Trade Commission of the Merger Movement*, Washington, D.C.: Government Printing Office, 1948, p. 35.
    United States Department of Economic Affairs, *International Cartels*, New York: United Nations Publications, 1947, p. 38.
11. *Newspapers*
    Chicago Daily News, April 22, 1957, p. 31.
12. *Encyclopedias* (Unsigned and signed articles)
    "Potassium," *Encyclopaedia Britannica*, vol. XVIII, 14th ed.
    Ferdinand Schevill, "Germany and the War," *The Encyclopedia Americana*, ed. A. H. McDannald, vol. XII (1946).
13. *Public Documents*
    Congressional Globe, 37th Cong., 1st. sess., July, 1861, p. 73.
    Council of Economic Advisors, *The Economic Report of the President Transmitted to the Congress January 16, 1952*, Washington, D.C.: Government Printing Office, 1952, p. 27.
14. *Manuscripts*
    McClernand MSS, McClernand to Lincoln, September 28, 1862, Illinois State Historical Library.
15. *Interview*
    Statement made to the author by Professor Thomas Brentwood, DePaul University, May 5, 1960.

Sample Group of Footnotes

Footnotes	*Comments*
1. Robert R. Aurner, *Effective Communication in Business,* Cincinnati: South-Western Publishing Company, 1958, p. 87.	1. First reference to a book.
2. Norman B. Sigband, "Writing the Annual Report," *Advanced Management,* XVII, no. 1 (January, 1952), 20.	2. First reference to a journal article.
3. Aurner, *op. cit.,* p. 63.	3. Reference is identical to footnote 1, except that a different page number is given.
4. Carl Van Doren, *Benjamin Franklin,* New York: The Viking Press, Inc., 1938, p. 137.	4. Reference to a book.
5. *Ibid.*	5. Reference is identical to footnote 4.
6. *Ibid.,* p. 173.	6. Reference is identical to footnote 5, except that a different page number is given.
7. Walter Blair and John C. Gerber, *Better Reading,* New York: Scott Foresman & Company, 1945, p. 48.	7. Initial reference to a book by two authors.
8. Edward Channing, *A History of the United States,* New York: The Macmillan Company, 1948, vol. II, p. 43.	8. Reference to a work made up of more than one volume.
9. Sigband, *op. cit.,* p. 21.	9. Reference is identical to footnote 2 except to a different page.
10. Channing, *op. cit.,* vol. IV, p. 185.	10. Reference is identical to footnote 8 except to a different volume.

11. George Goyau, "Normandy," *The Catholic Encyclopedia,* ed. John J. Wynne, vol. XI, pp. 104-107.	11. Reference to signed encyclopedia article.
12. United Nations Department of Economic Affairs, *International Cartels,* New York: United Nations Publications, 1947, p. 33.	12. Reference to a report.
13. "Potassium," *Encyclopaedia Britannica,* vol. XVIII, 14th ed.	13. Reference to an unsigned encyclopedia article.
14. "The A & P Suit," *Chicago Journal of Commerce,* September 20, 1949, p. 20.	14. Reference to an unsigned newspaper article.

Suggested Bibliographical Form

1. *One Author*
   Aurner, Robert R. *Effective Communication in Business.* Cincinnati: South-Western Publishing Company, 1958.
2. *Two Authors*
   Koontz, Harold, and O'Donnell, Cyril. *Principles of Management.* New York: McGraw-Hill Book Company, Inc., 1955.
3. *Several Authors*
   Shepherd, Hilton D., *et al.* (*or* Shepherd, Hilton D., and Others.) *Introduction to Modern Business.* Englewood Cliffs, N.J.: Prentice-Hall, Inc., 1955.
4. *No Author Cited*
   Title is moved directly to the left-hand margin.
5. *Editor of a Collection*
   Wixon, Rufus (ed.) *Accountants' Handbook.* New York: The Ronald Press Company, 1956.
6. *Editors of a Collection*
   Ireson, William G., and Grant, Eugene L. (eds.). *Handbook of Industrial Engineering and Management.* Englewood Cliffs, N.J.: Prentice-Hall, Inc., 1955.
7. *Translation of an Original Work*
   Allers, Rudolf. *The Psychology of Character.* Translated by E. B. Strauss. New York: The Macmillan Company, 1931.
8. *Portion of a Book*
   Eliot, T. S. "Religion Without Humanism," *Humanism and Amer-*

ica. Edited by Norman Foerster. New York: Farrar and Rinehart, 1930.

9. *Magazine Article*

   Sigband, Norman B. "Remedial English at the College Level," *Journal of Higher Education,* XXIII (May, 1952), 270-272.

10. *Report*

    Federal Trade Commission. *Report of the Federal Trade Commission of the Merger Movement.* Washington, D.C.: Government Printing Office, 1948.

    American Medical Association. *Medical Relations under Workmen's Compensation.* Chicago: American Medical Association, 1933.

11. *Newspapers*

    "The A & P Suit," *Chicago Journal of Commerce,* September 20, 1949, p. 20.

12. *Newspaper Article Without Title*

    Chicago Journal of Commerce, June 15, 1949, p. 7.

13. *Reference to Signed and Unsigned Encyclopedia Article*

    Encyclopaedia Britannica, 14th ed. Vol. VIII. Article, "Electricity."

    Schevill, Ferdinand. "Germany and the War," *Encyclopedia Americana.* Edited by A. H. McDannald. Vol. XII, 1946.

14. *Public Documents*

    Council of Economic Advisors. *The Economic Report of the President Transmitted to the Congress January 16, 1952.* Washington, D.C.: Government Printing Office, 1952.

Standard Abbreviations Used in Footnotes

In an effort to make the writer's job easier, a standard group of abbreviations has been compiled. The proper use of these may well save the student a great deal of time.

Singular	*Plural*	*Meaning*
ante		Before
bk.	bks.	Book
ca. (circa)		About
cf.		Compare
ch. (in law citation)		Chapter
chap.	chaps.	Chapter
col.	cols.	Column
comp.		Compiler
ed.	eds.	Editor
ed.	edd.	Edition
e.g. *(exempli gratia)*		For example

Singular	Plural	Meaning
et al. (et alii)		And others
et seq. (et sequens)		And the following
f.	ff.	And following page(s)
fig.	figs.	Figure
fol.		Folio
i.e. *(id est)*		That is
ibid. (ibidem)		In the same place
illus.		Illustrated
infra.		Below
l.	ll.	Line
loc. cit. (loco citato)		In the place cited
MS	MSS	Manuscript
n.	nn.	Note or notes
N.B. *(nota bene)*		Note well
n.d.		No date
no.	nos.	Number
op. cit. (opere citato)		In the work cited
passim		Here and there
p.	pp.	Page
rev.		Revised, revision
sec.	secs.	Section
ser.		Series
sic.		Inserted in brackets in quoted material to indicate that the quotation is literal, "battlle [sic]"
supra		Above (or see above)
trans.		Translated or translator
v.	vv.	Verse
viz. (videlicet)		Namely
vol.	vols.	Volume

QUESTIONS FOR DISCUSSION

I. Indicate the call number for each of the books listed below. Use the numbering system of your library.
  1. John Gunther, *Inside Latin America*
  2. Allan Nevins, *The Emergence of Lincoln*
  3. Lincoln Steffins, *The Autobiography of Lincoln Steffins*
  4. Carl Sandburg, *The People, Yes*

5. Samuel Eliot Morison, *Admiral of the Ocean Sea*
6. Leo Tolstoy, *War and Peace*
7. James Boswell, *The Life of Samuel Johnson*
8. Alexander P. De Seversky, *Victory Through Air Power*
9. S. I. Hayakawa, *Language in Action*
10. Berelson and Janowitz, *Reader in Public Opinion and Communication*

II. Below are given the call numbers of various works. List the name and author. The Dewey Decimal, Cutter, and Library of Congress numbers are given for each work and in that order.

1. 551.46
   C 32s
   Gc21.C3

2. 937
   G 439
   DG311.G5

3. 973.2
   An 565c
   E188.A572

4. 973
   B 455d4
   E183.7.B4682

5. 810.9
   P 26m
   PS88.P3

6. 910.4
   H 615k
   G530.T463

7. 550
   C 947d
   QE28.C8

8. 709
   V261a
   N5300.V33

9. 808
   P 45w
   PE1411.P4

10. 921
    W 317up
    E185.97.W315

III. Answer the following questions and *list the source* from which you drew the answer.
   1. How many students were enrolled in institutions of higher education in your home state in the year preceding this one?
   2. What work contains a thorough guide to reference books concerned with government documents?
   3. Who wrote the biography of Nathan Bedford Forrest which appears in the *Dictionary of American Biography?*
   4. Where is Dusseldorf? What is its population and what is it noted for?
   5. Find a biography of the president of your school. List the outstanding points in the biography.
   6. What is the first use of the word *commerce* that you can discover?
   7. What articles appeared in popular magazines on Douglas MacArthur during February, 1956?

8. List the articles concerned with report writing which appeared in various commerce magazines during the three months preceding this assignment.
9. How many passenger automobiles were registered in your state during the preceding year?
10. What newspapers are published in Albany, New York?

IV. Answer the following questions and cite the source from which you secured the answer.

1. What libraries in Chicago have a file of the *Journal of Marketing?*
2. List five articles which have appeared in popular magazines on the subject of guided missiles.
3. What pamphlets are listed in the *Vertical File Catalog* in the two months preceding this date on the subject of the federal government?
4. What articles have appeared in the *New York Times* newspaper during the first month of this year on the subject of the federal government and education?
5. List articles on business correspondence which have appeared in *Printers' Ink* during 1959.
6. Check the reviews on the last fiction or nonfiction book you read and note how many were favorable or unfavorable and the names of the original publications in which the reviews appeared.
7. List the subsidiaries of the Zenith Radio Corporation.
8. List the capital, population, and area of Finland.
9. Who wrote the article titled "Role of the Colleges in Nuclear Engineering Education," which appeared in *Journal of Engineering Education,* October, 1955?
10. Who wrote the article on the poet Edmund Spencer which appears in the *Dictionary of National Biography?*

V. Answer the following questions as briefly as possible.

1. How does a paraphrase note card differ from a quotation note card?
2. What are the specific reasons for taking a quotation note card?
3. Under what specific situations should a footnote entry be made?
4. In entering footnotes, under what conditions is *ibid.* used, and when is *op. cit.* employed?
5. Submit five critical note cards on books in your field of concentration.

VI. Choose any *one* of the following topics. Then go to the library and take notes on it. Use magazines or books for your sources, and for each source, complete a bibliography card. Submit a minimum of ten note cards on your topic.

1. Use of averages in reports
2. Use of pictograms in reports
3. Utilization of questionnaires to secure consumer opinion
4. Television as a sales promotion medium
5. Good will communications to business firms
6. Recruitment of executives by industry
7. Supply of engineers available
8. Automation in the auto industry
9. Memorandum reports
10. Employee profit sharing plans

VII. "Unscramble" the following entries and enter footnotes for each in the order given.

1. Vol. 32, no. 5, How to Measure the Results of Supervisory Training, March, 1956, L. David Korb, p. 379, Personnel
2. Same as footnote 1.
3. N. Loyall McLaren, Annual Reports to Stockholders, The Ronald Press Company, New York 1947, p. 39.
4. Accountants' Reports, The Ronald Press Company, New York, William H. Bell, 1949, p. 155.
5. Railway Age, August 1, 1955, Norman B. Sigband, vol. 139, no. 5, Look to Your Letters, p. 23.
6. Same as footnote 3 except page 145 was used.
7. Handbook of Modern Accounting Theory, Englewood Cliffs, N.J.: Prentice-Hall, Inc., p. 55. 1955, Edited by Morton Backer.
8. Career in Congress? The Wall Street Journal, April 2, 1956, p. 1 by James A. Reynolds.
9. New York, Appleton-Century-Crofts, Inc., Robert E. Tuttle and C. A. Brown, Writing Useful Reports, 1956, p. 38.
10. Same as footnote 9 except page 148 was used.
11. McGraw-Hill Book Company, Inc., Economic Problems of Latin America, edited by Seymour E. Harris, 1944, New York, pp. 151-153.
12. Same as footnote 9 except p. 175 was used.

VIII. "Unscramble" the following entries and enter footnotes for each in the order given.

1. Harper & Brothers Publishers, p. 55, New York, Florence Peterson, Survey of Labor Economics, 1951.
2. Readings in Economics, McGraw-Hill Book Company, Inc., New York, 1952, pp. 114-116 edited by Paul A. Samuelson, Robert L. Bishop, John R. Coleman.
3. Help Your Retailer and Reduce Your Marketing Cost,

p. 24, March 16, 1956, Murray Spitzer, Printers' Ink, vol. 254, no. 11.

4. Same as footnote 2.
5. Volume II, edited by Bernard F. Haley, A Survey of Contemporary Economics, 1952, Richard D. Irwin, Inc., Homewood, Illinois, p. 45.
6. Same as footnote 5 except vol. I., p. 153 was used.
7. Rollin G. Thomas, Our Modern Banking and Monetary System, Prentice-Hall, Inc. p. 10, 1950, Englewood Cliffs, N.J.
8. Same as footnote 5.
9. Monthly Labor Review, Feb., 1956, vol. 79, no. 2, Joseph P. Goldberg, A Survey of American Labor During 1955, pp. 150-151.
10. John T. Dunlop and James J. Healy, Richard D. Irwin, Inc. Homewood, Illinois, p. 180, 1953, Collective Bargaining.
11. Norman B. Sigband, Journal of Marketing, vol. XVII, The Cover Letter, no. 4, April 1953, pp. 424-427.
12. Same as footnote 11.

IX. Offer your criticism of the following cards. Cards 1 and 2 are bibliography references; cards 3 to 6 are note cards.

1.

> J. N. Ulman, Jr. and J. R. Gould,
> *Technical Reporting,* New York:
> Henry Holt and Company, 1959.
>
>
> This is a well-written revision of a standard book in the field. It is directed, according to the preface, to engineers and men in science.

2.

> Mildred S. Parten, *Surveys, Polls and Samples,*
> New York: Harper and Company, 1950.
>
> This is an excellent and very scholarly work. It
> is very detailed and would seem to be a required
> reference book for anyone in marketing or man-
> agement.

3.

> Tables in Reports   Johnson
>   p. 32
>
> It has been found unsatisfactory to use com-
> plex tables for reports directed to the consumer.
>
> Under most situations memorandum reports
> should be made up in duplicate.

4.

> Averages   Lyons
>
> Mean averages may be used to present data
> which are technically correct but may reflect an
> inaccurate interpretation.

5.

> Order of   ④
> presenting data   p. 84
>
>
> "In reporting information, simply follow a
> time sequence. Describing any process takes this
> order. . . . Similarly in telling how you carried
> out a project, you could put first the step you
> actually first took, and so on."

6.

> Graphic data
>
>
> "When using graphic methods of presenting
> data to the man in the street, it is wise to use
> pictographs [*sic.*]. Any cartoon-like representa-
> tion of that type has a wide appeal."
>   Martins
>   **Vol. I, p. 34**

X. Answer the following questions and list the source in which
you found the data.
1. What was the National Income for 1959, 1950?
2. List the president and vice-president of sales of the Zenith
   Radio Corporation.
3. List the number of passenger cars produced in 1952 and
   1959 by Plymouth, Ford, and Chevrolet.
4. List complete bibliographical information for four articles
   on report writing which appeared in 1958 or 1959.
5. State in one or two sentences the primary purposes of the
   book *Evolution of Wage Structure* by Lloyd George Reynolds and Cynthia Taft.
6. In what popular journal would the article "Six Steps to
   Executive Success" appear?
7. What daily newspapers are published in Los Angeles, California?

Chapter 3

The Use of Primary Sources

Many of the reports written today use primary source material as their basis. These primary sources may be company records, original letters or diaries, the data collected from interviews, questionnaires that have been completed, or the personal observations of a problem or situation.

When the report writer works with primary sources, he has an opportunity to use his own analytical abilities to the greatest degree. He has material which is original; no one else has revised, edited, or interpreted the data before him; and he may examine the information without encountering the prejudice or bias of an earlier investigator.

This is not to imply that secondary sources of information are not valuable. On the contrary, such material often serves as the foundation on which further investigation is based. The researcher should utilize both wherever possible.

Among the primary sources used extensively today are questionnaire and interview returns. The information gathered from these two sources often determines whether or not a product should be marketed, whether it would be advisable to distribute an item in a specific area, whether the employees of a factory are satisfied, or whether an item coming off the production line is up to standard. These are just a few of the situations where the opinions of the respondents are used in research.

Surveys which utilize questionnaires or interviews should be very carefully thought through. The planning begins with the question, "Who shall be surveyed?" Teachers? Housewives? College students? Businessmen earning $8,000 per year? Physicians? Lawyers?

Once the group or groups have been selected, the researcher

must determine what percentage must be questioned to insure the validity of the results. The *percentage* of the entire group selected is known as the *sample*. The "group" from which the sample is drawn is usually referred to as the *universe*. The sample may then be referred to as that *segment* or portion of the "universe" which will accurately reflect the opinions or attitudes of that universe.

SAMPLING AND SAMPLING METHODS

If the researcher desires to determine a specific fact concerning the 6300 employees in a factory, it is unnecessary to ask all of them the same series of questions. Experience has shown that if a representative cross section (the "sample") of the 6300 persons (the "universe" in this case) is taken, the results determined will be quite common to all. So too, it is not necessary to test every single sheet of steel in a day's production; a few sheets chosen from the morning and afternoon output and then tested will result in an accurate estimate of the quality of the entire lot. If the laboratory analyst takes a sample from a pharmaceutical preparation, she too will be able to evaluate the entire output. This in essence is what is done in sampling among people. The researcher evaluates a percentage of the group, rather than the entire group, and arrives at a conclusion. In that manner, large sums of money are saved, and a reasonable degree of accuracy is achieved.

Like everything else, sampling should not be done unless a careful plan or program has been established. The researcher should ask certain questions that will determine the various boundaries of the sampling process. Just exactly what information is desired? If one knows the answer to this question, he may more accurately decide where the sample should be taken and how big it should be. What is the scope of the problem? In other words, what age group, religious group, vocational group, social group, or economic group is being examined? If several groups are involved in the universe, the sample obviously must be chosen from each according to a specific plan. This may be on a ratio basis. If, for example, the universe is composed of 5000 lawyers, 3000 engineers, and 2000 accountants, then the sample surveyed might be 500 lawyers, 300 engineers, and 200 accountants, a ratio equal to the total number in each group. Of course, a completely different ratio may be desired.

Another question that frequently arises is, "How accurate must the results be?" Certainly, as the desire for accuracy increases, so too must the size of the sample. Generally speaking, you may be more certain your findings are correct if your sample is based on 5,000 questionnaire returns rather than 500 when the universe totals 20,000.

Another factor in accuracy is the extensiveness of the questionnaire itself. As the number of questions or categories in the questionnaire increases, so must the size of the sample. And, finally, the size of the budget that has been allocated for securing the data affects the accuracy since at times, the confines imposed by a small budget will restrict the size of the sample. These are a few of the preliminary questions which the report writer must answer before he decides how many, how much, and where the questionnaires shall be sent or the interviews taken.

Types of Samples

In a *random sample* the basic premise is that every member of the universe being sampled has an equal chance of being selected. Even in this simple definition there seems to be some controversy among various authorities. If one states that he will make a *random* selection of 300 names from the telephone directory, another person may point out that such a selection is not random; it is restricted to individuals who own telephones. Or if the researcher points out that he will select every fifth name in a voting list, does it follow that everyone in the group has an equal opportunity of being selected? These technical points are discussed in various statistics texts for those students who desire additional information on the topic. By and large, it is safe to say that a random sample may be secured in the following situation: Let us assume that the researcher wants to learn the attitudes of the voters of Centerville toward a new school bond issue. He could select the town's voting list as the universe and draw his sample from that directory of names. If the list contains 8000 names and the researcher decides a sample of 800 persons is needed, every tenth name should be selected. For the selection to be random, the researcher should write numbers from 1 to 10 on slips of paper and choose among them. If number 7 is selected by chance, then the seventh name on the list becomes the first name chosen, the seventeenth name the second, the twenty-seventh the third, the thirty-seventh the fourth, and so on until the total of 800 has been reached. In this manner, a random sample among the voters' list will be completed.

A *stratified sample* is sometimes referred to as a quota or proportion sample. In this case differences in classes or strata in the population are recognized and split into homogeneous groupings. Lawyers, physicians, teachers, or engineers may be separated into groups; or perhaps the groupings may be in such terms as professional persons, white collar workers, and laborers. Or the selection may be on the basis of race, religion, or economic or social status. In any event, segments are established, and from each of these a percentage is sampled.

Of course, the same percentage of each group must appear in the sample as appears in the universe being sampled. The value of such a system is quite apparent, for if persons of high and low economic status were mixed in a group and a *random* sample taken, the results might not be accurate if a larger number from one economic stratum were selected than from another. Stratified sampling is accepted among most statisticians as being reasonably accurate.

In *area sampling* geographical areas are surveyed. Specific segments of a city, a state, or the nation are recognized and samples taken of that area. The United States Bureau of Census often finds that for its gigantic undertakings such a sampling procedure is valuable.

In addition to these popular sampling methods, there are several others which the report writer may wish to investigate. There are *cluster, purposive, double, disproportionate, selective,* and other sampling systems.

Some time ago, the Business Information Division of Dun and Bradstreet conducted a survey of *Time* Magazine subscribers. The examination was to determine the age, education, occupation, position, and community activities of each member of the family surveyed. A complete mailing list of *Time* subscribers was turned over to the research agency and the sample drawn from it. The statement below illustrates the sampling procedures used:

1. *Original Sample*

The sample of names to whom the original mailings were made was chosen by selecting every 192nd name in a systematic manner from the list of *Time* subscribers. Because this list is arranged geographically by states and alphabetically by city within states there was automatic insurance that the sample was properly distributed by states. The actual number of cases selected from each city was within one case of the number expected to be attained on a proportionate basis.

Through the above selection process, a total of 6,404 names of subscribers was obtained. Examination of these names revealed that 166 subscription copies were addressed to institutions, libraries, businesses, or clubs. These names were deleted to yield the basic sample of 6,000.

2. *Sample of Non-Respondents*

After the 4,222 questionnaires had been received by mail, the names of 1,778 persons in the original sample of 6,000 remained. To insure a representative selection of non-respondents, every third name in this residual list was selected. This yielded 590 names. Then an additional 10 names were selected from this residual file to provide for a total of 600 names for the sample of non-respondents.[1]

This brief statement gives some indication of how sampling is carried through by a large firm.

The Reliability of the Sample

In taking any sample whether it is by mail, telephone, or in the field through interviewers, the report writer is especially concerned with the reliability of the results. On the basis of his findings, a company may spend hundreds of thousands of dollars on a new product or on a new package, or it may change a work system, purchase or sell machinery, select a plant site, or take action in a thousand different ways that are extremely important in a firm's operation. The researcher, then, is most concerned with the reliability of his findings.

As noted earlier, accuracy is dependent on the sample size. That size or number in the sample must be greater if the possibilities of different answers are greater. In other words, not so many questionnaires need to be sent out if the questionnaire has 15 questions as is the case if the questionnaire contains 40 questions. Then, too, as the desire for accuracy increases, so must there be an increase in the size of the sample taken. However, the researcher should be aware that a plateau may be reached after a specific number of replies come in. And regardless of how

---

[1] Business Information Division, Dun and Bradstreet, Inc., *A Sample Census of Time Subscriber Families,* April, 1950, p. 23. Reproduced by permission of *Time* Magazine.

many more questionnaires are evaluated, the increase in accuracy will not be significant. This is an extremely important factor from the point of view of the expenditure of money for research. If specific results are determined on the basis of 3500 questionnaires, and these results are not *materially* changed (for greater accuracy) by evaluating an additional 2000, there is little need for the extra expenditure of funds. In some instances a very high degree of accuracy is desired, and the increased number in the sample may be warranted.

Most basic texts in statistics illustrate various formulas which may be utilized to determine how many individual cases in the sample are necessary for a predetermined measure of reliability.

After all the basic requirements of good sampling procedure have been met—the purpose of the survey, the determination of the group to be sampled, how many are to be questioned, and the cost involved—then the actual examination may be begun. Of the various types of surveys which may be undertaken, the mail questionnaire is, perhaps, most frequently used. But before we can examine the questionnaire in the mail survey, we should look at the "cover letter" which almost invariably accompanies the questionnaire.

THE COVER LETTER [2]

In a study by the Marketing Research Committee, a statement concerning the cover letter emphasized that the letter itself is the most important of all auxiliary materials in a direct mail survey.[3] Certainly it will be agreed by anyone who has engaged in testing a situation by mail that a good cover letter will be of great assistance in convincing the recipient of the questionnaire that he should complete and return it.

Several basic attributes are common to the makeup of every cover letter if success is to be achieved:

1. The cover letter should be brief.
2. The purpose of the survey should be clearly and simply explained.

[2] See also Norman B. Sigband, "The Cover Letter," *The Journal of Marketing,* April, 1953.

[3] Albert S. Blankenship (ed.), "Questionnaire Preparation and Interviewer Technique," *The Journal of Marketing,* October, 1949.

3. The letter should contain a strong "You" attitude.
4. It is advisable to indicate a final due date for the questionnaire's return.
5. A copy of the results, if feasible, should be offered to the respondent.
6. The respondent should be assured that his identity will remain anonymous if he desires.
7. A warm friendly tone should be maintained and the letter should have a pen-and-ink signature.

Brevity in the Cover Letter

The cover letter to the questionnaire should certainly not contain a long discussion of the background to the survey, how the results may be utilized, or any other facts that are not vital to the problem. Even the directions on how to complete the questionnaire may be more advantageously placed at the top of the questionnaire itself rather than in the cover letter. The cover letter should contain only those statements which are necessary to explain the survey and persuade the recipient to respond.

Aim of the Survey

The aim or purpose of the survey should be included in the cover letter, for the respondent is entitled to know why he has been asked to spend anywhere from five to thirty minutes doing something for someone else. The *interested* recipient is more likely to respond; that interest may be aroused by pointing out, in the cover letter, the goals of the survey.

Then, too, most people like to feel that they are part of a project. When the report writer explains the purpose of his survey to the prospective respondent, he is certainly using good psychology. Experiments in education and in industry have proved repeatedly that when the individual knows why and for what purpose he has been assigned a task, his performance of that job is invariably more satisfactory.

The "You" Attitude in the Cover Letter

Our previous point leads almost directly into this discussion. If at all possible, the report writer should show the respondent how he (the respondent) may benefit from completing the questionnaire.

The respondent who is convinced that it is wise for him to complete the form is much more inclined to accede to the request of the researcher.

In business writing the "you" attitude has always come in for a great deal of discussion, for it is writing with the recipient's point of view in mind. The one who answers the questionnaire may not be particularly concerned with what the report writer's company will gain from the survey or how that company's products will be improved or services bettered; he is interested in what the survey might do for *him*. Note in the letters below how those at the left are concerned only with the company and how those at the right give the respondent a valid reason why he should spend his time answering the questionnaire.

Dear Sir:

Enclosed you will find a questionnaire which is being sent to all our dealers. It is concerned with the shipping of our products from our plant to your place of business.

In the past two years, we have noted some delay as well as pilfering in the shipments of our merchandise. Inasmuch as both of these factors vitally affect our profits as well as efficiency, we are now making an effort to determine where the faults lie, correct those faults, and thus save needless expense to our company.

We hope you will give this questionnaire your attention and return it at your earliest convenience.

Dear Mr. Dealer:

The Excello Corporation has recently become concerned with a problem which we feel you can help us solve. In the shipping of merchandise to you and other dealers, we have uncovered what we feel to be an unusual number of delays.

In an effort to get the merchandise to you in the most speedy manner possible and to insure that every order is complete as entered, we are conducting a survey. The results of this examination will bring you better over-all service. Good service in any business usually means better profits, and if we can accomplish that for our dealers, we will be most happy to do so.

If we may have this questionnaire returned, in the envelope provided, by June 5, it will help us get a new delivery system into operation by the first of July.

Thank you very much for your courtesy and attention to this matter.

Dear Sir:

You undoubtedly know that our corporation has manufactured over one hundred products for American druggists for the past seventy-five years. At the present time our board of directors has been seriously considering introducing to the market a hand soap containing a deodorant. Because there are several on the market, we are not sure that there is room for another; even a high-class, quality product. Inasmuch as the expenditure in research, packaging, and advertising would be tremendous, we do not want to enter into this until we have determined that it would prove profitable.

You can help us a great deal by entering your opinions on the attached questionnaire; your experience as a druggist will permit you to answer the questions easily and accurately.

May we have your reply at your earliest convenience.

Dear Mr. Druggist:

The Acme Pharmaceutical Corporation is coming to you for help. As you know, we have taken a great deal of pride in supplying the drug trade for the past seventy-five years with over one hundred pharmaceutical products. Recently, many of our dealers have suggested to us that there is probably room in the market for a high-quality and reasonably priced hand soap containing a deodorant.

We are, of course, concerned with the manufacture of such an item but only if it will return to you a fair margin of profit and will move rapidly off your shelves.

We are sure that the quality will be high, but we want to be equally sure that the market for such a product is available and that our druggists will benefit in the sale of every package.

May we, therefore, ask that you spend a few of your valuable minutes filling out the enclosed questionnaire.

If you will be good enough to complete the questionnaire and return it to us in the self-addressed stamped envelope by June 5, we will be most appreciative.

Thank you very much.

Along with the "you" attitude in these letters, an attempt has been made to "personalize" the message. The stilted, hackneyed, and rather formal approach has been pretty well eliminated from the letters on the right. And a further interest in the respondent has been illustrated by enclosing a stamped envelope.

This factor, the "you" attitude in a cover letter, is probably the most important of the seven points which have been listed.

Statement of a Time Limit

Unfortunately it is human nature to delay doing little jobs and especially so if the work is for someone else. Placing the questionnaire in the bottom of the basket and glancing at it periodically with a statement, "I'll have to get at that one of these days," has occurred to every businessman a hundred times. More often than not a month passes, and this time his observation might be, "Well certainly, it's too late to fill this thing out now; I might as well throw it away." This unfortunate result may often be avoided if the researcher requests that the questionnaire be returned by a specific date.

Sending Out Results

Whether the respondent should be offered the results of a survey is quite a problem. If sending out the results is not too expensive from the point of view of printing, handling, and postage, and if it may result in good will and a greater number of responses, the effort is warranted. In such a case every effort should be made to make it easy for the respondent to request a copy. This may be accomplished by a simple statement at the bottom of the questionnaire or in the cover letter, "If you wish a copy of the results of this survey, please check here."

Assurance to Respondent That Information Will Be Kept Confidential

Quite often a prospective respondent will not return a questionnaire if he knows he can be identified. This is especially true when the questionnaire contains several statements which might be termed "personal." In such cases it is wise to include a sentence which states, "You may be sure that your comments will be kept completely confidential," or "Please do not sign the questionnaire; we are interested only in accurate answers."

The Personal Tone

The cover letter that gives its reader a warm, friendly feeling is not easy to write; but any effort it takes is well worth while. Try to

THE ILLINOIS SOCIETY OF

Certified Public Accountants

208 SOUTH LA SALLE STREET   CHICAGO 4   ANDOVER 3-3518

Dear Member:

    We are asking your help!

    One of the duties of your Committee on Public Service &
Information is to evaluate and improve the effectiveness of the
Society's communications to members. As a part of this
responsibility, we want to find out whether THE ILLINOIS
CERTIFIED PUBLIC ACCOUNTANT and the NEWSLETTER are serving
you as they should.

    <u>The enclosed questionnaire will take less than 5 minutes
of your time to fill out</u>. Your answers, however, will be worth
a great deal to us. They will help us determine whether these
two publications are useful to you . . . whether they are giving
you the type of information you want . . and if not, what type
of information you do want.

    The questionnaire is <u>not to be signed</u>. We are not in-
terested in <u>who</u> thinks what. Our main concern is that you
tell us honestly and frankly <u>what you really think</u> . . . not
what you might think we want to hear.

    We are asking that all questionnaires be filled out
and <u>mailed by December 10</u>. A return addressed envelope is
enclosed.

    In the hope that you will help, please accept our thanks
in advance.

                  Sincerely,

                  JOHN P. GOEDERT
                  Chairman, Committee on
                  Public Service & Information

Enclosures: 2

Persuasive Cover Letter for a Questionnaire (Courtesy of The Illinois Society of Certified Public Accountants)

eliminate stereotyped and hackneyed phrases. A letter with a personal tone will arouse the respondent's interest and he may really want to fill in the questionnaire—and as accurately as possible.

Note how the letter reproduced above follows the various suggestions which have been discussed.

TYPES OF QUESTIONNAIRES

It has been previously indicated that questionnaires and interviews are frequently used in many fields today. Because of this, it is valuable for the student to examine the various types in detail so that he may use them competently in the future.

1. *The Mail Questionnaire.* Inquiries are sent through the mail to selected groups of individuals. These surveys are usually accompanied by a cover letter or note of explanation.

2. *Personal Interview.* An interviewer asks a respondent a specific series of questions and notes the respondent's replies on a questionnaire form.

3. *Telephone Interview.* The respondent is reached by telephone; questions are asked; and the answers are recorded during the conversation.

4. *Qualitative or "Depth" Interview.* A situation where the researcher permits the respondent to discuss in a rather informal manner the broad general topic of the problem.

5. *Personal Observation.* A person or item is observed and the behavior recorded on a standardized form. An example of this might be observing just exactly what women will do in purchasing a package of cereal. One will examine the weight, another the price, still another the premiums offered, etc.

There are advantages and disadvantages in each of the methods. Selection of one and not another depends on the product investigated, the individual survey, or the type of analysis being attempted. Rather than attempt a discussion of each of the types, it might be wiser to list the commonly accepted advantages and disadvantages and then discuss each in detail.

Mail Questionnaires

ADVANTAGES

1. The cost is normally less than that for a personal interview.
2. Information may be secured easily from widely separated geographical points.
3. A trial survey may be run to test the validity of the questionnaire. This involves sending out a relatively small quantity of questionnaires. If the replies which are received are as expected, the major mailing may be made.
4. Respondents will usually answer more frankly than they will in a personal interview. This is because of the assurance of anonymity that often accompanies the questionnaire.
5. The bias of an interviewer does not enter.
6. Those who answer may put more thought into their replies because the questionnaire will usually be completed during leisure time rather than "on the run" as is the case in some personal interviews.
7. There is a greater possibility of having respondents answer who are not usually easily accessible to the interviewer (those in high income brackets, senior executives, major government officials).

DISADVANTAGES

1. It may be calculated that each response will cost 20 cents provided a 50 percent return is received. However, if the response drops to 10 percent, the cost per return rises fivefold, sending the cost to $1.00 per returned questionnaire.
2. Very often those who return completed questionnaires feel quite strongly on the subject under discussion; either for or against. The percentage of returns from individuals in the middle group is sometimes not as great as from those who have emphatic opinions on the topic.
3. Normally the questionnaire must be brief to be answered.
4. It is difficult to determine whether the addressee actually answered it by himself, conferred with his friends or family, or had someone else complete it for him.
5. It is difficult to secure qualitative (comments and discussion) replies on the questionnaire form.

6. It is not always true that the respondents are representative of the list to whom the mailing was made.

Personal Interview

ADVANTAGES

1. The questionnaire may be more lengthy than in the case of the mail survey.
2. Topics which are taboo in the mail questionnaire may be discussed by a competent interviewer. These may involve religion, earnings, political sympathies, etc.
3. A more accurate sampling of the field may be obtained by this method.
4. The competent interviewer can bring in an answer where a questionnaire would fail.

DISADVANTAGES

1. Bias on the part of the interviewer may enter into the results.
2. Personal interviews are costly.
3. Answers may not be accurate nor carefully thought through if the respondent is interviewed when his time is limited.
4. Gathering personal interviews is a time-consuming task when compared with the time necessary to bring in an equal number of replies by mail.
5. The interviewers must be competent and efficient, or else the results may be of little value.

An examination of this partial list of advantages and disadvantages of the mail questionnaire and the interview survey reveals that they are both valuable in specific situations. It is impossible to say that one is superior to the other; each has its place and should be utilized when necessary, or a combination of both should be undertaken for the best results.

Telephone Interview

ADVANTAGES

1. Cost, especially as compared to the personal interview, is low.
2. It may be easier to reach individuals not readily accessible to

the interviewer. This might be the case with busy business executives or individuals who work during the day. Such persons may be telephoned.

3. Data may be obtained in a rapid and simple fashion.

DISADVANTAGES

1. The number of questions must be limited to two, three, or four.
2. No question can intrude to the slightest degree into the respondent's personal affairs. An immediate refusal to answer might be forthcoming if personal facts are touched upon.
3. The possibility of having someone other than the desired respondent answer is obvious (child, visitor, etc.).
4. The questionnaire must be short because of the time limitation.
5. "Busy" signals and "no answers" present additional problems.

Qualitative or Depth Interviews

ADVANTAGES

1. The wording and number of questions may be varied according to the needs and background of the one being questioned.
2. A greater number of questions may be asked than in the mail questionnaire.
3. This type of interview is excellent for determining what motivates individuals, their attitudes, and their interpretation of specific situations.

DISADVANTAGES

1. It is quite expensive to conduct a personal interview.
2. A relatively long time factor is involved in each case.
3. Because of the above two points, the size of the sample is usually restricted.
4. The investigator must be exceedingly well qualified.

Observation

In the case of the personal observation, it is difficult to list advantages and disadvantages because this procedure is so often a part of one of the preceding four methods of gathering information. It is used for counting traffic, noting what type of window displays usually attracts shoppers, how frequently individual attention is directed to an outdoor advertisement, what apparently motivates a shopper to buy one item instead of a similar product packaged by a different firm, and other problems of this nature.

In the various advantages and disadvantages that have been listed above, the student will note some overlapping and duplication. Obviously many of the creditable points are applicable to several methods, and the same is true of some of the items of criticism. The researcher is wise, before initiating his project, to evaluate carefully which of these methods would be most beneficial to him in his gathering of information. It may be that a combination of several methods would be the best procedure to follow.

PREPARING THE QUESTIONNAIRE

In the first three methods listed, the mail questionnaire, the personal interview, and the telephone interview, a specific listing of questions is drawn up. The researcher may request the respondent to answer all or some of them; but the important point is that there are specific questions to guide and control the interview.

Persons well acquainted with many avenues of research maintain that the composition of a *good* questionnaire is a most difficult task. There are so many items to consider: How many and how long should the questions be? Are the meanings of the questions clear? Are the questions "too personal"? How should the form be made up? Is every single word in every single question correctly chosen in reference to the prospective respondent? Etc.

It is quite impossible to arrange a complete list of suggestions for making up a questionnaire; but in the following pages a few notes have been made which may aid the report writer.

Suggestions for Formulating Questions

1. *The arrangement of questions should be logical and orderly.* The successful questionnaire has its questions arranged carefully so that respondents will be able to make their replies easily and without confusion. There is little logic in asking the respondent what type of auto tires he prefers in question four, only to determine by question nine that he doesn't own a car. Nor is there any reason to ask him to list his academic degrees in question three, if

inquiry number seven determines that he did not attend college. Such haphazard arrangement only encourages the individual to throw the questionnaire aside.

There is some psychological advantage in asking an easy-to-answer question in the beginning. If the respondent finds that it takes no great effort on his part to answer the first few questions, he will probably continue to work to the end. However, if those first few questions cause him difficulty, he may very well put the whole thing aside as being too much trouble. This presents a problem: Shall easy-to-answer questions be placed early in the questionnaire even if they are not in their most logical order? The type of project and the nature of the questionnaire will determine the answer.

2. *There should be good transition between the questions and, if possible, parallel wording.* Both of these factors will aid the respondent in "swinging along" from one sentence to another. With good transition he easily sees the connection between the questions and is interested in following them through to a logical end. Parallel wording actually makes it easier for him to understand the questions and thus answer them. Notice the similar beginnings in the first few words of the following questions and how they aid the respondent in "gliding" from one to another.

a. Have you purchased automobile tires in the past two years?
b. Have you checked the relative merits of various tire brands on the market in the past two years?
c. Have you suggested a specific brand of automobile tires to a friend in the past two years?

3. *Each question should be concerned with one factor only.* Where there is more than one major thought in a question, the respondent may misinterpret the meaning or answer with a mental reservation that is due to the secondary point.

"Do you prefer automatic transmissions in low-priced cars at a slight extra charge?"

In this particular question there are three factors to contend with: whether or not the respondent prefers automatic transmissions, low-priced cars, and extra charge. It may be that he does prefer automatic transmissions, but not in low-priced cars. Or it may be that he does not prefer low-priced cars in general, with or without automatic transmissions. And as for the extra charge, the qualifications on that point are almost innumerable. Of course, it is possible that the question may be listed in different ways which would recognize the various possible interpretations. The problem can be solved much more simply by asking each one of the three questions separately and then giving the respondent several choices from which he can make his preference known.

4. *The questionnaire should be easy to answer.* The actual content, wording, and number of questions may, if handled properly, make the questionnaire a simple task to complete. Too many questions should not be asked. Usually 15 to 20 are the maximum. However, there have been much more extensive questionnaires, cleverly constructed and laid out, which have received a very satisfactory return.

A common device is to set up several questions under one arabic numeral with subletters.

1. What style of residence do you prefer? (Check one.)

_____Cape Cod   _____Georgian   _____Other

_____Ranch style   _____Colonial

a. Do you prefer a basement in your home?

_____Yes   _____No   _____No preference

b. What type of fuel do you prefer to use in your heating system? (Check one.)

_____Gas   _____Coal   _____Oil   _____Other

With this method one can *list* 10 questions but actually ask 30 to 50. On the whole, however, you should not ask the respondent to expend too much of his time in completing a questionnaire.

Another way you can help him is to make the questions short and concise. Then, too, the researcher will do well to remember that his choice of words will frequently determine how easily the questions may be interpreted.

To send out a questionnaire to a typical cross section in an urban center and use such terms as depreciation, appreciation of money, sinking funds, and amortization of securities is foolhardy. The possibilities of the questions being misinterpreted and misunderstood are tremendous. If the sample being tested is made up of professional groups, the researcher can often score a valuable point for himself by using the terminology in the field. Trained engineers, physicians, and accountants will readily understand a vocabulary common to their area of specialization and probably feel that the researcher is working on a legitimate topic and knows whereof he speaks.

5. *Words with an emotional or colored connotation should be*

avoided. The use of such words as "liberal," "capitalism," "social-ism," "red," "isolationism," and a great many others concerned with politics, morals, and sex should be chosen with discretion.

6. *Questions should not be ambiguous.* The structure of the sentences, as well as the word choice, should permit no opportunity for misinterpretation on the part of the respondent. A question like "What kind of a car do you prefer?" may have the respondent asking, "Do they mean sedan, coupe, or convertible, or are they trying to find out whether I like a Ford, Pontiac, or Buick? Or perhaps it is the color they are after?" The question could be much more accurately phrased in such a manner as this:

What type of car model do you prefer? (Choose one.)
_____Sedan   _____Station wagon
_____Convertible   _____Other
_____Coupe

7. *Leading questions should not be asked.* Sometimes it is quite difficult for the researcher himself to recognize questions as leading. However, anyone who is competent in the field of questionnaire construction may serve to check what has been made up. Often the researcher is so close to the problem that he "reads into" his question the interpretation he hopes his respondent will draw. To make up intentionally leading questions is completely unethical, and the results obtained from such a questionnaire will only prove inaccurate and invalid.

To include the name of one brand item and exclude all others may lead the respondent to an answer he might not have offered. An example of this might be, "Have you purchased any General American Home Appliances in the last five years?" Of course, the question might be acceptable if the survey is concerned only with one company. Other examples which may lead the respondent to a specific answer because of pride or social position are found in these questions: "Do you buy the best cuts of meat for your week-end menu?" "Which of the best sellers listed below have you read?" "When attending plays, do you usually buy seats on the main floor?" In cases like these the respondent will often indicate biased and even fallacious answers. Care should be taken to avoid such situations.

The respondent may also be led into answers when the questions list only *some* of the possibilities. To inquire which type of face soap she prefers and then list only five brands will normally lead the respondent to check one of those suggested. This situation may be partially alleviated by putting a sixth choice labeled "other."

8. *If possible, "skip-and-jump" or involved rating questions should not be asked.* For the average person the "skip-and-jump" type of question is most difficult to follow and to comprehend. An example of such a question is one that reads, "If you have answered number 5 with a 'Yes' then skip numbers 7 and 8 and answer 9 and 10. If you have answered number 5 with a 'No,' answer numbers 7 and 8 and skip 9 and 10." It would have to be a most unusual situation for a respondent to answer questions of that nature willingly. It is equally unreasonable to ask the respondent to "Rate from numbers 1 to 10, in order of preference, the following factors." If the researcher tries to set up a complete list with 20 or 30 items to rate, the answers will be still more inaccurate. A certain amount of guessing will result and accuracy will be lost.

Sometimes the respondent is asked to assign percentage ratings to his own activities or to his expenditure of money or time. "What percentage of the day do you spend in leisure-time activities?" "What percentage of your yearly income is assigned for the purchase of newspapers, magazines, journals, and books?" On the average, answers to questions of this nature can only be guessed. And if the results are not accurate, the basic attribute of a good questionnaire is lost.

9. *In general, personal questions should not be asked.* If at all possible, the questionnaire should not contain inquiries that are concerned with age, income, sex habits, religion, church attendance or affiliation, the use of liquor, and points of similar nature. Many individuals will simply point out that "the answer is none of your business" and file the questionnaire in the wastebasket. However, the answers to some of these are sometimes extremely important. In the case of age and income, bracketed areas may be used:

Please indicate your average yearly income. (Check one.)
$2,000–$3,999 _____
4,000– 5,999 _____
6,000– 7,999 _____
8,000– 9,999 _____
Over $10,000 _____

In line with this discussion, many research directors have emphatically stated that the best way to get answers to personal questions is to ask them directly without subterfuge and without the type of question that permits an inference of the answer. There is much merit to this suggestion, but, like so many factors thus far commented on, the most important consideration is "who is the respondent?" Knowledge of that fact will usually lead one to a decision on whether or not or how a personal type of question should be presented.

10. *Questions involving memory or mathematical computations should be avoided.* Asking the respondent questions based on his memory is quite unfair, especially when the matter is of relatively minor importance. "At what age did you begin smoking?" "How often in the last two years have you purchased flowers from a florist?"

The desirability of asking questions involving mathematics or computations has already been touched on in the discussion on percentages. To ask a person for a figure which is indicative of his "expenditures for charity, less the amount he contributed to his church" is, under ordinary circumstances, unwise. Or to ask him how much he spent on any activity over a period of years not only involves the factor of memory but, of course, requires some computation. A question looking into the future should, if possible, be avoided. "How much do you expect to spend on recreational activities next year?"

11. *"Blanket-type" words should be avoided.* This point, in some respects, goes back to the discussion on word choice. Nevertheless, it is an error so common in the construction of questionnaires that it deserves special consideration. Words, or even questions, with broad general meaning or interpretation should be avoided. "Have you recently used tea?" "Do you expect to purchase a car in the near future?" "Do you occasionally purchase powdered dentifrice?"

In the first, the meaning of "recently" will vary from respondent to respondent. And in the second, he will ask, "What do you mean by 'the near future'?" And in the last, the meaning of "occasionally" may be open to discussion.

AUXILIARIES TO THE QUESTIONNAIRE

Several items may be termed auxiliaries to a standard questionnaire. The employment of them or even some of them is frequently

R·L·POLK & CO.

PUBLISHERS

Polk Building · 431 Howard Street · Detroit 31. Michigan

To the Lady
Of the House

Dear Madam:

      May we ask a favor?

          We have been asked by a client to gather some information on the use of detergents for washing woolens and other garments.

          Your answers to the attached questions are very important because you are part of the representative sample of people we are asking. The survey is anonymous, so that these answers are in confidence.

          Would you take just a moment to do this, right now if you possibly can?

          There is a postage paid envelope enclosed for your reply. Thank you very much for the courtesy.

                    Yours very truly,

                    R. L. Polk & Co.

                    H. H. Geddes
                    Director
HHG/eb   Research Department

P. S. The dime is a token of our appreciation of your help.

Questionnaire Cover Letter with Premium (Courtesy of R. L. Polk & Co.)

found to be of value in bringing in returns. The most common auxiliary, the cover letter, has already been discussed in some detail.

Very often the inclusion of a premium with the questionnaire will also help increase returns. In recent years, the premium has often been a discount coupon which may be applied on the purchase price of a product. Not uncommon also is the enclosing of money with an attached statement of some humor that contains the suggestion for its use.[4]

Cartoons on either the cover letter or bordering the questionnaire may induce an individual to take a rather light-hearted view of the situation and so complete the questionnaire. The humorous type of cartoon was used with a great deal of success by the Corning Glass Company.[5]

The use of serious cartoons, drawings, or illustrations will also increase the percentage of returns. This device often aids the respondent in understanding the question and consequently lessens the work that he is required to do. The Customer Research Division of General Motors has so successfully used this device that their questionnaires may frequently run an unusually large number of pages (24) for a questionnaire and still bring in a highly favorable percentage of responses.

On the other hand, it is interesting to note the comments of an expert on this topic. Mr. Thomas E. Ryan, Research Manager for *Time* Magazine, said:

> Contrary to most literature in the field, it has been our finding that a very plain questionnaire (that is, without color, illustration, or "cute" copy) pulls the highest return from the groups we measure. I rationalize this finding on the basis that an intelligent person is willing to give a few minutes of his time in furnishing information which he

---

[4] Crowell-Collier Publishing Company included a shiny quarter dollar in an envelope with its questionnaire several years ago. In tabulating the results, Mr. R. Robinson, Director of Research for the company, pointed out that they received 1000 replies out of 1666 questionnaires which were mailed (60 percent response). When they did not include the quarter, there was a response of 1000 out of 6664 mailed (15 percent response). Where the quarter was used, each response cost 65 cents; where it was not employed, each response cost 70 cents. Ray Robinson, "Five Features Help This Mail Questionnaire," *Printers' Ink,* February 22, 1946.

[5] "Cartoons Jump Returns on Business Questionnaires," *Printers' Ink,* January 16, 1948.

All together (including yourself), how many people in your home read TIME?

Children (under 18) _____   Men _____   Women _____

Is your copy of TIME passed along to others outside your home?   Yes ☐   No ☐

If "yes," how many persons do you estimate read your copy of TIME outside your home?

Children (under 18) _____   Men _____   Women _____

Do you ever refer to items from TIME in conversation with friends and acquaintances?

Yes ☐   No ☐

If "yes," how often is this likely to happen?   Frequently ☐

Occasionally ☐

Very seldom ☐

what sort of an impression does your mention of TIME seem to make? _____

_____

Just About You and Your Family

What is your full name? _____

Are you.. a man? ☐ or a woman? ☐

About how old are you?.............................. _____ years

Have you lived in your present hometown most of your life?   Yes ☐   No ☐

If "no," for how many years have you lived in your present town?   _____ years

in what town (city) and state did you spend most of your growing-up years? _____

_____

What schools have you attended? (Please list names of schools) <u>Grammar schools</u> _____

_____ <u>High schools</u> _____

_____ <u>Colleges</u> _____

_____

Do you hold any bachelor's or advanced college degrees?   Yes ☐   No ☐

If "yes," what degrees do you hold?   _____

Are you...................................... married?   ☐

single?   ☐

widowed, separated, divorced?   ☐

One page from a Five-Page Time Magazine Questionnaire Entitled "Portrait of a Time Magazine Subscriber" (Courtesy of Time)

probably considers valuable if, from the appearance of the request, the information is necessary and will be used for a serious purpose.[6]

A duplicate questionnaire, sent along with the original, which the respondent may keep in his file, may also be termed an auxiliary. Usually, the researcher will point out that if the respondent desires a copy of the findings, he may then compare his answers on the duplicate questionnaire with the tabulated results.

PHYSICAL LAYOUT OF THE QUESTIONNAIRE

The science of "packaging" has grown tremendously, and everyone is well aware of how important the appearance of a product is in its sale. Inasmuch as some measure of selling is involved with a questionnaire, its physical appearance is also very important. The questionnaire that is "crowded" on the page, carelessly mimeographed, and unattractively folded is well on its way to the wastebasket.

The questionnaire should be printed on a good grade of paper; yellow and pink seem to bring especially good results. The size of type should be carefully chosen; the questions should not be crowded together; generous use of "white space" gives the impression of few questions and plenty of room to answer.

If "please comment" questions are used, adequate space should be provided so that the respondent may write out his answer completely.

If possible, include sketches, pictures, or diagrams to help make the problem easier for the respondent to grasp.

In the matter of individual questions, the placement of the choices is important. If a list is given, the items at or near the top are most likely to be chosen. If they are set up in a horizontal instead of vertical fashion, the answers may be more accurate.

Which one of the sports listed below do you now engage in most frequently?

_____Tennis   _____Golf   _____Baseball
_____Fishing   _____Bowling   _____Handball

As for the dimensions of the questionnaire, there seems to be a wide variety of acceptable sizes. Many firms use the booklet form, others the standard 8″ x 11″ size, and still others use a type which

[6] Letter from Mr. Thomas E. Ryan, Market Research Manager of *Time* Magazine, to the author.

may be folded and sealed within itself so that the cover becomes the front of an envelope.

LARGE-SCALE USE OF QUESTIONNAIRES IN PRACTICE

Many large corporations have been using a variety of surveys over the years. Their purpose is to determine what the American buyer wants in his car, his home, his refrigerator, his clothes. One firm that has developed an outstanding research department is General Motors.

At General Motors some 20 to 30 surveys are conducted each year by the customer research staff. Their function is to determine what the motorist likes and dislikes in his car. To do that, mail questionnaires are usually employed, and they bring in anywhere from 2,000 to 5,000 returns each day and sometimes as many as 2,000,000 replies in one year!

Every question and questionnaire is examined and reëxamined before it is accepted. The questionnaires are very informal and use the language of Mr. Average Motorist: "leg room," "wraparound bumpers," "pick-up," etc. Attention to the question is secured by excellent sketches and illustrations and a variety of type styles: headlines, script, italics, boldface, marginal comments, and footnotes.

The research departments of other major automotive manufacturers, such as Ford or Chrysler, also carry through similar programs, as do most large corporations which manufacture products for consumers. The general consensus is that the questionnaire is an effective means of soliciting desired information. In the words of Mr. Rex Tullsen,

Perhaps the best evidence that the information developed by this staff—General Motors Research Staff—is considered of value by the executives is in the fact that we have been operating nearly a score of years, during which time a considerable sum of money has been expended . . . and the results of our studies have continued to justify the cost of getting this information.[7]

Careful research, based on surveys, will invariably result in profitable answers to the report writer. As the General Motors

[7] Letter to the author from Mr. Rex Tullsen, General Motors Customer Research Staff.

Covers of Questionnaires Sent to Motorists (Courtesy of General Motors
Corporation and Chrysler Corporation)

Research Department states, "An ear to the ground, an eye to the future." One way, as noted above, General Motors keeps that "eye on the future" is through customer research. In a letter to this author, G.M. explained its objectives and procedures in this fashion:

. . . As has been fairly evident for many years, the management of General Motors is very consumer conscious, and goes to considerable trouble to find out what people want, and then to provide the products that will suit their needs and desires. This applies not only to automobiles, but to practically all of the products we make, even down to such dull and unglamorous things as spark plugs.

We use a number of different methods to gather information. One that we use most extensively is the mailed questionnaire. This has been most effective for our own particular purposes. For one thing, we are able to select our "audience" by the make of car owned, year model, geographic location, etc. This is possible because the R. L. Polk Company compiles registration lists of all cars in the country. Thus we can get whatever kind of a sample we want. . . .

Sometimes the question arises as to just how many answers are needed to be sure that they are truly representative of the whole. That depends on a number of things, including the subject matter, the type of questions being asked, and the breakdowns that may be required. On this latter point a thing that is sometimes overlooked is that the total answers in a survey may be entirely adequate for a nation-wide picture, but completely inadequate if attempts are made to break the results down by areas, size of community, or whatever other separations might be desired.

By using mailed questionnaires we are able to ask everyone who receives one exactly the same questions in exactly the same way. Of course, we have to be very careful ahead of time to be sure that the questions are properly phrased so that everyone will interpret them in the same way, and in this respect we have a sort of motto that we use as a guiding principle. It goes like this—"It is not enough that a thing can be understood—it must be so clear that it simply cannot be MISunderstood."

A great many surveys are conducted through the means of personal interviews, and there are certain types of information which cannot be very well obtained any other way. Some companies use this method exclusively, with satisfactory results. As a matter of fact, we make considerable use of this method at auto shows to get public reactions to the new models before people have had a chance to buy them. . . .

In conducting any consumer surveys, it should be recognized that there are certain limitations—certain things that we cannot hope to find out with any degree of accuracy or dependability.

In our own case we consider the average car owner as an expert on the USE of the product, and it is in that area that we seek his opinions. . . .

You'd probably find it interesting to read through a batch of these questionnaires that have been returned. A common characteristic is that people apparently take considerable time and care in filling them out, because it is very seldom that anyone goes right down the line checking everything good, or even fair or poor. The response is a deliberative, thoughtful one, which makes it that much more valuable to us. . . .

A relatively new term has come into the picture recently—motivation research. Generally speaking, people doing this type of research attempt to analyze, in considerable detail, the buying habits of a relatively small number of people, and from that, reach conclusions as to why people buy, what approaches appeal to them, etc. In some cases this type of information has proved very helpful, but again there are pitfalls in case the sample is too small, or the conclusions inaccurate. Indirectly, we have been doing almost the same thing in every survey we do.

Our method of accomplishing it is to leave lots of room for people to write down any comments they may care to make. The cooperation we get on this point is exceptionally good; many of those who answer, write at great length about their viewpoints, their experiences, their reasons for liking or disliking various features, etc. When these are tabulated—an arduous job—it is almost equivalent to thousands of "Depth interviews" which would take infinitely longer to do. . . .

Naturally, we can't hope to get the final answer because public tastes are in a constant state of change. But to the extent that we can find out what they like, to that extent we can do a better job of giving people what they want—and incidentally, make it that much easier to sell the products that we make.[8]

INTERVIEWS AS A SOURCE OF INFORMATION

As has already been noted, interviews are quite frequently divided into three groups; the formal interview that closely follows a printed questionnaire, the qualitative (or depth) interview where broad general topics are discussed for the purpose of gathering attitudes and preferences, and the telephone interview.

In the first two cases, it is wise to communicate with the prospective respondent prior to the time of the interview. The knowledge

[8] Letter from General Motors Customer Research Staff to the author.

that he is to be interviewed usually prepares him for the general subject matter which is to be discussed and permits him to reserve a block of time for the interviewer. Many of the attributes of such a letter are similar to those that have already been reviewed in the discussion of the cover letter to the questionnaire.

Qualities of the Interviewer

Whether the interview that is to be conducted is of the formal or qualitative type, the competence of the interviewer is necessarily of primary importance. The interviewer should possess initiative and a pleasant personality; he should be objective, persistent, and tactful; and his appearance and humor should be excellent. These are a few of the essential qualities of the interviewer who questions all groups of people. But those individuals who must gather data from persons in professional fields or high executive position must possess further qualities.

If the interviewer is working in a specific field, such as the physical or biological sciences, he obviously must be fairly familiar with that area of knowledge, and he must possess an adequate vocabulary. He must be alert and able to elicit complete answers from individuals whose time is precious.

A magazine article concerned with improving interviewing techniques lists twelve factors which the writer of the article felt were important. Some of those mentioned were that the instructions to the interviewers should be complete and accurate, that the interviewer be told the complete purpose of the survey and the results, that the organization conducting the survey not expect the interviewer to complete an impossible number of calls or to secure answers to unfair questions, that the questionnaire itself which the interviewer uses must be good, and that standards for selecting interviewers and field men must be kept very high.[9]

Many firms find that perhaps the best solution to the problem of securing competent interviewers is to first hire persons with the necessary physical and mental attributes and then train them in the methods, goals, and work of the specific organization. This procedure tends to make the individual a specialist in the specific field. Surely an interviewer should not work on the problems of Munchie

[9] A. S. Bennett, "12 Ways to Improve Field Research," *Advertising and Selling,* December, 1947.

Breakfast Foods one week and bridge construction the next without careful preparation. Firms that conduct surveys for all "comers" find it necessary to switch from field to field. In these cases it is strongly recommended that the interviewer receive sufficient training to familiarize himself with the topic under consideration.

Conducting the Interview

The basis for a good formal interview is the questionnaire which the interviewer follows. The many factors which were suggested as qualities for the good mail questionnaire earlier in this chapter hold true in this case without exception.

The interviewer should begin his discussion with his name and that of his company, the purpose of the survey, and what part the respondent plays in the project. The questions themselves should then follow quickly and concisely. And although the interviewer should be a good listener, he should also retain control of the discussion at all times. Wordy digressions on the part of the respondent are valueless as a source of information and materially increase the cost of the individual interviews held. In such cases, tact is especially necessary in pointing out that the discussion should revolve around the respondent's preference in automobile tires and not the health of Aunt Emma. It goes without saying that the interviewer's attitude should be one of deep interest in the responses, and he should not appear to be merely completing an assigned chore.

Experience through the years has indicated to the Bureau of the Census of the Department of Commerce the most expedient methods for handling a large-scale survey. Because the survey will be only as good as the interviewers who conduct it, the Bureau has issued a variety of training manuals, instructional film strips, and directives to its interviewers and enumerators. The basic plan of training, as outlined in a letter to the author, follows this general procedure:

1. General orientation to the purpose of the survey or census.
2. Step by step explanation of the questions to be asked. Explanations of the concepts and definitions implicit or explicit in each question, and of the type of information sought. The instructor usually covers each point with reference to the manual, which contains a detailed explanation of each question, and may supplement the instruction with the use of film strips.
3. The technique of interviewing. In some of our training each inter-

viewer has an opportunity to fill out questionnaires in a "mock" interview or respond to a recorded interview situation. Film strips may also be used for further elaboration. . . .

4. How to canvass an assigned area, how to identify the persons or units within the scope of the survey, and how to determine which questions are to be asked. . . .

5. The recording of entries, order of asking questions, and acceptability of information offered by the respondent. The manuals are generally quite detailed on these points. . . .[10]

Note Taking During the Interview

Taking notes during the interview often becomes a problem for the researcher. In the case where the survey is based on twelve concise questions, the interviewer simply makes checks or enters a word or two on his interview form (or "schedule" as it is sometimes called) as he asks his questions. In those cases where it is necessary to draw forth comments which must be recorded or which will lead the interviewer to evaluate attitudes or preferences on the problem, some difficulties may arise. Most people have a natural tendency to become self-conscious when they perceive an individual assiduously recording their statements. Their replies are hesitant, their statements are chosen with great care, and, on the whole, they inhibit themselves.

These factors alone may give the interviewer replies which are not accurate. On the other hand, should a qualitative interview be conducted without the researcher taking notes? After the interview is over, can he accurately record the respondent's feelings without including such bias as he (the interviewer) possesses on the topic?

It is often suggested that when a general, overall viewpoint from the respondent is desired, the interviewer should wait until the discussion has been closed and then note his findings.

If the interviewer records answers during the discussion, he should not do it so completely as to be required to ask the respondent to repeat answers or "slow down so I can get it on paper."

It is sometimes suggested that partial answers be recorded on small pads of paper or in little notebooks or on other material that does not appear "official." When this is done, the interviewer

---

[10] Letter to the author from Morris H. Hansen, Assistant Director for Statistical Standards, Bureau of the Census.

can easily extend his findings from his brief and informal notes when the discussion has closed. Another idea that can be used with success is to have a stenographer accompany the interviewer. The former takes a seat in the corner of the room out of line of vision of the interviewer and the respondent and then proceeds to take stenographic notes on the discussion. The stenographer in such cases must be alert and sufficiently well trained to recognize material that should be recorded and that which should not.[11] And, of course, she should never interrupt with "What was that again?"

Setting up and using a tape recorder has also proved to be an excellent device for securing interview data. With the excellent machines now available, there is almost no recording noise to disturb the interview. Reels of tape that will run an hour or more are available as well as tape recorders that take up as little space as a hand camera.

Thus the method of recording data while interviewing should be selected with great care, and the primary considerations should always be: What type of interview is it? How long will it take? Who is the respondent?

Auxiliary Materials of the Interview

Here, as in the mail questionnaire, a few auxiliary items may improve the results of the findings. The letter of introduction which preceded the interview may be classed as an auxiliary, and proper identification cards or badges also help. Where there are several possible answers to a question, the respondent is often aided if he is handed a card on which the possibilities are listed, so that he is not forced to remember the various alternates that are presented. Where the interviewer is working on a problem that requires a response from memory, such as an advertisement of a product, an individual reproduction placed in the hands of the respondent is valuable. Where tangible items such as shoes or machinery are the topic, cutaway or miniature models should be available. Samples of the product, where feasible, also aid in gaining a response if presented at the beginning of the interview. Other auxiliaries to aid in the interview may be used if they will improve the results.

---

[11] This method was employed with success by some members of the U.S. Army Historical Section in Europe immediately after the termination of World War II. It was used in discussion of tactical and logistical problems with high echelon commanders of both the American and German armies.

OTHER PRIMARY SOURCES OF INFORMATION

In writing his report, the researcher undoubtedly will gather a great deal of information from the sources suggested above. Probably, however, he will find at least an equal fund of knowledge contained in various company records, manuscripts, and miscellaneous documents which have not been published.

Company Records

Company files may prove to be rich mines of information. It is in these records that the report writer can often find material that will assist him in his research. Of course, it is difficult to suggest methods for examining company records. What data are retained and how they are filed differ from one company to another. All that can be said is that the report writer should first familiarize himself with the company's filing system; the broad general headings that are used; what type of documents have been retained and what type destroyed; and what vital records exist from earlier surveys. With his knowledge of these facts, the researcher may determine if *somewhere* in company records there are data that will prove of value to him. Once the writer has determined that the company files can aid him, then he enters into their examination, using the accepted research techniques.

Miscellaneous Sources

Interviews with long-service employees and elderly officers of the firm frequently prove of value as sources of information. Discussion with customers or stockholders may give the researcher points of view from the "other side of the fence." But in both of these cases, the information may be colored by the long years of association with the company and perhaps may be heavily opinionated.

Not infrequently, visits to city historical associations, city chambers of commerce, and coöperating companies will also reveal data of value. Wherever the report writer must examine records that go back into the years, he must make allowances for economic, social, and political differences of the times.

The various primary sources that have been suggested in this chapter are, to a large extent, just the beginning. Once again, the report writer is reminded that his individual problem will determine his steps in research. The suggestions given, however, may be adequate to start him on the road toward the solution to his problems.

QUESTIONS FOR DISCUSSION

I. Answer the following questions as completely as possible.
1. What is meant by the term *sample* in research techniques? Cite an example.
2. Define and illustrate a *stratified sample*.
3. Secure the definitions for four different types of samples using a source other than this text. Cite the name of the source.
4. What is meant by the term *universe* as used in research techniques?
5. Assume that you have been assigned to write a research report on the effectiveness and value of advertising major kitchen appliances in magazines such as the *Ladies' Home Journal* and *Good Housekeeping*. You have decided to send questionnaires to a sample of the subscribers. Prepare the cover letter that will accompany your questionnaire. (Do not prepare the questionnaire.)
6. One of the suggested attributes of a good cover letter is the "you" attitude. Prepare a brief report on the "you" attitude by referring to several business English texts and/or magazine articles. Note your sources.
7. List the various types of questionnaires and interviews with which you are familiar, and then note three specific survey situations for each.
8. In the use of the mail questionnaire, it is sometimes said that an advantage is "The cost is normally less than that for a personal interview." Point out a situation where the cost might be higher than in a personal interview.
9. If you know your prospective respondents' social, economic, and educational levels, what specific factors should be taken into account when designing the questionnaire?
10. Why is it easier, and what principles must be followed, to secure answers on "taboo topics" (religion, money, sex, etc.) in an interview as opposed to a mail questionnaire?

II. Answer the following questions as completely as possible.
1. Would you recommend a telephone interview survey for a company which is interested in determining attitudes toward a political candidate? Why?

2. Investigate and write a brief report on a company that determines television program preferences through telephone interviews.

3. Your problem is whether or not you should place "easy-to-answer" questions first in the questionnaire. These questions are out of logical order. Defend your position or explain.

4. What criticism can you offer on the following question: "Do you prefer high fidelity recordings on a 33⅓ rpm record of symphonies or operas?" How would you revise it?

5. What factors should be considered in the physical appearance of a questionnaire?

6. List ten words that you frequently see used in newspapers or magazines that have strong emotional connotations in addition to their basic meanings.

7. What criticism can you offer of this question? "When a salesman presents two shirts, one for $5.00 and one for $7.50, do you select the more expensive one, feeling that the higher quality will compensate for the additional cost?"

8. Make up three questions that contain "blanket-type" words.

9. A recent questionnaire sent to office managers of large firms included a crisp dollar bill with the suggestion that the "wampum be used for a Deluxe Havana cigar." Do you feel that the recipient would be pleased and desirous of responding or that he would be irked by what he might consider a bribe for his services? Discuss.

10. Secure a mail questionnaire and offer a criticism of its (a) appearance and (b) make-up of the questions. Note all favorable and unfavorable aspects. If you cannot secure an actual questionnaire, you may wish to evaluate one that is reproduced in a marketing or management textbook.

III. Comment on the following cover letters to questionnaires.

1. Dear Sir:

At the present time I am a student in East Illinois State College where I am enrolled in a course in auditing. To secure credit for this course, I must write a paper concerned with auditing procedures of a large corporation. I have therefore chosen your company, and as you can see, I am badly in need of your help.

I have enclosed a questionnaire which I hope you will not discard. On the contrary, I hope you will complete it if you have time and return it to me.

Thanking you in advance for the trouble and imposition on your time.

2. Dear Customer:

Here at Excello office supply corporation, we periodically examine the services we offer our customers. Among the most important of these services are our delivery procedures to you and our other valued friends.

We are, of course, interested in getting merchandise to you quickly, efficiently, and in perfect condition. We have therefore undertaken to examine our methods of packaging and delivering your merchandise.

A few brief questions have been printed on the attached page. It will only take you a few minutes to check the appropriate boxes. And if you will add any relevant comments in the spaces provided, we will be most appreciative.

Because we expect to complete all necessary changes by the beginning of next month, may we ask that you return the questionnaire no later than September 20.

Our desire is to improve our service to you; toward that end, therefore, will you complete the questionnaire today.

Thank you.

3. Dear Former Student:

The School of Business is completing a survey of occupations, income, etc., presently enjoyed by all persons who have received degrees in the last five years from this University.

Please complete the 3-page questionnaire enclosed and return.

Hoping to hear from you.

4. Dear Madame:

You, like all American home makers, are interested in making your home an attractive, comfortable, and enjoyable place for your family.

The makers of Excello Soap know exactly how you folks feel, and we want to help you make *your* home the best in the city. We have, therefore, tried to help by sending you a giant 3-pound package of Excello Flakes which you will find to be excellent to use in a standard or automatic washer, or for cleaning dishes, floors, or walls.

We do hope you will enjoy using this FREE package, but there is a little favor we would like to have you do for us.

Enclosed with this letter is a brief questionnaire concerned with Excello Soap Flakes. Will you please answer the questions and return when completed. Further directions for answering will be found at the top of the questionnaire.

IV. Offer your criticism on the two questionnaires which follow.
  1. (The following questionnaire was sent to the personnel directors of 20 large corporations in an effort to learn about company problems concerning recruitment, training, and retention of female workers.)

    a. Do you secure many of your female employees through the classified "ad" section of the local newspaper?

                                                  Yes   No

    b. Do you frequently use the local school placement bureaus to secure women employees?

                                                  Yes   No

    c. Does your company have a training division for employees?

                                                  Yes   No

    d. What is the average number of months that women employees have been with your company?

    e. Do women who work in the offices remain with the company longer than women who work in the factory? If so, how many months more?

    f. Are many women employees secured through recommendations by other employees?

                                                  Yes   No

    g. What percentages of women employees have _____, _____, _____
              Elementary High school College
    education?

    h. Has your company experienced any shortage among women employees in 1959?

                                                  Yes   No

    i. Do your salaries compare____favorably or____unfavorably with similar industries?

    j. Explain company policies designed to keep female employees' morale high and attitudes toward the company favorable.

_____

_____

_____

2. (The following questionnaire was sent to owners of automobiles in an effort to determine what brand of gasoline they
   purchased, why they bought one brand and not another, and
   what motivated them in making purchases.)

   a. What is the name of your car?   _____
   b. What *year* model is your car?   _____
   c. What model type is your car (sedan,
      coupe, station wagon, etc.)?   _____
   d. What type of gasoline do you purchase in the various
      seasons of the year? Please check below for each season.

	Ethyl	*Regular*
Summer	_____	_____
Fall	_____	_____
Winter	_____	_____
Spring	_____	_____

   e. When you need gasoline do you (check one)
      _____stop at the first station you encounter?
      _____stop at any one of two or three brand stations?
      _____stop at a station that handles the *specific* brand you
           prefer?
   f. If you prefer one specific brand of gasoline, please list the
      brand name. _____
   g. If you cannot conveniently purchase that one brand, what
      will you select as the next most desirable brand? _____
      _____

   h. Please check the reason(s) (or fill in the reasons) why
      you prefer the gasoline listed in question f.
      _____It is cheaper.
      _____I receive free premium tickets or stamps.
      _____My car runs better when I use it.
      _____The service station employees of that company are
           very courteous.
      _____My car gets more miles per gallon when I use it.
      _____The service station employees of that company are
           more competent.
      Other reason(s) _____
      _____
      _____

   (If you do not buy one specific brand of gasoline consistently,
   skip all questions that follow.)

   i. Do you buy oil for your car at the same

station where you consistently purchase
, your gasoline?

	Yes	No

j. If not, why not? _____

_____

k. Do you have minor mechanical work
(such as brake or carburetor adjusting,
motor tune-up, head lamp repair, etc.)
done at the station where you consistently
purchase gasoline?

	Yes	No

l. If not, why not? _____

_____

PLEASE RETURN THIS QUESTIONNAIRE
NO LATER THAN DECEMBER 5

V. Write the cover letter and questionnaire for each of the following
problems.

1. Assume that you are the registrar of a large urban university.
You are interested in attempting to discover if those students
who work part time and carry a full load of courses receive
higher or lower grades and have a higher or lower grade point
average than those students who carry a full load but do *not*
work part time. You will survey the entire junior and senior
classes.

2. As a member of the research staff of WRXR TV you are attempting to find out how successful a documentary program
in American history has proved to be. The program has appeared at 8:30 P.M. every Thursday evening for the past ten
weeks. It is sponsored by a local dairy firm. Your survey
sample has been carefully selected from among the names
which appear on the registered voters' lists. The city has a
population of 1,200,000.

3. Your management firm has been engaged by the Michigan
Machine Products Corporation to examine employee morale
and opinions toward the company. The plant is relatively
new and modern, the wages compare favorably with industry
in general, and production is running at a high level. Nevertheless, there seems to be a feeling of resentment on the part
of the employees toward management and a generally low level
of employee morale. You have selected a proper ratio of employees from the groups of skilled, unskilled, office, and factory to survey. Prepare *one* cover letter and questionnaire to
serve all groups.

Chapter 4

Organizing and Analyzing the Data

After the report writer has carried through his research, he is faced with the task of converting the primary and secondary information into a finished report. That is certainly easier said than done. Most of us can only look at our stacks of note cards, completed questionnaire and interview returns, and miscellaneous data and say, "Where in the world shall I begin? And how in the world am I going to turn all this material into an interesting and worth-while report?"

Well, it is not a simple task, but neither is it a very difficult one. And the report writer can make his job easier by following a series of steps.

CLASSIFICATION OF DATA

Classification is the first task the researcher must complete if he is to move toward his goal of producing an effective report out of his collected data.

In the case of note cards which have been derived from secondary sources, the classification task is relatively simple. Each note card has its topic heading and is placed in the group that carries a similar designation; these similar groups may be clipped or held together with a rubber band. The collections of cards may then be arranged in the same order as the topics in the outline; in many cases, the topic headings on the cards will be the same as the headings in the outline.

The questionnaires, because they make up a homogeneous group, need no further classification as such. However, it is quite possible that the questionnaires must be placed in specific categories for further analysis. Such divisions might be the returns from specific geographical areas, particular social or economic strata, age classification, or some other logical breakdown. This particular task may be facilitated if these areas are recognized early in the survey and the questionnaires themselves are colored, notched, or marked to indicate the various sub-categories desired. Then when the researcher receives them from the respondents, he can quickly assign the questionnaires to the proper group without bothering to read each one at this time.

Schedules drawn from interviews may be classified almost exactly like questionnaires; the problems of classification in both areas are quite similar.

The end purpose in the classification of notes and note cards taken from secondary sources, data gathered from primary areas, and miscellaneous information which has been assembled is to arrange the material in the best way possible to facilitate analytical use that will result in a complete and thorough report. If the material which has been gathered can be quickly and easily utilized, the task of the report writer is made infinitely easier.

PRECODING

The device of precoding is sometimes employed in an attempt to save time and expense and increase accuracy during the process of tabulation of questionnaires. When precoding is accomplished, a number is assigned to each possible answer to every question and printed on the questionnaire. When the question is asked, the interviewer circles or checks the number on the schedule or questionnaire form which corresponds to the actual response given. In the process of tabulation, the quantitative answers do not have to be converted into specific numbers and *then* recorded, but only the numbers designated on the answer sheet need be used. Of course this precoding may be accomplished easily only when the questions are of the quantitative type or when the possibilities of answers have been predetermined. Thus if there are five possible answers to one question on a questionnaire, each answer receives a designated number from one to five, and that number is placed under or near that answer. In the tabulation there is no further editing that must be done on that question; the number corresponding to the respondent's choice is transferred to the tabulation sheet or recorded by the tabulating machine.

4. What brand of automobile do you presently own? (Check one; if you own more than one car, check all answers necessary or the same answer two or more times.)

Ford	____(1)	Plymouth	____(5)	Chevrolet	____(9)
Mercury	____(2)	Dodge	✓(6)	Pontiac	____(10)
Lincoln	____(3)	De Soto	____(7)	Oldsmobile	____(11)
Continental	____(4)	Chrysler	____(8)	Buick	____(12)
				Cadillac	____(13)

Other _____(14)

In the example above, the tabulator simply checks and notes that the answer to question 4 is number (6). Column six is given a credit on the tabulation sheet with a slash mark (/) or the proper item is punched on the machine (explained in more detail below). But the tabulator does not have to check a guide to see what number or letter has been assigned to the Dodge car; the designation is right in the question. Precoding can save a great deal of time in the tabulation job and will also aid in securing accuracy of results.

EDITING

Editing is the examination of the data and materials collected in order to make the necessary corrections of errors or adjustments in answers. A good definition was given in the *Journal of Marketing:*

> Editing is an important tabulating function; it acts as a first line of defense against bad interviewing, cheaters, carelessness in reporting the answers, and slips that pass in the field. It is a vital screening process that catches trouble at an early production stage before any serious damage is done.[1]

Those persons who have been designated to do the editing should be thoroughly familiar with the field. Under no circumstances should editing be carried on by relatively untrained, part-time personnel. The job of the editor is an important one and requires that he make decisions which may vitally affect the results of the survey.

In the editing process, similar instructions should be given to all

[1] Joseph S. Boyajy, "Tabulation Planning and Tabulation Techniques," *The Journal of Marketing,* January, 1948, p. 338.

those who are assigned to the job. Any notations that are made on questionnaires or cards by the editors should be accomplished with a colored pen or pencil; there should be no erasures, no cancellations of original entries, and no elimination of data without very careful thought. For quantitative data, the editors should standardize units of measurement into acceptable terms such as meters, feet, months, hours, pounds, etc.

For qualitative data, an attempt should be made to set up categories into which the various "please comment" answers may be assigned. The editor should also be alert to note inconsistent answers or unintentional errors which respondents sometimes make. Such changes, like almost all others, should be made on the original paper in colored pencil. Again it is emphasized that any changes the editor does make should be carried through with discretion.

The editor will also find that he must work out, to the best of his ability, illegible entries, confusing answers, and, often, he must reduce the impressive titles that people are prone to give to their prosaic jobs. The editor may find that the respondent has noted cents for dollars, hours for minutes, or years for months. He will also find that an occasional practical joker has completed a questionnaire and noted down ridiculous answers. Such a questionnaire should be completely discarded.

The editor should make every effort to secure a complete piece of data. Where blanks have been left, he should attempt to determine what the proper answer would be as indicated by the other replies. Or, in some instances, it might be wise for the editor to simply fill in "unknown" or "not applicable." For example, the respondent may not have answered the question which asks if he owns a television set, and yet on the next question he indicates that he has one with a 24-inch screen. Here is a task for the editor to correct. The editor may also find that a "check" question, which has been designed to prove the validity of an answer to an earlier inquiry in the questionnaire, does not carry a consistent reply when compared with the other. Here is another situation which may well require additional attention.

The editing of schedules from personal interviews may be easier than the editing of questionnaires. Surely it can be accomplished more expeditiously. The interviewer can actually do it without much difficulty while he is out in the field. At the conclusion of the interview he can easily note which areas have not been touched upon adequately and reënter that specific field with the same respondent or similarly grouped or classified respondents. And, of course, in the process of checking each of his interview schedules before submission to the headquarters office, he notes those which require additional work.

TABULATION

Once the editing process is completed, the results of the survey may be counted, or tabulated, so that the source material may be translated into data for evaluation, interpretation, and subsequent action. The actual mechanics connected with tabulation may be accomplished by either machine or manual methods.

Machine Tabulation

The first step in machine tabulation is to transfer the data which appears on the questionnaires, schedules, or other primary sources to cards which may be handled easily.

Various mechanical devices designed for these purposes are available on the market. Those manufactured by the International Business Machines Corporation and the Remington Rand Company are frequently utilized.

Both companies have perfected a series of machines which may be likened to a complete chain. These run from the unit that punches holes in cards (which correspond to specific items of information) to electronic calculators. When they are all utilized, a connected series of results becomes available; however, the use of one, two, or three of these machines is of inestimable aid to the report writer who is faced with reducing a mass of facts and figures to a few well-qualified conclusions.

Most of us have seen various types of these electronic devices on TV programs if nowhere else. We have watched some of these machines run through hundreds of cards in just a few seconds and select only those which carry specific information.

These electronic servants are in themselves complex, but they certainly make our work much simpler. Large corporations (and many small ones) now have many of their tasks, from their payrolls to their inventory control, completed by machines. The job is usually carried through much more quickly and accurately than when accomplished by an office full of clerks.

The first step in machine tabulation is that of punching the cards. I.B.M. uses a card that has 80 vertical columns with each column containing 10 digits, "0" to "9"; with space provided on the card for two additional numbers, "X" and "Y," if the need should arise. In other words, 960 items of information may be punched into one card.

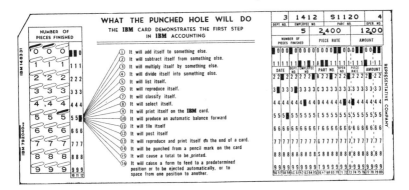

I.B.M. Card (Courtesy of International Business Machines Corporation)

Thus, if the researcher has 10,000 questionnaires, he must be equipped with 10,000 cards in which to punch the information. Each one of the 80 columns can, if necessary, carry specific information. For example, the first few columns may be given over to an identification of the social class, city, state, season of the year, sex and age of the respondent and other classification data. *Each* of the remaining columns may be identified with a specific question in the questionnaire. Thus, column 32 may stand for question 6 in the questionnaire. If the code for question 6 is 1 for "yes," 2 for "no," 3 for "sometimes," and 4 for "never," then a punch on number 2 in column 32 means an answer of "no" to question 6. Usually, only one hole is punched in each column used.

The key-punch operator records the data on the cards by referring to each questionnaire and transferring the information to the card.[2]

[2] The card itself may be designed to answer the needs of a specific situation, problem, or business although the illustration above indicates the basic makeup. As a matter of fact, cards sent out by a firm, which may ask for a

The first step in insuring accurate work at this stage is to select key-punch operators who are efficient and competent. But even with due care exercised, human errors may take place. Thus it is sometimes wise to run the punched cards through a second machine called a Verifier.

The two steps outlined above, punching and verifying, are the only manual operations necessary in the entire tabulation procedure. All other steps may be accomplished automatically.

From the Verifier the 10,000 cards may now go into the sorting and counting instrument. This machine will run the 10,000 cards through at the rate of 2,000 per minute.

In that process each card is dropped into one of the 13 compartments (the reader will recall there is room for 12 digits in each column on the card; the thirteenth space is reserved for "rejects"), and at the same time the number in each compartment is counted as well as the total number of cards run through.

Let us assume that the answers to question 14 are desired. The information punched into column 14 on each of the 10,000 cards corresponds to the answers made on the questionnaire to question 14. The electronic sorter is then set up for question 14 and all the cards are run through it.

If the respondent, in answering question 14, was asked to select one of eight different TV programs, then in precoding, each program would be given a number from one to eight. When the 10,000 cards are sent through the sorter, they are automatically separated into eight homogeneous groups for question 14. As the cards are separated, they are also counted. Thus the operator determines from the computers the number in each of the eight categories for question 14. As is now quite obvious, *all* the cards must go through the sorter each time a different column on the card (which corresponds to a different question on the questionnaire) is tabulated. Thus if 28 of the 80 columns have been used for questions, the cards must go through the counting and sorting instrument 28 different times.

I.B.M. has another tabulating instrument on the market called the Electronic Statistical Machine which not only carries through

---

subscription renewal, payment of an account, or some other task which requests that it be returned to the sender, often have advertisements across the face.

the same task as the sorter, but will also automatically type the tabulated data on posting forms.

In addition to the machines listed above, there are now many others which accomplish amazingly complex tasks electronically. The speed and efficiency with which they can perform extremely involved operations seem almost magical.

Hand Tabulation

This tabulation, like the machine variety, must follow a definite plan for best results. The questionnaires, or whatever the primary source happens to be, must first be sorted into a logical breakdown arrangement. This may be by specific area or combination such as geographical, economic level, or sex. Inventory or transcription sheets should then be prepared for the actual tally. Most of the tabulation errors occur between the time the data are seen by the eye and recorded by the hand; thus every effort should be made to set up a sheet which is as easy to handle as possible. Spacing between columns should be generous, the printing of various headings clear, and the width of the entire sheet not too great. Because the eye is accustomed to traveling "across," the headings should be placed in that fashion and the quantities, to follow the natural movements of the hand, should be set up vertically. If it is necessary to record a large amount of material, it is much wiser to set up several sheets rather than use one of unusual width.

The actual tallying of the data is best accomplished with two or more competent individuals working together. If one person is required to read the original source material and also enter quantities on the data sheet, errors may very likely occur. However, if one person reads and another records, the operation moves much more easily. In tallying the information, a diagonal line is usually found to be an adequate mark and a time-honored four diagonals crossed by a single line (⧅) is very satisfactory for indicating units of five. After the material has been tallied, it may be recorded on posting sheets.

EVALUATION OF TABULATED DATA

Before the researcher can begin to interpret the results of the data which have been tabulated, he must make certain that the survey actually measured what it was designed to measure.

The validity of answers can be checked by observing a sample of respondents to determine whether they actually do what they said (on a questionnaire) they do. Then, too, the validity of the answers can be checked by including nonexistent possibilities in the answer columns of the questionnaire. Quite recently when a researcher included the names of several novels which had not been written under the question, "Which of the following best sellers have you read?" a good percentage of the respondents not only checked those which were actually on the market but several which were not as well.

One will also find that many persons have a consistent tendency for overestimating their accomplishments in areas such as academic grades or offices held. Thus it is wise to check replies against objective records if possible.

A further step in evaluation might be an attempt to compare the results of the survey with the results of a different type of survey made in the same field. This may be done by checking questionnaire results with interview responses; if all phases of the survey are relatively equal, the responses should indicate a correlation. And, of course, the validity of a piece of research may be indicated by looking at the results of the survey and comparing those results with actual subsequent events.

INTERPRETATION OF DATA

The data have been gathered, counted, checked, and examined. What do they all mean? In answer to question 4, 1850 responses were "yes," 4865 responses were "no," and 2540 people said "sometimes." Question 7 drew twice as many "blue" answers as it did "red." In question 10, 850 respondents indicated they would walk a maximum of four blocks to a food store and 2560 said their maximum would be three blocks.

What does all of this mean?

To determine what it *does* indicate, we must INTERPRET the results of our findings.

Interpreting the data is one of the most important steps in arriving at a final, acceptable conclusion of the problem which the researcher has undertaken. However, interpreting the information which has been gathered is not an easy task and can hardly be accomplished effectively by a novice; there are specific qualities that the competent individual must possess to qualify him for the job of interpreting the data. It is certainly unwise to make expenditures of major sums of money for gathering information from a variety of primary and secondary sources and then have an unqualified person make inaccurate recommendations on the basis of the data. Therefore, it is valuable to set up certain criteria as a basis for the choice of the interpreter.

He should be skilled, competent, and well versed in the field in which he is working. He should be a patient individual who is not content with superficial research but who demands of himself and his field force thorough analysis and investigation into all primary and secondary sources of information which are available. His viewpoint should not be narrow; he should be able to see the broad aspects of his findings. He should have good organizational ability so that he can readily integrate the results of the qualitative comments with the quantitative facts. Only such a man may qualify to interpret the data and make recommendations which may involve the expenditure of thousands of dollars for a new plant site, a new package for a product, the opening of a new store, or the introduction of a new item on the market.

In the process of interpreting the data, the researcher must continually strive to avoid:

1. Showing bias or prejudice
2. Assuming that because some aspects of two or more situations are similar, all aspects are
3. Arriving at conclusions on the basis of inadequate evidence
4. Assuming that one situation is the case if the data prove that a second situation is not
5. Making recommendations on inadequate data
6. Comparing information or facts which are not really comparable

As an example of the care one must exercise in the interpretation of data, let us examine the chart on page 106 carefully.

On the surface, an analysis of the data would seem simple and the interpretation obvious. We might say that those students who register for Saturday classes and evening classes are more ambitious, brighter, and harder working than those students who are

A RANDOM SELECTION OF 600
STUDENTS FROM THE FRESHMAN, SOPHOMORE,
AND JUNIOR LEVEL CLASSES OF STATE COLLEGE

Class Group	Enrolled in Regular Classes Only (number)	Enrolled in Saturday and Night School Classes Only (number)	Average Grade Level (by percentage of group) for the Spring Semester of 19—									
			A		B		C		D		F	
			R	SN	R	SN	R	SN	R	SN	R	SN
			%	%	%	%	%	%	%	%	%	%
Freshman	99	99	5	20	10	25	50	50	20	5	15	
Sophomore	101	102	7	18	13	32	45	45	25	5	10	
Junior	99	100	5	19	15	34	53	41	15	5	12	1

R—regular class.
SN—Saturday and night class.

enrolled in regular classes. But this is only an *assumption*. It may be:

1. That Saturday and night classes are easier
2. That the regular classes are more difficult
3. That the instructors' standards for regular classes are different from the standards of instructors of the Saturday and night classes
4. That students in regular classes do not work as hard
5. That students in regular classes are quite dull

And we could go on and on with what the data *seem* to indicate. But the vital factor to recognize is that with the information given, we *do not* know if any of the assumptions *are* valid. Perhaps all we can say from the facts given is that students who register for Saturday and night classes average (for this group only) higher grades than those students enrolled in regular classes. And we can probably add that additional study is indicated.

Scope of the Interpretation

It is quite important that the researcher decide how great an area his interpretation will encompass. Shall he simply point out in very brief statements what the various percentages indicate? Or shall he go further and discuss the implications which one may draw from the findings? It may be that the interpreter feels that his task is not completed until he not only interprets the statistical data, and discusses its implications, but also offers recommendations. There is even one additional step that he may wish to take, and that is to point out in detail how his recommendations may best be carried through into actual practice.

It is important, therefore, that the report writer decide early in his work just exactly how far he intends to go in his report; will it carry merely an analysis or will recommendations for future action be included? And if recommendations are submitted, in what detail will they be offered? These are some of the decisions he must make in the writing of the report.

PRESENTING RECOMMENDATIONS

This is perhaps the easiest step after the report writer has gone through all those which have been previously considered. If his sample of primary and secondary material is adequate, his editing competent, his evaluations fair, and his interpretations valid, then the recommendations will follow easily. It may be that the report writer will feel that his suggestions should be given in greater or lesser detail; this is largely dependent, of course, on who the reader is and what scope the report intends to cover. For some readers, merely listing recommendations will prove adequate; for others a detailed plan for each suggestion made must be offered. If the entire survey has been undertaken by a private firm, the initial contract and the fee paid will indicate whether the survey is to offer recommendations and, if so, to what degree these recommendations should be handled. It may be that the suggestion is to install several new machines or the recommendation(s) may go further and indicate exactly how and where in the plant the machines should be located, what lighting should be provided for their operation, how many people should operate the units, and what the rate of pay and production level of the employees should be.

But even in such a case as the one discussed immediately above, the researcher must first establish tentative conclusions and recommendations. As in some of the earlier steps, he should constantly check himself to be sure that his concluding statements are based on a sufficient quantity of facts, that they are accurate, unbiased, and representative of the data gathered. He must note whether or not the authorities in the field seem to agree with his findings and whether his recommendations are feasible and would work out in actual practice. If the researcher can answer "yes" to these conditions, he can then honestly set forth his conclusions in detail and submit them as a major section of his report.

QUESTIONS FOR DISCUSSION

I. Answer the following questions as briefly as possible:
1. How and why would you precode the following questions on a mail questionnaire? Assume that you expect approximately 20,000 responses.
   a. Please complete the following questions:
      Age_____   Marital status_____
      Rank_____   Highest degree received_____
   b. In what theater(s) of operation have you been stationed? (Check one or more.)
      European_____   South Pacific_____
      African_____   Korean_____
   c. Year of initial entrance into U.S. Armed Forces_____.
2. As an editor, what changes, if any, would you make in the answers given to the following questions?
   a. Do you own an automobile?   _____   _✓_
                                   Yes   No
   b. What year model is it?   *1960*
   c. Check the style.
      Convertible_✓_   Station wagon_____
      Sedan_____   Other_____
   d. Which type of steering does your car have? (Check one.)
      Power steering_____   I don't know_____
      Regular steering_____
   e. Approximately how many years did you have the car immediately prior to the one you now possess?   *1 year*
   f. How many miles was *that* car (the one which you owned prior to your present model) driven before you traded it in?   *60,000 miles*

Answer the following questions as completely as possible:
   a. Do you expect to attend college on graduation from high school?
                          _✓_   _____
                          Yes   No

b. Have you chosen a specific career toward which you would like to work?

Nursing
_____   _____
Yes   No

c. Have you made application for admission to any college or university?

Illinois State
_____   _____
Yes   No

d. What type of college or university would you *prefer* to attend?

Illinois State

_____   _____   _____
Public   Private   Other

e. Have you or will you apply for a scholarship or grant for your higher education?

_____   _____   _____
Yes   No   Don't know

II. What conclusions may be drawn from the following article, quoted from a daily newspaper?

Last week, as world tensions mounted and the various leaders in the world centers growled at each other, there seemed to be a definite reaction within our economy.

By coincidence or not the Department of Defense awarded 575 million dollars in new contracts for aircraft and arms. Industries associated with national defense, such as communications, transport and electronics announced new programs of labor recruitment, over-time schedules, and full scale production lines.

The stock exchanges also reacted strongly to the barbed words which the world's leaders were directing at one another. All industrials went up an average of 6 points during the week of February 12-19. Chemicals rose about 10 points and electronics 14 points during the same period. The Dow-Jones average certainly gave the investor a good opportunity to applaud.

In Washington, the Senate . . . .

III. Given the following data, what interpretations would you make after an analysis? What conclusions can be reached?
1. Five thousand housewives living in the northeastern section of the United States were interviewed. They were questioned regarding their preference for color in soap and the shape of the bar.

Average Family Earning Per Year	Color of Soap Preferred by Largest Percentage	Shape of Bar Preferred by Largest Percentage
$3000–$3500	Pink	Oval
3500– 4000	Green	Oval
4500– 5000	Blue	Square
5000– 6000	White	Oval
6000– 8000	White	Oval
Over	White	Oval

2. The names of 4000 children were selected at random from among those who had come into Illinois and enrolled in the freshman year of high school. These children came from eight different states.

State of Origin	Number from Each State	Average of Grades at the End of Four Semesters (in percent of total no.)				
		A	B	C	D	F
Alabama	510	15	20	40	15	10
North Carolina	490	25	25	30	10	10
Kentucky	495	10	15	50	10	15
Michigan	520	20	20	40	5	15
Indiana	505	20	25	25	15	15
Wisconsin	480	15	5	50	25	5
Iowa	525	30	5	50	10	5
Florida	475	15	20	50	5	10

3. Is there any correlation between grades received and participation in extracurricular activities?

Student Number	Average Grade	Participation in Activities				
		Baseball	Football	Track	Band	Other
1	A	√		√		√
2	A		√	√	√	
3	B	√	√	√		
4	C			√		
5	B	√	√	√		
6	A		√	√	√	
7	C			√		
8	C		√		√	

Chapter 5

Outlining the Report

How many times in your life have you been thoroughly irritated with a speaker or writer because "he never did get to the point"? He rambled here, digressed there, and introduced irrelevant materials at every turn. And as a result, you left the lecture hall in disgust or you cast aside the magazine or book you were trying to "wade through."

What often irritates us in the piece of writing we read or the lecture we hear is the lack of organization in the material presented. The "point" is lost somewhere among the illogical examples, the unrelated materials, and the cloudy arguments.

All of us enjoy reading or listening to a carefully thought through and clearly presented piece of exposition. It reflects the thinking of a well-organized mind. Using planned procedures will assist us in attaining the faculty of being well organized. The outline, of course, is an excellent example of planned procedure.

Those persons who have no patience with outlining and who indicate, "I put it in proper order as I speak or as I write," are really offering a weak excuse for their own lazy attitude. That individual's report must usually be written several times before it is finally acceptable. Or if he submits his report, which has been written without the help of an outline as a guide, it usually reflects confusion and lack of organization.

THE VALUE OF AN OUTLINE

There are three primary reasons for making up an outline:

1. To insure that the final report is well organized and presented in a logical manner.

2. To insure that each part of the report is given the emphasis it requires. By arranging information in outline form, it is easy to see and check the *relative* importance of one item to another.
3. To insure that the report writer does not expend more time and effort on a report than is necessary. An examination of the points listed in the outline quickly tells the researcher what areas to eliminate or what to add.

The above three reasons are discussed in detail in the pages which follow.

Organizing and Planning the Report

From our initial thoughts and our tentative outline, we build our plans. Often our ideas, while in the developmental stage, change. And so we revise the outline. But we also examine the outline carefully and critically, for it is the plan, the blueprint for our finished report. It serves the same purpose as the architect's blueprints. The construction engineer would not begin to think of the building's wiring requirements *after* the bricks were laid; he demands that the plans be completed for all construction and utilities *before* the first brick is cemented in place.

The report writer can check his outline; does the plan for the report seem well organized? Is it logical? If his answer is an unqualified "yes" and the other attributes of a good outline are present, then he may begin writing his report. It is just as necessary to have a complete plan for the report before writing as it is to have plans before starting the construction of a building. Notice the few points listed below and the lack of logic they reflect:

ADVANTAGES AND DISADVANTAGES OF VARIOUS TRANSPORTATION
MEDIA FOR MOVING HEAVY-DUTY EQUIPMENT

Railroad
  Accessibility
  Low cost
  Safe handling
Truck
  Scheduling problems
  Low cost
  Rapid delivery
  Personnel
    Possible union conflict of qualified drivers
    Wage scales

Automobile
  Difficulty of handling
  High cost
  Rapid delivery
Air Freight
  Coördination problem of truck and plane
  High cost
  Rapid delivery

From the title of the problem, it would certainly seem to be illogical to even consider transporting heavy-duty machinery in automobiles. The introduction of such a section can only result in having the focus of attention lessened in considering various feasible possibilities. Then, too, why the section on "Personnel" under the "Truck" heading and nowhere else?

DEVELOPING LOGICAL ORDER

The well-organized report depends almost entirely on a second phase of logic in outlining: the development of the plan through logical order.

Pick up almost any sample of good exposition and read it. Almost invariably you will find that the author has used one of the following methods in developing his topic:

Temporal or Chronological. Beginning at a logical date or time and moving forward to illustrate growth and development or moving backward to illustrate the historical background or significance of a situation, product, or institution.

Geographical or Spatial. The report might begin at a point and move east, west, or in whatever direction seems most logical. The movement might also be *within* a plant or office building. But ordinarily the discussion would not jump from New York to Los Angeles to Chicago back to New York, etc., without good reason. So, too, discussion of the production line would probably not be followed by discussion of the office, then back to production, over to personnel, then to transportation, and back to personnel. Ordinarily one division of the plant would be examined, then another, and then another. "Jumping" back and forth, in most instances, would upset the organization of the report.

Simple to Complex. It is often wise to introduce your reader to more complex procedures after he has gone over simple ones. By first explaining the advantages and disadvantages of several simple inventory control methods, the reader will be more likely to understand and evaluate more complex systems.

General to Specific. Here the writer might proceed logically from a discussion on the value of testing all new employees to the specific tests given to applicants for clerical, mechanical, research, and sales jobs.

Specific to General. This obviously is a reversal of the above; the general comments or conclusions follow the discussion of specific cases.

Functional. Here the items, individuals or groups, are discussed according to their logical functions. First all the personnel concerned with sales might be evaluated, then those in the accounting division, then purchasing, etc. Or the functions of all the ceramic units, then the plating, and finally the packaging machinery would be presented.

These are merely some of the ways a report may be organized. Any one of these would probably result in a logically developed outline.

Checking the Relative Importance of One Section to Another

On occasion we have read a piece of material and wondered why the author spent "eight pages on this and only half a page on that." For some reason we were sure that such a division was not wise because both items seemed to be of about equal importance. Had an outline been made first and then checked, perhaps the disparity would have been apparent to the writer.

ALLOCATION OF ADVERTISING BUDGET

Newspaper
    Papers and dates available
    Cost
    Readership analysis
Magazines
    Magazines and dates available
    Cost
    Readership analysis
Radio
    Time periods available
    Cost

Programs available
Listening audience analysis
Television
Time periods available
Cost
Networks
Programs available
Possibility of originating own program
Listening and viewing audience
Competitors' programs
Local, national, and other hookups
Use of kinescope programs
Technical problems of using TV

Quite obviously, if the written report follows the outlined pattern above, the section dealing with television will receive much more extensive treatment than the other three. On the basis that all four advertising media should receive equal consideration, the reader may very well attach greater importance to the television section of the report than it deserves. However, the solution is simple: if the researcher formulates an outline and examines it, he will immediately note the disparity among the sections. It is surely easier to correct this situation in the outline stage than to discover it after the written report has been completed. Revising an outline is simpler than rewriting a report.

Saving Time Through Making an Outline

After the report writer has checked, weighed, and evaluated his outline, he can proceed to write his report. It is not necessary for him to wonder if he should now write up this section or that, if he should secure additional evidence for that portion, if he should extend or cut down the explanations at this point, and *ad infinitum*.

Once every portion of the outline has been tested and found satisfactory, the report writer need only move ahead with the writing task. He is satisfied that the outline is logical, orderly, and that its points are in proper relative proportion.

FORMULATING AN OUTLINE

The outline begins in the writer's mind when he contemplates the areas he will cover in his report. When the researcher determines his objective, the scope of his report, and who his reader will be, he has undoubtedly established his major points. When these are transferred to paper, the initial or tentative outline has been formulated. Normally all the major items in the report will be found in this initial outline.

As research continues, topics should be jotted down in a listing. Once the items are assembled, they can be examined and grouped under the major headings previously recognized. Of course, additional major topics may be added as research continues. The report writer should have no hesitancy in changing, revising, adding to, or deleting from the outline.

Let us assume that you have been requested to write a report on Office Personnel for the executive echelon of your steel corporation. You have decided to cover:

I. Recruitment
II. Training
III. Salary
IV. Office Policies

As you carry through your research, you find that you have information in the following 22 areas:

Effectiveness of newspaper advertisements in securing personnel
Company sponsored training programs
Present salary policies
"Coffee break" policy
Salaries paid by competing companies
Employee training in university evening classes
Local salary averages
* Subsidiary companies
Office dress policies
Securing personnel by visiting graduating high school classes
Training programs directed by consultants
Training conducted by department heads for personnel under their
    direction
Employees secured through recommendation by present personnel
Formal class sessions in training program
Determination of a salary formula
* Hospitalization statistics of present employees
Mailing to local schools of brochures describing job opportunities
Conference type of training programs
Radio "spot announcements" describing job opportunities

* Vacation plan systems of railroads
Sick leave policy
* Annual report to employees

A hasty glance at the topics listed above indicates that each of the items may be placed under a Roman numeral heading with the exception of those marked with an asterisk. These, quite probably, would have no place under the four headings. Now is the time, while the outline is being formulated, to discard those points which are unrelated. Without an outline, discussion on these might have been included in the written report. Think of how that would have upset the continuity of the report's message that supposedly is to deal only with recruitment, training, salary, and office policies.

The remaining points would then be organized in the following manner:

I. Recruitment of Office Personnel
   A. Newspaper advertisements in securing personnel
   B. Securing personnel by visiting graduating high school classes
   C. Employees secured through recommendation by present personnel
   D. Mailing to local schools of brochures describing job opportunities
II. Training of Office Personnel
   A. Company sponsored training programs
   B. Employee training in university evening classes
   C. Training programs directed by consultants
   D. Training conducted by department heads for personnel under their direction
   E. Formal class sessions in training program
   F. Conference type of training programs
III. Salary of Office Personnel
   A. Present salary policies
   B. Salaries paid by competing companies
   C. Local salary averages
   D. Determination of a salary formula
IV. Office Policies for Personnel
   A. "Coffee break" policy
   B. Office dress policies
   C. Sick leave policy

Organizing the outline is really an excellent exercise in logic. It is not difficult to see what topics belong under major headings, but often there is a question in the process of subdividing the secondary points. The time to check it is when the outline is being formulated, *not* when the report is being written.

COMPARISON OF AIR, RAIL, AND BUS TRAVEL TO NEW YORK

Considerations in Air Travel
   Cost first class
   Cost air coach
   Luggage
      Weight restriction
      Restriction on number of pieces
   Time of trip first class
   Time of trip air coach
Considerations in Rail Travel
   Cost first class
   Cost rail coach
   Luggage
      Weight restriction
      Restriction on number of pieces
   Time of trip first class
   Time of trip rail coach
Considerations in Bus Travel
   Cost first class
   Cost of coach
   Luggage
      Weight restriction
      Restriction on number of pieces
   Time of trip first class
   Time of trip coach

In the simple outline above, it is obvious that the major headings are considerations in air, rail, and bus travel. In the first, the sub-headings are cost, luggage, and time. Of these, only one—luggage—is broken down still further. Set up in outline form, it is easy to see that "weight restrictions" and "number of pieces" fall *under* "luggage" and should not be treated as separate topics. On the other hand, the researcher might ask himself if the report should go into such detail on "luggage" and *not* on any of the other topics. If he can defend such action, then he should proceed.

The important factor to keep in mind is to place subordinate points under the proper headings and thus to treat them as minor points when the report is being written. Finding a "spot" for all the items is not always a simple assignment. Some headings, obviously necessary, will not seem to fit logically anywhere; or they will appear to be partial duplications of others, or they will not be quite important enough to deserve a separate heading but too important to treat as a division of a main category.

There can be no doubt that designing a logical, well-balanced outline is a job that requires good analytical ability. And there can be no doubt, also, that the quality of the outline will almost invariably reflect the quality of the written report.

POINTS TO REMEMBER IN MAKING UP THE OUTLINE

It would not be difficult to make 25 suggestions for preparing an outline. However, as we grow in experience, we each develop our own system and follow those suggestions which have proved themselves within our own academic or business efforts. Some of these suggestions are discussed briefly in the following pages; they are all designed to secure better organization within the outline and, finally, a better written report.

Numbering System

A logical numbering system within the outline permits the reader to recognize immediately the relative importance of one item to the next. Almost any logical system of numbers, letters, symbols, spacings, or combinations of these may be used in the outline.

NUMERALS AND LETTERS

Using a combination of numbers and letters is probably the most popular system today. The major heads are indicated by Roman numerals, capital letters are used for subtopics, and Arabic numerals and lower case letters are then employed. If further divisions are required, Arabic numerals and lower case letters are used again and enclosed in parentheses.

I. _____
  A. _____
  B. _____
    1. _____
    2. _____
      a. _____
      b. _____
        (1) _____

(2) _____
    (a) _____
    (b) _____

II. _____
  A. _____
  B. _____
    1. _____
    2. _____

III. _____

Note that each subordinate point is indented a specific number of spaces. In actual practice, an outline using this system might look like this:

AN ANALYSIS OF THE EFFECTIVENESS OF COLLECTION PROCEDURES USED BY THE BRYANT CORPORATION

Object of the Survey
I. Methods Used in Collecting Delinquent Accounts
  A. Collection correspondence
    1. The single letter
    2. The collection series
  B. Personal contact between delinquent account and Bryant Corporation
    1. Telephone
    2. Bryant representative visiting homes of delinquent accounts
  C. Commercial collection agencies
    1. Those using only direct mail
    2. Those using agents
    3. Those using a combination of mail and agent
II. Analysis of Effectiveness of Methods Used
  A. Percentage of collections against losses
    1. Correspondence
      a. Chicago area ratio
      b. National ratio
    2. Personal contact
      a. Chicago area ratio
      b. National ratio
    3. Collection agencies
      a. Chicago area ratio
      b. National ratio
  B. Cost per dollar collected
    1. Correspondence
    2. Personal contact
    3. Agencies

III. Recapitulation of Survey
IV. Recommendations

DECIMAL SYSTEM

This method is used very frequently by engineers, and it does have a distinct advantage in that every single point in the outline has a separate number.

1. _____
   1.1 _____
   1.2 _____
      1.21 _____
      1.22 _____
         1.221 _____
         1.222 _____
2. _____
   2.1 _____
   2.2 _____
3. _____
   3.1 _____
   3.2 _____

In referring to an item using the "numeral-letter system," it would be necessary to say "3 under B in II." However, in the decimal arrangement, a simple "1.221" would place the item immediately.

INDENTING

This method of outlining without using numbers is frequently used effectively in making short outlines. However, it has definite disadvantages; it does not accurately reflect the rank of the various items and there is no simple way to refer to the topics.

_____
  _____
  _____
    _____
    _____
      _____
      _____
  _____
  _____

Logic in Subordination

1. *Overlapping in Topic Headings.* By carefully evaluating the individual points in the outline, the writer can avoid needless repetition and overlapping in the final report. Note the lack of logic in the list of headings which follow:

    I. Consumer Demand for the Falcon
   II. Consumer Demand for the Chevrolet
  III. Consumer Demand for the Sedan
  IV. Consumer Demand for the Chrysler
   V. Consumer Demand for the Station Wagon

If the researcher follows the outline above in writing his report, he will be required to discuss the various Falcon models (sedan, convertible, station wagon, etc.) under his first point and the cars (including the Falcon) manufactured by different companies under his third point. This will lead to repetition and a lack of logic when the final report is written.

2. *Orderly Development.* Another consideration in the outline involves the relative organization of points. Clarity and coherence are lost when topics are widely separated which are logically related. When setting down initial ideas, related points may not be grouped as logically as possible, but later evaluation should clarify the relationships.

DEVELOPMENT OF TASTY FOOD CHAIN

    I. Initial Plans for Self-service Stores, 1922
   II. First Store Opened in Chicago, 1923
  III. Chain of 12 Stores Operating in Chicago, 1925
  IV. Effect of Stock Market Crash on Chain's Financial Condition, 1929
   V. Total of 24 Stores Operating in Chicago, Detroit, and New York, 1927
  VI. Depression Period of Contraction, 1929-1932
 VII. Gradual Expansion from 18 to 22 Stores, 1931-1936

A brief examination of the above will quickly reveal several facts which are certain to upset the continuity of the final report. Note how the time factor moves back and forth in IV and V and again in VI and VII. It might be wiser to progress smoothly year by year. Then, too, VI and IV both cover portions of the depression years. Thus, correcting the outline will result in a more logical report.

3. *Evaluation of a Single Topic.*   Under ordinary circumstances a single topic should not be subordinated.

USES OF JET PROPULSION

I. Missiles
  A. Ground to air
  B. Air to air
  C. Ground to ground
II. Satellites
  A. Space satellites

If "space satellites" is the only category under "satellites," why subordinate it? When one point is subordinated under a single head, it is likely that either the major head has simply been restated or that other subordinate points do exist but have not been considered and noted.

Proportion in the Outline

Although cases may certainly arise where there would be a dozen subpoints under Roman numeral II and only three headings under III, these would be unusual. Usually, there will be some consistency in the number of points under the Roman numeral headings and the major subheads.

I. _____
  A. _____
    1. _____
    2. _____
  B. _____
  C. _____
    1. _____
    2. _____
II. _____
  A. _____
    1. _____
    2. _____
  B. _____
    1. _____
    2. _____
      a. _____
      b. _____
      c. _____
      d. _____
      e. _____
  C. _____

In the example above, examine topic 2 under B in II. It has so many more subdivisions than similar headings that it might be well to determine if it should be changed to a separate capital letter heading and thereby receive different treatment in the written report. As the outline appears above, the report writer might devote as much space in the report to a third-level subpoint as to a complete Roman numeral section. This would most likely result in a lack of proportion in the report that would confuse the reader. Here again, correction of the outline is much easier and wiser than trying to correct the report after it is written.

Parallel Wording

Parallel wording of similarly designated points aids in interpretation and helps in thought relationship from the outline to the report. Consistency of word choice and sentence structure for coördinate headings should be followed where possible. In the example below, note how Roman numeral III, although of equal importance to I, II, and IV, is a bit difficult to grasp because of the change in wording. It would be simple to revise it and achieve parallelism.

   I. The Economic Background for the Revolutionary War
  II. The Social Background for the Revolutionary War
 III. Philosophical Theories Also Entered into the Patriots' Arguments
 IV. Political Background for the Revolutionary War

Parallel Development

Topics of relatively equal importance should be treated under similar headings in the outline. Thus when the report is written from the outline guide, the reader will find that items which are at the same levels are treated more or less equally.

If the following outline were used as a guide to write a segment of a report, the reader might well wonder why "Competent personnel for unit assembly" was treated *under* "Production Line Problems" in Roman numeral II but was handled as a separate major topic under Roman numeral I! Notice that the subject of "Repairs" is also handled differently in I as compared to II.

Tubes Versus Printed Circuits in Component 31A

I. Use of Printed Circuits in Component 31A
  A. Availability

    B. Cost
    C. Competent personnel for unit assembly
    D. Repair problems
    E. Public acceptance
II. Use of Conventional Tubes in Component 31A
    A. Availability
    B. Production Line Problems
       1. Breakage
       2. Competent personnel for unit assembly
       3. Excessive time for tube installation
    C. Cost
    D. Public acceptance
       1. Public attitude on repairs
       2. Advertising to promote acceptance

In the outline above, topics in similar areas should probably be given similar designations through equal subordination. If the writer follows a faulty outline in writing his report, the reader may feel that the report is illogical and unbalanced. The outline which appears below seems to have parallel development and will probably result in a clearly developed report.

A COMPARISON OF FACTORS INVOLVED IN
SHIPPING COMPONENT 31A FROM SAN DIEGO OR SAN FRANCISCO

 I. San Diego
    A. Railroads
       1. Lines available
       2. Cost
       3. Convenience
          a. Time schedules
          b. Spur tracks
    B. Trucking companies
       1. Trucking companies available
       2. Cost
       3. Convenience
          a. Time schedules
          b. Loading docks
II. San Francisco
    A. Railroads
       1. Lines available
       2. Cost
       3. Convenience
          a. Time schedules
          b. Spur tracks

   B. Trucking companies
     1. Trucking companies available
     2. Cost
     3. Convenience
       a. Time schedules
       b. Loading docks

FORM OF THE OUTLINE

The outline usually consists of a title, a thesis statement, and the list of topics. The thesis sentence states in as concise and pointed manner as possible the objective of the study. The outline is then presented as a listing of topics or sentences.

Topic Outline

Each heading in a topic outline consists of a few words or a short phrase. This type is especially valuable for short reports. It also is valuable because it permits the researcher to jot down headings without giving attention to careful sentence stucture.

AN ANALYSIS OF FACTORS TO CONSIDER IN THE SELECTION OF A
SITE AND THE CONSTRUCTION OF A NEW PLANT

PROBLEM: Shall a new plant be constructed in Peoria, Illinois, by the Excello Corporation?

Introduction
  (Items to be manufactured, projected size of plant, number of employees, and level of production contemplated.)
  I. Transportation Facilities
    A. For raw materials into plant
      1. Rail
      2. Truck
    B. For finished products to market
      1. Rail
      2. Truck
    C. For employees from home to plant
      1. Local public transportation
      2. Automobile
  II. Availability of Raw Materials
    A. Metals
    B. Woods
    C. Plastics
    D. Other necessary materials

III. Tax Regulations
    A. State
    B. Local
       1. Property
       2. Product
       3. Others
IV. Labor Supply
    A. Skilled production personnel
       1. Availability in local area
       2. Wage rates
    B. Unskilled production personnel
       1. Availability in local area
       2. Wage rates
    C. Professional personnel (engineers, chemists, and physicists)
       1. Availability in local area
       2. Wage rates
    D. Administrative personnel
       1. Availability in local area
       2. Wage rates
    E. Office personnel
       1. Availability in local area
       2. Wage rates
 V. Labor Relations
    A. Organized unions in area
    B. Relationship of labor to management in similar industries in area
VI. Other Factors
    A. Climate
    B. Water supply
    C. Fuel supply
    D. Topography

Obviously this type of outline has several commendable features. It can be made up very rapidly; words, phrases, and even sections can be shifted easily, and it can be tested quickly for proportion, clarity, unity, and emphasis.

Sentence Outline

Each point in this type of outline, whether it is a major heading or a subordinate point, is a complete sentence. Normally, of course, each sentence will probably serve to designate a section in the report. There is one caution, however, that may be given to the report writer who is a novice in the field, and that is to avoid the common pitfall of turning a sentence outline directly into a report by the simple expedient of inserting transitional words and phrases between the points in the outline. In such reports, the skeletal outline "shines through" with such inadequate words as "moreover," "secondarily," "in addition to," and reflects little credit on the writer.

AN ANALYSIS OF ADVERTISING MEDIA

USED BY THE ACME CORPORATION

PROBLEM: To determine the relative value of advertising Acme products in three media during the present fiscal year.

I. An evaluation of newspaper advertisements placed by Acme was carried through.
  A. An analysis of advertisements placed in daily newspapers with a circulation between 50,000 and 200,000 was completed.
  B. An analysis of advertisements placed in daily newspapers with a circulation between 200,000 and 500,000 was completed.
  C. A comparative analysis between Group A and Group B on two bases to determine the value of each was completed.
    1. A presentation of facts on cost of advertisements in Group A and Group B was completed.
    2. A presentation of facts concerning results on returns on advertisements which have appeared in Group A and Group B magazines was completed.

II. An evaluation of radio and television advertisements placed by Acme was completed.
  A. An analysis of 15-minute news programs placed by Acme over three different radio networks was completed.
  B. An analysis of 15-minute news programs placed by Acme over three different television networks was completed.
  C. A comparative analysis between radio and television advertising on two bases to determine the value of each was completed.
    1. A presentation of facts on cost of advertisements in radio and television was completed.
    2. A presentation of facts concerning results on returns on advertisements which have appeared on radio and on television was completed.

III. A recapitulation of the results of advertising by Acme in the three areas was completed.
  A. An analysis of expenditures in the three media was completed.
  B. An analysis of results in the three media was completed.

The report writer should not usually attempt a sentence outline for most of his work; generally a topic outline will serve his needs.

However, when a long, complex, and extremely important subject is to be discussed thoroughly, a sentence outline should be carefully made. Some researchers prefer to develop their sentence outline from a topic outline.

A FINAL WORD

After the outline has been completed, the researcher should check it for accuracy and completeness:

Are all major headings of the same order (chronological, geographical, etc.)?
Have duplicate headings been eliminated?
Are the headings in the proper levels of importance? Have minor topics been subordinated properly?
Are all the statements clear, parallel in development and wording, and concise?

If the report writer receives an affirmative answer to these questions and is satisfied in the other areas discussed in this chapter, he may proceed to the next step—the writing of the first draft.

QUESTIONS FOR DISCUSSION

I. Evaluate the following outlines. Are they logical and proportional? If not, what suggestions would you make?
1. I. The Ranch Style House
   A. Advantages
      1. No stairs to climb
      2. Modern in design
      3. Large roof area adds to construction cost
   B. The Cape Cod style house
      1. Utilized to a large extent in New England
      2. Utilizes space to excellent advantage
   II. The Colonial Style House
   A. Advantages
      1. Two floors make for low construction cost
      2. Limited lot size needed
   B. Disadvantages

2. A. Trees for new communities near urban centers
      1. The Chinese elm
      2. The sugar maple
      3. Advantages of the above

B. Evergreens for new communities near urban centers
   1. The Japanese yew
   2. The various types of yews
      a. Upright yew
      b. Spreading yew
   3. The juniper

3. 1. The engineer's liberal education
      1.1 Necessary courses in the humanities
      1.2 Courses in the social sciences
      1.3 Physical science courses
      1.4 Social science courses
         1.41 History
         1.42 Economics
         1.43 Geography
   2. The engineer's professional education
      2.1 Courses in general engineering
         2.11 Mathematics
         2.12 Physics
         2.13 Mechanical engineering
      2.2 Courses in concentration area
         2.21 Electrical engineering
         2.22 Ceramic engineering
         2.23 Structural engineering
         2.24 Civil engineering

4. I. Directions of Communication in Industry
   A. Upward
      1. Purposes
         a. To inform
         b. To suggest action
   B. Downward
      1. Purposes
         a. To direct
         b. To inform
         c. To issue orders
   C. Laterally
      1. Purposes
         a. To inform
         b. To suggest

5. I. Construction of the Peabody Plant
   A. Labor supply

        1. Skilled
        2. Unskilled
    B. Cost of construction
        1. Interior plant requirements
        2. Exterior plant requirements
        3. Miscellaneous requirements
    C. Time schedule
        1. Initial ground clearing and excavation
        2. Foundation, utilities installation, and exterior brickwork
        3. Interior finishing
  II. Construction of the Shelley Plant
    A. Labor supply
        1. Skilled
        2. Unskilled
    B. Cost of Construction
        1. Interior plant requirements
        2. Exterior plant requirements
        3. Miscellaneous requirements
    C. Time schedule
        1. Initial ground clearing and excavation
        2. Foundation, utilities installation, and exterior brickwork
        3. Interior finishing

6. 1. The conventional American automobile
    A. Cost (initial)
    B. Passenger space
    C. Upkeep (gasoline, insurance, normal maintenance)
  2. The foreign sports car
    A. Cost (initial)
    B. Passenger space
    C. Upkeep (gasoline, insurance, normal maintenance)

II. Arrange the following headings in what you feel is the most logical order. Subordinate those points which require such treatment.

1.   Steps in Writing a Report
Evaluation and interpretation of the data
Tabulation of the data
Gathering information from sources
Choice of a subject
Primary sources of information
Editing the first draft

Utilization of charts, tables, and graphs in the report
Limitation of the topic
Writing the final draft
Purpose of the study
Making a tentative outline
Secondary sources of information
Writing the initial draft
Drawing up a final outline

2.   PREPARING FOR AN EXAMINATION
Reviewing lecture notes
Supplementary reading
Note taking on supplementary reading
Reviewing required reading notes
Preparation of examination materials
Preparation of pens and pencils
Group discussion for review purposes
Answering possible questions
Preparation of slide rules and table of numbers
Formulation of possible questions
Reviewing supplementary reading notes

III. Answer the following questions briefly.
   1. Discuss three different orders of development. Which one (and
      why) would be most effective for the topic, "The Growth in
      Size and Cost of the Federal Government"?
   2. What is meant by the statement, "Before writing the report,
      always make an outline; it can save time and work"?
   3. What is meant by the statement, "The outline must be an
      elastic guide"?
   4. What are the disadvantages of a sentence type of outline?
   5. What is the difference between "parallel wording" and "parallel
      development"?
   6. Outline an assignment made by your instructor.

IV. After carrying through a limited amount of research make up a
    tentative outline on one or more of the following subjects.
   1. Development and printing of pictures
   2. The value of possessing a good vocabulary
   3. How to fish in the winter
   4. How to train a dog
   5. Wood into paper
   6. Growth and specialization in the engineering profession
   7. Growth of motion and time study in industry
   8. Advantages of various consumer-directed advertising media.

V. Outline the following articles, allowing yourself 30 minutes for each one.

1.   Do You Know How to Listen? [1]

Lydia Strong

> The problem is not one of getting men to talk.
> The problem is one of getting leaders to listen.
> —Carl F. Braun, *Management and Leadership*

"So you're doing a study on how to listen?" said an executive we interviewed. "That's a great project, really interesting and worth while. I've done a lot of thinking about listening. Let me give you some of my ideas."

And he proceeded in rapid-fire fashion to describe how he gets other people to listen to *him!*

Our friend mistook the topic, because his mind shied away from the very thought of listening. His feelings were extreme, but not really unusual. Most of us do tend to fidget while the other fellow has the floor. If the subject is boring we drift away to our own affairs. If it interests us, we concentrate on what we're going to say as soon as we can get a word in edgewise. . . .

Half-listening is like racing your engine with the gears in neutral. You use gasoline but you get nowhere.

Fortunately, listening can be learned. Few accomplishments pay higher dividends in efficiency, productivity, and personal satisfaction.

Success in management hinges on ability at problem-solving. Most problems must be solved with people—quite often, people who have highly individual points of view. And in working with people, no tool rivals skilled and sympathetic listening. . . .

Swift Company workers said of successful foremen, in interview after interview: "He listens," or "I can talk to him." A disgusted worker said of another foreman: "He knows it all. And he don't know nothing! 'Why don't you tell me?' says he. But if I try to, he won't let me tell him." . . .

INGREDIENTS OF SUCCESSFUL LISTENING

A few basic principles have been discovered. Of these, perhaps the most essential is that listening is an active process. Figuratively or literally, too many of us "sit back and listen."

[1] Lydia Strong, "Do You Know How to Listen?" *The Management Review,* August, 1955. Copyright by The American Management Association, Inc.

This attitude may work well for music, but we need to "sit up and listen" when we're trying to take part in communication. A good listener's mind is alert; his face and posture usually reflect this fact. He may further show his interest by questions and comments which encourage the speaker to express his ideas fully. If you've ever tried—as who hasn't?—to talk with a poker-faced, bored, silent listener you can readily appreciate the difference.

Another essential is to develop ability at four different levels of listening skill. The first level is to make sense out of sound: that is, to distinguish the speaker's words. The second is to understand what he is saying.

Neither of these skills is quite as simple as it sounds. Spoken words can be mumbled—and jumbled. And the same word may have quite different meanings to different hearers. This is not surprising when you realize that the 500 most commonly used words in English have 14,070 dictionary meanings!

In *The Second World War,* Winston Churchill tells of a long argument that developed in a meeting of the British and American Chiefs of Staff Committee. The British brought in a memo on an important point and proposed to "table" it—which to them meant to discuss it right away. The Americans protested that the matter must not be tabled, and the debate grew quite hot before the participants realized they all wanted the same thing.

Or connotations can shade a word's original meaning. To an executive, the word "efficiency" probably connotes increased results from the same expenditure of energy. To a worker it may mean pay raise or pay cut, layoff or promotion, depending on his own, his family's, and his friends' experiences.

The third level of listening is to tell fact from fancy—in other words, to evaluate a statement. The fourth, and highest, is to listen with imaginative understanding of the other person's point of view. Psychologists call this listening with empathy. It's an essential skill in supervision. But it takes courage to listen with empathy. As psychologist Carl R. Rogers has explained: "If you really understand another person . . . enter his private world and see the way life appears to him . . . you run the risk of being changed yourself. You might see it his way; you might find yourself influenced in your attitudes or your personality."

"LISTENING" WITHOUT HEARING

To stave off this frightening prospect we erect barriers to understanding.

One such barrier is listening intellectually, for the verbal statement alone. We all know better; for if only words mattered, why bother to hold interviews or conferences? Why not do all the work with memos? The answer, of course, is that industry continues to use time-consuming face-to-face communication because nothing else will take its place. The speaker's tone, gesture, posture, and facial expression may reinforce, amplify, or even contradict his verbal statement. Listening without observing is like getting the words of a song without the music.

Bias is a second barrier to communication. It takes many forms. We may decide just from looking at a speaker or listening to his voice that he has nothing to contribute. This could be true, of course, but it is exceedingly unlikely. External factors like the shape of a person's nose, the curl of his lip, the cut of his clothes, or the pitch of his voice may be quite beyond his control. At all events they're not likely to tell us much about the worth of what he has to say.

Or some word, phrase, or idea may so cut across our prejudices that we just stop listening. The speaker says: "We've got to stop making widgets. . . ." This is a sore point with you, this widget fight. So you call him an enemy, and you either interrupt or stop listening. Anyway, you don't hear the end of his sentence, which is ". . . until Tuesday, because the shipment of raw materials was delayed."

A more subtle, harder-to-spot form of prejudice is to distort the speaker's presentation, hear only those parts of it that seem to support our point of view. A movie reviewer writes: "What a stupendous waste of the fine actors and great story, which could have made this one of the year's outstanding films!" The ad quotes him as saying: "Stupendous . . . fine actors . . . great story . . . one of the year's outstanding films!" Cutting out just a few crucial words turned the criticism into praise. We're all adept at this kind of cutting.

Nobody can free himself completely from all forms of prejudice. The best we can do is to expose ourselves to facts as often as possible, and to try to allow in advance for subjective kinks in our point of view.

SOME OTHER PITFALLS

A frequent block to good listening is boredom. Your thought speed, it has been calculated, is four or five times the usual speed of speech. If you're not deeply interested, if the subject matter seems too simple, or if the speaker is on the dull side, you tend to go off on your own private mental tangents. There are times, of course, when inattention constitutes the best possible form of self-defense. But if you do have a purpose in listening, you can stay on the same track as the speaker without slowing down to his pace. Use your spare time to get clear in your mind what you hope to learn, and listen specially for this. Try to anticipate the speaker's next point; review the points he has made already; weigh his evidence. Watch his expression and movements to get the fullest possible understanding of his point of view.

Apathy sets in also when the subject matter is too difficult, or when the speaker fails to make himself comprehensible. If circumstances permit, you can help yourself and any other participants by asking the speaker to be more clear.

Among the more damaging forms of non-listening is pretended listening. You may fool the speaker by nodding and grunting from time to time, but you can never fool yourself. Face the facts squarely. You either have or have not a reason for listening. If yes, and even if the reason is only an inescapable social pressure, listen; you'll get into difficulties if you don't. If no, make an excuse and go away.

Experts have suggested certain procedures which will help you improve your listening. The first is to do some preliminary practicing, as when listening to speakers on television and radio. Try to sort out the speaker's main theme from his digressions, irrelevancies, and supporting subject matter. Try to evaluate his argument. Notice any words or statements which touch off your antagonism or sympathy. Note also any propaganda techniques: appeals to prejudice, use of stereotyped symbols, statements which are cleverly worded to sound logical even though they're not.

When the speaker has finished, write a single paragraph giving his main idea and supporting evidence and stating why he has—or has not—made out a convincing case. If you do this with a group of friends, the group members can compare reactions. This practice, incidentally, will make you a more skillful speaker as well as a better listener.

If the arrangements for a meeting are up to you, provide the best possible physical conditions. Seats should be close enough to hear without straining; face to face for an interview, arranged in a circle or square for a conference. Try to exclude distracting noises and interruptions. If notes must be taken, have pencil and paper ready. It pays to prepare yourself mentally and emotionally for listening. Give some thought to the subject of the meeting. If it's controversial, try to recognize your own prejudices and your possible private goals.

Once the meeting starts, your newly acquired listening skills come into play. Again, you listen for the main points and supporting propaganda appeals. But use this material with, not against, the other person. Chances are you'll be working with him for a long, long time.

Let's say that a person whose point of view is opposed to yours makes a ridiculous, indefensible statement. On a debating team you'd pounce on the statement, make the man look foolish. But the purpose of this meeting is cooperation, not competition. A brief pause will give the speaker a chance to correct himself without feeling humiliated.

Interruption and contradiction should be used only sparingly. But in a small meeting or interview a timely question may help the speaker make himself clear, or may bring him back to the point if he has strayed.

Taking notes may be unavoidable. But you'll do well to keep them as brief as possible. Your time is better spent in concentrating on the speaker.

2.   BRIEF SUGGESTIONS FOR SPEECH IMPROVEMENT

You have frequently noticed the close correlation that exists between the good speaker and the successful executive. Successful businessmen speak clearly, forcefully, and easily.

It is of course true that these men have had more opportunities to speak than some of us; but it is also true that *you* must develop a faculty for speaking. There are dozens of situations that illustrate to you most pointedly how necessary the attribute of good speaking is. In a job interview, can you hope to "land" the position if you merely sit and answer the personnel manager with a "yes sir," "no sir," or "I believe I can." Hardly. He probably has all your academic and experience background down in black and white. He would like to know you; your personality, your character. But he can't learn if you don't talk!

As a salesman, can you express yourself easily to your customers? Can you explain a new idea clearly and forcefully to your supervisor? In both cases the "pay-off" to you will be in dollars and cents.

If you are the sales manager, can you stand up at a board meeting and convince the directors that such and thus is necessary and the expenditure should be made?

The men engaged in commerce and public life today know the inestimable value of possessing commendable speaking abilities. But—as we said earlier—many know, but do not possess.

Actually, there is no reason "not to possess." There is no magic, no inner quality, no "born with the gift" ability to speaking satisfactorily. One may learn, and learn quite easily. You need only concentrate on the few suggestions in the following paragraphs and then practice, practice, practice and then, practice some more.

One of the basic steps is adequate preparation. If you are well prepared, you are confident you will not suddenly run out of ideas or be embarrassed by a question from the audience. Knowledge about the subject will give you confidence in yourself which makes for easy speaking. In preparing your topic you should investigate all the information on it which has been delivered in either a written or verbal fashion. Primary as well as secondary sources should be examined. Authorities in the field should be interviewed.

Also in the process of preparation, carefully printed notes with your topic headings should be composed. These, of course, will be used during the speech when a casual glance will indicate the next topic to be covered. You should prepare your visual aids before your speech so that valuable (and embarrassing) minutes are not wasted trying to make the "darn contraption" work. Chalk should be handy if you contemplate using a blackboard for diagraming. And slips of paper should be inserted in the proper place in the book to avoid, "now just a second; I saw it someplace around the middle of the book."

In the process of research, in preparing your topic, you will probably encounter the arguments that may be raised in opposition to your statements. If you have an opportunity to recognize those arguments *before* your talk, you can more easily prepare a rebuttal should questions be raised.

In addition to preparation, you should make certain your verbal delivery is effective. Your enunciation of words should be clear and your pronunciation equally perfect. The tone of your voice should rise from your chest cavity and not spill forth nasally from your nose nor in a scratchy, superficial manner from the upper throat. Your volume must be carefully controlled to the size of room and audience. Surely it shouldn't "blast" people from their seats nor should it be too soft. Both require an effort to hear on the part of your listeners, and few people will make that effort.

One should also keep in mind physical movement on the platform. Jingling coins or keys, tossing a piece of chalk, tapping a pencil, and pacing back and forth are all disturbing mannerisms and should be avoided. However, the value of a good hand gesture at the proper point is very effective. A smile is also excellent in its place. But the best gestures are not practiced; they are spontaneous and inserted on the spur of the moment. Those are "natural" and they usually prove most effective. One thing is definite; the speaker should not inhibit his gestures.

As for the organization of the talk, that is a point of major importance. If you have carefully followed all other suggestions, but your organization is faulty, the impact your address has on the audience will be slight.

The arrangement of sub-topics must be logical so that the listener may follow your points easily. The entire speech must contain the quality of unity, or a "oneness," without irrelevant digressions and anecdotes. Coherence should be present; it is the careful interconnection and transition of thoughts and ideas. Finally, in your organization, you must watch your emphasis. Before you deliver your talk, you should decide where, how, and what points you will emphasize.

Emphasis may be secured by simple repetition of facts, or key words, or statements. It may be secured by the choice of colorful or image arousing words or by simple proportion. That is, giving an important point the major portion of your delivery time.

These four points; preparation, delivery, movements and gestures, and organization are only a few of the important factors the experienced speaker tests himself on. There are others, such as tone, inflection, rate, word choice, etc. However, the four that we have discussed are "musts." But to talk and study them is not enough. One must practice and practice.

Practice in the front room, in the yard, in front of your mirror; anywhere! Your speaking ability will only improve with practice.

Chapter 6

Tabular and Graphic Presentation in the Report

In writing your report you will often find that the best way to present some of your data will be by the use of some type of graphic aid. This is especially true when you wish to call your readers' attention to a variety of statistical facts.

There is probably nothing more irritating or exasperating to the individual who is examining a report than to try to compare, contrast, or interpret dozens of statistical facts which are sprinkled among the sentences of this paragraph, the preceding one, and another one four pages back. Trying to keep specific sums in mind while looking for previously mentioned comparative figures is a difficult and tiresome job.

How much simpler it is for the reader, and much more palatable too, when he finds all the statistics that are relevant to a particular problem presented in one figure. Whether the facts are presented in a chart, graph, or table, they are usually easy to analyze and compare.

In the few pages which follow, a discussion of the various types of graphic aids is given, but because space is limited, the presentation is not detailed. However, there are dozens of excellent books, reports, and studies on this subject which are easily available to you. An examination of some of them will certainly prove to be a profitable supplement to the comments contained in this chapter.

CONSIDERATIONS IN GRAPHIC PRESENTATION

The only real justification for the use of illustrations in reports is that they assist in the interpretation and clarification of the text material. Properly chosen, carefully drawn, and accurately presented, they can make many of the statements which appear in the body of the report more meaningful. In utilizing graphic representation to assist you in presenting your data, you should avoid making your report a collection of tables and charts with little or no explanation or interpretation of the data. On the other hand, the reader's progress will be laborious indeed if the sentences in page after page of text are crammed with statistical facts, and no attempt is made to clarify the presentation with a table, chart, or graph. A happy compromise is to use a chart, table, or graph where it will prove meaningful and valuable to the reader; then interpret the data in as many sentences as required.

The Reader of the Report

In choosing a type of graphic presentation, consideration of the reader is very important just as it is in other phases of report writing. It would be ridiculous to place a complex logarithmic chart or a Lorenz curve on the *Daily Gazette's* Homemakers' Food Page, illustrating the rise in the price of coffee. It would be just as silly to use a pictogram to help explain to a group of nuclear physicists a complex series of experiments concerning radioactive fallout.

If the prospective reader of your report will appreciate analyzing and comparing five different but related situations on *one* chart, that is what should be used. If your reader would find it much more interesting and understandable to compare a *sketch* of a large money bag with a small one, then that should be utilized. One of your first considerations, therefore, should be: what type of reader will examine this illustration? This point would seem to be so apparent as to require little or no consideration. Not infrequently, however, one finds illustrations in a report that do not match the complexity or simplicity of the material being presented and the audience expected.

Analysis of the Material

A second consideration before choosing the graphic illustration is the material that it is supposed to interpret. Information that is complex and involved in itself should not be represented in a simple illustration or sketch. Conversely, there is no point in taking some little fact and presenting it in an unnecessarily complicated table or chart. In either of these cases the suspicion of the

reader will probably be aroused, or he may assume that an attempt
has been made to delude him. Of course, it is recognized that unscrupulous individuals have attempted to "sugarcoat" a particular
situation by presenting figures that may be "technically" correct
but which may be misinterpreted. Let us say, for example, that
Company Blank had a debt of $85,000 last year which was serious
but not dangerous. This year's debt of $98,000 has the company on
the verge of bankruptcy. If these two facts were presented side by
side as two stacks of dollars, one slightly larger than the other,
with no other reference or interpretation, this would certainly be unethical. Darrell Huff in his book, *How to Lie with Statistics,* discusses
in a very entertaining, yet eyebrow-raising, fashion what can be
done and what has been done with statistics to delude the reader.
However, the point that is being made here suggests that the report
writer carefully evaluate the nature of his material and the type
of reader for whom he is writing before deciding on the graphic
aid which will best present his data.

The Position of the Illustration

Where is the chart, table, or graph placed? Should it be in an
appendix at the end of the report, in a footnote at the bottom of
the page, or within the text itself? There is no specific answer, for
the situation determines the placement of the figure. Most frequently the illustration should be placed within the text of the discussion if it is directly relevant to the material. If the reader finds
the table within the discussion, he can more easily examine it,
make reference to it, or go back to it as he reads the report. Explanatory sentences within the report should direct the reader's
attention to the specific illustration so that he may easily correlate
the written information in the sentences with the statistical data
presented in the figure. If the information in the illustration is of
a supplemental nature to the discussion that is being carried
through, then the figure might most advantageously be placed in an
appendix. However, the report writer should assign his illustrations to an appendix only after careful consideration. Often that
portion of the report is ignored by many readers because of the
trouble usually encounterted in "flipping" back and forth from a
page in the report to the appendix at the end and then back and
forth again.

At times a small chart or graph may be placed in a footnote if the material is concerned with the discussion but is not vital to it. However, this is a rather unusual procedure and is not recommended very often.

In general, the most effective placement of a chart, graph, or table is right within the pertinent discussion with explanatory or interpretive comments preceding and following the illustration.

USE OF TABLES

For the report writer who has a great deal of statistical information to present there is probably nothing more valuable to use than a table. For the reader who is required to interpret a great deal of information, the same is true. This particular type of graphic presentation has a great many advantages:

1. Materials may be listed concisely.
2. One heading at the top of a column may serve for dozens of facts presented.
3. Material which the reader may be required to refer to frequently may be found easily in a table.
4. Comparisons between and among data may be made quickly.
5. Information may be assimilated by the reader much more rapidly when presented in tabular form than if it were dispersed within sentences in the body of the text.

In making up a table there are several basic requirements to keep in mind.

1. Column headings should be clear and concise.
2. Standard terms should be used for all unit descriptions, whether they concern linear measurement, sums of money, or weights. Thus, if exports for a dozen nations are listed, there should be an attempt made to convert dollars, pounds, francs, yen, or lira to one specific monetary value. Of course, an explanatory note should be appended to the table.
3. Figures to be compared should be placed on a horizontal plane because this is the usual way our eyes travel in reading.
4. Tables should always be neat and orderly with plenty of white space within the body and surrounding it to avoid a crowded appearance.
5. Tables should be self-explanatory.

6. Tables should be titled clearly, and the source of data used should be indicated.
7. Tables should be numbered consecutively so that any reference to the table made in the text may be facilitated.
8. The listing of items should follow a logical sequence which may be chronological, alphabetical, quantitative, or geographical.

No. 155.—Institutions of Higher Education—Enrollment, by Type of Institution and by Sex: 1956 and 1957

[Enrollment in thousands. Opening (fall) enrollment of degree-credit students. Includes estimates. Includes data for Territories and possessions]

TYPE OF INSTITUTION	1956				1957			
	Total	Male	Female	First time students enrolled	Total	Male	Female	First time students enrolled
All institutions [1]	2,947	1,928	1,019	723	3,068	2,003	1,065	730
Universities	1,346	963	383	250	1,373	984	390	242
Liberal arts colleges	777	434	342	200	827	463	364	205
Independent professional schools:								
Teachers colleges	278	133	145	72	295	141	153	75
Technological schools	95	89	5	21	98	92	6	20
Theological schools	35	29	6	5	36	29	6	5
Other	68	54	14	13	71	56	14	14
Junior colleges [1]	348	226	122	163	370	238	132	168

[1] Excludes enrollment in 35 two-year institutions devoted wholly or principally to the training of technicians or other semiprofessional personnel.

Source: Department of Health, Education, and Welfare, Office of Education; *Opening Enrollment in Higher Educational Institutions, Fall.*

A Short Statistical Table (United States Statistical Abstract, **1958,** Table No. 155)

Note that in the table illustrated above, the data are easy to read, interpret, and compare—the basic attributes of almost all tabular presentation.

A detailed discussion of the use of this type of graphic presentation is contained in the book *Bureau of the Census Manual of Tabular Presentation* by Bruce L. Jenkinson.[1]

Types of Tables

Some authorities in the field of graphic presentation list three types of tables: spot, special-purpose, and reference. However, all three follow the same basic principles.

The *spot table* is usually placed within a paragraph and is not normally numbered:

[1] Bruce L. Jenkinson, *Bureau of the Census Manual of Tabular Presentation,* Washington, D.C.: Government Printing Office, 1949.

It therefore appears that salaries have increased in a very steady manner since 1940. If this continues, we can expect to be making wage payments in 1970 of about double that of 1940.

		Weekly Wage	
Year		*Men*	*Women*
1940		$ 70.00	$ 60.00
1950		90.00	80.00
1960		115.00	105.00
1970	(projected)	140.00	120.00

Because we must accept these figures as being reasonably reliable, it would certainly be wise if we began making plans now for increases in our product's price.

The *special-purpose* table contains a relatively small amount of data. These facts are clearly titled so that comparisons may be made easily.

Automobile: Standard 8-cylinder Model	Average Miles Secured per Gallon (with HXH Additive)		
	0 to 20,000 Miles	20,000 to 40,000 Miles	40,000 to 50,000 Miles
A	12	12.2	14.5
B	14	13.5	15.5
C	12	12.5	15
D	18	18.5	21
E	19.5	19	21
F	17.5	17	19
G	16	16.5	19.5

The *reference table* usually contains a large amount of data in several columns. Because of its size and the amount of data it contains, it is frequently ruled.

GRAPHIC PRESENTATION OF DATA

The value of graphic presentation of statistical data is also outstanding. The vivid effect gained by a graph, chart, pictogram, or sketch has several advantages over the listing of the same material in the expository section or body of the report.

The graphic illustration may be attractively displayed; it is usually understandable at a glance, and it may be readily interpreted. Charts and graphs save time and space because large amounts of statistical data can be quickly visualized, and dramatic differences in data may be brought to the reader's attention with forceful impact. When Stockholder Jones reads in his annual report that his company's taxes in 1935 were so many digits as compared with the taxes of this year of even more digits, he may not be impressed to the extent that the report writer desires. Stockholder Jones sees so many series of numbers in his newspapers, magazines, and at work that the impact of the tax figure may not reach him. If, however, he is permitted to examine two stacks of dollars, one for 1935 and one for this year, the disparity in their sizes may startle him into an awareness that the report writer will find desirable. The same effect may be achieved with a chart or graph, as well as with a pictogram.

Charts and graphs have some limitations. Normally, they cannot depict as much data as a table. Then, too, only approximate, rather than very detailed and specific facts, may be presented.

TYPES OF CHARTS

Charts usually employ vertical or ordinate lines and horizontal or abscissa lines, spaced equidistant from each other, as the basic figure on which data are entered.

Curve Charts

In the curve chart, each point under consideration is usually located in reference to two variables; most frequently, one is a time factor and the other is the quantity or sum involved. Once the various points have been plotted on the graph, it is a simple matter to connect them into a line which becomes a curve. Thus this chart is very valuable, for it presents a continuous situation along with variations in quantity. Trends in activity, at different periods of time, may be appreciated easily. In addition, a single chart has the advantage of depicting different but related data by the use of multiple curves. Care must be taken, of course, to distinguish among the curves presented. A broken, solid, light, heavy, dash, and other lines may be used on one chart to differentiate among the facts considered. The information, explaining which type of line refers to what fact, is normally placed in a box. This legend may appear directly on the face of the chart or immediately below it.

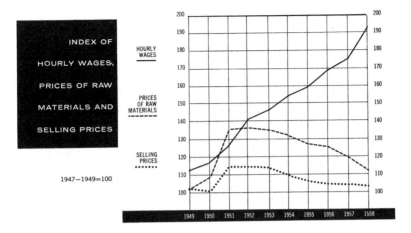

A Typical Curve Chart (Monsanto Chemical Company Annual Report, 1958)

Band Charts

A band or "strata" chart is very similar to a simple curve chart except for various shadings. This hatching or shading should go from dark at the zero line to lighter and lighter shades as the eye moves upward. A key, made up of small blocks, each one properly shaded and identified, should appear at the bottom of the chart. It is not recommended that the legend be printed right in the bands.

A rather serious disadvantage of this chart is that it offers a very general picture; detailed and specific facts can hardly be plotted.

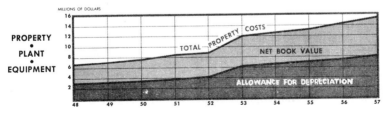

Band Chart (Brown & Bigelow 62nd Annual Report)

Ratio Charts

This type of chart is plotted on ratio paper or semilogarithmic paper. This particular type of illustration may be used for comparing *ratios* or *percentages* of change, whereas arithmetic scales (used in almost all other charts, measure *amounts* of increases or decreases. When changes in percentages are constant in two series being presented on the same ratio chart, the differences between the two consecutive points in the two series should be equal. For example, Bank A has $800,000 on deposit, and Bank B has $200,000 on deposit. On a specific day, Bank A has an additional $80,000 deposited and Bank B receives $20,000. If these two figures, $80,000 and $20,000, were plotted on ordinary charts, the disparity of four to one might be so great as to appear rather incongruous and, perhaps, might force the line right off the illustration. However, using a ratio chart, the task becomes much simpler because the *percentage* of new deposits to holdings is the same in both cases. In other words, the ratio of increase is constant for both institutions; equal changes in *percentages* would reflect equal changes on the vertical axis.

Bar Charts

The use of various types of bar charts conveys information to the reader quickly, easily, and graphically. Bar charts may be found in almost every level of written expression from daily newspapers to highly technical articles. This is because they are extremely flexible and may be readily adapted to almost any field and level of reader.

Comparisons among bars, in any one chart, are usually made on the basis of length. Bars are not usually varied in two directions: length and width. In an attempt to denote changes in two areas with *one* bar, confusion on the part of the reader may result, and, in addition, the appearance of the chart may seem to be peculiar.

In the ordinary chart the bars should be sufficiently wide and properly colored or shaded so that they stand out clearly. Frequently a specific color is employed for each of the years represented and a particular shading for the factors involved. Bars are sometimes given a tridimensional effect for the sake of interesting appearance and, of course, they may be arranged in either a horizontal or vertical plane. However, when the factor of time enters into consideration, the bars are customarily drawn in a vertical position and the illustration is sometimes referred to as a "column chart." The distance *between* the bars varies, but it is usually one-half the width of a *single* bar.

When a chart is drawn on a horizontal plane, it follows a similar pattern to the vertical. In the former, the numerical designations may be placed along the top of the illustration. If the horizontal chart is rather long and wide (because of the many bars presented), the horizontal numerical designations may be placed at both the top and bottom of the chart to facilitate reading and interpretation.

Grouping of bars or columns is often carried through to picture changes in two or more categories from one time to another or to offer a contrast among the categories in a single time period.

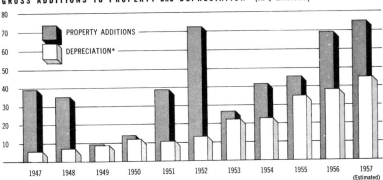

GROSS ADDITIONS TO PROPERTY and DEPRECIATION* (in $ millions)

*DEPRECIATION INCLUDES: DEPRECIATION, OBSOLESCENCE, AMORTIZATION AND DEPLETION.
1955, 1956, 1957 INCLUDE LION OIL.

Bar Chart Drawn on a Vertical Plane (Monsanto Chemical Company Annual Report, 1956)

Component Vertical and Horizontal Charts

These charts are constructed like any "solid" bar chart except for hatching or shading to indicate different data. As in the case of the band charts, the shading should proceed from dark to light, and a key, made up of properly hatched blocks, should be drawn in at the bottom of the illustration.

Sales of Vehicles, Fairmont Agency

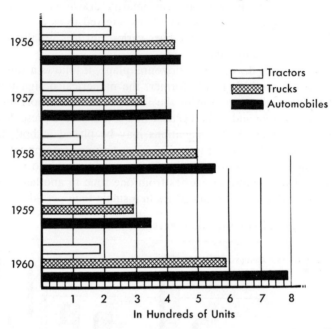

Bar Chart Drawn on a Horizontal Plane

How each dollar was spent in 1960

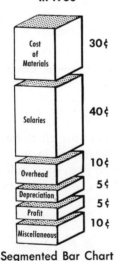

Segmented Bar Chart

Segmented Bar Charts

A segmented bar chart is often used to aid in the graphic presentation of information. When this is done, the total bar represents 100 percent of the data and various portions of the whole are indicated by segments in proper proportion to the percentage the information reflects.

This segmented bar chart may be drawn on a horizontal or a vertical plane. In a great many respects, this type of illustration is very similar to the "pie" or circle chart (discussed below) which also is segmented into proper percentages to make up the whole.

CENTRAL TENDENCIES OR AVERAGES

Averages are frequently employed in the presentation of quantitative statistical data where it is desired to indicate central tendencies and/or characteristics of a group or a series of figures.

The term "on the average" is used frequently and, by many persons, rather loosely. Those individuals who are not familiar with the different types of averages sometimes make misleading statements quite unintentionally. It is, of course, always necessary in report writing to indicate to the reader whether the mean, median, or modal average is under consideration.

Mean Average

The mean average is probably utilized more than the other two. It may be arrived at by simply adding the factors involved and then dividing the total by the number of cases under consideration. The answer is the mean. The disadvantage of this system is immediately apparent on simple examination. If, for example, the report writer points out that Stores A, B, C, and D rang up gross sales for a specific week of $9,800, $10,400, $10,900 and $44,500, respectively, the mean average for each store would be almost $19,000. Thus, to state that the average sales of each of the stores was $18,900 would be technically correct, but most certainly a distortion of the true sales situation for each store.

Median Average

Use of the median average is a little more accurate. In this situation, the factors are arranged in ascending or descending order according to the most logical scale for the items: size, weight, number, distance, etc. The middle factor is then chosen to indicate the median. Thus, 15 is the median in the following group; it is fifth in position from low to high or high to low: 2-5-10-12-15-18-21-23-26.

Modal Average

The modal average is utilized to indicate the typical members

Thus in the following table, the modal average would be $45 per week:

WEEKLY EXPENDITURES FOR FOOD
FOR A FAMILY OF THREE

Families Checked	Expenditures per Week
A	$40
B	45
C	25
D	35
E	45
F	60
G	45
H	50

Ordinarily the use of central tendencies may be of some value when it is known that the reader of the report will usually be "the average man." On the whole, however, charts, graphs, and tables are usually more effective—especially when the report is directed to individuals whose training permits them to interpret statistics easily.

FREQUENCY DISTRIBUTIONS

The use of this device is especially valuable where a large number of cases is involved, and the investigator desires to know which situation occurs with the greatest frequency. In checking questionnaire returns, interview schedules, or examination results, a tally is often made.

A distribution may be prepared by using a tally sheet and noting each case under its proper designation. From the data on the tally sheet, mean, median, and modal averages may be derived and, in addition, graphic illustrations of the information may be constructed. The report writer can thus make up a histogram which is a graphic bar chart presentation of a frequency distribution. From the histogram a frequency polygon can be drawn by the simple expedient of tracing a line to each bar in the histogram.

Those persons working in market research often convert their raw data into distributions. Some trends in consumer demands and

CLASS GRADES: MID-TERM EXAMINATIONS

Grades	Student Scores
100	//
95	////
90	////// /
85	////// ////// /
80	////// ///
75	////// /
70	////
65	///
60	//
55	/

Mean Average: $3795 \div 47 = 80.7$
Median Average: (47 cases) $= 80$
Modal Average: $= 85$

preferences, retail markets, and the influences of price, package design, advertising, etc., may all be drawn from the tabulated data.

SKETCHES AND PICTOGRAPH CHARTS

Pictograms

The use of various types of pictograms has risen tremendously in recent years. They have proved to be very popular because of the effective manner in which they transmit information to the individual who may not have the capacity nor the inclination to analyze and absorb the more technical and detailed representations found in formal types of charts.

The use of figures is admirably suited, in many cases, to newspapers, popular booklets, and other media that the average citizen utilizes. When a figure, such as an automobile, airplane, man, house, dollar sign, is employed, the character itself is made to represent a specific numerical value or measure. To a great many readers this use of symbols to transmit information, rather than a line or a bar on a graph, usually makes the problem more easily understandable and impressive.

Quantities should be represented by symbols of *uniform* appearance and size. They should be equally spaced without scale values or lines. The sketches should be simple so that a subjective interpretation is not made. For example, if a pictogram of "Automobile

WELFARE: ITS BENEFICIARIES

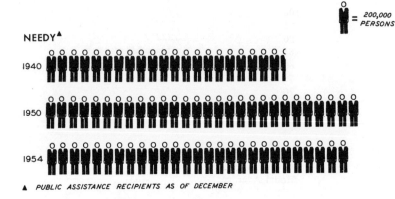

A Simple Pictogram ("Toward Better Government," Report for 39th
Annual Meeting, National Industrial Conference Board)

Production in General" were to be presented, it would be unwise to
draw a series of what appeared to be sleek, highly expensive cars.
The reader may interpret the information as "Production of Expensive Cars Only" rather than "Automobile Production in General."

You should utilize this method of graphic presentation with
discretion. Obviously these pictogram types of illustrations lend
themselves to the presentation of simple data which are directed
to a specific type of reader. As indicated above, pictograms are
often used in the daily papers, annual reports to stockholders,
booklets or reports to employees, and in similar situations. However, the more technical report, which you are usually engaged in
drawing up, will normally utilize a table or line graph more effectively.

Geometric Figures

The use of geometric figures, although quite popular, has frequently received heavy criticism. This is because such figures are
used by some writers to indicate size or quantity, whereas others
utilize it to represent *cubic area* or *volume*. One can easily grasp

the difference in the length of two lines and translate those lines into the magnitude or sum involved, but interpretation is not so easily accomplished when *volumes* are considered. Frequently, the average reader's eyes cannot accurately measure cubic dimensions, and an error in analysis may turn out to be serious.

If you use a geometric figure in your report, indicate clearly whether or not it represents volume. Conversely, when you encounter such figures in your reading, determine exactly what the author wishes to convey.

Pie and Circle Charts

As noted earlier, the "pie" chart is very similar to the segmented bar chart, for it also represents 100 percent of the information involved. The report writer may designate portions of the circle, which have been reduced to specific parts of 100 percent, to indicate specific data. Dividing the circle into accurate segments may be facilitated by utilizing a protractor, marked in degrees, to "cut the pie." The item considered (taxes, salaries, depreciation, etc.) should be noted within the boundaries of its segment as well as what percentage of 100 it depicts.

It is not wise to present two circles for comparative purposes if

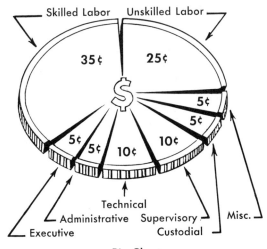

How our salary dollar was spent

Pie Chart

the percentage figures have *not* been marked within the segments or immediately outside the circle and adjacent to the associated part. Slight differences in segment size may be difficult for the reader to ascertain if he is not guided in his interpretation by the statistical values involved. As was the case with geometric figures, an individual's visual analysis of a figure may not be accurate. However, if the numerical percentages are noted within or just outside the segments, the data become clearer to the reader.

The term "pie chart" has, in recent years, come to be applied to much more than the circular diagram alone. One now sees a specific product of a company (such as a bottle cap, a cracker, an automobile, a bar of soap, etc.) cut into portions, the whole of which equals 100 percent.

Map Charts

Where geographical factors or spatial relationships are involved, data may be illustrated easily by the use of a map chart. City, state, county, continent, hemisphere, or world maps may be used. By shading, cross-hatching, dotting, or coloring, specific geograph-

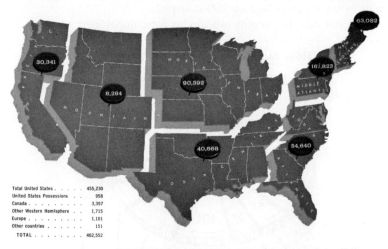

Total United States	455,230
United States Possessions . .	958
Canada	3,397
Other Western Hemisphere . .	1,715
Europe	1,101
Other countries	151
TOTAL	462,552

DISTRIBUTION OF JERSEY SHAREHOLDERS • *Registered holders of Jersey stock now total more than twice the number in 1950. For many years there have been Jersey owners in every state in the nation. Their distribution by regions of the United States is shown above and, to the left, where they live in other parts of the world as of the end of 1957. Owners include not only individuals but educational institutions, foundations, churches, pension funds, and insurance companies.*

Map Chart (Standard Oil Company, New Jersey, Annual Report, 1957)

ical areas may illustrate graphically the facts under discussion.

Dots are most frequently employed when numerical quantities are involved. One dot may then represent 10, 100, 1000, or as many units as the report writer may desire. Population statistics are often presented by the use of this device.

Tiny figures or pictorial symbols are also employed; they are placed on the map so that the reader may readily understand what that specific geographic area has to offer. Some of the more common figures that one sees are animals, oil well derricks, airports, factories, corn plants, and bundles of wheat.

"Exploded," Schematic, and "Cutaway" Drawings

These are all methods of giving the reader a clear view of surface and subsurface areas of a piece of equipment. "Exploded" drawings are especially valuable in technical writing because they depict the component parts of a piece of equipment.

A sketch which gives the reader an understanding of the interior of a mechanical device or piece of equipment is called "a schematic." Sometimes the term is used to indicate an electrical circuit drawing, but more frequently it refers to a sketch showing the interior of an item. A cross section of an item, illustrating the interior, is often referred to as a "cutaway."

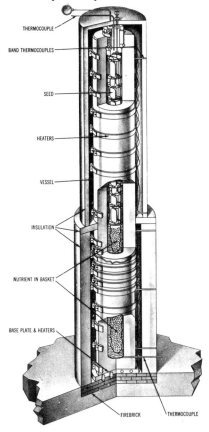

A "Cutaway" or Schematic Drawing of a Western Electric Pilot Plant Vessel with Insulation and Heaters (R. A. Sullivan, "Growing Quartz Crystals," The Western Electric Engineer, April, 1959, p. 5)

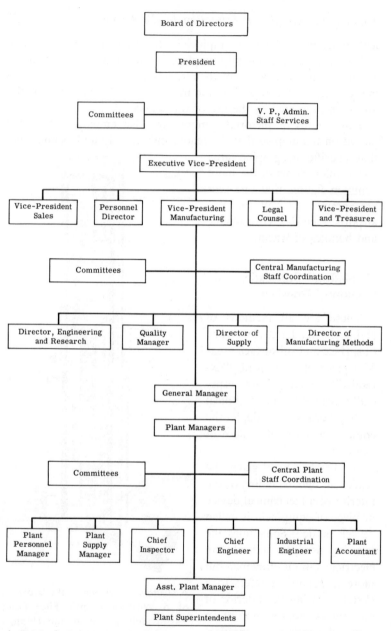

A Typical Organization Chart of an Industrial Corporation (Ralph Currier Davis, *Industrial Organization and Management*, 3rd ed., New York: Harper & Bros., 1957, p. 161)

Organizational Charts

With the administrative machinery of many corporations becoming more complex, the need for employees to understand a clearly defined line of command is very important. When all personnel (except for the lowest echelons) in an organization know exactly where on the "ladder" they stand, friction is often avoided.

This is true in governmental agencies as well as the giant corporations which control several subsidiary firms.

Photographs

Perhaps the greatest value in the use of a photograph is that it can prove the truth of an assertion as no other type of graphic illustration can. If you tell your reader that laboratory tests prove that a specific piece of rotating equipment loses water because it is too shallow, you need only photograph the machine in operation as the liquid flies out to prove your point. If you contend that certain cement supports crack under specific conditions, you can verify your statement by a photograph.

If, on the other hand, you wish to prove how attractive, effective, beautiful, or graceful your item is when used under normal conditions, you may accomplish your objective with a photograph.

Of course, there are some disadvantages, but they are relatively minor. A photograph will present what is *not* significant as well as what is in the same picture. In such cases the unimportant part of the photograph can be "trimmed" out but that may cause the reader to ask, "what has been cut?" Another disadvantage is that colors cannot usually be employed in photographs as effectively, accurately, and inexpensively as they can in charts or sketches. Also, a photograph, unlike a "cutaway" drawing, cannot very well illustrate the section of an item which lies between the exterior and interior surfaces.

Flow Charts

The flow sheet, flow chart, or routing diagram has become very valuable in industry. For the administrator or worker who may not be familiar with a production process, the path to follow in routing information from one division of the company to another, or the

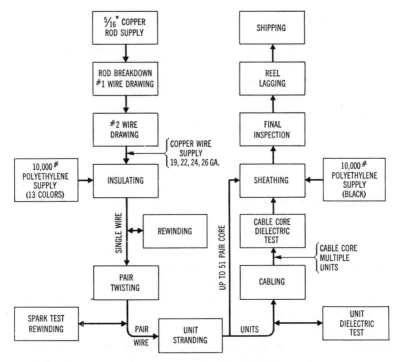

A Flow Chart—A Block Diagram Showing the Sequence of Manufacture for Exchange Area Cable (B. C. Ellis, Jr., and J. F. Strohecker, "The Point Breeze Expansion," The Western Electric Engineer, July, 1958, p. 15)

flow of money payments or receipts, this type of chart provides a dramatic and easy-to-understand picture. Different colored lines or arrows easily and quickly tell the reader the direction of movement.

There may be a good deal of exaggeration to the old phrase concerning one picture being worth a thousand words, but everyone will agree that there is value in presenting certain data in graphic form. The effect on the reader is usually excellent: the information is easier to grasp, more interesting to examine, and simple to comprehend and retain.

There are several points you should keep in mind when selecting and presenting your illustrations.

CHOICE OF ILLUSTRATION

After you have decided to present a segment of your data graphically, carefully consider before making a choice among a table, chart, graph, or pictogram. Evaluate the complexity of the statistics and the level of your reader. Tables and graphs are especially valuable where comparisons are important; pictograms are excellent for visual impact; schematics are superior for illustrating equipment interiors, and so they go—each type with a specific advantage for a particular situation.

READABILITY AND ANALYSIS

The physical appearance of each illustration should not only be attractive but it should lend itself to easy analysis and comparison.

Tables should be carefully ruled, clearly titled, and accurately documented. There should not be so much data as to require extremely long columns which in turn make reading difficult.

In graphs or charts, a reasonable amount of information should be presented, but not so much that the curve lines or bars become very numerous, complex, or confusing to interpret. Here, as with all illustrations, captions should be carefully drawn up and informative sources of data should be indicated clearly.

All graphic illustrations should be numbered consecutively within each chapter so that references to them can be made easily.

Where your reproduction process permits, color should be used. Contrasting colors for different curve lines, bars, map locations, and pictograms all assist in understanding and comparison.

TRUTHFULNESS

Of course, graphic aids should be accurate in the story they tell. At times, however, one encounters a chart or graph which may be "technically" accurate but actually dishonest. Some examples of this have already been cited and many samples may be found in *How to Lie with Statistics*. The figure which follows, for example, has omitted a 20-year span apparently to save space but actually to hide an extremely bad era in the company's history.

Sales
(In Thousands of Units)

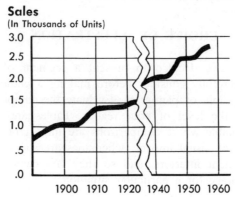

NUMBER AND USE OF ILLUSTRATIONS

Do not use so many illustrations that your reader will become bored and ignore several, nor so few that important facts are lost because they are not presented graphically. If you are positive that a chart or graph will add to the understanding of your comments, design and construct one.

When you use graphic aids to supplement explanatory statements in your report, integrate one with the other. Your statements should point out to the reader the high points represented in the illustration. And the graphs or charts, conversely, should substantiate or emphasize statements in the reports.

ILLUSTRATIONS SHOULD BE MEANINGFUL

At times we are so completely familiar with our topic and the relationships of the data that we forget that our reader may not see as much in our material as we do. For example, it may be unwise to present a chart which lists the following for the current year: 50 men in administrative jobs in the company, 650 in production, 20 in maintenance, and 40 in sales. What do these figures mean? With what should they be compared? Perhaps the sales department is greatly overstaffed with 40 men and production running critically low with 650!

The illustration should contain adequate data or comparative information for valid interpretation and understanding.

For many readers, a simplification of the statistics presented will often make the illustration more meaningful. Rather than indicate that the city now owes $58,675,500, it might be wiser to state (or represent in a pictogram) that every man, woman, and child in the city owes $350!

It is usually better to have your chart indicate that "80 percent of our employees own their own homes" rather than "12,600 of our employees out of 15,750 own their own homes."

In every case, make your presentation as meaningful as possible.

QUESTIONS FOR DISCUSSION

I. Present the data in the following problems in any tabular or graphic form which you feel is the most appropriate.

1. The Bryson Corporation spent 5¢ on machinery depreciation in 1959 compared to 6¢ in 1960. In 1959, 35¢ of every dollar went to pay salaries. This figure was 34¢ in 1960. Taxes took 22¢ in 1960 but only 20¢ in the previous year. Cost of materials came to 30¢ in each dollar in 1959 and 32¢ in 1960. Plant expansion accounted for 4¢ in 1960 and 7¢ in 1959. Net profit went from 3¢ in 1959 to 2¢ in 1960.

2. Draw a simple organization chart of a club, organization, or society of which you are a member.

3. The number of transistor model 34A radios produced by The Monarch Company's three plants varied widely during the years 1958, 1959, and 1960. The Jackson plant produced 85,000 in 1958, 95,000 in 1959, and 110,000 units in 1960. This was far below the Harrison plant's production of 150,-000 in 1958, 175,000 units in 1959, and 225,000 transistors in 1960. For some reason the Fairview plant's production rose and fell during the same three-year period. In 1960 Fairview was down to 140,000 units compared to 210,000 in 1959 and 190,000 in the year previous to that.

4. The average rate of pay per hour for skilled punch press operators at the Monarch Company (since the firm was established) is as listed below and on page 164. Week-end and holiday pay were not included.

1958	$2.90
1957	2.65
1955	2.40
1953	1.90
1954	2.40
1959	3.10

1956	2.55
1952	1.65
1951	1.55
1960	3.15
1950	1.40

5. In question 4 above, list the (a) mean average, (b) median average and (c) modal average.
6. Make a schematic or cutaway sketch of any simple instrument such as a fountain pen, automatic pencil, or stapler. Title and label all parts.
7. During last year the Clear Tone Bell Company had four outstanding quarters of sales among its five models. The Colonial had a rather consistent sale of 25,000 units in each quarter except the third when sales went up to 40,000. The Georgian Bell, a slow seller, had a record of 15,000 units in each of the last two quarters of the year as compared to 10,000 in the first quarter and 12,000 in the second. The Contemporary line sold rather well with 18,000 in each of the first three quarters and 16,000 in the last quarter. The Moderne rose steadily in each quarter with sales of 16,000, 18,000, 20,000, and 24,000 units in the year. The most surprising change took place with the Hostess Bell. It started out with 35,000 units in the first quarter and ended the year with double that or 70,000. However, in the second quarter only 40,000 units were sold and the third quarter was just 5,000 units above that.
8. The number of single dwelling homes constructed in the United States in the year 1958 was 900,000 compared to 1,250,000 in 1959 and 1,500,000 homes in 1960.
9. Student use of library books and periodicals for the 1959-1960 academic year was as follows:

	Books	Periodicals
College of Law	115,000	21,000
College of Commerce	190,000	23,000
College of Engineering	125,000	20,000
College of Liberal Arts	270,000	32,000

As compared to the previous academic year, the College of Law showed a 2 percent increase on book use and a 4 percent drop on periodicals. The College of Commerce records indicate no change in use in 1958-1959 compared to 1959-1960. The College of Engineering figures for book use for 1959-1960 were 4 percent below 1958-1959 and 3 percent less for periodicals use. There was a 5 percent increase in the use of both books and periodicals during the 1959-1960 period compared to 1958-1959 for the Liberal Arts College. In the statistics given above, faculty and interlibrary loan use were not included.

10. The Jet Transport Airlines presents its safety record by two different methods. No major injury or fatality took place on any of its flights during the years 1957, 1958, 1959, and 1960. In those years 2,700; 3,900; 4,900; and 6,100 flights, respectively, were flown.

Jet Airlines flew 2,500,000 miles in 1957; 4,000,000 in the next year; 7,500,000 in 1959; and 12,000,000 miles in 1960.

II. Carry through the assignments listed below.

1. Submit two samples each of a table, line graph, bar chart, and pie chart. Cut these out of magazines, reports, or newspapers. Mount and identify and cite source for each.

2. Follow the directions in problem 1 above for three pictograms and a map chart.

3. Submit two examples of simple tabular or graphic presentation and two of a complex nature. Evaluate the logic of each, noting the source, the intended reader, and the accuracy of the level chosen.

4. What specific advantages are there in using a table rather than a graph for presenting a large quantity of statistical data?

5. When should tables in a report appear in an appendix? When should they appear within the report?

III. Present the data in the following problems in any tabular or graphic form which you feel is the most appropriate.

1. Assume that a class of 48 students enrolled in English 361 and received midterm grades ranging from 68 to 95. Assume 48 grades within that range; make up a frequency distribution on the basis of the data. Convert the frequency distribution into a bar chart. Label all work.

2. Present the following information to (a) stockholders and (b) company executives. Each company dollar is spent as indicated.

	1959	1960
Salaries	$ .35	$ .37
Cost of materials	.40	.38
Depreciation	.02	.03
Net profit	.03	.02
New machinery and equipment	.05	.07
Plant construction	.12	.10
Miscellaneous	.03	.03

3. The following enrollment figures were presented by the Registrar of Central College at a recent faculty meeting.

Year	Full-Time Students
1945	2300
1950	5000
1955	4500
1960	5300
1965 (Projected)	6000
1970 (Projected)	7000

The above figures do not include students classified as "special."

4. Production of the Arco Lamp has climbed steadily during the past five years. In 1960 it was 90,000 units; in 1959 and 1958, 70,000 units; and in 1957, 55,000 units. In the first year of production, 1956, exactly half as many units were produced as in 1960. This is an interesting comparison with the Reflecto Lamp which had a production rate of 25,000 in 1956; climbed 5,000 per year in 1957, 1958, and 1959; and jumped to 75,000 in 1960. In the case of the French Admiral model, production declined from 90,000 units in 1956 to 60,000, 50,000, and 25,000 in 1957, 1958, and 1959, respectively. The year 1960 was the worst for the French Admiral when production dropped to 6,000 units.

5. The Kendall Electric Company produced a large number of relay switches in 1959 and in 1960. Inasmuch as 1959 was the first year in which production was carried through, the results are little less than surprising.

In the classification of "over 750,000 dozen," the 1959 production of the TL100, TL200, and TL 300 was 800,000, 850,000, and 900,000 dozen units, respectively. For the same type of units in 1960, the production was 900,000 dozen units of the TL100; 950,000 for the TL200; and 1,300,000 for the TL300.

In the classification "300,000 to 750,000 dozen" the RS300 sold very well for 1959. In that year the production of RS300 was 525,000 units and 700,000 for 1960. The RS200 numbered 400,000 for 1959 and 450,000 in 1960. The RS100 had a total production rate of 350,000 in 1959 and 400,000 in 1960.

When the 1960 figure only is compared with the production figures for similar units turned out by the subsidiary Marquette Company, the range varies. For the TL100 and TL200, production was up 2 percent for Marquette. For the TL300 it was down 3.5 percent. In the case of the RS100, RS200, and RS300, production of the Marquette Company ran 2 percent, 3 percent, and 5 percent, respectively, more than the Kendall Corporation.

6. Make an organization chart of your college beginning with the dean.

7. Compare the cost of the standard United States Food Basket for 1940, 1950, and 1960. You may assume contents and costs. The presentation is for the "Homemakers' Page" of a major city newspaper.

8. Using the same data as in question 7 above, present the information graphically to the "Economic Council" of the International Bankers' Association.

9. The earnings of seven executives are listed below for last year.

Mr. Stevens	$ 8,500
Mr. Brooks	9,000
Mr. Martin	9,500
Mr. Jameson	70,000
Mr. Schlesinger	80,000
Mr. Gilroy	9,000
Mr. Johnstone	15,000

What specific cautions would you recommend to the reader (and why) if these figures were presented as (a) mean, (b) median, and (c) modal averages.

10. The Acme TV Corporation advertising expenditure figures for January compared dramatically with February of this year. For January in areas 1, 2, 3, and 4, $18,000, $4,000, $16,000, and $21,000 were spent respectively. In February, area 1 and 2 each spent $15,000, whereas $30,000 was expended in area 3 and $37,000 in area 4. Making any assumption you wish, explain these figures to the stockholders of the corporation.

Chapter 7

Drafting the Report

One of the most difficult problems that the report writer must solve is how to present material which is often formal, complex, and factual in an interesting and readable style. Obviously no one would expect a detailed and analytical study of a corporation's personnel problem to read like a thrilling western. On the other hand, there is no reason why it must be as dry as dust, as formal as a starched shirt, and as cold and stiff as a 5-foot icicle.

The writer is faced with a major task when he sits down to write his report. He must transfer what seems to him to be a mountain of data into a readable piece of exposition. His ability to communicate his ideas is now put to the test. If he has learned the techniques of written communication, the task will not be hard; but if he cannot communicate with ease and facility, the job is most difficult.

The ability of the educated person to communicate is a vital one—not only in writing reports but in other avenues of written expression as well. This was demonstrated quite dramatically when the results of a General Electric study were released. That corporation published the results of a survey which was conducted among some 24,000 of its employees holding degrees. One of the questions asked of these college graduates was: *What areas of college study have contributed most to your present position of responsibility with the General Electric Company?*

Of those respondents who had degrees in fields *other* than engineering, "English Communication" was listed as their most important subject in college. Of those who had engineering degrees, "English Communication" was listed second in importance after mathematics. It is, of course, interesting that mathematics is also a communication tool.

This information is cited merely to reëmphasize the well-known fact of how important the ability to communicate is to persons who occupy positions of leadership. The report writer certainly realizes this fact. If he is not as adept as he would like to be, he can improve by applying some of the basic principles of good writing techniques to his own efforts.

This chapter and the one which follows will be concerned with many of the basic factors involved in written communication. Profit by the suggestions made and practice by writing as many reports as you possibly can; you will be gratified with the results.

WORDS

Ideas and Words

Have you ever heard someone say, "I've got the ideas for this project, but I just can't seem to put them into the right words." I suppose most of us have said this at one time or another, and yet we so often do not recognize the depth of the statement. If ideas are to be of value to mankind, they must be communicated. If that communication is not clear; if it is garbled or confused; or if it is incomplete; the value of the idea is diminished appreciably or even lost.

If we do not communicate our ideas with as much force and clarity as we would like, we should seek the reason. Mr. A. M. Sullivan, one of the officers of the respected commerce journal, *Dun's Review,* made some excellent comments in an article entitled "Words—Precision Tools." He introduced his discussion with the following statements:

> The most annoying person I can think of is the verbal parrot who says, "You know what I mean. You know what I mean," and you know that he hasn't the capacity to express himself. The next worse bore in dialectics is the person who says, "In other words," and gives repeated evidence of his inability to convey a precise meaning, mood, or condition.
>
> Precision in meaning is probably the greatest single need in meeting the problems of religion, politics, and economics in any day, and especially in our day. . . . when misunderstanding is the result of our

lack of skill in putting words together, then the fault is ours, and the fault is serious.[1]

Because ideas are made up of words, it is certainly wise to examine our fund of words as well as our use of them. Words are the building blocks and the foundation of ideas.

Ideas and Vocabulary

Obviously if the report writer is to express his ideas easily and clearly his supply of words must be adequate. If he is constantly "at a loss" for words, the expression of his ideas will be impaired. It is therefore of value for each of us to have some idea of our vocabulary level. If we find, after taking one of the many standardized tests which are available, that our vocabulary level is not as high as we would like, we should make every effort to raise it.

Enlarging a vocabulary is not a difficult task—but it does require work. It is not enough to read widely among excellent pieces of literature; words that are new to the reader must be copied from the source and then checked in the dictionary for usage, denotation, and connotation. After that a conscious effort must be made to use them again and again in verbal and written communication. It is in this way that a new word becomes part of our permanent "using" vocabulary.

Some persons have found one or more of the "vocabulary building" paperback books, hard cover volumes, and manuals to be of value. There are several on the market from which to choose, and the cost is nominal. Many individuals carry small notebooks in which they record new words. However, it should be remembered that "recording" is of little value, if "using" does not occur.

In every instance, a conscientious and determined effort on the learner's part is necessary if he is to expand his vocabulary. Mere reading or hearing new words will not be especially fruitful. New words, like new skills, are not usually absorbed through the process of osmosis. They must be consciously and conscientiously assimilated.

Word Connotation and Denotation

In using words, a careful distinction should be made between what the word suggests to the listener (connotation) and what it

[1] A. M. Sullivan, "Words—Precision Tools," *Dun's Review,* October, 1952. Reproduced by permission of Dun & Bradstreet, Inc.

actually means by definition. Thus the word "horse" means "A large, solid-hoofed, herbiverous quadruped" (denotation); however, if the same animal is described as a "nag" it suggests a completely different picture as compared to "stallion" or "thoroughbred" (connotation).

To different people and in different contexts, words have distinct emotional and imaginative meanings (connotation). Although the denotation of the following words is "payment for services," the connotations differ: fee, stipend, wage, salary, honorarium, pay, compensation, emolument, remuneration.

Certainly the surgeon receives a *fee,* the laborer is given *wages,* and the stenographer is paid a weekly *salary.* These words are not interchangeable; their connotations differ. We associate *fee,* not *wages,* with a surgeon; we pay our secretary a weekly *salary,* but we do not award her an *honorarium* or pay her *wages.*

Thus in writing our reports, we must choose words for their proper denotations and connotations. As in many other areas, the words we choose are largely determined by who the reader will be.

Differences in Word Levels

When we speak of word levels or levels of usage, we usually refer to the dictionary classifications: standard, colloquial, obsolete, archaic, illiterate, slang, dialectal, and technical. Words which are standard do not carry any special designations in the dictionary; other words are labeled colloquial, obsolete, or in any of the other ways noted above.

STANDARD WORDS

When writing a report which is directed to a company's client, standard words should be chosen and presented in a formal style. For example, you might say: "It is a matter that should not be permitted to exist under present economic conditions." However, the same idea could be communicated in an interoffice memo in an *informal* manner: "It's a matter that shouldn't be permitted to exist under present economic conditions."

TECHNICAL WORDS

Obviously technical words should be employed by professional personnel engaged in specialized activities. When an engineer, physician, lawyer, chemist, or physicist writes for his particular reader, he must use the language of his field. If he does not, he will find it almost impossible to express himself concisely and accurately. Can you conceive, for example, how a physician might express the following idea *without* using a technical vocabulary:

> The role of the hypothalamus in regulating water balance centers principally in the *supra-optic nucleus.* It is possible that some cells of the paraventricular nucleus also participate. The axons of these neurons pass down the infundibular stem and branch to form a dense meshwork among the pituicytes, ...[2]

COLLOQUIALISMS

These words are acceptable in informal conversation and writing.

The airlines have a difficult time with reservations because of the many *no shows.*

If you're really serious, we can clean out the *dead wood* by the end of the week.

SLANG

These words should not be used in any formal writing and are acceptable only very infrequently in informal situations.

Those *hoods* (hoodlums) threatened to *knock off* (to kill) Mr. Byron.

DIALECTAL WORDS

These words should not ordinarily be used because their meanings are familiar only in specific regions of the country.

OBSOLETE AND ARCHAIC WORDS

These words should not be employed in writing; however, they are found in dictionaries to explain statements written in earlier periods.

ILLITERACIES OR VULGARISMS

These words should not be used except in reproducing dialogue.

"We ain't got no money."

---

[2] *Ciba Clinical Symposia,* vol. 8, no. 4, p. 136.

These then are some of the word classifications found in every standard dictionary. The report writer will usually employ standard and technical words in a formal writing style.

Perhaps the most important fact in word usage is to match the words to the reader. An explanation of the mechanics of a bond issue will be presented differently, depending on whether the reader is a stockholder, an employee, or a member of the company's board of directors. The words chosen must be at the appropriate level.

Word Usage

Clarity and exactness in the presentation of ideas are dependent to a large extent on the care with which the words in the idea are chosen. A skilled artisan or a competent technician is extremely careful of the tools or instruments he chooses when he undertakes to complete a specific task. Certain tools are made for specific jobs, and certain words are "made for" the best expression of specific ideas.

"What's the difference," asks a college freshman, "if you use words wrongly or inaccurately, so long as your meaning gets across? Isn't it just splitting hairs to quibble about the precise meaning of a word?"

His is a widespread attitude these days, and there are several possible answers to it. The most obvious, of course, is that in many cases the meaning *doesn't* get across if the wrong word is used—and thousands of people have had to go to court to straighten out grammatical errors.

Equally important is the fact that useful words are lost to the language if they are persistently misused, and this results in an impoverishment of speech.

The other day I was reading an article on television in which the writer mentioned the large staff required for a certain program—ending with the phrase, "the enormity of the operation."

Now "enormity" does not mean size alone, but a large wickedness, or an outrageous act or offense.

"Enormous" means size alone, but if we keep using "enormity" for this meaning, then we have lost a useful word to describe some particularly heinous offense.

Also in this category are the two related words "masterly" and "masterful." We find them used almost interchangeably in most speaking and writing; but "masterful" means domineering and arbitrary and haughty, while "masterly" means "with superior skill and power."

By ignoring the distinction between these two words, we gain nothing and we rob the rich tool chest of our national vocabulary. It is just as though a carpenter called a screwdriver an awl, and began using the screwdriver to do the work of an awl. . . .

It is not prissy or pedantic to object to these misuses, for a language reflects the powers of thought and discrimination of a people. When a civilization begins to disintegrate, its language shows the first signs: the fall of Rome was preceded by the decay of the Latin tongue in its everyday usage.[3]

If we want "illusion," we should not use "delusion"; if we mean "farther," we shouldn't use "further"; and if the correct word is "uninterested," then "disinterested" should not be employed. A careless choice of words certainly seems to reflect careless thinking.[4]

SENTENCE SENSE

Choosing words with care and precision is vital in expressing ideas clearly. Once selected, the words are linked together to form sentences, and these sentences convey our ideas. Sentences may make a statement of fact (declarative), ask a question (interrogative), issue a command or request (imperative), or express strong feeling (exclamatory).

Sentences are also classified on the basis of their internal structure: simple, compound, complex, and compound-complex. Using these different types in various ways permits us to secure variety and interest in our writing style.

Simple Sentences

These are composed of one complete thought—not a fragment or a portion of an idea, but a complete idea.

John went to the bank.

Betsy went home.

Compound Sentences

A compound sentence contains two or more simple sentences or two or more complete thoughts.

[3] Sydney J. Harris, columnist, General Features Corporation, 250 Park Avenue, New York. Reprinted by permission of the author.
[4] See Chapter 24 for a list of words frequently misused.

Robin went to school, and Shelley went to the library.

Robert Brennen registered for Report Writing 361, but his friend, James Pierce, signed up for Business Letters 211.

Complex Sentences

A complex sentence contains one independent clause or statement and one or more subordinate clauses. The dependent or subordinate clause is *not* a complete thought but depends on the main clause to convey its full meaning.

When the flat tire was noticed, we immediately stopped the car.

I was disappointed to find that supper was rarely ready when I came home.

Compound-Complex Sentences

This type of sentence is made up of one or more independent clauses and one or more dependent or subordinate clauses.

Before I arrived at the factory, Bob had set up the punch press, and Mr. Graham had begun to stack the sheets of steel.

Using just one of the types of sentences listed above results in a deadly and monotonous writing style. Examine the two examples below and then the revision. The contrast is striking.

USING SIMPLE SENTENCES ONLY

An analysis of sales for the month of December is interesting. The sales volume of December of this year is much higher than the sales volume of December of last year. Sales are up 14 percent.

This may be explained easily. The reason is probably our new TV program. The program began in October. Results have been good. November sales were up 6 percent. This is in comparison to November of last year.

One item in our line had the greatest rise in sales. It was

USING COMPOUND SENTENCES ONLY

An analysis of sales for the month of December is interesting and indicates that the sales volume of December of this year is much higher than the sales volume of December of last year.

Sales are up 14 percent and this may be explained easily. The reason is probably our new TV program, and this program began in October. The results have been good, but November sales were up 6 percent and this is compared to November of last year.

USING SIMPLE SENTENCES ONLY (*Continued*)

women's blouses. Most of our TV advertising concentrated on our blouse line. A free pair of nylon hosiery was given with each blouse purchased. This was done in December.

A conclusion may be reached. TV advertising focusing on a single line is wise. This is better than TV advertising which presents several lines. A free item also seems to boost sales. This plan is recommended for January and February sales promotion.

USING COMPOUND SENTENCES ONLY (*Continued*)

One item in our line has had the greatest rise in sales and this item has been women's blouses. Most of our TV advertising concentrated on our blouse line and a free pair of nylon hosiery was given with each blouse purchased, and this was done in December.

A conclusion may be reached, and that is that TV advertising, focused on a single line, is wise. This is better than TV advertising which presents several lines; also a free item seems to boost sales. This plan is recommended for January and February sales promotion.

USING A VARIETY OF SENTENCE TYPES

An analysis of sales volume for the months of November and December of this year indicates a rise of 6 percent and 14 percent respectively compared to similar months of last year. This is doubtlessly due to our new TV program which was begun in October.

Women's blouses reflected the greatest rise in sales because our TV advertising concentrated on this item, and a free pair of nylons was given with each blouse purchased. Certainly our most effective sales promotion is achieved when our TV advertising emphasizes a single item which is "tied" to a free gift.

This type of promotion is recommended for the first two months of the approaching year.

It will certainly be agreed that the version using only simple sentences is monotonous, childish, and deadly. The second attempt, using compound sentences, achieves a singsong, seesaw effect where every idea presented has the same value; nothing is emphasized.

The last attempt has a variety of sentence types. The paragraphs display some flexibility, there is variation in structure, interest is achieved, and greater clarity is secured. It is also important to note that the last example, certainly superior to the first two, has only 97 words as compared to 155 words in the simple sentence example and 172 words in the compound sentence version. A fact to ponder: the best of the three had only slightly more than *one-half* the words of the other two!

In writing your reports, you should use a variety of sentence types to achieve interest and clarity. And keep in mind the value of conciseness. If your report is ten pages long and you cut it to seven and still convey the *same* ideas, you will have improved the writing style. A short story, a movie, a novel, or a speech that moves rapidly and without extra words to its climax or important facts is always more interesting to the reader or listener. Sentences that include extra words, unrelated ideas, or illogical construction usually lack unity and coherence.

Wordiness in Sentence Structure

Unrelated ideas and extra words should be eliminated; if they are permitted to remain, they will obscure the meaning of the sentence. Every word in every sentence should contribute to the objective of securing a clear idea.

WORDY: In an analysis of the questionnaire returns, which came in over a three-week period, it was found that most of the respondents, who, by the way, were in the Huntington rather than the Radcliffe area, preferred that kitchen appliances be white, rather than any one of the three pastel colors listed.

BETTER: An analysis of the questionnaire returns indicated that white, rather than a pastel color, was preferred for kitchen appliances. (If other facts are deemed important, they may be presented in separate sentences.)

WORDY: The little girl who was selected for the leading role became, as so many children of that age, very excited at the prospect of appearing before a large audience which would be examining her performance very critically.

BETTER: The little girl who was selected for the role became very excited at the prospect of appearing before a large audience.

WORDY: It would seem that the drop in sales in southern Illinois of model 230, which you know utilizes the same frame as our older model 105, is due to the unusual labor conditions in the Rockmount area that are caused by the closing down of the King Coal mines. Many men are out of work, and, consequently, economic conditions are poor.

BETTER: In southern Illinois, sales of model 230 have decreased. This is undoubtedly due to the poor economic conditions in Rockmount caused by the closing down of the King Coal mines.

Always write as concisely as you possibly can. It is true that it requires more effort on the writer's part to present a report in 1500 words rather than 2000, but the effort is worth while. The report is easier to read, more interesting, and more sharply focused on the points of importance.

During World War II, when Winston Churchill was the Prime Minister, it is said that he presented an important war message after his introductory comment, "I am sorry this communication is so long, but I did not have time to write a shorter one."

Sentence Clarity

Of course, there is more to good writing than choosing words correctly, using a variety of sentence types, and being concise. The sentences which make up the report must be clear. There should be no ambiguity, fogginess, or confusion in the interpretation of each sentence.

Confusion in Sentence Sense

We have all read sentences that are so confused in their meanings that they have made us laugh. Perhaps we have never written any that are as ridiculous as the following, but sometimes they do slip in, and when that happens, the reader of our report turns his attention to this glaring error. It is similar to the case of the individual who dresses perfectly in tuxedo, matching shirt, and tie and then slips on tennis shoes instead of the black footwear required. Everyone's attention is focused on the error; everything else about this perfectly groomed individual fades into insignificance. So, too, with a glaring error in an otherwise well-written report: the spotlight is placed on the ridiculous sentence.

If the report on the punch press is satisfactory, send it at once.
(Send what? The report? The punch press?)
If the report is satisfactory, send the punch press at once.

The mother rebuked the child when she made an error.
(Who made the error? The mother? The child?)
When the child made an error, her mother rebuked her.

To fly efficiently, the competent mechanic should check the plane
before each trip.
(Will the mechanic fly? Or will the plane?)
To insure that the plane will fly efficiently, the competent mechanic
should check it before each trip.

In the cases above, a simple revision will make the sentence clear and acceptable. In most instances, all that is necessary is to move the descriptive (or modifying) words closer to the word or words to which they refer.

The careful and precise use of words and sentences, certainly helps us complete a satisfactory report. There are additional factors such as the tone of the report and its unity and coherence which we will examine in the next chapter.

QUESTIONS FOR DISCUSSION

I. Cite the differences in connotation of the following words which are listed in a thesaurus as synonymous.

1. Director
   Manager
   Superintendent
   Overseer
   Taskmaster

2. Skilled
   Dexterous
   Adroitness
   Knack
   Talent
   First fiddle

3. Respect
   Consideration
   Deference
   Approbation
   Homage
   Reverence
   Veneration

4. Attentive
   Advertent
   On the job
   Observant
   Absorbed

5. Meal
   Repast
   Spread
   Mess
   Picnic
   Banquet
   A feed

6. Child
   Papoose
   Kid
   Brat
   Bambino
   Urchin

7. Traveler
   Transient
   Commuter
   Tourist
   Wanderer
   Vagabond
   Nomad

8. Woman
   Dame
   Nymph
   Matron
   Maiden
   Lady

II. Make such changes as you feel are necessary in the following passages so that they are readily acceptable in a formal report.

1. A careful look-see at the plant's interior revealed that some major changes would be necessary in the heating and ventilating system. Also the machines will have to be shuffled around if the new production line is to get going by the first of the month.

   As far as the office space which is provided for the office brass is concerned, that seems more than adequate. However, we've got a real knotty problem on the employee locker situation and a corker to get over on the loading docks. In addition to this an office will have to be provided for the medic's Florence Nightingale. But I think the architect we got can handle it easily; he really seems to be on the ball.

2. The problem as far as the market is concerned is whether or not John Q. will pull another switcheroo on us and not go for the chrome. Of course, I doubt that will happen because our questionnaire boys have been out tapping the market. What they learned would seem to indicate that we can finalize our plans on our new Kitchen Helper appliance line.

   There is one other show we've got to place under the microscope and that's the appliance store dealer. You know he's the boy who can make or break our summer line. We've got to give him a sales pitch built completely around the old green lettuce approach. If we don't, you can bet your bottom dollar that Ace Appliance Manufacturers will be in there taking over from us.

3. We have a situation in the plant which is somewhat disturbing. At times we have need for a research engineer in our particular field. However, we do not have one. We would have a problem if we hired one for full-time work. There is not always enough work for one man. However, we sometimes need one. In the past, we have hired a consulting research engineer. This has proved to be expensive.

   In the past three years we have used consulting engineers. The yearly fees have averaged $4800. A full-time man would not be much more costly. His salary would be about $8000 per year. He could of course carry on full-time research. We are expanding. We are also growing. For all these reasons I recommend that we hire a full-time man. He should be a qualified research engineer. He should be trained in our field.

4. An examination of our correspondence indicates that it leaves much to be desired from the standpoint of courtesy, completeness, and conciseness; this was definitely proved by the communication consultant who spent several days with us and examined our carbon copies and showed me the wide differences which exist in the quality of our letters from very

poor to excellent and with no relationship to the level of the writer in the company.

It is therefore my recommendation that said consultant, Mr. Barnett, by name, be engaged to run a series of classes for all administrative and office personnel for the express purpose of securing better quality letters, with emphasis on conciseness, and also to visit all interested personnel at their desks for conferences in the general area of improvement in written communication as well as such other areas which are associated thereto and furthermore that he be available to us for such other work and advice that we require and which lie within his field.

5. The relationship which exists betweeen employer and employee is one of paramount importance in industry today. When this relationship is on the beam, all parts of the factory hum along smoothly. However, one should not assume that good relations will result, hocus-pocus, from adding another buck to the pay voucher or seeing that each Joe and Jane has a turkey in the pot for the Thanksgiving holiday.

No; good relations requires more than pay and fringe benefits. It is necessary to recognize the dignity of each employee and treat him like a respected person. It is also vital to keep him informed of what goes on in the company; what the firm's goals are and where it expects its arrows to land. It is not unwise to explain policies; how they are formulated and why they were arrived at. Too often decisions for the employees to carry through seem to come from the wild blue yonder without purpose or reason.

III. Make any changes which you feel are necessary in the following sentences to make them acceptable for use in a formal report.
   1. The present situation in sales puts all of us up in the clouds.
   2. The unexpected exigencies which have arisen give us all cause for some stimulated cogitation.
   3. It would seem, by and large, that all similar cases which arise, in reference to the situation under discussion, should be handled promptly, quickly, and expeditiously.
   4. We have investigated the credit of the Armstrong Company and we found that their credit is not all it's cracked up to be.
   5. We feel that you will agree that under the circumstances when payments are not made as requested on the invoice, and throughout the furniture industry, that good relations cannot be maintained.
   6. Although Mr. Martin always looked through rose-colored

glasses, I believe he had good reason for his optimism in this case.

7. One need not make rash statements if one only checks the projected figures and if one takes into account the market situation.

8. Under similar business situations, we should batten down the hatches, furl the sails, and make preparation to buck the storm.

9. Anyone not on the beam in this organization had better drop his ballast and hit the silk as soon as possible.

10. An investment in the Aceland Corporation is as good as gold and as solid as the pyramids.

11. Although the Johnson Corporation and the Melton Corporation both were involved in extensive research work for the government as well as all of industry, I felt that it wasn't fair that the Johnson Corporation should make an extra charge. However a good job was done by both and I awarded the contract to the one which did the best job. Therefore when you write to the company for information, you will be wise to mention our name.

12. The legislation was brought up at the conference as well as the wage contract, and it was felt that it should be handled as the first order of business.

13. Although the salesmen gave the campaign all they had and really turned on the big push in June, the results were rotten.

14. Profits and wages must both be considered carefully, but if a company does not watch its step, attention to it is not given and then difficulties for the company arise.

15. Although the salesforce was lethargic and lackadaisical in their efforts, the unusual, outstanding, and superior qualities of our, as yet unmatched, product helped the sales record to soar to unheard of heights.

Chapter 8

The Report in Final Form

Writing the report in its final form is both a simple and a most difficult task. As paradoxical as this may seem, it is essentially true.

Writing the report is simple because the researcher *has completed* the time-consuming and difficult tasks of gathering information, analyzing it, and interpreting it. Now, only the final job is left and that is to write the report using the material which has been gathered.

But presenting the report may also be most difficult if the writer has not mastered the techniques of good composition. The experienced report writer is aware of the qualities of tone, style, unity, emphasis, and coherence. He can apply these almost out of habit as he writes. Because of this he can concentrate on the presentation of his message. However, for the report writer who must constantly check his grammar, diction, rhetoric, tone, and style, as well as the content of the report, the job can be *most* difficult.

TONE

The tone of the report reflects the writer's position toward the problem under discussion and his attitude toward the reader. There are several factors which are involved in tone which merit examination.

Objectivity

Whether the report writer works on a problem for a week or a year, he cannot help but become involved intellectually and

183

emotionally. Try as he might, it is difficult to maintain an impersonal and completely objective viewpoint when he writes the report. Although many authorities maintain that objectivity is necessary, it must be recognized that everyone does build up prejudices as he cogitates on a controversial issue. Therefore, for us to categorically state that the report writer must be completely neutral is ridiculous.

On the other hand, there is no reason why the report writer cannot attempt to be as impartial as possible.

A tone of objectivity may be achieved by presenting both sides of an issue, citing advantages and disadvantages, displaying facts pro and con, and eliminating, insofar as possible, personal reactions and viewpoints.

Positive Tone

Wherever possible a positive rather than a negative tone should be used in writing the report. A positive statement speaks of pleasant and desirable objectives; it indicates what can be done. The negative is the opposite and arouses in its reader's or listener's mind an unfavorable association with the product or service. Here are some examples of what is meant:

NEGATIVE	POSITIVE
We hope you will not be dissatisfied with the enclosed report.	We are sure you will be pleased with the enclosed report.
We do not believe you will have much trouble or difficulty putting our recommendation into operation.	We are sure that these recommendations, when put into operation, will result in increased production and higher employee morale.
Because of a variety of unforeseen difficulties and complications, it will be impossible to complete the report before April 21.	We are happy to tell you that the report will be delivered immediately after April 21.

In writing the report, the writer should strive to organize his statements in a positive fashion. The reader's reaction to them will be much more favorable. There is, however, some value to the use of a negative tone as is so frequently displayed in modern advertising. We sometimes encounter advertisements that arouse an unpleasant association in our minds by asking if our "tires are safe from blowouts" or if we are "in danger of vitamin deficiency," and others of a similar nature. But in almost all cases where a negative problem is used, a positive *solution* is emphasized and dominates the advertisement. So far as we are concerned, in the general area of report writing, almost all statements should be presented in a positive manner.

Friendly, Natural Tone

There is no reason why a report should be "stuffy," stiff, and filled with hackneyed phrases. It is true that the writing style should be formal, but it can also be friendly and the word choice can be natural. Although the topic of word choice is discussed elsewhere, the reference in this case is to the entire tone of the report which is drawn from the choice of words and the writing style.

This natural tone is evident in a National Broadcasting Company report entitled "How Television Changes Strangers into Customers." Here are a few quotations from the actual report. Notice how friendly and "relaxed" these statements are:

> You can't expect people to "ask for it by name" if they've never even heard of the name. So your very first step in creating customers through advertising is to make people *aware* of your brand name. . . .
> It's not enough for people to be aware of your brand name. They must associate it with your cigarette, your cleanser, your cereal, etc. The moment they see or hear your name, they must get a mental picture of your product. . . .
> A slogan is a capsulated sales message—a single, compelling reason for product purchase. Advertising which impresses the slogan on consumers is an important step in the pre-selling process. Television, which delivers the message to the mind through sight and sound and motion, has a rich talent for selling the slogan. . . .[1]

It would be a simple matter to have written the above sentences in a stiff and pompous manner, but how much more readable they are in their present form.

The "You" Attitude

The "you" attitude is sometimes defined as "an awareness of the reader or listener's point of view." Writing with such a point of view in mind can certainly contribute to the tone of a report.

---

[1] Reproduced by permission of the National Broadcasting Company, Inc.

In the report issued to employees or stockholders, it is wise to speak of "your company," "your profits," "your corporation's growth." When the reader is involved in the report, he will usually give it his undivided attention.

"We" Attitude	"You" Attitude
This corporation has had an excellent year and the directors are very gratified at the profit margin.	Your corporation has advanced during the past year and strengthened its position.
The executives have undertaken a new policy of management-labor relations. They have established a representative group from labor and from management which meets once each week for the purpose of discussing common problems of interest to improve profits.	With the conscientious assistance of employees from all levels, a conference group has been established which meets periodically. Its primary purpose is to improve management-labor relations for the advancement of the company and each of its employees.
In addition, the top echelon of the company, after extensive research and analysis, has outlined a new compensation schedule for its level to match the percentage increase recently granted to the hourly workers.	In addition to improved services for employees, wages and fringe benefits have increased as well as the profits which are returned to stockholders.

Notice in the "we" attitude section the frequent references to the executives' work, the executives' company, and the executives' profit. Certainly the approach used in the "you" attitude paragraphs will prove much more acceptable to the employees to whom the report is directed.

Although it is not always possible to write from the reader's viewpoint, an attempt should be made in that direction whenever possible. As long as the report writer knows the approximate social, economic, and educational backgrounds of his readers, he should write with their best interests in mind.

STYLE

Style is an intangible quality of all writing. Although it is difficult to define, we often say that style is the author's manner of expression, the way he "puts sentences together," his sense of humor, the color and liveliness of his statements, and his overall presentation. We have often said that this writer's style is dull and this author's style is interesting; his articles are lively, hers are entertaining, and his are persuasive. These are all descriptions of writing style.

Obviously style, which is just as much a part of expository writing as it is of narrative, involves many qualities: choice of words, objectivity (both of which have been discussed earlier), conciseness, persuasiveness, coherence, unity, and emphasis.

Reports need not be dull and deadly as they are so often said to be. They can just as well be lively, interesting, and even entertaining. A General Electric booklet has this to say about writing style:

> We know from experience at General Electric that too many of our younger employees say to themselves before spreading their wings for a flight with words: "But if I write that report the way I *feel* it should be written, my boss will think that I am a child." If an engineer, for example, is testing an insulating material and it chars and smells like burned string beans, we can think of no reason why he should not say so.
>
> Our business world needs young men whose minds are packed with facts, but with the boldness of imagination to release them in a form that is easy and pleasant to take.
>
> We have on our desk copies of *The General Review* and the *Scientific American*—both written for thousands of top-flight engineers and scientists. The editors of both magazines know that factual reporting is necessary so that their readers, who are so brilliantly expert in many fields, will have confidence in the authority of their articles. But they know, too, that men and women, whatever their job or profession, are willing to begin and stay with an article only if it is well written. Only you can guess how many books and articles you have thrown aside after tasting the first few paragraphs. Everyone who reads and listens is so very human.
>
> Without interested readers, whether the magazine is *Scholastic* or *Scientific American*, its survival depends upon the skill and labor-of-love that editors and authors lavish upon it. Your survival . . . depends upon your ability, desire, and courage to put your best foot forward in a world that will judge you by your words as well as your actions.[2]

A college professor, writing in a bulletin recently, felt similarly. He pointed out that report writers may be "trained to write tech-

[2] "Why Study English?" a General Electric Educational Publication.

nically perfect prose but hideously colorless documents." He goes on to recommend that "personality" be injected into the report, that variety in sentence structure be employed, and that a well turned phrase be used wherever possible.[3]

Conciseness

One of the most valuable qualities of writing is conciseness. Know what you are going to say, say it, and stop! There is nothing as distracting to the reader as irrelevant material and "padded" details in a report. The very essence of a report is conciseness; the busy executive who requested the report in the first place looks for that quality along with accuracy, completeness, clarity, and objectivity.

The report that is concise will be much more interesting to the reader. Shorn of all unnecessary verbiage, details, and illustrations, it will move to its focal points much more rapidly and directly. A recent essay commented on brevity in writing in this fashion:

A report of three thousand words may be brief, and a 100-word memo may be long. . . .

To use too many words to communicate one's thoughts is a sign of mediocrity, while to gather much thought into few words, clearly and accurately, stamps the person of executive genius. . . .

When Churchill was directing Britain's war effort he wrote a memo containing this dictum: It is sheer laziness not compressing thought into reasonable space. . . .

Alas! there are many people who think that if they are dull enough and laboured enough they will sound scholarly. They take an ordinary proverb, like "Early to bed and early to rise makes a man healthy, wealthy and wise," and they change it to "Early retirement is a significant factor in one's physical development, pecuniary success and intellectual stature." . . .

Good style is not reached by such tortuous ways. . . . Ornamentation wearies the eye and deadens the mind. . . . Every word that can be spared from the purpose and plan . . . is hurtful if it remains.[4]

Persuasiveness

A persuasive style should be utilized in only those reports which are designed to induce action. However, the reader of the report

[3] L. D. Wyld, "Report Writing Need Not Be Dull," *Collegiate News and Views*, May, 1959.

[4] "On Writing Briefly," *Monthly Letters*, published by the Royal Bank of Canada, Montreal, Canada, July, 1956.

must be persuaded on the basis of the facts presented; an emotional appeal is unwise. Arguments for and against, statistics pro and con, and factual data reflecting the various facets of the problem should all be presented. The reader should be persuaded by the logic of the details.

Unity

Unity is the quality of oneness in writing. Each sentence should focus on a single idea; each paragraph should develop its specific topic; each section should develop a definite aspect of the entire report. In this way every sentence, paragraph, and section contributes to the unity of a report.

The report writer must check his material carefully and eliminate any fact that is not relevant to the subject matter. Without regard to the time spent on research and the effort expended on gathering the data, he must slash it out if it is not completely germane to the topic. In this way the clearly stated purpose of the report may be achieved. Thus when each sentence, paragraph, and section is checked and found to be unified, the whole report will, perforce, reflect the clear and logical development of its purpose.

The competent writer knows from experience that one of the most important aids in securing unity in a report is having a good outline for guidance purposes. The outline which has been carefully developed and checked, and which is rigidly followed in the writing process, will assist tremendously in securing a report that reflects unity.

Coherence

Coherence is usually interpreted to mean the interconnection of ideas in writing and the clarity of their presentation.

An orderly arrangement and development of ideas assists the reader in assimilating the thoughts of the writer. Coherence is secured by the judicious use of transitional words, phrases, clauses, and sentences. These give a cohesive and integrated quality to the writing that keeps the material "flowing" smoothly from one idea to another. Thoughts are not presented as pieces and parts; they are related one with the other and all together progress logically toward a specific conclusion.

Sentences are usually linked to one another through the use of transitional words and the orderly development of ideas. Paragraphs "flow" into one another through the employment of short statements or sentences that indicate to the reader the relative association of ideas.

The same technique may be carried through for the various sections of the entire report. In such a case, transitional paragraphs are used to "tie" one section of the report to the next; all paragraphs then lead to the clearly defined purpose of the report as a whole.

Coherence, as mentioned above, also means accuracy and clarity of writing. This involves the careful choice of words, the correct construction of sentences, and the correct use of all other basic factors involved in achieving a piece of writing that is easy to understand and a pleasure to read.

Emphasis

The wise report writer is careful to emphasize the important segments of his report. Because many reports are persuasive in nature, this is a vital factor in report presentation. Emphasis may be secured by a variety of methods.

Perhaps the most effective is simple *proportion*. Giving more space to a particular aspect of a problem will draw special attention to it. Certainly if four pages are spent examining housing and only a half-page is devoted to transportation, communication, and safety, it is obvious that the writer is focusing his spotlight on housing.

Placing certain ideas at the beginning of a section or the beginning of the report will usually result in special reader attention. This second device, *placement,* may be employed profitably within *sections* of the report as well as the report as a whole. Placing a topic sentence or a thesis idea in a strategic position will often produce the emphasis desired.

The use of *dramatic words* or *colorful phrases* may be used to draw the reader's attention to key ideas. This is rather frequently used in advertising directed toward the consumer. However, it is not recommended as a particularly effective device in report writing.

Repetition of an important fact also helps emphasize it. To mention it once and then again, in a different way, brings it to the direct attention of the reader.

Then there is the *writing style* itself. It is wise to use complex sentences and place the main idea in the independent clause. Parallel sentence structure helps; building one thought on another to reach a climax may also be utilized. The use of strong, active, colorful words and carefully selected similes and analogies are also used to secure emphasis.

In addition to these, there are various *mechanical methods* that may be utilized to emphasize ideas in the reports. Capitalization of all the letters in a word or a series of words is one method. Underscoring the statement that is to be emphasized is another. The use of italics, colored ink, sketches, and cartoons may also be utilized. Emphasis is secured by indenting key ideas and centering them on the page with plenty of white space around them. The reader will certainly give special attention to an idea that is presented in a paragraph and then dramatized in a table, chart, or graph.

All in all, it is best to secure emphasis in as natural and unassuming a manner as possible. The most potent emphasis is secured by the impact of an idea. When ideas which are important are presented logically and clearly, they will secure the emphasis which the report writer desires.

WRITING THE FIRST DRAFT

After the report writer has gathered his material, tabulated and interpreted it, outlined his report, made tentative plans for tabular or graphic illustrations, and completed other necessary tasks, he is ready to proceed to his last step: the writing of the report. With the purpose and objectives of the report clearly in mind, he is ready to begin.

He should be as sure as possible that he has all the data necessary to complete the report. Of course, this is not always possible, and the writer will find "holes" and "spaces" that require additional research and filling in. However, it is always disconcerting to the writer, when he is intent on transferring "Roman numeral III" in the outline into interesting prose in the report, to stop and fill in some research "gaps."

Indeed, when the researcher sits down to write his report, he should be so familiar with his topic that all he needs are his outline, his notes, his statistical data, and pencil and paper.

When working on a rather extended report that will require more than one draft, the researcher should attempt to get his thoughts and findings on paper as quickly and as coherently as possible. The editing or polishing of the report may be put off until the time the final copy is drawn up. At this first stage in the writing process, the researcher is wise if he concentrates on getting his ideas down on paper as completely as possible.

The Writing Environment

In putting the first draft of any extended composition on paper, it is certainly important to concentrate and write in a quiet, comfortable place without the distracting influences of radio, phonograph, or television within hearing or "tempting" distance. In addition, it is advisable to have a good-sized desk or table on which to spread note cards, an adequate supply of paper and pencils, an excellent dictionary, and a thesaurus.

There are distractions to be found whether a student writes a report at home or an employee writes one in an office. We are all aware of the disturbing factors at home, but at work the clattering of typewriters and filing cabinets, the jangling of the phone, and the interruptions by other office personnel are equally annoying. In any event, once these have been taken care of by finding a quiet place to work, the report writer can begin the composition of his final product.

Unless the report is very extensive, sufficient time should be allocated so that most, if not all of it, can be written at one time. This is certainly important. If the writer is absorbed in his report topic, he will have a message to deliver and it is this desire that leads him into putting his ideas down on paper with force and clarity. The report is a complete account, a whole story, an entity in the writer's mind, and that is the way it should be put on paper. Everyone has had the experience of beginning to write on a topic, then being interrupted, and finally attempting to return to it. Efforts to gather the train of thought at a later time are often difficult, and continuity and coherence are often lost; surely the drive to create is not as pressing as it was before the interruption.

The Writing Technique

Each section of the report should be written in an orderly fashion. After having introduced and developed the first section, noted in the outline as Roman numeral I, the report writer should then move on to the second phase. With his note cards arranged in a logical manner, and his outline before him, the task is usually a simple one; he need only go through the same steps taken previously: arrangement of the notes, correlation with the outline, integration of graphs and charts—and section II is developed. By using such a method, the writing of the report progresses smoothly and easily with the writer's complete attention being concentrated on the specific section being expanded. Transition from one phase to the next in a report will normally be incorporated. However, if it is felt by the writer that transition between two sections is not satisfactory, it is of no great moment, for that factor will be corrected in the editing. This same philosophy applies not only to transition but to word choice. If it is felt that better words could be chosen—though they are not at hand at the moment—to provide a clearer meaning or more accurate connotation, that task too should be put off until the final editing when the thesaurus and the dictionary can be used. In this first draft, the intention of the writer should be to write rapidly and creatively. If an attempt is made to polish a paragraph by reading, rereading, revising, and correcting, the continuity with the following paragraphs may be lost, and the net result is a lack of continuity in the entire report.

REVISION AND CORRECTION OF THE FIRST DRAFT

Obviously, the basic purpose of the report is to communicate ideas, findings, and recommendations to the reader as accurately and clearly as possible. Achieving this purpose is directly dependent on how well the report is written and the validity of the statistical facts presented. If there are flaws in wording, imperfections in sentence structure, poor coherence, faulty organization, or any factor that seriously impedes the free communication of ideas, that report needs revision. There can be no doubt that regardless of the excellence of the material gathered and the conclusions which it emphatically brings out, if the written presentation of the material is awkward and faulty, the effect on the reader will be materially lessened.

Those individuals who have not had too much experience in report writing are usually somewhat amazed at the many revisions which are necessary. The most hardy soul may well be staggered by the multitude of constructive suggestions which he and his critics can make relative to this first draft. It is hardly conceivable that the initial copy would be so excellent as to make some rewriting unnecessary.

But this reworking of the first draft should not deter the ambitious report writer. Many of the world's great authors have pointed out that the major portions of their writing time have been expended not on the original writing but on the revision of it. Many years ago, Robert Louis Stevenson epitomized the comments of successful authors with the statement, "When I say writing, O believe me, it is re-writing that I have chiefly in mind." And someone else made the statement to the effect that good writing is 1 percent inspiration and 99 percent perspiration. The report writer will find that the creditable end product of his work will come from revising, rewriting, revising, and rewriting again.

If the report is of an extended nature, and time and working conditions permit, the writer should make every effort to permit a day or two to pass between the composition of the first draft and the editing of the final copy. It is unwise to read the paper over for the purpose of inserting corrections immediately after the first draft has been sketched out. The reason for this is obvious to anyone who has done any writing. The writer is so thoroughly immersed in his subject matter that whatever he finds on his paper will appear to be excellently written and perfectly clear. What happens, of course, is that the author knows the topic so well, and what he wishes to say, that after it is written, he reads into the paper what he wishes to find.

A short period of time should be allowed to pass to permit the report—as well as the writer—to "cool off." It is during the reading at the later date that the author may well say, "Why in the world did I say this?" or "How could I have constructed such an awkward sentence?" It is at this later time that the report writer can look upon his original material with a much more objective attitude and thus discern errors that would not have been immediately obvious. And, of course, it is during this reading that the individual should be analytical just as in the period of roughing out the initial draft, his primary aim was to be as creative as his data permitted.

STEPS IN THE EDITING PROCESS

Editing our own material for the purpose of improving the over-all presentation is not an easy task. As noted above, there is probably a psychological factor which helps to dull our analytical ability when we search for imperfections in our own completed efforts. But search we must. If any sentence is found to be the least bit awkward or confusing, it must be rewritten; if a word does not say exactly what the context demands, it must be slashed out and a substitute found. There can be no hesitancy, no fear, no compunction on the report writer's part. He must strive to improve, regardless of the amount of "surgery" that is required on the initial draft.

In analyzing his first copy, the report writer should check for each of the qualities discussed earlier. A vital factor is unity: Are there any statements that are not relevant, any digressions, any points which are not germane to the subject? If so, they must be cut out. Every sentence, every table, every chart must contribute directly to the development of the problem.

And what of coherence? Does the paper have an integrated quality that keeps one section "flowing" into another? If not, check the transitional words, clauses, and sentences with the objective of improving the interconnection of ideas to give the report a cohesive quality.

Because most reports suggest some action to the reader, they are persuasive in tone. Good persuasion requires proper emphasis. For this quality, the writer should check the proportions of space given to the various aspects of the report, the "positioning" within the report of vital topics, and the use of topic headings, under-lining, and capitalization.

Clarity is still another specific quality that the writer should check. Short paragraphs with key topic sentences are important. Specific terms, not generalities, should be employed as well as the exact word in the exact place. Lively words, similes, analogies, and figures of speech all aid in giving a report color and vitality.

The following excerpt is an example of how a rather stodgy, dull segment of a report can be improved:

THE FIRST DRAFT

It is interesting to glance at the Acme and Excello Corporations and their trade figures following World War II. Acme had an average export figure of about 150,000-200,000 tons per year from 1952 to 1959. This was on about a par with export tonnage of Excello who has also enjoyed a brisk trade and which got its start just after World War I. The Excello Corporation, just as an item of possible interest to the reader, was known as the Columbian Corporation during the period 1895-1910. It was given this name in honor of the Columbia Exposition which was held in Chicago during 1893. To this date, the statements, invoices and stationery of the Excello Corporation still carry this message in small type: "Formerly known as the Columbian Corporation."

However, during World War II, Acme picked up a small metal scrap company (directed by the government during the war) in Cincinnati, and after this little deal was made, Acme moved ahead of Excello. In 1955 Acme shipped 325,000 tons and 400,000 in 1956 and 1957. Then up to 490,000 tons in 1958 and well over 600,000 in 1959. Excello could not keep up, for it exported between 150,000 and 200,000 tons for every year between 1955 and 1959 except 1957 when the picture rose to 225,000 tons. It should be noted

THE REVISION

An analysis of the export tonnage of the Acme and Excello Corporations reveals several very important factors.

Both companies enjoyed a similar export figure of about 150,000 to 200,000 tons per year from 1942-1946. But, as noted earlier, this figure dropped as it did with all exporters in the field during World War II when shipping space was only available for the transport of vital materials.

The competitive picture between Acme and Excello changed quite drastically following World War II. This was the period to expand, and Acme bent every effort in that direction. It purchased from the War Assets Administration a government surplus plant at a relatively nominal fee. It was the addition of this factory that permitted Acme to outrace Excello for the export market in the field. The table below vividly illustrates the situation:

Tonnage Exported

Year	Acme Corp.	Excello Corp.
1955	325,000	150,000
1956	400,000	180,000
1957	400,000	225,000
1958	490,000	170,000
1959	620,000	200,000

These figures are not only the result of the expansion or contraction of the companies' production, but are also due to the quality of the administrative per-

THE FIRST DRAFT (*Continued*)

that the administrative leadership in the two companies was of a different caliber also.

The Excello firm has had as its director, Mr. Barton T. King, who became the leader of that company in 1930 and who has had a long association with the firm in a variety of different positions many years before that date. Mr. King was known as a conservative individual whose basic philosophy in business (although he has many and varied interests in the area of fishing) was probably conditioned by the conservative post-depression years of the United States. In the case of Acme, . . .

THE REVISION (*Continued*)

sonnel heading the corporations.

In the case of Acme, Thomas R. Manning, a forward-looking, experienced and hard-hitting executive, took the office of president in 1955. He brought with him, several top echelon. . . .

A comparison of these two passages illustrates that with very little time and effort, a section of a report may be made much more interesting, more readable, and more effective after it has undergone simple revision.

The Presentation and the Appearance of the Report

There can be no doubt that regardless of how excellent is the analysis, how thorough is the investigation, and how detailed are the statistics, the report will not have served a particularly valuable service if the person for whom it is intended does not peruse it carefully. The actual appearance of the report will often determine not only whether it will be carefully read but also the mental acceptance or rejection of the paper. This is a rather intangible factor but existent nonetheless.

If the report is made up of large block paragraphs, crowded tables and charts, and is inefficiently and carelessly typed, it will not be attractive to the reader. As a matter of fact, one glance at such an affair will have a bad psychological effect on the reader's mind. If, on the other hand, the report has short paragraphs, clear headings, plenty of "white space," an attractive binder, and a good appearance in general, it will be favorably received.

A few of the ideas that the report writer might keep in mind in the presentation of his report are these:

TOPIC HEADINGS

The busy business executive likes to be able to read his communications rapidly. If the report writer will set up headings and subheadings, the reader will perforce know what to expect in the paragraphs that appear below the headlines.

Furthermore, with these headings the reader may quickly glance through the entire document and immediately note what areas have been covered; he need not read the text at this time if he does not wish to, for the topic headings give him the clues that he

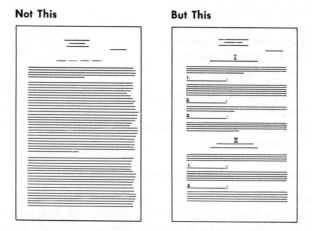

wants. Another advantage that results from the use of this system is the ease with which the executive may find a specific section of the report; he need not read and digest several pages, but he may quickly leaf through the paper, looking for only the topic heading he is interested in at the moment. Compare, for example, in the figure above, the page on the left with that on the right.

Certainly these diagrammatic sketches emphatically indicate the value that careful layout has for any reader.

TABLES, GRAPHS, AND ILLUSTRATIONS

In another chapter, much has been said concerning tables and graphs. Perhaps, however, a few notes on the presentation of figures may bear repetition because of the importance of the subject. The report writer is again reminded that when circumstances permit he should attempt to alternate text with figures, for when several pages of either are presented it is quite difficult for the reader to follow and/or "backtrack" on the cross references. For example, if figures 8, 9, 10, 11, 12, and 13 are presented one after another and then the report writer has several pages in the text referring back to each of the figures, it is most difficult for the reader to follow the references. It is much wiser to present an illustration and then offer what explanations may be necessary in the text; then go on to the next illustration and back to the text, etc.

The report writer should make every effort to see that those illustrations he does offer the reader are made up in the most attractive form possible under the circumstances. It is certainly foolish to spend a great deal of time and effort compiling statistical data and then to present them in a table or figure that has been haphazardly planned.

APPENDIXES AND SUPPLEMENTS

The report writer will frequently find that he has information which he strongly feels the reader should have access to. If the researcher includes it in the text of the report, however, it may upset the continuity of the exposition. This may be due to the fact that although the material is concerned with the topic of the report, it is not completely relevant. If these data are short, they may be offered to the reader in a footnote. If, however, they are rather extended and contain statistical facts, charts, figures, and tables, then it is probably wise to place them at the end of the report and refer to them as Appendix A or Appendix B.

Another situation where the writer finds the use of appendixes and supplements valuable is when the report he is presently working on is largely based on the findings given in an earlier study. This may be the case when a recommendation report is being prepared. Much of the material may be based on an earlier examination report. The latter may well be included, for reference purposes, in an appendix of the recommendation report.

BINDINGS AND COVERS

A binder or cover not only improves the appearance of a report but also aids in the handling, filing, and general use of the report. A cover should be used when the report is made up in several copies and is being distributed to various individuals in different organizations as well as when it is distributed to several people within one organization.

There are a variety of bindings on the market which may be used. These range from the hard cover spiral bound affairs to the very inexpensive file folders. If a concern or a department within a company writes a great many reports for its own use or for clients, it is wise to choose a standard cover and color with the name of the firm imprinted. The specific title, purpose, and date may be typed in the space provided. This lends a certain amount of uniformity and dignity to the reports submitted.

REPRODUCING THE REPORT

Typing the report is basically a mechanical function carried on by a competent stenographer. The author of the report, however, should make sure that the report is typed on a good grade of paper, that sufficient numbers of copies are being made, and that the carbons are clear and distinct. The typist should check to see that the typewriter keys are clean and the ribbon fresh.

These little points hardly fall within the scope of the report writer, but he should be cognizant of them and quick to call the attention of the stenographer to careless work.

Where a number of copies of the report are required, there are a dozen different methods of reproduction which may be used: mimeographing, multilithing, planographing, as well as various printing processes.

QUESTIONS FOR DISCUSSION

I. The following sentences violate the qualities of objectivity, positive tone, interest, clarity, and "you" attitude. Make whatever changes are necessary to correct these faults.

1. Although we have not proved this fact through research, it is our unbiased opinion that the consumer market will accept the R-32 enthusiastically.

2. As indicated in the foregoing statement and as per your earlier request, we have taken the matter under advisement, and we wish to state that at the first opportunity, we shall advise as to legal action.

3. We feel that purchase of the Brown and Bryant machine will not result in difficulties nor ill-will.

4. Although the survey was made prior to World War II, we feel that there has been little change in the earning level of the average production worker.

5. It was a clear case of industrial growth: in 1957 we produced 275 complete units. This was nowhere near the figure in 1959 however when our production was 25 percent over 1958 which as you well know, topped 1957 by 50 units.

6. We believe it would be wise for your firm to seriously consider eliminating your "Protap" Line which has been cutting into our profits and our sales.

7. In regards to yours of the 17th, we herewith submit said report in triplicate.

8. It is of interest to examine the reports of previous years and note that in 1958 our net profit was $27,000 (which did not include $12,500 put aside for contingencies but which might be included) which was 25 percent less than the books showed for the next year but which was 20 percent less as compared with the previous year. Next year, 1961, and in 1962 we shall go higher.

9. Although we have had trouble with the A-9 automatic switch in the past, I know that its performance now will not be unsatisfactory and troublesome.

10. Although the task may seem insurmountable on first examination, we at Blakely have achieved a solution which cannot be duplicated by any other firm, under any other conditions.

II. Make changes in the following sentences to correct violations of the principles of conciseness, persuasiveness, coherence, unity, and emphasis.

1. We strongly urge that your firm begin operation of the Patton System. However, we also know that you are an old line conservative firm that hesitates to move forward. For that reason, we feel that you may wish to try the System on approval.

2. On our first effort we found that the consumers were very receptive. The product was not designed for high heat resistance. Sales went up during May.

3. Time is a factor for consideration in the marketing of this product. But there are others to consider such as price, appeal of the package, quality, and advertising. Of these, you know, the most important is the package. This is the most vital of all. However, quality cannot be overlooked.

4. The labor supply is limited during our present peak season of October and November. Of course we can all remember back to 1957 during our busy season when it was virtually impossible to hire engineers. However to get back to the

present problem; we have sent two men out to recruit graduating seniors from the six technical colleges in the area. We
have already been assured of ten men.

5. The production of units 32 and 33 is down drastically. The
   trouble is in the punch press department. It is operating much
   too slowly. Of course the answer is simple. Equip all machines
   with safety devices which they do not now have. The workers
   can't be blamed for working slowly without them. Last year
   our production of the items in question was higher but not
   much. Action is necessary.

III. Assume that each of the sections below has been taken from the
initial draft of a report. Go over each, editing and revising where
necessary. Submit a finished or final draft for each.

1. In direct observation of consumer purchases, several very
   interesting facts were discovered. These facts were carefully
   substantiated by other facts discovered in a similar test situation in New York last year.

   On March 15, 16, and 17 of this year, trained observers
   were stationed at 12 Excello Food Marts distributed throughout the Los Angeles area. One man or woman was assigned
   to each Excello store. In six of the stores our 5-foot Deluxe
   display stand was placed near the check-out counter. In the
   other six stores, our 2-foot stand with flashing red and yellow
   blinker was placed near the check out counters.

   In Stores 1, 4, 8, and 11 (see addresses of each below) the
   stands were approached (by consumers) between 2000 and
   2500 times in the three-day period. In Stores 2, 6, 7, and 9
   approaches averaged between 2500 and 2800 times in the
   same period and for Stores 3, 5, 10, and 12 there were between 2900 and 3500 approaches made. Sales of our product
   varied from 300 units to 1250 units in the same period. Sales
   in Stores 2, 8, 4, 7, 9, and 12 were 750, 800, 820, 850,
   1050, and 1250, respectively. In Stores 1, 6, 5, 3, 11, and 10
   sales were 300, 350, 400, 475, 620, and 700, respectively. It
   should have been noted above that in Stores 2, 4, 7, 8, 9, and
   12 the 2-foot flasher display stand was utilized. It would therefore seem that correlation exists between sales and the flasher
   type unit.

2. We can now see that the decision to combine the office forces
   of the two companies was not a wise decision especially
   in the way it was handled by the new controller. It was
   handled in an arbitrary manner by the controller. It is true
   that the two companies, before their merger, handled similar

products but the method of office operation was vastly different. For example, The Bryson Company utilized electronic accounting machines almost completely whereas The Exacto Corporation used bookkeepers, accountants, and ledgers exclusively. At The Exacto Company, a typing pool was utilized but at Bryson it was not utilized. Each executive was assigned a secretary and the office had a number of stenographers. In addition one company (I do not recall which one) had a "coffee break" policy and the other did not. Exacto had a different salary classification than Bryson. Etc.

All of these differences were difficult to settle agreeably and to make hard and fast decisions, as did the controller, was no answer. Consequently, morale fell, the resignation rate rose appreciably, and efficiency of office operation dropped appreciably.

What is now needed is a careful analysis and then a reorganization of the existing system. If handled competently, an appreciable change will take place.

3. It was conclusively determined that a change in the package design would have no affect on the sales of Pradese. This was determined by a thorough statistical review. See Appendix II.

The only factor which would seem to indicate very strongly an affect on sales is *price* and *size* of package.

Accepting these two items as facts, then the following recommendations are made. These recommendations are that the price to the consumer should be below 20¢ per package. This recommendation would also be in keeping with competitors' prices which are all slightly below twenty cents per package. The second recommendation is to increase the size of the package to a full 16 ounces. This recommendation is also made with the competitor in mind. Brands A, B, C, and D have packages with 14, 14, 16, and 16 ounces each. Our package size of Pradese has always been 12 ounces.

It is strongly recommended that these recommendations be followed.

4. This survey reveals that the amount of support provided for the roof of the structure is completely inadequate. See Appendix III for specific data. The load bearing beams are not adequate in size and henceforth developed cracks. See photographs in Appendix IV. The result was that deep, penetrating cracks opened in the roof on the exterior unbeknownst to the maintenance staff. Consequently when snow fell into the cracks, froze, melted, and froze, the expansion and con-

traction, caused further damage until water began to drip through and into the space separating the theater's ceiling from the roof. The ceiling, of course, became damaged very much and cracks spread thru-out it.

The long and the short of it, is that the present beams must be removed, new trusses and supports, preferably of steel (see Appendix V for specific recommendations), be put in and the whole job redone properly. This should be done within 10 or 12 days to prevent further major damage.

IV. Carry through the following directions as assigned.

1. Write a first draft of a paper (500-800 words) on "The Utilization of Reports in the Field of Management" (or Government, Engineering, Marketing, Science, etc.). When you have completed the assignment, submit it to a colleague for his editing, revision, and evaluation.

2. Write a first draft of a paper on "The Ability to Communicate Effectively as a Factor in Advancement in The Field of Management" (or Government, Engineering, Marketing, Science, etc.). In this instance, edit, revise, and evaluate your own paper. You will be wise to make your changes in a different colored ink.

3. Secure a corporate annual report or a government report. Select any page of discussion, paste that page on a large blank sheet, and then make such written changes or corrections (on the blank sheet) as you feel are necessary to improve the presentation.

4. Using the same report as above or a copy of the *Wall Street Journal,* select five examples of interesting and vivid writing style. Each example should be three or four sentences in length.

5. Complete the same assignment as number 4 above but this time use a professional journal in your major area of interest.

Chapter 9

Short-Form Reports

In commerce and industry, the short-form report is among the most frequently utilized of all types of written communication. Brief reports "flow up and down the line" throughout the day in most American corporations. Among others there are memorandum, letter, progress, periodic, credit, examination, and recommendation reports. In most cases, these reports are quite brief, running from a half to three or four pages in length. Some of them are even completed on a form and all the report writer is required to do is to fill in a few statistics or a simple series of comments.

Basic Attributes of the Short Report

The same principles of composition are followed in writing the short report as are pursued in completing any type of written communication. The organization of the report should be carefully planned. Because of the report's brevity, it is not always necessary to have an introduction or summary. This is especially true in the letter and memorandum reports.

Word choice, clarity of writing, the profitable use of topic headings, correct graphic and tabular presentation, and attractive appearance are all important considerations in presenting the report.

LETTER REPORTS

The letter report is similar in many respects to the business letter. The length of the letter report is approximately one to three pages; it—like the business letter—also appears on letterhead stationery and often uses an inside address, salutation, and signature.

However, there are differences, too: the tone and style of the letter report are usually more formal. It may carry a "To: From: Subject:" type of heading instead of the usual inside address, and it usually utilizes more graphs and tables than does the everyday letter.

Although the tone of the letter report is factual and formal, it is still written from the viewpoint of the reader and it does reflect a helpful and considerate attitude.

In the example below, notice the differences between the report and a letter. The inside address of the letter report has been omitted, the usual signature section (which includes the company name in upper case type, the written signature, typed signature, and title) is changed, and there is generous use of topic headings and tables.

WESTRIDGE REALTY and MANAGEMENT COMPANY
1955 East Granville Avenue
Chicago 21, Illinois

October 15, 19—

To: Mr. Harold Miller, 1750 North Brent Avenue, Los Angeles, California

FROM: James T. Randolph, Manager, Westridge Realty and Management Company

SUBJECT: Report on Building at 1420 East Oak Street, Chicago 26, Illinois

Following is a report on the property which you recently inherited from the late George P. Barnes. As you may know, Westridge Realty has managed this piece of Chicago property for Mr. Barnes for almost 14 years. It has been a pleasant and mutually satisfactory relationship which this firm would be happy to continue.

History and Description of Property

This building was constructed in 1939 by Thor Builders Corporation. The three-story building contains 4 five-room and 2 six-room apartments plus 4 stores on the ground floor. (See photograph enclosed.) It is a steel beam building with face brick on all four sides. The building was constructed for Mr. Arthur Fleming who sold it in 1945 to Mr. Barnes for $95,000. Mr. Barnes made an initial payment of $40,000 and secured a $55,000 mortgage from the Prudential National Bank of Chicago. The final payment on this mortgage was made in 1957. The building is now free and clear of all encumbrances.

Occupancy

The occupancy record of the building has been excellent. Since 1946 (termination of World War II), the flats have been rented almost continuously. No apartment has been vacant for more than one month since that date.

The stores have enjoyed a similar record. In three of the stores, the same tenants have maintained occupancy since 1946. The fourth store was vacant for 2 months in 1951 and for one month in 1956.

Repairs

On the whole, the building has required very few repairs since its construction. A new roof was put on in 1949 by River Roofing Corporation. In the same year major repairs were carried through on all back porches. In 1953, because of increased electrical demands on the tenants' part, additional wiring was brought in. This is now adequate to handle all modern electrical appliances and air conditioning equipment.

Present Condition

The building is in very satisfactory condition. However, some work is necessary and should be done within a year. This is listed below together with approximate costs.

Tuckpointing	$1,800 (approximate)
Painting of all hallways and landings	400 (approximate)
Carpeting for hallways and landings	600 (approximate)
New sidewalk (50 feet)	700 (approximate)

Income

	Rental per unit per month	Yearly Income
2 apartments (6-room)	$140	$3,360
2 apartments (5-room)	100	2,400
2 stores (30′ x 80′)	150	3,600
2 stores (40′ x 80′)	200	4,800
Total Yearly Income		$14,160

Expenses

	1959	1958
Fuel	$2,400	$2,500
Taxes	1,085	1,150
Scavenger Service	160	160
Decorating	800	650
Janitor Service	2,600	2,800
Electricity	150	160
Repairs	1,200	400
Insurance	290	315
Landscaping	60	90
Total Yearly Expenses	$8,745	$8,225

Location and Neighborhood

The building is located on Chicago's north side. It is about two blocks from public and parochial elementary schools and about a half mile from a public secondary school. Shopping and transportation are both within a three-block radius. A public park is less than half a mile distant.

The neighborhood is largely residential. Single family dwellings predominate with a few flat buildings in each square block. The neighborhood is well established; the residents are conservative, hard-working individuals who take great pride in the appearance of their homes and gardens.

Conclusion

On the basis of the information given above, it is recommended that you retain possession of the building as a very profitable parcel of income property. The return is satisfactory and the expenditures for repairs should remain very low for some years to come. The appearance of the building is excellent.

We shall, of course, be happy to continue to manage this property at the prescribed fee of 5% of gross rental payments. A certified statement will be provided twice a year from the "Thomas Downs, C.P.A.'s" accounting firm.

If, on the other hand, you would prefer to sell this building, I am sure such a transaction may be carried through; buyers are available. I would suggest that initially a price of $115,000 be placed on the property. Certainly, a minimum of $105,000 could be secured. The standard fee for sale would be 5% of the gross price.

We shall be happy to cooperate with you in any way that will prove of value to you.

Sincerely yours,

James T. Randolph
Manager

JTR/rs
Encl.

Notice in the letter report above the slight difference between its tone, style, and opening and that usually found in a business letter. The overall presentation is somewhat more formal; however, the "you" attitude, positive tone, clarity, and courtesy are all evident. The frequent use of topic headings and the method of statistical presentation all assist the reader.

The letter report which follows uses the mechanics normally associated with the business letter. However, the tone and style are still quite formal.

George R. Frame
Management Consultants
121 West La Salle Street
Los Angeles 21, California

November 8, 19—

Mr. Robert T. Hall, President
Hall Leather Corporation
2121 South Jackson Boulevard
Los Angeles 8, California

Dear Mr. Hall:

In your letter of October 8, 19—, you requested that a brief survey be carried through of the production facilities of the Hall Leather Corporation. The purpose of the examination was to determine whether or not a more intensive study should be undertaken and changes in procedures recommended.

What Was Done

A three-man "job and production" analysis team visited the plant from November 2 to November 4, 19—. A time study was conducted on piece-rate and hourly-rate employees. Production of products was observed and the arrangement and layout of the manufacturing lines were checked.

What Was Found

Compensation standards were found to be rather outmoded in comparison to methods now widely used.

The plant layout, which was initially made in 1945, is not as effective as it might be. Although new machines and processes were introduced in 1955, plant layout was not changed.

What Is Recommended

It is recommended that a thorough study be carried through by the George R. Frame Company. The purpose of such an examination would be to recommend a more efficient employee compensation system and improved production methods.

Conclusion

If this proposal meets with the approval of the Hall Leather Corporation, a contract, covering the assignment discussed above, will be submitted no later than November 15, 19—.

Sincerely yours,

Shelley T. Robin
Executive Vice President

STR:fp

These are typical examples of letter reports. It is quite obvious that they are similar to business letters in some respects. However, the report writer should note that the letter report, unlike the business letter, does not usually try to sell, persuade, adjust, or inquire. It is primarily an information document that is formal in tone and style.

MEMORANDUM REPORTS

In intercompany communication, there is probably nothing—except conversation—which is more frequently utilized to transmit ideas than memoranda. These brief messages move *within* companies; it is not very often that a memorandum is sent from an individual in one company to a person in another firm. When one considers the pressures, complexities, and the number of echelons in modern industries, it is a wonder that verbal communications are able to retain as much accuracy as they do in traveling from one person to another. But just because it is so easy for verbal messages to become garbled in transmission, industry has recommended more and more frequently that they be put in written memorandum form.

Blank memo sheets often carry the admonition—in bold, black letters:

WRITE IT—VERBAL ORDERS DON'T GO
PUT IT IN WRITING NOW
MAKE IT A MATTER OF RECORD—WRITE IT
WRITE IT OUT FOR ACCURACY

Use of the Memorandum

When a brief message contains some detail and requires precision of expression, a written memo should be used. Of course, there are those persons who have become "memo happy," and the little yellow half-sheets fly from their desks like the leaves in an autumn windstorm. This is an abuse of the use of the memo. However, the memorandum can be used effectively:

1. To transmit information that requires a written or permanent record.
2. To transmit data which may be easily confused (statistics, complex details).
3. To transmit the same information to many people.
4. To make a record of policies or decisions which have been reached by an executive or a group at a meeting.
5. To give committee members a summary report of a meeting's business.
6. To confirm, as a matter of record, a decision or agreement which has been reached.

Attributes of the Memo

Although the make-up of the memorandum varies from company to company, in general it should:

1. Discuss one subject only.
2. Be very concise.
3. Dispense with a formal inside address, salutation, complimentary close, and signature.
4. Indicate in the heading the subject and the recipient's and sender's names.

The body of the memorandum is single-spaced with wide margins to aid in reading. If a second page is necessary, it should be numbered. Sometimes a memo may be initialed.

Memoranda may be written on printed memo forms or blank sheets of paper. The former usually have the "To, From, Subject, and Date" headings and lines printed in. However, it is easy enough to fill this information in on a blank sheet.

The size of the paper is usually 5½ inches x 8½ inches although an 8½ inches x 11 inches size memo sheet is not very unusual. Some firms have their memo pads so prepared that one or even two carbons are written or typed along with the original.

ERLEE CORPORATION

Interoffice Memorandum

To	M. Grant, Sales Manager	Date	Oct. 20, 19—
From	R. Erlee, President	Subject	Monthly Meeting

A meeting of all department heads will be held at 2:00 P.M. on November 2, 19—. The tentative topics for discussion are
  1. New winter line
  2. Christmas promotion of the Erlee Jacket
  3. Other business as suggested

R E

MEMORANDUM

Intercompany

Date: March 5, 19—   Subject: Coffee Break
To: All Department Heads   Copy to: R. Grant, Treas.
From: R. Pierce, President   G. Feltt, Exec. Ass't.
                                         M. Kelt, Trning. Div.

Recent informal surveys have indicated that some of our employees are extending their coffee break time appreciably. It is suggested that a bulletin be posted in each department reminding all workers of the times allotted for this privilege. The "Employee Handbook" may be quoted.

Although most memo reports remain within the company, they are also sent from one firm to another. However, this is not usual and when reports do go "out," they are usually sent in a more formal manner than as a memo.

MEMORANDUM

To: Midtown Shoe Sales
         111 West Lincoln Street
         Springfield, Texas

From: American Shoe Corporation
         5 East Fifth Avenue
         New York City

Subject: Sales Promotion Aids

On March 1, 19— a new policy concerning dealer sales aids will be instituted. It is designed to benefit all dealers through increasing their sales, profit margin, and customer relationships.

It is hoped that you will avail yourself of many of the services outlined below; we at American Shoe are eager to assist you.
   1. A new series of store pennants will be available on the 15th of each month. These will be available free.
   2. Window display posters will be mailed out to those dealers who

request them. These posters will be available every other month.
3. Window display aids, such as plastic models, "back-to-school" display items, toy animals, etc., will be used by our window trimmers. All display materials remain the property of American Shoe Corp. Each dealer may have his windows trimmed 6 times per year free of charge.
4. Each dealer may secure a supply of booklets for either counter or mail distribution. It is contemplated that booklets will be made available four times each year: September "back to school," Easter Shoe Sale, Christmas Holiday Special, and Summer Styles.

We feel sure that all dealers who avail themselves of these services will find an appreciable increase in their sales.

Tone of the Memo

Sometimes the writer, in his efforts to secure brevity, will complete a memo whose tone is rather curt and abrupt. Regardless of how brief the message is, there is always time and place to be courteous. The following message to all foremen, which issues a directive but gives no reason for the action, will certainly be interpreted as brusque and discourteous:

Beginning Monday, April 20, no employee will be permitted to borrow any shop tools for home use.

Brevity is important but never at the cost of losing employee good will.

PERIODIC REPORTS

Periodic reports are summaries of the activities which have taken place in a department or area during a *specific* block of time. They are on-going reports which are completed and submitted at a predetermined periodic interval of time. That time span may be daily, such as the report completed by the bread wagon or milk wagon driver; it may be weekly, such as those filled out by the paymaster or newsdealer. Or it may be a monthly report which the general manager expects to receive from each of his department heads. And it may be a yearly report, such as the stockholders' and employees' annual report.

One of the most important functions of management is decision making. However, decisions are not made "out of a clear blue sky."

They are made only after careful thought and the examination of pertinent records. Very often, these records—as indicated above— are the periodic reports received from various departments and personnel. After examining these, the average manager, supervisor, or director will make a decision.

It is obvious that the contents of these reports must be clear, accurate, honest, and complete. The general manager cannot be an expert in personnel, sales, credit, production, and finance. He must rely on the content of these reports, and from the data given, he must reach decisions and issue orders. Not infrequently, the recommendations made in one report will conflict with those in another.

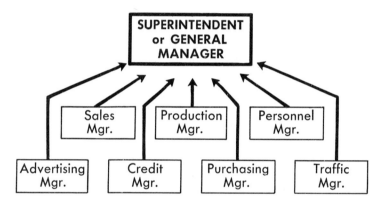

Typical Flow of Monthly Periodic Reports

The recipient must examine the data and reach a decision; if his choice is correct, he is applauded; if it is wrong, he may be discharged. But he must use the reports as the basis for the conclusions he reaches.

It is quite possible that the credit manager may recommend a tighter money policy because of a recession; the sales head, however, may suggest "easier" credit which will help attract new outlets and dealers. It is up to the general manager to make decisions not only on credit, but also on personnel, sales, production, etc. As these periodic reports come in, they are read and evaluated and then decisions are reached on the basis of their content and the recommendations which have been made.

These are vital decisions that have serious consequences; it is imperative that the reports on which the decisions are based are accurate and valid in content and clear and concise in presentation.

Specific Attributes of the Periodic Report

If this report is to accomplish its major purpose, the following items should be noted:

1. Adequate statistical data should be presented, where necessary, to substantiate statements made.

2. The facts and figures presented in graphic or tabular form should be easy to *compare*. Ordinarily, figures for the current period should be presented with comparative data for the reader's scrutiny. It may seem that a profit of $65,000 is very good for the period covered by the report. However, if comparative data for comparable periods show a profit figure twice as large, it may very well be cause for concern. Figures by themselves are often revealing only when *comparisons* are possible.

There is sometimes a question as to what data to use for comparative purposes. If the sales volume for March is given in a table, should the comparative sales volume be for February or should it be for March of the previous year? The answer varies with the company and type of business. It would seem silly to compare the sale of winter clothes for October with September; it would be much more logical to use October of the previous year. Sales of bathing suits in June should be compared with the previous June; however, it would be logical to compare gallons of water used in May with the quantity used in April. In many cases it is helpful to contrast the current period with the previous period in this year and the same period in the previous year.

Sales Volume
(in units)

Product	December 1959	November 1959	December 1958
Model 221	6,850	6,780	5,950
Model 222	12,750	12,150	10,800
Model 421	25,600	25,100	23,750
Model 422	28,750	26,500	21,150

3. In presenting statistical data which cover an extended period of time, any dramatic rise or fall should be explained by the report writer. The reader will certainly notice the unusual deviation and he expects and deserves an explanation. After all, it is presumed that the man who writes the report is an "expert" in the field; if he does not explain the change reflected in the figures, who should?

4. The mechanics of the periodic report should permit easy reading and assimilation. Topic headings and subheadings should be used generously; tables and graphs should be neatly presented and the entire report should be as concise and as brief as possible.

MIDWEST CLOTHING CORPORATION

141 West Oak Boulevard
Milwaukee, Wisconsin

Monthly Sales Report

To: Mr. Burton Grames, President

From: Robert J. Smith, Sales Manager

Date: October 5, 19—

Summary

Contrary to expectations and the financial forecast, sales in the month of September exceeded the forecast made at the beginning of the year. The new plaid "mother-daughter" (#221) line moved especially well. It is felt that the high level of sales will continue in the months to come.

An adjustment in production should be made to take care of the steady decline in the "Little Miss Honeybun Sweaters" (#324).

Although there has been some turnover in sales personnel, it is not an unusual situation.

It is recommended that special attention be given to advertising our new college plaids in the areas in which institutions of higher education are located. It is felt that this line has not been sufficiently exploited by Midwest.

Sales Volume

Sales for the month of September have held up very well. The increase over last year is appreciable and indicates that our emphasis on quality and service is wise.

Sales Volume
(in dozens)

Item	September	August	September Previous Year
Plaid 221			
Size 1-3	300	250	220
3-6x	550	575	525
7-14	625	600	600
Pre-teen	650	575	600
Juniors	600	550	575
Misses	500	450	475
Plaid 222			
Size 1-3	600	550	575
3-6x	900	850	875
7-14	900	850	875
Pre-teen	1100	1050	1000
Juniors	1200	1150	1100
Misses	1000	950	1000
Sweaters 324 (all sizes)			
The Starlight	1800	2300	3200
The Arizona	2700	2500	2300
The Californian	3500	3000	2500

As has been expected, the Starlight sweater has dropped drastically in its sales. There can be no doubt that the "turtleneck" type of collar is no longer accepted as a popular style among young women.

The Tartan Plaid (221) seems to be especially popular, and its sales are increasing steadily.

Sales Personnel

Salesmen

Sales Area	September	August	September Previous Year
1	12	12	10
2	9	8	8
3	13	18	16
4	16	12	12
Totals	50	50	46

The rather drastic changes in sales personnel in Areas 3 and 4 are due to the changes in district boundaries. District 3 no longer includes Indiana and Michigan. These two states were made a part of our District 4. The eight sales trainees hired in July are still in the Milwaukee office. All will be assigned on October 15, except one man who will be released.

Advertising

The program suggested by our advertising department has certainly worked out very well. It is suggested that space in *College Girl* and *Today's Miss* be continued.

Recommendations

1. It is recommended that the Starlight sweater line be discontinued as of January 1.
2. The Scottish Thorn Plaid designed by Miss Joan Lyons is most attractive and should be considered seriously for next year's line.
3. The budget for advertising might well be raised; sales seem to rise appreciably with increases in our advertising.

Robert J. Smith
Sales Manager

The sample periodic report above is typical of the type that is written each month by the head of a department. It is possible that these monthly reports may also be reduced to a form which may be filled in. However, even when it is typed on regular stationery, it is wise to follow the same general order of headings each month.

PROGRESS REPORTS

Progress reports relate the successive stages in the development of a project. They are frequently utilized by corporations to tell their stockholders what advances have been made in the development of construction, research, expansion, or marketing operations.

Cities which are in the process of expanding a filtration system, a network of roadways, a housing development, or a similar public works project will often issue a progress report to the citizens of the area.

Research agencies or associations are often required by the terms of a grant to submit a report on the advances or progress made on a problem. Quite obviously, this is vital if a request is made to continue or expand its assistance. A report for the director of a research project is also necessary if he is to evaluate the work which has been done, plan further investigations, and correct or revise plans which are being followed.

In industry, progress reports are utilized frequently. Firms that have groups of personnel working on various projects (such as auditing teams, construction crews, and engineering survey units) almost invariably require that reports be submitted to the central office summarizing the work which has been accomplished. An accounting team sent out to the Excello Corporation to survey and revise a payroll system may very well find that it is involved in a six-week assignment. At intervals during this period, the team director must report. The head of the accounting company, or his general manager, is eager to determine what progress the team has made, what problems have been encountered, and approximately how much more time the job will require.

A series of progress reports reflects the history of a complete project and may serve as the basis for a formal report or for the future organization of a similar project. A progress report may also tell the general manager of problems which can be solved much more easily while the work is going on than later when the job has been completed. The report can also discuss other areas *now* and suggest changes which can be made more economically at this point. These might be revisions in design, plans, expenditures, or construction. However, the primary purpose of the progress report is to keep the interested party, company, or supervisor apprised of the work that has been completed.

Types of Progress Reports

Unlike periodic reports which are on-going, progress reports are submitted only during the period that the project is being carried through. For this reason there may be an *initial* progress report, the *regular* progress reports, and a *terminal* report. The first or initial report spends a good deal of time orienting the reader to the purpose and objective of the operation. The regular progress reports simply report on the activities completed during a specific period of time. The terminal progress report is the last one submitted on a project and is, consequently, written as a summary of the entire project.

The Mechanics and Organization of the Progress Report

Some companies have a form which their employees use to report work completed. Very often these will carry a form heading with space for "fill-ins":

MARLAKE PUBLIC ACCOUNTANTS

Date: _____
Progress Report No. _____
Period Covered _____
Company _____
Job Assignment _____
Personnel Assigned _____

_____
_____

There are a dozen other forms used by various types of companies. Sometimes they follow the "To: From: Subject:" style with space to indicate the period covered by the report. At other times, the report utilizes the most logical mechanical arrangement for the particular situation involved and is then typed. Whatever form is used, it is always wise to remember that the title of the project and the period covered by the report should be clearly and prominently indicated.

The organization varies slightly according to the nature of the assignment and whether or not the report is initial, regular, or terminal. On the whole, however, the divisions of the report usually follow a logical plan, such as this:

I. Purpose and Objective of the Project
II. Summary of Earlier Work Accomplished
III. Detailed Account of the Period Covered by This Report
    A. Work accomplished during this period
    B. Methods used
    C. Difficulties encountered

IV. Conclusion
  A. Next step or steps scheduled
  B. Forecast of completion date
  C. Recommendations (if necessary) for changes or
     revisions in plans

  There can be any number of variations to this but the above plan
can serve as an effective guide.

ROBERT M. BLENDER AND ASSOCIATES
Certified Public Accountants
212 North Madison Avenue
Los Angeles, California

November 21, 19—

SUBJECT: PROGRESS REPORT # 2, For Period November 12-20, 19—.

TO: Mr. James R. Blake, Supervisor
           Robert M. Blender and Associates

FROM: Mr. Peter R. Pryor, Team # 5

FIRM: National Toy Plastics Corporation
           651 East Glenview Street
           Los Angeles, California

Introduction

  Although sales of National Toy have risen approximately 800 percent over its 1946 figure, accounting methods and systems have not
changed appreciably since that date. On November 2, 19— Team #
5 was assigned to the National Toy Plastics Corporation for the purpose
of surveying and improving all accounting procedures.

Summary of Earlier Work

  Progress Report # 1, covering the period November 2 to November
12, outlined the systems and procedures recommended and carried
through for:

Accounts Payable
Accounts Receivable

As of this date, the recommended innovations are working out very well and the accounting department of National Toy seems very pleased.

Detailed Account of This Period

During the period covered by this progress report, two areas were revised:
Payroll System
Inventory Control and Costing System

Payroll System

In conference with the paymaster, controller, and other responsible persons, the following methods and principles in employee compensation were agreed on:

1. *Supervision.* The issuance of all payroll checks shall be under the direct supervision of the treasurer.

2. *Payment interval.* Checks shall be issued bimonthly on the 15th and 30th of each month.

3. *Method of payment.* All employees will be paid by a new form payroll check supplied by Grace Check Forms Company (see sample attached). These checks will include a stub for the employee's possession which will show the following items:
   a. Gross pay
   b. F.I.C.A. deduction
   c. Income tax withheld
   d. Other deductions
   e. Net pay

4. *Funds for payroll.* A special bank account has been set up for the sole purpose of covering payroll checks. The treasurer is to draw a check on the regular bank account twice each month for the purpose of covering the payroll demands.

Inventory Control and Costing System

A perpetual inventory account has been set up under the direct supervision of the comptroller. The following procedures are to be carried through:

1. *Purchase orders.* All purchase orders are to be made in triplicate: one each to purchasing, receiving, and controller.

2. *Shipments received.* All merchandise received will be checked under the supervision of the head of the shipping department. A copy of each order received will go to the comptroller and purchasing department.

3. *Materials for production.* All requisitions for materials are to be sent to the storage department where the request will be filled. Copies

of the requisition will go to the comptroller and purchasing department.

4. *Costing of jobs.* All materials will be charged to specific jobs on a first-in, first-out pricing system.

5. *Materials record.* Inventories will be credited in quantity and price only upon receipt of the storage department's copy for each item. Requisitions for re-ordering will be sent to the purchasing department when any item reaches 30 percent of maximum quantity.

6. *Physical inventories.* Actual counts of merchandise will be made once a year, one week prior to the end of the fiscal year. Any differences between actual and physical inventory will be debited or credited to the proper profit or loss account.

All work was accomplished according to normal accounting procedures and systems approved by our company. No difficulties have been encountered during this period. Evidently the treasurer, who displayed some antagonism to this survey during the November 2-12 period, has recognized that his attitude was immature and unwarranted. His cooperation during this later period was excellent.

Conclusion

The next and final step will be according to the recommendations made in the memorandum of October 24. It is contemplated that this assignment will be completed on the expected date of December 6. No recommendations are offered at this time.

Peter R. Pryor, Head, Team # 5
Lawrence T. Sterne
Marvin Lessor

QUESTIONS FOR DISCUSSION

I. *Letter Reports.* Write a letter report on the basis of the data given in each of the following problems.

1. Assume that you have applied for a position and the personnel director has requested a letter report from you detailing your work experience. You are to include jobs which you have held which are related to the one for which you are making application as well as those which are unrelated. Note duties, compensation, period worked, and the benefits and values which you secured from the position.

2. Assume that you have acted as Mr. Norton's investment counselor for the past 15 years. You have recently been in-

formed of his death and the fact that he has willed all his stock to a younger sister, Mrs. Ella Mason. Mr. Norton's attorney has suggested that you send a report to Mrs. Mason telling her of her stock inheritance.

You have decided to give her a list of the stocks which you presently hold in Mr. Norton's name as well as the earnings during the previous year.

Stock	No. of Shares	Purchased at	Present Level	Earnings for Previous Year
U.S. Metals	150	40	60	7%
California Aircraft	50	18	16	–
Becker Electronics	25	75	90	5
Atlas Equipment	75	45	40	9
American Transport	100	70	95	6.5
New York Telephone	200	51	61	8.1

You can also have the stock transferred to her name if she will forward the proper probate form to you. You may also wish to give her some advice on which of the stocks to sell and/or retain.

Your fee for your service is 2 percent per year of the total stock value.

3. Assume that your firm has four representatives in Latin America handling your store display cases. You manufacture very attractive units which are suitable for use in drug and jewelry stores, women's and men's clothing shops, and in other retail establishments. You have 12 different units each equipped with fluorescent lights, sliding glass doors, interchangeable shelf levels, and other modern features. All cases are available in either blond oak or dark mahogany.

You have just returned from visiting each representative and some of the data gathered on each is given below. You may add any additional facts you wish in a letter report you are to submit to the board of directors of your firm, The Castle Case Company.

You may wish to suggest that various steps be taken: withdrawing your product from one or more of the representatives or lending capital to any. You will also probably wish to report on sales volume, attitude, size of company, competence, etc.

Enrico and Company, Buenos Aires, Argentina.

Sales for year: $175,000

Company facts: A large firm handling all types of retail store fixtures. Progressive and hard working staff. Well capitalized with an excellent credit rating. Firm is rapidly expanding and has high potential.

Latin American Fixture Company, Havana, Cuba.

Sales for year: $12,000

Company facts: This firm is owned, managed and operated by one man, Miguel Vastro. He also represents American and German camera companies. He is not very familiar with our product and is obviously not very interested in building the sales of Castle Case. His credit rating is poor.

Modern Display Fixture Company, Santiago, Chile.

Sales for year: $110,000

Company facts: This firm is run by J. Hernandez, a young college graduate who has studied business administration in the U.S. He is a very hard-working person. He has a representative display of our cases in his place of business. He also represents an American electric fixture firm. This company enjoys an excellent rating; however, at the moment it is in need of funds. Senor Hernandez requested a $15,000 loan as well as $25,000 worth of merchandise on a consignment basis. His certified financial statement is attached.

Metropolitan Suppliers, Mexico City, Mexico.

Sales for year: $225,000

Company facts: This firm is wholly owned and operated by M. Valesquez. He has been established for 25 years and is the leading store fixture and industrial furniture dealer in Mexico. The company is in an excellent financial position and enjoys a high credit rating.

4. Write a letter report to the dean in charge of student affairs. Give him a complete account of the social activities of your club, fraternity, or sorority for the last academic year. He is probably interested in membership level, financial gains or losses, admission or ticket charges, and any unusual facts or events. You may assume any data necessary.

5. Assume that your firm is considering the rental of a vacant store

located at 2150 North Granville in San Diego, California, as the twenty-first unit in a chain of hardware stores in the Southern California area. Write a letter report to the company president of the West Coast Hardware Chain giving him the results of your investigation. He will probably want facts covering the following areas:

Description of store: width, depth, type of fixtures, heating, and general description.

Other retailers in immediate vicinity: number and type of stores in two-block area.

Traffic: pedestrian and vehicle level.

Neighborhood: type of residences (homes, apartments, hotels), stability of neighborhood, income level, etc.

Finance: cost of remodeling, rental, and related facts.

Business potential: competition, need for hardware store, and other facts in a brief market analysis.

You may make any assumptions in the above areas which you feel are reasonable.

6. Write a report for the student counselor on your study habits. He is probably interested in the methods of study you use, the time devoted to each subject, and the system you use to prepare for examinations.

II. *Memorandum Reports.* Write a memorandum report on the basis of the data given in each of the following problems.

1. Send a memorandum to each of the other participants in this morning's sales meeting. Specific action was taken in several areas and it was agreed that:

a. The Montclaire sweater line would no longer be produced after July 1.

b. Six sales trainees would be hired to begin work on June 15. They would all be secured from the marketing department of Center College.

c. Prices of the Miami line would be dropped 5 percent in an effort to increase sales.

Assume that you are the company sales manager.

2. Send a memo to the production supervisor. As the head of the adjustment department you have been disturbed by the large number of complaints you have received from your customers (furniture dealers) on the Moderne Coffee Table. These complaints involved the brass and mosaic insets. They are not always exactly level with the tables' tops and are often loose. These complaints have only been coming in during the last 30 days.

3. A safety and accident report is due from each of your 15 factory department heads on the fifteenth of the month. Although today is June 20, you have not received reports from the packing, punch press, and shipping departments. Send each of these three department heads a memo reminding him of his oversight. You are the company personnel director.

4. As the executive vice-president of the Fink Frame Company, you often make a casual inspection of the factory area. During your visits in the past month you notice that almost all departments began "clean-up and check-in" operations at about 4:40 P.M. When the bell rings at 5:00 P.M. almost all workers leave the plant. Actually company policy and the union agreement indicate that work on the line is supposed to cease at 5:00 P.M. The financial loss to the company for a 20-minute period (with 1800 workers) is appreciable. Therefore, a memo to each of the 26 foremen seems to be in order.

5. On Tuesday, May 20, the King and Queen of England will be in Washington as guests of the President and the United States Government. You have just been informed through Executive Order #107 that all federal employees in your department are to be given a half-day off beginning at noon. Send a memo to your 12 department heads informing them officially of this action.

6. On your inspection trip to the Midvale Housing Project, which your firm is constructing, you notice that the medicine cabinets for each of the 80 apartments have been delivered three weeks early. They are now stacked at the building site. Each unit is in a cardboard carton but this protection is inadequate for outdoor storage. Continued rain, falling debris, and playful children are all hazards to these units which cost $60 each. A memo to the construction supervisor suggesting that the cabinets be moved into the finished basement area or covered with a tarpaulin would be wise.

7. Department B has recently been given an additional assignment which involves wiring the A32 relay unit. This wiring assignment was given to Section 3 of Department B. However, several of the workers in the section have been complaining that the illumination level for the work is inadequate. In your capacity as production engineer, send a memo to the vice-president requesting that a consulting illumination engineer be engaged to make a survey of the department's lighting requirements. You have used Mr. W. Frank of the Production Management Company for this purpose in the past. His work proved satisfactory.

8. Among the 68 typists in your department, there are approximately 18 who are classified as temporary. A Civil Service Examination for typists is scheduled for November 7. Send a memo to each of the 6 section heads informing him of the examination.

III. *Periodic Reports.* Write a periodic report on the basis of the data given in each of the following problems.

1. You are the manager of one of the Disc Record Company stores. On the fifteenth of each month each of the 32 store managers is required to submit a monthly sales and personnel report. Your store is number 12 and is located at 6820 North Francisco in Chicago. The report for June 15 to July 15 is now due.

   Statistics in sales volume for the three areas of sales—records, phonograph accessories, and phonographs—should be cited. Record sales are usually split into popular, classical, jazz, and miscellaneous. A special sales promotion on Clear Tone Records during the first two weeks in July boosted sales appreciably.

   During the period, you had two full-time clerks and three part-time clerks. Your stock seems well balanced except for Latin American tunes. They do not seem to sell very well in your store and perhaps a large quantity should be returned to central storage. There also seems to be a theft problem. In the same period, four transistor-type radios disappeared from counter display racks.

2. You are the engineer in charge of research at the Freeton Corporation. Your department has four graduate chemists, one man who is a specialist in physics, and yourself. Submit your monthly report to the president on the activities of your department.

   Projects Completed
   a. Development for production of a felt and cork gasket for use in the Navy 232 Missile. The gasket complies with Naval Specification 2134R.
   b. Development for production of a lubricating oil to be used effectively at temperatures up to 5000° F. This carries the present designation of Product 30712.

   Projects in Process
   a. Development of a timing device to release lubricating oils at predesignated times while a missile is in flight.
   b. Development of a no-leak gasket which contracts and expands with adjoining metal parts during severe temperature changes.

Routine Projects

   a. Forty-five tests were carried through to measure quality level of company manufactured products.

   b. Seventy-five tests were completed on items under consideration for purchase by your company.

Other Factors for Consideration in the Monthly Report

   Cost of research

   New equipment needed

   Future projects

   Personnel

3. As the controller of the American Automotive Accessories Company you are required to submit a monthly report on your department's activities. You may assume all necessary details around the following major areas as well as any other which you feel should be included for the month of March.

   a. All accounts are billed by electronic billing machines.

   b. Your machines made up 40,000 invoices.

   c. A total of 24,000 invoices were mailed out.

   d. A total of $860,500 was received and credited against the proper accounts.

   e. A total of $950,000 was charged against accounts.

   f. Delinquent accounts totaled $32,500.

   g. Court action is being taken against five companies.

   h. Losses for the month in uncollectible accounts totaled $4,500.

   i. Twenty-five new accounts were opened.

   j. All payroll accounting for the company is completed automatically. Checks for a total of $48,500 were prepared.

   k. Checks for accounts payable totaling $580,000 were prepared.

   l. Your staff of three accountants, four bookkeepers, and nine clerks remains unchanged.

   m. New inventory control system begun.

4. Write a sales report for the month of March for the American Automotive Accessories Company. Sales for the month totaled $115,000 which was $10,000 more than March of last year and $5,000 over February of this year. These sales are split among Group One (radios and heaters), Group Two (chrome muffler pipes, headlamp trim, mirrors and hood ornaments), and Group Three (ash trays, clocks, lighters, map holders, and various dashboard mounted items).

Your total inventory for the three groups amounts to $165,000. This figure is $10,000 higher than February and $20,000 less than March of last year.

Your salesmen number three with two trainees working in the office. This is the same as last month. Last year during March you had four salesmen and no trainees.

The outlook for the future is good. You feel that automobile air-conditioning units will enjoy a major jump in sales and you would recommend that this item be stocked heavily and promoted intensively.

You may assume sales, inventory, and all other figures for each group or item if you desire.

5. As a government motor vehicle department head, you are required to submit a monthly report to your bureau chief. Complete the report for August. You may wish to include all the information given below, or less, or add to it.

	August	July	August of Last Year
Received for Assignment			
Passenger sedans	89	85	90
Jeeps	12	15	14
Trucks	18	18	14
Turned in for Credit			
Passenger sedans	82	70	85
Jeeps	10	12	12
Trucks	12	16	12
Miles Traveled			
Passenger sedans	85,000	80,000	110,000
Jeeps	8,000	10,000	12,000
Trucks	12,000	12,500	10,000
Gas and Oil Used (gallons)			
Passenger sedans	7,500	7,300	8,000
Jeeps	820	890	910
Trucks	1,400	1,450	1,250
Repairs—Hours Spent in Labor			
Passenger sedans ⎫			
Jeeps ⎬	600	650	700
Trucks ⎭			
Repairs—Cost of Parts			
Passenger sedans ⎫			
Jeeps ⎬	$1,800	$2,100	$3,050
Trucks ⎭			
Staff			
Drivers	42	36	47
Mechanics	4	3	4
Administrative	2	2	2

6. Complete a periodic report in your major field of study. Assume all facts necessary. Submit it for a specific month but include all necessary comparative statistical data for the same month in the previous year as well as the preceding month of the current year.

You may assume that you are a sales, personnel, advertising, production, or credit manager. Or you may wish to assume that you are a government department head, an industrial, mechanical, electrical, or civil engineer. If none of these lies within your field of interest choose your own.

IV. *Progress Reports.* Write a progress report on the basis of the data given in each of the following problems.

1. Write a report to your parents regarding your progress in college. Note the courses completed, the grades received, costs and expenses, difficulties encountered, housing, and future plans.

2. As the accountant in charge of Team D of the Robert Wellington Accounting Company, submit your second progress report. You and your two team members have been working at the Caroline Candy Company for three weeks as part of a projected six-week assignment.

The Caroline Candy Company has used the same accounting procedures since 1946 although their sales have increased about 400 percent and their staff size has almost tripled.

During the first and second week, your team has revised the accounts payable and receivable departments. Automatic equipment has been installed and personnel trained.

In the period covered by this report, the payroll system has been revised. Employee checks will be issued twice each month instead of weekly. All deductions will be made and a complete record stub issued. Overtime pay must be verified by the signature of department heads. Payment for negligent breakage of equipment will be automatically deducted ($5.00 per check maximum) rather than billed to the employee to be paid at his convenience.

A new inventory control system (FIFO) was begun the day before the report was written.

If your team is to finish on schedule, the assignment of another man seems to be necessary.

All personnel of the Caroline Company have coöperated with the exception of the accounting department head who still seems antagonistic and disgruntled.

3. Write a report detailing the progress which has been made at

the Stone Steel Company. This is your terminal report, the fifth submitted in a ten-week period.

In this time span you have supervised the installation of new machinery and illumination fixtures, a revision in the production lines, and a change in the compensation pattern. This has all been carried through in the fabrication department.

In the period covered by this report (previous two weeks) all the new lighting fixtures were installed. All other areas (installation of machinery, production line, and pay changes) were completed to the Stone Company's satisfaction during the earlier period.

There were 480 new fixtures installed; of these 390 were 4-tube fluorescent units and the rest were 2-tube units. Each unit was of a recessed type, with safety plastic cover, instant start feature, and equipped to handle 80-watt tubes.

The level of illumination rose an average of 20 percent. Employees' morale seemed to rise, and the production rate has gone up by 12 percent.

All work agreed to in the original contract should be completed by 5:00 P.M. today.

Mr. Stone has questioned you on whether or not your management firm has ever done any consulting work regarding the establishment and revision of employee communications such as orientation booklets, house organs, and monthly bulletins.

4. Your firm has the contract to install new street lights in the city of Burlington, Montana. You are in charge of this project. You have already submitted two progress reports to your Chicago headquarters. Submit the third in what is expected to be a series of six.

You have completed all installations in three of the eight sections into which you have divided Burlington. In section three (completed in this period), 240 standards No. 212 were installed, wired, and completed. In the lot of 250 standards delivered by Maywell Trucking Company, six were badly damaged and were not used.

Your next installation will be made in section four where you expect to encounter some difficulty and delay. This is because the section involved includes the Burlington business district.

Assume any necessary data.

5. Because you have been the manager of one of Stanford's biggest shoe stores in New York for five years, you have been asked to

help establish and "break in" a unit to be opened within one week in Springdale.

You have been in Springdale for two weeks and you are to submit your initial progress report to the Company's president.

In the two weeks you have been in Springdale you have carried through the following:

Staff

Hired a store manager; Mr. Robert Cain, five years' experience, competent and pleasant. Salary of $8500 per year plus bonus as per paragraph 25, compensation rate booklet.

Hired three full-time shoe clerks;
Mr. John Taylor, $6000 per year
Mr. Wayne Lexo, $6000 per year
Mr. George Murphy, $6000 per year
All the above also receive commission as per usual procedure.

Hired one woman to handle handbags, hose, and miscellaneous;
Miss Ella Strange, $5400 per year

Hired one part-time porter ($25.00 per week) and two part-time stock clerks ($30.00 each per week)

Advertising

Newspaper "ads" contracted for. See attached schedule for six-month period.

Fliers and handbills prepared for delivery the day prior to grand opening.

Three television sets were purchased to be used as Opening Week Door Prizes (bill enclosed).

Window posters, streamers, and flags secured.

Work Accomplished

All shoes ordered have arrived from central warehouse except children's play line 21.

Carpeting, fixtures, and decorating have arrived or have been completed.

Work to Be Accomplished Prior to Opening

All merchandise must be stocked, windows trimmed, and private opening and luncheon held for chamber of commerce members.

Obstacles or Problems

None with the exception of the register. This item may not be delivered until the morning the store is scheduled to open. However every effort is being made to secure earlier delivery.

Chapter 10

Short-Form Reports (Continued)

CREDIT REPORTS

In any literature concerned with credit, most readers are amazed at a frequent opening statement: "Approximately 75 to 80 percent of all business carried on is on the basis of credit." To many persons this comes as a surprise because their transactions for food, clothing, gasoline, etc., are almost always cash. The average individual may well wonder where this amazing 80 percent figure comes from.

The answer lies in the areas of credit which may not often occur to Mr. John Q. Public: bank, investment, commercial, retail, government, international, and others. The credit tied up in these areas runs into billions of dollars each year. It is for this reason that we can say, "Eighty percent of all financial transactions are carried on a credit basis." However, we all know that no firm or government agency will grant a "line of credit" without first investigating the reliability of the requestor. The information on which the decision to grant or not grant is contained in a *credit report*.

As can well be imagined, hundreds of thousands of credit accounts at all levels are opened or closed daily. This action is often taken on the basis of the credit report. Therefore, these reports must be written clearly and concisely so that accurate decisions may be made in a matter of minutes.

However, credit reports are not only written to evaluate the credit position of an account. Purchasing agents examine them to determine whether or not a particular firm is sufficiently stable and should be given an order; sales managers select prospective customers from such a list; and law firms and businesses use them when contemplating company relationships.

Most credit reports have been reduced to a form which is filled in. This is true at the consumer as well as the industrial level. However, the credit report form usually has adequate space for comments which the investigator is required to complete. These statements should be concise, clear, accurate, and unbiased. This is not the place for opinions, theories, or definitely stated prognostications. The purpose of the report is to indicate as accurately as possible how good or poor a credit risk the applicant is.

The credit report tries to answer the investigator's classic "C's": Capital, Capacity (of the business to do business), Character (of the applicant), and Conditions. In addition to these areas, there may very well be others which vary according to whether the applicant is an individual or an industrial corporation.

In the case of the report on a commercial account, areas such as "fire hazard," "payment record," "history," and "method of operation" are included. For the consumer applicant, information on "place of employment," "other creditors," "mortgage," etc., are requested in addition to the "C's" listed above.

Reports on Retail Applicants

Throughout the United States there are dozens of excellent credit agencies which issue reports to clients concerning the consumer who desires credit. Many large firms operate their own credit departments which handle many of the functions of the credit agency. However, more and more firms are turning to an agency which so often does a quick, efficient, and accurate job of gathering, processing, interpreting, and presenting data on the applicant.

In Chicago, for example, The Credit Bureau of Cook County has data on approximately 3,000,000 individuals and firms in the Chicago metropolitan area. A merchant can make a telephone call to the bureau and request credit information on Mr. Joseph R. Brown. In approximately one minute the businessman is given several vital facts. He may, if he wishes, have that supplemented by a written report which is mailed out shortly after the telephone request is received.

In this type of report, the businessman is told from what firms the credit applicant has made purchases in the past and whether or not he met his obligations promptly. In addition he is given routine information on the applicant's place of employment.

In the more detailed reports, as one might assume, the specific areas evaluated are marital position (married, separated, divorced, single; number of children), employment record, income, property holdings, credit record, legal record (convictions, liens, etc.), and social habits and associations.

Industrial or Commercial Credit Reports

There are many firms which specialize in gathering data and reporting on business firms. This service has grown so rapidly that many fields now have a credit agency which specializes in one specific area, such as lumber, woolens, transportation, foods, etc.

Most of these reports follow a rather general pattern in their mechanical make-up and organization:

Identification: Company name, address, code number, and list of personnel.

Rating: Code number and/or letter.

Summary or Synopsis: This covers the entire report and may be part of the rating section.

History: A discussion of the company's background including personnel, management, legal involvements, and other relevant data.

Operation-Location: Comments on the firm's policies and practices, number of employees, inventory, type of sales (cash and/or credit), and the advantages or disadvantages of its location.

Fire Hazard: Record of fires, condition of buildings and nearby structures, fire losses suffered and insurance payments made.

Financial Statement: Comparative facts on assets and liabilities, an analysis of the data and the results of current investigations.

Trade Investigation: Comments from suppliers on highest level of credit granted, how much is owed, terms of sale, manner of payment (discounts, prompt, slow).

Each of these sections, or others if the report is so designed, should carry a clear, capitalized heading. The comments made should be specific and factual. General statements, if at all possible, should be avoided. If it is necessary to qualify a statement, the words should be chosen with care. Obviously it would be dangerous to say, "Mr. Bryan will pay all outstanding debts by September 1, 19—," if it is more accurate to state, "Mr. Bryan indicated that he will pay all outstanding debts by September 1, 19—."

It is wiser to say, "Mr. Flanger stated that to the best of his knowledge no firm in which he had a financial interest had gone into bankruptcy," rather than to write the fact *without* the qualifying statement, "Mr. Flanger stated. . . ."

Be as specific and as factual as possible. Do not say, "Mr. Larkin has been an officer in the Fairmont Corporation for many years," if you can say, "Mr. Larkin became the treasurer of the Fairmont Corporation in June, 1947. In 1955, he was promoted to executive vice-president, a position he now holds."

The credit report writer should choose all his statements with care for he must remember that a company's future will often depend on the interpretation given to the comments in the report.

Dun & Bradstreet Credit Reports

Among the best known of the credit reporting services at the mercantile level is Dun & Bradstreet, Inc. It is said that this firm is the world's oldest and biggest commercial credit organization.

The Dun & Bradstreet Reference Book contains a listing on almost 2,900,000 companies, corporations, and individuals! This enormous 4,000-page credit guide is revised and published six times each year. To keep it up to date, Dun & Bradstreet makes over 6,000 changes in ratings every single day.

To determine what credit rating Brown's Butcher Shop or U.S. Steel should have, Dun & Bradstreet has 2,000 full-time and 22,000 part-time credit reporters who interview businessmen and make notes during the day. These data and others funnel into one of the 150 offices Dun & Bradstreet maintains. The information is carefully analyzed and integrated into the proper records. When one of Dun & Bradstreet's 80,000 clients requests credit information on the Bryant Brass Corporation, the data are available almost immediately.

Types of Dun & Bradstreet Reports

Most of the credit reports are submitted to the client who requested them as a *synopsis* report. This brief, factual report contains a rating; a brief synopsis of the history, operation, and loca-

Dun & Bradstreet Credit Report

tion of the company; and financial information and payment record. An *analytical* report may be secured on larger firms. This report is a detailed analysis in the areas listed above as well as background data on the guiding officers of the company. In this report, a good deal of information is listed on the business and personal activities of the individuals discussed. Some of this may be extremely detailed, noting the person's academic and extracurricular

Dun & Bradstreet, Inc.   *Report*   RATING CHANGE

JONES, ROBERT

CD 12 NOVEMBER 3 1955
INFANTS WEAR

SPRINGFIELD, OHIO
PAGE 2

Interviewed on November 3, 1955, Jones said that until recently he has been handicapped by a heavy inventory and consequently has been slow in meeting bills. By retaining all earnings, beyond withdrawals for living expenses (about $75 a week), working capital has been built up to a point where, according to Jones, payments in September and October were all met fairly promptly. However, accounts payable are now stated to be between $4200 and $4500 as the result of some further seasonal increase in inventory since August 31, and he is again slow in meeting some trade bills.

The following comparison of sales for 1954 and 1955 was submitted by Jones:

	1954	1955
8 months thru August 31	$ 21,475	$ 24,792
September	2,686	2,360
October	4,262	4,314
November	3,238	—
December	8,516	
	40,177	

It can be seen that during 1954 about 8 percent of the annual volume was transacted in November and 21 percent in December. Jones expects on this basis to do about $3500 in November 1955 and $9500 in December. Should this sales budget be met and inventories be reduced to normal January requirements, Jones anticipates that there will be sufficient cash available to meet January 10th obligations promptly.

PAYMENTS

HC	OWE	P DUE	TERMS	NOV 3 1955	
350			EOM	Ppt	Sold 7 yrs to date
350	159		8-10 EOM	Ppt	Sold yrs to date
250	250		8-10 EOM	Ppt	Sold 1946 to 11-49
200	90		8-10 EOM	Ppt	Sold Occasionally
150			EOM	Ppt	Sold yrs
600	200		8-10 EOM	Ppt-Slow 30	Sold 1947 to date
400	300		EOM	Ppt-Slow 15	Sold yrs to date
300	300		EOM	Ppt-Slow 15	Sold yrs to date
300	100	45	2-10 EOM	Ppt-Slow 30	Sold 11-48 to date
212	163	80	1-10 EOM	Ppt-Slow 60	Sold 1945 to date

11-3-55 (192 158)

Dun & Bradstreet Credit Report (Continued)

record, his date of marriage, minor and/or major encounters with the law, and many other facts which would do credit to an F.B.I. report.

In addition to these two standard types, Dun & Bradstreet also offers the following specialized reports:

Key Account Service which answers specific questions about key customers whose sales, collections, or inventory problems are not usual.

Municipal Reports analyze the financial operations of cities, counties, and states for investors, manufacturers, and buyers.

Foreign Service Reports are issued on buyers and sellers in some 49 foreign markets. These reports are made by trade analysts familiar with the language, business operations, and conditions of the country with which they are concerned.

Fire Insurance Reports are prepared for the use of fire insurance companies and underwriting agencies.

Specialized Reports are issued in various areas to answer a particular problem.

The standard report is usually printed on a form which has a distinctive color line across the top sheet. Red indicates "special notice" (read immediately, the company is rising or falling rapidly); rust means a rating change has taken place but it is probably not vital; green stands for a rating which has not been changed. It is these credit reports, written at various levels by a variety of different agencies, which help the wheels of industry to turn smoothly. Without them, innumerable problems in the conduct of business would arise.

EXAMINATION REPORTS

An examination report is often classified as a short-form report. However, there are occasions when it is extended and formal in nature. But whether long or short, the principles on which it is based and written are essentially the same. Although these fundamental concepts of gathering, interpreting, and presenting data have been discussed earlier, a brief review of those and related factors in connection with *this specific type* of report may be of value.

The examination report may vary in length from a 100-word analysis of a customer's complaint to a 1000-page report of a Congressional investigation. This report may cover:

1. Materials—such as raw materials and their possible use, new synthetic compositions, and other items subject to laboratory analysis or experimentation.

2. A process or system—such as an analysis of a manufacturing process or an accounting system.

3. An industrial or commercial situation—such as low sales volume or lack of wholesale or retail product acceptance.

4. Personnel—such as employee production rates, morale, and human relations.

In different companies and in different situations this examination report is titled by various names. It may be called an analytical report because its basic function is to analyze a situation; it may be an inspection report that gives the results of direct observation; it may be an experimental report based on laboratory procedure; it may be an evaluation report that compares two or more products of a similar nature; it may be an investigation report which presents the results of a detailed investigation. But whatever it is titled, it still presents the results of an examination.

Unlike the progress or periodic report, the examination report does not summarize routine activities; it does reflect the results of *new* investigations and information.

Attributes of an Examination Report

It is not unusual for a company to pay $5,000 for a report on several of its production processes or $2,000 for an analysis of its employer-employee relationships. A municipality will spend $20,-000 for a survey of its traffic, housing, or planning problems. In all these cases, the employing agency receives a report which represents untold hours of investigation, analysis, and interpretation plus the experience and knowledge of many competent persons. Whether the report is six pages or sixty in length, it is all that is received for the $5,000 or $20,000 check. That report, therefore, must be good.

It should be complete and should tell the reader in detail exactly what steps in the examination were taken, what methods of investigation were utilized, what was discovered, and what implications may be drawn from the findings.

It is not adequate that the writer indicate that most of the women surveyed prefer pink packages; he must indicate what type of sample was used, how many women were sent questionnaires, what percentage responded, what method of tabulation was utilized, and what percentage responded in what way.

He should remember that he is writing a report of an examination; he must, therefore, report on every important step in his investigative procedure for the benefit of the intelligent readers who will peruse his report and ask, "how?" "why?" and "what was the purpose?"

In addition to being well-written, complete, detailed, and clear, the examination report should be attractively typed or printed with plenty of "white space" to aid in reading. Meaningful charts and tables should be presented, and correctly designed supplementary sections (such as a letter of transmittal, table of contents, an appendix, and a bibliography) should be included.

The Organization of the Examination Report

Heading. This section of the report varies. Most companies have agreed on a heading that suits individual needs. However, the most frequently utilized introductory information employs the "To: From: Subject:" idea. In other cases, the formal title page arrangement (see Chapter 11) is preferred.

Title. The title should give a clear picture of the nature of the project:

An Inspection of the Old South Mine and Its Safety Features
An Analysis of the Accounting Procedures of the National Plastic Toy Corporation
A Survey of the Buying Habits of Urban College Students

Summary. This should be a brief synopsis of the entire report which contains the outstanding findings of the survey.

Purpose or Objective. A clear statement of the reason for the examination should be listed as well as the objective which the examiner hopes to achieve.

Scope of the Report. Here the writer states exactly what areas were examined and refers to the original agreement made. This often helps to avoid misunderstanding. If the report writer indicates that the original assignment requested that the survey include an investigation of payroll procedures, accounts receivable, and accounts payable, then the employing agency (or employer) cannot expect the report to contain an analysis on inventory methods or cost control.

Body of the Report. This section, as indicated earlier, may cover one page or a hundred. It follows the suggestions made earlier concerning layout, headings, clarity of organization and discussion, graphs, etc.

Conclusions. The conclusions might well be indented and numbered. They should be clearly substantiated by the material offered in the body of the report.

Recommendations. An examination report will almost always present a list of recommendations if such is warranted. The amount of detail in the recommendations varies according to the report, the writer, and the procedure followed. Quite often, simple statements such as the following are made:

> Improved illumination should be installed in Department B.

or

> Approximately 12 fixtures, each holding four 48" fluorescent tubes, should be installed in Department B.

However, a detailed recommendation indicating the specific types of fixtures required, their placement, and the wiring diagrams would ordinarily appear only in a recommendation report.

Appendixes. The appendix should contain material that clarifies, substantiates, or elaborates on various segments of the report. The information contained in the appendix usually proves helpful to the reader, but is often not vital to the clear understanding of the report.

Each segment in the appendix should be clearly titled and attractively presented.

AN EXAMINATION REPORT OF THE TRAINING FACILITIES OF THE UNITED STATES METALS CORPORATION

Purpose of the Survey

The purpose of the examination was to determine and report on the various training facilities carried on by the United States Metals Corporation in its three major locations: New York, Chicago, and Los Angeles. At the present time, training programs are operated independently at each location. This survey presents a report on the various methods used currently; brief recommendations are also presented.

Research Techniques Used in the Examination

In an effort to secure necessary data the following research methods were utilized.

1. Questionnaires were sent to a selected sample of employees and administrative personnel. (see Appendix I for a copy of the questionnaire and the statistical analysis of the sample.)
2. Interviews were held with key officers at the New York headquarters to determine their viewpoints on training. In addition, interviews were also carried on with administrative and supervisory personnel at the company branches in New York, Chicago and Los Angeles. (See Appendix II for a copy of the interview schedule and statistical analysis of the sample selected.)
3. Observation. The director and various members of the survey team attended classes and conferences which were being carried on in each of the three locations.
4. Secondary research. Reports on the training programs of various American corporations were read, discussed, and analyzed by the survey team members.

Summary

The survey of the three headquarters indicated that wide disparity exists in expenditures, quality of instruction, course of study, and numbers of employees participating.

Because of the heterogeneity of the three programs, the best interests of the company are not served, nor are the results commensurate with the expenditures which are made.

A Review of the U. S. Metals Training Programs

Training Facilities in New York

The training facilities carried on in New York were well organized and rather extensive. From time to time the entire program was given aim and direction by conferences held between the personnel director of the New York office and the head of the industrial training division of New York State University. The basic philosophy of this program seemed to emphasize the need for developing potential administrators and supervisors for the New York headquarters.

Training began on a more or less formalized basis in New York in 1945; it was expanded materially in 1953 and has continued without interruption since that date.

Administrative Training. There was no training of administrators prior to 1956. Since that date, however, various small and unconnected programs have been carried through by engaging consultants from neighboring universities to come in and meet with corporation officers. During the past year a formal course in executive duties and control was established. Each person in the management echelon with the exception of vice-presidents has attended.

Supervisory Training. During the past three years all individuals in the New York office occupying positions of supervision have taken a course in human relations offered by New York State University. This course has been held in a company conference room and has been taught by an instructor from the industrial relations department of the University. These classes have been held during the evenings and not on company time. Payment was on the basis of regular tuition assessments.

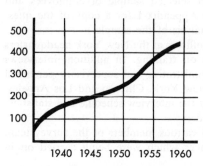

Personnel Trained in New York Program

Professional Training. Any employee of the U.S. Metals Corporation holding a professional type of degree, such as accounting, engineering, chemistry, and so on, has been permitted to register for one graduate course per year in any accredited university in the area. The entire cost of tuition was underwritten by the New York headquarters. It is suggested that all courses be "job related."

Office Personnel Training. The New York headquarters has offered a consistently detailed program for this particular group. Classes have been held during company time and in company facilities in the following training areas:

Personnel management
Business writing
Office practices

In these three areas various qualified consultants have been hired to instruct the personnel selected. A definite attempt has been made to give all individuals an opportunity to avail themselves of this training.

Skilled Personnel Training. This has been quite unorganized. New York has, from time to time, attempted to set up some programs with various unions. In 1958, a six-month course for tool and die apprentices was carried through with the cooperation of the full-time skilled artisans employed. A similar program was attempted in 1957 with union electricians and plumbers. In all cases, however, there seemed to be differences of opinion and some friction, not only between management and labor organizations, but also within the locals themselves. All training in this area has been discontinued.

Training Facilities in Chicago

The training program carried on by the Chicago office has been quite complete and fairly well organized. Although not as extensive as the New York effort, it nevertheless has provided instruction for a large percentage of interested personnel.

Administrative Training. The Chicago office has carried through no formal training program for administrators. There are, however, several individuals on the administrative level who have availed themselves of the "graduate business program for executives" of Chicago University. This is a credit program leading to advanced degrees.

Supervisory Training. All personnel in the Chicago office who hold supervisory positions have taken three courses: "How to Deal with Others," "Report Writing," and "Job Supervision." Each of these courses met for thirty hours in the company offices. A fourth course in verbal communication and conference leadership is now being planned for the same group. Professional consultants were employed.

Professional Training. The Chicago office permits all employees who hold degrees to register for a maximum of three graduate level courses each year at any accredited college or university. The entire tuition cost is met by the company provided grades of "B" or better are attained.

Office Personnel Training. The Chicago Branch of U.S. Metals has held twelve courses for this group since 1957. Six of the courses have been in business writing and six in office practices. The classes have been conducted by consultants in the area and have been held on company time and in the company building. In addition, one person is retained from Illinois Central University for the purpose of improving all written communications which leave the company. This individual spends approximately 15 hours a week reading duplicates of letters and reports and consulting with the employees who have written them.

Skilled Personnel Training. There has been no attempt to carry on company-sponsored training activities for skilled personnel.

Training Facilities in Los Angeles

The training program carried on in Los Angeles by the U.S. Metals Corporation has been negligible. Unlike New York and Chicago, various formal programs have not been instituted and what has been carried through has been relatively superficial in nature.

Administrative and Supervisory Training. In both of these areas there have been no planned programs of any type. In 1958, a weekly staff conference was instituted for the purpose of discussing "improved employee relations." These meetings were held each Monday morning for almost six months. However, after the third month attendance began to drop drastically, and two months after that, the program was terminated because of a lack of participants.

Professional Training.   Since 1956, the Los Angeles office has established a budget of $1,500 per year to pay for graduate level tuition. This nominal amount was exhausted by either March or April in each year and additional application on the part of professionally trained employees was rejected because of a lack of funds. Considering the many excellent graduate level training institutions in the Los Angeles area, the loss was significant. There can be no doubt that many of our technical personnel left the company and joined one of the many aircraft corporations whose educational training programs are well known for their liberal policies.

Office Personnel Training.   The Los Angeles center has maintained a full-time individual since 1955 who is charged with the training and improvement of communications. He has counseled employees, trained new personnel, and held classes periodically in the areas of business writing and verbal communication. The results of this program have been excellent and reflect credit on the individual in charge.

Skilled Personnel Training.   There has been no instruction in this area with the exception of electricians. Local 105 has been most cooperative in attempting to secure additional on-the-job training for its apprentice personnel.

Cost Analysis of the Three Programs

It is most difficult to give any accurate breakdown on what each of these training programs cost the Corporation. However, the figures which follow include an approximate estimate for:

Employees' time
Tuition payments
Consultants' fees
Supplies and books

In no case were outside facilities leased for training purposes; therefore, no cost was assessed when company conference rooms and offices were utilized. The table which follows is self-explanatory. However, a more detailed breakdown of expenses is available in Appendix III.

As is noted from the above table, the disparity among expenditures is startling. The amounts of money spent by Chicago and New York exceed that of Los Angeles in both years by an extremely large percent-

Cost Estimate for Training Purposes

	New York		Chicago		Los Angeles	
	Current Year	Last Year	Current Year	Last Year	Current Year	Last Year
Administrative	$15,500	$ 4,500	—	—	—	—
Supervisory	3,500	3,000	$ 9,000	$ 8,000	$ 800	$ 500
Professional	21,000	18,000	23,000	18,700	1,500	1,500
Office Personnel	12,500	8,500	14,800	12,600	8,000	8,000
Skilled Personnel	1,200	1,400	—	—	900	900
TOTAL	$53,700	$35,400	$46,800	$39,300	$11,200	$10,900

age. This is not to imply that one situation is more favorable than another. It is merely a fact that should be examined.

Conclusions

The following statements are obvious from the data which have been presented and are further substantiated by the various tables found in the appendices.
1. Major differences in expenditures exist in the three centers.
2. The training among the three centers is completely uncoördinated.
3. The level of training in the three centers is unequal; some of it is on a high professional plane, other training is hit or miss, very informal, and in many cases, of little value.
4. Unequal company training background contributes to the difficulty of transferring personnel from one city to another.
5. Efficiency varies from one center to another and is somewhat influenced by the training which is or is not available.

Recommendations

The following recommendations are listed very briefly. Further discussion and a much more detailed series of points for each recommendation offered will be presented in a formal recommendation report, if such is requested.
1. A training director for the three centers should be appointed. This individual should occupy a position at the top management level.
2. An assistant training director should be appointed for each of the three locations.
3. A complete training program should be prepared one year in advance and with the cooperation of educational consultants drawn from leading business schools. These men should meet from time to

time at the discretion of the individual named in No. 1 above. Their duties would be to establish curriculum, standards, and procedures. A formal evaluation of the program should take place once each year.
4. The training offered at each of the three centers should supplement what is available at neighboring institutions of education. Where specific courses are available at nearby colleges and universities, employees should be urged to register for those. When specialized training is desired (specific programs which are not available as formal courses), consultants should be brought in to the company itself. In other words, U.S. Metals should not get into "the education business" except when necessary. Universities and colleges are normally better equipped with facilities and faculty to carry through a more efficient job.

RECOMMENDATION REPORTS

Most examination or analytical reports conclude with a series of recommendations. Normally, however, these recommendations are presented briefly and concisely. It is only when the reader is told exactly how to put the recommendations into complete operation, that we have a recommendation report.

This report has as its purpose the improvement of a policy, a situation, or a procedure. Because the emphasis is on improvement, reference is made toward what weaknesses an examination revealed and how the suggested course of action will change the situation.

The organization of the recommendation report usually follows a plan such as the following:

Introduction. This may establish the objectives and purpose of the report. It refers to the examination which served as the background for the recommendations presented. At times it is feasible to include the report of the examination in an appendix of the recommendation report so that the reader may, if he wishes, review any section that served as the basis for a recommendation.

Summary. A brief synopsis of all recommendations is then given.

Body of the Report. The recommendations should be clear, complete, and accompanied by all the necessary visual aids. These might include floor plans, wiring diagrams, plant layout drawings, wage-scale formulas, and any other data which will assist the reader.

Conclusions. Those that are necessary should be presented. A "Forecast" section may also be included.

Recommendations

1. Because there is inadequate personnel to handle the evening rush hour crowd (see Appendix II, copy of examination report dated November 23, 19—), the following recommendations are made:

   Each day the entire lamp and electrical supplies section (Department B) should be closed from 4:00 to 5:00 P.M. All personnel should be transferred to the food and grocery department (Department D) to assist in handling the evening crowd.

   The manager of Department D should be given temporary supervision of all personnel working in sections 1, 2, and 3 of Department B. He will thus maintain his position of authority. The 14 persons from Department B should be assigned to assist in Department D as follows:

Section Number	Number of Sales People
1	1
2	2
3	2
4	3
5	2
6	4

   It is possible that some personnel of Department B may be reluctant to work in Department D, even on a temporary basis. In such cases, a "person-for-person" transfer may be worked out with Departments A or C. However, every effort should be made to avoid this.

2. The present customer parking facilities should be revised to secure greater convenience for the store's patrons. The diagram attached (figure 3) presents a solution to the problem. As will be noted, a concrete dividing strip is recommended, an extension of the parking area proper, and a rearrangement of car stalls. The detailed plans are presented in Appendix III attached.

In almost all cases, the recommendation report gives a specific, comprehensive, and detailed plan for a new process, procedure, or system.

A REPORT RECOMMENDING AN INCREASE IN PRODUCTION RATE
OF THE STEVENS STOVE CORPORATION

Introduction

During the period November 15-25, 19—, an examination and an investigation were made at the Stevens Stove Corporation for the purpose of determining the reasons for the decline in production. A copy of that complete examination may be found in Appendix I of this report. The examination report contained a series of recommendations. By authority contained in the letter of January 18 of Mr. Thomas Fareman, Vice-President of the Stevens Stove Corporation, the detailed recommendations and plans for implementation are presented below.

Summary

As a result of the examination, a series of detailed recommendations have been made. These provide for the purchase of new high-speed punch presses, the installation of safety devices, improvement in the level of illumination, a change in the compensation plan, and a revision in the employee use of the cafeteria.

It is felt that most, if not all, the production problems presently encountered will be alleviated or eliminated when the recommendations made here are carried through.

Recommendations

As indicated in the basic examination report (see Appendix I for a copy) of the Stevens Corporation, the serious decline in production was traced to Department H. For that reason the recommendations which follow are concerned with that particular department although certain statements apply to other departments in general. These will be indicated during the presentation.

Recommendation 1:

Machinery

Of the eighteen punch presses in Department H, twelve were purchased prior to 1940. The production rate obtainable on these twelve is far below accepted production standards today. It is recommended that at the earliest possible date, twelve Smith and Barton punch presses, Model 261B, be purchased for Department H. The installation of these machines should be in conformity with the floor plan suggested (see Appendix II). The six Crane and Green punch presses which the department presently possesses should be retained. However, their position in the shop should be moved in accordance with the floor plan included with this report. (See Appendix II.)

In addition, the six Crane and Green machines should be immediately equipped with the No. 21 Peterson safety plates. These may be purchased from the Peterson Gear Corporation in Madison, Wisconsin. When this is carried through, all machines in Department H will possess adequate safety devices. The fact that the machines in this department heretofore operated without this necessary feature undoubtedly contributed to the relatively slow production rate carried on by the personnel in this department.

Recommendation 2:

Illumination

Much of the work in Department H is of a precision nature. Yet the level of illumination is below that in other departments where meticulous work detail is not carried on. In addition, Department H does not have the advantage of any natural lighting. Lighting throughout the remainder of the plant is quite adequate. It is recommended that eight fluorescent strips be installed in the department in question immediately. These strips should each contain four units each holding four 48-inch fluorescent tubes. This will result in adequate footcandles of illumination for the precision work involved as recommended by the engineer who handled this segment of the examination.

It is further suggested that as a safety feature, these strips be recessed into the present ceiling or that a false ceiling be constructed. The fixtures should be fitted with translucent, unbreakable covers. The exact position of the strips and the wiring diagrams are presented in the plans enclosed. (See Appendix III.)

It is further suggested that the colors of the walls in Department H not be gray, slate gray, brown or the other dark hues which have been heretofore used. Light pastel colors in a flat base paint should be utilized.

Recommendation 3:

Wage Rates

At the present time the operators in Department H are paid on a flat wage rate basis. This, of course, does not motivate the men, increase productivity, or generate a competitive spirit.

It is suggested that a "base-rate-plus" plan be instituted on the first of next month. This procedure is satisfactory to Union Local 107 which is the labor organization involved.

The "base-rate-plus" plan has the advantage of rewarding those men who work rapidly and competently. It provides wage incentive which heightens interest and improves morale. There is no additional cost to the company when weighed against production level. As a matter of fact, Stevens Corporation will benefit from such a program.

The specific wage rates for new personnel in Department H as well as those having 5, 10, 15 and 20 years' service is laid out on the wage-rate chart attached. (See Appendix IV.)

Recommendation 4:

Plant Facilities

At the present time all personnel except executives of the Stevens Corporation have a lunch hour time period between 11:45 A.M. and 12:30 P.M. The plant is housed in an H-shaped structure. Department H occupies the lower portion of one leg and the cafeteria is at the upper portion of the other. Because of this location factor, the personnel of Department H invariably arrive at the cafeteria last. Three problems are immediately obvious:

1. Personnel of Department H are at the end of the cafeteria line.
2. The choice of food is relatively poor by the time these men arrive at the serving tables.
3. Only scattered seats are left in the cafeteria, thus preventing the personnel of this department from sitting with one another.

It is therefore recommended that the lunch period in the Stevens plant be staggered according to the pre-arranged schedule. (See Appendix V for a complete plan of the schedule.)

Such a program would certainly be much more equitable than the one presently followed and would give the personnel of Department H a feeling that they were not "the step-children" in the factory.

Miscellaneous

The results of the other areas that were investigated indicated that the personnel in Department H were reasonably competent, emotionally stable, and satisfactorily oriented to their jobs and company. There can be no doubt that if the recommendations made above are put into operation at the earliest possible date, production in this department will rise materially and the company as a whole will benefit appreciably.

Estimate of Cost

A detailed breakdown of the costs involved in carrying through the recommendations made is contained in Appendix VI. These include machinery, equipment, labor and supplies. The gross figures, however, follow.

Cost Estimates

12 Smith & Barton punch presses, Model 261B, @ $12,500 each	$150,000	
Minus: Trade-in value of 12 T & W 1231 presses (obsolete) @ $500 each	6,000	$144,000
6 Peterson No. 21 Safety Plates and related equipment, $250 each		1,500
8 fluorescent strips, $200 each		1,600
TOTAL		$147,100

Estimate of Production Increase

On the basis of the present production rate of Department H, it is estimated that a significant increase would be effectuated when the recommendations made above are put into practice. The results of that increase as measured in production rate are reflected in the following graph.

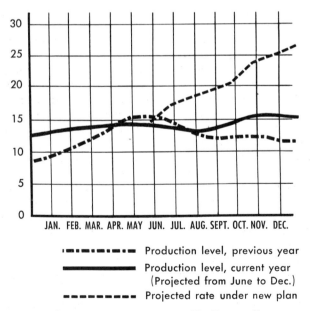

Production Rate—Department H—Current Year

Conclusion

For maximum results, it is suggested that recommendations 1, 2, and 3 be carried through within 30 days; recommendation 4 can be instituted within one week. The over-all results will be reflected in higher morale and increased production.

QUESTIONS FOR DISCUSSION

I. *Credit Reports.* Write a credit report on the basis of the data given in each of the following problems.
 1. Mr. Martin Blake has applied to the Ballantine Department Store for the purchase of a Clear Tone TV and Hi Fi combination which sells for $495. The department store has requested your company, Consumer Credit Rating, to submit a report on Blake.

 You have secured the following information, some or all of which you may wish to include in your report.

 Martin Blake is married and has three children, 12, 10, and 9 years of age. He has been employed by Raley Meat Packers for eleven years. He is a foreman in the shipping department and earns $490.50 per month. His wife works on week ends in a neighborhood candy store. It is estimated that she earns about $110 each month.

 The family has lived in the same 5-room apartment for seven years. Current rental is $110 per month.

 Blake owns a 1959 Ford on which he is making payments of $30.00 per month. Other payments are Maxwell Jewelers, $10.00 per month; family physician, $10.00 per month; and Ace Appliance Store, $15.00 per month. A savings account is maintained at First Federal Bank. All accounts report that Blake's payments are made promptly.
 2. Consumer Credit Rating has been asked by the Keeler Auto Agency for a credit report on Joseph King.

 King lives in a 30-year-old home with his wife and four children. The house still has a $3,000 mortgage and is not clear as King reported. This mortgage is held by Surety Savings Corporation. Payments are $90.00 per month which cover principal, interest, taxes, and insurance.

 Joseph King has worked for Belton Milk Company for six years as a driver. He earns $480 per month and not $600 as he reported. His wife does not work.

 Belton Department Store reports he has been delinquent on payments made on a bedroom set. Karton Kredit Jewelers reports a $60.00 balance on a ring set which he purchased for his wife 12 months ago. No payment has been made in 3 months. King served 18 months in the state penitentiary in 1946-1947 for theft. Mr. King's children are 1, 3, 5, and 7 years old. He was married in 1950. King has a savings account in low three figures at North Side State Bank.

3. Submit a commercial credit report on the Nabor-Hood Grocery and Meat Market located at 2100 West De Soto Drive in Albany, Illinois. The store has been owned and operated for five years by Neil Bankcroft and his wife. The financial statement of the store as of August 31 of this year follows:

Assets		*Liabilities*	
Cash	$ 1,800	Accounts Payable	$ 2,000
Merchandise	14,500	Due on Loan	1,200
Fixtures and			3,200
Equipment	3,000	Net Worth	16,100
	$19,300		$19,300

Net profit for the year was $5,850; monthly rent and utilities, $170; fire insurance carried, $18,000.

The above balance sheet is accurate and has been verified. Neil Bankcroft is 47 and his wife 45 years of age. Bankcroft was a chain store food manager for seven years before he purchased this store. The payments due on the store were completed three years ago. Bankcroft attended the University of Illinois. In his sophomore year he married. The Bankcrofts have two sons, both of whom now attend the University of Illinois School of Engineering. Bankcroft assists them with expense money each week.

From 1942-1946 Bankcroft served in the Army from which he was discharged with the rank of captain.

No court litigation or suits were found listed against Bankcroft's store.

The store handles a medium grade line of merchandise. All transactions are on a cash basis. Canned merchandise, fresh fruits and vegetables, frozen foods, and fresh and smoked meats are sold. Customers are all local residents. Bankcroft, his wife, and a delivery boy constitute the entire staff. The store occupies the lower floor of a two-story building. A four room apartment is above the store and is occupied by Mr. and Mrs. Bankcroft and their 13-year-old daughter. The store is modern, has a 35-foot front and a 90-foot depth. Sales approximate $6,300 per month.

Bankcroft indicated that he is finally completing payments on very heavy medical expenses incurred as a result of an auto accident three years ago. However, his sales have been going up, especially since he started to distribute Homemakers Savings Stamps three months ago. He also feels that his inventory should be reduced to give him a more fluid position. There is a rumor that the Tastee Food Chain is considering the erection of a super market in the 2300 block of De Soto Avenue. Bankcroft's payment record follows:

HC	Owe	P. Due	Terms	Payments	History
$700	$350	—	2–10 EOM	Ppt.	Sold 3 years
850	—	—	2–10 EOM	Discounts	Sold 2 years
600	300	—	2–10 EOM	Discounts	Sold 2 years
1200	650	—	2–10 EOM	Discounts	Sold 5 years
500	150	—	2–10 EOM	Ppt.	Sold 1 year

His rating is E2.

4. Submit a commercial credit report on the Jordan Drug Store located at 1500 West Dearborn Street in Los Angeles, California. This store is located on the corner of a busy intersection. The corner is a bus transfer point and traffic is heavy. The store is modern in design with windows on Dearborn and on Asbury Street. The store has a 50-foot front and a 100-foot depth. All standard brands of merchandise usually found in a large city drug store are available. However, no food or ice cream is served. An effort is made to concentrate on prescription service. The area immediately surrounding the store is a busy shopping district. Week-end business is especially heavy. The store was originally opened as the Becker Drug Center by the present owner's uncle, Bryant Becker, in 1929. Mr. Becker operated it successfully until November, 1946 when he sold it for a nominal sum to his nephew. At that time the name was changed.

Jay Jordan was born on June 27, 1920. He went to pharmacy school and graduated in 1943. The same year he entered the Army and was discharged in 1946. In 1945 he married an Army nurse, Betty Burness. He worked for Mr. Becker for several months and then purchased the business.

A financial statement as of June 30 follows:

Assets		Liabilities	
Cash	$ 2,400	Accounts Payable	$ 4,500
Merchandise	12,000	Loan from White	
Fixtures and		Drug Corp.	2,500
Equipment	5,000		7,000
Accts. Receivable	5,000	Net Worth	17,400
	$24,400		$24,400

Jordan is an aggressive young man who has tremendous plans for growth. At the present time he is attempting to secure the store next to his, break through the wall, and enlarge his own operation. He enjoys the complete confidence of the sales and credit managers of the three major wholesale firms supplying him. His hobby of sailing is very important to him. He owns a 24-foot sailing boat. His gross sales average about $9,500 per month. He works on a very small profit margin, but he feels it is necessary to maintain superiority over his nearby competitor, Economy Drugs. His payment record follows:

High Credit	Owe	Terms of Sale	Payments
1. $1,500	$ 700	2-10 net 30	Disc.
2. 2,500	800	2-10. net 30	Disc.
3. 7,000	3,000	2-10 net 30	Disc.
4. 2,500	500	2-10 net 30	Disc.
5. 1,500	—	2-10 net 30	Disc.
6. 4,000	2,000	2-10 .net 30	Disc.

II. *Examination Reports.* Write an examination report on the basis of the data given in each of the following problems. Use any graphic or tabular representations which will assist you in your presentation.

  1. You have been asked to examine the advertising activities of your company to determine the effectiveness of the present program in comparison with the cost. You are a research assistant to the president.

  You have limited the area of your research to newspaper, radio, and television.

  Company records reveal the following advertising costs in the three media listed.

	January	February	March	April
Newspaper	$80,000	$85,000	$95,000	$90,000
Radio	45,000	80,000	80,000	85,000
TV	10,000	20,000	60,000	60,000

Newspaper advertising consisted of one-quarter- and one-half-page ads placed in the *Chicago Bulletin* and *Gazette*. Radio advertising consisted of two 15-minute news programs per day in January, and this was increased to include a one-half-hour evening entertainment program in February, March, and April.

  Television advertising during January and February consisted of spot announcements only. In March and April a 15-minute children's program at 4:00 P.M. was added.

Company records for sales of your product (cold meats, wieners, and smoked ham) follow:

	Chicago Only	Chicago Suburbs
January	$4,200,000	$ 800,000
February	4,300,000	950,000
March	4,900,000	1,250,000
April	5,200,000	1,300,000

You sent out 15,000 questionnaires to a selected sample of housewives in the Chicagoland area. Almost twice as many respondents were aware of your 15-minute children's program as compared to the radio programs. Most of the comments on the TV program were favorable as to its entertainment value and level.

Approximately 3,000 interviews were held with shoppers in food marts throughout the same area. In almost all cases, responses favored the TV program, and 40 percent of those interviewed said it led them to select your company's products.

An interview schedule and questionnaire, with data tabulated for each question, may be attached to the examination report.

2. The mayor of your city has requested that the Department of Traffic attempt to relieve the downtown congestion in some way. The head of the department has asked you, one of the traffic engineers, to make a complete examination of the situation so that recommendations may be made on the basis of accurate and reliable findings. You completed an examination in the areas listed below. Your findings are included.

Private Automobile Traffic

Approximately 100,000 autos move into the downtown area between 7:45 and 8:30 A.M. Most of these vehicles carry one passenger only. Almost 90 percent of this number attempt to leave the downtown section between 4:30 and 5:15 P.M.

Truck Traffic

Additional early morning congestion is brought about with the entry of 10,000 to 15,000 trucks between 6:00 and 8:00 A.M. These deliver merchandise of all types to the downtown stores. Most of these are out of the downtown section by noon.

Public Conveyances

Subways bring in approximately 400,000 individuals between 7:30 and 8:45 A.M. Trains of six cars each operate efficiently and move into the area every 2 minutes. They operate below street level.

City owned buses bring about 120,000 people into the downtown area between 7:30 and 8:45 P.M. However, they are big and unwieldly and the number of accidents with cars and trucks is amazingly high. In addition, their noxious fumes do not make them very popular.

Parking

Parking of automobiles is not permitted in the downtown area between 8:00 A.M. and 6:00 P.M. each day. However, there are many violations of this. In addition trucks are constantly parked while deliveries are completed.

Traffic Routing

All traffic moves in both directions on all downtown streets.

Business Firms

Interviews held with the managers of 80 downtown stores revealed a general drop in sales supposedly due to the reluctance of shoppers to come into the downtown area and "battle the traffic."

Shoppers' Reaction

Interviews were held between 10:00 A.M. and noon with 500 women in the downtown section. The general reaction to the 10 questions asked was that almost all disliked the inconveniences and crowds when one came into the center of the city for shopping purposes. Interviews were also held with an additional 800 women at four different suburban shopping centers. Almost all indicated their pleasure at being able to drive within a block of the department store or shop desired, no trucks and busses to "battle" and, free parking areas to use.

Other Cities

Brief surveys of three other downtown sections in three urban centers brought out several interesting facts.

Two cities did not permit autos into the downtown sections between 7:00 and 9:00 A.M.

All truck deliveries must be completed prior to 6:00 A.M. Where busses were used, their routes were carefully controlled. Street traffic in all three cities in the downtown sections was on a one-way basis. Traffic violations by either motorists or pedestrians were dealt with severely. Tickets for infractions of regulations were issued immediately. (Assume any necessary statistical facts, as well as additional data, where required.)

3. Your corporation has recently purchased the Dayton Automatic Dishwasher Company. This has been a Dayton family-owned corporation for 40 years. No changes in management have been contemplated, and Mr. T. Dayton remained as company president.

However, a superficial inspection by the industrial relations director of your company, American Industries, turned up several disturbing factors. Supervisory personnel were not sure of their duties nor responsibilities. Foremen did not command or receive respect or coöperation. The personnel of the offices and factory seemed to be made up of dozens of cliques. Rumors, some of them quite vicious and destructive, filled the air. Employees seemed to take no pride in factory housekeeping. Aisles in the factory were cluttered, the cafeteria was messy, and the plant grounds were littered with cigarette and candy wrappers.

You, as a member of the industrial relations department of American Industries, have been asked to examine the situation in detail and submit a report of your findings.

Findings

There is no clear organizational plan of management authority and responsibilities at Dayton. Mr. Dayton seems to give most of the orders, and almost every company action or decision must clear through his office.

Mr. Dayton frequently overrules directives issued by managers and/or foremen after such decisions have been announced. He also has purchased machinery, signed contracts, and refused orders without consulting with or even telling the department managers involved. Mr. Forbes and Mr. Burton, Dayton's two sons-in-law, hold positions of vice-president of sales and production respectively. These two men are not on speaking terms with each other, and neither one knows very much about the business. Forbes came from the printing industry two years ago, and Burton came directly from college.

The last time a meeting of department heads was held was 18 months ago. The foremen have never met as a group. There is no orientation program or guidance booklet for new employees. The company makes no attempt to communicate in any formal manner with its 2300 employees. Company-wide meetings have never been held; there is no company newspaper or house organ. Bulletin boards are not used. There are no company-sponsored recreational programs of any kind.

The pay rate throughout Dayton is excellent and is well above the average of the industry.

(Assume any other facts for this examination report which you feel are necessary.)

III. *Recommendation Reports.* Write a recommendation report for each of the problems listed below.

1. Write a recommendation report on the basis of the examination report data in problem 1 of section II above.
2. Write a recommendation report on the basis of the examination report data in problem 2 of section II above.
3. Write a recommendation report on the basis of the examination report data in problem 3 of section II above.
4. Write a report to the dean of your college recommending a plan of acceleration for outstanding students. He will probably want specific facts concerning credit hours, tuition charges, courses to be taken, and method of student selection.
5. A large steel corporation (or department store) has offered to coöperate with your school's placement bureau in providing part-time work for junior- and senior-level students. Many students are eager to secure jobs which will provide them with funds and give them experience in their major areas of concentration. The student government has been asked to prepare a report for consideration by the placement director of the university and the personnel manager of the firm.

   Submit your recommendations in the form of a report. Take into account the various job areas, method of student selection, number of hours of work permitted in relation to course load carried, training programs, and other factors.

Chapter 11

The Long Formal Report

Whether the field is management, marketing, engineering, science, sociology, or government, the extended formal report is encountered frequently. These reports are almost always analytical in nature, although they may also present a record of events or activities.

Formal extended reports have been called by a variety of other designations:

Research reports
Inspection reports
Examination reports
Evaluation reports
Analytical reports

This list can be expanded; but other titles would simply refer to similar types of reports. Regardless of what these extended reports are called, however, they follow a rather general pattern in their makeup.

The elements which appear in the long report are not precisely set down; they often vary from company to company. In the pages of this chapter which follow, the sections of the long report will be discussed and explained. However, it would be a very unusual report which would contain every part listed.

COMPONENTS OF THE LONG REPORT

The Cover

The cover of the long report not only offers protection but also indicates pertinent information. By listing the title, author, company

AN ANALYSIS OF

VIEWER REACTIONS

TO

THREE TELEVISION COMMERCIALS

Prepared
for the

FLAVOR-FULL BEVERAGE CORPORATION

Sales Department

Prepared
by the

RUSSELL ADVERTISING AGENCY

Market Research Department

Chicago, Illinois

June 5, 19__

A Sample Formal Report Cover

```
                                                              PRD-121
```

EDUCATIONAL RELATIONS INFORMATION BULLETIN

WHAT THEY THINK OF
THEIR HIGHER EDUCATION

A report of a survey of the opinions
of 13,586 college-graduate
employees of the General Electric Company,
evaluating their own college experience
as preparation for career success
and leisure satisfaction.

EDUCATIONAL RELATIONS SERVICE

GENERAL 🄶🄴 ELECTRIC

Cover of a Formal Report (Courtesy of General Electric Educational
Relations Service)

name, and date, it assists the librarian, the firm's file clerk, and
the reader. In addition to these data, the cover may also cite a
volume and report number (if it is part of a series), the firm's
insignia or trademark, and possibly the distribution list.

The information typed or printed on the cover should be taste-
fully and carefully arranged. The spacing should be balanced; the

type size should not be too large; and the color of the printing and its overall arrangement on the page should be conservative. Modern styling can be used to good effect, as can an illustration cleverly depicting the company's product or identifying symbol. The covers of the long report may vary in thickness from that of a file folder to the heavy, stiff fiberboard type. Many firms have their own special binding and hole-punching machines. This is a relatively inexpensive process, especially for the firm that produces a good many reports for its clients or for intercompany use. Some organizations have the covers made up by a bindery firm. These hard cloth covers are imprinted in the same manner as a book.

Title Page

The title page should not only present the necessary vital information concerning the report, but it should also possess an attractive, neat, and well-balanced appearance.

The spacing of the data should be planned and centered on the page. The type face should be conservative in size and appearance. Upper case (capital) type should be used for major headings; upper and lower case type may be employed for subheads or for the supplementary data which are presented.

The title page of a report should have several specific attributes:

The title should be brief and interesting.

The title should not be repetitious.

The title page should cite for whom the report was written.

The title page should indicate the author or issuing agency.

The title page should list the date.

The title of the report should give the reader a clear idea of the subject of the report. Intriguing and curiosity-arousing titles should not ordinarily be used except for reports directed to groups that would appreciate such an approach. "Crossroads at the Compton Corporation" is hardly acceptable, and "Tailored to Traynors" would be equally unwise. An improved title for the first might be "An Analysis of the Compton Corporation's Accounting Procedures." The other might be "The Traynor Corporation's Personnel Practices" (An Analysis of Pay Structure, Fringe Benefits, and Training).

As indicated in the second example, a title may be extended and clarified either in a supplementary subheading or in an added

ANALYSIS OF

PROFIT SHARING PROGRAMS

IN INDUSTRY

Prepared for:

American Spring Corporation

Director, Personnel Division

by

Brandon and Brandon

Management Consultants

Chicago, Illinois

July 20, 19__

A Sample Formal Report Title Page

parenthetical statement. Negative phrasing and unnecessary words should be avoided. Usually, thought and trial and error will produce a short, explanatory title.

After the subject has been presented, the recipient should be indicated whether that might be an individual, department, division, company, or government agency.

Report Prepared for:
John C. Higgens, General Manager
Higgens and Higgens Building Contractors

Report Submitted to:
Sales Division
Arrow Metal Manufacturing Company

The writer or issuing division should be listed next. If the report has been prepared by an individual, his capacity within the company should be indicated to lend authority to the report. Of course, the recipient of the report need not always precede the writer; the positions may be reversed.

At the bottom of the title page the report writer should list the name of the issuing company, the place of publication, and the date. Where the company name has been listed elsewhere on the title page, it may be omitted at this point.

Sometimes there are other items which appear on the title page in addition to those listed above: trademarks, addresses, name of individual whose critical or supplementary comments are attached, and a notation if the report is part of a series.

The back of the title page may list copyright data or the number of the legislative act authorizing the report.

Letter of Authorization

No investigation of major importance is begun without proper authorization. This usually is formally given in a letter of authority. Such a message will generally cite the meeting, conference, or legislative action approving the appropriation of funds for the investigation and compilation of the report.

The more specific the letter is, the easier is the task for the report writer. The letter of authorization should make a clear statement of the problem, the area or scope of the investigation, the limitations of the survey, and how the results will be utilized. When the precise boundaries are established, the report writer's time is conserved; he does not expend his energies investigating, analyzing, and examining data which are not definitely and specifically pertinent to the problem.

May 18, 19—

Mr. Conrad Melton, Sales Manager
Contemporary Design Lamp Company
333 West Michigan Avenue
Chicago 21, Illinois

Dear Mr. Melton:

This is to authorize an investigation to determine the feasibility of establishing a West Coast division of our firm.

As you know, our firm's products have enjoyed an extremely favorable reception in the Midwest. The trend on the West Coast also seems to favor furniture of modern design, and it is possible that our company would find it profitable to establish a West Coast plant and distributing center.

On May 15 of this year, the Government Surplus Division offered a Los Angeles factory for sale. It was fully described in Circular 105, a copy of whch is enclosed. Bids must be entered with the Surplus Division no later than July 15. For that reason, I would like to receive a report from you no later than July 8.

I would suggest that you use as many of your staff men as you feel are necessary to carry through this investigation. In addition, you may wish to secure the services of a professional research consultant. You may draw vouchers for necessary expenses on our "Account D."

To aid you in deciding whether or not to recommend the purchase of the plant and grounds, I would suggest that the scope of your investigation cover the following topics in detail:
   1. Labor
   2. Physical plant (interior)
   3. Physical plant (exterior)

4. Transportation
5. Source of raw materials
6. Potential market
7. Local regulations
8. Tax structure
9. Financing
10. Utilities available

It would probably be wise to have a detailed outline prepared for each of the 10 points listed above. The limitations established by the outlines may be discussed at a conference scheduled by you for this week. I, of course, shall be happy to attend.

Cordially yours,

Louis Lyons
President

LL:fp
Encl.

In the letter above, the scope of the problem is clearly established. The investigation of the ten topics listed will be limited by the outlines which are drawn up and approved. It may be that the outlines for "labor" or "transportation" will contain five subpoints; it may be that they will contain fifteen. But at least, the investigator assigned will know specifically what areas to cover.

The letter of authorization is not usually included in the formal report although it is invariably referred to in the message which transmits the report. On occasion, however, especially in government reports, the letter of authorization is reproduced at the beginning of the formal report.

Letter of Acceptance

The assignment offered in the letter of authorization may be accepted, rejected, revised, or changed in a letter of acceptance. This letter may present certain conditions or stipulations regarding time, fees, or the scope of the investigation. This letter is rarely reproduced in the formal report.

Letter of Transmittal

Unlike the letters above, this one, which transmits the report to the recipient, almost invariably appears with the formal report. Sometimes the information which appears in this letter may be presented in the "preface" or the "foreword" to the report. But whether it appears in a letter of transmittal, a foreword, or a preface, it serves the purpose of telling the reader something about the authority for the project, the scope and purpose of the examination, and other background data which assist the reader in recognizing the various facets of the problem under discussion.

The letter of transmittal must be written with careful consideration of the reader. The tone, language choice, and depth of detail of background data will all be dependent on the reader—who he is. If the reader is a company stockholder the approach will be different than if he is the executive who authorized this research project. If the reader is a technically trained engineer, the report must be written differently than if the reader is a business executive whose background has been in management only.

The content of the letter of transmittal normally covers the following items:

The authorization of the project. A sentence or two should refer to the original piece of communication which established the investigation. Sometimes the relevant section is quoted directly from the letter of authorization.

The purpose of the investigation and the report is then stated. This section tells the reader what the report hopes to accomplish, what the reader might find of specific interest, and just where in the bigger pattern, this particular segment (or report) fits.

The scope and limitations of the report are indicated next. The listing of the main topics that the report covers will effectively tell the reader the report's scope. This is usually wise because if the reader is told what to expect, he will not be disappointed because of inadequate data nor overwhelmed with a great deal of material.

The limitations will also help the reader evaluate the report. If the boundaries which are imposed by time, money, the research facilities available, and legal restrictions are cited, the reader will be assisted in weighing the report.

The sources used in gathering data may be cited. To state that information was gathered from "company records, the Lincoln Chamber of Commerce, and observation" is totally acceptable. If the sources are extensive, the bibliography should carry the listing.

Specific references to certain segments of the report may be wise if it is desired that the reader understand unusual conditions or give special attention to a particular portion of the report.

Conclusions and/or recommendations may also be included in a letter of transmittal. These can be set forth very briefly because they are usually contained in greater detail at the end of the formal report.

Acknowledgment of assistance may be cited in this letter also. This act of courtesy should be accomplished in a brief, dignified manner. This is not frequently done in a letter of transmittal, but where an individual or a group has given unusual aid to the report writer, an acknowledgment may be made.

The final paragraph of the letter of transmittal often indicates that the report writer is available to answer questions, carry through further research, and, in general, is desirous of assisting in any way possible in the future.

July 6, 19—

Mr. Louis Lyons, President
Contemporary Lamp Design Company
333 West Michigan Avenue
Chicago 21, Illinois

Dear Mr. Lyons:

As authorized by your letter of May 18, 19—, an investigation was undertaken to determine whether or not a bid should be submitted on the Los Angeles plant offered for sale by the Government Surplus Division.

You will find that the attached report and its exhibits reflect the detailed findings of an intensive survey in the areas suggested by you:
1. Labor
2. Physical plant (interior)
3. Physical plant (exterior)
4. Transportation

    5. Source of raw materials
    6. Potential market
    7. Local regulations
    8. Tax structure
    9. Financing
   10. Utilities available

It should be noted that because of the limitations imposed by the dead-line date, the study of several of the areas listed above was not as detailed as I would like to have carried through. Nevertheless, the findings are accurate and reliable.

I would like to call your special attention to the section devoted to financing. The Western National Bank and Trust Company is pre-pared to offer a 20-year mortgage for the required amount at a very favorable rate of interest.

The data cited in the attached report were secured from the Los Angeles Chamber of Commerce, local municipal offices, the state division of employment, personal observation and interviews, and secondary sources which have been documented in the report.

From the data gathered and the cost estimates available, it is recom-mended that the plant be purchased. Detailed recommendations may be found in the report.

I am sure you will find adequate data in the report so that you may arrive at a definite decision. It was a pleasure for me to carry through this investigation, and you may be sure that I shall be happy to par-ticipate in securing additional data for this project or others with which our company is concerned.

                                    Sincerely yours,

                                      C. Melton
                                      Sales Manager
CM:fs

The letter of transmittal above is somewhat long; the letter is frequently much shorter.

Mr. Lester Jameson, President
Illinois Metal Manufacturers
333 North Jackson Boulevard
Chicago, Illinois

Dear Mr. Jameson:

As authorized in your letter of March 28, I have carried through an examination of credit policies to consumers as administered by our dealers.

The information was gathered from interviews, a questionnaire survey and company records. I believe you will find all the information necessary to formulate any changes in policy which you feel are desirable.

If, at any time in the future, I can be of further assistance, please do not hesitate to call on me.

Sincerely yours,

Bernard Lapidus

BL:mp

    Letters of transmittal may also be in a memo form with the typical "To: From: Subject:" type of heading.

Table of Contents

    This section of the formal study is prepared after the entire report has been typed or run off as a first copy. The table of contents usually lists chapter and/or section headings, minor subdivisions, and page numbers for the divisions. Each heading is indented properly and agrees with the designations in the report itself.

    When a letter and numeral organization pattern is used, it is the same as that employed in the outline. The major head is a Roman numeral, then capital letters, Arabic numerals, and small letters. Numerals or letters of the subheads, as listed in the table of contents, are placed directly under the first letter of the preceding heading.

REPORT ON INTERIOR PHYSICAL FACILITIES OF PLANT X

TABLE OF CONTENTS

REPORT ON TRANSPORTATION FACILITIES AVAILABLE TO PLANT X

TABLE OF CONTENTS

Following the table of contents, a list of tables may appear. This agrees with the same general pattern of the table of contents. The headings are derived from the table captions. This section may be followed by a list of figures which offers reference information on charts and graphs.

LIST OF TABLES

LIST OF FIGURES

Foreword and Preface

There is not very much difference between a foreword and a preface. Either of these is usually found in a book; however, the letter of transmittal performs almost the same function in a report. When used in a report, the foreword or preface usually indicates the need and purpose of the survey, its general scope, the method of organization, and other necessary factors. It is possible that a single work may have a foreword written by the organization sponsoring the investigation and a preface written by the person who

foreword

THIS study, prepared under the direction of the Consultant—Educational Research, is the culmination of a long-time interest on the part of many components and individuals in the General Electric Company in those features of a college education which lead into the development of managerial and professional skills and responsibility, and to subsequent personal satisfactions of a related nature. In brief, it was a careful attempt to have college graduates in the General Electric work force evaluate their higher education.

The purpose of the study was twofold. It was hoped that the results, made available to the administrations and faculties of institutions of higher learning, might assist them in guidance and curricula planning. Simultaneously, these results should be useful in testing and revising the Company's machinery for recruiting and manpower mobilization. So far as can be determined, no similar study of a comparable sample has ever been conducted.

The source of the data has to a marked extent been the thoughtful comments of the college-educated men and women of General Electric. At the time of the survey, this group numbered more than 24,000. Today the number approximates 27,000 individuals. The responsible positions which they occupy continue with each passing year to call upon an interesting and complex blend of skills and academic disciplines, both technical and nontechnical.

It is hoped that the study will make a contribution to the task of educating men and women for rewarding and useful careers in industry and to the complementary task of mobilizing and utilizing them to the greatest advantage of individuals and Company alike. In a real sense it continues the long period of co-operation between the colleges and universities of the nation and the General Electric Company.

Kenneth G. Patrick

Manager—Educational Relations

An Introductory Foreword from a Formal Report (General Electric Report "What They Think of Their Higher Education." Courtesy of General Electric Educational Relations Service)

actually carried through the research and wrote the report. In such a case, the foreword would explain the broad purposes of the project, whereas the preface would introduce the reader to the report.

PREFACE

As America steadily moves forward in its quest for easier, cheaper and more efficient methods of communication, the United States Telephone Corporation moves with it. Our Corporation constantly strives to improve the facilities it offers the American public. Although U.S. Telephone has maintained a constant research program in the plant located in Bentryville, Missouri, it now finds those facilities inadequate.

There is definite need for a new research plant which will supply adequate facilities for divisions that will experiment and develop new products for the American consumer, industrial firms, and the U.S. Department of Defense.

For that reason a detailed investigation of possible plant sites in Scottsvale, Maryland; Springfield, Illinois; and Traline, New York; were carried through. This study presents the results of those findings.

The entire investigation was materially aided by the generous assistance of Professor Homer T. Allen of the University of Detroit. His extensive knowledge and competence were of outstanding value. In addition, the advice, help, and suggestions of Dr. Robert T. Wade and Dr. Martin B. Sand, both of the College of Illinois, were deeply appreciated by the author.

Acknowledgment

Usually an expression of gratitude for assistance received is contained in the letter of transmittal or, as in the case above, in the preface to the study. On occasion, however, it appears as a separate section.

ACKNOWLEDGMENT

This study was materially aided by the generous financial assistance received from the Bankcroft Foundation. The grant permitted a much more intensive and detailed study to be carried through, and the results thereby achieved greater reliability.

To Dr. Robert T. Miller, Chairman of the Economics Department of Chicago College, a deep debt is owed. His constant counsel, encouragement, and suggestions proved very valuable. Appreciation is also extended to George T. Moody and Richard C. Allen, both instructors in the same department.

Thanks are also accorded to the following companies which generously opened their company files to the research team:

American Steel Corporation
Metalkraft Fabricators
Indiana Tool Company
Rowe-Radcliffe Corporation

The tables, charts, and other graphic aids were drawn by Mr. Leo Maxwell. His analytical ability and competence are reflected in the outstanding illustrations presented.

Summary

The summary is a concise review of the entire report. It is designed to give the reader an understanding of the significant and outstanding facts of the report without having to read the entire study.

Although the terms *synopsis, abstract, digest, brief,* or *review* are often used, their essential characteristics are the same as a summary. Of course, there are specific differences between, for example, an abstract and a summary, but their purpose of giving a concise view of an extended work is the same.

The summary of the report should be a crisply worded statement that gives the reader specific facts and information on the problem, its scope, the method of investigation, and, most important of all, the findings and recommendations for action. These points (listed above) may very well serve as an outline for the summary.

The specific qualities of the summary are most important to keep in mind; if they are not followed, the summary may become a rather boring review that really wastes, rather than conserves, the busy reader's time.

The summary should be written very concisely. Of course, this is true of any piece of writing, but here it is especially vital. The reader who finds your summary verbose will have little patience with your report.

The proportion in the summary should be accurate. Minor sections in the report should not be treated in detail nor should the vital sections be handled superficially.

The tone of the summary should be formal, penetrating, and objective.

The length of the summary obviously depends on the length of the report. The former may run from a few paragraphs to several pages. In any case, topic headings may be used to assist the reader.

SUMMARY

On January 15 of this year, it was decided at a meeting of the board of directors that the manufacturing facilities of this corporation be expanded. After a thorough investigation of plants available for purchase, it was concluded that the factory in Avondale, Missouri, most closely suited our needs.

The subject of transportation of raw materials to the plant and finished products away from the factory and to consumers needed intensive study. The report which follows this summary explains the findings in detail.

Rail Facilities

The Avondale plant has two rail spur lines which run to the loading docks. These spurs are in excellent condition as are all the loading docks except for minor repairs which are necessary.

Freight rates for bringing raw materials to the plant and transporting the finished products to our three distribution points are in conformity with government rate regulations. It is important to note, however, that service by the Baltimore and St. Louis Railroad is extremely favorable for this plant.

Commuter service for employees who might reside in St. Louis is also fast, efficient, and inexpensive.

Trucking Facilities

There are six local trucking firms which are available to serve the plant. Their prices are all similar, but on a tonnage basis, the rail freight rates would be consistently more advantageous for our purposes.

Two primary highways and three secondary roads all run within the immediate plant area.

An excellent combination to serve the local as well as the more distant market is the truck-rail service offered by the Baltimore and St. Louis Railroad. This "piggy-back" arrangement has a most attractive rate schedule.

Water Transport Facilities

The wharf facilities of the Avondale factory have obviously not been used in years. Extensive repairs costing approximately $28,000 are necessary before loading and unloading can be accomplished.

Once that is carried through, however, the Barton Barge Line is prepared to offer extremely favorable freight rates on bulk chemicals, coal, lumber, and other commodities.

Recommendation

On the basis of the initial cost of the plant, its favorable location to market, the excellent labor market available, and other factors discussed in detail in Company Reports 210 and 211, the purchase of the Avondale plant is strongly recommended.

TEXT OF THE REPORT

The body of the report naturally accounts for the bulk of the study. It is in the body or the text that the background to the problem is explained, the scope defined, the method of investigation listed, the source cited, the presentation of the information made, and the analysis and interpretation of the data given. Finally, the author offers his conclusions and recommendations.

Broadly speaking, the report contains the (1) introduction, (2) discussion, (3) conclusion and recommendations.

Introduction

The introduction tells the reader what the subject of the report is, what data were gathered and how, the purpose and scope of the investigation, and all the background information necessary to orient the reader properly.

Obviously, every introduction is different. Where the report does not have a summary, letter of transmittal, preface, or other introductory data, the introduction is very complete. Where prefatory information is given elsewhere, the introductory section of the report may be shorter.

It would be an unusual introduction which would contain all the following items, but many of them might very well be included.

Authorization data for the report
The problem which brought about the report
History of the problem
The scope of the investigation
The limitations of the survey
Purpose of the investigation
Methods of gathering data

Sources of primary data
Sources of secondary data
Methods used in tabulating the data
Methods used in measuring the reliability of the data
Definition of terms
Brief statement of the results
Brief statement of conclusions and recommendations
The general plan used in presenting the report
The *authorization* data, even when mentioned in the letter of transmittal, might, as a matter of record, be referred to briefly in the introduction.

The *problem* which the firm has encountered should be reviewed for the reader. If he has a clear understanding of the problem, he can better appreciate the objectives and scope of the survey. The *history* of the situations leading to the problem or the history of previous relevant investigations will also prove of value to the reader.

The *scope* of the investigation should be clearly outlined. If the reader understands right at the beginning that rail, truck, and water freight facilities were investigated, he will not be disappointed or irritated not to find a discussion of air freight facilities.

This investigation was specifically designed to evaluate the freight facilities, rates, and services of rail, truck, and water transportation which are available to the Avondale plant. Because of the high cost of air transport, that medium was not examined.

The survey was limited by reason of time (July 5 to July 10). Under more favorable circumstances, additional time would have been permitted.

When the survey has specific *limitations* such as time, assistance, data, money, or coöperation, they should be cited. In the paragraph above, this has been done.

The *purpose* of the survey should be explicitly and specifically stated. This may be indicated in a sentence or two. This, too, is a matter of protection; there should be no opportunity for the reader to misconstrue the purpose of the report.

The purpose of this report is to present data, conclusions, and recommendations concerning the advisability of accepting or rejecting the Fairfax Corporation's bid to place this firm's loading docks and freight handling platforms in satisfactory condition.

The *method of gathering* data and the *sources* of primary and secondary data should be explained. If a questionnaire study was carried through, the method or mechanics in the survey should be explained. The reader should be told what type of sampling method was employed, how the recipients of the questionnaire were chosen, the time interval between mailings, the *editing* and *tabulating process* used, and other pertinent data. It may make quite a difference to the reader if he learns that all results were machine tabulated, or hand tabulated, or if an "outside" agency did all the counting of the quantitative data.

If secondary sources were also used, the reader should again be told how and where. All of this can be done briefly; it permits the reader to evaluate the researcher's method of investigation.

The report writer must also explain how and why he secured *reliability in his survey.* If a specific number of questionnaires were sent out or interviews held, the researcher should explain the statistical significance and why the findings may be presumed to be valid. This also permits the reader of the report to measure the work of the writer.

It was also assumed that sufficient persons would respond to 2,000 questionnaires in each group to permit a 95 per cent level of confidence. Once the figure of 2,000 had been decided upon, it became necessary to select a specific number of persons from each of the cities which the College served. On the basis of the most recent population census, a figure was designated . . . so that a . . . ratio among the cities was maintained.

Where terminology is used which is common and well known in a specialized field, but which may not be familiar to the reader, *definitions* should be presented. This might be true for a medical investigator who would present the result of his research to a foundation from which he had received a grant.

The introductory portion of the report may also (although not very frequently) present a brief statement indicating the results of the survey, the conclusions reached, and the recommendations offered. Finally, the reader may be told the general plan used in presenting the report. If he knows that a general discussion is presented first and that all statistical data may be found in appendixes, he will be oriented toward the report's organization.

The Discussion Section of the Report

The discussion portion of the report is, of course, *the* report. It utilizes most of the space of the report and requires the greatest expenditure of time on the part of the report writer.

The explanation of the discussion section which follows in this chapter is brief because so much has been commented on in other divisions of this book.

It is in the discussion section of the report that the writer presents his information, evaluates it, interprets it, and indicates the relationships and significance of various ideas.

Essential facts are made clearer by the use of tables, charts, graphs, and diagrams.

It is also in this section that the report writer is so careful of organization. He assists his reader by major and minor type headings for each new section. And he writes, edits, and revises to secure the best possible piece of exposition.

All in all, the presentation of the discussion portion of the report must utilize many of the devices, crafts, viewpoints, and techniques discussed in the earlier chapters.

Conclusions and Recommendations

The last portion of a formal report is concerned with the conclusions which are drawn from the discussion section. Usually both conclusions and recommendations appear in one segment of the report; at times, however, each is quite extensive and is given a separate division in the report.

A summary of the entire report also appears quite frequently. If this is done, the summary (discussed earlier) should be a series of concise statements. Nothing should appear in the summary which is not discussed in detail in the body of the report.

The conclusions should be based on clear analysis and logical interpretations of the material presented in the report. If the report is not an examination type of survey, but is entirely informational, there is little or no need for a conclusion; a summary will do nicely. However, almost any other type of report profits from a conclusion section.

When it is utilized, it may be presented as either a series of points or in a discussion fashion. In either method, the conclusion should be clearly substantiated by the material in the discussion portion of the report. The following is an excerpt from the conclusion section of a report on the possible purchase of an available plant at Elsinore.

CONCLUSIONS

1. The heating plant at the Elsinore factory is in satisfactory condition except for approximately 70 feet of steam pipes.
2. The illumination facilities at the plant require replacement. The present incandescent fixtures should be replaced with fluorescent units which will result in a higher level of illumination.
3. The power plant produces adequate electricity for all present and contemplated future needs.
4. The ventilation system is in satisfactory working order.
5. The present facilities for water are satisfactory. However, if an air conditioning system is installed, which uses large quanties of water, a new heavy-duty water pipe will have to be laid from the plant to the present city supply mains.
6. The present overhead truss supports of the Elsinore plant are not properly set up for the installation of overhead traveling cranes.
7. The cafeteria equipment in the Elsinore plant is outmoded.

The sample above illustrates the statement type of conclusion section. The discussion form elaborates in a little greater detail on each point and is presented in paragraph form.

The recommendations follow from the discussion in the report and the conclusions reached. It is important that the recommendations be directed toward accomplishing the purposes of the investigation. For that reason they should be as specific as possible.

The recommendations which appear in an investigative report are usually statements suggesting action. However, the details of carrying through the suggestions are not usually indicated except in a formal recommendation report. For example, a recommendation at the end of an analytical report may state that all incandescent light fixtures should be replaced with fluorescent units. But it would not, ordinarily, indicate the type, position, number of, and wiring diagrams for the new fixtures; this would appear in a recommendation report. Most usually, however, the recommendation section would be similar in nature to the following excerpt from the recommendation section of a report.

RECOMMENDATIONS

1. That the Elsinore plant be purchased for the agreed price of $660,000.
2. That the incandescent fixtures be replaced by fluorescent units.
3. That a new water main be provided immediately for eventual use in an air conditioning system.
4. That overhead supports be installed. These should be of adequate size to easily handle three No. 204 Grantley Overhead Cranes.
5. That the Industrial Kitchen Equipment Corporation be engaged to bring the Elsinore employee cafeteria to a high level of convenience, comfort, and efficiency.

These recommendations, like the conclusion items, may also appear in paragraph form and be discussed (in either form) in greater or lesser detail.

Regardless of what form they take, the recommendations should be carefully thought through and presented. They should be substantiated by adequate data, and they should be reasonable in the action they propose. It is ridiculous to make suggestions which would require unusual efforts or expenditures or would be, in some way, out of reason with the situation.

SUPPLEMENTARY SECTIONS OF THE FORMAL REPORT

There is usually some material which is relevant to the formal report but is not so vital as to be included in any of the three parts (introduction, discussion, conclusion and recommendations) of the report. Among those which may be found in the supplementary portion are the appendix, bibliography, and index.

The Appendix

This section is frequently found in the long formal report. It may contain a variety of items such as:

Graphic representations
Tables
Copies of questionnaires
Copies of interview schedules
Blueprints
Schematic diagrams
Tabulation statistics

Testimonials
Glossary of terms
Mailing list data
Other reports associated with the one presented
Maps

These are some of the items which may be found in appendixes. Whatever is used should supplement the data in the report. The items placed in the appendix should be numbered so that when reference is made to them in the body of the report, confusion will be avoided. Sometimes each item is placed in a separately numbered appendix. Whatever system is used, specific designations should be employed for easy reference.

The Bibliography

The list of primary and secondary sources used should be listed at the end of a formal report. The method of citing books, magazines, documents and other sources is noted in Chapter 2.

The Index

An index is rarely used in a formal report unless the study is long and complex. The index assists the reader in finding particular portions of the report as quickly as possible. It cites page references for names, facts, places, ideas, important statements, and key thoughts.

The easiest way to make up an index is to use 3" × 5" cards. Each idea, fact, name, etc., should be noted on a card with the page number on which it appears. The cards should then be alphabetized and the index typed from them. The index is made up after the report is typed or after the printed copy is submitted as galley proofs. The researcher should use index cards generously; he should never try to get more than one idea on a card.

A sample formal report is given on the following pages.

AN ANALYSIS OF

LABOR AND THE LABOR SUPPLY

OF

FREEMONT, MISSOURI

Report Prepared by:
Robert Pembroke
Executive Vice-President
Sterling Metal Manufacturers

Submitted to:

Robert T. Sterling, President
Sterling Metal Manufacturers

Sterling Metal Manufacturers
Chicago, Illinois
October 17, 19___

STERLING METAL MANUFACTURERS

2250 South Washington Street
Chicago 18, Illinois

MAin 3-1313

October 17, 19___

Mr. Robert T. Sterling, President
Sterling Metal Manufacturers
2250 South Washington Street
Chicago 18, Illinois

Dear Mr. Sterling:

As authorized by your letter of October 3, 19___, a survey of Labor and the Labor Supply of Fremont, Missouri was carried through. This was done in connection with the possible purchase of the plant available in Fremont.

The purpose of the attached report is to present a clear picture of the Fremont labor situation in the following areas:
    Present labor supply available
    Unions and labor relations
    Wage rates
    Sources of labor supply
    Use of labor by industries in area
    Community facilities

It should be kept in mind that research and investigation were somewhat limited due to the two-week time limit imposed. It is nevertheless felt that the enclosed report gives an accurate and valid picture of the labor situation.

The sources used in gathering the data were the Fremont Chamber of Commerce, local employment agencies, official city records, the current *United States Abstract,* administrators of Fremont's major companies, educational directors, and bound copies of the *Daily Fremont Gazette.* On the basis of the labor survey made, it is strongly recommended that the plant available in Fremont be purchased.

ii

The investigation was carried through with the competent and able assistance of Mr. Donald T. Wright of the personnel office and Mr. James R. Blaine of the president's office.

I believe you will find that the data in this report are adequate and valid, and will permit you to reach a reliable decision concerning the matter in question.

It was a pleasure to direct this study. I shall be happy to carry through further work or answer any questions if the need arises.

Sincerely yours,

Robert Pembroke
Executive Vice-President

RP:fp

Summary

At the present time Sterling Metal Manufacturers is evaluating three different plants which are available for purchase. It is contemplated that one of these will be selected.

The report which follows is concerned only with the labor and labor supply of the plant located in Fremont, Missouri.

The city of Fremont is a growing, prospering city that is rapidly attracting industry. In addition to the smaller firms located in Fremont, there are also Afco Photographic Equipment Corporation, Burns Battery Company, and the Bunting Brass and Foundry Corporation.

The present labor supply in Fremont would prove very adequate for Sterling's needs. Some slight shortages might arise among the skilled, technical, and administrative categories. However, transfers from the main plant would alleviate or eliminate this problem.

Union-management relations in Fremont have been consistently favorable since the end of World War II.

Wage rates in all categories compare favorably with present levels existing in the Chicago plant and office.

Fremont possesses excellent sources of labor in all categories. The public and private secondary schools, the private business schools, the colleges, and the city and its environs will prove fertile sources for necessary personnel.

Other firms practice stable, ethical employment policies.

The city possesses very commendable public and private recreational services as well as adequate housing, educational, and religious facilities.

On the basis of the labor survey carried through, it is strongly recommended that the Fremont plant be purchased by the Sterling Metal Manufacturing Company.

Introduction

Obviously, "Labor and the Labor Supply" is one of the most important factors to consider before Sterling Metal Manufacturers can seriously consider the purchase of the Fremont Plant. Although it is expected that an appreciable number of key personnel will have to be brought in from the home office and factory in Chicago, the bulk of the employees will have to be secured from the city of Fremont and its environs.

Other reports in this series have been prepared on the internal and external plant facilities, transportation, tax structure, source of raw materials, the potential market, and other vital areas of interest. This specific report, however, deals only with Labor and the Labor Supply.

This survey is concerned with six topics concerning labor:
1. Present labor supply available
2. Unions and labor relations
3. Wage rates
4. Sources of labor supply
5. Use of labor by industries in the area
6. Community facilities available to labor

Sources of data have been cited as footnotes and indicated in a general way in the letter of transmittal.

Background Data on Fremont, Missouri

A detailed study of the city of Fremont, its history, growth, industries, transportation, cultural and recreational facilities, sociological backgrounds, and other necessary data are cited in the appropriate report. However, a few notes follow which are specifically related to the topic of Labor and Labor Supply.

Fremont, Missouri, is a city of 78,000. It is estimated that approximately 30,000 individuals are presently available for active positions.

The city has one parochial and four public secondary schools. One of the public schools is vocational and technical in nature. The State Teachers College, the Missouri College of Engineering, and the Fremont Branch of the State University are all located in the City of Fremont.

Major industries located in Fremont are the Afco Photographic Equipment Corporation, The Burns Battery Company, and The Bunting Brass and Foundry Corporation. These organizations employ approximately 850, 1,275, and 1,500 employees respectively.

1

Present Labor Supply Available

A careful survey of the local employment agencies, the Fremont office of the State Employment Office, and the Fremont Chamber of Commerce indicates that an appreciable number of persons, in all work categories, is available for employment.

The shortages which exist, as measured against the possible requirements of Sterling, are not serious. The number that is short in the

TABLE I. City of Fremont: Individuals Available for Employment, October, 19—

Category	Approximate Number Available	Approximate Number Required by Sterling Metal
Skilled	30	80
Technical	50	60
Administrative	20	40
Clerical	95	75
Production	375	350
Unskilled	375	50
Miscellaneous	75	20

skilled, technical, and administrative categories may be made up quite easily by transfers from our main plant and office.

Unions and Labor-Management Relations in Fremont

Sterling would be concerned with the following unions if the Fremont Plant were purchased:

Local 121, Truckers
Local 423, Production and Maintenance
Local 325, Tool and Die

From discussion with the directors of the industrial relations department of Afco, Burns Battery, and Bunting Brass and Foundry, it was determined that the unions listed above were most equitable and fair. The union leaders concerned are ethical gentlemen who obviously have the best interest of their members in mind, and also recognize the needs of management.

Conferences called by either labor or management concerning pay rates, fringe benefits, or grievances have been very successful. Meetings are usually held in the Fremont Community Center and have been conducted in a professional manner. Since the end of World War

II, there have been four union-sanctioned strikes and one wildcat strike. The fact that only five strikes have occurred in Fremont (each of a relatively short period) since 1946 is very encouraging.*

TABLE II. Strikes Called in Fremont

Local	Date Called	Date Settled
Local 121	March 15, 1947	March 30, 1947
Local 423	April 8, 1948	June 5, 1948
Local 121	November 7, 1949	November 27, 1949
Local 325	March 21, 1956	April 25, 1956
Local 121 (Wildcat)	December 5, 1958	December 8, 1958

Wage Rates

On the whole, present wage rates in Fremont are approximately 5 percent below wage payments made in the Sterling parent plant and offices in Chicago, Illinois. The only exception to this is in the area of skilled workers whose wage rates are approximately 8 percent above those being paid in our Chicago factory. This higher level is probably due to the demand in Fremont for skilled machinists, tool and die workers, and steamfitters. However, the number of artisans available in these categories should increase appreciably after next month. At that time the first class of the Fremont Industrial High School is due to graduate.

If employees are transferred from the main plant and office, certain minor wage adjustments will be necessary to maintain equity among our old employees and those hired in Fremont.

See Appendix I for a complete tabulation of wage rates in all categories.

Source of Labor Supply

There seem to be six primary sources of labor in the Fremont area:

1. Those who are presently unemployed. These individuals are registered for the most part with either private employment agencies or the State Employment Office.
2. Other industries in the area. There is always a small number of employees in all categories who find their present place of employment unsatisfactory. We can expect to secure a small number in this fashion; conversely, we shall also lose some for the same reason.

* Issues of the *Daily Fremont Gazette*, January 1, 1946 to present.

3

3. Influx into Fremont from the surrounding rural areas. We can expect approximately 20 to 30 rural persons each month to apply for production and unskilled positions. As the farms become more and more mechanized, the need for farm help decreases. Persons falling into this position, frequently migrate to the nearest urban center.
4. Secondary schools in the area will be a constant source for production and semi-skilled help. As the Fremont Industrial High School grows, we will have more and more applicants for the skilled positions. The other public and parochial high schools should provide us with clerical and secretarial personnel.
5. The two, small, privately owned business schools should be fertile sources for stenographers and office girls. Both of these schools (Fremont Business School and The Fremont Office Training School) have acceptable courses of study and commendable entrance requirements.
6. The Missouri College of Engineering has assured this investigator that it would cooperate completely in helping Sterling secure adequate technically trained graduates. These college-trained men could fill available engineering positions in our company and take care of our needs in the "technical" category.

The Fremont Banch of the State University would assist us by supplying competent accounting, management, and marketing personnel.

All in all, the possible sources of labor for the projected Sterling plant in Fremont are very good.

Use of Labor by Other Companies in Fremont

The number of individuals working for the three major companies in Fremont is given above under "Background Data."

In the three major firms in Fremont, wage rates, fringe benefits, working facilities, and other factors are all reasonable, ethical, and fair. It is doubtful that more than a small percentage would leave Afco, Burns Battery, or Bunting Brass for Sterling. This is certainly desirable, for it is an important factor in building a stable community.

Community Facilities Available for Present and New Residents of Fremont

Housing. The housing situation in Fremont is most satisfactory. Rental units are constantly available in 3 and 6-flat building units. Modern, unfurnished apartments (4, 5, and 6 rooms) are for rent at an average of $17.00 per room per month.

4

There is a limited number of furnished and unfurnished homes available for rent or purchase. The prices seem very fair.

In Fremont itself and on its northern border, new building developments are in progress. Well-built, brick ranch style homes on generous lots are available at $13,000 to $25,000. According to price, these vary from 5 to 7 rooms, 1 to 2 baths, full basement, and finished recreation rooms.

Sterling employees transferring into Fremont would find housing to suit their needs and desires.

Education. Fremont's elementary and secondary schools have been rated very high by the Midwest Accrediting Association. The present tax rate provides for excellent physical facilities, a very good teacher-salary scale, and a sound academic program. A referendum held two months ago was passed and thereby provided funds for a new 600-student elementary and 1200-student secondary school. Both will be constructed next year.

The colleges in the area have already been detailed.

Religious Facilities. The religious groups in Fremont and its environs cooperate excellently. The religious leaders questioned (Protestant, Catholic, Jewish, and Seventh Day Adventist) indicate that there are more than enough facilities presently existing to satisfy any reasonable population influx into the area.

The city has 13 churches of various Christian faiths and 2 small Jewish temples.

Recreational Facilities

Public. Fremont has excellent public recreational facilities. There are three public parks in the city. Each of these is provided with baseball and football fields, tennis courts, a modern well-equipped field house, and beautifully landscaped grounds.

Each of the field houses has basketball courts, swimming pool, small auditoriums, fully equipped woodworking and art rooms, and classrooms.

One of the parks has a small zoo, another a conservatory, and the third a golf course.

Fremont has a main library building and two branch libraries.

The civic auditorium is used for cultural and political meetings from time to time.

A small natural history museum is maintained in Fremont Hall on the State University grounds in Fremont.

Private. There are more than enough private recreational facilities in Fremont. The bowling alleys, movie houses, private golf course, and swimming pool were visited on various occasions. Prices were found to be reasonable and service excellent. In no cases were crowds encountered or "Sorry, sold out" signs displayed.

In addition to those facilities mentioned, there are a number of attractive, well-supervised supper clubs, bars, and restaurants available.

Conclusions

If our firm, Sterling Metal Manufacturers, were to purchase the Fremont plant, an adequate labor supply would be available for present and projected needs.

Amicable union-management relations would most probably be carried on.

Wage rates in all categories in the Fremont area are equitable. The future source of labor is assured by reason of schools, population distribution, and normal population mobility.

Coöperation with other companies in the Fremont area may be expected to be most satisfactory based on their present labor policies.

Recommendations

On the basis of the labor supply, conditions, and policies, the purchase of the Fremont plant is strongly recommended.

If such purchase is carried through, it is recommended that our Chicago employees be apprised of the fact at the earliest judicious date. A request should then be made for applications from those interested in transfer who are in the skilled, technical, and administrative categories. This should be carried through as early as possible because of the time required for family relocation.

APPENDIX I

Fremont Industrial Area, Current Wage Rate, November, 19—

Comparative Analysis

	Fremont Wage Rate	Sterling's Chicago Plant and Office Wage Rate
Skilled	Per Hour	Per Hour
Tool and die	$3.30	$2.95
Machinists	3.45	3.20
Electricians	3.25	3.05
Carpenters	3.40	3.15
Punch press operators	3.05	2.95
Other	3.15	2.90
Production	Per Hour	Per Hour
Assemblers	$1.45	$1.55
Coil winders	1.65	1.75
Other (average)	1.45	1.55
Clerical	Per Week	Per Week
File clerks	$55.00	$55.00
Stenographers	65.00	70.00
Typists	60.00	60.00
Unskilled	Per Week	Per Week
Loaders	$57.50	$57.00
Miscellaneous (average)	57.00	55.00
Miscellaneous	Per Week	Per Week
Guards	$65.00	$68.00
Elevator operators	60.00	60.00
Service employees:		
Male	55.00	57.00
Female	50.00	52.00
Technical Engineers	Per Month	Per Month
Class I	$375.00	$375.00
Class II	425.00	450.00
Class III	475.00	490.00
Administrative	Per Month	Per Month
Class I	$400.00	$425.00
Class II	450.00	475.00
Class III	550.00	575.00

QUESTIONS FOR DISCUSSION

I. Set up a title page for a formal report for each of the problems given below.

   1. A report was prepared in New York, New York, on November 17, 1960 for the President of the Solinger Biology Supplies Corporation by the Biology Department of Cranbrook College. The subject of the report concerns the utilization of white mice for cancer research at Cranbrook.

   2. A report was prepared by the Chicago Electronic Research Company for Mr. T. Carrol of the Cartun Radio Supply Corporation. The report was completed during this current month in Chicago and concerned the utilization of printed circuits in color television receivers.

   3. This report concerned a cost-of-living analysis for American families stationed in 18 European and Near Eastern countries. It was completed in Washington, D.C., last month and was prepared by the Research Division of the Department of Foreign Affairs for the Director of the same department.

   4. This report was completed in St. Louis, Missouri, by the Kenilworth Construction Corporation for the Director of the Civic Opera Association. The report contains suggestions for renovating, remodeling, and increasing the capacity of the Civic Fine Arts Building.

II. Offer your criticism of the four letters which appear below.

   1. Letter of authorization:

Dear Mr. Johnson:

You are hereby authorized to direct a survey to determine the advisability of whether or not this corporation should extend its production into the kitchen appliance field.

As the executive vice-president of this company, you may request the participation and assistance of any department heads which you feel could contribute to this project.

May I suggest that you concentrate your investigation on mixers, toasters, waffle irons, automatic knife sharpeners, and related items.

Your complete report, together with recommendations, is requested for the September 15 meeting of the board of directors.

                         Sincerely yours,

                         Julian Solinger
                         Chairman of the Board

2. Letter of authorization:

Dear Mr. Clock:

You are directed to undertake the immediate investigation of opening a branch store in Lambson, Iowa.

This suggestion was made by a group of the officers at the last board meeting. As you know, we have already opened eight new branch stores this year which I think is more than we should have. I strongly feel that one more will really put us in "over our heads." Nevertheless, I want you to carry through a completely objective investigation on whether or not we should take this risk.

Please follow your usual procedures in drawing funds for research. I know you will carry through a thorough and efficient job.

Let me have a complete report within 10 days.

Sincerely,

Robert Blainges
President

3. Letter of transmittal:

Dear Mr. Faxon:

As authorized by your memorandum of March 24, an investigation has been completed concerning the possible change in our package design. You will find specific recommendations made in the accompanying report.

The investigation included a questionnaire survey of 20,000 families, interviews with 3,000 shoppers, and investigation into other primary and secondary sources. It is felt most definitely that the findings are completely reliable.

If additional information or details are desired, I shall be most happy to coöperate. Please do not hesitate to call on me.

Cordially yours,

Robert M. Lange
Research Director

4. Letter of transmittal:

Dear M. Palleton:

When you asked me to submit a report on whether or not we should purchase the small Midville Carton Company, my immediate statement was that it would be a poor investment.

Just as I expected, the investigation proved me right. All the facts are attached and I'm sure you'll come to the same conclusion that buying this outfit would be a poor move.

Yours truly,

Leo Meddleton
Vice-President

III. Write a letter of authorization or transmittal according to the directions given. Assume any necessary facts in addition to those given.

1. Prepare a letter of transmittal to accompany your report which covers an investigation on market acceptance of a line of electric table clocks in a completely modern design. The report is directed to the president of the company from the research director. The sources were interviews, questionnaires, women's magazines, and articles by interior decorators.

2. Write a letter authorizing your sales manager to investigate the sales potential of handling a line of plastic toys by your chain of grocery stores. He may carry through the investigation under his personal direction or hire a research agency.

3. Send a letter to your West Coast vice-president authorizing him to evaluate the suggestion of putting all of his accounting procedures on electronic machines. You would like the results of his survey within 60 days.

4. Transmit a report to the city engineer giving him the results of your investigation of the quality of construction of the new Weston Secondary School. Shortly after it was completed by the School Construction Corporation, deep cracks in the masonry developed, plaster breaks occurred, the entrance steps dropped 4 inches, etc. Your private engineering consulting company was asked by the city engineer to prepare and submit a report. You secured information from testing and checking the building and sending various samples to the research laboratories of the Washington College Technology Center.

5. Your department head in a federal government office has requested that you examine the advisability of hiring girls for part-time secretarial work in an effort to relieve the help shortage which exists. You have carried through your investigation by checking with potential employees, nearby schools, and companies which are using or have used this system. Write the letter of transmittal for this report.

6. Complete a letter of transmittal which will accompany a report on the urban family's acceptance of the "compact" sport-type car in comparison with the more conventional American models. Your sources of information were mail questionnaires, depth interviews, and magazine articles. The report has been prepared for the chairman of the board of Moderne Motors.

IV. Write a complete formal report on any one of the 25 topics listed below or one which your instructor assigns. If you are permitted to choose your own topic, submit the title and a brief, tentative outline for your instructor's approval. You will be told which of the following sections (or all) are required in your formal report. Your instructor may wish to suggest the length of the report.

The Cover
Title Page
Letter of Transmittal
Table of Contents
List of Figures
Preface
Acknowledgment
Summary
Text of the Report
   Introduction
   Discussion
   Conclusion
   Recommendations
Appendix
Bibliography
Index

1. How accurate is market research of the American consumer?
2. Industry's suggestions for a college of commerce curriculum.
3. Industry's suggestions for a college of engineering curriculum.
4. Why colleges should establish training programs and major fields of study for federal and/or state government service.
5. The relationship between students' employment and participation in extracurricular affairs, and grades received.

6. The potential sales of FM radio receivers in automobiles.

7. Solar energy as a source of heat for homes of the future.

8. A comparison of the quality, effectiveness, and repairs required of printed circuits and conventional tube circuits in television receivers.

9. An analysis of the accident rate on tollways as compared with conventional highways.

10. The American suburb—future garden or slum.

11. Auditing procedures and recommendations for the _____ _____ Company.

12. What programs college students (or any other selected group) prefer to watch on TV.

13. A report on the use of profit-sharing programs in companies in the United States.

14. The value of weekly bulletins to employees as a device for motivating interest in the company.

15. An analysis and comparison of the advertising programs of _____ and _____ department stores.

16. A report on customer preference of the present package and another one (which you should design for the survey) for _____ product. This may be a package of any food, automotive, or household product.

17. Earning potential for a member of the _____ profession as compared to the _____ profession.

18. The advantages (or disadvantages) of a C.P.A. continuing his education to secure a law degree.

19. A comparison of LIFO versus FIFO inventory control systems.

20. The use of transistors in the missile program.

21. An analysis of the effectiveness of the written and verbal communication systems of the _____ company.

22. Methods of new employee orientation in five selected companies.

23. The need for electrical (civil, mechanical, ceramic, etc.) engineers by industry in the next five years.

24. Automation on the American farm.

25. Does factory automation cause widespread unemployment?

Chapter 12

Report Writing in Specialized Areas— Accounting, Management, and Marketing

Elsewhere in this book the point has been made that a report is a report regardless of whether it is written in the field of government, accounting, or engineering. The principles of organization, analysis, interpretation, and composition are quite similar. However, there are some distinct differences in the make-up and viewpoint of a report in one field as opposed to a report written in a different area. For those students who are specializing in a specific field— accounting, marketing, management, government, or engineering— the relevant section in this chapter, or the next, may be of interest.

ACCOUNTING REPORTS

Accounting reports may be divided into two basic types: the internal accounting report and the report written by independent public accountants for their clients.[1]

Of course, the basic elements of any report—clarity, accuracy, and conciseness—are found in both types, but dissimilarities also exist. The format, purpose, and, to some degree, even the language in a report written within a company differs from one written by an independent accountant *for* a company.

[1] There are several excellent sources in the field of accounting reports: J. Palen, *Report Writing for Accountants*, Englewood Cliffs, N. J.: Prentice-Hall, Inc., 1955; R. Wixon (ed.), *Accountants' Handbook*, New York: The Ronald Press Company, 1957; J. K. Lasser (ed.), *Standard Handbook for Accountants*, New York: McGraw-Hill Book Company, Inc., 1956.

Internal Accounting Reports

Internal accounting reports are designed specifically to assist management in the areas of planning, coördinating, and controlling. They are directed to the individuals in the policy-making echelon, the coördinating executives, and the supervisory personnel.

FUNCTIONS OF THE INTERNAL REPORT

It is true that a primary function of any report is to inform. However, in the case of the internal report, the data which is presented should be important from management's point of view. In most instances, the internal accounting report may fulfill one or more of the following necessary functions:

1. *Income Statement.* A presentation of the results of operations for a firm, or a division of it, for a specific period of time.
2. *Balance Sheet.* This is a statement which reflects the financial condition or position of a business (or any part of it) at a specific time.
3. *Application of Funds Statement.* The sources of working capital and its uses are presented for a given period. When this report reflects only the movement of cash, it is called a cash flow statement.
4. *Trend Report.* This compares two activities for a specific period of time. The relationship of the increase of bad debts to the rise in sales would be an example.
5. *Analytical Report.* This report analyzes various areas such as cost and volume to secure a better understanding of gross profit.
6. *Cost Report.* This is perhaps one of the most frequently utilized and vital internal accounting reports. It summarizes information related to production and distribution costs in an effort to arrive at accurate decisions in the area of price, production, and labor.
7. *Deviation or Exception Report.* This report compares actual operating results or financial position with a predetermined budget to recognize and act on significant deviations.

The internal accounting report is one of the most important of all management tools. Executives may utilize it as a basis for policy-making decisions which are designed to increase sales, eliminate or alleviate problems, or simply to control the various activities of a complex business enterprise.

FORMS OF INTERNAL REPORTS

Almost every one of the report forms examined earlier in the text is utilized by accountants for internal reports.

1. *Form Reports.* Usually a blank form used for recording original data of a statistical nature.
2. *Memo Report.* A brief report which contains a record of the activities of a conference, announces information for general or limited circulation, or informs interested personnel of decisions which have been made.
3. *Letter Reports.* An infrequently utilized internal report which covers a limited scope of activity.
4. *Progress and Periodic Reports.* Covers a specific period of time regularly (a monthly sales report) or reports the progress achieved in a limited area (production department).
5. *Formal Reports.* A detailed analysis of a major operation. This report is usually supported by appendixes, schedules, and exhibits.
6. *Oral Reports.* These are often made by the accountant and submitted to various levels of management or the board of directors.

PRESENTATION OF THE INTERNAL ACCOUNTING REPORT

Every effort should be made to present an attractive, well-planned internal accounting report. Tabular and graphic illustrations should be chosen and designed with care. Typing, layout, and headings should be completed neatly and competently.

In the case of tables, the accountant should follow the suggestions made in the section on tabular presentation or the rules of his own firm. In addition to the usual cautions concerning the title, headings, and columnar arrangements, the accountant will probably want to observe the present trend of "rounding off" numbers and omitting cents in the tables which appear in internal reports for some purposes.

The data presented should be accurate and complete; however, for several reasons care must be taken to avoid an excess of technical detail:

1. Members of the management group are not always sufficiently familiar with the accounting system to permit a thorough understanding of it.
2. Terminology of the accounting department may be used in a different context in the management area.
3. Details are a matter of record; management's function is to achieve an *overall* view of business and coördinate the various areas in the company.

Totals by themselves are often of little value for management purposes. Therefore, in addition to the current data, information from previous, corresponding periods should be included to enable the reader to make comparative and percentage analyses.

Reports Submitted by Public Accountants

The public accountant must be especially adept at writing clear, accurate, and comprehensive reports. Although his examination of a client's books may require days or weeks of effort, the result of the examination is contained in a report. Often this is the only tangible product which the client receives in return for his fee. It is in this report that the accountant has an opportunity to transmit the pertinent information which he has gathered in his assignment.

There are several reasons why a company will prefer to have a report of its activities written by an independent source rather than by its own accountant.

A supplier or creditor will obviously place more reliance on a financial report and opinion of X Company which has been written by an independent auditor than on a statement prepared by an officer of the X Company.

Secondly, an audit conducted by a public accountant tests the honesty and competence of the firm's employees. In addition, an "outside opinion" helps substantiate the claims made to stockholders. Then, too, the suggestions and viewpoints of a disinterested source are often valuable in revising or initiating policy or procedural changes.

It is easy to understand from this the magnitude of the accountant's responsibilities to his own company, the firm on whose books he may be working, and the organizations which will be reading the report he prepares. The accountant must be fair to his client and keep in mind the ethics of his profession. Of course, his report should never result in the firm's creditor, supplier, or banker reaching a more favorable analysis of the company's condition than that which actually exists. It is for this reason that the accountant's opinion should be prepared and read with care.[2]

THE READER OF THE REPORT

Unlike the accountant who submits an internal report to a specific reading group (usually management), the report submitted by the public accountant is often read by a variety of persons. Some of the readers who may peruse and analyze this report are:

Company stockholders
Company employees
Securities and Exchange Commission
Union leaders
Prospective investors or purchasers
Security analysts
Credit rating agencies
Credit grantors
Banks and investment houses
The clients who engage the accountant

It is difficult to write a report which will be at the proper level for everyone among such a variety of readers. Nevertheless, it is a job which must be accomplished. The report writer must exercise careful judgment regarding the quantity of detail presented, the level of complexity of the report, and the word choice he uses in his discussion.

TYPES OF PUBLIC ACCOUNTING REPORTS

In recent years, reports prepared by public accountants have more and more frequently been designated as one of the following: special purpose, short form, or long form.

Special-Purpose Reports. These reports are often of a confidential nature and, of course, are written in a great variety of areas. Most often such reports are rendered to cover specific as-

[2] The accountant's opinion is discussed later in this chapter.

pects of financial statements or other areas like rentals, bonuses, unexpected losses, etc.

This special report is also submitted on occasions when the firm's accounting procedures do not follow customary formulas. At other times the accountant, who is familiar with the activities of other firms, may suggest (in report form) a procedure to one company which has proved successful in another organization.

Short-Form Reports. This report is sometimes referred to as the condensed report. It usually contains a financial statement and a one- or two-paragraph explanation concerning the scope of the examination and the accountant's opinion of the statements.

The short-form report typically presents financial facts as concisely as possible. It is used for publication or examination purposes by readers who do not desire or request a detailed account.

Long-Form Reports. This report contains detailed schedules and statements which offer adequate data for intensive analysis and comparison. The two groups which most frequently utilize this report are the following: (1) Companies which grant credit. Their examination of the long-form report takes place prior to the granting of a credit line. (2) The management echelon of the company for which the report was written.

DIVISIONS OF THE LONG-FORM REPORT

Although every long-form report may not have each of the sections listed below, most of them will have all or several.

1. *The Balance Sheet.* This is a statement of the financial position of a company at a specific time in a company's operations.

Because so many firms are now owned by thousands of shareholders, there has been a real effort in recent years to make the balance sheet more understandable to persons who do not have an accounting background.

In some cases, the title has been changed from "Balance Sheet" to "Statement of Financial Condition." Other terms such as "What we own" and "What we owe" have replaced the more technical "Assets" and "Liabilities." And, as indicated earlier, comparative figures, ratios, and percentages are often presented to make trends more meaningful to the reader.

The amount of detail in a balance sheet depends on who the reader is. If the statement is to appear in an annual report, it has much less detail than if it is intended for management's examination.

But whether the balance sheet is highly detailed or condensed, it should disclose the company's financial position accurately.

2. *The Income Statement.* This is sometimes referred to as the profit and loss statement, statement of operations, or statement of earnings. This analysis reflects the operations of a firm for the period which the report covers.

Persons who are not familiar with accounting procedures should keep in mind that the income statement reflects the operations of the enterprise for a specific period (usually a year); however, it is not wise to reach formal decisions on such a limited period. For example, an income statement for one year may not be very favorable, although the trend for that firm for the preceding ten years indicates that the company's position is improving. That interpretation may be far more accurate than the one-year picture.

In this section of the long-form report, the amount of detail also depends on who the reader is.

3. *Retained Earnings Statement.* This financial record is sometimes called the earned surplus statement and reflects the changes in the retained earnings for the period being reported on. In actual practice today, the income and retained earnings statements are frequently combined into one.

4. *Other Financial Statements.* In addition, the following financial statements are among a long list of others which may be found in the public accountant's reports:

a. Statement of source and application of funds. This accounts for *changes* in working capital for a specific period.

b. Statement of cash receipts and disbursements. This is often found in special-purpose reports.

c. Statement of income available for special purposes. This is prepared to take care of specific agreements such as a bond issuance or financing not previously provided for.

d. Statistical statements. These employ statistics to reflect ratios or trends for some special purpose.

e. Statement of affairs and/or realization and liquidation. This is prepared for firms which are or have been required to liquidate their assets.

f. *Pro-forma* financial statements. These are prepared *as if* certain transactions had occurred during the period.

g. Supporting schedules. Additional data are often presented in the form of a schedule to verify, substantiate, or support information in the body of the long-form report.

5. *Opinions*. The public accountant's opinion usually attests to the "fairness of the financial statements, their compliance with generally accepted accounting principles," and related facts. However, these opinions and their use are often misunderstood. It is sometimes thought that the accountant who writes the opinion (also referred to as a certificate) is assuming responsibility for the content as well as the accuracy of the financial statements. Actually, the substance of a financial statement is management's representation. The *form* of the statement is usually suggested by the accountant, but his work is based on the facts available to him in his audit. It is for these reasons that the competent accountant takes great care in the wording of his opinion and whether it is "qualified" for various reasons or "unqualified."

Where the auditor has found that certain limitations do not permit him to make as complete an examination as he would like to, he should attach a "qualification" or condition to his opinion. This may occur, for example, if the accountant does not find it possible to examine the accounts of a branch office or subsidiary plant. In some cases, the auditor may render no opinion at all or "disclaim" an opinion in the financial statement. However, many accountants will offer no opinion rather than a "disclaimer of opinion." Offering no opinion is a generally more favorable action for the client.[3]

The accountant's opinion is one of the most important tools he possesses; he should use it with care, discretion, and attention to the highest ethical standards of his profession. The following four examples of opinions are suggested by the American Institute of Accountants:

UNQUALIFIED OPINION (Standard Short Form)

We have examined the balance sheet of X Company as of December 31, 19___ and the related statements of income and retained

---

[3] A recent survey of the American Institute of Accountants covered 7000 reports filed with a number of banks. An analysis of the survey indicated that 48 percent of the reports presented an unqualified opinion, 21 percent were submitted with a qualified opinion, 11 percent disclaimed an opinion, and the remaining 20 percent offered no opinion or disclaimer. (Howard F. Stettler, *Auditing Principles*, Englewood Cliffs, N. J.: Prentice-Hall, Inc., 1956, p. 587.)

earnings for the year then ended. Our examination was made in accordance with generally accepted auditing standards, and accordingly included such tests of the accounting records and such other auditing procedures as we considered necessary in the circumstances. In our opinion, the accompanying balance sheet and statements of income and retained earnings present fairly the financial position of X Company at December 31, 19__, and the results of its operations for the year then ended, in conformity with generally accepted accounting principles applied on a basis consistent with that of the preceding year.

QUALIFICATION AS TO SCOPE—UNQUALIFIED OPINION

We have examined the balance sheet of X Company as of December 31, 19__ and the related statements of income and retained earnings for the year then ended. Our examination was made in accordance with generally accepted auditing standards, and accordingly included such tests of the accounting records and such other auditing procedures as we considered necessary in the circumstances; however, it was not practicable to confirm accounts receivable from government agencies, as to which we have satisfied ourselves by other auditing procedures.

In our opinion, the accompanying balance sheet and statements of income and retained earnings present fairly. . . .

QUALIFIED OPINION

We have examined the balance sheet of X Company as of December 31, 19__ and the related statements of income and retained earnings for the year then ended. Our examination was made in accordance with generally accepted auditing standards, and accordingly included such tests of the accounting records and such other auditing procedures as we considered necessary in the circumstances.

In our opinion, except as to such adjustments as may result from final determination of litigation as explained in Note 1, the accompanying balance sheet and statements of income and retained earnings present fairly. . . .

DISCLAIMER OF OPINION

In accordance with the terms of our engagement, we did not follow the generally accepted auditing procedures of communicating with debtors to confirm accounts receivable balances and of observing the methods used by your employees in determining inventory quantities. Because of these limitations, the scope of our examination was not sufficient to permit us to express an opinion on the accompanying financial statements taken as a whole.[4]

The Accountant's Writing Style

In recent years the accounting profession has intensively examined the ability of the accountant to express his ideas in writing. This analysis comes with good reason for the accountant has been accused—often with good cause—of an inability to transmit his findings into clear statements of fact. A consultant in communications for one of the nation's largest accounting firms said:

> We are faced with the same difficulties that business and industry face in a complex world: the simple fact that unless our skill in communicating keeps pace with our increased professional knowledge and experience, our clients are just not going to be able to make the fullest use of our services.[5]

Obviously, there are dozens of methods which may be utilized by the accountant to improve his communication skill. In addition to courses and instruction in report writing, there is nothing as effective as frequent practice carried on under a competent, sympathetic, and understanding "accountant-critic."

How the accountant secures this facility is of little import; it is vital, however, that he possess it.

REPORTS IN MANAGEMENT AND MARKETING

The reports written for personnel at the management level in industry follow the pattern recommended in the earlier chapters of this book. The same is true for the marketing report. Many marketing reports are prepared by advertising agencies for their clients. These are very often quite elaborate in their make-up and in their style of presentation. Hard, printed covers, fold-out transparent display sheets, colorful graphs and charts, and superbly typed or printed text are all quite commonplace. However, the principles which guide the competent writer in his research, analysis, and written presentation have all been discussed earlier in the book.

[4] American Institute of Accountants, *Forty Questions and Answers About Audit Reports,* 1956, pp. 17-20.

[5] George de Mare, "Communicating—A Realistic Program to Improve Writing Ability," *The Price Waterhouse Review,* June, 1958, p. 53.

Nevertheless, some of the basic concepts of both of these reports, management and marketing, are briefly outlined below.

Management Reports

Management reports are used in planning and controlling activities in large corporations as well as in motivating executive activities.

A corporation grows and becomes stronger when the decisions made by management are accurate and profitable. These decisions are only as sound as the foundation on which they are built—the management report. When the report is poor, the foundation is unstable, and the decisions may be faulty.

Reports for top management are vital to check on whether or not policy is being carried out as directed, to measure personnel performance, to evaluate costs, and to facilitate planning for future operations.

NUMBER OF REPORTS

One of the dangers in reporting to management is that more communications may come in than the executive can read, analyze, and act on. More than one company president has felt that he was about to drown in a "sea of reports." Charles Redfield in *Communication in Management* cites the case of the executive who had 1500 letters, reports, forms, and other material requiring his personal attention moving across his desk each month. And this did not include a backlog of telephone calls to be made, interviews to be held, and other matters requiring his decisions. If top management is to do a good job, only the most vital reports should be submitted. And, of course, they should be expertly written.

FUNCTION OF REPORTS SUBMITTED

Executive leadership is strengthened when the reports submitted are of excellent quality. They must be brief, accurate, and with adequate data for the level to which they are directed.

Elizabeth Marting in *Reports to Top Management* describes the report systems used by Burroughs, Carrier, Koppers, Ford, and other companies. In every case, the functions of planning, controlling, and directing are largely carried through on the basis of what is said in the report.

A recent survey of corporation executives who are responsible for formulating policy indicated that they wanted reports with the following qualifications:

1. Comprehensive—but not too detailed.
2. Comparative—a comparison of data with previous results. The use of tables and charts, illustrating percentages and ratios, are especially valuable for this.
3. Standard in form—easy to assimilate.
4. Concise, accurate—vital qualities, of course.
5. Timely—must be realistic.
6. Forward-looking—sufficiently analytical to offer recommendations for future action.

In every progressive firm, the reporting function is recognized as the basis for proper management control, direction, and planning.

Marketing Reports

The field of marketing is concerned with finding the best possible methods of increasing the sale of products. This frequently requires the intensive analysis of the potential buyer and the product.

When an advertising agency undertakes to find out the best method of selling Crunchie Munchies to some five million television viewers, it has a formidable job on its hands. Such a research task involves dozens or hundreds of people who question thousands of potential consumers, researchers who examine mountains of data, and still others who search for answers to scores of questions. Weeks of digging, analyzing, and interpreting lie behind the finished report presented to the management of the Crunchie Munchie Company. That report must be good; if it is not, it can only reflect on the quality of the work behind it.

When the Crunchie Munchie Company pays $40,000 to the advertising company for its research, all it receives is a report. But, as indicated above, that 50-page report represents thousands of hours of work. That effort must be fairly, competently, and accurately presented in a well-written report.

In both of these areas—management and marketing—as well as in many others, the basic principles and concepts discussed earlier in the text must be applied.

QUESTIONS FOR DISCUSSION

I. Write a report on any one of the following topics or one suggested by your instructor. Attempt to limit the report to 3000 words. Utilize tabular and graphic aids where possible. Submit the title of your report, its purpose, and a tentative outline of it to your instructor for his approval.

MARKETING

1. An analysis of consumer buying habits of name brand appliances in the suburb of _____
2. What really motivates the middle-income American to purchase a foreign sports car?
3. An analysis of the reasons for frequent dress fashion changes among American women.
4. Is there a need for "built-in" obsolescence?
5. The future market for home freezers.
6. How valuable as a trade stimulant are savings stamps distributed by food chains.
7. Consumer retention of facts in the _____ TV commercial.
8. Compensation systems for company salesmen.
9. The rise in the standard of living and changes in the consumer buying habits.
10. Psychological devices in TV selling.
11. A sales analysis of _____ products.
12. A ten-year projection of sales in the infants' wear field.
13. The growth of the two-car family.
14. A ten-year projection of railroad passenger travel.
15. The effect of airplane mishaps on passenger travel.
16. Consumer acceptance of "instant" coffee.
17. Consumer acceptance of canned carbonated beverages.
18. Does today's home buyer prefer a basement or not.
19. The importance of the package in the sale of _____.

MANAGEMENT

1. An analysis of the effectiveness of the wage incentive systems of three companies.
2. Methods used by three corporations in training supervisors in the area of human relations.
3. The effectiveness of a program in communicating ideas at the _____ company.

4. Incentive pay systems in industry.
5. Methods of plant layout.
6. Securing additional production area in a crowded plant layout.
7. A job evaluation program in the _____ industry.
8. Setting up a quality control department in a small factory.
9. How thorough is "100 percent" inspection?
10. Measuring the effectiveness of a company house organ.
11. Cost reduction methods in a small-appliance manufacturing company.
12. Production control at the_____company.
13. Color dynamics and production level at three companies.
14. Measuring employee morale.
15. The value of the "outside consultant" in solving management problems.
16. Requirements for effective management conference leadership and participation.
17. Handling the "extended" coffee break period.
18. The value of an organized employee recreational program.
19. Standard vacation period versus the staggered system.
20. Company owned and operated cafeteria versus an outside cafeteria service.

ACCOUNTING

1. An audit report of the_____company.
2. Setting up a cost procedure for the _____ company.
3. The advantages of a machine accounting system.
4. Accountants' training programs among three major accounting companies.
5. The responsibilities of the controller in a large corporation.
6. A suggested cost accounting system for the _____ company.
7. A suggested inventory control system for a medium-size manufacturer of home appliances.
8. A financial analysis of the _____ Corporation.
9. The C.P.A. certificate as a factor in the income level of accountants.
10. An analysis of the accounting curriculum of a selected group of 12 schools of business.
11. The growth of machine payroll accounting methods.

II. Answer the following questions as concisely as possible or carry through the directions listed.
    1. Secure a report submitted by a public accountant and discuss

the various sections in an oral report to the class. Eliminate all company names prior to your discussion.

2. Analyze the thoroughness of the accounting sections of two annual reports.

3. Why is it absolutely imperative that the accountant today express himself clearly, concisely, and accurately in his reports.

4. What specific differences exist in the accounting report as compared to almost all others in business and industry?

Chapter 13

Report Writing in Specialized Areas— Engineering and Government

In two additional areas, reports follow a rather specialized pattern: engineering and government. In both cases the basic principles of report writing are followed, but in addition, there are several specific factors which should be kept in mind when completing reports in either of these fields.

ENGINEERING REPORTS

The business report may be prepared for the technical or nontechnical reader. If it is written for an individual in the latter group, such as a stockholder or an employee, it is often presented as a relatively simple piece of exposition. This is not usually true of the engineering report. More often than not, it is directed to a person who has technical background. This makes the author's job easier, for he may write about a technical subject using the vocabulary of his field and directing his comments to the reader who possesses a clear understanding of complex problems.

Thus engineering reports are usually written by engineers for engineers or for those persons who possess engineering "know-how."

Classification of Engineering Reports

Engineering reports are classified differently by various authorities. Rose, Bennett, and Heater in *Engineering Reports* listed the memorandum, descriptive, analytical, inspection, test, progress, and recommendation reports.[1]

[1] L. A. Rose, B. B. Bennett, and E. F. Heater, *Engineering Reports,* New York: Harper & Brothers, 1950.

Agg and Foster classified engineering reports into the purposes they serve:

Operation Reports. Used to determine the cost of operation, quantity, or quality of a manufactured item. In describing an operation within a factory, plant, or on a project, the economic aspect is emphasized.

Construction Reports. This report reflects the progress and cost of construction.

Preliminary Reports. This piece of exposition is submitted to interested parties prior to the beginning of a project. It will indicate whether the project is feasible, its contemplated cost, and its expected results.

Reports on Design. This may suggest a design or indicate a preferred type of a design for a particular project.

Research Reports. A presentation of the data involved in the development of a project.

Reports on Failure. A report which attempts to fix the cause for failure.

Reports on Tests. These reports may be routine or special depending on the test described. If the report covers an extensive test, the report will be complex and detailed; if the project is a simple one, the report will be brief and uninvolved.

Valuation Reports. This is an analysis of a project which sets forth the major findings and value achieved.[2]

These are some of the more popular designations for reports in engineering. As indicated above, companies have different names for the same types of reports. However, these are merely changes in designations and should not disturb the report writer.

Presentation of the Report

Because the engineer usually directs his report to another technically trained individual, there is every reason in the world why he should maintain his presentation at the appropriate level. Not only should the word choice be made with the engineer in mind, but also the tables, charts, and graphs should be designed on the same basis.

It is true that it is difficult to make technical reports entertaining reading, but on the other hand, there is no reason why complex subjects must often be confusing, unorganized, and difficult to analyze and interpret. Engineers have gained a reputation, valid or not, for having difficulty presenting their ideas in clear, interesting sentences, but there is no reason why this must be continued. In recent years technical schools and industry have directed their attention toward writing improvement programs. The results, as measured by the excellence of articles appearing in recent technical journals and the high caliber of reports completed in industry, attest to the progress made.

Every engineer, early in his career, recognizes that data which are not adequately recorded have little value for the future, except to the person who carried through the original work. The experiment, the study, the analysis are not really completed until the results have been written down for the future use of the engineer and/or his colleagues. This is basic to research—building new findings on what has been previously determined and recorded. If the record is not complete or is inadequate, much time, effort, and research expense may be wasted.

An article on report writing which appeared in the *General Motors Engineering Journal* concluded with these statements:

> Success in engineering, as in all other organized undertakings, depends as much on the ability to present an idea convincingly as it does upon the ability to perform experiments and calculations. The most miraculous discovery in the laboratory is not a contribution to the store of knowledge until the results are recorded and transmitted to others. A written report is often the only record which is made of the results that have come out of years of thought and effort. It is used to judge the value of the engineer's work and serves as the foundation for all future action on the project. If the report is written clearly and precisely, it is accepted as the result of sound reasoning and careful observation. If the report is poorly written, the results presented in it are often dismissed as the work of a careless or incompetent worker. Most engineers can become good writers if they will put the same thought and effort into this phase of their work as they do in conducting their experiments.[3]

This quotation is an accurate and vital appraisal of this important area of engineering activity. In today's rapidly moving technical society, the engineer is called upon to write reports on his find-

---

[3] R. A. Richardson and C. A. Brown, "How to Organize and Write Effective Technical Reports," *General Motors Engineering Journal*, September-October, 1955.

ings to a much greater extent than ever in the past. This is a natural result in our world of ever increasing complex technological changes. And as the field of engineering constantly expands, the student must give more of his educational time to the technical areas and less to the vital topic of communication. Yet he must communicate effectively; he has this obligation to himself, his colleagues, and society. This is a dilemma which the engineer can solve by first recognizing the importance of communication in his work and then directing his efforts toward developing a facility in the presentation of his ideas.

The excellent journal, *The Western Electric Engineer,* had this to say about written communication and the professional engineer:

All things considered, an engineer will find the best reason to write about his work is the fact that the most significant effect of writing is to improve the writer, even if his writing is never read. In accepting the discipline of recording his thoughts in clear and generally understandable language, the engineer will emerge from his writing chore with a better and clearer arrangement of his own knowledge than when he began. And inevitably, as a man commits his own thoughts to paper, he develops a curiosity as to what others may have written about the same or related subjects. Hence, writing often stimulates the writer to increase his knowledge.

If on no other basis than its value as an effective method of personal and professional development, the self-imposed discipline of frequent writing recommends itself to the thinking engineer who has more than the minimum interests in his profession.

The engineer is particularly fortunate in the fact that he has an excellent subject to write about—namely his work—and a well-defined readership that is interested in his subject—namely the large body formed by the other members of his profession. However, beyond this proximate objective, the engineer-author will in time discern broader areas of common interest, affecting larger groups of people.

Now it appears that, far from forbidding his entry as an author into the area of literature of power, the exigencies of a society in which technology is assuming increasing value require of the engineer that he concern himself more intimately with the important non-engineering and non-technical interests that are being affected as a result of his work, and that he reflect this concern in his writing.

It isn't enough any more that an engineer design, develop, and manufacture a better mousetrap or a louder firecracker. His responsibilities must include a regard for the effect his work will have on patterns of social life, on economic balances, on relationships between social groups. The climate of modern society, more than ever before, invites the engineer to apply the fruits of his training and experience to the main issues of the day, to think about them as deeply as his intellect will carry him, and to express the substance of his thought in clear and unmistakable language.

If the engineer accepts this invitation and develops the habit of committing his thoughts to paper with the primary purpose of analyzing and composing his own thinking without regard at first for the publishability of his writing, it is almost inevitable that in time both the content of his thought and his skill at giving it expression will so improve that he will find it difficult to escape publication, and in broader areas than encompassed by technical or professional journals.

Most important, if he has held to this primary and worthwhile purpose, when his writing is published, it will be eminently worth the reading.[4]

There is little to add to these comments concerning engineering reports which has not been covered in the earlier chapters of this book. The basic fact, however, may well be stated again: The engineer's job in the shop, laboratory, or field is not complete until he has submitted a clearly written report of his activities and findings.

GOVERNMENT REPORTS

As in the case of other reports in specialized fields, those submitted by various governmental units—federal, state, county, city— are based on the fundamental principles of effective communication discussed earlier. But government reports, like accounting or engineering reports, are specialized. Because of this, there are some important differences which the report writer in this field will want to examine.

In addition to the federal government, there are some 137,700 independent government units which have authority to impose, collect, and spend revenue.[5] These consist of school districts, towns, municipalities, counties, territories, states, and miscellaneous governing bodies. These groups have expenditures amounting to mil-

---

[4] Michael J. O'Leary, "About Writing" (an editorial), *The Western Electric Engineer*, January, 1958.

[5] J. K. Lasser (ed.), *Standard Handbook for Accountants*, "Reports to Meet the Needs of Public Officials," by Stephen A. Derry, New York: McGraw-Hill Book Company, Inc., 1956, section 5, pp. 41-71. This is an excellent article and is recommended for further reading on the subject.

lions of dollars; the need for them to prepare accurate reports is obvious.

The report rendered to the public is different from the one submitted in business in an important aspect: the former is *not* concerned with profits. It does attempt to measure efficiency in expenditures and the benefits achieved for the taxpayer.

Since the termination of World War II, there have been many revisions in the content, style of presentation, and format of public reports. Perhaps the most drastic changes have taken place in the reports issued by city managers. Many municipalities with this type of government have submitted excellent, factual, informative reports.

The Reader of this Report

The public report, like the annual report, is often read by different groups. It is written for three primary audiences: (1) the citizens of the community, (2) public administrative officials who may be either above or below the level of the individual signing the report, and (3) investors and bankers. Obviously, writing a report for so varied a readership is difficult. But the situation is further complicated by the variety of "publics" which fall into the first group. Some of the citizens are very intelligent, perceptive, and analytical; others are apathetic and unconcerned. Attempting to write a single report for readers of such heterogeneous backgrounds and interests is indeed a trying task.

This has raised a real problem for the individuals who are required to assemble the data and present an acceptable document. An annual report for a municipality, county, or state, must contain complex, detailed, and involved financial data. If such statistics are omitted, the report becomes suspect and a hue and cry is raised. But why include dozens of pages of financial information if they will be examined by only a few interested citizens, a number of responsible public officials, and a relatively small group of investors? The public, in general, wants some overall evaluations of the current budget, a few pictures illustrating the progress made on the new highway and filtration plant, and a comment or two on public safety, taxes, and schools.

For these reasons, there seems to be a trend toward issuing either a "popular" annual report and/or a financial report. The former is distributed to interested citizens; the financial report is written primarily for investors, prospective investors, and financial institutions.

Who Writes the Report

Legal statute usually requires that reports be submitted by the directors of towns, cities, counties, and states as well as the heads of major divisions within those units. Technically of course, the mayor, county commissioner, or whatever the interested party's title is, signs the report. It is prepared, however, by his staff or, more and more frequently of late, by a professional management or accounting firm.

In every instance, the person who is given the responsibility for preparing such a report should also receive the authority and budget needed to do the job properly. It should also be made clear to the department and divisions contributing information that their complete coöperation with the report writer must be given willingly.

Quite often "lip-service" only is given to the individual who is trying to secure necessary facts and statistics. Perhaps this might be due to the inherent qualities of a democracy. But if a thorough and unbiased report is expected, the person charged with writing it should have free access to all necessary sources of data.

Planning a Report

Because the information in a report is drawn from many sources, early and complete planning is essential. The first step in producing a good report is to assign a specific individual to the task. This person should then be given *authority* along with the responsibility for the production of the document. All too often someone is told to produce the report but is not given a position of sufficient authority to demand and receive all necessary data from department and bureau chiefs. Thus, when the appointment is made, there should be a clear understanding among all department and bureau directors that they are to coöperate with the report writer.

One of the most important steps in planning the public report lies in the initial directive from the mayor, city manager, or person in charge to all department heads. This bulletin must make it clear to all concerned *what, why, when,* and *to whom* data are to be submitted—and point out that no exceptions will be tolerated. The writer of the public annual report will find that among his best sources of data will be newspaper clippings, editorials, newspaper photographs, and the various bulletins and reports issued throughout the year by the departments within the governmental unit. For this reason, files should be set up well in advance of the report's due date.

The purpose and objectives of the report should be discussed with the department heads; they should know what material the report writer wants and how and when he would like to have it submitted. Of course, the arrangements should be based completely on coöperation and not on pressure from above.

The size of the staff required to produce a public report varies. In small communities, one individual working on the report on a part-time basis can usually do a good job. However, in large cities with populations of a half million or more, the task requires the full-time efforts of one or two people. Statistics, photographs, and information must be gathered from many different departments and correlated into meaningful facts.

Writing Style

The report should be written in an interesting and understandable manner for the citizen to whom it is directed. If one of the important objectives of the report is to motivate the citizen to read it, every effort must be made to make it an attractive document.

If it is at all possible, the usually complex financial section should be presented in terms that are simple; the public report is not directed to C.P.A.'s; it is for the average, interested member of the community.

The writer should think in terms of presenting "performance" rather than "object" financial statements. Mr. Doe will be more receptive to spending $10,000 for "Polio vaccine to keep our children healthy" than he will if the same expenditure is listed as "Preventive medicine; inoculation program." The same is true of "To keep our streets and boulevards clean and attractive" as compared to "Sanitation of road network" or "For providing fresh, pure water" as opposed to "Filtration and purification of water system."[6]

The indexed titles of the sections of a Boulder, Colorado, report also strive to motivate reader interest:

[6] Norman B. Sigband, "Put 'Bang' in Your Annual Report," *School Executive*, June, 1953.

1. You are influenced by city   GROWTH
2. You depend upon public   PROTECTION
3. You demand   WATER
4. You require   SEWERS
5. You drive on city   STREETS
6. You request   OTHER SERVICES
7. You pay   TAXES AND FEES
8. You expect   COMMUNITY PROGRESS
9. (Back cover) If you need   FURTHER INFORMATION[7]

Throughout the public report, the writing style should be from the citizen's point of view. The writer should speak of "your elected officials," "your streets," "the facilities of your community," and use similar terms designed to arouse interest and improve readership.

Make-Up of the Report

Attractive human interest photographs of public works and services should be included. Whenever possible, people utilizing the items or services should appear in the picture. Although there may be reason to display a small-size picture or series of them of the government or municipality director and his cabinet members, there is no reason (as is often the case) to have full-page photographs of a dozen public officials.

Simple and attractive tables and graphs add much to reader understanding and appreciation of trends. A good quality of paper stock should be used. The type and format should be attractive, modern, and easy to read. Color should be used as generously as the budget permits.

The size of the report should preferably be approximately 6″ × 9″, but in no case more than 8½″ × 11″. A larger size report is difficult to file, with the exception of the tabloid newspaper form. The smaller size lends itself to easy handling and filing and can be read conveniently on the bus or the train by Citizen Smith.

The length of the report should vary according to the size of the city and the number of services discussed plus the writing style of the author. Derry, however, indicates in his article that a population of about 5,000 may require a 10-page report whereas a 50-page report may be necessary for a city of 800,000 and more.

[7] J. K. Lasser (ed.), *op. cit.*, section 5, p. 60.

Attributes of the Government Report

Two authorities feel that the public report must be complete enough to allow the reader to form a conclusion as to the usefulness of a particular service to the community.[8] This requires a discussion of the various services the municipality or public body offers the citizens. The report issued by any public agency, whether it is a municipal bureau or a state or federal government, should follow similar principles:

1. The writing style should be interesting, easy to read, clear, and written at a level that permits every adult in the community to assimilate its contents easily.
2. The report *should* contain financial data relative to income and expenditures. These figures should be interpreted and explained in as direct and simple a manner as possible. Other necessary facts, in addition to finance, should also be presented.
3. The report should be attractive in format and design. The size of the type should encourage reading, and the colors should enhance the report's appearance. Photographs should be attention-getting; graphs, charts, and tables should be simple and meaningful and the overall layout should be pleasing. Paper stock should be of good quality.
4. The report should be distributed according to a carefully conceived plan. In an attempt to secure the widest readership for the smallest number of copies, the guide for distributing the report must be planned carefully.
5. All major division chiefs should receive a copy, as well as interested professional personnel and citizens throughout the community. Where it is financially impossible to provide every citizen with a copy, the report may be made available by sending copies (in a hard cover binder) to all of the community's churches, temples, libraries, schools, civic organizations, health offices, and other sources where relatively large numbers of citizens gather from time to time.
6. If a report is sent to each family, it may be distributed at town meetings, made available at city offices, sent out with utility or tax bills, or delivered by Boy Scouts or some other citizen group.

[8] Clarence E. Ridley and Herbert A. Simon, *Specifications for the Annual Report*, Chicago: International City Managers Association, 1948, p. 27.

Of course, each of these methods of distribution has its advantages and disadvantages. If each citizen is sent a copy, the expense may be prohibitive and the number who will read the report is really quite small. On the other hand, many interested persons may not attend a town or city meeting. And having reports available only at a central location certainly restricts distribution.

7. In an effort to place this information before *every* interested citizen as inexpensively as possible, some communities are now printing their annual reports in issues of the city newspapers or presenting the information on local television or radio outlets.

8. The report should be honest and factual. All important legislative, administrative, and service activities should be presented and discussed. Those areas of activity which have not fared too well, or where problems exist, should be presented and discussed frankly.

Organization of the Public Report

Most public reports are roughly divided into the six following areas:

1. Introduction
   Cover
   Title page
   Letter from chief executive officer
   Table of contents
   Directory of officials
2. Service
   Police
   Fire
   Public works
   Public utilities
   Education
   Housing
   Library
   Welfare
   Recreation
3. Legislative and General Administration
   Legislation
   Administrative actions

4. Supplementary Services
   Correctional and penal
   Legal
   Judicial
   Clerical
   Treasurer
   Taxation
   Miscellaneous
5. Financial
   Balance sheet
   Listing of sources of income and expenditures
6. Future Plans
   A resumé of the activities, plans, and construction
   projects planned

The titles and subtitles listed above cover the areas often found in a public report. However, the order may be different and the number of sections may be larger or smaller. It is understood also that some of the areas listed are more related to a report at one level than another. What may be part of a municipal report may not be contained in a county report; what may appear in a report from the level of state government may not be useful at the federal level.

Discussions of the Sections

1. *Introductory Section.* The cover of the report should carry an eye-catching illustration or photograph. It should have life and interest: children rushing into a new school building, cars flashing over a new bridge or freeway, or adults using recreational or sporting equipment in a new park or stadium all serve to capture the reader's attention. Under almost no condition, as is sometimes done in municipalities, should the cover carry a posed picture of a politician.

The title page should contain all necessary information: report title, issuing agency, period covered, and other vital facts. The letter of transmittal from the mayor or some other executive should summarize the report and transmit it to the people.

If the report is about 15 pages or more in length, a table of contents should be provided.

A list of public officials and their office telephone numbers should be published also. As a supplement to this, it is often bene-

Annual Report
and
Statement

City of Wilmington, Delaware
June 30, 1958

Cover of a Public Report (Reproduced by permission)

ficial to present an organizational chart illustrating the lines of authority and the various branches of the government.

2. *Services.* In this portion of the report, the writer should review the activities for the year of each department: police, fire,

welfare, educational, and all the others. This presentation, wherever possible, should have a factual and statistical basis and should permit the reader to make an analysis of the figures of the annual period reported on compared with previous years. Some discussion of future plans of the service departments may also be made.

3. *Legislative and General Administration.* This brief section summarizes the year's work of the legislative and administrative branches of the city, county, or state.

4. *Supplementary Services.* This area (licenses, taxes, legal, etc.) should be handled in the same way the major services sections were presented. In some public reports, all services, major and minor, appear in one division.

5. *Financial.* A simplified but complete balance sheet should be presented. An effort should be made to avoid as much of the technical financial terminology as possible, but this section should nonetheless be complete.

In addition, there should be a clear statement of the sources of funds and the expenditures. It is recognized that for a large city, such a presentation might require dozens of pages. In such an instance, a summary financial report might be included here with the detailed financial statement available to those who desire a copy.

In each case, the balance sheet and the statement of income and expenses, as well as comparative statistical data for previous years should be presented to the reader.

6. *Future Plans.* With our burgeoning population, cities, towns, and states are growing "in every direction." No public government, if it is cognizant of its duty, can permit this growth to take place without a plan.

For this reason, it is necessary to apprise the interested citizen of future plans, problems, and costs. Experience has proved that freeways, schools, filtration plants, and water systems which have been constructed without adequate thought, counsel, and discussion sometimes result in disastrous situations.

Types of Public Reports

There is a variety of methods which are used to present the public report. Most are printed in any one of the following manners: booklet, brochure, self-mailer, mimeograph summary, leaflet, or newspaper supplement. Visual presentations are also becoming more and more popular; the television report has found a great many adherents. Films and slides have also proved useful, and lectures and radio reports are used from time to time.

Richmond, California, issued a 6″ × 9″ calendar-report. It was arranged by weeks with 54 pages in all. Each page lists the days and dates of the week along with a brief explanation of a community service.[9]

The annual report of the Board of Public Works of the City of Los Angeles is a 153-page document.[10] It contains many excellent organizational charts, attractive photographs, detailed financial figures, and clear and well-written explanations.

The cover of the Milwaukee report has the title "Roads to a Better Milwaukee" printed across a background of roads.[11] The report opens with a heading, "The Route of Good Government." Throughout the report, road signs and references to correct travel intrigue the reader and keep him interested in the subject matter. All in all, this appears to be an excellent report.

Richmond, Virginia's report has the attention-catching title of "Five Years of Progress." It is filled with interesting photographs, clever graphs, and well-written copy.[12]

The annual reports of Dallas and Los Angeles appear in spiral binders and follow the format, to some extent, of a corporation annual report. They are both attractive and very readable.[13]

During 1959, the mayor of the city of Chicago appeared periodically on the area's educational television channel. He attempted to summarize the activities of various city departments and to inform the viewers of some of the city's contemplated projects and plans.

Federal Government Reports

A brief note concerning federal government reports is in order when one considers the multitude which are issued and the mountains of invaluable data which they contain.

[9] "New City Calendar Is Also a Municipal Report," *American City,* February, 1956, p. 22.

[10] For period July 1, 1952 to June 30, 1953.

[11] 1950 Report of Milwaukee.

[12] "A Report to the Citizens of Richmond, 1948-1953."

[13] "Annual Report, Los Angeles, 1952," and "Annual Report of Dallas, 1953-1954."

Government reports fall into two broad classifications: there are those which are for public and professional use and are printed by the Superintendent of Documents and sold for a nominal fee. These are written by highly skilled persons. The other large group of reports comprise those which are prepared for limited or restricted circulation and may be informational and/or analytical in nature.

Each year the federal government finances over $2½ billion worth of basic and applied technical research. The Office of Technical Services was established in 1950 to permit interested persons, private laboratories, and business firms to use the results of much of this research for their own purposes and in the national interest.

Government research, although emphasizing national defense, has developed products and processes in metals, ceramics, chemicals, electronics, atomic energy, plastics, leather, instruments, lubricants, and in many other fields.

The Technology Division of the Office of Technical Services releases 300 to 600 new reports each month. This adds to the thousands in stock which have previously been prepared by such agencies as The Atomic Energy Commission, Naval Research Laboratory, Signal Corps, Army and Naval Ordnance Laboratories, Wright Air Development Center, Air Force Cambridge Research Center, and the Civil Aeronautics Administration.

Reports having wide interest are reproduced and sold for very nominal fees by the Technology Division. Over 200,000 such reports are sold each year. Those in very specialized areas are deposited with the Library of Congress and may be secured in microfilm or photocopy.

Several publications from the Office of Technical Services announce the reports which are available:

U.S. Government Research Reports. A monthly catalog which lists and abstracts all reports released by OTS for the one-month period.

Technical Reports Newsletter. A monthly publication that gives detailed reviews of new reports which are of interest to small and medium-size firms.

Catalogs of Technical Reports. Compilations of reports in many specialized areas such as transistors, adhesives, rubber, etc.

AEC Reports Price List. A semiannual publication of AEC reports available from OTS.

The tremendous value of the technical reports issued by various government agencies is being recognized by thousands of technical personnel. It is to the great credit of the Department of Commerce that these materials are made available in such a convenient and inexpensive manner.

QUESTIONS FOR DISCUSSION

I. Answer the following questions or carry through the instructions given.
    1. Use *The Industrial Arts Index* and *The Applied Science and Technology Index* to secure a list of articles on the subject of written communication (reports, technical articles, etc.) and the engineer. Read as many of these as are available to you and submit a report on them. Document your paper.
    2. Why is it so important for the engineer to be able to communicate his ideas clearly and concisely in reports written for individuals and groups outside his professional area?
II. Write a report on any one of the following topics or one suggested by your instructor. Attempt to limit the report to 3000 words. Utilize tabular and graphic aids where possible. Submit the title of your report, its purpose, and a tentative outline of it to your instructor for his approval.

ENGINEERING

1. A critical analysis of printed circuits in radio transmitters.
2. The use of ceramics in electrical components.
3. The use of direct distance dialing systems in telephone communication.
4. Production savings in the use of prefabricated housing.
5. A comparison of water filtration methods as utilized by representative urban centers.
6. Techniques available for utilizing sea water for human consumption.
7. Overcoming the sound problem in jet aircraft.
8. The technique of strip mining.
9. A chemical analysis of _____.
10. The history of synthetic materials.
11. The major problems in the construction of the Mackinac Bridge.
12. Suggestions for low-cost housing in urban centers.

13. The design of _____ should be changed.
14. Major problems encountered in color television program transmission.
15. Major considerations in urban renewal.

III. Answer the following questions or carry through the instructions given.
1. Secure two city annual reports (from communities of similar population levels) and compare their organizational make-up.
2. What is the effect on the reader of a public report which is "citizen-centered" and which utilizes photographs of children, schools, and community activities?
3. What are the problems in the distribution of public reports? How may these be solved?
4. Compare a federal report with a state report written in a similar area (roads, education, health, etc.).
5. What can be done to make Citizen Smith demand, read, and react to public reports?

IV. Write a report on any one of the following topics or one suggested by your instructor. Attempt to limit the report to 3000 words. Utilize tabular and graphic aids where possible. Submit the title of your report, its purpose, and a tentative outline of it to your instructor for his approval.

GOVERNMENT REPORTS

1. Changes in the make-up and content of the reports of the city of _____, 1920-1960.
2. Methods of report distribution in three urban centers .
3. The responsibility for writing and preparing the annual report in the city of _____.
4. The relative effectiveness of the municipal printed booklet report as compared to the report published in the local newspaper.
5. A report on the health facilities of the city of _____ for the year 19___.
6. A report on crime rate of the city of _____ for the year 19___.
7. Judicial operations of the city of _____ for the year 19___.
8. Penal operations in the state of _____ for the year 19___.
9. City vehicle license assessment methods in 10 cities each of over 500,000 population.
10. Reporting to the public by television at the federal, state, and local levels.

Chapter 14

The Annual Report

The annual report is the result of the growth of American industry. As corporations became more complex, and the number of shareholders increased, the need for a report of activities grew.

When our nation was young, the affairs of the relatively few companies which did exist were in the hands of individuals. The owner of a company was responsible to no one except himself. Whether he worked or not, whether he made a profit or not, whether his business increased or not—these and a thousand other details were his affair only; he reported only to himself.

But as time progressed, the demand for his product increased and customers became more numerous. No longer was this maker of wagons able to handle all the orders he received. It was necessary for him to request that other artisans join with him to produce his wagons. As the company prospered, the need for additional capital became apparent. Because the firm was obviously a good risk and the interest paid on the borrowed money was attractive, lenders were easily available. However, the lenders now had a stake in the business, and they wanted a statement of account on the firm's progress, its financial position, and its future plans. Certainly this was not an unreasonable request, and compliance with it demanded that a report be presented.

The situation at the present time is the same although magnified thousands of times over. The giant corporations in America today are largely financed by lenders; now the lenders sometimes number hundreds of thousands of individuals, each of whom owns shares of stock. Like the lenders of long ago, they also expect and deserve to receive a report on the corporation's activities. Today we call the lenders "shareholders"; what they secure to attest to their investment in the firm, we designate as "stock." And the account of the activities which the company sends out, is the "annual report." According to an article by Weston Smith, an authority on annual reports, the Borden Company issued a report in 1858 and American Telephone and Telegraph released one in 1885. The practice was strongly encouraged by the New York Stock Exchange in 1900 when it requested that all companies applying for listing print an annual statement. In 1902 U.S. Steel issued a detailed report. Monsanto Chemical and Swift and Company followed shortly thereafter. Mr. Smith indicates that:

> The next acceleration in the trend toward modernized reports came between 1920 and 1930, and most of these were the elaborate and colorful statements issued by public utility holding companies during the pyramiding era. These selling documents—and that's what they were—proved to be the best tool in the stock salesmen's kits. Another gain was scored following the passage of the Securities and Exchange Act of 1934, but it took the stimulus of World War II, and the fact that the cost of picturesque annual reports came largely from excess profits taxes, to bring this document to the fore as a medium of effective communication.[1]

Since 1934 the Securities and Exchange Commission requires that annual reports be issued to shareholders by all corporations listed on the stock exchange. This must be done within 120 days after the close of the fiscal year. Most states have similar requirements. For example, Ohio Code Section 8623-64 provides:

1. At the annual meeting . . . every corporation . . . shall lay before the shareholders a financial statement consisting of:
   a. a balance sheet containing a summary of the assets, liabilities, stated capital and surplus of the corporation as of a date not more than four months before such meeting. . . .
   b. a statement of profit and loss and surplus, including a summary of profits, dividends paid. . . .
2. The financial statement shall have appended thereto a certificate signed by the president or . . . a public accountant . . . to the effect that the financial statement presents fairly the position of the corporation. . . .[2]

[1] Weston Smith, "The Progress in Stockholder Relations," *Financial World,* January, 1950.

[2] "Corporate Annual Report Requirements," issued by Reuter and Bragdon, Inc., Pittsburgh, Pennsylvania, 1950, pp. 3-4.

Corporation Annual Reports (Courtesy of Standard Oil Company, New Jersey, 1958; Container Corporation of America, 1957; Sperry Rand Corporation, 1956)

Thus it is obvious that one of the reasons that annual reports are issued is that it is required by law. However, this has become somewhat incidental; the purposes of the annual report today are varied, vital, and interesting.

PURPOSES OF THE ANNUAL REPORT

Perhaps its most important purpose is to give the owners of the company (the shareholders) a report on the activities of the corporation. The stockholder wants to know about the progress of the company, its financial structure, its profits, union-management relationships, expansion of facilities, new product development, etc. When he knows about these, he will be more interested in the company and this interest, if properly handled, can improve good will. The chairman of a major American corporation expressed it in this fashion:

First and foremost, of course, the report is an accounting to stockholders.

The importance of stockholders, not alone to our individual companies but to the entire economy as well, is apparent to all of us, I am sure.

Stockholders' money started the wheels going around in all the companies represented by this audience. That may be an obvious point, but it's remarkable how obvious things can be in this world and never be fully appreciated.

Stockholders are a source of additional capital for companies. That is, if they are satisfied stockholders.

Stockholders are no doubt an influence in the purchase of securities by others. Research among stockholder groups shows that people often buy stock on the advice of friends and relatives who are also owners of stocks. People recommend to others only that which they like themselves.

Stockholders, naturally, are capitalists. The informed owners of a business can be powerful supporters for the principles of free enterprise. If they are not informed, their effectiveness is weakened.

But most importantly, stockholders are people. In their thoughts about business, their reaction to companies, their attitude toward the achievements of American enterprise, they represent public opinion. There is no better group to spread the true and vital facts about American business.

Certainly the annual report is the fundamental medium of communication between the company and those who own its stock. It seems to me that this medium should be used to its fullest advantage.[3]

Another important function of the annual report is to inform the employees of the activities of the firm. Here is an excellent opportunity to raise employee morale by not only telling labor *about* the company, but writing the report in such a way as to show the reader the company's indebtedness to its employees. When the worker knows that his efforts are appreciated, and when he knows about the plans and operations of the firm, he will surely feel closer to it and take greater pride in its progress.

Then, of course, the annual report informs a host of different reading groups about the company. The officers of many of the firms that do business with Company A are very much interested in the report; bank directors, credit men, and various types of analysts are also concerned. Investment and brokerage firms examine the reports very carefully not only for themselves but for the thousands of investors they represent.

The government reads the report as part of the company data on which tax figures are computed; the general public is often interested as are newspaper financial editors, educators, and competitors.

For all these groups, the annual report fulfills the purpose of offering information and building good will.

TYPES OF ANNUAL REPORTS

Some companies issue an annual report to stockholders and another to employees. The separate report to employees has some advantages if properly handled; however, it is often subject to the question, "Why did the firm's officers issue us a *different* report? What are they trying to hide? What are they trying to 'softsoap' us into now?"

Although there is little reason to legitimately ask that question today, it may have been valid a generation ago when some firms did attempt to delude the worker.

[3] Response of Frank W. Abrams, Chairman of the Board, Standard Oil Company (New Jersey), on receiving the gold Oscar of Industry for the best 1948 annual report at *Financial World's* Ninth Annual Awards Banquet, New York, October 31, 1949.

The justification for issuing a separate report for employees is clearly obvious. It is often felt that because the interests of the employee are different from that of the stockholder, the subject matter should be different. The employee's report, some executives feel, should primarily concern itself with topics of vital interest to the worker: wages, bonuses, future expansion or contraction, fringe benefits, and company-union relations. It is also felt that the employee would like to know about the product he manufactures, who buys it, and in what capacities it is used.

In designing and writing the employee's report, some companies have assumed the workers' intellectual and educational level to be low and have produced the report from that point of view. That may have been true years ago, but certainly not now. The error of producing a report at the "comic book level" for employees is discussed more completely in the chapter on employer-employee communications.

The interests of the stockholders are concerned with dividends, profits, assets, liabilities, surplus funds, the company's future, and related information. However, the thinking, loyal employee is also concerned with these topics. As a matter of fact, there seems to be little reason not to issue one report for both groups.

On the other hand, there are real dangers in separate reports. As noted above, the act itself is suspect; both groups may wonder what is being hidden. Union leaders would be quick to notice and exploit unfair or unfavorable material which might appear in one and not the other. And employees may resent the inference that they aren't bright enough to be given copies of the "regular" report. It is always wise to flatter a reader by overestimating his intelligence rather than underestimating it and "writing down" to him.

MAKE-UP OF THE ANNUAL REPORT

What goes into an annual report?

This is a question that is much easier to ask than to answer. Think of the multitude of activities that every giant American corporation engages in, and you have some concept of the task that lies before the annual report author. With no effort at all, he can easily fill hundreds of pages, recounting company activities for one year. Most of his readers are interested in the financial affairs of the company; some are concerned with future plans; the employees who read the report are looking for this and other information.

It is easy to see that the writer has an unenviable job. He must write for several different reading publics; he must include sufficient data so that he will not be accused of omitting vital facts. Yet he must not write so much that he is accused of being "long-winded." He must do all this in a maximum of about 50 pages and in a writing style that combines formality, wit, clarity, friendliness, and also builds good will and business.

Every company, in recent years, has made efforts to assist the recipient in the reading of the report. Sometimes little summary booklets have been sent along with the report or even booklets on "how to read the report." The Minneapolis-Honeywell Company used a 12-page booklet for that purpose.

Some of the topics that should be considered for comment or displayed numerically are:

Consolidated balance sheet
Statement of income and profit and loss
Auditor's certificate
Research
Management-employee relations
Community relations
Future plans
Brief history of the company
Individual department operations
Company publications
Statistics on stockholders
Statistics on employees
Company fringe benefits
Employee training and development
Thumbnail biographies of executives
Organization chart
List of auditors and duties
Legislation affecting the company

These are some of the topics that might be included for either general or detailed analysis in the report.

As for the various sections of the report, the following should be considered:

Title page
List of officers

GENERAL
MOTORS

FIFTIETH

ANNUAL

REPORT

YEAR ENDED DECEMBER 31,

1 9 5 8

CONTENTS

GENERAL   MOTORS   CORPORATION

Table of Contents of an Annual Report (General Motors Annual Report,
1958)

President or board chairman's letter
Summary of the report or preface to the report
Review of company activities
    Finance
    Research

    Expansion
    Management-labor relations
    Company product development
    Financial statements
    Employees, numbers, benefits, and policies
    Plants and products
    Auditor's certificate
    Miscellaneous and conclusion
    Many annual reports have other sections in addition to these
and many reports cover much less.

The President's Letter

    This is usually the first "official" part of the report. It is certainly
one of the most important. It is through this letter that hundreds or
thousands of small stockholders really establish their relationships
with the company. To many of these individuals, scattered in small
rural towns, major urban centers, or on the farms of our country,
the giant corporation is a million miles away—not only in distance,
but in understanding.

    The president's letter addressed to "Dear Stockholder" can be a
vital factor in public relations. If it is stiff, formal, and difficult to
understand, its effect on the reader is obvious. If it is friendly and
natural in tone and displays a strong "you" attitude, it will certainly receive a much more favorable reception from the reader.[4]
Just a word here and there helps break down the forbidding aus-
terity formerly found in many reports. The titles, "Your President
Reports," "A Message About Your Company," "Your Company
Chairman's Message," all attempt to start the annual report off on
a friendly basis.

    What about the length of the letter? There seem to be two
sharply divided viewpoints: One group advocates the short, crisp,
friendly letter that is one or one-and-a-half pages long and the

---

[4] The Broadway hit play, *The Solid Gold Cadillac*, which was made into a
movie, humorously depicts what friendly communications sent to stockholders can do. In this delightful comedy, a young office employee is
assigned the task of improving company relations. In no time at all she is
corresponding with hundreds of stockholders: trading recipes, inquiring about
illness, and answering questions of all kinds. When a proxy battle is fought,
the majority of the stockholders happily sign their votes over to the letter
writer who in turn "winds up" as the corporation's chief executive.
Fanciful? Yes, but with important implications also!

R. F. BENSINGER   B. E. BENSINGER

The year 1957 witnessed the most dramatic forward surge in the history of your Company. Activities in all three areas of our business were successfully expanded. The automatic pinsetter was the principal factor in the increase in sales and was a substantial contributor to net income. We can say that 1957 saw the first real fulfillment of years of research, development and planning, but equally gratifying was the growth of business in our newer fields of education and defense.

The record in the following pages speaks eloquently of the past year. However, the Brunswick organization looks toward the future. Our goals will be attained only through our continuing program of vigorous and creative effort. Heretofore, in the recreational field, we have concentrated our interest on indoor activities; now, the acquisition of MacGregor Sport Products Inc. opens the door to a large vista of outdoor recreation.

Past expansion and the prospects of further growth have been taxing the capacity of our two United States plants. The acquisition of a new production facility in Kalamazoo, Michigan, will provide needed manufacturing and warehousing space with room for future expansion.

In recreation, education and defense, Brunswick is firmly established in three fundamental activities of the American people. We are confident that 1958 will again mark further progress in our growth and prosperity.

March 1, 1958

R. F. Bensinger
Chairman

B. E. Bensinger
President

**An Example of a President's Letter of Transmittal in the Annual Report
(The Brunswick-Balke-Collender Company Annual Report, 1957)**

second group favors the lengthy communication of many pages. In the case of the brief message, the narrative portion of the report usually follows immediately. In the extended letter, the company activities are noted in detail within the communication. Although the former is found more frequently, the longer recapitulation is not unusual. The letter of transmittal in the Minneapolis-Honeywell report published in 1957 covered 15 pages and included comments on various areas: financing, company operations such as residential heating and air conditioning, commercial building market, controls for industry, aeronautical and ordnance activities, Canadian and foreign operations, research, engineering, and a forecast.

But whether long or short, this narrative portion, covering the various company activities, should give the reader a clear and comprehensive (though not a complicated and detailed) picture. The order of their presentation should be logical. It might begin with the company's financial position, then treat dealer relationships, management-labor relations, research, new products, plants and plant development, and conclude with foreign operations. Wherever possible, narrative passages should be supplemented by charts or graphs that will assist the reader in understanding.

The Financial Information

The financial position of the company, as reflected in the annual report, is the most important section for most stockholders. The earliest annual report presented only financial data to the stockholders' most obvious question, "Is the company making money and, if so, where is it going?"

A simple consolidated balance sheet is often inadequate to present the true picture of the complex financial structure of the modern corporation.

A consolidated balance sheet, carefully prepared, can reflect a valuable financial picture of the firm. Because of its right-and left-hand series of entries, it is wise to place it on two pages and give it the center double spread of the report. One report presented three summaries of the company's financial activities: first, a consolidated summary which reflected investments in plants and properties, funded debt, and stock retirement; funds for future capital expenditures; the decrease in cash and securities; and increases in receivables and inventories. Then followed a statement of profits and losses and dividends paid. The third exhibit recounted increases and/or decreases in assets and liabilities.[5]

The annual report writer might consider presenting exhibits and statistics in the following financial areas:

Balance sheet	Distribution of income
Operating statement	Capital expenditures
Auditor's certification	Working capital
The company's financial position	Payroll
The earned surplus statement	Schedule of value of plants and
The capital surplus statement	properties
Sales	Investments
Earnings	Depreciation and depletion
Dividends	Income other than from opera-
Taxes	tions
Reserves	Net worth[6]
Financial highlights	

An excellent explanation of the financial portion of the annual report is given in almost 50 closely written pages of the American Management Association's research report, *Preparation of Company Annual Reports*.[7] This is recommended to anyone engaged in the preparation of the annual report.

The writer must also be concerned with the financial narrative as well as the financial statistics. The American Management Association says:

The financial narrative may turn out to be of even greater importance than the conventional financial statements. It can serve: (1) to amplify; (2) to explain the nature and significance of changes in financial data and policy; (3) to draw attention to the bases of valuation, alternative accounting treatments, contingencies, and unusual situations; (4) to describe the relationship of the various data to one another; (5) to discuss the prospects; (6) to indicate qualifications usually stated in footnote form. In short, it can touch on matters which cannot be expressed satisfactorily in the figures themselves. In all these ways the narrative can throw additional light on the condition of the company.

Specifically, the financial narrative may include a discussion of im-

[5] K. C. Pratt, *Company Annual Reports to Stockholders and Employees*, Hamilton, Ohio: The Champion Paper and Fibre Company, 1948, pp. 28-29.
[6] *Ibid*.
[7] *Preparation of Company Annual Reports*, American Management Association, Inc., Research Report Number 10, New York.

portant items and changes on the balance sheet and income statements. . . .

But the financial narrative should omit self-evident and obvious commentary. . . . Nor should the commentary be trite or too lengthy and detailed. If possible, it should be woven around a central subject, or at least some connecting links and continuity.[8]

The Nonfinancial Narrative

This portion of the annual report is of primary interest to the stockholder who has little interest in complex accounting terms and "no head for figures."

Topics which should be considered for comment are those concerned with the following five areas.

1. *The Company Itself.* A few brief sentences summarizing the development of the company and its historical background are often of interest to the new stockholder as well as the old. The traditions and early progress and difficulties may be recounted.

The reader is certainly interested in the market acceptance of the company's products. Illustrations of the items and their use in either the home or in industry may also be presented. The advertising and sales promotion programs should be summarized. Research and new product development might be recapitulated for the stockholders who are certainly interested in the future outlook of the firm. Company plants, their locations, products, and facilities should be listed and pictured. These are just a few of the activities of the company itself which might be discussed along the lines suggested.

2. *The Company and Employee Relations.* Various employee benefits such as pension plans, insurance programs, vacation policy, sick leave policy, stock buying plan, and employee profit-sharing might be presented. Employee training and development might well be examined. Many firms have very generous and far-reaching plans which include the payment of evening college tuition and sponsorship of classes during and after work hours.

The number of employees and some indication of average earnings should be recounted as well as safety and health records, retirements, and a recapitulation of the number of long-service employees.

One of the most vital factors in this area concerns management-

[8] *Ibid.,* p. 29.

labor relations. A frank and clear account of labor contract agreements, strikes, and bargaining sessions should be listed. To ignore vital or troubled periods in the year's activities is unfair to the reader. That reader, who has probably heard something about the labor difficulty, expects to find some explanation. If he finds nothing, he may have good reason to be skeptical of the *entire* report.

3. *The Company and Its Management Personnel.* A list of the top executives, their photographs, and brief biographies are usually included. Certain policies might be included as well as future plans for adding or reducing the number of officers.

4. *The Company and Its Stockholders.* It is always of interest to the small stockholder to learn how many persons, just like himself, own shares in the company. He might also be interested in their geographical distribution, the average number of shares they hold, and other general information.

5. *The Company, Its Policies, and Its Contributions to the Community.* Here is an opportunity for the corporation to explain its viewpoints concerning its responsibilities and obligations in our economy, competition, free enterprise, government control or direction, community housing and education problems, taxes, labor relations, and other activities involving the corporation and the society in which it exists.

A recent annual report states:

Be a good citizen wherever we serve.

This we accomplish by accepting our full share of leadership in civic affairs and of social responsibility, knowing that the good results of these activities flow through the community to our employees and eventually back to the Company. . . .

The last of our four standards—corporate citizenship—is sometimes not fully apparent or understood. One example of its application is the modest help we are giving to some 35 privately-supported colleges and universities in Illinois. We regard these fine accredited institutions as important business assets because they are a major source of our future managerial talent. In turn it is appropriate that we assist them. . . .

Our Bell System series of Science Films . . . is an example of our efforts to help educators . . . encourage more young people to prepare themselves for science careers. . . . [This is] also . . . the purpose of the Student Science Fair program. . . .

These are matters germane to the basic management function of operations and profit. Call them public relations, citizenship, or what you will, they are examples of an important element of our Company's guiding principles of management.[9]

WRITING STYLE AND THE ANNUAL REPORT

One of the most frequent criticisms of annual reports has been concerned with the way they are written. Abstruse, complex, involved, mumbo-jumbo, gobbledygook—have been some of the descriptive terms applied. And can the critics be blamed? This sixty-six word sentence should be criticized:

> Thus, for the year . . . this corporation has made progress, to some extent that is, in its fields of manufacturing by introducing a system of internal control that is resulting in a definite saving in overhead expenditures that have not yet been reflected in declared dividends for the stockholders, but will, at the discretion of the company directors, be announced in the not too distant future.[10]

However, the writing style of annual reports of recent years has shown tremendous improvement. There has been a real effort made to make the stockholder want to read his annual report.

An article in *Advanced Management* suggests that the writer check his report on the basis of the questions summarized below:

1. Is the report interesting?
   Does it have a "you" attitude? Ample use of meaningful tables and charts? Unity of subject matter?
2. Is the report understandable?
   Is the word choice at the proper level for the stockholder? Are the sentences clear and easy to understand?
   An investigation on the "readability" of annual reports, using the Rudolph Flesch (author of *The Art of Readable Writing*) formula, produced some interesting facts. In 26 annual reports, the level of reading understandability ranged from *fairly difficult* to *very difficult*. As for the words in the reports, a large proportion were beyond the fluent comprehension and language experience of 75% of the U.S. adult population.[11]

---

[9] From the President's message, *Annual Report,* 1957, Illinois Bell Telephone Company.

[10] Norman B. Sigband, "Writing the Annual Report," *Advanced Management,* January, 1952, p. 20.

[11] See S. Pashalian and W. J. E. Crissy, "How Readable Are Corporate Annual Reports?" *Journal of Applied Psychology,* August, 1950.

The report writer must choose his words with care and construct his sentences to insure clarity; there can be no hint of ambiguity.
3. Is the report easy to analyze and interpret?

Although this point is primarily concerned with the statistical data presented, it also has reference to the composition. There can be no doubt that in some reports statements are intentionally made in a very abstruse manner so as to make interpretation difficult. However, it is the figures with which we are primarily concerned.

The consolidated balance sheet should not only reflect all the necessary statistical data, but the terminology should be easy to interpret. It is often just as easy to use a simple group of words in place of a highly technical accounting phrase. Certainly the statements, "The cost of human energy," and "The cost of tools wearing out," are as acceptable as "wages, salaries, depreciation and depletion."[12]

For accurate analysis, it is *imperative* that the report writer offer comparative data. To present this year's figures only may be almost meaningless unless the reader is provided with some basis for comparison. The statistical data for the previous year is not adequate; there should be information on at least the previous two years for the reader to examine. Some reports, in recent years, have presented comparative data going back a full ten years. And one authority, Weston Smith,[13] feels that "at least ten years" should be provided.

The American Management Association establishes three similar criteria for good reporting: completeness, interest, and clarity of expression. The areas covered by these three are quite obvious and need no further explanation. However, in our easy understanding of the three terms, we must be careful not to accept them and pay only "lip service" to what they mean. We must constantly keep the stockholder-reader in mind.

PRODUCING THE ANNUAL REPORT

Although the production of the report is a technical task, the report writer must know enough about it so that he will not be "caught short." He should know the different levels of expense

---

[12] Sigband, *op. cit.*
[13] Weston Smith, "Design Factors to Help Improve Annual Reports," *Printing News,* May 21, 1949.

involved in different printing processes, what can and cannot be be done with photographs, how much time the printer must have to produce 300,000 three-color reports, and a host of other details.

Responsibility for Production

One person must be made responsible for the annual report. It is unwise to have half a dozen different executives making decisions since this will only lead to a conflict. One person must be placed in charge; he must have the authority to make final decisions on content, makeup, printing production problems, and distribution. Of course, there is no reason why he cannot work closely with a committee, but when there is disagreement, it should be clearly understood that a two-week delay for discussion is not necessary. Mr. Blank can and should state—right or wrong—the action that will be taken.

The first step in production is the determination of what shall go into the report. Once that is decided, the department heads concerned should submit their contribution by a specific date. Of course, the greatest care must be exercised on the accounting department's, comptroller's or treasurer's portion. The financial review must be scrutinized with meticulous care.

Establishment of a production schedule is vital. Precise dates should be set down and pictures, charts, photographs, financial statements, and narrative portions should be submitted when indicated. One laggard among the contributors can throw the entire schedule into confusion that will result in nasty tempers, recriminations, and several cases of "management ulcers."

Covers should be dramatic but not ostentatious. Good taste can be a quality of a compelling, colorful cover. It should reflect the key product or service of the company.

Several reports have used novelty covers to emphasize their products. The Ohio Match Company's cover was made to look like a match book cover; Burgess Battery's annual report was cut out in the shape of a flashlight battery; a wallpaper company used one of its designs on the cover. Since 1952, the Manhattan Shirt Company report has been cut in the shape of a shirt-clad torso.

On the whole, an attractive, colored cover printed on good stock is very effective.

Size of reports varies from 3″ × 5″ to 9″ × 12″. The small ones are designed to be slipped into a pocket and read when leisure

Annual Reports in a Novelty Design to Simulate the Company's Product
(Burgess Battery Company Annual Reports, 1952, 1953)

time is available. Too often, however, they are simply forgotten or lost. The most popular and effective size is $8\frac{1}{2}'' \times 11''$.

This size permits easy filing and wide pages for unbroken columns of statistics. The text in this size page should be broken into two columns to enhance appearance and readability.

Type faces should be chosen with the overall style of the report in mind. One family of type faces may be used or at most two different types may be used to suppplement and/or complement one another in the report. Several different types will clash. Dignity and clarity in reproduction should be important considerations in the choice of type.

Tabular and graphic presentation can improve the reader's understanding of the report and also aid the report's appearance. The tables, charts, and graphs should be made up by experts who will consider the reader and the material to be presented before deciding on the type of graphic illustration. A good table or chart can effectively supplement (or even supplant) several pages of text. It can add tremendously to a report. (The details of graphic illustration are presented in Chapter 6.)

Photographs can be used most effectively. There is no better way (except samples) to acquaint the stockholder with company products than clear, expertly arranged photographs. Color pictures are invaluable for giving the reader a view of company plants, operations, and officers.

Layout and headings should be carried through with thought. Layout, giving careful attention to design qualities, will help give the report balance and continuity. Headings help the reader find items of interest and are useful for quick reference purposes. Headings may be in color printing, a large size of type, bold face type, or italics.

DISTRIBUTION OF THE REPORT

It goes without saying that every stockholder is supposed to receive a copy of the report. Quite obviously, the mailing lists should always be kept up to date.

Today, however, most reports are distributed much more widely than this. Because the report is frankly recognized as an important public relations document, many companies have directed it to a variety of publics. Naturally, special care in the writing and layout of the report is necessary due to the fact that others, in addition to stockholders, will read it.

Some of the groups that receive corporation reports are:
Company employees
Company suppliers

Officers of banks and investment houses
University administrators and faculty
Community leaders
Officers of service groups
Government agencies
Newspaper editors
Business journal editors
Legislators
Radio and television station directors
Clergymen
Librarians

A form cover letter may accompany the reports. It should, of course, be written with the particular readership in mind.

As for the quantity distributed, in some cases it is staggering. It is estimated, for example, that the 1,000 leading U.S. corporations distributed over 40,000,000 copies of their reports in 1957![14] By 1959 the figure was up to 50,000,000.[15] General Motors had a press run of a million for 1957, and American Telephone and Telegraph Company distributed 1,825,000 copies![16]

Some firms have purchased newspaper or magazine space where a condensed version of the annual report is displayed to the reading public. Other firms have used a film which reports on the year's activities.

THE TREND IN ANNUAL REPORTS

Among the many changes in industry since 1940, none is more dramatic than the revisions in the company annual report. An article in an issue of *The Reporter of Direct Mail Advertising* was appropriately titled, "Today's Annual Reports Are Really 'Reporting.' "

The big trend is towards making the annual report much more than a private financial accounting for select shareholders. For today's owners of industry are millions of people with different interests, in all walks of life. Modern annual reports are edited for them . . . telling company stories dramatically. With added attention to art, color, and

[14] "From Dance Cards to the Ivy-League Look," *The New Yorker,* May 18, 1957, p. 76.
[15] *The New York Times,* May 13, 1959.
[16] "From Dance Cards to the Ivy-League Look," *op. cit.*

slick magazine or book presentation, today's best annual reports can serve a multiple purpose:

1. They present a detailed report of operation to all stockholders.
2. They tell the over-all company story, or history . . . becoming a dramatic promotion piece for selling prospective shareholders (and sometimes customers as well).
3. They are used as a general public relations tool to keep the public informed of the firm's progress in a competitive marketing era.
4. They sometimes help solve specific corporate problems.

In short, today's annual reports are really "reporting." They are diversifying their content and appealing to a broader audience. They are becoming more . . . "external" . . . to win new friends, shareholders and customers. And they are doing it with better, more interesting content and visual presentation.

The emphasis is on clearer copy and more pleasing presentation. The demand is from the stockholding public.[17]

The yearly annual report survey and competition sponsored by *Financial World Magazine* has probably been the strongest single factor in the improvement of reports. In 1941, Weston Smith, formerly a *Financial World* editor, instituted the first survey. By 1958, some 5000 reports were accepted for judging by the *Financial World*.

It is difficult to say which is directly responsible for the tremendous improvement in the caliber of annual reports—the *Financial World* surveys or the corporations' awareness of what an effective public relations document the annual report can be if properly presented. Glancing at almost any 20 reports selected at random and printed in 1940, one is impressed by the drab, dry, forbidding nature of the booklets. By the 1950's most of these reports were colorful, attractive, and readable.

The *Financial World* survey, directed by Weston Smith, has grown each year since 1941. Each report that is entered is subjected to an initial screening covering the president's letter, the narrative section, comparative financial statistics, and design and production. Those passing this screening (only 2000 of the 5000 submitted in 1957) receive a merit award. The reports selected are then carefully evaluated by a competent group of judges. The best report in each of 97 industrial classifications (everything from "air conditioning" through "cosmetics," "paper products,"

[17] "Today's Annual Reports Are Really 'Reporting,' " *The Reporter of Direct Mail Advertising*, November, 1957, p. 30.

"pulp and paper," "stove and furnace" down to "waterworks") receives a bronze Oscar. Then silver Oscars are awarded to the best annual report in each of six broad classifications, such as transportation, public utilities, and consumer goods. From these six, one gold Oscar is awarded to the annual report as the "Best of All Industry."

Industry's interest in communicating with stockholders is reflected in the caliber of today's annual reports. These reports are steadily improving by giving the reader more information in an attractive, comprehensive, and readable fashion. Here is one area of communications in industry that has advanced tremendously during the twentieth century.

QUESTIONS FOR DISCUSSION

I. Answer the following questions as concisely as possible.

1. In recent years annual reports have become more detailed, colorful, and elaborate. What do you think are some of the reasons for this?

2. Large sums of money are spent by corporations in printing and distributing the annual report. It is sometimes argued that these funds should be paid to stockholders in the form of dividends and the vital facts in the report should be mimeographed on a sheet or two of paper. How do you feel about this and why?

3. List what you think are the purposes of the annual report. Choose an annual report and indicate specifically why and where those purposes are and are not met. Submit the annual report together with your comments.

4. Using the same annual report, evaluate its letter of transmittal. Be specific in your comments.

5. An executive recently said, "An annual report which does not present financial data for at least three years preceding the one being reported on, is suspect. Comparisons are vital for clear understanding." Can you explain the reasoning behind the executive's comment?

6. Evaluate an annual report on the basis of its readers. Point out specifically why you feel the report is or is not written at the proper level.

7. Thousands of annual reports sent out to stockholders by American corporations are never even opened, much less read and studied. Can you make a suggestion on how this expenditure can be avoided and good will maintained?

8. What are the advantages of giving one person the authority and responsibility for producing the annual report?

9. Borrow or secure three or four annual reports from one company. Try to get them spaced about 5 years apart and going back about 20 years. Comment on the specific differences and the trends which you find among them.

10. Conduct an informal survey among 20 different stockholders who receive one or more annual reports. Attempt to determine which, if any, section of the annual report they read most intensively. Explain your findings.

II. Answer the following questions according to the suggestions made.

1. Using the *Business Periodicals Index* as a guide, review as many articles as possible on the annual report which have appeared in the last two years. Present a brief report on your findings.

2. Present a panel discussion on the *Financial World* annual report award contest for this year and last. Secure copies of as many award-winning reports as possible. Analyze and discuss these for your group.

3. Assume that you are the chairman of the board of a steel corporation that has 65,000 employees. Write two letters transmitting your annual report. Direct one letter to company stockholders and the other to employees.

4. Secure an annual report and offer your criticism of the tabular and graphic aids presented. You may wish to point out how they fulfill their specific purposes, how they can be improved, and which ones might be added.

Chapter 15

Communicating with Employees

It takes two to speak the truth—one to speak and another to hear.

—Thoreau

"Say, Joe, did you hear that the company was going to close down this plant in ninety days and concentrate all production in the St. Louis factory?"

"Why no, Tom, I didn't know that. But if it's so, they certainly should have told us. I'm quitting and getting a new job just as soon as I can!"

Actually, the corporation had no intention of moving or closing the plant at all. These were merely rumors that a worker had mistakenly begun. But they did travel like wildfire among the employees.

Sometimes the information that is passed along on the production line, in the cafeteria, in the washrooms, out in the parking lot, and at the bowling alley is accurate; often it is not.

When the information is accurate and important for the employees to know, a precise method of communication should be established; a "word-of-mouth" system is not satsifactory. However, the "word-of-mouth" system will exist when no direct and formal system of communication is available. Almost invariably, when a group of persons is interested in a particular situation and they are not informed of the facts, someone in the group will supply information—accurate or inaccurate. Therefore, one of the most important reasons why a system of communications to employees is vital is that it is a strong deterrent to the spread of inaccurate and harmful rumors.

NEED FOR A COMMUNICATION PLAN

The problem of managerial control becomes more complex as America's industries expand, diversify, decentralize, and merge. Employees accomplish a better job when they know *why* their job is necessary and when they know *how* and *through what avenues* their company functions. They work more efficiently and productively when they have some picture of the organization's past activities and future program and when they are aware of the function of the different echelons, different divisions, different departments. When the employee possesses knowledge about the company and its activities, he will obviously be better informed and as a result he will probably be happier, more coöperative, and certainly more loyal.

Every employee, almost without exception, wants to know about his company. He wants to know about the company's history, its "ups and downs," its future plans, its profits, its losses. He wants to know about the firm's products: how they are made, who buys them, and facts on the competitors. He wants to know about company organization and policies and how they affect him and all the other employees. And most important, of course, he wants as much information as possible on his job and where it fits in in the event of strikes, layoffs, expansion, or contraction. The more an employee is told about the company, the more it will become *his* company.

In addition to providing the worker with information about the firm, the employer has an obligation to provide his employees with as much data as possible concerning basic facts and principles in economic, social, and cultural areas. Management benefits when employees understand how a corporation operates, what a shareholder is, the dangers of inflation, the results of overproduction or underproduction, the individual's responsibility to his community, and the marvelous cultural heritages we all enjoy. Many companies subscribe to a "rack service" which offers employees a variety of information booklets in these various areas.

The important factor is to keep employees informed. It is not enough for a company to indicate that it believes in a policy of communicating with its employees and that it distributes magazines and bulletins; it must put this policy into practice in every sincere way possible. An interesting little story which illustrates this is contained in the booklet, *Effective Communication in Industry.*

A CHRISTMAS STORY

But no matter how genuine and useful a personnel policy may seem, as written, it is worse than useless, in fact, when its words are denied by top management behavior. In the communication of policies, not only inconsistent action, but even silence at a crucial stage of developments, may make nonsense of written words. This inconvenient fact was clearly illustrated in a non-unionized company that included in its policy system a specific commitment for two-way communication on all matters of importance to employees. Other policies stressed consideration of the sense of mutual responsibility and loyalty between management and every employee.

For a number of years it had been the company custom to give all employees a Christmas bonus. This check was presented with ceremony at the annual meeting, the only occasion on which the president talked to all his employees as a group. He usually forecast business opportunities for the coming year, discussed major new developments and with fulsome expressions of esteem, expanded on his liberal intentions for employee benefits.

During 1947, the company experienced production difficulties that necessitated extensive layoffs. These diminished the total work force so much that the remaining fifth of the former group were all people of long service. While the arrangements for the annual meeting were going forward, there was much speculation as to whether the Christmas bonus would be paid as usual. Management made no statement on this point.

When the president got up to make his customary speech at the meeting itself, he appeared ill at ease. He seemed to find it hard to go through his annual routine, and made no reference whatever to the bonus, which was not given out.

This failure to discuss the matter of the bonus with the employees belied the company policy of two-way communication. The Christmas bonus was a "matter of importance to employees." The communication policy committed management, before making a decision, to hear what the men had to say about omitting it. Otherwise they could only complain *after* the event; a response that needed no "policy" to permit it.

After the meeting there was a general feeling of disappointment. Some members said they had expected this all along. A few clung to the forlorn hope that the bonus would be included in the usual weekly pay envelope; given out on Wednesday, which fell this year on Christmas Eve. When the extra check was not forthcoming, they went to their foremen to inquire whether there had been some mistake. All that day, and on the day after Christmas (Friday, when they had to work as usual), the grapevine buzzed with accusations, rumors, and forebodings. But most revealing of the damage done to morale was the comment of one member in a group long noted for its loyalty to the company president: "If he'd said he couldn't pay, I'd have understood. If he'd told us everyone had to pitch in and work harder, I'd have been glad to do it. But I can't help thinking less of him since I saw he didn't trust us."

Top executives in this company seemed unaware that their policy system was repeatedly belied in action. And they apparently never recognized this inconsistency between words and behavior as the origin for the deep-rooted suspicion and resentment that was gradually built up in the minds of employees. . . .[1]

It is important for management to know what the employees think, how they feel, and what they want. It is only when management knows the attitudes, desires, and needs of the workers that it can follow a plan of action that benefits both employer and employee. The company executive who says, "Oh, *my boys* know that I have their best interests in mind," is voicing a statement that industry recognizes today as being completely ridiculous. Thousands of corporations have established formal procedures for communicating with their employees. At the same time management is attempting to have the employees communicate "up the line" as well. Obviously, the latter is a much more difficult system to establish; employees do not ordinarily have the printed devices to distribute (such materials as brochures, reports, and bulletins) that the company has.

In any event, the purpose of this chapter is to explore some of the methods of two-way communication within a company. Although many of the references which follow are associated with some of America's large corporations, it should be understood that the principles apply to all firms whether large or small.

OBJECTIVES OF A COMMUNICATION PROGRAM

The objectives of a communication program have already been alluded to in a rather broad and general fashion. Although differ-

[1] Paul Pigors, *Effective Communication in Industry,* New York: National Association of Manufacturers, 1949, pp. 38-39.

ent corporations have slightly different communication goals, most of them are quite similar. The General Motors Corporation, for example, has summarized its objectives in company-employee communication as:

To INTEREST the employee in his job, in its importance, and in doing it better.

To FOSTER loyalty to and pride in the company and its products.

To DEVELOP an urge to make working for the company a lifetime job.

To EDUCATE the employee in the benefits of the company, its progressiveness, and its fairness in wages and working conditions.

To INFORM the employee on company problems and how he can help solve them.

To PERSUADE employees of the company's interest in human values and its acceptance of social responsibilities.

To COUNTERACT the unrest sown by those who profit most from misunderstanding.

And finally (by extending publications into the home), to DEVELOP the same attitudes on the part of the families of the employees.[2]

The broader purpose of communicating with employees was noted in a letter written by V. K. Proctor, Director of General Motors' Employee Programs Section. Mr. Proctor said:

Our purposes in communicating with employes are many. We must communicate with employes if they are to know: what we want them to do; why we want them to do it; why it is in their best interests to do it in this way. These are merely the immediate objectives. On the longer term, we know that we get best performance only by appealing to and building: interest, understanding, loyalty, pride, team spirit, and so forth, with our people. You do not achieve that by being a sphinx. The only way is to communicate with the people directly involved.

Communication, as the old saw goes, is not a one-way street. You have to let and get your employes to communicate. Unless you do, you will lose out on important information and viewpoints; you will tend to become fat, inbred, complacent and self-important. Furthermore, people listen a lot better if you occasionally give them a chance to say what is on their minds. . . .

At the local level, written communication with employes is achieved through the plant papers, posters and other bulletin board pieces, and occasional letters from general managers on holidays and other appropriate occasions. Approximately 35 of our plants and divisions now

[2] Milton E. Mumblow, "Employee Communications: A Number One Job," *American Management Association,* No. 127 (October, 1950), 16.

publish their own plant papers, ranging from a simple mimeographed sheet on to a glossy publication and on a schedule ranging from once a week to once every two months. . . . A quarterly news packet prepared in Central Office for local editors attempts to keep the editorial standards high and provide some reprintable thoughts and ideas. . . .

One of the major media emanating from Central Office is our Information Rack Service, a field in which we were a pioneer. . . . We publish also, on approximately a monthly basis, a simple management leaflet which goes to 30,000 persons including most members of supervision. Under the name, *GM Personnel News,* this little magazine centers mainly around key personnel changes from here, there and everywhere. . . .

As new employe benefit programs are introduced or older ones revised, we naturally make a point of getting this information in the hands of those people concerned. The medium is usually a special booklet mailed to the employes' homes to insure that other members of the family have an opportunity to become aware of its contents. Special booklets of this nature cover such benefit areas as group insurance, pension plans, Blue Cross and Blue Shield, unemployment compensations, etc. . . .

Also in the area of employe communications is a series of posters which we ourselves prepare for use in the plants and divisions. On a one-poster-a-week basis, they cover such subjects as safety, good housekeeping, careful workmanship, waste, absenteeism, teamwork, etc. These multi-color posters are for use not only on plant bulletin boards but also suspended in frames out in the plant work areas where employes can see them from their job locations.[3]

The Chrysler Corporation has similar objectives for its employee communication program. To achieve its goals, Chrysler utilizes some eight different media: biweekly newspapers (thirteen different editions for as many units and divisions), personnel newsletter, employee bulletins, posters, executive announcements, newsletter news service, executive bulletins, and bulletin board notices.

The viewpoint of the Ford Motor Company on employee communications is quite similar to what has already been said:

In companies the size of Ford it is an easy thing for the individual employe to become just another name on the payroll unless definite plans and programs are established which are directed at making our employes feel as if management of a company recognize the importance of treating them as individuals. . . .

---

[3] Letter to the author from Vern K. Proctor, Director, Employe Programs Section, General Motors Corporation.

Some years ago Mr. Henry Ford II summed up the purpose of our employe communications program in these words:

"It is certain that uninformed people can't have good morale, if only for the simple reason that people fear what they don't know about —things like skeletons in the closet."

We feel it to be axiomatic that when we have a condition of high morale among our employes, the chances are pretty good that productivity, quality, costs and the like will be more efficient. . . .

Our most important means of communication are the 29 employe newspapers located throughout the country wherever there are Ford plants. For the most part, these are monthly, eight-page tabloids. The only exception is the parent newspaper (the Rouge News) published every two weeks covering the greater Detroit area. Circulation is approximately 100,000.

Without exception these papers are all mailed to the employes' homes, both because we feel families have an interest in the Company and to prevent waste and loss normally associated with plant distribution.

For many items which do not coincide with the publication date of the newspapers, the Company employs a series of bulletins. The Company's teletype network is used to transmit such information to all manufacturing and assembly plants, sales offices and parts depots. It is reproduced in bulletin form locally according to instructions received from the Central Office. . . .

In addition to the above, we publish regularly two special publications, a bi-monthly news letter with information of particular interest to salaried employes only and a management publication, distributed monthly, which is concerned with management-labor matters.

As the occasion demands, we are geared to prepare and publish special booklets, pamphlets, brochures and letters.[4]

The Du Pont Corporation has a complex and thorough employee communication program.

We might break down the purpose of communicating with employees in this way: (1) To make clear the duties of a job; (2) To make clear the method or methods by which the duties are to be carried out; (3) To convey the reason or reasons for assigned work; (4) To acquaint employees with employee benefit plans; (5) To let each employee know, from time to time where he stands; (6) To acquaint employees with general Company policies; and (7) To keep employees up to date on Company progress in all of its major functions.

[4] Letter to the author from Anthony M. Menkel, Jr., Acting Manager, Management and Employe Information Department, Ford Motor Company.

By accomplishing these aspects of communication, it is believed that employees, in general, will derive maximum benefit from their occupations and will render a most efficient service to the Company. . . . On general Company practices . . . we use many devices for communicating to employees. Here are some examples:

1. Annual Report—Each year a leaflet containing highlights is distributed to all employees. A full copy of the Annual Report is available to each employee on request.
2. We have a program known as "How Our Business System Operates." This program presents economic facts of business and is participated in by all employees on a discussional basis. The program is brought up to date from time to time and repeated.
3. Movies pertaining to the Company as a whole or various aspects of it, such as benefit plans, are shown to employees usually during working hours.
4. A Foreman Visitation Program brings to headquarter's offices, foremen from plants throughout the country, at which time they meet management people in Wilmington and learn more about general Company policies and practices.
5. Our Public Relations Department publishes a magazine, "Better Living," which informs employees on many subjects related to the Company and its people. This department also supplies information to our plant papers, which is of interest from a general Company standpoint. . . .

Most specific information requested by an employee is available in the unit where he is employed. If not, it is a function of supervision to obtain it and see that the employee receives it, assuming the request to be a reasonable one.

One of the most important facets of communication is letting an employee know where he stands. It is Company policy to schedule performance reviews with each employee at regular intervals.

Another approach to this subject is embodied in attitude surveys in which employees answer questionnaires anonymously, but which frequently bring out areas of information on which employees need to be better informed.[5]

Many companies indicate that although their communication program is designed to be "two way," the information that moves from the employee to the company is not very well organized. As a matter of fact, it is limited, in most cases, to the "Employee Suggestion System." Obviously, this is an area that needs inten-

---

[5] Letter to the author from L. A. Wetlaufer, Assistant Manager, Employee Relations Department, E. I. Du Pont de Nemours & Company.

sive work; information must flow up with accuracy and consistency if management is to make intelligent decisions concerning employee attitudes.

COMMUNICATION MEDIA USED BY MANAGEMENT

The House Organ

Of the various communication pieces utilized by management and distributed to employees, none has gained wider use in recent years than the house organ. Thousands of companies presently publish them with the hope that they will be carefully read by employees.

House organs—or company magazines, as they are frequently called—come in all shapes, sizes, and philosophies. Some are inexpensively reproduced by a mimeograph process and are designed to be read and discarded; others are printed on excellent paper stock and are filled with lovely color photographs and perfectly executed tabular and graphic illustrations.

PRESENT STATUS OF "HOUSE MAGAZINES"

The number of house magazines issued in the United States today is difficult to estimate; however, it is safe to assume that there are between 8,000–10,000 different ones published. The circulation of these publications is without a doubt greater than the daily newspaper total, and the cost of publication is a staggering $500,000,000 per year. Distribution of 50,000 copies per issue is not uncommon and in major corporations such as General Motors, Standard Oil (New Jersey), and Western Electric, the figure is many times higher. A large proportion of these are so attractive in format and so interesting in content that they are also distributed to thousands of customers, stockholders, and/or friends of the company.

PURPOSE OF THE HOUSE ORGAN

The obvious purpose of management in sponsoring house organs is to improve morale and build *esprit de corps* among the employees. It is an attempt to foster the idea of "one big happy family" regardless of the employee's position within the company.

Corporate House Organs (Standard Oil Torch, **November, 1958**; Caterpillar Tractor Co. News and Views, **January-February, 1957**)

In addition to building this democratic concept, the magazines strive to give the employee an idea of the various segments of the corporate enterprise, acquaint him more intimately with the company's organization and personnel, and explain the functions and objectives of the various divisions.

Management is usually very desirous of "explaining the company" and its activities, and it is felt that the average employee will be much more receptive to assimilating information of this type if he finds it in an employees' publication rather than a company booklet.

TYPES OF PUBLICATIONS

A booklet published by one of America's large paper corporations indicates that most house organs fall into (1) standard magazine size; (2) tabloid size; or (3) pocket size.[6] In the first group, the most popular size is $8\frac{1}{2}'' \times 11''$, although $7'' \times 10''$ is frequently used. Most of these are printed by letterpress or offset lithography; mimeographing is not often utilized. Color is being used more and more to add interest and improve the appearance of the publication.

The magazine size is usually more attractive to the reader than the tabloid or pocket size and will probably be retained by many employees.

The tabloid or newspaper size company publication is not used as frequently, and, unlike the magazine type, it seldom uses color and has no cover. Of course, it is not usually saved by the employee or his family but, like a newspaper, is read and discarded.

The pocket affair ranges in size from $6'' \times 9''$ down; $5'' \times 7''$ seems to be especially popular. Its chief advantage, naturally, is its convenience. It can be slipped into a coat or jacket pocket and read while riding the bus or waiting in the cafeteria line. The ease with which this may be carried home or retained until leisure time is available is a very real and important advantage. Many of these, using color, photographs, and illustrations wisely, are among the most attractive and dynamic company publications.

CONTENT

The nature of the material in house organs varies from company to company. However, this type of publication seems to contain: (1) organizational news and tidbits, (2) formal technical and nontechnical articles, and (3) a combination of both.

"Newsy" House Organ. This approach concentrates on items

[6] K. C. Pratt, *House Magazine Layout,* Champion Paper and Fibre Company, Hamilton, Ohio, 1952.

of news concerning company employees. It has a very liberal al-
lotment of photographs depicting graduation exercises, retirement
dinner testimonials, army promotions, weddings, vacation pleasures,
and so on. In each case company employees and/or their families
are involved.

If the company is a vast enterprise, such a magazine is usually
split into sections corresponding to the firm's divisions. From time
to time, such a publication also carries a letter from the company
president or chairman.

Certainly a publication of this nature strives to build employee
morale and *esprit de corps*. The vice-president is pictured with a
string of fish; but on the next page, a company janitor is photo-
graphed holding an 18-pound muskie. In this way a feeling of
democracy might be secured. This idea, of course, is that regardless
of our differences in positions, we both work for the same company
and both have our pictures in the same "family" magazine.

Such a publication does build a community of interests and com-
radeship among the employees. On the other hand, however, there
are obvious disadvantages. Many technically and analytically
minded employees will soon refer to this publication as a gossip
sheet; they will see little benefit to themselves in reading it and
they may quickly discard it. Then, too, if the organization is large,
the magazine must be split into divisions; the readers may only
peruse the single section that applies to them. Another disadvantage of this type of magazine is that it cannot publish all
the graduations, all the trips, and all the happy events of all the
employees. Some people will be missed and they may be resentful.

The "Combination" House Organ. This magazine includes
several articles of general interest. These may be concerned with
areas of activity within the company: an account of a new product
the firm is developing, a description of a new plant, an analysis of
a government activity and its influence on the company, and other
areas that would have a definite interest for the thinking employee
but not have so technical a nature as to appeal to a limited segment
of the work force.

In addition, this type of publication also reserves a section for
employee news: promotions, weddings, births, etc.

This type of house organ is probably the most popular of the
thousands which are published in America today. It discusses various aspects of the company that are of interest to management and

labor, and it builds company spirit by acquainting the employee intimately with the activities of his company. These activities may be concerned with the firm's growth as well as with incidents in the personal life of individuals or with company affairs, such as an award-winning suggestion, an act of heroism, or a major promotion.

The "Journal" Type of House Organ. This type of publication contains a series of articles which are informative in nature and of *general* interest. They may be concerned with public affairs, governmental activities, international situations, and social or cultural conditions. *The Lamp,* a quarterly published by Standard Oil of New Jersey, is an excellent example of this type.

Such a publication has dignity and performs a public service through its educational contributions. Naturally, it is frequently distributed to many persons in addition to the company employees.

These are a few of the types of house organs which exist. Where a company is very large, it may issue one of each type listed. At Western Electric, for example, a tabloid for each of its major divisions is printed, along with the magazine, *WE,* and the technical publication called *The Western Electric Engineer.* Naturally, a complex publication arrangement of this nature may be maintained only by very large corporations.

Time Magazine, in a pointed article, clearly indicated how American corporations are also utilizing their house organs to keep pace with the printed communication media of labor.

Industry in the U.S. will spend an estimated $135 million this year to put out about 10,000 house organs aimed at strengthening ties— and improving communications—between worker and employer. The industrial publications range from crudely mimeographed sheets in small plants to handsome, slick-paper magazines by big corporations, such as General Motors' Life-size *G. M. Folks* (circ. 500,000), and the *DuPont Magazine.*

Despite the immense outlays for company publications, a growing number of industrial editors are worried. They are well aware that many of the company publications are doing a poor job compared to the hard-hitting crusading of some 500 national, regional and local papers published (at far lower cost) by labor unions. Complained Koppers Co. President Fred C. Foy: "Union publications are fighting with both fists—fighting in unity and sometimes with complete lack of regard for the Marquis of Queensberry rules. . . . The question is whether management will get in the ring too or lose the battle for the minds of its employees on an editorial TKO."

A "Journal" Type of House Organ (Standard Oil Company, New Jersey, The Lamp, **Spring, 1959**)

Why are so many company publications in danger of losing this battle? The chief reason is that the majority deliberately pull their punches. Unlike union papers, which thrive on dispute and energetically exploit any issue that affects the worker's welfare, most house organs concentrate on personal notes and chitchat. They not only shun controversy but steer clear of any stories on company policies and problems. A recent survey of 75 house organs in the Los Angeles area showed that only 15% made any attempt to communicate management plans and policies; almost all the rest were filled with social and personal items.

Actually, surveys by Westinghouse and other corporations have shown that employees are least interested in personal items. What they want is stories on such subjects as the company's plans for the future, its employee benefit program, new orders for the company. Union officials recognize the failure of many companies to use their publications effectively. Said an Omaha A. F. L. leader: "There are so many ways the company could put their point across. If they'd come out in their house organ and explain why they're going to do this or that, who's going to be affected by a layoff, and how long it would last, then the employees would be able to make their plans. More often than not, they'd be willing to cooperate."

One reason company papers put out such a bland diet is that they are too often published by employees on loan from personnel and advertising staffs who have no newspaper experience. Furthermore, they have no contact with top management, have no idea of what goes on in the president's office. Some editors, in turn, often show an ostrich-like attitude to important stories. . . .

More and more corporations are changing the editorial content of their magazines in an effort to keep the employees up to date on all aspects of the company. For example, some 30 monthly tabloids published by the Ford Company for its U.S. plants give detailed reports on union negotiations. On-the-job grievances, once the exclusive domain of the labor press, are now thoroughly aired by companies such as Milwaukee's Line Material Co., which devotes an inside cover each issue to employees' complaints and answers. General Electric runs columns of answers to employees' questions on company problems and policies. Republic Steel uses its house organ to give employees a graphic breakdown of profits, has backed it up with a do-it-yourself picture story on cutting costs. Some corporations, such as Westinghouse and Standard Oil Co. of Ohio, regularly devote space to broad economic and political questions, e.g., private v. public power.

But many companies still hold back, fear that employees will lose faith in the corporate publication if management tries to express its

views or discuss union-management problems. Yet, polls of employees
by both management and unions have shown that, in general, employees put more faith in what they read in company publications
than they do in union papers. And publications which have dropped
the social notes in favor of stories on corporate problems have found
that their readership has jumped. Concludes one company president:
"In many companies, we just haven't given employees a chance to
hear both sides of the question. It's about time we started to do it."[7]

Annual Reports to Employees

One of the most effective pieces of employee communication is
the annual report. It is not usually the same annual report that is
issued to stockholders. It is written specifically for the employees
who help make the profits for the firm, not for those persons who
share in the profits of the firm.

Many large corporations are now utilizing this method to inform
their employees of factors in the companies' growth, financial position, new product plans, expansion programs, labor relations, and
a host of other vital areas.

The organizational plan is similar to that of the stockholders'
annual report. However, it usually has a "team" approach. The
letter from the president to his employees is written on a person-
to-person basis that attempts to impart information and arouse a
desire to further advance "our" company.

Recently there has been a good deal of discussion on whether it
is wise or not to issue one report to the stockholders and a different
one to the employees. Is there any reason to believe that the level of
communication must be different?

Many employers feel that the makeup should be different since
the average stockholder will understand "depreciation, funded
debt, and reserves" more easily than the average employee. Of
course, there is no "pat" answer on this. However, there is absolutely no reason to "write down" to the employee. As a matter of
fact, this might be an excellent way to antagonize him; he may well
resent what he considers a child's edition of the annual report.

On the other hand, there is good reason to have a separate report
for both stockholders and employees, but the level should be

---

[7] "Telling the Employees," *Time,* September 19, 1955. Courtesy *Time*;
copyright Time Inc., 1955.

proper. In the average industrial plant, the employee will appreciate receiving a separate report provided it is written for him about his company. One firm has produced a "comic strip" type of affair that has various "foldouts," cartoons, and broad generalizations. This would seem to be an insult to the average employee when he compares it with the dignified annual report submitted to the stockholders.

If the company has several thousand foreign-born employees, the solution is not a childish annual report for all workers. It is wiser to issue a bulletin type of report in the foreign language for those employees who would prefer it. The others should receive a report written at the proper technical (but readable) level.

Basically, then, it is felt that it is wise to issue a separate annual report for employees and stockholders. The former should be at least as detailed and technical in nature as the stockholders', but it should be written from a completely different point of view. It must be presented as "our company's liabilities," "we accomplished this," and "it is expected that we may undertake further expansion." The annual report for employees should be written in an interesting, informative manner about "our" company.[8]

Handbooks

In today's industrial society, the corporation is an extremely complex unit. Not only is its organizational structure vast, but its policies are frequently numerous and specific. No longer can the new employee sit down with the "boss" and learn in a few minutes what he may expect from the company and what the company may expect from him.

Today the new employee wants facts on the pension program: What percentage does he contribute and what does the company add to the "pot"? What may he expect per month if he retires at 60? At 65? And what happens to the money if he dies before retirement? And what special benefits do his children receive if they are under 21? And what portion is returned to him if he leaves the company?

And this is just one area. What about sick leave? Vacation privileges? Stock-buying plans? Employee profit sharing? Hospitaliza-

[8] This topic is discussed in Chapter 14.

Company Orientation Booklets for Employees (Brown & Bigelow, A Design for your Future; **The Brunswick-Balke-Collender Company,** In Business with Brunswick; **Ford Motor Company,** Going Places with Ford; **Illinois Central Railroad,** This is Our Railroad)

tion and surgical benefits? Educational training at company expense? Work hours? Overtime pay? Equipment breakage responsibilities? Credit union? Promotion policies? Salary schedules? And there are many more questions concerning what the company expects of the new employee and what he may expect from the company.

No, the "boss" can hardly take the time to answer all the questions and certainly another employee can rarely do a complete job. The answer, industry has found, is the company handbook— not a pamphlet of "rules and regulations" but a booklet explaining the rights and privileges of employees and the policies of the company.

The writing style should be friendly and natural, not commanding or dictatorial. The discussion revolves around "your company" and "our firm." The handbook not only attempts to inform the employee, but it also tries to build the worker's pride in the company; it endeavors to give him a feeling of security so that he will want to stay with the firm in the years to come.

The physical makeup of the handbook is most important. It should be so executed that the employee would desire to retain it. Certainly if an employer thinks it unimportant to provide a stiff cover, good-quality paper, clear printing, and attractive presentation, why should he expect an employee to keep the booklet carefully for future reference?

The handbook should be small, neat, and appealing in its appearance. The cover should be hard and the title clearly printed on it. It is wise to speak of "Policies for the Employees of the Acme Corporation" rather than "Rules and Regulations for the Employees of the Acme Corporation." Or it might be well to title it "Facts about Our Company," or "Welcome to Acme."

The handbook should make liberal use of color and reflect care and thought in planning and layout. The writing style should be much like other employee communications: friendly, natural, interesting, vital, clear, and at a dignified level.

Although the handbook cannot always present the precise details of a particular area, it can give the employee general information and tell him where he may secure "the fine points." For example, the handbook may not be able to explain the intricacies of a company stock-buying option plan based on differences in wage rates, market conditions, years of service to the firm, and the amount already held, but it can tell the employee whom to see or what company bulletin to read to secure the answer.

Some of the topics covered in the average handbook are these:

Company background and history	Layoff and resignation policies
Lunch and break periods	Policies regarding company equipment and records
Vacation privileges	Sick leave
Health services in the plant	Social security and pension benefits
Medical examinations	
Compensation:	Hospitalization and surgical benefits
Weekly	
Overtime	Advancement and promotion
Bonus	Safety rules
Labor organizations	Visitors
Recreational facilities:	Absences
Clubs	Use of company facilities
Sports	Suggestion systems
Hobby groups	Company publications

Today most employees beginning a job with a new firm expect to receive a handbook. Once they have the booklet in their hands, they feel the security we all enjoy when we know what we may expect from others and what is expected of us.

Letters to Employees

An outstanding characteristic of the letter—its personal touch—makes it one of the most valuable devices of communication to employees. Here is a message that is addressed to production worker John Anderson, and to John Anderson alone. It is true that it may be a form letter with a "printed" signature, but it was delivered to Anderson's house, it was in a sealed envelope, and it was directed only to Anderson. John Anderson will certainly recall the contents of this message in much more detail than if the same data appeared in a company bulletin that was inserted in each employee's pay envelope or slipped into every locker.

What is more, his family may read the message and discuss it. In this manner, activities of the firm become a matter of family concern.

A publication of the United States Chamber of Commerce lists a series of advantages that letters from management to employees possess:

1. Everyone likes to receive letters.
2. A letter carries its message directly to the person for whom it is intended.
3. There is always something personal about a letter, even when the person who receives it knows the same letter is being sent to others.
4. A letter can be timely. It can be built around a certain event or development.
5. A letter can drive home one point at a time. The next letter can drive home another point.
6. A letter can be made to appeal to the emotions as well as to the intellect. You can get closer to a person in a letter than you can in a printed statement.
7. A letter from the company is something a man is likely to show to his wife, and to talk over with her.
8. You can get out a letter in a hurry if need be.
9. Letters are economical.[9]

There are dozens of excellent opportunities for writing letters to employees. It is wise to welcome new employees to the firm with a letter; to explain company profits, employment policies, cutbacks in employment, or plant expansion; and simply to thank employees occasionally for their coöperation and efforts.

TONE OF THE LETTER

The tone of the letter should be natural and friendly; never pompous or patronizing. It should be informal, not stiff. It should be positive, not negative. It should be written from the employee's point of view, not the employer's.

POOR: Herewith enclosed as per monthly custom, a missive from the company's executive officer.

BETTER: Here is a message from one of your co-workers at the Excello Motor Corporation.

POOR: We hope that our firm will not encounter difficulties in the coming year.

BETTER: We feel certain that the approaching year will be a successful one for Excello.

[9] Chamber of Commerce of the United States, *How to Strengthen Employee Loyalty with Letters*, p. 3.

POOR: We are sure you are interested in the strides the company has made under its executive leadership.

BETTER: It is a pleasure to report that our firm has moved forward due to the combined efforts of every employee of Excello.

The letter should be personal, interesting, truly informative, and sincere. The examples given below demonstrate these attributes. From John L. McCaffrey, President, International Harvester Company:

To All Harvester Employees:

Several weeks ago I wrote you a letter about the condition of our Company's business. Many of you have been good enough to write back and give us your ideas. We really appreciate that and I want you to know it. The problems of this business are not just management's problems. They affect all of us and we want you to take an interest in them.

Naturally, my letter didn't answer all the questions you had in mind. No one letter could do that. Besides, we had to guess at what you would like to know. The only way we can be sure is for you to tell us. Maybe we won't always be able to answer your questions but we surely will try. So feel free to ask whatever is on your mind.

You might be interested to know that every letter I received from an individual employee has been answered, if the employee signed his name. Some employees didn't sign their names. I suppose they thought their bosses might not like it, or I might not like it, because some of them disagreed with me. People have been disagreeing with me all my life. They still are. One of the good things about our Company is that nobody has to agree with the president just because he's the president. I have learned a lot from sincere people who disagree with me.

Don't be afraid to ask what you want to know. Don't be afraid to sign your name. Nobody in this Company is going to get mad at you or penalize you for speaking your honest thoughts.

All of us need to understand our business better. We need to understand each other better. We are all in the same boat and we will go forward or backward together. So we want you to know how the management thinks. We sincerely want to know more about what you think. If you have questions, let's have them. You have a right to know about our business.[10]

Sincerely yours,

(Signed)

John L. McCaffrey

[10] *Ibid.*, pp. 20-21.

From John S. Coleman, President, Burroughs Adding Machine Company:

Dear Mr. Blank:

It is a real pleasure for me, on behalf of every member of the Burroughs organization, to welcome you to the oldest and best-known company in the business machine industry.

Perhaps you already know something about Burroughs, but here are a few things that might be of special interest, now that you are one of us. Our over-all job is to design, make, sell and service high quality precision machines used for all types of accounting and figuring work in the business world. At present, the demand for Burroughs products is the greatest in the Company's history.

Burroughs is truly a team in operation. Our engineers design new products and improve existing ones; people in our manufacturing plants build the highly intricate machines to satisfy the needs of customers; our salesmen study business methods and systems and sell our machines to firms throughout the world; our servicemen take their technical skill into the customers' offices to maintain the machines in top operating conditions; our executive, administrative and office staffs plan operations and do the necessary paperwork to keep the organization running smoothly.

You will find that every one of the thousands of men and women who make up our organization has an important part to play. They are a fine group of people who believe that Burroughs is a "better place to work." Because they like their jobs, they remain with the Company a long time. In fact, at least half of them have been here for more than ten years and many families have been represented in Burroughs for generations.

Burroughs has always been known for its steady employment and its high wages and salaries. Pay for legal holidays is not new to Burroughs; it has been in effect more than ten years. Payment of time and one-half or double time for overtime was started more than forty years ago, and vacations with pay, twenty years ago.

Since 1915 the Company has provided life insurance free of charge for its employees. Christmas and New Year's Eve are half-holidays with pay, to give you time off for last minute personal affairs. In the plant you will find modern cafeteria service and the best first aid facilities.

As a member of the Burroughs Company, you and your family are entitled to the privileges of the Burroughs Farms, a recreational center located on a wooded lake near Detroit. The facilities of the Burroughs Farms are maintained by the Company for the convenience and enjoyment of all members of the organization and their families.

You undoubtedly want to know something of your chances for advancement. It has always been our policy to give everyone an equal opportunity, depending upon his ability and interest in his work. The people who have moved forward in the Company have been chosen because they have shown that they can do a better job.

We in Burroughs are interested in you and all the people who work with us, interested in your ideas and your problems. We believe in freedom of expression and whenever you have any suggestions concerning yourself or your work, feel free to discuss them with your supervisor or other members of management.

I mention a few of the things Burroughs does for employees because I thought you might want to know how the Company feels about its people. I am also attaching the official statement of our policy, to assure you that Burroughs will always endeavor to be a "better place to work."

Again I want to welcome you as a member of the Burroughs organization and to give you my personal good wishes.[11]

> Sincerely yours,
>
> (Signed)
>
> John S. Coleman
> President

As indicated earlier, the tremendous value of letters lies in their personal quality. We normally direct more attention to a letter addressed to us than we do to a printed booklet, bulletin, or brochure.

The Pay Envelope Insert

Many firms have found that a message inserted in the pay envelope, along with the employee's check will be read carefully by the employee. This method of communication is certainly direct and effective. However, the company which utilizes pay inserts must be aware of two rather obvious factors. If every single pay envelope carries an insert, the employee will soon begin to feel that the messages are not vital, and he will give them only a cursory glance. Secondly, the firm should not present more than one idea on a pay insert. As soon as the insert becomes a bulletin announcing everything from the company picnic to contemplated plant expansion, its value is lost.

[11] *Ibid.,* pp. 4-5.

Pay inserts can be valuable if they are kept brief and pertinent and if they are used infrequently.

The Company Bulletin Board

Here is one of the most direct lines of communications between company and worker. Unfortunately, many firms ruin the value of the board. They permit it to become cluttered with stale and out-of-date notices. Or they will fill it with dull and uninteresting announcements that are merely cut out of other sources.

MECHANICS OF BULLETIN BOARD MAKE-UP

To be sure that employee bulletin boards do a good job, they should be located where they will be read. Good positions may be found near cafeterias, locker rooms, employee lounges, and elevator entrances.

The material on the boards should be changed once or twice a week. News items should be mounted attractively. Pasting a notice on a piece of colored construction paper provides a colorful background. Keep the board well lighted. Use clever art work where relevant: pointing fingers, dollar signs, bowlers, company products, and other decorations which add vividness to an announcement. Keep all notices up-to-date and vary the type of information.

EFFECTIVE USES OF THE BULLETIN BOARD

The bulletin board may be used for the following purposes:

1. To explain some of the financial activities of the company. These might be concerned with internal affairs, such as expenditures for machines, salaries, improvements, and expansion. External affairs, such as mergers or financial relationships with other companies, are also of interest to employees.
2. Safety records, incidents, rules, and suggestions may be announced on the bulletin board.
3. Basic economic facts may be presented. Information on taxes, cost of living, and local, state, and federal governments is of interest. Information on expenditures on housing, education, and defense are also of value.
4. Recognition of outstanding work or suggestions of employees should be posted as well as employee milestones measured in years of service.

| **FORD** MOTOR COMPANY | **EMPLOYE** Information Bulletin |

Starting Monday, March 3, the cost-of-living allowance
for Ford hourly employes is increased from 19 to 22 cents per
hour. The new amount is based on the Bureau of Labor
Statistics Consumer Price Index for January 15. The allowance
also is used in determining overtime, shift premiums, holiday,
vacation and call-in pay.

The Company's cost-of-living allowance has added 41 cents
per hour to wages for hourly employes since it was started in
1950. From June, 1953, through January, 1958, Ford has paid
hourly employes nearly $136 million in cost-of-living payments.

- 0 -

3/4/58

An Employee Bulletin (Courtesy of Ford Motor Company)

5. Union-management affairs may be announced on the company bulletin board and thus reflect a spirit of coöperation.
6. Notices of training programs and courses may also appear on the bulletin board.
7. Company teams and sports contests should receive management recognition.

These are only a few of the uses for the bulletin board; it can be a very effective and inexpensive device for employer-employee communications. A brochure from the United States Chamber of Commerce suggests several important "Don'ts."

Don't let the newspapers beat your bulletin board to press with announcements of changes in company policy or other news affecting employees. Tell your employees first.

Don't run the bulletin board haphazardly. Have someone with imagination responsible for maintaining it. Empower him to ask for news from the president to the janitor. Empower him to do this on company time.

Don't fill the board solidly with printed matter. Liven it up.

Don't make it too dignified. It needs to be human, with a lot of humor.

Don't let the items get out of date.[12]

Rack Services

This particular device of employer-employee communication began to grow rapidly in about 1948. It is a system of communication that is perhaps best described by its very name: rack service. Pamphlets covering a wide variety of fields are placed in metal racks. These pamphlet receptacles are then located at various stations in the plant where each employee may find it convenient to stop and examine the titles and help himself—cafeteria style—to those he finds of interest.

The subject areas that the pamphlets fall into are cultural, recreational, inspirational, historical, scientific, mechanical, economic, social, health, safety, and family. The pamphlets may run about 12 to 18 pages and are almost invariably attractive in format.

These booklets are always very informative. In just a three-month period, Western Electric employees could read pamphlets on the United nations, Thomas Jefferson, Paul Cézanne, Wood-Working Tips, How to get More Mileage from Your Car, and others. Each of these was well written and excellently illustrated. The booklet on Cézanne, for example, contained 13 full-color reproductions, and the text was written by the Curator of Paintings of the Metropolitan Museum of Art of New York.

[12] Chamber of Commerce of the United States, *Your Company Bulletin Board,* Washington, D.C.

Rack Booklets for Employees (How to Practically Drown-proof Your Family **and** The Meaning of Profits, **courtesy of General Motors Corporation;** Count Down to Survival, **courtesy of Western Electric Company; and** The Law Is on Your Side, **courtesy of Western Electric Company and March Press, Inc.)**

Large corporations maintain their own departments to write or edit the pamphlets; smaller companies may subscribe to a service. In such cases, deliveries are made and the racks are stocked by an outside agency.

General Motors estimates that in 109 months it distributed over 149 million copies of 625 different booklets through approximately 2,000 racks. Because the GM objectives for its rack service are so similar to all companies' purposes, they are cited here:

1. To keep employees well informed on the economic facts of life.
2. To offer health and hygiene education.
3. To help employees become happier, better adjusted individuals.
4. To build goodwill for the company.
5. To develop in employees the habit of looking to the company for reliable information.[13]

Perhaps the most agreeable factor to employees in all rack services is the voluntary aspect of the programs. The worker may pick and choose; he may take a copy or not; there is no "boss" present to see whether he does or does not. Then, too, the subjects are usually of interest to others in the family and this also motivates the employee to make a choice.

This chapter has discussed some of the types of employee communications. There are others, both formal and informal, which are utilized by various companies.

The editor should remember that whether the communication piece is a mimeographed "hand-out" or a beautifully printed brochure, it should have several specific attributes: it should be interesting, personalized, honest, accurate, adequately illustrated, well-written, and, above all, it should encourage two-way communication.

But a good system of communications does not just happen. It must be carefully organized, planned, and worked at. When this is done, the free flow of ideas throughout the company can be secured, and employer-employee relations are thereby improved.

QUESTIONS FOR DISCUSSION

I. Answer the following questions as concisely as possible.
   1. Can you cite and explain an example where no specific verbal or

[13] An announcement titled, "The GM Information Rack Service in Brief," dated, January 1, 1958.

written communication on a subject took place but yet an exchange of information nevertheless occurred? One example might concern the instructor who says absolutely nothing about the final examinations which have been scheduled by the dean for all classes during the week of June 2.

2. Is it true that when people know or are told about a situation, good or bad, they can "face up" to it more easily and rationally?
3. If a major state university contemplated publishing each month a house organ type of publication for its faculty, would you recommend the "newsy," "combination," or "journal" type? Why?
4. Do you think corporations should or should not issue separate annual reports for its employees? Defend your stand.

II. Carry through the requests made in the questions which follow.

1. Submit a house organ and a criticism of it. Your evaluation should note what sections are commendable as well as those which should be improved. In making your criticism, keep in mind the cost of printing, the reader, and other vital factors.
2. Assume that you are the president of a furniture manufacturing company that has 5500 employees. Write the introductory letter for the employee orientation booklet. Remember to attempt to motivate them so that they will read the entire booklet thoroughly.
3. Using the necessary indexes to periodical literature, secure a file of sources on the "rack booklets" supplied to employees by industry. Read those articles which are available to you and then present a report on "rack services."
4. Although the company orientation booklet clearly indicates that gambling is not allowed on company property, there is definite evidence that it is going on. Write a bulletin on this subject which will be posted on bulletin boards throughout the plant.
5. Mr. Ralph Smather, company executive vice-president, will retire on March 15 after 40 years of service with the company. Write an article on this topic for the company news magazine and another article for the weekly management-level bulletin. Mr. Smather began as an office boy, rose to foreman in the plant, production supervisor, personnel director, vice-president in charge of sales, and, finally, executive vice-president. Mr. Smather will receive a company pension of $25,000 per year.
6. Each issue of your monthly house organ has a column titled "Safety Pays." Injuries to workers are listed in this column with a statement explaining how the accident might have been avoided if proper precautions, such as wearing safety shoes, safety glasses, etc., had been taken. Last week Baker Brown suffered a com-

pound fracture of his left arm. The injury was entirely due to the mechanical failure of his press machine to operate properly. How would you handle this news item? Write it up.

7. A small branch plant of your corporation located at Martinville was closed down three weeks ago. It was 160 miles from the main plant; it employed 1675 people. The Martinville plant manufactured table model radios. The factory had been losing money for 18 months. In any event, the action of closing the plant has caused many rumors and lowered morale in the main plant. Write an article for the monthly company magazine explaining the situation. As far as can be seen at the present, production and employment level at the main factory will remain unchanged.

Chapter 16

Technical Writing

In our highly complex society, marvels such as color television, jet aircraft, and long-distance telephone dialing are looked upon as commonplace. Complex computers, interplanetary travel, and solar energy as a source of fuel hardly raise an eyebrow. Yet the magic these phenomena are able to perform is due to the meshing and coördination of thousands of infinitely complex working parts.

Someone was responsible for creating, developing, and perfecting each part. But as long as the idea remained in the mind of the technical artist, it could not be brought to fruition for the benefit of mankind. Somewhere along the line it was necessary to describe, explain, and clarify the functions and purposes of the transistor, the cathode tube, the vaccines, so that they could be mass produced, manufactured, integrated, and sold. Hundreds of persons, some with technical background, some without, had to understand the functions of the piece of technical apparatus or scientific advance before it could be accepted and produced.

In other words, the technical man must *communicate* his ideas to others so that the value of his invention or idea may be realized. This is done through *technical writing*—a specific type of written communication.

In today's industrial world, the need for technical writers continually increases. An article in *The Wall Street Journal,* entitled "What-Is-It Writers with Technical Skill Spin Out Short Story," had this to say in part:

WHAT-IS-IT WRITERS WITH TECHNICAL SKILL
SPIN OUT SHORT STORY

Firms Bid High for Engineers with Literary Bent;
Costly Devices But Costlier Words

Hysteresis motor stator insulation tester experts take note: There's a company willing to pay you $8,500 a year if you can explain what it's all about.

The company is combing the country for 15 literary-minded engineers who can turn out training manuals for this and other complex instruments.

And dozens of other companies are doing the same. The reason for the hunt is simply this: The hectic pace of technological innovation is creating an enormous demand for training pamphlets, operating manuals, parts catalogues and other technical documents. The demand is so large, in fact, that technical writing is getting to be a good-sized business. . . .

The Government estimates it spends close to $250 million annually for the preparation of technical works. Sperry Gyroscope Co., a division of Sperry Rand Corp., has enlarged its publications department from 20 men in 1941 to close to 300 now. Glenn L. Martin Co., maker of the Matador guided missile, started from scratch three years ago, and now has a staff of 279 turning out technical literature. . . .

International Business Machines Corp. has a multi-million-dollar contract with Uncle Sam to manufacture computers for the SAGE radar warning system; it also has contracted to turn out the necessary publications.

To produce the technical manuals, I.B.M. set up a special task force of 160 men, including 75 technical writers, at its new Kingston, N.Y., plant. This team, after nine months of work, sent out the first set of manuals a few days ago.

Each set contains more than 20,000 pages of data, and will fill a 12-foot-long bookshelf. I.B.M. will make up 1,000 different sets before it's through. . . .

"Publications Engineers," as one company calls them, usually get equal if not higher pay than technical men in more conventional fields. Top salary for an experienced writer ranges from $8,000 to $12,000, with editors receiving more. . . .[1]

This type of writing is characterized by its careful choice of technical and scientific language, its formal tone, its impartial

[1] *The Wall Street Journal*, December 4, 1956.

approach, its accuracy and conciseness in its presentation of facts, and its use of graphic aids. Technical writing is most frequently found in:

Technical descriptions of a piece of equipment

Descriptions of a process

Abstracts

Each of these will be discussed and illustrated in this chapter. However, the first step in discussing a complex, technical topic is to make sure that all persons concerned have a clear concept of the meanings of the terms employed. For that reason, it is often wise to utilize definitions in technical material where necessary.

THE SENTENCE DEFINITION

When the meaning of a term is presented in one statement, it is referred to as a sentence definition. At times, one statement becomes rather long and involved and in such cases it is wiser to secure clarity by splitting it into two or three shorter sentences.

Normally, the sentence definition contains the term to be defined, the group (or genus), and the discriminating statement (or differentia). The item to be defined is first placed in a large classification referred to as the group or genus. The differentia attempts to distinguish the item from the others in the same genus. Thus a sentence definition of a telephone might be:

The telephone (the term itself) is a communication device (the genus) which transmits and receives sound through electrical impulses through the medium of wire (differentia).

It is easy to see that many items fall into the genus of "communication device." There are television, radio, recorders, signal flags, blinker lights, and others in addition to the telephone. The technical writer's task, therefore, is to differentiate among the telephone and the others. This is done by indicating, through the differentia, that the telephone "transmits and receives sound through electrical impulses through the medium of wire." This cannot be said about television, radio, recorders, signal flags, or blinker lights.

The following examples might be used as samples of technical writing:

Item	Genus or Class	Differentia or Discrimination Statement
Fountain pen	A hand device used for writing messages or symbols. . .	which possesses a self-contained ink supply which automatically flows to the point.
Spark plug	A mechanical accessory of an internal combustion engine. . .	having two electrodes separated by a tiny arc gap across which the ignition system current discharges, forming the spark necessary for combustion.
Mortar	A military cannon or piece of artillery. . .	that is usually muzzle loaded and which throws a projectile limited distances at relatively low velocities. The course of the projectile may be at high angles.
Jeep	A motor vehicle. . .	that is multipurpose, with cross-country ability, an 80-inch wheelbase, quarter-ton capacity, weighing about 2200 pounds, equipped with four-wheel drive and capable of 60-mile-an-hour speed.

In all the examples given, the suggested routine has been followed: identifying the object as a member of a genus or class and then differentiating it from the other members of its class.

THE EXTENDED OR AMPLIFIED SENTENCE DEFINITION

Many objects or processes are of such a level of complexity that a simple sentence or statement will prove quite unsatisfactory to the reader. He will have unanswered questions concerning the function or application of the item under discussion. It is in these instances that the writer is wise to add a sentence or two which will further clarify the situation.

Chromatic Dispersion. The splitting of a white beam of light into different wave lengths, or frequencies (colors), by the action of a heterogeneous medium or by a surface which the light strikes at other than a normal angle. A classical illustration is seen in the spectrum produced by passing a light through a prism . . . different wave lengths are refracted to differing degrees by the same refracting medium, the highest-frequency waves (violet) being refracted the most, the lowest-frequency (red), the least, with a sliding scale of refrangibility between these two extremes. The scale of refrangibility, however, does not have a constant relation to the frequency of the wave, since differing wave-lengths behave differently according to the quality of the medium, so that the scale of refrangibilities for the wave-lengths will differ in differing media.[2]

In the illustration above, the author has gone beyond the simple sentence definition in an effort to answer the reader's questions of "how" and "under what conditions."

Any definition may be made clearer by using the following techniques:

1. *Illustrations and examples* of how the item or process works.
2. *Physical description* of the item defined.
3. *Analysis* of how a process works.
4. The *effect* a process may have on or in a given situation.
5. Offering of a *comparison or contrast* with a known item.
6. A *negative analysis* to indicate what the process or item does not do. This should be done after indicating what functions it can carry through.
7. Using a *diagram, sketch, picture,* or any visual device is a great aid in giving the reader a "picture" of the item or the manner in which the process works.

Of course, there is a variety of other methods in addition to these which would assist the writer in amplifying his definition. Sometimes a combination of two or more of the methods suggested above are used.

The technique that is employed and the depth of the definition is often predicated on the topic under discussion and the background of the reader. The following expanded definition was written for a specific group.

The die casting machine of today is a far cry from the laboriously hand-operated device with which this industry made its humble start

---

[2] Thomas G. Atkinson, *Oculo-Refractive Cyclopedia and Dictionary,* Chicago: The Professional Press, 1944, p. 82.

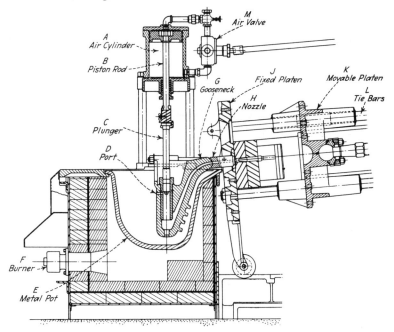

"Hot-Chamber" Die Casting Machine

shortly after the turn of the century. Most of the machines in modern die casting plants are almost completely automatic, with all major parts power-actuated. The rapid improvements of recent years in die casting machine design have not only greatly accelerated production speeds, but have assured the attainment of the utmost in properties.

The machine used in die casting zinc alloys is known as a "hot-chamber" machine. This machine utilizes a pressure chamber with an air, or hydraulically, operated ram. In die casting the zinc alloys, a supply of molten metal is kept in a holding pot at one end of the machine, with a cylinder and ram—or plunger—submerged to drive the required amount of zinc alloy automatically into the die cavity for each "shot."

The machine used in die casting aluminum, magnesium and copper alloys is known as a "cold-chamber" machine, in which the metal is ladled into the pressure chamber for each shot. This procedure is necessary in die casting the higher melting point alloys because these metals would pick up iron if left, in molten form, in. contact with an iron holding pot or plunger. This iron pick-up not only would cause

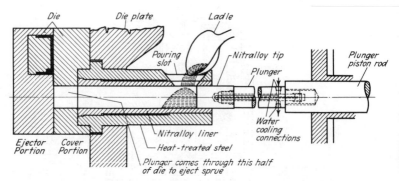

"Cold-Chamber" Die Casting Machine

the plunger to freeze in its cylinder and result in a short pot life, but it would affect the properties of the die castings produced.[3]

Position of the Definition

Because technical writing is usually directed to the reader with a scientific background, the definition may be included in the text of the discussion.

However, if the writer feels that the definition may break the continuity of the exposition or if the reader does not have a technical background, it may be wise to place the definition of terms in footnotes, in a glossary, or in an appendix to the report.

In any case, the writer, knowing his reader and the type of report he is presenting, will be in the best position to place the definition.

DESCRIPTION OF A PROCESS

In our highly technical society, it is vital that those who are concerned with developing and improving machinery and methods understand and appreciate the advances made by their colleagues. Like so much of technical and scientific writing, this is necessary to avoid duplication of effort and to build on top of the work of others. The technical man especially must know how a job or task

[3] Reproduced by permission of American Zinc Institute, Inc., 60 East 42nd Street, New York 17, New York, "Zinc Die Casting—Molten Metal to Finished Part," p. 7.

is carried through or in what manner a piece of machinery operates. This, then, establishes the two types of descriptions with which we are concerned:

1. The process where an individual plays the primary role. (Welding metals, developing photographs, making a hi-fi cabinet, carrying through a laboratory experiment, landing an airplane, etc.)
2. The process carried through where the functioning of a machine plays the primary role. (The work of a computer, the operation of a fuel injection unit, the functioning of an aircraft mounted radar, etc.)

Description of a Process Involving an Individual

In this particular description, it is probably wise to split the piece of exposition into four or five specific sections:

The introduction
A list of equipment and/or materials
Specific description of the action
Conclusion (if necessary)
Summary or recapitulation (if necessary)

THE INTRODUCTION

The introduction to the description should give the reader some indication of (1) what the process is, (2) the qualifications of the individual who performs the process, (3) why it is carried through, and (4) a bird's-eye view of the entire affair.

In describing what the process is, the first consideration must be the level of the reader. If the description of wiring a telephone switchboard is directed to a high school sophomore, one approach is used; if it is written for a college senior majoring in electrical engineering, a different path is followed.

The introduction might also indicate who performs the process. It is helpful for the reader to know what educational or experience backgrounds are necessary to perform the process under discussion. To carry through the process of blood analysis might not be too difficult to describe or even to do, but the educational background that a hospital or laboratory technician receives is important for an understanding of the implications of the blood findings.

Describing a new process of reinforcing concrete would be valuable and interesting to a structural engineer but might be boring or unclear to a high school music teacher. For all these reasons, the technical writer should clearly state who should perform the process he is describing.

Thirdly, in the introduction, the technical writer should tell the reader why the process is performed; what is its purpose, its objective. Of course, the "why" is often made clear in the definition or in explaining who carries through the job. For example, there would be no point in indicating why one roasts a piece of venison; the purpose is obvious. However, it would certainly be necessary to indicate that the purpose of taking a soil sample is to test the soil acidity and chemical content. Likewise, the writer should not only explain how to "ground" a power line but why.

Then lastly in the introduction, it is often a good policy to give the reader some idea of the entire process, or a "bird's-eye view." Perhaps this goes along with the old teaching precept of:

> First tell them what you are going to tell them.
> Then tell them.
> Then tell them what you told them.

Of course, this overview should be a very brief glance at the entire operation. Sometimes this is given in the mechanical fashion of a listing, but it nevertheless serves the purpose of preparing the reader for the step-by-step description of the entire process.

THE LIST OF EQUIPMENT OR MATERIAL NECESSARY TO CARRY THROUGH THE PROCESS

Although this listing does not have to appear as a separate section, there are certain advantages to noting the necessary instruments or pieces of apparatus immediately after the introduction. To stop periodically in the explanation of a process to introduce and describe a piece of equipment or material often interrupts the continuity of the exposition. It is usually wiser to present your listing first, as is the case in the following examples:

The equipment required to perform the assembly of a six-volt automotive storage battery includes:
A container
Plates
Separators
Lugs

Plate straps
Connector straps
Terminal posts
Vent plug
Sulphuric acid
Distilled water

The equipment necessary for a gas welding operation are:
One cylinder of oxygen
One cylinder of acetylene
Gas pressure regulators, gauges and connections
Two lengths of colored hose with adapter connections for the torch
  and regulators
A wrench for tightening connections
Welding goggles
Welding gloves
A safety flint and file gas lighter
A caustic soda solution
A wire brush
A fire extinguisher
A welding or filler rod
The material to be welded

THE STEP-BY-STEP EXPLANATION OF THE PROCESS

This portion of the description of the process requires the most space. This is the body, the central portion, the detailed explanation of each step.

As the process is explained, each step is taken up in chronological order. The writer should not only explain the action but also the results which may be expected from the action. This tells the reader what he can expect after carrying through the action. When the reader knows what the expected results are for each step or series of steps, then he can quickly recognize a situation which arises that is not according to plan.

The presentation should clearly indicate to the reader when one major step has been completed and another begun. This can be done by either using topic headings or simply stating "first," "second," etc.

One of the best devices the technical writer can use to assist his reader in understanding is the utilization of illustrations. Cutaways, diagrams, sketches or charts, if properly presented, all help the reader in assimilating the explanation of the process.

The type of illustration and the depth of detail in the explanation are predicated on who the reader is. Normally, however, a technically trained reader will be the one for whom a technical description is written.

All in all, each step must be clear and well-written; so completely so, as a matter of fact, that the reader must be able to *visualize* the action in the step under consideration.

CHLORIDE CONTAMINATION

General

This supplement covers the procedures to be used in the quantitative measuring of equipment chloride contamination in the Toll Crossbar Shop by the functional Inspection Organization. The technique used is the method developed by the Bell Telephone Laboratories.

Materials used in this test such as silver chromate paper, filter paper discs, reagents and other chemical supplies are to be obtained from the Chemical Laboratory Dept. 8267-1. The comparator to be used for measuring the diameter of the spots is the Pee Gee Pocket Comparator or equivalent, obtained from the National Tool Co., 1120 Madison Avenue, Cleveland, Ohio.

Scope

Measurements should be made on all frames prior to prepacking and shipment with the following exceptions: Trunk Frames 4.69F, S.F. Signalling Frames 4.69W and any miscellaneous frames that do not have adjustable apparatus.

A similar check should be made on frames and units as they are turned over to Inspection on a random sampling. At least three frames and three units should be checked each day.

Materials Required

Concentrated Reagent Grade Ammonium Hydroxide is necessary for extracting the chloride salts from the switch springs.

Extraction discs, 5/16 inch in diameter, punched from Schlicter and Schull No. 576 filter paper are necessary for the extraction step.

A spot plate, made by drilling conical indentations with only the conical end of a ⅜″ twist drill in Lucite, Plexiglas, or other nonwettable plastic, is necessary. The plastic used should be tested to determine that no chloride ion is extractable from the plastic by contact with concentrated ammonia or sodium nitrate solution.

Tweezers.

A pipette calibrated to deliver 0.05 ml.

1 molar Reagent Grade sodium nitrate solution in distilled (chloride free) water.

A fine tipped capillary pipette (as per sample left at Kearny).

Silver chromate impregnated paper. This paper is prepared by dipping Whatman #1 Filter paper in a solution containing 1.57g Reagent Grade silver nitrate, 360 ml. ethanol and 40 ml. distilled water.

The dipping is done by drawing the paper through the solution in a continuous motion. After dipping, the paper is hung in a dark room to dry. The bottom edge should be gently blotted to prevent a high concentration of salt along the edge.

The dipping is repeated (after paper has dried) in a solution containing 1.37g sodium chromate in 500 mil. distilled water. This second dipping operation should be done without any hesitation, the paper being lowered into the chromate solution at constant speed (about 10 cm/sec.).

The paper is immediately rinsed in 3 successive pans of water and again dried. The paper is cut so as to discard the areas of obviously variable density. The paper must be stored in nearly air tight containers in the dark. The paper should not be touched with fingers in the areas to be used in the determination.

A magnifying comparator is used for measuring the diameter of the bleached spots.

Solutions containing 0.5, 1.0, 2.0, and 4.0 micrograms of chloride ion per 0.05 ml. should be prepared for standardization of the paper.

A frame for holding the silver chromate paper should be constructed.

Procedure

The basis of the method is the areaometric determination. In this scheme, the quantity of material sought is measured by the area of impregnated paper which reacts with the material sought. Under ideal conditions the square of the diameter of the spot is proportional to the quantity of ion being determined.

The frames should be sampled so that the springs most likely to have received the largest amount of contamination will be extracted. At least two determinations should be made on each frame.

The ammonium hydroxide should be placed in a small beaker provided with a watch glass cover. The cover should be left in place except when dipping a disc. Extraction of the chloride is accomplished by dipping a *single* 576 filter paper disc in *fresh* (should not stand open for more than 2 hours) concentrated ammonium hydroxide and placing the disc on the contact spring in such a manner as to have as great an area in contact as possible and yet cover the outermost parts of the spring. The opposite side of the spring from the contacts is used. Care must be taken not to use the same spring for more than one extraction. The disc is allowed to remain in contact until practically dry. The disc is then transferred to a *clean* (wash with soap and water) spot plate. Every series of extractions should be preceded and followed by one or two blanks. The blanks are prepared by dipping a disc in the ammonia and then placing them on the spot plate.

The discs are allowed to dry completely before proceeding with the leaching. The last blanks will be the best indication of complete dryness.

Leaching is accomplished by measuring 0.05 ml. of 1 m sodium nitrate into each disc on the spot plate. Make sure that each disc is submerged in the solution. The batch is allowed to stand at least 1 hour and not more than 1 3/4 hours. While standing, the plate should be protected from dust or other chloride containing foreign material.

After standing, the solution is taken up in the small pipette. Great care should be exercised to recover as much solution from the paper as possible.

The silver chromate paper is then placed in its holder. The tip of the pipette is then placed in gentle contact with the center of the exposed paper area and a gentle puff of air or tap is applied to start the capillary flow of solution into the paper. The flow must be allowed to continue without further air pressure (unless the flow is interrupted). Some pressure must be maintained between the pipette and paper to avoid flooding.

The silver chromate paper must be allowed to dry before the spots are measured.

The average diameter of the spots is measured with the optical comparator.

Calibration of the paper is done by running 0.05 ml. of the standard solutions into the silver chromate paper and plotting the square of the diameter versus the amount of chloride. This plot should be linear or nearly so. Each different batch must be calibrated separately and a batch should be recalibrated if more than 2 weeks have elapsed since the previous calibration.

The spot on the back of the paper is usually less ragged and therefore, more easily measured. If calibration is carried out measuring the back of the paper, the back may be measured in the analysis.

The average of the major diameter and the diameter at right angles to the major diameter should be taken as a measure of the area of the spot.

To record data in accordance with the present accepted standard of micrograms of chloride ion per square centimeter, rather than per unit area, the final relay and switch readings should be multiplied prior to recording by a factor of two (2) and three (3) respectively.

Limits

All frames and units having readings of 5.0 or below 5.0 micrograms per square centimeter shall be considered conforming.

All frames and units having readings in excess of 5.0 micrograms per square centimeter shall be deferred from shipment, immediately notifying the Functional E of M Organization for disposition.

If four or more micrograms per square centimeter is found on any one frame or unit, the E of M should be notified and measurements on three frames and three units prior to pre-packing and shipment shall be made daily until notified by the E of M to do otherwise.

Recording of Results

The information required is as specified in the TX Contamination Record Form.

The E of M Contamination Report Form is compiled from the analysis of the fiscal period Contamination Record Forms. The report should be forwarded to the Functional E of M Department by the second day of the fiscal week following the week tests are made.[4]

The Conclusion and Recapitulation or Summary

After you have offered a thorough explanation of a process, there may be no need to write a conclusion or offer a summary. On the other hand, you may wish to state in a concluding statement the importance of the process, how it fits into a larger project, or what its particular value is in a larger study.

Offering a summary or recapitulation is also of value when a specific series of steps has been followed with meticulous detail and you wish to have your reader keep the order clearly in mind. Then, too, it is often helpful to recall to the reader's mind the vital points which were followed in the process.

The technical writer will find that his ability to write a creditable description of a process will be very valuable. There are countless occasions when he will be called upon to explain technical activities to his colleagues, his administrators, or the general public. He must always keep in mind, however, that a description of a process is not a "how-to-do-it" guide. Although it may contain instructions on how to carry through a project, it also tells the reader who com-

[4] Reproduced by permission, *Manufacturing Handbook, No. 18,* Western Electric Company, Inc., Engineer of Manufacture, Kearny.

pletes the activity, why it is carried through, and the importance or function of the action.

The writing of the second type of process, where the functions of a machine play the primary role, is essentially the same as the type discussed above.

WRITING THE ABSTRACT

The abstract is one of the most important sections of the report simply because it is the most frequently read by the executive to whom it is directed. Whether it is referred to as a summary, a digest, or an abstract, it still serves the same purpose—that of summarizing the report in the fewest words possible for the conservation of the reader's time.

Although it may be a sad blow to the ego of the report writer, he must recognize that his abstract will be read more frequently and more attentively than his report. As a matter of fact, it is not an infrequent occurrence for the busy executive to read only the summary or abstract, the conclusion, and the recommendations of the reports he receives.

The technical writer has frequent use for abstracts. Not only does he make up an abstract of the report he writes, but he must also prepare abstracts of technical articles for his own notes and future reference and also for the colleagues with whom he is working.

All the tenets of good writing must be followed religiously and scrupulously in writing an abstract. There is no room for wordiness, digressions, or illogical organization in an abstract. Of course, the same is true in other writing efforts, but when the material is longer (than an abstract), the errors of digression, verbosity, and irrelevancies are not as noticeable as they are when they appear in an abstract. Conciseness, therefore, is a key quality in the writing of this type of exposition. Every word must count; every phrase must be necessary.

Before the report writer undertakes the writing of an abstract, he must be completely familiar with the material. This is one of the most important steps. *Complete familiarity with the content* of the basic article, its organization, its items of emphasis, and its point of view are requirements if the report writer is to write an accurate abstract.

A frequent error that is made in writing an abstract is to summarize *each* paragraph of the original. Certainly to read a paragraph, condense it, read the next, and then condense that, is unwise. The original article undoubtedly contains paragraphs of transition, illustration, and example. Material of this type may have no place at all in the abstract.

The writer must read the entire article carefully, make notes on the vital material, and then write the abstract using his notes, outline, and the original as his foundation material.

The abstract should also reflect the organizational pattern of the original article. If the original author used a chronological or geographical sequence in his article, the writer of the abstract should do the same. This is also true of emphasis. The abstract should not give major importance to a point that is given only minor treatment in the original.

Clarity of expression is vital in writing the abstract. Be especially careful of word choice, sentence structure, and overall presentation.

Types of Abstracts

Abstracts are usually divided into two groups. One is *descriptive* which simply tells the reader the *topics* which are covered in the original article. The second type is more truly an abstract. It not only indicates the topics but also summarizes each one in adequate detail. This is sometimes referred to as an *informational* abstract.

Length of the Abstract

To state what the length of an abstract should be is foolhardy. Some authors advise that an abstract should be about 20 percent of the length of the original material. Other writers suggest everything from 5 percent to 25 percent. But to follow any figure is dangerous because you may be writing an abstract of a very wordy article or one that is extremely concise in its presentation. What, then, happens to the 10 or 20 or 30 percent figure you are trying to follow?

The safest course is to read the original carefully, familiarize yourself with it intimately, make your notes, sketch your outline, and then write the abstract as concisely as possible, choosing the words and approach that will appeal to the particular type of reader who will use your summary.

Perhaps, too, the writer of the abstract should keep Abraham Lincoln's advice in mind. When that President was asked how long a thoroughbred colt's legs should be, Lincoln replied, "Long enough to reach the ground." We might rephrase that and say that the abstract should be long enough to cover the material concisely and clearly.

The following two examples are abstracts published by a technical journal.

Optimum Noise Performance of Linear Amplifiers (Haus and Adler, p. 1517)—This paper introduces an important new measure of the noise performance of any given type of linear amplifier. This measure takes into account not only the impedance of the source connected to amplifier input and the noise figure of the amplifier, but also the gain of the amplifier stage. By taking gain into account it is able to deal with the case where feedback is applied to an amplifier, a situation in which former measures of noise performance broke down. This new measure of noise thus makes it possible to specify the best noise performance achievable with any type of amplifier. Perhaps the most important property established by the new noise measure is the fact that a cascade of amplifiers of different types cannot have an excess noise figure at high gain that is better than that obtained with amplifiers of the "best" noise class alone.[5]

Unmanned space ships capable of orbiting about the moon have passed from the realm of science fiction and are now an acknowledged goal of the near future. If we wish to place instruments on board and telemeter information back to earth, what will be the requirements for the radio system? If we figure on a 10 watt transmitter aboard the vehicle operating at 2250 mc, a 500 kc bandwidth receiver, and make certain reasonable assumptions concerning the characteristics of other parts of the system, it turns out we can readily span the 260,000 miles with a 4.8 foot antenna on the vehicle and a 60 foot receiving antenna on earth. However, if the same ship is to orbit about a nearby planet some 100 million miles away, the problem becomes more formidable. The transmitting antenna will have to be increased to 60 feet in diameter, the receiving antenna to 84 feet, and the receiver bandwidth reduced to one kilocycle. These and other requirements imposed on the system probably could not be met by presently realizable techniques. However, there seems little doubt that the kinds of improvements that are needed to make a planetary telemetry system feasible will be well

[5] "Scanning the Issue," Institute of Radio Engineers, *Proceedings of the IRE*, August, 1958, p. 1461. Reproduced by permission.

within our capabilities in the near future. (H. Scharla-Nielsen, "Space Ship telemetry," *IRE Trans. on Telemetry and Remote Control,* June, 1958.) [6]

An example of a more extended and complete abstract of a technical article is the one that follows. This abstract is taken from a paper entitled "Capacitance Measurements in Terms of Time."

Early Western Electric Company methods of measuring the electrical characteristic "capacitance" of a capacitor were by means of microfarad meters or capacitance bridges.

Over the past 25 years, modifications of the microfarad meter have been used. This modification utilizes segments on the face of the meter to which the pointer makes contact by electro-mechanical means to operate external circuitry to accept or reject the product tested or to direct the product automatically in one of several channels. The test time required for a meter of this type is approximately three seconds.

The capacitance bridge may be designed for high accuracy measurement, but the relatively long test time required and circuit switching problems involved for automatic testing make this method undesirable for high level production testing.

Additional facilities required for increased production levels necessitated faster testing than could be accomplished with traditional methods.

A survey of the commercial test equipment field revealed no equipment having the necessary capabilities; therefore, development work proceeded with the following design objectives:

1. Accuracy to approximate that of a precision capacitance bridge
2. Testing time to be one-quarter second or less
3. Adaptable to mechanization
4. No moving parts subject to the "wear and tear" of multi-shift shop use

Several methods of approach to accomplish these objectives were considered.

Since time is one of the basic units that can be measured accurately and at high speed, development work centered around a suitable means of measuring capacitance in terms of time. The resistance-capacitance relationship ("time-constant") of a capacitor charged through a resistor is a very exact time interval. A method was devised to start an electronic counter which counted its own internal precision pulses when the capacitor on test began to charge through a resistor. The

[6] "Scanning the Transactions," Institute of Radio Engineers, *Proceedings of the IRE,* August, 1958, p. 1545. Reproduced by permission.

counter then stopped when a predetermined voltage level on the capacitor was reached. By the proper selection of circuit parameters, the time interval measured by the counter will be the value of the capacitance on test.

This new method of measuring capacitance by the time-constant relationship meets the design objectives, and has resulted in substantial labor saving. This method with digital read-out, has opened a new field of potentialities applicable to other forms of testing in similar electronic problems.[7]

TECHNICAL DESCRIPTION

Technical descriptions are written on a variety of different simple and complex items: mechanical devices, nonmechanical objects, miscellaneous pieces of equipment, physical facilities, weather conditions, or a piece of construction.

In every case the purpose of this type of writing is to give the reader an accurate, visual picture of the object and at the same time tell him what its purpose is.

Because most of us have read and discussed literary descriptive writing, it might be wise for us to note that it is vastly different from technical description. Literary descriptive writing attempts to give the reader the emotional as well as visual picture of the object or situation. It tells the reader not only how the item looks, feels, and smells but also the emotional, psychological, and physical effect it produces. The technical description limits itself to a formal word picture of the object under discussion. Thus, an air conditioner, utilized on a hot, sultry day, might be "a magical box bringing blessed, cooling relief from the stifling, unbearable, blanket of sticky, hot humidity that enveloped the city." The technical description might simply indicate that "it was a ¾-ton air conditioning unit using a standard compressor and capable of adequately cooling an average household area of approximately 400 square feet."

The technical description is usually part of a longer piece of writing or a report, which may appear prior to the presentation of data, analysis, conclusions, and recommendations.

[7] This abstract was written by the author of the original article: Harry R. Shillington, "Capacitance Measurements in Terms of Time," *The Western Electric Engineer*, July, 1958.

Organization of a Technical Description

Any good description begins with a definition of the object to be described. Next, a general description—size, shape, materials— follows. Thirdly, a more detailed description of the component parts is given, and, finally, there is a concluding or summarizing statement.

The definition which is given should indicate what the object is and its purpose. What has already been said about definitions also applies here.

The best conveyor is an endless moving belt for transporting materials horizontally or on an incline up or down. The drive pulley is at the head end or at an intermediate point along the return run. A take-up, located preferably just behind the drive pulley, adjusts the tension in the belt. The load is discharged over the head or at any point along the carrying run by a plow scraper or a "tripper."[8]

Following the definition, a brief overview of the object may be given. This general "bird's-eye view" helps the reader to visualize the relationship of the component parts.

Detailed Description of Parts

With this general picture in mind, the reader is now better prepared to appreciate the component parts. This part-by-part description follows a logical pattern. Each part of the device is introduced, defined, and described. In other words, the description of each part is similar to the technical description of the entire device: an introduction, a definition, a detailed analysis, and perhaps a conclusion.

The parts should be presented in a logical order. In some cases this might mean listing one part, then the part that works with it or activates it, and so on, through the entire device. In another case, it might be more logical to present the exterior parts of the device first and then those on the interior. In a different situation it might be wise to describe the major part and then the minor ones that contribute to the functioning of the central unit. In any case, the writer, considering his device and his reader, should choose a logical presentation of the parts.

[8] Reprinted with permission from W. G. Hudson, *Conveyors and Related Equipment.* Copyright 1954, John Wiley Sons, Inc., p. 205.

In describing each part, it is a good idea to give the following information:

Its name and function
Its size and shape
The material from which it is made
Its relationship to other parts and to the device as a whole

The technical writer must always be aware of the danger of a mechanical, uninteresting presentation of one part, then the next, and then the next, always following the four steps listed above. The solution, in part, is variety in word choice, differences in depth of detail, and change in the order of the information presented

Of course, the writer understands that many of the usual and expected parts of a device are not described. These might be screws, bolts, braces, rubber cushions, and other miscellaneous parts. If a very special and unusual type of screw or brace is used, it probably should be included in the description. Ordinarily, however, these items of attachment, support, or separation are taken for granted.

The following is a portion of the technical description of a skip hoist taken from the book, *Conveyors and Related Equipment*. It is important to note that several illustrations and much of the original discussion do not appear below. This was done to conserve space in this book.

The Skip Hoist

In simplest form the skip hoist consists of a guided bucket raised and lowered by a cable attached to a hoisting machine, with provision for loading the bucket at the lower point of travel and discharging it at the top of the run. The path of travel is determined by the guides. . . .

Applications and Limitations. The outstanding advantages of the skip are: its few moving parts; its ability to handle material which contains large lumps or is abrasive or corrosive; and its adaptability to high lifts and large capacities. With high lift and large capacity the first cost will, as a rule, be less than for any other type of mechanical conveyor. The skip is easily adapted to the formation of reserve storage as an auxiliary function either through a by-pass at the head or by an intermediate discharge point to form a pile, on the far side of a track hopper, which is then spread out and reclaimed by a bull-dozer, caterpillar crane, or drag scraper. . . .

Types. There are three types of skip hoists: . . .

Loading. Each type may be loaded by an automatic loader which controls the flow to the bucket. The three general types of such loaders are: . . .

Control. There are two control methods: . . .

The Hoist. This is the all-important part of a skip hoist, and it has reached a high state of development by various manufacturers. . . . The grooves are machined and polished. The heavy drum shaft is carried in three anti-friction bearings, two of which are arranged to take end thrust. The intermediate shaft is mounted in two anti-friction bearings which permit centering of the herringbone gears. The high speed shaft has two anti-friction bearings which will take any end thrust from the floating armature of the motor. All bearings are automatically lubricated, and outside bearings are sealed. The motor is either a direct-current compound-wound or an alternating-current high-torque squirrel cage, connected to the reducer high-speed shaft through flexible coupling which forms also the brake wheel of the solenoid brake. The traveling cam limit switch is connected by chain drive to the intermediate shaft. The base is a rigid welded steel frame with the joint between the upper and lower halves of the gear housing machined for an oiltight fit. This description serves to indicate the careful engineering entering into the modern skip engine.

The Bucket. Skip buckets are of heavy steel plate in the form of an open-top rectangular box. They are rated in cubic feet waterlevel capacity with the bucket vertical. In a skip having a flat, inclined path the working capacity of the bucket is reduced. Four flanged wheels guide it along the runway. As a rule, the leading pair is set to a narrower gauge than the trailing pair so that when the bucket approaches the dumping point, the forward end moves horizontally while the trailing end continues upward until the bucket reaches the discharge position. The "bale" or yoke is pivoted and extends slightly above the top of the bucket, where connection is made to the hoist cable. If loading is automatic, suitable steel roller arms on the front plate of the bucket engage the loader at the approach to the lower end of the run. . . .

The Counterweight. As the bucket of the counterweighted skip enters the dumping rails at the top of the lift and tilts, much of the load is taken off the hoist cable. As the counterweight at this moment has nearly reached the lower limit of its travel, brackets are provided to lift off part of the weight sections and maintain balance. This is called the "compensating counterweight." A spring connection between counterweight and cable reduces the shock when starting and stopping.

Cables and Sheaves. The cables are the vulnerable part of a skip

hoist and should be of the highest grade obtainable. Sheaves should be
of ample diameter. If the cables show damage from bending, a replacement with a cable of larger diameter is useless. . . .

    Capacities and Power Requirements. . . .
    Comment. . . .
    Maintenance. . . .[9]

In most cases a concluding or a summarizing statement after each
part is unnecessary and might result in a boring and verbose presentation. Such a statement might be in order, however, for the
primary part of a device.

Amount of Detail

The detail with which each part is described is naturally dependent on what purpose the description is supposed to serve and who
the reader is. Obviously, if the description of the device is going
to be read by an engineer who wishes to improve on the function
or design of the item, it should be highly detailed. If it is meant
for one of the firm's business managers, it might be rather general.

Use of Illustrations

Here, as in many other cases, the use of a cut-away drawing, a
sketch, a schematic, or a table or chart might aid the reader tremendously in his understanding of the device described. Every effort to
improve the appearance of the report should be made. Excellent
visual representation, variety in type size and style, and attractive
binders will all assist you in securing for your report the readership
which it deserves.

Concluding Comments on the Technical Report

An excellent and brief statement on the preparation and importance of the technical report is contained in the booklet, "Technical
Writing."

A report is frequently the only permanent thing that comes out of
an investigation. It is false economy to skimp on a report which represents the spending of anywhere from ten to a hundred thousand
dollars and years of time. We have examples of developments where
large sums were spent and valuable information was obtained without
ever being adequately reported. It has then been necessary to duplicate
expensive and time-consuming work years later when the information

[9] *Ibid.,* pp. 53-69.

was badly needed to solve some immediate problem. In many types of projects we are dealing with ideas and broad generalities rather than specific devices, and these must be put in such a form that others may use the experience. Work not adequately reported has no permanent value except for the one person who originally did it.[10]

QUESTIONS FOR DISCUSSION

I. Answer the following questions as concisely as possible.
  1. Why is there a much greater demand for technical writers today than there was 15 years ago?
  2. One authority insists that good technical writing is based on precise sentence definitions. Comment on this point of view.
  3. Quote two sentence definitions from your textbooks and point out the class or genus and differentia or discrimination statements in each. Cite your source.
  4. What specific attributes should the introduction in the description of a process possess?
  5. What are the different patterns which may be followed in writing a conclusion in a description of a process?
  6. What specific factors should the technical writer keep in mind when writing an abstract?
  7. Submit a technical description taken from one of the journals in your field of concentration along with your criticism of it. Your criticism may be based on the requirements for technical description which are listed in this chapter.
II. Criticize the following sentence definitions.
  1. A seagoing freighter is a ship which carries goods.
  2. A tractor is a piece of farm equipment used in the fields.
  3. A briefcase is a leather container, usually rather flat in nature, easily portable, and designed to carry papers.
  4. A compass is a magnetic device which indicates the directions on the earth.
  5. A speedometer is a mechanical device which measures an auto's speed.
  6. A station wagon is a four-wheeled vehicle, similar to an auto but designed to carry more than the usual number of passengers and/or merchandise.
  7. A rocket is a self-propelled physical agent.
  8. A tomato is an edible fruit, usually red in color, about the

[10] Thomas O. Richards and Ralph A. Richardson, *Technical Writing,* Detroit: General Motors Corporation, n.d. (Reprint of a paper given at the Conference for Teachers of English in Technical Schools, 1941), pp. 10-11.

size of a human fist, pulpy in texture and possessing a high liquid content.

III. Submit a sentence definition for each of the terms listed.

1. Salt	6. An automatic toaster
2. Thermostat	7. Calculus
3. Generator	8. Stationery
4. Profit and loss statement	9. Fog
5. A ball-point pen	10. Coffee

IV. Write a description of a process of any of the following or one assigned by your instructor. Attempt to limit your discussion to about 1000 words. Include any graphic or visual aids which will help clarify your discussion.

1. The process of auditing the books of a small retail establishment.
2. Developing and printing photographs.
3. Water filtration for human consumption.
4. The process of market research to determine consumer desires.
5. The process of testing the strength of concrete.
6. The process of "tuning up" an automobile motor.
7. The process of _____ (fill in a chemical reaction).
8. The process of running a motion and time study on a specific job.
9. The process of testing a television set to determine the cause of malfunction.
10. The process of selecting a sample of television viewers for a program evaluation.

V. Criticize the following abstracts.

1. This article is very interesting and gives a clear picture of what is involved in using transistors in guided space missiles. Of course the article is rather general in nature because it only deals with transistor utilization in declassified missile systems.

It is unfortunate that the author's strong bias in favor of conventional tube systems forces him to constantly depreciate the value of transistors. However, those of us who have had clear evidence of the efficiency and reliability of the transistor know that he is all wrong.

J. R. Rallie, "Transistors in Space," *The Journal of Electronic Components,* June, 1959.

2. This brief article discusses one of the most controversial topics in public school education: How should gifted children be handled?

Three methods of educating this student are discussed.

First the author lists *acceleration* and points out the advantages of placing the child in a challenging class. Acceleration also keeps the student from becoming bored and frustrated. However, he is usually grouped with older children who may be ahead of him socially and physically; both factors which can lead to personality maladjustment. Then too there may be areas of play or learning which he will never be exposed to.

Enrichment of the gifted students' curriculum has also been attempted. This permits the child to remain with his social group while he carries through advanced work. However, few teachers can find adequate time to formulate a good program. Often teachers assign "busy work," somehow believing this is enrichment.

Special classes or schools is a third method discussed by the author. This places gifted children of equal abilities in the same environment thus maintaining a challenging situation. Of course it is a very expensive arrangement.

These three areas of handling gifted children are discussed carefully by the author.

F. P. Anton, "Educating Gifted Children,"
American Education Journal, May, 1960.

3. This particular piece of exposition examines the relative merits of using natural gas or electricity as the major agent in industrial air-conditioning units.

The author lists the advantages and disadvantages of each system. These reactions were secured from 30 plants' engineers who were interviewed according to a carefully devised questionnaire schedule.

For those plant engineers who are considering the installation of air-conditioning equipment, this article is "required" reading.

F. Levin, "Gas vs. Electricity in Industrial Air
Conditioning," *The Engineers' Monthly*, February, 1960.

VI. Criticize the following descriptions of a process.

1. The Process of Distilling Water

Distillation is a simple process in which a liquid is converted into a vapor (usually by the application of high temperatures), and the vapor is then condensed back to a liquid.

In the distillation of water, the objective is to remove various components, such as calcium and lime, from the liquid. The result is relatively pure water which can be used in a wide variety of medical, chemical, and pharmaceutical operations.

Almost anyone of reasonable intelligence can distill water; no special technical skills are required.

The apparatus needed is inexpensive:

A retort   Stopper
Condenser   Collecting container
Bunsen burner

The first step in the process is to place the water to be distilled in the retort. Using a rubber stopper, the condenser is attached to the open end of the retort. This attachment of condenser to retort should be above the water level. The condenser should be so designed that vapor which turns into liquid may drain into a recovery vessel of some type.

Heat is then applied to the retort through some mechanical means such as a bunsen burner or gas or electric heat source. The temperature is maintained at a level sufficiently high to cause the water to boil. As this reaction takes place, vapor rises which circulates through the condenser. The ambient air around the exterior of the heat exchanger causes the vapor to condense. This condensate then drains into the recovery unit or collecting container.

This process may be continued until the desired quantity of distilled water is obtained. If a large amount must be secured, the process may be speeded up by placing the condenser completely in a medium such as water or oil which will expedite the operation of vapor into liquid.

A final word concerns the method. If the water is to remain pure and distilled, the operator must be sure that foreign or contaminated materials are not easily added to the distilled water.

2. The Process of Gas Welding

The process of gas welding joins metal parts by fusion. This fusion takes place after heat is applied to the metals, causing them to melt and flow together, thereby forming a single piece of metal. Because this process of welding requires skill and care, it should be attempted only by a competently trained person.

The equipment and material necessary for carrying through this process include a cylinder each of oxygen and acetylene, pressure regulators, gauges and connections, colored flexible hose, goggles, welding gloves, a safety flint and file gas lighter, a wrench for tightening connections, a caustic soda solution, wire brushes, a filler or welding rod, a fire extinguisher, and the material to be welded.

The first step is really preparatory to the welding operation.

This includes connecting the regulators to the cylinders, and the hoses to the regulators. The tanks are attached to some object so that they will not tip over.

The hoses are then connected to the gas regulators on one end and the torch on the other. Soapy water is then applied to all joints to detect any escape of gas.

After the leak test, the proper tip is selected for the welding torch. The tip is chosen with consideration of the thickness of the metal to be welded.

The next step involves preparation of the materials to be welded. It is usually sufficient to clean the material with a caustic soda solution. Loose particles, dirt, and chips may be scraped away using a wire brush. Sandblasting will remove a coat of paint or varnish. The edges of the metal to be welded are then beveled down to an angle of about 45 degrees.

The welder then lights the acetylene by using the safety flint and file gaslighter. He then turns on the oxygen and regulates the flow from both tanks to achieve a good cone of flame. Of course the welder has his goggles and gloves on during this operation.

The welder now carefully lowers the torch and welding rod toward his work area. Both the metal surface and welding rod should then be heated and the molten metal flows into the groove. The molten mass is permitted to fill the groove until the latter is slightly higher than the surface of the metal. The welder than moves along the entire seam until the length has been completed and filled.

When the entire area has been covered, the operator should inspect it for any imperfections. If none are found, the job has been completed and the weld may then be ground down to a level surface with the use of a grinding wheel.

The process of gas welding is really quite simple. The one factor to be kept clearly in mind is the need for care and caution in handling the torch. It can be a very dangerous tool.

3. The Process of Color Coding Plastic Wire

Cables used in telephone central offices contain hundreds of wire conductors which must be identified and connected to their corresponding terminals. To take advantage of the superior qualities of plastic—which is replacing textiles as insulation for wires used in these cables—a way had to be found to color code the plastic. The use of solid colors alone wouldn't do the job since there were not enough different colors.

Some time ago, Bell Telephone Laboratories suggested a coding system of colored dots and dashes, and asked Western Electric to develop a means of applying these markings.

Our engineers decided to place the coding operation at a point where the wire emerges from the extrusion machine with a hot, semi-hardened coating of polyvinyl chloride . . . before it reaches the cooling trough and take-up reels. Since coding had to be done at a speed of over 2000 feet per minute —to match that of the production line—the relatively slow contact printing devices then available were not satisfactory. In addition, contact printing itself was undesirable because the coding instrument might damage the soft plastic as it came from the extruder. In short, there were no machines available that would code plastic insulated wire at the extrusion speeds required by Western Electric.

The basic problem in developing a high-speed coding machine was how to apply the marking ink. Initially, trials of a modified paint gun apparatus proved futile due to inability to control the size and location of the ink markings.

A concept for a new machine employing rotary ink ejectors was finally developed. These are hollow motor-driven disks, having removable rims into which .018″ holes are drilled in desired combinations.

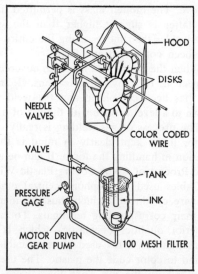

Schematic Drawing of a Color Coding Unit (The Western Electric Engineer, **July, 1958**)

To color code both sides of the wire, two of these spinning disks are placed in tandem and the wire passes between them. It passes close to the outside rim of each disk and ink fed into the hollow of the disks is forced out in radial streams, impinging on the plastic wire coating. By varying the arrangement of holes in the rims it is possible to apply various combinations of dots to the rapidly moving wire. Dashes are recorded by drilling holes in the rims so close together that the dots on the wire merge into a dash before the ink dries.

By simply changing the rims, it is possible to switch from one code to another. To shift ink colors, the system is flushed with a cleaner and the new ink added. The ink supply can be varied to suit the speeds of the wire and the disks.

The development of this machine permits the production of color coded plastic insulated wire at high extrusion speeds. It is one more step in the constant improvement of telephone equipment made by Western Electric as manufacturing and supply unit of the Bell System. This is another example of the way Western Electric's engineering ingenuity continues to bring you dependable telephone service . . . at low cost.

"How to Color Code Plastic Insulated Telephone Wire at 2000 Feet per Minute," *The Western Electric Engineer,* July 1958, p. 50.

Chapter 17

Oral Reports and Conferences

Foremen, superintendents, department heads, administrative officers, specialists, and many other individuals in commerce and industry are required to carry on verbal communication with individuals and groups throughout the day. Much of this communication is made up of directives and reports. It is on the basis of these that day-to-day activities are carried through, important decisions are made, and vital actions are taken.

There are dozens of opportunities each day for the man who aspires to be a leader, or is now in such a position, to use oral communication in a simple, direct, natural, forceful, and effective manner.

Unfortunately, there are many people who have a vast fund of training and knowledge; yet when called upon to speak or participate in a conference or to discuss matters with a group of men, they can only fumble, bumble, and stumble around. These persons suffer by comparison when contrasted with accountants, engineers, or executives whose oral communication is fluent, forceful, and effective.

When an individual expresses himself convincingly and persuades others to accept his point of view, he is practicing important qualities of true leadership. It is for this reason that adeptness in oral communication is so important to the young person who aspires to be a leader in commerce or industry.

In today's busy world there are many opportunities to utilize the different forms of oral communication: speeches, formal discussion groups, interviews, conferences, and oral reporting. Ability to communicate well in all these situations will prove gratifying and profitable. When the effective speaker convinces an audience, he enjoys almost immediate satisfaction. But in addition to this obvious advantage, the speaker gains in confidence in himself. The ability to speak effectively builds one's assurance in himself as almost nothing else does.

But it takes more than assurance and confidence to make a good speaker. It takes a great many attributes, some of which will be discussed in the pages which follow.

PRINCIPLES OF SPEAKING

The Message or Content of the Talk

The audience expects the message to be worth while, interesting, clearly presented, and logical. Regardless of how excellent the delivery of the talk may be, if the content is shallow, unimportant, misleading, or poorly organized, the speech will prove unsuccessful. No amount of skill in voice projection, use of gestures, or excellence in other areas of delivery can compensate for, or hide, an empty message. The message must be worth listening to. If it is of value to the audience, it should be delivered in the most effective manner possible. If it has little or no worth, there is no point in dressing it in the false cloth of excellence in presentation. The audience is never "taken in."

Study the background of your listeners so that your talk will accomplish a specific purpose. It may clarify a situation, analyze a problem, introduce new data, answer questions, or explain a process.

The address should be grounded in the experiences of the members of the audience. There is little point in citing examples involving office procedures and home ownership if your audience, by and large, works in factories and lives in apartments. Experiences which are used in the talk should be meaningful to the listeners; they should be presented from the point of view of the audience, and in the vocabulary level that the group will appreciate.

The message must be honest in content, valid in its conclusions, and reliable in its recommendations. There should be adequate factual evidence to substantiate your statements, and the organization of the talk should be logical and clear. The speech that possesses these qualities will reflect the integrity of the speaker

and will hold the attention of the audience and command its respect.

The Speaker and His Attitude

It is interesting and somewhat surprising how an audience evaluates the personal qualities of a speaker. Although the address
may be concerned with one topic only, every listener will form
some opinion of the speaker's personality, his generosity, his kindness, his honesty, his understanding, and his character. How are we
aware of these intangibles and how do we arrive at judgments in
these areas when the talk is concerned with "Free Trade and
Europe"? The answers are many and complex; suffice it to say,
however, "Speech is revealing as is no other activity."

The speaker must possess a good attitude toward the people in
his audience. He must respect them as individuals and he must
appreciate their point of view. If he thinks disparagingly of the
group he addresses, that fact—regardless of how well he tries to
hide it—will be apparent. The speaker must have a desire to meet
his audience on common ground, to speak to them on matters of
mutual interest, and to inform them on topics of importance.

The speaker must always keep in mind that the content of the
talk is what the audience is interested in; they are not especially
concerned with the speaker. Any attitude he displays, voluntary or
involuntary, of self-superiority, sarcasm, or boredom will obviously
detract from the message, and the primary purpose of communication is lost. The speaker who receives from his audience penetrating
comments of agreement or disagreement on his topic may feel sure
that his message, and not the man, dominated the talk.

The speaker has a definite obligation to say something important and meaningful to his group. He should never talk for the
sake of talking, even if it is only for 15 minutes; with 50 people in
the audience he would be using 50×15 minutes or more than
12 hours—an inexcusable waste of time.

The audience expects the speaker to be a man of many qualities:
he should be an individual who possesses high integrity, a pleasant
personality, an optimistic outlook, poise and confidence in himself,
sincerity in his attitude, interest in the group, and a dynamic
approach to the problems presented.

The Appearance of the Speaker

The speaker who holds himself erect, walks energetically, looks alert, smiles occasionally, and dresses well commands the respect of the audience.

The speaker whose posture sags does not impress his group with his energy or alertness. He should stand erect and walk confidently to and on the platform. Slovenly posture habits are associated with careless physical and mental habits.

His clothing should be suited to the occasion; a business suit for most occasions; formal wear when that is appropriate; sports clothes when they are in order. In every case, the garments should be neat and clean. Centering a tie, adjusting the collar on a blouse, or tugging at a jacket are all activities that will catch the attention of the audience and detract from the message.

The Presentation of the Topic

As in the presentation of all reports—oral or written—a primary consideration is the listener or reader. The speaker must always be sure that he has a clear conception of the attitudes of the listeners, their sympathies, and their interests. If possible, something about their economic, intellectual, and social level should also be known. With such knowledge in mind, he can plan his speech more effectively; it isn't enough that the speaker know what topic he is going to talk on, he must also know what approach his audience will appreciate.

Perhaps you have heard the story of the successful investment counsellor which illustrates this point. This gentleman was asked to deliver a talk at the city college. He chose as his topic, "Basic Principles in the Purchase of Stocks and Bonds." Because he was requested to speak at the college, he assumed his audience was made up of young college students who had little background in investment finance. However, when he arrived, he found that it was Alumni Day at the school and he was expected to address men who had become quite successful in business. Obviously his initial plan had to be revised completely; he could still speak on stocks and bonds, but he would now be required to approach it from a completely different angle.

The speaker who knows the desires, wants, aspirations, and

needs of the group and then directs his talk in line with these, will usually find that his address will receive a favorable reaction.

Organization of the Communication

Good organization is good organization regardless of whether it is applied to written or oral communication. What has been said, therefore, in the earlier chapter on outlining applies here just as well.

Briefly, however, the speaker should:

Decide on the *purpose* of the speech, conference, or meeting.
Select the *thesis* of the talk.
Check the *limits* of the topic to insure that it is not too broad (establish the scope).
Make an *outline* of the talk.
Gather *data* using available primary and secondary sources.
Plan *visual aids*.

As noted above, the speaker should decide in the early planning stage of his talk what its purpose will be. Will he try to convince his audience? Persuade them? Inform them? Or what?

The theme or thesis of the talk should also be decided on as early as possible. If the purpose of the talk is to motivate the assembled salesmen of the firm to sell more, the theme may be one of many. Perhaps the speaker could use the core idea of additional financial return for the salesmen; or he might suggest that more sales would result in a stronger company; or the theme running throughout the talk might be that the salesman with the best record would win a promotion to a staff position.

A strong recognizable theme is vital to a good talk; it provides continuity and firmly impresses the key idea on the listener.

The next step is to check the limits or scope of the topic. If the subject is too broad, the treatment will be general and superficial. If it is too narrow, the interest of the audience may be lost. It must follow a reasonable path. As noted in the chapter on outlining, a topic may be narrowed by imposing chronological, geographical, or other limitations on it.

The speaker should then make up his outline, dividing his talk into introduction, body, and conclusion.

The introduction should show the members of the audience their relationship to the topic, and it should also arouse their interest. The body should develop and explain the subject matter, and the conclusion should summarize and emphasize key points.

The outline of the talk should be prepared and then revised as data are added or cut out.

Now the speaker must gather ammunition to substantiate and strengthen his comments. Like the author of a written report, he must use his primary and secondary sources as profitably as he can. The same techniques should be used as suggested in the chapter on "Gathering Data."

Notecards should be made up, according to the outline form, for reference during the talk.

In the final evaluation, the speaker will usually have several instances where visual aids will prove of value. These may be models, charts, or diagrams which can be displayed on the platform.

This discussion covering the purpose, thesis, limits, and outlining of the talk plus data gathering and planning for visual aids all points up one important factor in oral communication: *preparation—preparation—preparation*—insures a good talk.

Use of Visual Aids

The use of visual aids will assist a speaker in securing a very effective presentation.

When we *listen* to an explanation of an idea or a device, we will usually assimilate what the speaker wishes us to grasp. However, when our hearing is supplemented by visual representation of the item under discussion, understanding is greatly increased. The eye finds it easier than the ear to transmit to our brains the relationship of parts to a whole. Even "points to remember" listed by the speaker on a board or a large sheet of paper are a help to the people in the audience.

Although the speaker encounters some slight additional work in arranging visual aids, this is well worth the effort. Often it is the visual aid which makes the difference between the speaker's achieving his objective or not.

Among the many devices which may be used are blackboard illustrations, pictures, posters, actual products, models, movies, slides, mock-ups, and drawings on large sheets of paper.

The experienced speaker knows that there is a precise time to display his visual aid. If it is visible before the time needed, the audience concentrates on it while the speaker is covering a different topic; thus the attention of the group is lost. Then, too, when the attention of the listeners is directed to it, it is no longer something new to be examined, and the desired impact is lost. Thus the aids should be available for showing at the precise time they are desired.

When displayed, they should be easily visible to every member

Utilization of Visual Aids in an Oral Report

of the audience; size should be adequate and the position on the table or easel favorable.

If facts are to be written out, it is wise to print the data on large sheets of paper and place them on an easel or affix them to the board at the most effective moment. Ideas may be written on the blackboard while the speaker is talking, but at best, it is not recommended. There are few speakers who can write as they talk and keep the attention of the group. To turn your back on the audience as you write on the board is an unwise procedure, for eye contact is thereby lost and often audience interest as well.

One lesson a teacher or speaker learns early in his career is never to pass out display articles or printed matter while talking. Almost invariably the attention of most of the members of the class or audience focuses on the material distributed. Not only has the speaker "lost" his listeners, but frequently several will begin a discussion concerning the item and disturb not only the speaker but other members of the group as well.

In every case of using visual aids, be sure that *you* dominate the platform; permit your audience to examine the visual aid, but never get yourself into a position where the audience subordinates you to the visual aid.

THE DELIVERY OF THE TALK

Up to this point we have considered briefly the preparation for the talk and, to a lesser degree, the content. Now a brief discussion of the delivery is in order.

Choice of Words and Word Use

It has been frequently pointed out that a primary purpose of communication is to transfer ideas. And ideas are made up of words; therefore, our supply and use of words must be excellent, for if they are not, the idea suffers. Words have precise meanings, and as has been said elsewhere in this text, the *exact* word should be used in the *exact* place. The more extensive your vocabulary is, the easier is the task of saying exactly what you wish with fluency and confidence.

In speaking before groups you must be sure that your choice of words will be easily understood by the listeners. So often we become so deeply involved in our own areas of specialization, from plumbing to surgery, that we forget that the meanings of our specialized words are not known to everyone. Analyze your audience before speaking to make sure that the vocabulary you use is clear to them. Do not hesitate to cite analogies or related incidents which will add clarity to the idea you are presenting.

Certain words arouse emotional reactions among most of us. Words like *strike, labor leader, scab, agitator, communist, liberal, delinquent, psychotic* may evoke a controversial reaction among some listeners or may be defined much differently by some people as compared to others. They may arouse prejudice, build support, or evoke opposition.

The speaker should also use as many descriptive words as he can to help his listeners not only in their understanding but also in their visualization of ideas.

We must always keep in mind that words in themselves, and one by one, have little value. Placing several well-chosen words in a series helps us express our *ideas;* they are the *tools* with which we transfer our ideas to others. To convey ideas effectively the exact words must be chosen and delivered.

Pronunciation and Enunciation of Words

Pronunciation of words should be accurate and according to the standard found in a reputable dictionary. If more than one pronunciation of a word is given, the speaker should use the one accepted by or familiar to the audience. Affected pronunciation of words, or what might be construed by the audience to be affected, should never be given.

When the sounds of vowels and consonants are produced clearly, good enunciation is achieved. The sounds for words are the result of the different positions formed by the tongue, teeth, lips, and shape of the mouth. The sharp and exact use of these physical properties produces clarity in the enunciation of words.

Careless or sloppy enunciation is usually the result of sheer laziness in the use of the mouth, tongue, and lips. The good speaker opens his mouth, moves his lips, places his tongue against his teeth, and carries through all necessary oral movements with energy and accuracy.

Enunciation of "yeh" for "yes," "dontchathink" for "don't you think" and "we're gonna" for "we are going" is the result of careless, lazy speaking habits.

It is also possible that poor enunciation is the result of a physical incapacity, such as missing or malocclusion of teeth, a cleft palate, and other conditions. When such is the case, medical or dental attention is required.

However, when poor enunciation is the result of negligent speaking habits, then it should be corrected. The audience, as it listens to continued carelessness in speech, can only reflect on the speaker's competence.

Voice

Much of the reaction of the audience to a talk is dependent on the speaker's voice. A voice that is pleasant in tone, adequate in volume, and interesting in the variation of its timing in delivery will certainly prove to be an asset to the speaker.

VOLUME

It is obvious that if the speaker wishes to have his ideas accepted, the audience must be able to hear him easily.

The volume should be adequate so that every member of the listening group, whether he is sitting in the first row or the last, can hear the speaker "comfortably." If the voice is too low, listeners must strain to hear, and that is undesirable. Many persons will soon find the action too much effort and simply give up.

If the volume is too great, it is uncomfortable for the audience. Too often, if the voice directed at us is too loud, we feel we are being shouted at, and again we lose interest.

The volume should be carefully modulated and pleasant. This is not an easy feat to achieve but it can be done through practice and thought.

One of the most important factors in volume is *variation*. Interest may be achieved by the raising and lowering of voice. However, this should never be mechanical nor affected. More volume should be achieved spontaneously, and it should be related to the immediate idea being presented. Heightened interest may also be achieved by lowering the voice, but here, too, it should be a natural sequence to the idea being conveyed. The speaker who pounds on the table as he raises his voice to a shout or lowers it to a conspiratorial level—for no good reason at all—soon loses his audience.

PITCH AND RESONANCE

The speaker's voice that is pitched too high is not easy to listen to; it is often the result of tenseness, emotion, and strain. Sometimes, in an effort to make himself heard by everyone in the audience, the inexperienced speaker may raise the level of the pitch so that his voice soon sounds like a screech, but his volume is not raised appreciably.

The voice that is pleasantly and adequately pitched usually functions in the individual's middle range. If your voice has a tendency to rise when you speak before a group, you would be wise to start at a conveniently low level.

An important thing is to check your voice pitch periodically.

Practice in rooms of various sizes; have your friends listen to you and offer constructive criticism as to pitch.

At the same time, you should strive to improve your resonance. As the vibrations from your voice resound within your chest and head cavities, resonance results. Resonance may be achieved by speaking "from your chest" rather than "from your throat."[1]

ACHIEVE A NATURAL AND CONVERSATIONAL TONE

A voice that is friendly, natural, and conversational carries with it a warmth that is persuasive and convincing. Any affectation, any hint of superiority, any artificiality will certainly result in an unfavorable attitude on the part of the audience.

Probably the best way to achieve a friendly and natural tone is to believe in your audience and in what you are saying to them. There is no better way to secure this than through the natural friendliness which arises spontaneously among people of good will.

Rate of Delivery

One of the most important factors in securing effectiveness in the communication of your ideas is the rate at which the message is delivered.

If you speak rapidly, your thoughts become difficult to follow. The listener must constantly strive to keep pace with you; he is on the "edge of his chair" all the time. If, on the other hand, you speak very slowly from the beginning to the end of the talk, he may become bored, irritated, or inattentive; his mind may dwell on topics other than the one being discussed.

Speak with verve and vitality; not too rapidly, not too slowly. Your ideas must be expressed fast enough so that the members of the audience must give you their attention in order to assimilate the facts you present.

Rate of delivery is also dependent on the subject matter, the audience, and the speaker. Some topic areas, because of their complexity, require more time in delivery. Audiences also vary with their ability to "stay with the speaker." And, of course, the speaker himself may be rather slow or fast in his overall activity.

However, the speaker can control his rate of delivery if he con-

[1] The mechanics involved here are explained in detail in almost any standard speech textbook.

centrates carefully. He should speak with vitality and freshness, but he should also be aware of how much interest he can secure by the judicious use of variety in rate. An audience that has become somewhat apathetic or unresponsive will become alert if the speaker dramatically slows or increases his rate. But this variation should always be predicated on the content; you cannot suddenly speak rapidly or slowly, with interest and excitement in your voice, if the subject matter does not warrant such a delivery.

Variation is an important key for the speaker who wishes to maintain the interest of his audience.

A speaker who is not familiar with his own rate should time himself by reading from selected passages. Most people find a rate of about 150 words per minute easy to deliver and also pleasant to listen to.

Gestures and Posture

Movements of your head, hands, face, shoulders, or any part of your body while you speak may be classified as gestures.

Gestures are an invaluable aid in helping us express our ideas. Think of how difficult it would be to give directions, or explain how to carry through a particular process, without using gestures.

The movement of your hands, your eyes, your face, all help tell your story and convey your moods. Perhaps the most important fact in achieving meaningful gestures is to make them natural and spontaneous. Nothing looks so ridiculously stilted or artificial as planned and planted gestures which appear at precise moments in the delivery of a talk.

The speaker should forget his inhibitions and gesture freely, naturally, and spontaneously according to his desires. However, he should not gesture to the point where the audience can only concentrate on the many and varied movements he exhibits. When this occurs, the dominant theme of the talk is subordinated to the variety of movements made.

Posture is another factor the speaker must keep in mind, for in this category also the audience "grades" the man on the platform.

What would your impression of the speaker be if you sat in the audience and reflected on the slouched, careless posture of the man in front of the group? You might assume that the individual's ideas and principles were as slovenly as his posture. When you stand erect and vigorous on the podium, you command attention. Certainly your speech can hardly be forceful or enthusiastic if you lean, lounge, or slump.

Not only should your stance on the platform be firm and straight, but the same should be true of your movements before the group. When you walk to the stage or to the front of the room, stride forward with confidence and assurance. If you are sitting on the platform and you are called to the rostrum, move with vigor and energy.

Eye Contact

This simple speaking device can be of great assistance in securing the attention of your audience. Visual contact is nothing more than "looking into the eyes" of various members of your listening group.

Choose various persons in different parts of the room and look directly at each from time to time. When you do this, you find yourself talking to individuals and not at the audience in general.

Looking directly at members of the audience keeps them alert and intent on what you are saying. They will concentrate on your comments and respond by reflecting, in their own eyes and faces, the interest they feel.

Poor visual contact can be very damaging to the speaker who wishes to convey his ideas. Think of instructors you have had or speakers you have heard who have gazed out the window, stared at the floor, or "attached their eyes to their notes" as they spoke. You soon lost interest; you might just as well have been listening to a tape recorder or a record. The point of the matter is that the audience feels that the speaker has little interest in the topic or the group if he does not look at his listeners. The quality of directness is lost.

But the speaker who looks at his listeners arouses their interest and captures their attention. Such an audience is compelled to maintain close contact with the speaker.

PRESENTING THE ORAL REPORT

Although the world of commerce and industry utilizes written reports at every turn, the oral report is almost as popular. Oral reports are given to directors, managers, committees, conference participants, work teams, and other types of individuals or groups. A written report is often the basis for the oral presentation, but there are some definite differences and some similarities in the preparation and composition of each.

Evaluate the Listeners

Here, as in the case of the written report, you will be required to adapt your content, word choice, visual aids, and organization to the type of listener in your audience. All of these factors, and others, will vary according to whether your group is made up of the salesmen, the directors, the engineers, or the stockholders of the Excello Television Corporation. Analysis of the listening group is, therefore, your first step.

Once you know the educational, economic, and social interests and backgrounds of your audience, you can prepare your oral report intelligently. However, you must have this information; it will determine what types of sources you should use, how you will organize the talk, and how and where you will place your emphasis.

Visual Aids

These must also be prepared with great care. The graphs or charts should be clearly understandable to the listener. If a complex bar chart should be utilized, make it up, but if this particular audience would be more likely to appreciate a group of pictograms, then this should be employed.

You should be sure that your visual aids are clearly visible to every member of the audience. A wise idea is to check this fact before you give your report. You should actually take your charts into the room, mount them, and then determine if they are clearly visible from all parts of the room.

Hand-outs

Sometimes you will find that your report will include facts, figures, or statistics that are quite involved. In such cases it might be wise if each member of your group had the information on a sheet of paper in front of him so that he could readily refer to it as you speak. This is certainly easier for the listener than if he is required to stare at a blackboard that is 50 feet in front of him.

The same is true of samples of equipment or products. If everyone who is listening to you can actually feel, assemble, take apart, or in any way examine the item for himself, he will gain much more than he will if he must look at the one you are holding.

Methods of Oral Report Presentation

The way you present your oral report should be determined by several factors: the level of your audience, its familiarity with the topic under discussion, and how much printed information, if any, you have distributed or will give out during the talk.

READING THE ENTIRE REPORT

At times it may be necessary for you to read the entire report. This occurs when you must secure accuracy. However, this method is not recommended unless you have no alernative.

If the report is rather extensive, it will be most difficult for you to sustain the continued interest of the audience. Reading to a group can be a deadly experience for both, especially if the speaker launches into a boring monotone.

Therefore, you should avoid this method, if possible. If it is necessary for you to read the report, do it with spirit, feeling, and understanding.

Go through the report before you present it; underline all words and phrases you wish to stress and emphasize. Know which words and phrases are to be read in groups. Indicate on your manuscript where your pauses should be short, where long. And perhaps the most important factor is not to read too rapidly. It is much more difficult to grasp the meaning of spoken statements than those which are written. If the reader is not sure of the meaning of a printed statement, he can go back over the material. But, of course, this is not possible when you listen to a talk being delivered. For these reasons, the speaker should deliver his message slowly and carefully.

THE ORAL REPORT

The straight oral report is usually much more effective than any other type. This is very much like a speech and permits the speaker to use visual aids, maintain good eye contact, and enjoy freedom of movement. Regardless of how well the report has been prepared for oral delivery, it is still wise to have a few prepared cards which list the main topics. As the speaker finishes one topic, he can quickly and easily go on to the next after a rapid reference to his note cards. Of course, the speaker must be very well prepared if he is to deliver this type of report successfully. He should know all the points thoroughly as well as statistics which he will cite. Nothing breaks the continuity of a presentation as much as the delay caused by the speaker who fumbles around trying to find "that slip of paper" that contains his statistics. In every case, thorough preparation is the key to the successful presentation of an oral report.

ORAL SUMMARY OF A WRITTEN REPORT

Giving a summary of a written report is not as simple as it may seem. The speaker must prepare a careful abstract of the entire written report. He must be sure that in the specific span of time allotted to him, he covers the essential facts in the report and substantiates the recommendations which he makes.

Conciseness, careful selection of details, and excellence of delivery are absolute necessities in this type of presentation. Here, too, the speaker will probably find that note cards listing the key points will assist him in making this type of oral report.

THE CONFERENCE METHOD

The conference is an excellent device to analyze a problem, pass along information, or establish policy. It may be as simple and informal as a "bull session" among a group of students or as delicately complex as a high-level meeting among the heads of several nations.

In business and industry the conference is one of the most effective methods of pooling the ideas and experiences of several people for the purpose of solving various company problems. When utilized in commerce, it cannot be informal or haphazard; it must be planned and organized with accepted procedures and clearly defined objectives.

Most organizations hold a variety of conferences each day. There

may be meetings among the management echelon, the sales directors, the men engaged in research, the engineering and planning
personnel, and others. In all cases, ideas are exchanged and decisions reached. In every instance it is necessary to plan the group
meeting carefully, for conferences can be very wasteful if not
properly arranged and directed.

The men who participate in conferences are frequently among
those who receive the best salaries in the firm. If each of the 15
men attending is compensated at the rate of four dollars an hour,
and two and a half hours are spent in discussion, the company has
spent $150 on the meeting. This figure is exclusive of other costs
which are incurred. But whether the cost is $50, $150, or
$550, a good deal of money is spent. If the conference is un-
planned, it will probably be unproductive and the money spent
(let alone the time) will be wasted.

There are other unfavorable results which may be the end product of an inefficient conference. If any group of intelligent men
meet to discuss a topic without first establishing a plan—arguments,
confusion, delays, bickering, and general ill will may result. In
such a case, the company would have gained more by not having
the meeting at all.

However, there are no mysteries involved if a successful conference is to be held:

The participants must feel the need for the conference.

The "climate" must be friendly.

The objectives and plan of the meeting must be clearly defined.

The participants must be prepared.

The leader must be competent.

The Need for the Conference

The participants in a conference must feel that a need exists for
the meeting. Everyone in industry is busy and short of time—or at
least this is what everyone says. Therefore, when a man spends
two or three hours at a meeting, he wants to be sure that the time
will be profitably used. Thus, he must be convinced *before* he attends the conference that there are problems to solve, decisions
to reach, or recommendations to make.

It is sometimes wise to indicate the nature of the discussion on
the memo announcing the time and date of the conference. This

permits thought and preparation before the meeting takes place.

Another method is to prepare a mimeographed form which lists the problem (drop in sales, safety problems, new plant or machinery purchase, change in administrative policies, etc.), the time and date for the meeting, and a roster of those men who will attend. With this information in hand, each of the participants can begin his preparation and increase his knowledge of the topic by research and informal discussion at lunch with other participants.

The conference leader can also visit each of the participants before the meeting and briefly discuss the topic; the need for the scheduled conference is then emphasized.

Or it is possible to open the meeting with a discussion of the problem, thereby establishing the need. However, this may not permit time for preparation on the part of the conferees.

Regardless of what method is used, the participants should be convinced that a real need for the conference exists, that it is not being held to satisfy someone's whim or desire.

The "Climate" of the Conference

The atmosphere of the conference should be friendly and agreeable. Antagonism, hard feelings, and disagreeable attitudes should not be brought into the conference room. The meeting is not the place to get rid of such feelings, "get even," or display an "I'll show them" attitude.

If problems or situations are to be examined objectively, there must be a desire on the part of the participants to coöperate with one another and share ideas and knowledge.

This requires that everyone's ideas be listened to and respected. All members should feel free to speak and voice their opinions, even though these may disagree with the opinions of the manager or boss. Every participant must feel that valid contributions will not only be heard, but if they are accepted, they will be acted on. It is very frustrating for conferees to spend several hours planning, discussing, and recommending action to the employer if their suggestions will not be followed. Morale drops and future conferences are looked upon as a waste of time because "the boss does what he wants regardless of what we suggest or how often we meet."

Every effort should be made to promote a friendly, coöperative atmosphere among the participants.

The Objectives and Plan of the Conference

Before the conference takes place, there should be a clear understanding of the objectives. The discussion will vary if the objective
is to find the reasons for the drop in sales or if the objective is to
find methods for increasing sales. It is true that both topics are
related, but they nevertheless should be discussed separately and in
proper order.

The plan for the conference should also be established, insofar as
possible, before the meeting. This is usually the conference leader's
task.

The plan should include the objectives and an outline to cover
the scope of the discussions.

Objective: To develop an effective method for employer-employee
communications at Martin Metals Company.
  I. Discussion of the Present Informal Word-of-Mouth Plan
      A. Advantages
      B. Disadvantages
 II. Methods Used by Excello Manufacturing Company
      A. Pay envelope inserts
      B. Bulletin board notices
III. Methods Used by Farmington Brass Company
      A. Weekly news sheet
      B. Bulletin board notices
 IV. Methods Used by Bricmont Tube Company
      A. Monthly printed report
      B. Monthly plant meetings
  V. Possible Plans Which May Be Used at Martin Metals Company

Additional Materials
      A. Blackboard
      B. Samples of communication media used by other companies for
         distribution to conference participants
      C. Cost figures (approximate) for weekly news sheet and
         monthly report if utilized by Martin Metals Company

This is a brief "working plan" which the conference leader may
use as a guide. Of course, the discussion may move to other related areas, but the leader should make an effort to see to it that
these topics are covered in the time allotted for the meeting.

In addition to these plans, arrangements should be made for

proper seating, demonstration materials, films, and viewing equipment if they are to be used, and all other details which will assist in providing for an efficiently run meeting.

Preparation of Participants

It is sometimes said facetiously that a conference is a pooling of ignorance out of which emerges misconceptions. This may be true if everyone who attends has not prepared for the meeting and comes "to find out" or to insist that his point of view—right or wrong—be accepted.

However, if the participants are informed of the plans and objectives of the meetings, and requested to prepare, they will do so. By carrying through necessary research in company records and in secondary sources, by interviewing key employees, by observing a production process, by visiting another plant, and by a hundred other methods, they can come to the meeting well prepared.

It is often wise to ask the participants to prepare a written brief, outline, or series of points to bring to the meeting. There is nothing that helps all of us to organize and crystallize our thinking as much as the requirement of writing it down. Ideas which seemed logical and clear often become hazy and nebulous when we write them out.

The conference leader can help his participants prepare by sending them a mimeographed copy of the working outline. Of course, none of the points should be phrased as though a conclusion has been reached: "Why Plan A is impossible to accept" or "Why Plan B is completely workable" are not acceptable. The guide should be an impartial list of points together with a statement of the problem, the objectives, and a list of those invited to the meeting.

The Conference Leader

It is not necessary for the conference leader to be an expert in the subject being discussed. He should be rather an expert stimulator and director of discussion. Any man who can be a good impartial chairman and manager of disputing men, can keep them cool and friendly, has the requisites for success as a conference leader. Knowledge of the subject is worthwhile, but is not so important as clear, impartial thinking and the ability to exercise skillful control of men. The leader has the function of seeing that everyone contributes and that no one monopolizes the time of the group. He also controls the intensity of the discussion lest feelings be aroused which interfere with clear thinking. If a member of the group tries to show up other members, it is the leader's task to handle all the parties to such a situation, so that the case is seen in its true relation to the problem being discussed.

The conference leader is never a teacher or lecturer. He does not tell the group how to think; he does not tell the group what to think; he does not dictate the results of their thinking; he does not have a program of his own to put over. Most of all he does not set himself up as an authority on the matters being discussed, nor permit others to appeal to him to settle their disputes. He does not enter into the discussion save to summarize or to re-direct it; neither does he correct misstatements made by the members of the group, though he may call attention to a questionable point or statement so that the group will not miss the importance of a situation or accept a significant error as truth.

The conference leader must avoid talking too much. Experience has shown that the more a leader talks, the less the members of his group will talk. If the leader is well prepared, his material carefully selected, his questions well planned, a minimum of talking on his part will be necessary.[2]

This is a brief definition of a conference leader taken from an excellent booklet titled, "A Guide to Successful Conference Leadership." This pamphlet points out many other factors which those of us who have worked with industry have found to be vital in developing conference leaders.

The conference leader is the key person in a successful meeting. His is a most difficult task and requires a great deal of tact and thought. The leader who is competent will guide the conference to group decisions and action. This is not easy to do when ten to fifteen men are assembled. Some of them know a good deal about the topic; others know little. Some are domineering and forceful; others weak and pliable. Some are objective and unbiased; others are narrow-minded and intolerant. Some are reticent in voicing opinions; others won't permit anyone else to speak. Some are aggressively antagonistic; others are courteously conciliatory. Working with all these diverse personalities, the leader must try to secure agreement and coöperation.

[2] "A Guide to Successful Conference Leadership," New York: American Management Association, Inc., 1948, pp. 3-4.

The booklet mentioned above lists the personal qualities of a conference leader that are well worth noting:

He must be a clear, rapid thinker.
He must possess ease of expression.
He must possess analytical ability.
He must be impersonal.
He must not let prejudice influence his leadership.
He must be patient.
He must be tactful in handling people.
He must have poise and self-restraint.
He must possess a sense of humor.[3]

It is certainly agreed that finding all these qualities in one person is a difficult task. However, the conference leader who is aware of the need for these attributes can strive to secure those he does not possess and practice those he does have.

The leader is the key figure in achieving a successful conference. He must be able to handle sensitive topics easily; he must hold the attention of the group; he must say very little but he must direct the thinking into the proper channels; he must be tactful to the individual who "must" talk constantly; and he must redirect the antagonistic or resentful comments of an individual into fruitful and profitable channels.

The leader probably has most of his difficulty with the person who constantly disagrees with his conferees—but only for the sake of disagreeing. The leader should try to refrain from answering, correcting, or directing the disagreeing conferee. In every possible case, the leader should let the conference participants handle the situations which arise.

Conference Procedure

There is nothing as irritating and as wasteful of time as the conference which "goes in circles" and accomplishes nothing. A fruitful conference is largely the result of careful planning, competent direction, and helpful coöperation.

Because a friendly atmosphere is desirable, the participants might begin the meeting by introducing themselves. Each person should give his name, department, and any other data which might be appropriate. Everyone's names should be printed with a heavy

[3] *Ibid.,* pp. 5-6.

A Conference in Progress

black crayon on folded cards which may be used as informal paper "name plates."

The item under discussion should be presented by the leader and clearly defined, if this is necessary. The scope of the conference should be listed, and the plan for covering the topics should be presented.

The Physical Plan for the Conference

One of the best ways to stifle a potentially successful conference is to schedule it for a small stuffy room, provide 12 chairs for the 15 men invited, and forget the ash trays, blackboard, and note pads.

The conference room should be light, well ventilated, and comfortable. Seating should be arranged so that all participants are clearly visible to each other. Extra facilities, such as movie cameras, screens, and rolling easel boards, should all be easily available.

Every meeting should have a specific time limit. If it is scheduled for 1:00 P.M. to 3:00 P.M., it should begin and end at the times designated. Few busy executives will appreciate returning to their desks at 4:30 P.M. when they have already told their secretaries that the meeting will be concluded at 3:00 P.M.

Terminating the Conference

We all need to secure a satisfying feeling of accomplishment when we complete any work. In the case of a conference, a good summarizing statement can accomplish this task. The conference leader or a perceptive member of the group can do this. The specific problems discussed may be listed, together with the major solutions offered. Then the courses of action proposed might be listed with a brief statement of the one accepted. Finally, members should be reminded of their assignments (if any) in relationship to the conference problem. And, of course, no conference should close without a word of commendation and appreciation from the leader.

QUESTIONS FOR DISCUSSION

I. Answer the following questions as concisely as possible.
   1. Although a speaker may address a group on "The Dangers of Inflation," his attitude toward the members of the audience and his estimation of them become quickly apparent. Can you explain how this is possible?
   2. Why should the speaker have knowledge of the economic, social, and educational level of the audience before addressing it?
   3. List the steps in the organization of an oral communication to a group. Begin with the decision of purpose of the talk.
   4. What would be the specific steps in the organization of a talk delivered to a group of recent alumni from the college of commerce or the college of engineering on "Recent Trends in Research in Engineering (or Commerce)"? The talk is to be given to about 250 men and women and has been limited to 30 minutes.
   5. Why are excellent visual aids so important in a good verbal presentation?
   6. In what specific ways can a chart which is carelessly made up, incomplete, and barely visible detract from a talk?
   7. Does voice tone have any effect on the reception a talk receives? Contrast the pleasant, clearly audible, properly pitched voice with the high, piercing, "scratchy" one.

8. Why should the speaker attempt to vary rate of delivery and volume level in his talk?

9. What are the disadvantages of distributing "hand-outs" during a talk?

10. A chief executive of a major corporation pointed out recently that a series of six conferences which were held by his management personnel cost the company $4000 "in time." How could he arrive at such an astounding figure?

11. In what specific ways can a conference leader prepare for a conference?

12. What can conference participants do in preparation for a conference?

13. List several personal attributes of the conference leader. Explain why each is important in an actual conference situation.

14. Although a young graduate just entering the field of commerce, government, or engineering has little opportunity to address groups or participate in conferences, it is still recommended that he develop skills in the areas of verbal presentation. Explain why.

II. Prepare and deliver a two-minute talk on any one of the following topics.

1. Why I chose _____ University.

2. Why I enjoy (detest) watching _____ on TV.

3. The importance of accounting (engineering, marketing, etc.) in our modern society.

4. Why I admire _____ (teacher, statesman, or sports figure).

5. The laugh was on me.

6. Why foreign language should be taught at the elementary school level.

7. Why I enjoy fishing (golfing, swimming, boating, etc.)

8. Why every man should spend 5 minutes a day thinking of his good fortune.

9. A movie I would (not) recommend.

III. Prepare and deliver a 5-8-minute talk on any one of the following topics. Complete any necessary graphic aids to utilize during the talk. Submit an outline of your address to your instructor.

1. Why (why not) the college curriculum in engineering (accounting, management, etc.) should be increased to five years.

2. A new plan for government foreign assistance.

3. How to improve the health standards of a large segment of our population.

4. How medical care costs can be lowered.

5. How to avoid slum areas in major urban centers.

6. How to make all *toll*ways into *free*ways.
7. Why we must give additional financial support to care for our aging population.
8. Why higher education should depend on TV instruction to a greater extent.
9. Understanding the stock market.
10. The true facts behind the so-called engineer shortage.
11. How the advertiser deludes (informs) the American consumer.
12. The problem of the four-day work week.

IV. Hold a 30-minute conference involving one of the following problems. Select 12 members of the class and assign each one to a specific role playing category as called for by the problem. As the conference leader, prepare an announcement for distribution prior to the conference which states the problem, purposes, questions to be discussed, and other data which you feel are necessary.

1. A fire in a section of the factory closes down production in Department C. What can be done about the 120 men and women who worked in that department? Assign the conference members to three groups: management, labor representatives, and the heads of Departments A, B, D, and E.

2. For several years, employees have been permitted to borrow company-owned tools on weekends for do-it-yourself projects. However, some tools are broken and often the employees do not return the items on Monday mornings. This has held up production. Hold a conference to decide on a change in the former system of lending out tools. Assign the conference members to two groups: management and employee representatives.

3. Your firm has a contract to complete the construction of a 25-story apartment building by October 15. By beginning work at 6:00 A.M. and finishing at 7:00 P.M. during the summer you can speed production and make up for the time lost during a protracted and unexpected March storm. Although workers are allowed overtime pay, you will still benefit financially if you can meet your construction deadline. However, several tenants' associations in the neighborhood have complained about the noise and racket which exists from 6:00 A.M. to 7:00 P.M. six days a week. Call a conference and assign the members to three groups: the tenants' associations, your contracting firm, and the corporation which is having the 25-story building constructed.

4. For two years your firm has been developing a color, transistor, printed circuit, television set which has a maximum width of 4 inches. Your advertising has given the public a hint that this

would be available in December. It is now October and to your complete surprise, a competitor has announced a set similar to yours which is available for immediate purchase from local appliance distributors. Assign your conference members to three groups: your company's management echelon, your organization's market research division, and your firm's advertising agency.

5. Employees have complained that they were not sufficiently informed about company policy, operations, and goals. They usually indicate that they "don't know what the score is"; that the supervisors and superintendents treat them in the same way they treat the machines; that they aren't told why they should carry through certain directives but are just told to complete them. After some investigation, you find that this attitude seems to go "up the line." Foremen feel similarly toward superintendents and the superintendents seem to harbor the same attitude toward top management personnel. This seems to be a major problem in communication break down which could become very serious. Assign your conference members to the groups which you feel should be represented. Perhaps this problem calls for two conferences, each having different group representatives in attendance.

Chapter 18

Reporting on Yourself—
The Letter of Application

INTRODUCTION

Here is one of the most important reports you will write in your entire life—a report on yourself. This report may very well be responsible for your securing a much better position than you now have or it might be instrumental in helping you to acquire your first job.

This letter of application can be a very vital instrument in making your everyday life, and that of your family, more comfortable and enjoyable. The letter can do this by helping you secure a job with a higher income and perhaps improved working conditions.

Those persons who complain about their jobs—but do nothing —deserve little sympathy. In many cases they can improve their situation by sending out letters of application. But it cannot be just any letter of application; it must be a letter of application that is excellent in every detail. No lower standard than excellent should be considered, not only for your own satisfaction but also to prove that your letter (and therefore you) is far superior to the letters of others who are bidding for the same job.

THE COMPETITION YOU FACE

When the personnel director of a large corporation or the employer of a small company places an advertisement in a trade journal or newspaper, he hopes to receive a great many replies.

More often than not, their desires are realized and the mailman may deliver anywhere from 25 to 200 replies. Naturally, what governs the number of replies is the type of job, the personnel available, and the labor market which exists. But in good times or bad you will have competition. And most of it will come from people who already have jobs and wish to improve their status, rather than from those who are seeking their first appointment. For that reason, and also because you want to give this prospective employer the best impression of your abilities that you can, you should write a letter of application that reflects the highest possible credit on you.

Put yourself in the reader's chair. Yesterday he placed an advertisement in *The Daily Gazette* for an accountant who has a bachelor's degree and some experience. Today's mail brings him approximately forty replies. The first envelope he opens contains a neatly typed, two-page letter of application for the position. The next letter is rather similar. Both of these he puts aside for further consideration. The third letter is scrawled almost illegibly on both sides of one sheet of paper. What does he do with that one? What would you do? Of course it goes into the wastebasket.

And so they go; some are neat, well organized, clearly and concisely written, and thoroughly informative. Then there are those that are incomplete, messy, illegible, and completely unsatisfactory.

Does the reader associate the letter with the competence and personality of the prospective candidate? Of course he does. You would too. Here is a letter that is carelessly and negligently written and composed. What kind of an employee will the author of that letter make? Certainly you can only conclude that such a person would turn out to be a poor accountant, a careless engineer, or an unorganized office manager.

Remember that until the employer meets you in person, the picture he has of you is derived from your application—your letter *is* you. You must strive to make that picture an excellent one, and you can do it by making your letter of application one of high caliber—a letter that will be added to the group written by those persons who are slated to be interviewed!

Steps in Writing an Application Letter

If you were about to take a very important step such as purchasing a new home, taking a trip to Europe, selecting a college, or purchasing a car, you would first sit down, plan the steps, and evaluate the pros and cons of the move. Trying to secure a job is certainly as important, if not more so, yet it is amazing how frequently that action is not carefully thought through.

Perhaps the first step is to make a self-appraisal—to take inventory and determine your assets and liabilities, your accomplishments and abilities. Secondly, you must examine the market to find out what is available, what the salary ranges are, and what firms seem to be expanding or contracting.

If your decision is to attempt to secure a position by answering likely advertisements (instead of writing to a company on the chance that there is an opening), then you enter your third step. That is the careful reading of "ads" and the selection of one or more attractive listings to answer.

The fourth step is to match your abilities with the advertisement's demands and then, fifth and finally, you write the letter.

First Step—Self Appraisal

This self-inventory or self-appraisal is not meant to be deeply analytical. All that is required here is that you sit down and examine your educational and experience backgrounds critically. There is no point in applying for a cost accounting position if you have had no courses or practical work in that area.

Continue to look; perhaps the three years of college Spanish qualifies you to answer the attractive ad for a sales correspondent. The advertisement indicates that the company concerned is in the export-import field doing most of its business with Latin America.

You should not forget your minor field. If it was finance and your major area was accounting, check the bank advertisements carefully. Now, what about experience? Think carefully. Perhaps a job you held on a part-time basis three years ago can now prove of value.

There is another important aspect to this self-appraisal. It should definitely help you to recognize some of your likes and dislikes. As you take this inventory, it will bring to mind the job you held last summer in an advertising agency. Your task was mechanical, uninspiring, and lacked self-satisfaction as far as you were concerned. For eight hours a day you tabulated answers on questionnaires. Or another person would recognize that he disliked and was unsuccessful in a part-time selling job he had. Still another will recall the content of a specific class he had in psychology. He found the material boring, insipid, and dull. On the other hand, it is just as important to appreciate those assignments and areas of activities which were very satisfying and challenging.

It is recognized that in all these cases, the satisfaction or dissatisfaction might have arisen from a deeper cause than cited; but a good self-appraisal should bring out certain fundamental truths. If Jack, three years ago, was unsuccessful selling at the retail level, he should try it again only if he can honestly recognize that definite changes in his personality and abilities now make such an assignment acceptable.

Those people who might not be able to see some of these likes and dislikes might be wise to take a few tests that would indicate their occupational preferences, aptitudes, and personality profile. Many companies have prospective employees take such a series before a job offer is made to the applicant.

Second Step—Examining the Market

After you have examined your own abilities and have decided what type of a job you would like to secure, then your next step is to find out what is available.

The advertisements in newspapers and trade journals are the obvious initial sources to check. Then, if you are a college senior, or an alumnus of an institution of higher education, you might visit the school placement bureau. In almost every instance, such placement services are as effective or superior to private employment agencies. And a further consideration is that their services are usually *gratis* to students or former students.

Private and public employment agencies should also be checked. When you work with the former, make sure that you clearly understand the schedule of fees before you sign. Public employment agencies, sponsored by cities and states, are also doing excellent jobs.

You should check the job announcements which are received by your school placement bureau from city, state, and federal civil service agencies. Some large firms also send out bulletins announcing their job needs and the dates their personnel and recruitment representatives will visit your campus and interview prospective candidates.

Read your newspapers—especially the financial section—for news of companies which are expanding their facilities, merging with other firms, or preparing to open new plants in your area.

Check with your instructors, friends, and the businessmen you may know about job opportunities.

In the past few years, publications have appeared annually which are specifically written for the job candidate. Three of these are *Career for the College Man, Career for the Experienced Engineer and Scientist,* and *College Placement Annual.* The *College Placement Annual* lists some 1400 companies. There is a detailed discussion of each firm, in what job areas they may need applicants, and to whom and where to write.

Third Step—Reading the Advertisement Offering the Job

To be favorably considered for a job, you know that your abilities will have to match the job's requirements. It is for this reason that you should read the advertisements or job bulletin with meticulous care.

There is no point in answering an advertisement that specifies "eight years' full-time experience required" if you are a 21-year-old recent college graduate. Why apply for a job that demands "experience required in supervising a minimum of 50 office personnel" if your most taxing supervisory work involved two junior library clerks? On the other hand, you must be equally careful that you do not apply for a job that will not utilize your abilities to your highest potential.

Selecting the advertisement may have some pitfalls if the applicant is not careful. Learn to read advertisements; analyze job announcement bulletins. Watch out for high-pressure advertisements that scream in bold, black type:

Are you a hard worker who needs more than $500 a week? If so, we have a job for you. Etc.

Do you need $15,000 a year or more? If you are competent, we can get together. This company etc.

It may be that such advertisements are perfectly legitimate and acceptable. However, it is suggested that you move with care and caution when you deal with the companies involved. By and large, a recent college graduate or one who has been out of school for a few years would be wiser to concentrate his efforts on advertisements such as the following.

ACCOUNTANT. Recent college grad, with major in accounting. Some exp. valuable. Must be free to travel periodically. Lg. firm, unlimited opportunity, many benefits. Reply in detail giving age, exp., ed., other background data. State salary desired. Box 7122	ENGINEERS needed by large corp. engaged in guided missile research for U.S. Gov't. No exp. necessary. Heavy math background desirable. Reply listing complete educational information, other training, and personal data. Replies held in confidence. Box 6321
Bus. Adm. major with degree. Large company needs office manager. Some supervisory exp. helpful; knowledge of men's apparel desirable. Salary $425 to $490. Write in detail. Box M212	Trainee wanted by large advertising corp. Must have degree in field and thorough educ. Attractive salary paid for 3 mth. training period. Must be bright and interested in copy and layout work. Give educ. backgrd, ref. and other data. Box 981

There are other types of advertisements that are primarily designed to attract executive personnel. Such ads are often found in trade journals, on the financial page, or in specific sections of newspapers. In all cases, the advertisement you decide to answer should be carefully selected and meticulously examined in preparation for the next step.

Fourth Step—Matching the Job with the Applicant

One of the most satisfying experiences for both employer and employee is to match the right man with the right job. Not only is the worker happier when he is working in a position for which he is competent, but the employer is also. The latter knows that such an employee will be more coöperative, productive, and satisfactory.

For these reasons you must analyze what you have, what they want, and then "match 'em up."

If the advertisement requests a person who has "education *and* experience," and you have both, present them with emphasis. If an export-import house advertises for an office manager who can correspond in Spanish, and you have that ability, note it prominently. In every case, examine your own background carefully in an effort to find those qualifications which are noted in the advertisement. Perhaps a good procedure is to list on a sheet of paper what the advertisement demands—the most important qualities (as indicated in the ad) first and then the other qualifications below them. Next to the list of requirements list your qualifications which "match up." If there is good balance between the two listings, you are ready to write your formal letter of application.

Fifth Step—Writing the Letter of Application

After you have completed these preliminary steps, you are ready to secure your job by a letter. Two types of letters of application are usually recognized: the solicited and the unsolicited. When you reply to a newspaper or trade journal advertisement, a printed job announcement, or a bulletin board notice, you are sending in a solicited letter of application; someone is soliciting a reply from you. When you choose a company, or ten companies, any one of which you would like to work for, and send in a letter on the chance that your services could be utilized, you are using an unsolicited type of letter of application.

There are, obviously, advantages and disadvantages to each. In the case of the solicited letter of application, the major advantage is that you know that a job, or jobs, do exist. Then, too, you have an opportunity to evaluate several ads and choose one that appeals to you and matches your qualifications. The big disadvantage is competition. There is no way of knowing how many replies may be received in reply to an attractive advertisement; your letter may be one of 25 or 50 or 100. Many of the competing letters will be excellent and they will be bidding for the same level of attention as yours. This is all the more reason for you to complete the best possible job you can in your letter.

In the case of the unsolicited letter of application, the big advantage is that you will not be competing with a great many other persons. Your letter, because it may be the only one of its type received on a specific day, will be read and carefully evaluated. Then too, you will be writing to companies you know something about rather than to "blind ads." For this reason you can talk about a particular company, its background, and how and why you are interested in working for it. The obvious disadvantage is that you have no assurance that a job exists or whether or not the firm is adding to its complement of personnel. However, that disadvantage should not dissuade you too much. Many large corporations may hire you even though they have no immediate opening. Experience has taught them that if no need exists for your talents today, it may arise next week or next month because of normal turnover of personnel. On such an assumption, large companies are inclined to hire you today and begin your training immediately.

THE FORM OF THE LETTER

The people in commerce and industry who will read your letter are usually very busy. They are most desirous of reading a letter of application that is clear, concise, and well organized. For that reason, the next few pages will be concerned with a discussion of three different forms for the letter: the one-part letter of application, the two-part letter of application, and the job brochure. Examine each one carefully and note the advantages and disadvantages as they apply to your particular situation.

One-Part Letter of Application

In this particular case the writer presents in one letter a resumé of his personal qualifications, education, experience, references, and miscellaneous data. This normally requires two, and not infrequently, three, typewritten pages. Naturally this makes for a rather long letter. However, if it is well written and topic headings are used, it is rather easy to read through. In the two examples below, you will note that one uses topic headings; the other does not.

Dear Mr. Barnett:

In June of this year I shall graduate from the Dawson College of Engineering. At that time I shall receive a Bachelor of Science Degree with a major in Electrical Engineering. Knowing that your firm is one of the leading producers of electronic components, I took this opportunity to write. I am applying for an opening on your staff which might exist.

The four years I spent at Dawson College were productive and profitable for me. The classes in which I was enrolled were taught by experienced, competent teachers. I especially enjoyed those classes which emphasized the development and production of transistors and printed circuits. I took as much work as possible in this area and this should prove of value to your company. Because I did not wish to become too narrowly specialized in engineering, I took a great deal of work in the humanities and social sciences also. In this way I learned something about people and how they act and react. I am sure this will prove of value to me in getting along with other employees and supervisors. During the last two years of my high school career and for the four years I spent in college, I worked each summer. The purpose of such employment was to supply me with funds to get along through the regular school year.

During the summers of 19– and 19–, I worked for A and T Metal Corporation. I served as an office and file clerk; although the job did not challenge me, I nevertheless found it interesting. During the first two summers while at college, I worked on the Inter-State Highway Project as an assistant to the chief engineer. It was my job to file and organize blueprints, complete the forms on new employees, take and transmit messages, and act as a "man Friday." For the last two summers, I have worked for the State Highway Commission as an assistant on a surveying team. In all these jobs, I have found it easy to get along with my co-workers and I have been invited to re-apply for a full-time position.

I am 22 years of age, 5' 11" tall and weigh 185 pounds. I am in excellent physical condition. I am unmarried and live at home with my parents and a younger brother. The following people know me well and would be happy to forward an evaluation on request.

Prof. Thomas R. Bane
Department of Electrical
  Engineering
Dawson College
Dawson, Illinois

Richard T. Blaine, M.D.
Doctors Building
Dawson, Illinois

Mr. Guy T. Rounder, Director
Illinois Highway Commission
Springfield, Illinois

Judge Homer T. Browne
Illinois State Court House
Springfield, Illinois

I would greatly appreciate an opportunity to come in and discuss my qualifications in additional detail. Please call Hemlock 2-4812; I am available for an interview at your convenience.

Sincerely yours,

Box 721R
Chicago Daily
Chicago, Illinois

Dear Sir:

This morning's issue of the *Chicago Daily* carried your advertisement for an experienced accountant who has a good educational background. I fit that description to a "T" and would appreciate it if you would evaluate my qualifications for the job.

Education

In June of 19— I graduated from Denton College with a Bachelor of Science Degree in Commerce. My major field of concentration was accounting and my minor field was marketing. While I was in school, I completed all the basic courses in accounting plus two in auditing, two in cost, one each in inventory control, taxes, budgeting and machine accounting. My work in marketing concentrated on sales, which should be of value to your company. Upon graduation, I was elected to Nu Sigma Pi, in recognition of the A- academic average which I maintained.

Experience

During the last two years of high school, I worked as an office boy at Burkhart and Burkhart, C. P. A.'s. It was this job that motivated me to carry through my studies in the field of accounting. While in college I worked part-time and summers for various accounting firms. Among these were Smithfield Public Accountants, Marks and Roberts, and Redfield and Redfern.

After receiving my degree, I continued on with Redfield and Redfern as a junior accountant. I remained there until June 19—when I received a better offer from a former employer, Marks and Roberts. I am now employed by this firm and find that most of my work consists of audits which take me out of town quite frequently. My desire to remain in the city, as well as to improve my status, prompts me to consider a change at this time.

Adaptability

I have always found it easy to work with others, both in school and on the job. I enjoy new assignments and quickly adapt myself to a change. I am sure that you would find that I could integrate myself easily and quickly into your present work force.

Personal

For a young man 27 years of age, I feel that I have secured a variety of valuable educational and work experiences. I am married and the father of two boys; one is 2 and the other 5 months of age.
I am in excellent health and enjoy golf, reading, chess, and my family.

References

I have spoken to the persons listed below and they have assured me that they will be happy to offer an objective, written opinion of my capabilities and personality.

Mr. Robert T. Marks, Pres.	Dr. Dwyer T. Dwyer, Chairman
Marks and Roberts, C.P.A.'s	Dept. of Accounting
110 W. Michigan	Denton College of Commerce
Westfield, Minnesota	Denton, Minnesota
Mr. James Smithfield, Partner	David Rattner, Attorney
Smithfield Public Accountants	Marks and Roberts, C.P.A.'s
1515 East Lansing Drive	110 W. Michigan
Westfield, Minnesota	Westfield, Minnesota

I am sure an association between us would prove mutually valuable. I would appreciate an opportunity to discuss my background in more detail with you. I can come in for an interview at your convenience. During the day I may be reached at Barton 2-0031, ext. 241. My home phone is Hazelcrest 5-0555.

Sincerely yours,

The two letters given above are well worth your close examination. They are both, of course, examples of one-part letters of application. Notice that they are quite long and that it does take some time to read through them. However, the second one, addressed to Box 721R, is definitely easier to read and refer back to because of the topic headings which are used.

If the reader wishes to recheck the applicant's experience, he can find that section quickly. If he is curious to determine the writer's age, he can find that rapidly by glancing under "Personal." However, in the first example (addressed to Mr. Barnett), it is necessary to read through the entire letter to find specific sections. This is due to the fact that topic headings are not utilized.

On some occasions the one-part letter without topic headings might be wise to use. This would be very true in a case where an advertisement states "experience desirable but not necessary." If the applicant has no experience, he would be unwise to use the topic heading form because his lack of experience would become magnified through the blank space under such a heading. It is safe to say, however, that in most cases where a one-part letter of application is used, topic headings are valuable and add a great deal to the visual appearance as well as the reading and understanding of the letter.

Two-Part Letter of Application

We have already discovered that the one-part letter has the disadvantage of being relatively long. This, coupled with the fact that most businessmen are short of time, makes the two-part letter valuable under many conditions.

The two-part letter itself consists of a short "cover" letter which emphasizes the main selling points of the applicant and a reference or data sheet which presents a detailed account of his background.

The two-part letter possesses a great many advantages. First of all, it does not take as much time to prepare as the one-part letter. The data sheet can be made up once and then the same form used again and again with such minor changes as may be necessary for different job applications. Because the cover letter is usually quite brief, it can be completed in a minimum of time. As for the reader, he finds the data sheet easy to refer to either on initial reading, subsequent reviews, or at the time of the interview.

The appearance of this letter is still another advantage. With a little planning, the layout of the cover letter and the data sheet can be easily balanced and made visually attractive. With the precise headings of the data sheet and the brief, pointed exposition contained in the cover letter, the reader will probably assume that the writer is a clear thinking, well-organized individual—and such an assumption will probably be correct.

The Cover Letter should open with a specific reference to the job and then go on to review briefly the applicant's qualifications. In this review it is important to emphasize the major selling point the writer possesses. This should be done to the extent that the reader's interest is aroused, and he will be motivated to turn to the data sheet for additional details. In other words, it is not enough to say, "I am well qualified for the job." You should say, "I am well qualified for the job by reason of three years' part-time experience in the field of accounting and a bachelor's degree from Dawson College with a major in the same area. Details of my education and experience are listed on the attached data sheet."

The cover letter, like the one-part letter, should also close with a specific and definite request for an interview.

The Data Sheet should be well organized and should contain approximately seven different sections:

Your job objective
Major qualifications
Experience
Education
Activities and organizations
Personal data
References and a photograph

Headings should be capitalized and/or underlined; subpoints should be indented, and adequate white space should be provided to give the data sheet a neat, uncluttered appearance.

Under education, the school attended most recently, from which a degree was received, should be listed first. Secondary school background may then be noted very briefly.

Courses in your major and related fields should be listed; other courses may be mentioned if such action seems wise.

In the case of experience, you again list your most recent job first unless a job held earlier is directly related to the one for which application is being made. You should indicate whether the job was full or part-time, when it was held, and the duties involved.

College, civic, and social organizations may be listed under activities. Membership in professional organizations should be listed. Honor groups, special awards, and recognition might also be indicated.

Under the heading, "Personal Data," physical details, hobbies and sports, and draft status are usually given. There is a question in the minds of some personnel counselors whether it is necessary or even wise to list parentage, church affiliation, and race. In some states, information of this nature may not be requested on the application blank.

It is usually suggested that a maximum of five and a minimum of three references be listed. Of these, two (or one) should be work references, one academic, and one personal. Identify your refer-

ences to the most advantageous degree possible for your own benefit. It is not enough to list:

> Thomas R. Barton
> Dawson College
> Dawson, Minnesota

The reader may ask who Mr. Barton is? Is he an assistant in the
library? A clerk in the bookstore? A helper in the lab? Certainly
it is better to say:

> Dr. Thomas R. Barton, Chairman
> Marketing Department
> Dawson College
> Dawson, Minnesota

The photograph should be of good quality and should be a
"portrait type" rather than "full length." Snapshots should ordinarily not be used.

Study the examples given below; perhaps various sections of
each might suit your purposes.

Sample cover letters in the two-part letters:

Mr. Ralph T. Snyder
Personnel Director
Richmond Steel Corporation
221 South Melborne Drive
Los Angeles 27, California

Dear Mr. Snyder:

For the last few years I have been following the growth and expansion
of the Richmond Steel Corporation. I have read, through newspaper
accounts, information about your outstanding programs and policies.
I would like to work for such a progressive company; if you will
review my qualifications, I think you will agree that I can prove of
benefit to your firm.

My primary objective is to work in your industrial relations department. My background for such a position is education, experience,
and interest. Next month I shall receive my degree from The State
University where I majored in management and concentrated on industrial relations and labor relations. I have worked on a part-time
basis in the personnel department of a plastics corporation. During
my last two years of college I was employed (also on a part-time
basis) in the office of one of our large west coast unions. Details of
these jobs, my education and other information may be found on the
attached data sheet.

I know that I could do a good job for Richmond, and I would appreciate an opportunity to discuss my background with you. I can come to your office any time at your convenience. I may be reached every afternoon at Essex 2-2910, extension 21; or any evening at Dickens 3-9753.

Sincerely yours,

Raymond Warren

Box R421
Dawson Daily News
Dawson, Illinois

Dear Sir:

Your advertisement for a competent secretary with some office experience caught my attention immediately. I believe I have the qualities for which you are looking.

Two years ago I completed the two-year secretarial program at Dawson Junior College. At that time I was able to take dictation at the rate of 120 words per minute and transcribe at the rate of 65 words per minute. Since then, I have improved my skill in these areas. In addition to my secretarial science program, I took courses in business law, accounting, office management, business writing, English composition, and others. This fall I expect to take the Certified Professional Secretary examination.

Since leaving school I have been working in a "two girl" office where I take dictation, handle correspondence and billing, take telephone orders from customers, and complete other routine assignments. I feel that I have gone as far as possible with this firm; I now want to join a company that presents opportunities for advancement.

On the attached data sheet I have listed many details concerning my education, experience and background. Please wire or call collect; I shall be happy to meet with you and present my qualifications in additional detail.

Sincerely yours,

Dorothy T. Malone

Box 229T
Los Angeles Daily Sun
Los Angeles, California

Dear Sir:

Your advertisement requested a "new engineering graduate who has ideas, ambition and is not afraid of hard work." *I am that man.*

Seven months ago I received my degree in engineering from the University of California's College of Engineering. Since that time I have been working for Dudley Aircraft in their equipment division. As you may have heard, Dudley is merging with Bankcroft in 60 days. I therefore feel that it would be wise for me to seek a new assignment at this time.

Two awards from the Dudley Suggestion Board in just six months' time will prove I have "ideas." One of my suggestions involved a new processing system of an electronic component. This is expected to save the company upwards of $4,000 each year. As for "ambition," I can point to four years of part-time work while attending college and two promotions within six months at Dudley.

Details of this and other information are listed on the attached data sheet. However, it only tells part of the story. May I come in, at your convenience, and tell you more? My phone number is Normandy 4-1649.

Sincerely yours,

Richard M. Watson

Box 256
Chicago Morning Sun
Chicago Sun Building
Chicago 4, Illinois

Dear Sir:

Today's *Morning Sun* carried your advertisement for an "accountant trainee who has a collegiate background and a desire to work." With my educational background, practical experience, and desire to make accounting my life's work, I am sure I can be of value to your company. Please review my qualifications.

In approximately two weeks I shall receive my Bachelor of Science degree from Dawson University's College of Commerce. My major field of study was accounting and my minor area of concentration was finance. In all courses I maintained an A— average and was elected to Mortar and Key in my senior year.

For several years I have worked at a variety of part-time jobs and for two summers, plus other time, as an accounting clerk. This was done to assist me in covering my collegiate expenses. I am sure this will indicate to you that I am a young man of maturity and responsibility.

I served in the R.O.T.C. while in college and am therefore not subject to the draft. Beginning this Fall I plan to take evening work in preparation for the January C.P.A. examination. In the years to come I expect to further my education, on the graduate level, with additional evening school attendance.

I would appreciate an opportunity to discuss my background, salary, and future possibilities with your company. Please call me at Sheldrake 3-3325 to arrange for an interview. I shall be happy to come in at any hour you suggest.

Sincerely yours,

David Harrison Roebuck

DAVID HARRISON ROEBUCK
221 South Madison Avenue
Chicago 23, Illinois

Sheldrake 3-3325

Job Objective

Professional position as an accountant with a large corporation. Eventual objective to serve as comptroller of a large firm.

(*Photograph*)

Major Qualifications

University background in accounting and finance.
Experience in the field of accounting and retailing.

Education

Bachelor of Science Degree in Commerce, Dawson University, Dawson, Illinois, June 19—.

Courses in Accounting

Elements and Principles of Accounting	Budgeting
Interpretation	Specialized Accounting
Advanced Theory and	Auditing Theory
Practice	Auditing Practice
Cost Accounting I and II	Taxes I and II
	Consolidations

Courses in Related Fields

Business Finance	Business Report Writing
Money and Banking	Conference Leadership
Credits and Collections	Marketing Theories
Management and Personnel	Office Management

Experience

Cantrell and Cantrell, C.P.A.'s
110 South Washington Street
Chicago 3, Illinois
    Summer of 19—
    Duties: Routine accounting work, ledger posting, and proofreading of auditing reports.

Illinois Accounting Associates
10 North Dearborn
Chicago 3, Illinois
    Part-time (after class) Jan. 19— to June 19—.
    Duties: Ledger posting and routine office work.

Other part-time jobs involving retail sales, door-to-door selling and work as a camp counsellor.

Social Activities and Organizations

Mortar and Key (honorary commerce fraternity)
Vice-President, Senior Class
Student Council Officer
Member of Dawson Debating Team

Personal Data

Physical details: age, 23 years; height, 5′ 11″; weight, 175 pounds; health, excellent.

Hobbies and interests: swimming, tennis, chess and wood working.
Church: Unitarian
Parentage: third generation American of English descent.
Draft status: not subject to draft because of R.O.T.C. service in college.

References

Mr. Robert T. Cantrell, C.P.A.	Mr. Harold T. Crane
110 South Washington Street	Vice President
Chicago 3, Illinois	Illinois Accounting Associates
	10 North Michigan
	Chicago 3, Illinois
Dr. Wilbur T. Shanks, Chairman	Judge Richard T. Hart
Department of Accounting	County Court House
Dawson University	Dawson, Illinois
Dawson, Illinois	

The Job Brochure

This particular device is not usually recommended for the recent college graduate or the young man or lady who has held a job for a relatively short period of time. Because of its very nature it is designed for an individual who has had a good deal of experience and training.

The job brochure is a folder that contains a number of pages. Separate sections are given over to a detailed presentation of jobs held, duties performed, salary received, and related data. Educational and practical training are also outlined in detail as are army experience, civic assignments, results of aptitude and personality tests, copies of letters of recommendation, and collateral information.

A recent college graduate usually does not have adequate background to fill a job brochure. Even when he triple spaces and leaves extra wide margins, there still is not enough background to fill more than three or four pages. The result is a rather "empty-looking" folder. In most cases he would be much wiser to use a two-part letter of application.

THE PARTS OF THE APPLICATION LETTER

In every letter of application you write you should strive to
Arouse interest

DESCRIBE background
VERIFY qualifications
REQUEST an interview

Arouse Interest

Because the average personnel man or employer finds that most letters begin with the usual hackneyed statement, he is delighted to find one that is friendly, natural in tone, and somewhat different.

A beginning that is fresh, interesting, and mentions the possible value of the applicant to the firm (a "you" attitude) will motivate the recipient to read on. The dull, stereotyped letter that starts "This is in reply to your advertisement which appeared . . ." or "In reply to your request for a secretary, I am taking the liberty of . . ." has little, if any, value. Use a beginning that is new, fresh, sincere, and interesting.

INQUIRY BEGINNING

These are especially valuable because they may be utilized if you are not sure that a job does exist.

Do you have an opening for a well-educated and experienced secretary?

Are you looking for a recent college graduate who majored in advertising and wants to start at the bottom and work his way up?

Do you need an accountant whose education and experience emphasized auditing? If so, let me present my qualifications in detail.

Your advertisement said you were going to add two junior engineers to your staff this spring. Won't you please consider my qualifications for one of the openings?

SUMMARY TYPE OF BEGINNING

It is sometimes wise to begin with a recapitulation of your outstanding qualities and thereby interest your reader.

Two years as a tax accountant with Brayer and Brayer, a Bachelor of Science Degree from Dawson, a pleasant personality, a conscientious nature, and a desire to work hard are some of the qualifications I can offer for the job you have available.

Abilities to type and to take dictation are superior; knowledge of office procedures, equipment, and machines is excellent; common sense and personality more than satisfactory; and ability to act as a Girl Friday, priceless.

Part-time work in surveying, bridge construction, and drafting plus a degree from the University of Springfield in engineering certainly seem to qualify me for the job you described.

I have some experience, a thorough education, a desire to work hard, and real ambition to move forward in advertising.

Unusual Beginnings

Interest may be aroused by an unusual and clever beginning. However, the writer should be careful that his opening is not looked upon as too clever or too "cute." Of course, a lot depends on who the reader is. An applicant looking for a job in advertising might be wise to use a beginning that reflects his ability to come up with a clever, original opening.

A popular song, but *not* for me is, "I Don't Want to Set the World on Fire," because the truth of the matter is—I really *do.* Let me tell you why I think I can.

Qualification	*Circle one*			
Accounting experience	Ⓐ	B	C	D
Accounting education	Ⓐ	B	C	D
Ability to work hard	Ⓐ	B	C	D
Ability to get along with others	Ⓐ	B	C	D
Ability to increase company business	Ⓐ	B	C	D

Could you leave your office for a two-week vacation without a worry in the world? You *can* if you hire me!

"There's gold in that boy," said my dentist after he finished working on me. He was kidding, but you can find out how true his statement really is by hiring me immediately.

Narrative or Story Beginnings

This type of beginning has the advantage of presenting a story that most readers will want to finish. A key quality here is truthfulness and sincerity.

Ever since I took my first course in bookkeeping in high school, I knew that I wanted to make accounting my life's work.

In June of 1954, during my Army service, I was asked to assist a group building a temporary bridge. I was amazed to see the logic and preciseness involved. Almost immediately I requested a transfer to the Engineers where I continued to work on technical assignments. Immediately after my discharge, I entered Springfield College of Engineering and four years later received my degree. Today, I am just as enthusiastic about engineering as I was that day in June. The attached data sheet. . . .

It was a bolt out of the blue when Mr. Martin, Personnel Director of Ajax Oil Company, asked me to serve as the Executive Secretary to the firm's president. However, that was four years ago, but perhaps I'd better start at the beginning.

REFERENCE BEGINNINGS

A point of contact often gives the writer an entree to a job or at least arouses the reader's interest by reason of the name or incident that is mentioned.

Mr. James T. Graph, who spoke to our Management Society last March, told me, after his address, that your firm would be interested in securing several management trainees this June.

Mr. Conway, director of our University Placement Service, told me of your firm's interest in securing a competent and efficient secretary.

When my uncle, Mr. Robert Wayne, visited us the other evening, he told me that you might be in need of several student engineers to work on the new state highway your firm is building.

These are a few examples of the different types of openings which may be employed to arouse interest. The important points to remember in any opening in that first paragraph are these:
1. Be sincere, original, natural, and friendly.
2. Emphasize a "you" attitude—tell your reader how you will be able to be of benefit to his company; indicate how his firm will profit by employing you.

Describe Background

Your reader will invariably desire specific information on your qualifications for the job. In this second section of your letter you should be sure to present your educational background, your experience, personal qualities, attitudes or interests which are relative to the position, and personal data.

A question often arises: should experience or education be presented first? The answer is this: describe and discuss that qualification which is most vital for the job or which places you in the best light. If the job requirement is "at least two years' experience" and you have it, say so emphatically, clearly, and concisely. You may then go on to a discussion of education. If the advertisement states, "Outstanding journalism graduate desired" and you have that qualification (and a Phi Beta Kappa key to prove it), say so immediately.

If the position requests applicants with some experience, and you have none, present your education early in the letter and exploit that as much as possible. A problem sometimes arises in how forceful you should be in stating an attribute which you possess. The danger, of course, is to have one of your statements interpreted as boastful, self-centered, and egotistical.

Too Boastful: It was not long after I started at Whartons that things settled down in their office and a system of handling the payroll logically was introduced.

Better: Shortly after I started work at Whartons, I suggested that the payroll be handled by a modified I.B.M. method. This suggestion was followed and is in use today.

Exaggerated: It is safe to say that McDonalds never really realized its potential until I introduced and carried through a hard-hitting, original, and attention-catching advertising program. It is now an outstanding furniture outlet due to my efforts.

Better: Because McDonalds is located in the center of several growing suburbs, its potential was obvious. I was placed in charge of the store's advertising program and in a nine-month period, its sales rose almost 60 percent.

Present each area as an individual unit beginning with the one which reflects the most credit on you. Be specific, accurate, and brief. The qualifications which are most intimately associated with the job should receive the greatest detail.

Vague and General: For two years I worked in the office of Markulum Fruit Company.

Specific and Detailed: For two years I worked as the office manager of the Markulum Fruit Company. In this capacity I supervised the work of three stenographers and two secretaries, made up office budgets, computed all salesmen's commissions, and handled the office I.B.M. payroll accounting tasks.

Your descriptions should always be handled as positively as possible. Rather than stating what qualifications you do not have and what tasks you cannot do, it is always wiser to indicate what you are capable of carrying through. In as many instances as possible, make your statements positively rather than negatively.

NEGATIVE: Although I do not have a full two years' experience, I did work for Kramer Brothers for eighteen months.

POSITIVE: For a year and one-half, I worked at Kramers where I learned and handled every office procedure which the firm practised.

NEGATIVE: Although I have not actually audited accounts myself, I believe my education has given me adequate training for such work.

POSITIVE: The two courses in auditing which I took in college were taught by men who are active in the field; the problems introduced and the methods used were practical and realistic. For this reason, I feel that I could handle competently. . . .

Do not be reluctant to discuss your personal desires, attitudes, and interests in relationship to the job. If you feel deeply and sincerely about the role of advertising in this modern world, say so. If you find accounting "vital, compelling, and engrossing," do not hesitate to say as much. Notice that the following letter (one-part letter) is specific, positive, sincere, and pleasant to read.

Dear Sir:

Your advertisement in today's *News* indicated that you wanted a recent college graduate who was attracted by the challenge of advertising and who possessed the ability to create ideas and then carry them through in the most practical way possible. Well, Mr. Box 271R, I *am* that person.

Educational Background

In June of this year I received my bachelor's degree from Dawson University with a major in advertising. I found every course in that field very interesting and profitable. Although I needed only twelve courses in advertising, I enrolled in seventeen and three of these were on a graduate level. I enjoyed them and came out with an A- grade average in my major field. In addition to these, I completed a variety of other courses in the field of marketing as well as courses in business law, report writing, world affairs, psychology, and philosophy.

Creativity

The attribute of creativity is certainly vital if one is to rise in the field of advertising. I believe that I possess that qualification as evidenced by my past performance. During my junior and senior years at Dawson, I served as the yearbook editor. In both of these years I evolved the theme for the issue, was responsible for securing publicity, and directed its production. The first issue under my editorship won the National Collegiate Yearbook Bronze Award for creativity, content, and production. The next issue won first place and the Gold Award.

I was also responsible for the theme used in decorating our fraternity house for Homecoming this year and last. In both cases, we won first place on campus.

Experience in Advertising

For the last two summers I have been employed by Dramer and Dramer, Advertising Associates. Although my particular assignment was largely clerical, I did have an opportunity to assist in production and layout. I was also able to observe the copy writers and their work, the sales and account executives, and the general functioning of a large agency.

Personal Background

I am now 22 years old, single, and in excellent health. I am 5' 11" tall and weigh 180 pounds. I am a practicing Protestant and live with my parents in a Chicago suburb. I enjoy all sports, good music, and interesting books.

References

I am sure the men listed below will be able to give you an objective and accurate evaluation of my personality and abilities.

Dr. Charles T. Morris, Chairman   Dean Howard T. Rassner
Advertising Department   Dawson Universtiy
Dawson University   Dawson, Illinois
Dawson, Illinois

Mr. Frederick Dramer   Judge Leon R. Leoford
Vice-President   Minnesota Supreme Court
Dramer and Dramer   111 South Prairie
111 North Huron   Minneapolis, Minnesota
Chicago 3, Illinois   (personal reference)

I do feel that I can serve as a valuable employee in your firm. I am sure that when you know more about my background, training, and personality, you will agree. I would appreciate an opportunity to come in and talk to you any time at your convenience. Just telephone Cedercrest 5-5151 or write to the address listed below.

Sincerely yours,

Notice several qualities in the letter above. It specifically lists factors of education and experience; it is positive and confident, though not boastful; it is clear and well organized; and its appearance and layout make it easy to read.

EDUCATION

Describe your education, emphasizing your major field of concentration in relationship to the description of the job that is offered. Name the specialized courses, the methods that were used in their presentation, any outstanding faculty members you worked with, and your grade average if it will reflect credit on you. Remember to list those supplementary courses which will add to your value in business, science, or engineering. Such fields as economics, marketing, business law, management, report writing, and business letters are important to list.

EXPERIENCE

Try to relate various aspects of your work background to the specific demands of the position for which you are applying. In listing previous places of employment, note the type of work you did, when you held the job, and the duties you performed.

In some cases, you can relate college assignments or associations with the job; or you may be able to do the same thing with civic, army, navy, or air force activities in which you have engaged.

Experience is one of the best "selling points" you can offer for a job. If you have not held a job directly related to the one for which you are applying, search your background for some activity, other than education, which can be utilized. If you do have experience, either full or part-time, present it in the most favorable light possible.

PERSONAL QUALITIES AND HISTORY

As indicated earlier, make an effort to let your reader know something about your personality: how well you get along with others, how hard you work, whether you carry through even when obstacles are encountered, your sense of humor, and how well you accept constructive criticism.

The trick here is to list activities and work in which you have engaged which are evidence of commendable personal qualities. This is more effective than making a statement of your abilities yourself. It is usually wiser to let the personnel man draw his own conclusions from your comments than for you to state bluntly that you possess them.

TOO FORWARD: During my senior year in college, I acted as editor of the year book, was vice-president of the Campus Voters' League, and played first violin in the University orchestra. This was in addition to carrying a full course load and receiving top grades in each. This should certainly prove to you that I am a hard-working individual who can adeptly handle a variety of activities with competence and efficiency.

BETTER: My grades for a full course load have been near the top of my class during my senior year. This was accomplished while I served as editor of the yearbook, vice-president of the Campus Voters' League, and played first violin in the University orchestra.

Employers usually want to know something about your age, marital and draft status, height, weight, nationality, interests, and hobbies. In a one-part letter of application, these data may be covered in two or three sentences; in a two-part letter, the information is listed on the data sheet.

Verify Your Qualifications

There are several different parts of your letter which help prove that you do possess the qualifications which you have listed. Obviously, the jobs you have indicated under your "Experience" heading do this. For this reason, you should be precise in listing the exact names and addresses of the firms for which you have worked.

Your degrees and diplomas accomplish the same thing for you in the area of education. Indicate the month and year in which certification was received and from what institution.

In listing references, present a minimum of three and a maximum of five. At least two of the larger number should be work references. Personnel directors indicate that they are especially concerned with these. Next in importance to the prospective employer are academic references, and finally the names and addresses of persons who can evaluate your personality and character should be given. Be sure to identify your references clearly by title and capacity.

Some applicants have a file made up of samples of their work and copies of letters of commendation. Either or both of these can prove of value, but they should not be mailed with the initial letter of application unless requested. Frequently they can be presented to better advantage at the time of the interview.

Request An Interview

Although it is true that the letter of application may secure a job for you, it is probably more accurate to say that it will secure an interview. How you conduct yourself at the interview may determine whether or not you get the job. Your real purpose in the letter of application, therefore, is to arouse sufficient interest in your reader so that he will ask you to come in for an interview. Therefore, you should make your request definite and friendly.

I have education and experience in the field of accounting; may I tell you about this in detail at an interview?

What I listed above is just part of the story; may I come in at your convenience and tell you more about myself? I can be reached during the day at Financial 8-4000, extension 32, or in the evenings at Cedercrest 4-4047.

I shall be in New York during the period of December 22 to January 2. May I come in to see you, at your convenience, and tell you more about myself?

In every case try to convey the impression that your letter tells only part of the story (and so it does) and that you have more details to add; that is the reason why you want the interview.

Avoid timid, half-hearted, negative, or weak requests such as these:

May I have an interview, please? Perhaps you have some questions. (timid)

I think I may be able to do the job. Please call me if you agree. (negative)

I think I may like the job and would like to hear more about it. (half-hearted)

In every case, make it as easy as possible for the prospective employer to get in touch with you. List your address clearly and, if possible, note your phone number.

IMPORTANT FACTORS IN THE LETTER OF APPLICATION

There are three overall areas that are important for the job applicant to be aware of while writing his letter: (1) the mechanics of the letter, (2) the attitude of the letter, and (3) personal factors.

Mechanics

Stationery. The stationery used should be 8½″ × 11″ good-quality white bond. This is a serious business letter and there is no place for paper that would not ordinarily be used in an office situation. Social size paper with designs and patterns, fraternity insignia, or school names should not be used.

Company paper where you are now employed or have been in the past is certainly not acceptable. Personnel people may feel that if you wrote on your present employer's paper, you probably wrote on his time as well, and certainly you would do the same in a new situation.

If you have a dignified personal letterhead on stationery about 7″ × 10″, this is acceptable.

Young ladies should be sure to avoid use of scented, social size paper that has a liberal imprinting of "hearts and flowers" in the margins.

Typing. Every letter of application *must* be typed. If you do not own a typewriter, you should borrow one. There is no alternative; your letter must be typed. Typing improves the appearance of the letter greatly and, of course, makes it much more readable.

In several areas, legible writing is extremely important. This is true in accounting, nursing, or other areas where a misread number or word may prove very costly. For this reason, advertisements may sometimes state, "reply in your own handwriting." If you write very clearly, you may reply as requested; if your writing leaves something to be desired, you might consider typing the letter and enclosing a sample of your writing. Such a sample may consist of a short essay written on your field of work.

Placement on the Page. The letter should look neat, attractive, and inviting. The typing should be of high caliber with no "strike-overs" and few erasures.

The margins should be generous; never crowd the information on one page if a second page will enhance the letter's appearance. Leave adequate room for a clear signature; do not "squeeze it in" on the bottom of a page.

Be sure your own address, city, state, and phone number are conveniently indicated. The upper right-hand corner of the first page may be used or a block typed out at the left-hand margin and immediately below the signature.

Assist your reader by using topic headings, such as "education," "experience," "personal data," and "references."

Take special pains with the data sheet if you are using a two-part letter of application. Balance the various sections on the page, use headings in capital letters for each section, and do not crowd the data which are presented.

Diction and Grammar. This topic hardly needs any comment. Sentence structure, spelling, word use, punctuation, and other qualities of composition must be perfect—no more, no less—just perfect.

As one personnel manager remarked,

We don't expect a literary masterpiece, but we do expect a college level letter. Anyone who is careless about the composition of one of the most important letters he will write in his entire life would hardly be careful of our accounts and customers. When we hire a custodian or truck loader, we expect one type of letter; when we hire a graduate accountant or engineer, we expect another.

This area could be discussed for pages, but there is little point in doing so. There is only one evaluation of the letter's composition qualities that is acceptable, and that is "perfect."

The Attitude in the Letter

The tone and attitude of the letter have already been mentioned briefly in other areas. However, it is so vital that once again the applicant is reminded that the tone of the letter should be friendly, frank, and natural. The attitude displayed should reflect a sincere desire on the part of the writer to do a good job and prove to be of real value to the firm.

Avoid boasting, timid, or shy statements and negative or trite comments and exaggeration. Just be yourself; say what is in your heart as directly and exactly as possible.

Personal Factors

Salary. If the advertisement does not request a comment on salary, skip it. This sensitive topic can be discussed at the interview much more advantageously.

If the advertisement does read "state salary desired," then you should discuss it in your letter. There is no point in ignoring the advertiser's request. It is true that you may be involved in a bit of a dilemma, for it is often felt that a figure too high or too low will eliminate your letter and you from further consideration. However, there are three possible solutions which might be considered:

1. Bracket your salary. On the basis of my education and experience I feel that a salary of $395 to $425 per month would prove equitable.
2. State and hedge. A salary of $425 per month would be satisfactory. However, I am primarily concerned with associating myself with a firm which recognizes hard work and competence. I am sure that an equitable salary may be reached at the time of an interview.
3. Indicate that you will accept his fair offer. As for salary, I shall be glad to accept the going rate which your firm has established for the position.

The suggestions above are predicated on the fact that you know approximately what a job in your field, based on your background, should offer. By your senior year in college you should be well aware of this; if you are not sure, a few minutes spent with your school's placement director or an instructor in your major department should prove very profitable.

However, if you indicate in your letter that "any salary will do" or that "salary is completely secondary," you will not usually arouse the respect of the prospective employer. If you do not place value on your own services, it is difficult to expect someone else to do it for you.

Religion and Race. This is an especially delicate area. Unfortunately, there are still many narrow-minded individuals (and, alas, companies also) who will not consider an applicant if his religion or race is not "acceptable." From this point of view, everyone may be a member of a minority group if the person doing the hiring does not approve of that group.

What to do? What to do?

There are placement counselors who say, "Mention it in the first letter; don't waste his time or yours." There are others who say, "State nothing on this score if no request is made. He will learn of your background at the interview and may suddenly recognize how wrong he has been about your group. Not only will you benefit, but also everyone of your religion or race."

The only thing you can do if your group has been subjected to bias more than others, is to let the circumstances, situation, and your heart guide you. There can hardly be a better solution to a problem involving human nature that is influenced by many deep-seated viewpoints.

Draft Status.   Service in the armed forces is now such a usual procedure for every young American man that it should be commented on in the letter if such information is requested in the advertisement. Most large firms are quite ready to hire, train, and employ you until the time you enter service and then reëmploy you as soon as you are discharged.

If you have completed your tour of service, then that fact should be included in your letter of application.

THE INTERVIEW

The interview is what you hoped your letter would secure for you; this is what you have been looking for—an opportunity to tell this prospective employer, in detail, about yourself and give him the time to evaluate your personality, attitudes, appearance, and general make-up.

It is really quite surprising how many people will take four or five hours to plan, organize, write, revise, and edit a letter of application before they are satisfied with it; yet these people will walk into an interview without spending five minutes preparing for it.

One of the nation's university placement directors had this to say about the interview:

Key to the entire recruitment process is the interview. Here, in a twenty-minute period are made or broken the opportunities for further consideration by the employer. Good impressions don't happen. They are created by careful advance preparation.[1]

Know What You Want

You should have your abilities carefully organized in your mind when you walk in for an interview. You should know specifically what job you want and what others you could handle.

An accepted theorem in the personnel field is that a person who says, "I can do anything," usually can do nothing . . . or at least, nothing very well.

Sit down and take stock of yourself, your education, and experience. Can you handle general accounting procedures? How about cost? Budgeting? Auditing? Have you had enough exposure to management to enable you to work in some phase of that field if an offer should be made which would prove attractive?

Perhaps there is no immediate opening in accounting but the company does need a sales correspondent. How many courses have you had in business writing? And how does such a proposal strike you?

Know what positions you can fill and what you cannot or will not. Review your qualifications so they will be fresh in your mind and you will be able to substantiate immediately your competence for a specific opening.

Know About the Company

Prior to going in for your interview, you should gather as much information as possible about the company. This will not only permit you to carry on an intelligent conversation with the interviewer, but it will indicate to him your sincere interest in knowing about the company.

You should have some information about the products the company manufactures, how long it has been in business, where its main and branch offices are, the names of its parent or subsidiary firms, the organizational plan of the company, and the buyers of its products. Some of this information you will not be able to secure, but even if you have data in only a few of the areas, it will assist you in evaluating the company and help you in carrying on a discussion.

[1] *College Placement Annual,* 1958, p. 11. Statement by F. Y. Mitchell, Director, Appointments Office, Duke University.

Some of the sources which you may utilize to secure background information on a company are *Standard and Poor's Corporation Records, Moody's Investor's Guide, Moody's Industrial Manual, Moody's Public Utility Manual, Moody's Transportation Manual, Moody's Municipal and Government Manual,* and *Thomas' Register of American Manufacturers.*

The local library probably has a file of annual reports from major companies and you may find one from the firm that you are going to visit. If it is a local company, the library may have a brochure or two which the company has issued.

Prepare Several Questions

There are several reasons why you should prepare a half dozen questions to ask the interviewer:

1. Certainly you want to know something about the company's policies and regulations for your protection. Why affiliate yourself with a firm whose plans and policies are not agreeable to you?
2. Asking several penetrating questions of the interviewer will be evidence of your own maturity and desire to be selective—both commendable qualities.
3. While the interviewer is answering your questions, you will have an opportunity "to catch your breath," compose yourself, evaluate your earlier answers (for possible revision), and prepare other questions.

Some of the questions which will reflect your own critical analysis and which are perfectly acceptable to ask are these:

1. Who are some of the major buyers and users of the firm's products?
2. What is the firm's policy on promoting employees who demonstrate merit and competence?
3. Is the business seasonal or cyclical? ("Am I just being hired for the busy season?" is what you are getting at.)
4. What fringe benefits does the company offer?
5. How old is the firm? What percentage of its employees are "long-service" people?
6. Will my position entail traveling?
7. Can you tell me more about the duties of this job and the

nature of the organization in that department and in the company?

8. Are "outsiders" often brought in for supervisory positions or is the firm's policy one of "promoting from within"?
9. Does the firm support some type of educational program for its employees?
10. Does the company offer its employees any stock-buying plans or similar programs?

Of course, you will be able to think of others, and the time and situation will determine which ones you will ask and which you will not. Naturally you will not go into your interview with any of these written down on paper; they should appear to be spontaneous and related to the immediate subject under discussion.

In every case watch the word choice and the content. It would surely be unwise to ask about vacations early in the interview, although you could ask about fringe benefits. You would not inquire immediately about raises, although you might ask about the company advancement policy. These should all be carefully thought through, evaluated, and prepared.

Appearance and Manner

The topic of dress, personal appearance, and conduct at the interview has been so frequently and thoroughly discussed on other occasions as to require little additional mention here.

Suffice it to say that young men and women should always present themselves at an interview in a well-groomed, conservative fashion. Jackets should be buttoned, and clothing and accessories should be in good taste.

Your posture, while sitting, should be erect and your general manner one of alertness and interest. Your features should be alive, vital, and active. Do not forget to *look* pleasant. Smile; don't "freeze up." Laugh if the occasion calls for it, and in all cases, act natural but always in "good taste."

Be aware of your verbal communication. Speak in complete, carefully enunciated sentences. Choose your words carefully; watch your grammar; discard slang, "yeh's," and any trace of "dese, dem, and dose."

In other words let your manner and appearance reflect the polished executive type which you one day will certainly be.

The interview is what you have been striving for, shooting to achieve, hoping to secure. Make the most of it through planning, preparation, and thought.

FOLLOW-UP LETTER

At a recent convention of the American Business Writing Association, a personnel director related a very interesting incident. He said,

A year ago we advertised for a mature, experienced woman to become our office manager. We wanted someone to supervise 30 girls, take care of office details, supervise billing, correspondence, etc. It took us two weeks to narrow the field down to two; either of whom would doubtlessly prove satisfactory. For some reason I decided on Miss A, perhaps because she was born and raised in the city and knew of the growth of the Company. However, that afternoon I received a cordial note from Miss B, thanking me for the time I had given her in three interviews, telling me of her continued interest in the job, briefly recapitulating her major qualifications, and asking me to select her for the position.

Well, what would *you* do? Of course, I selected Miss B. She had demonstrated courtesy, interest, and a real desire for the job through her little note. In other words, she had followed through.

And that is what a brief follow-up letter *does* demonstrate: *courtesy* and thanks for the time spent at the interview, *interest* in the firm and the position, and *desire* to secure the job.

Writing a follow-up letter seems to be such a logical and natural thing to do, and yet personnel directors indicate that they rarely, if ever, secure a note of this nature. Why not? What is so difficult about taking a few minutes to express appreciation and interest? The answer is difficult to find, but the facts are not. This we know —few people write such a letter following an interview and if you do, it will most certainly be read and thought about.

Qualities of the Follow-up Letter

This letter should be brief, sincere, and sent out immediately after the interview is held.

Brevity is a prime ingredient of this note. It should recall the interview or letter to the reader's mind; it should briefly recapitulate the major qualifications of the writer; and it should emphasize the applicant's continued interest in the position.

Dear Mr. Barry:

Once again I want to thank you for the time you spent with me on Monday, June 10, telling me about the opening your firm has for an accountant.

Now that I know more about the job and the company, I am more than ever sure that I would like the position and that my abilities and background would prove of value to your firm.

You may recall that I have a degree from Dawson with my major in accounting, as well as two years' part-time experience with Frank and Harris, C.P.A.'s. This, coupled with my interest, will certainly help make me an asset to your organization.

I shall be happy to again come in and discuss this more thoroughly with you. Just call ORchard 6-0754.

Sincerely yours,

Dear Mr. Forsythe:

The time you spent with me last Tuesday was certainly appreciated. The description of the position of assistant to the marketing research director was clear and complete.

Now that I have had an opportunity to weigh all my qualifications with the needs of the job, I am sure that my services would prove of real value to the Archer Steel Corporation.

My degree in marketing, my interest in research, and my desire to find out what motivates people, all "add up" for consideration as assistant to your research director. I hope your evaluation will result in approving me as the man for the job.

In the meantime, if you would like additional information, or if you would prefer to see me for further discussion, please call JUniper 8-8073.

Sincerely yours,

Besides brevity, the follow-up letter must be sincere. If it sounds "trumped up," overenthusiastic about the job, or too flattering toward the firm, it will receive little or no attention. Write briefly, say what you have to say, and stop.

Finally, in the follow-up letter, remember to be prompt. Send it on the same day or the day following the interview. If you wait much longer, the job may be filled or perhaps someone else's letter will receive the attention you hoped yours would get.

This then is the letter of application—one of the most important letters (unless you propose by mail) you will write in your life. Do a good job; plan carefully; work hard. It may mean the difference between holding a routine job or a challenging one, between $7,000 a year and $17,000, and between working in a rut or at your highest potential.

QUESTIONS FOR DISCUSSION

I. Criticize the following beginnings for letters of application. Explain why you feel some are good and others are not.

1. This is in answer to your ad which appeared in the Sunday *Banner.*
2. Someone said, "There's always room at the top," and that's where I would like to go with your company—to the top.
3. You can stop looking now; I'm the man for the job.
4. A competent accountant should have a minimum of four years of collegiate education, some work experience in the field, and a desire to work hard. I fill all these qualifications; please consider me for the job.
5. Mr. Sharpe of The Helmut Advertising Agency suggested that I write you about a possible opening on your staff.
6. Have you ever said, "Oh, if I only had a girl Friday who could handle *all* the office details"? If you have, your girl Friday has arrived.
7. "Sure we're full, but I'm positive we can find room for one more," was what the circus ticket taker would say. I'm hoping you'll reply the same way after you finish this letter.
8. Your advertisement requested an aggressive, sales minded young man with some college training in marketing. Please read my application and note how well I fit your requirement.
9. Check, check, check was all I could say when I found your ad called for a young lady with collegiate background, ability to type, and a very pleasant personality. Why don't you check, check, check my letter of application so that you can now evaluate my qualifications in detail?
10. An audit of my enclosed profit and loss sheet will convince you that I would be a decided asset to your firm.

II. Criticize the following one-part letters of application. Be specific in your comments.

1.

Dear Mr. Grant:

I understand that you are looking for a full-time accountant for your offices. You can stop looking *now;* I am the man for the job!

In June of this year, I shall graduate from Columbus College with a major in accounting. Although I do not wish to seem boastful, I think you should know that I maintained a B average in accounting, was 21st in my graduating class, and I was generally well thought of by my professors.

Although I have no practical experience in the field of accounting, I know that the courses which I had in college should be adequate for your purposes.

I am 21 years of age, healthy, and eager to start work at a good salary immediately. I shall list references for you at the time of an interview. Please call me at HO 5-1931 to make arrangements.

Sincerely yours,

2.

Dear Mr. Powers:

I was deeply impressed with the talk you delivered on May 17 to the Marketing Club of State University.

The challenges, ideas, frustrations, and advantages of the field of advertising left me breathless. For almost four years I have prepared myself for a career in advertising which would lead me toward the goals you listed. Please evaluate my record so that you may see for yourself that I would be a valuable asset to your company.

Education

In my four years at State, I have taken 14 different courses in the Department of Marketing with most of these in the specific area of advertising. In addition, I have minored in English, a field which has made me tremendously aware of the techniques and requirements of good writing style. I have also taken courses in shorthand and typing so that I could serve in a secretarial capacity as well.

While attending State, I was a member of the Women's Political Club, the Band, and Beta Theta, a national sorority.

Experience

During my four years at State, I have always held a part-time job which has helped pay my tuition and living expenses. For two years I worked in the main library and for an additional two years I worked for Graduate Typing Service, a small company which specialized in preparing graduate dissertations.

Capacity

I am a young lady who likes to work with people; I have always found that most individuals are pleasant and easy to get along with. I enjoy sports, good music, and unusual foods. I am in excellent health, 23 years of age, and unmarried.

References

The people which I have listed below will be happy to give you a fair evaluation of my capabilities.

Mrs. E. Spore, Dean of Women   Prof. Alfred Tryte, Chairman
State University   Department of Marketing
Administration Building   State University
Chicago, Illinois   Chicago, Illinois

Mr. Robert Hallecke, Owner   Winslow Graft, M.D.
Graduate Typing Service   109 South Baxter Road
104 North Jackson Street   Chicago, Illinois
Chicago 41, Illinois

I am sure that if you will allow me a few minutes of your time, I can give you many other facts on my background which will prove that I will be of benefit to your company.

Hopefully yours,

Marcia Lord

3.
Dear Sir:

Your advertisement in the Sunday *Tribune* called for a young engineer who had some experience in electronics and a degree from an accredited school. I fill the requirements to a "T."

My *education* consists of four years of training at Illinois Technical College. At this school I majored in electrical engineering and took as many courses in mathematics as I could. I have also taken three graduate courses in their evening division as I am desirous of securing a master's degree in the area of advanced electronics.

My *experience* should prove advantageous in the job you describe. For three summers I worked with the Continental Telephone Company which, as you probably know, is the supplier of telephone equipment for the Rocky Mountain Phone and Telegraph Corporation.

Since my graduation from Illinois Technical, I have been employed as a junior research engineer at Northern Switch Corporation. Although the work is interesting, opportunities for advancement are very limited. The job you describe seems like a real challenge for a hard-working conscientious young man—I'd like to be that young man.

Will you, therefore, call me at Sheldrake 3-8825 to arrange for an interview? At that time, I can give you additional details on myself, list references, and tell you how I can serve your company effectively.

Sincerely yours,

Robert Washburn

4.

Gentlemen:

This is in answer to your advertisement for a business administration graduate who is interested in a trainee position.

I shall graduate from Carton College on the 10th of next month with a Bachelor of Science degree in Commerce. My major area of concentration was business administration and my minor area was accounting. In addition, I have had courses in business writing, marketing, management, history and other areas, all of which have helped to round out my education.

I began working part time when I was a junior in high school and have continued that pattern. During the summers I was employed full time. All my earnings have been used for my educational expenses. I am sure that this will indicate to you that I am a young man of maturity and responsibility.

I would sincerely appreciate an opportunity to come in and

speak to you. At that time I could list references, give you additional facts on my work and educational background and answer any questions which you may have. Please call me at Harrison 3-3434.

Sincerely yours,

Byron Blakee

III. Criticize the following cover letters for two-part letters of application.

1.

Dear Sir:

Your advertisement in yesterday's *Gazette* was of real interest to me because I think I shall be of real interest to you.

A college education, two years of experience, and a desire to associate myself with a company that desires a hard-working man are all plus factors in my favor.

Please check my attached data sheet to determine how well I meet your requirements. I shall be pleased to come in for an interview if you have any questions.

Sincerely,

Robert Famper

2.

Dear Mr. Burnee:

I was delighted to learn from our placement director that you are looking for a junior accountant for your company. For some years I have heard wonderful things about your accounting company; now I would like to become a player on your team.

This June I shall receive a Bachelor of Science Degree in Commerce from Preston College. I majored in accounting and had ten different courses which are listed on the attached data sheet. In addition, I took approximately 21 hours in the area of business administration.

During my four years at Preston, I worked part time and

summers for Salem and Salem, C.P.A.'s. Through this job I was able to pay my school expenses and gain valuable experience.

However, I didn't permit school and work to monopolize all my time. I was active in the Accounting Society, Young Citizens League, and Theta Beta Gamma.

Additional details may be found on the attached data sheet. Please call me at Orchard 7-8654 to arrange for an interview. I shall come in at any time that is convenient for you.

Sincerely yours,

Peter P. Price

3.

Dear Mr. Gail:

"At last," I said to myself when Dean Frale handed me my degree last week. Now, I thought to myself, I could go ahead with a long-time ambition of attempting to secure an assistant buyer's job with Pame and Johnson.

All my life, I have found Pame and Johnson the most exciting store in the world. For years I have said to myself, "That's the place I want to work."

I hope you will feel the same about me when you finish reading the attached resumé of my background. Details of my education, experience, a list of references, and personal information are all carefully set down.

Please call me at Washington 2331 to arrange for an interview. I know I can serve Pame and Johnson excellently in that assistant buyer's position.

Sincerely yours,

Margaret Paine

4.

Dear Mr. Green:

You may recall that you spoke to the Young Engineers Club at State Technical Institute late last year.

I was deeply impressed with your address and the comments you made about your architectural company.

Here at State Technical, I specialized in architecture and became especially interested in school building and church design. Thus, when I heard that your company specialized in these areas, I thought I would write and apply for a junior position.

In just four weeks, I shall receive my engineering degree from State Tech. I have enjoyed my work and I was elected to Theta Sigma, honorary Engineering organization, in my senior year.

During my summers I worked on various construction projects so that I could gain practical experience to supplement the theory of the classroom.

On the enclosed data sheet I have listed my education, major courses, extra curricular activities, references, and other facts with which I am sure you are interested.

I would appreciate an opportunity to come in and speak to you about a job with your firm. Please call me and let me know when it will be convenient for you to permit me to come in for an interview.

Sincerely yours,

James R. Stevens

IV. Criticize the following data sheets.

1. Robert T. McKinley
   1212 South Jackson Drive
   Los Angeles 34, California
   Olympic 5-3124

Education   (*Photograph*)

   Bachelor's Degree from California State College, 1959.
   Additional graduate work at California State College, 1960.
   Major Field: Advertising
   Minor Field: Management

Experience

   Blake and Martin, part time, 1957-1958, clerk-typist.
   Johnson and Johnson, part time, 1959, assistant office manager.

Hartnell and Associates, full time, 1959—present, copy writer.

Personal

Age: 27
Marital Status: Single
Draft Status: Not subject to draft; service obligation completed.
Health: Excellent
Height and weight: 5'10"; 175 pounds.

References

Furnished on request.

2. Henry T. Malley
   480 South Crescent Dr.
   Chicago 3, Illinois
   Lincoln 9-0303

      (*Photograph*)

Age: 24
Height: 6'1"
Weight: 185 pounds
Health: Excellent

Job Objective

To secure a position with a firm that recognizes hard work so that I can rise to a management position within a reasonable length of time.

Major Qualifications

Education and experience in the field of accounting.

Experience

Part-Time: Price and Warren, C.P.A.'s, 1956-1958.
             Maling Accounting Associates, 1958-1960.
             Both of these positions gave me valuable experience in inventory control, cost accounting, and auditing.

Education

Bachelor of Science, 1960, Illinois State College
Associate in Arts Certificate, 1958, Chicago Junior College
Major Field: Accounting
Minor Field: Management

Extra-Curricular Activities

President, Accounting Club, 1959.
Captain, Illinois State Track Team.
Hobby: Wood carving, chess and bridge.

References

Prof. Thomas Haymes
Department of Accounting
Illinois State College
Washington, Illinois

Thomas Price
Price and Warren, C.P.A.'s
1518 S. Kenneth
Chicago, Illinois

Randolph Maling
Maling Accounting Associates
122 East LaSalle Street
Chicago, Illinois

Dr. Frank Fedder
185 South Dearborn
Chicago, Illinois

V. Carry through the following assignments.
 1. Choose an advertisement from the classified section of a news-
    paper and complete a two-part letter of application. Choose an
    advertisement that you would sincerely answer if you were in
    a position to do so. You may make no assumptions concern-
    ing your education or experience which are not true except
    one. You may assume that you have just recently graduated
    or you are about to graduate from college and you possess
    the credits and courses which accompany your degree or certi-
    ficate.
 2. Repeat the assignment above except this time write a one-part
    letter of application.
 3. Send out an unsolicited two-part letter of application. Assume
    that you will graduate within three weeks.
 4. Assume that you have had a one-hour interview with the per-
    sonnel director of a firm of your choice. Send him a follow-up
    note to the interview.
VI. Answer any one of the following advertisements which have been
    taken from the Sunday issue of the *Sun-Gazette*.

Acc't wanted. Interesting job,
good pay, must have college degree. Experience helpful but not
essential. Reply in detail, state
salary. Box RL 102

Electrical engineer for West
Coast aircraft company. Excellent salary and fringe benefits.
Write immediately giving complete background. MX 103

Competent executive secretary wanted. Must have excellent typing and office ability. Willing to handle vice-president details on own initiative. Exc. pay; gd. working conditions. Reply to Box 3212

Sales trainee wanted. College education in mkting helpful. Must be aggressive and pleasant. Exc. opportunity for right man. Box TR 331.

Engineer wanted by electronic machine corp. Experience on computers helpful but not necessary. Unlimited future for bright young man. Degree required. Age 23-27. Reply Box ER21

Ass't buyer wanted in dress dept. of major woman's store. Young lady 25-30 desired with some exp. Good pay, exc. fringe benefits, 5-day week. Write Mrs. Adams, 121 State St., New York.

Part II

Business Letter Writing

Chapter 19

Mechanics and Principles of Letter Writing

In our modern world of business, science, industry, and government, the business letter accomplishes several vital purposes. Under all circumstances we hope that it will build good will for the company or agency which originates the message. Secondly, we assume that it will convey a message regarding a specific matter of importance that is related to the sender and the receiver. And finally, we know that it will serve as a record for many years to come of a transaction or a proposal.

When a business letter is incomplete, discourteous, or confusing, it does not accomplish its primary purposes. Then time is lost, money is wasted, and tempers become short. The few brief chapters which follow will present and discuss the principles of letter writing which will assist the writer in securing the three purposes, listed above, in every letter sent out.

MECHANICS OF THE BUSINESS LETTER

Through the years the format of the business letter has changed according to the needs of the times and the desires of the writers. The paragraphs which follow, concerning the general make-up of the letter, are offered to the reader as *suggestions*. The comments are not meant to be rules; they are merely suggestions. Almost every company has its individual preferences on how it wishes its letters arranged, how the inside address shall be typed, and what particular format shall be used in the layout of the entire letter.

For the person who is interested, it is a simple matter to secure in any one large urban center, 50 or 60 manuals published by individual firms. These all tell the company's employees just exactly what the firm recommends when a letter is typed and directed to a customer or client. Frequently these manuals differ from one another regarding the suggestions made on the mechanical aspects of the letter. But there is no arguing with the manuals because they do reflect the viewpoint of the company. There is considerable variation among firms in the type of inside address or layout that is preferred. Therefore, the statements which follow should not be interpreted as hard and fast rules. They are merely suggestions on the mechanical aspects of the business letter which have been generally accepted.

FORMS OF THE BUSINESS LETTER

Business today utilizes a variety of different forms in the typing of its letters. Among the most popular are the block, the modified-block, and the full-block forms. The illustration below will give you an idea of the format that is usually followed for these three.

A further modification on the full-block form has been suggested

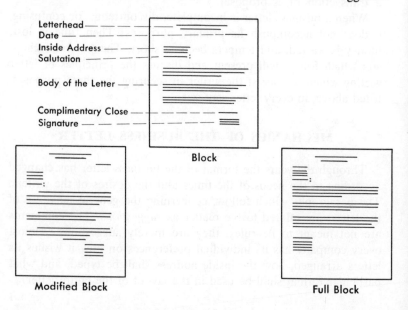

Letterhead
Date
Inside Address
Salutation

Body of the Letter

Complimentary Close
Signature

Block

Modified Block

Full Block

for some years by the National Office Management Association. This organization has recommended what they call a simplified letter form.

It will be noted in the illustration of the simplified letter form both the salutation and the complimentary close are omitted. The reasoning behind this is probably obvious: inasmuch as most people agree that the "Dear Sir" and "Yours very truly" have very little meaning, why should they be used at all? Furthermore, time is saved and, consequently, office expense. This particular form, however, has not been readily acceptable to most American companies. It is rather unconventional, and many firms are reluctant to break the habits of years of correspondence.

Simplified Letter

In addition to these, there is the indented form, which has become almost completely obsolete. Typing a letter and envelope in this style requires that the typist space more carefully and spend additional time on the mechanics of the letter. This again increases office expense.

Indented Form   Executive Form   Hanging Indention

There is also the letter form which places the inside address immediately below the signature section and along the left margin of the page. This has been used for many years by various branches of the federal government; in many cases industry has followed suit because, as one executive put it, "Why place the inside address at the top of the letter when no one really reads it except the filing clerk." There is some logic to this statement.

The hanging indention form has been used rather infrequently by most companies because of the care necessary in typing the entire letter. It can be appreciated, from looking at the illustration above, that one misplaced line, going out to the margin when the line should be indented, can be disastrous. The only correction for such an error would be to retype the letter.

These are just some of the forms which are used by companies today. Whichever one you utilize is largely up to you or the firm which employs you. However, the letter writer should be consistent and never use one form in part of the letter and a different form in another.

PARTS OF THE BUSINESS LETTER

For purposes of discussion and instruction, the business letter is usually divided into six parts. Each of these will be explained very briefly; however, the reader should again keep in mind that these statements are merely suggestions.

The Heading

The heading is usually said to consist of two parts: the letterhead and the date. The former can be one of the most important factors in a letter, and most companies in the United States today have come to realize the value of an attractive letterhead. The sheet of stationery which carries a large, awkward, and poorly printed letterhead design certainly does not reflect a firm whose taste and dignity are impressive. On the other hand, the neatly spaced and attractively printed letterhead which may or may not carry an illustration of the company's product or factory site may favorably impress the recipient of the letter.

Styles in letterhead design have changed through the years. Three or four generations ago the letterhead was filled with impressive scroll work, photographs of the company officers, and ornate printing embellished with curlycues and flowing capital letters. As time went on, the ostentatious nature of letterheads disappeared, and today many have become so conservative as to be almost severe in their appearance.

The individual who is interested in drawing up a letterhead for his own company or revising the one which presently exists may secure the services of any one of the large paper corporations which specialize in this field. Most of these firms have staff artists who will design a letterhead on the basis of instructions or their own ingenuity. In addition, these same companies will be happy to supply most interested parties with letterhead "design kits" which are made up to give the prospective stationery purchaser ideas for his own letterhead. Graph paper, sample letterheads, and a variety of different types of stationery are included for inspection. But whether the letterhead is designed by a professional in the field, an advertising agency, or yourself, it should include *who, where,* and *what.*

The *who,* of course, is the name of the company; the *where* answers the questions: street location? phone number? and cable address? The type of product and/or what the company makes or what the service is that the company offers, is the answer to *what.* Nothing is more disturbing than to receive a letter from the Excello Corporation located at 1221 North Michigan Boulevard in Chicago, Illinois, and not have the least idea whether the company manufactures locomotives or whether it offers an accounting service.

Many firms utilize the bottom portion of the sheet of paper for some of their letterhead information. It is often felt that this space is completely wasted and a listing of the company's products or its address at the bottom of the page is of real value.

The second part of the heading is the date. It is recommended that it be typed in either of the following two methods:

> August 4, 1960
> 4 August 1960

Both of these are widely used by America's industries today. The second method grew out of government use during World War II. Because there is so much to recommend it, it has been widely accepted. It is certainly unwise to have the date typed as either 1-6-60 or 1/6/60. Not only does this seem to be discourteous through its haste, but also it may result in confusion. In European and Latin American countries where this numerical method is used, the day always precedes the month, which is the converse of the system accepted in America. It is easy to see the difficulties and misunderstandings which might arise when this numerical system is used.

The Inside Address

The inside address should contain all the information necessary to insure that the letter is directed to its intended recipient. The data in the inside address are usually repeated *in toto* on the envelope. Most secretaries feel that all of the vital information in the letterhead of the letter which is being answered should appear in the inside address. There is some disagreement on this point because a letterhead may sometimes include a suite number, the name of a building, and other information which may not be vital in the inside address. However, the recipient's name, his title, his department, the name of his company, street address, and the city and state should be indicated.

Here are a few suggestions on the make-up of the inside address: The recipient's title should always be utilized whether it is *Mrs., Mr., Captain, Doctor, Reverend or Admiral.* Each of us has a title and it should be used. If the individual has an office or a capacity, that should also be noted. Abbreviations should be utilized sparingly and only if the company specifically desires that they be used. Street numbers with the exception of *one* should be indicated as numerals. Street names from First to Tenth Street should be spelled out. From 11th street on, numerals should be used. The zone should follow the name of the city.

Dr. Robert T. Mason, Dean
College of Commerce
Central State College
101 North Main Street
Centerville 3, Ohio

Miss Joyce Gilmere
One North Jackson Drive
New York 3, New York

Dr. Robert James, Director
Cancer Research Clinic
Mercy General Hospital
109 West Fifth Avenue
Los Angeles 3, California

Mr. Robert T. Harlow
2121 West 63rd Street
Chicago 5, Illinois

Mr. Peter M. Downs, Ass't Manager
Personnel Department
Fairfax Corporation
103 West Madison Avenue
San Francisco 5, California

Miss Bertha Fine
21 South 121st Street
Albany, New York

The Salutation

The salutation, or the third part of the business letter, has become rather standardized throughout American industry. For the male singular, it is *Dear Sir;* the plural is *Gentlemen. Dear Sirs* is now obsolete. In the feminine, *Dear Madam* and *Ladies* are used. The *Mesdames* is outdated. But superior to these is the recipient's name. *Mr. Burton, Miss Johnson,* or *Mrs. Kennedy* are all preferable to *Dear Sir* or *Dear Madam.* Most of us like to see our name in print and our reaction to a letter is much more favorable if that letter begins with our name rather than *Dear Homeowner, Dear Friend, Dear Occupant,* or *Dear Sir.*

There is a trend among those persons who are attempting to make the business letter less formal, to begin the letter with a salutation phrase such as *Thank you, Mr. Brown* or *It was a pleasure, Mr. Green* or *We were sorry, Miss Benton.* These openings seem, as one letter writer says, "To get the piece of correspondence off to a running start." In all cases these short phrases appear in the same position in the letter as the salutation.

The Body

The body of the letter and its make-up are largely determined by the type of letter under consideration. Because the remaining chapters in this section discuss the different types of letters, we can omit such treatment for the moment.

The Complimentary Close

This section of the business letter has, like the salutation, become almost completely standardized. Perhaps the most popular forms are *Truly yours, Yours truly, Sincerely, Sincerely yours,* and *Yours sincerely.* The term *Cordially yours* seems to be gaining in popularity. *Respectfully yours* should be used only under those conditions which warrant such a statement.

As in the case of the salutation, there has been a movement to make the complimentary close more meaningful and personal. Toward that end some companies close their letters with phrases in reference to their product or service. Some which have been used are *Buy an Excello today* or *Yours for the best in home fur-*

nishings or *Truly an excellent restaurant*. The novelty of these as well as their content often make a favorable impression on the reader provided the author does not become "Too cute" or clever in the make-up of the complimentary phrase.

Signature

There is probably more variety in the make-up of the signature of the business letter than in any of the other five parts. Some companies utilize a two-part signature; others a three- or four-part signature. On the whole a four-part signature is usually recommended. This should consist of the company name, in upper case type, the written signature of the author, his typed name, and his title. Whether these four parts are arranged on three lines or four is immaterial. They usually appear in one block; however, it is not uncommon to find the typed name of the author at the left margin. Below are some typical examples of acceptable signature forms.

ACME STEEL COMPANY

Robert Smyth

Robert Smyth
Sales Manager

PEACOCK JEWELRY
COMPANY

Peter Jay

Peter Jay, Comptroller

JOHNSON MACHINERY
COMPANY

Burton Brice

Burton Brice: BG

Credit Manager

MISCELLANEOUS FACTORS IN THE MAKE-UP OF THE BUSINESS LETTER

The Attention Device

Frequently in industry we would like to have one individual or a department in another company receive and process our letter. Perhaps Mr. Johnson at the Acme Corporation knows that we always ship by Baltimore and Ohio Railroad, that we invariably purchase quarter-inch brass tubing, or that our orders should invariably be sent out C.O.D. For reasons such as these we may direct our letter to Mr. Johnson's attention. This has an advantage over sending the letter directly to him, for if it is addressed to Mr. Johnson at the Acme Corporation and he is no longer with that company, or he has been transferred, that letter will be *returned* to the sender or *forwarded on* to Mr. Johnson. However, if we send it to the company, but to Mr. Johnson's attention, and he has left the company or has been transferred, that letter will be processed by his replacement. Thus the distinct advantage in using this device, is that whether or not the individual to whose attention the letter is sent is with the company, the letter will be opened and read.

The position of the attention line often varies according to the company. Most frequently it may be found in any one of the following places:

Superior Fixture Company
121 East Harrison Avenue
Chicago 3, Illinois

Attention of Mr. T. Roberts, Treasurer

Gentlemen:

Martin Scientific Instrument Company
1115 East Fifth Avenue
San Diego 3, California

      Attention of Miss Brice

Gentlemen:

Superior Rug Corporation
21 East Jackson Boulevard
Chicago 7, Illinois

           Attention of Mr. Ransom, President

Gentlemen:

Lakely Hotel Corporation
2150 West Roosevelt Avenue
Milwaukee 6, Wisconsin

Gentlemen: Attention of Mr. J. Lakely, Treasurer

Whenever the attention device is used in the inside address, it is also noted on the envelope of the letter. Some firms consistently abbreviate the word *attention* to *Att:* or *Attn:*. Typing the word out completely is preferred.

The Subject Line

In an effort to tell the reader what the nature of the letter is or to eliminate a good part of the information normally contained in the first paragraph, the subject line is used. Like the attention device, it may appear in a variety of different places in the upper portion of the letter. It is most usual, however, to find it in the middle of the page "on line" with the salutation or on the right side of the stationery opposite the inside address.

Matson Cartage Company
1418 West Albany Avenue
Newark 3, New Jersey

Gentlemen: Subject: Your shipment of May 12, 1960

Banner Wholesale Grocers
15 East Hoover Avenue
St. Louis 3, Missouri

                    Subject: Your invoice of May 5, 1960

Gentlemen:

Mr. Robert Thomas
Modern Metal Company
1500 West Filmore Drive
New Orleans 3, Louisiana   Subject: Your check of June 7, 1960

Dear Mr. Thomas:

It is easy to see that the use of the subject line can be of real assistance to the reader of the letter as well as to the clerk who is required to secure the file of correspondence and attach it to the letter for the one who will take action on it.

Identifying Initials and the Enclosure Line

Most firms request that the typist place her initials in the lower left-hand section of each letter. These are usually typed in either upper or lower case immediately to the right of the dictator's initials and separated from them by either a slash or colon. Because it is usually apparent who dictated the letter, the dictator's initials have been omitted more and more frequently in the last few years. However in some companies, the department head signs all letters although they may actually be dictated by any one of the six different members of that department. In such cases the initials of the dictator do not correspond with the initials of the signer of the letter.

TR/RB	SH:MT
FG:sm	GL/ps

The enclosure device is used whenever some other item such as a check, deed, or invoice is sent along with the letter. In business the word *Enclosure* appears immediately below the identifying initials. If there is only one, then just the word *Enclosure* is noted. If there is more than one enclosure in the envelope, the word is followed by the numeral indicating the number of enclosures. In government correspondence the enclosures are usually identified, so that if one is withdrawn, the recipient may be made aware of that fact.

BL:mm	ST/RB
Enclosure	Enclosures 3
GH:SM	LM:JM
Enclosures 2	Encl.
1. Deed to property	
2. Tax assessment bill	

Punctuation

In referring to the date, inside address, complimentary close, and signature, we sometimes speak of open and closed punctuation.

Open punctuation is used almost exclusively today and it requires no end-of-line punctuation. This obviously saves time in typing and therefore it saves money. Closed punctuation, which is not used very often, is recognized by a comma at the end of each line and a period at the end of the last line. This applies to the inside address, salutation (which uses a colon), and the complimentary close.

A frequent exception found with open punctuation is that the comma is used after the complimentary close. An example of closed punctuation follows:

June 6, 1960.

Mr. George M. Burt,
2121 South Forsyth Avenue,
New York 3, New York.

Dear Mr. Burt:
....
....
Yours very truly,

An example of open punctuation follows:

Tasty Beverage Company
2400 West Michigan Avenue
Fargo 3, North Dakota

Gentlemen:
....
....
Very truly yours

BAKER BOTTLE COMPANY

Peter Brown, President

PB:lm
Enclosure

Stationery

Stationery, like the letterhead, may be discussed at great length. However, in our case, space does not permit us to do that. Briefly however, the choice of stationery should be dictated by good taste and cost. A good quality paper will last longer and impress the recipient favorably. Of course there is the problem of office waste to consider also. Buying expensive paper so that it may be doodled on, formed into paper airplanes, or taken home to be used as scratch paper hardly seems wise. And yet we know that less than half the letter stationery purchased for American offices actually leaves the company as business letters. For that reason many firms are now buying several different grades of paper. The most costly is used by the executive personnel and less expensive grades are utilized for general work. In all cases, a good grade of bond, consistent with the purpose, should be secured. Here, as in the case of letterhead design, the paper manufacturing companies will be happy to offer samples and advice.

PRINCIPLES OF BUSINESS LETTER WRITING—
A BAKER'S DOZEN

Although it would take no great effort to list and discuss a score of principles for letter writing, limited space requires that we consider only the most important thirteen. These principles are the very heart of successful letters. Although the letter writer should not violate any of the suggestions made concerning mechanics, the result of deviation from the suggestions will not usually be serious. Certainly a firm will not gain or lose a customer if the address is typed 210 West Fifth Avenue rather than 210 West 5th Avenue; nor will it make much difference whether or not the complimentary close has a comma at the end of it. On the whole, any variations in the form of a letter will not deeply affect the business transaction.

However the same cannot be said when the *principles* of letter writing are not followed. The mechanics of a letter may be perfect, but if a tactless statement is made or a paragraph is incomprehensible, the business relationship between the parties will undoubtedly suffer. It is for this reason that the student should not only familiarize himself with the principles of letter writing, but he should also read as extensively as possible in this area.

1. The Principle of Completeness

As we probably know from other discussions, the business letter is an expensive instrument. In an efficiently organized company it is estimated that each letter costs approximately $2.30 to produce. When letters are sent out which are not complete, it means that the firms which receive them must write back and request additional information. The company which originated the correspondence is then required to write another letter often containing the information which *should have* been included in the basic communication. It is not unusual to find that 10 percent of a company's correspondence is taken up with supplying supplementary data which should have appeared in the initial letter. Not only is there a waste of money involved, but also good will suffers. Every letter should be checked for completeness before it is signed.

One sure way to secure completeness in your own writing is to organize and plan before the letter is dictated.

2. The Principle of Organization

Before any letter is written or dictated, a careful plan should be made. Normally we refer to this plan as an outline. Where and in what form the outline is made up, is not too important. What is vital is that some organizational plan be carried through. Notes may be placed in the margin of the letter to which the writer is replying, or a formal outline may be drawn up on a separate sheet of paper. Regardless of what system is used, however, the letter writer should set up a plan before he begins to communicate his ideas. The informal notations made below constitute a perfectly good plan for the letter which Mr. Briceson is going to dictate within the hour.

1. Acknowledge his November 15 request for credit.
2. Explain present credit system.
3. Imply the refusal.
4. Sales appeal on the Traverse Line.
5. Friendly close.

Such a listing of points can be extended and made more complete, or it can stand as it is. The most important factor to remember is that *some* plan must be made for every letter if the principle of organization is to be followed.

3. The Principle of Directness and Simplicity

Letters which are easy to understand and simple and direct in their statements are usually the most successful. Pompous phrases, extended sentences, and roundabout wording all present barriers in attempting to achieve clarity and force in writing.

Poor: Your letter of March 15 was received and examined with care and precision, and it was noted that your interest in our rust-resistant paint was a direct result of your careful and assiduous attention to an article which was written with great effort by one of our engineers for the technical and scientific journal titled *The Modern Engineer.*
Improved: Thank you for your recent inquiry concerning our rust-resistant paint.

The letter writer should not go too far in making his sentences simple and direct. If he does, he may find that all of his writing is made up of simple sentences which give his letter a child-like quality. He should use complex sentences primarily but keep them short and to the point.

4. The Principle of Short Paragraphs and Short Sentences

The letter writer should make every effort to keep his paragraphs down to a reasonable number of lines. The sheet of stationery which carries two, heavy block paragraphs, each of which has 25 lines,

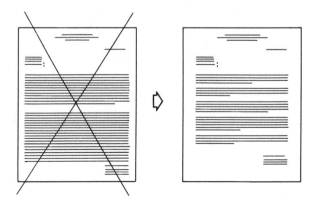

is unattractive and uninviting. The reader is repelled by what appears to be a big job. If possible, the number of lines in a paragraph should be kept to eight or ten.

Sentences also should be relatively short. When a sentence goes on for 140 words, it is difficult for the reader to remember and retain the primary ideas. A good rule to remember is: *one idea— one sentence.* Here again there is some danger that the writer in an effort to keep his sentences short will make them all simple. This is no solution to the problem, and it results in a letter that sounds as though it were written by a second grader. Present your ideas in clear sentences which are in the neighborhood of ten, fifteen, or twenty words each.

5. The Principle of Attractiveness

In our modern world today, we are duly impressed by appearance. Towels which are packaged in an attractive plastic case somehow seem to be of better quality than those thrown helter-skelter on a counter. Even a phonograph, fountain pen, or piece of jewelry somehow gains in quality when it is packaged attractively and is not one of dozens in a pile of similar items. The same is true of the business letter. A piece of correspondence that is neatly and perfectly typed and attractively placed on the paper with plenty of white space around it, impresses the reader favorably. He must feel that a letter like this can only come from a company that is well-organized and considerate of its customers and vitally concerned with its products. A letter that is haphazardly arranged on the page and contains a half dozen strikeovers and several sloppy erasures can only reflect poorly on the company which permits it to be mailed out.

Every letter should be examined before it is signed. The typing should be perfect; the placement on the page should be attractive; and a generous amount of white space should be allowed. When this is not true of the letter you are about to sign, you should return it to the typist without compunction on your part. She need only receive two or three of these back for retyping, and you may be sure that her future efforts will be much more satisfactory. By taking such action on your part, you will be doing your company a service and giving the typist a lesson in an important area of business communication.

6. The Principle of Correctness

The qualities of good grammar, coherence, unity, and emphasis have all been discussed earlier. They canot be overemphasized in letter writing. A mistake in English "jumps out of" the business letter in which it appears. Every one who has worked in an office has had the experience of seeing a letter passed from hand to hand or posted on a bulletin board because it contained a gross error or an illiteracy. A sentence like "If the report on the engine is satisfactory, send it at once" can result in an unnecessary freight bill if the receiver of the letter should send the engine when it was actually the report that was desired.

Every letter should be checked to make sure that it is correct. It is immaterial whether an error is your fault or the typist's; as long as your signature is on the letter, *you* are responsible.

7. The Principle of the Natural Style

For some peculiar reason the personality of many persons changes when they write or dictate a letter. So often the style of the letter becomes curt, sterile, and cold. Sometimes this is thought to be "business-like," but actually such reasoning is fallacious. There is no reason in the world why one should not write as he speaks. The same warmth, sincerity, and desire to be of assistance should be extended in the business letter as would be extended if the customer or client sat next to the writer's desk or stood across the counter from him.

Poor: Received yours of the 15th and beg to state that merchandise requested on your order No. 241 has been shipped as per your instructions. All merchandise complete with the exception of quarter-inch brass rods, catalogue No. 27273, which are presently out of stock. Item has been back ordered.

Better: Thank you for your recent order of May 15. It is always a pleasure to hear from our steady customers.

All the items which you requested except one have been shipped via Illinois Central Railroad and should arrive at your warehouse no later than June 1st.

Item 27273, quarter-inch brass rods, is temporarily out of stock. Because of its high quality and low price, it has sold exceptionally well, and the demand for it has been greater than we anticipated. We have, however, wired our Boston warehouse and they are sending us a quantity of this item by air express. Your request will be filled immediately thereafter and shipped.

Please call or wire us collect if this arrangement is satisfactory with you.

It is true that the second letter is longer, more costly, and more time-consuming than the first. But there can be no comparison between the warmth and sincerity of the two. The immediate reaction of most individuals to the first letter would be to attempt to secure the brass rods from another source. Certainly that would not be the case with the second. The reader must feel that the writer has a sincere desire to work with him. And that reaction is due entirely to the natural tone which is evident throughout the longer of the two letters.

In securing this natural and personal style and tone, the letter writer should attempt to eliminate as many stereotyped expressions as he can. Not that they are all bad; one or two may be used with good effect in a letter, but to fill a piece of correspondence with one meaningless phrase after another is ridiculous. Some of the words and expressions to be avoided are these:

As in the above	Enclosed please find
According to our records	Esteemed order
Advise	Hand you herewith
As per	Hereby acknowledge
At hand	In accordance with
As the case may be	Per
At an early date	Previous to
Attached hereto	Prior to
Attached please find	Persuant to
At earliest convenience	Permit me to say
Avail yourself of this opportunity	*Re* or *in re*
Beg to state	Recent date
Beg to remain	Take this opportunity
Contents noted	We wish to state
Contents duly noted	Would say
Due to	Would suggest

These are only a few of many archaic expressions that are used by the person who has no desire to give his letter the sincerity and originality it deserves.

8. The Principle of Conciseness

Keep your letters concise. Whether this requires three pages or three lines makes little difference. The important thing is to say what you have to say and then stop. Brevity is a valuable attribute, but conciseness is a more important one. The brief letter which contains ten lines when six would be adequate is not concise. A three-page letter which *requires* three pages to carry its message is concise.

9. The Principle of Courtesy

This is such an obvious factor that we often overlook it in the haste and pressures of business. It is better to say "Please send the reports by May 15" rather than "Send the reports by May 15." And it is just as easy to use the words *kindly, thank you,* and *may* as to avoid them. We are all well aware of what a magic word *please* is and when it and others like it are used with sincerity, they can assist us to an extensive degree in our letter writing problems.

10. The Principle of Speed

The letter writer who says, usually with some pride, "It seems to take me forever to get a good letter out; I've got to write a rough copy, revise it, edit it, and then dictate it—and even then when the typist brings it back, I find that it must be rewritten," has much to learn. The cost of such a practice is tremendous. If two men in an office are each paid a salary of $500 a month, and Mr. A. completes 25 letters a day, while Mr. B turns out 50, their rate of pay is far from similar. If all things are equal, it is easy to see how Mr. A. who turns out half as many letters as his colleague receives double the pay. And in addition, the company suffers many other expenses.

The best way to secure speed in business letter writing is to organize your thoughts, decide on the primary purpose of your letter, and make up an outline. With such a plan, you will find it easy and simple to compose and dictate letters rapidly.

11. The Principle of Tact

The person who possesses the quality of tact has the most vital attribute necessary in carrying on good relations with others. It has been defined as saying the right thing at the right time in the right place. But like most definitions, this one is much too simple. Frequently statements are made that are accurate in their meaning but untactful when interpreted. To say to a customer that he has "failed to indicate the color desired" or "We have received your letter in which you claim" may be completely accurate, but thoroughly untactful. Here we come to grips with word connotation and the meanings we have given to certain expressions and phrases.

POOR: You failed (or neglected) to list the color of dress desired.

BETTER: You inadvertently did not list the color of dress you desire; or Please list the color of dress desired and it will be sent out immediately.

POOR: We received your letter in which you claim we did not ship the jackets.

BETTER: Your letter of March 15th, concerning the Ace Jackets, was received.

POOR: We were surprised to hear that you did not find our Automatic cutter satisfactory.

BETTER: We received your letter concerning our No. 571 Automatic Cutter.

POOR: If you will read the book of instructions, you will find out that a child can operate our Excello Cleaner easily.

BETTER: Complete satisfaction with your Excello Cleaner may be achieved by following the suggestions made in the enclosed booklet of instructions.

In any discussion concerning tact in writing, difficulty is almost always encountered when a definition of tact is attempted. Perhaps it is nothing more than speaking and writing to individuals as you would expect them to speak and write to you.

12. The Principle of the "You" Attitude

Of all factors in business writing, the "you" attitude probably receives the most attention. Extended definitions are presented and scholarly discussions are carried through. Reduced to its simplest form, it is often said to be "communicating with the other person's point of view in mind." But to say this is not enough. For the result may be a series of insincere statements. Mr. Louis Baldwin wrote an article on the "you" attitude some years ago and he pointed out that among other things it was "an attitude." This is most accurate, for if one does not possess the proper attitude of understanding, sympathy, and appreciation for the other person, he can never really achieve a sincere and effective "you" attitude. Compare the two letters which follow. Notice how the one on the left is concerned only with the writer's interests, desires, and profits, whereas the one on the right makes a sincere effort to understand and appreciate the reader's position.

Dear Mr. Locke:

We are very much concerned with the new shipping container that is being used to bring our fine products to your store. As you probably noticed, we used a cardboard container for many years. However, in January of this year, we switched to a combination of plywood and steel strap which is much more costly to us.

In an effort to find out how effective this new package has been, and in our own best interests, we ask that you carefully check the contents of the deliveries made to you during this week and for the next ten days. Then complete the questionnaire which is enclosed with this letter.

We know that you will want to assist us, and we shall look forward eagerly to the receipt of the completed questionnaire.

Dear Mr. Locke:

In our effort to bring our dealers the best possible products at the lowest possible prices, we are constantly carrying through research. Because we are aware that our customers are desirous of receiving their merchandise in perfect condition, we are especially careful of the shipping containers used. Early this year we switched to a new plywood and metal strap box, which we thought would be easier for you to handle, store, and open.

We would appreciate it if you would give us the benefit of your years of experience and tell us, on the enclosed questionnaire, how the new container has worked out. We know that packages of merchandise in excellent condition sell more rapidly and thereby increase the profit margin of our dealers. We want to be sure therefore that every package you receive from us is as perfect as when it left our shipping department.

Will you, therefore, take the time to complete the enclosed questionnaire and return it no later than June 27? We will deeply appreciate your coöperation.

This is a brief discussion on the "you" attitude. You are reminded that if you will always make an effort to appreciate the viewpoint of the person with whom you are communicating, you are on your way to achieving this most important quality. It takes imagination, understanding, sympathy, and a desire to work with others on a friendly basis to achieve it. But regardless of the effort, the "you" attitude is well worth including in all your written and verbal contributions. It is certainly as necessary at the highest levels of intergovernmental affairs as it is in getting along with your customer, wife, neighbor, or child. To some extent it was summed up many years ago with a statement, "Do unto others as you would have them do unto you."

13. The Principle of the Positive Tone

In almost all situations, we like to learn about pleasant actions rather than unpleasant; we like to hear about what can be done rather than what cannot. It is for these reasons that large stores do not have sections titled "Complaint Department." Such a heading would motivate most individuals to think, "This must be a store that has a great deal of difficulty if it must establish a special department to handle complaints." However, the sign which reads "Adjustment Department," or "Customer Service Department," causes most persons to think of satisfaction and service.

What would your reaction be if after paying the television repair man $35.00, he said, "I sure hope this set doesn't continue to give you trouble"? You would indeed be skeptical of the caliber of his work. However, if he is an ethical technician who knows he has done a good job, wouldn't it be wiser to say, "Now that your set has been repaired, it will perform satisfactorily."

Because "tone" is so intimately associated with individual reactions and the interpretations we give to words, it is difficult to define. It is probably accurate to say that a negative tone arouses an unpleasant mental association with the product or service under discussion. Think of this definition as you read the following examples:

NEGATIVE: I hope you won't have trouble with your new Worksaver Washer.

POSITIVE: I know the efficiency and quality of your new Worksaver Washer will provide you with many extra hours of leisure time.

NEGATIVE: We do not think you will find our prices unreasonable.
POSITIVE: We are sure you will find our prices reasonable.

NEGATIVE: We don't think you will be dissatisfied if you stock our new line of merchandise.
POSITIVE: We know that when you stock our line you will find that it sells rapidly and results in a very satisfactory margin of profit.

NEGATIVE: We will hold up your shipment until we receive your payment.
POSITIVE: Your order has been processed and shipment will be made immediately after we receive your check.

An unpleasant or unfavorable mental association is aroused by each of the negative examples given above. In almost every instance in letter writing, you should use a positive approach.

There are exceptions to this, however, which are found in modern advertising. Not infrequently the advertiser *wishes* to arouse an unpleasant picture in the prospective purchaser's mind. For this he uses a negative suggestion. Then he quickly introduces his product or service which offers a positive solution. Examples of this are found in the advertisements for insurance ("if something should happen to you tomorrow, will your wife and children be provided for?"), personal hygiene products ("do you offend those around you?"), safety situations ("what would happen if, at high speed, your tires blew out?"), and others. However, these are not usual situations. On the whole, you should look to the past, comment on the present, and evaluate the future with optimism and confidence. Mention pleasant prospects and indicate what *can* be done rather than what cannot. Always attempt to arouse favorable associations.

QUESTIONS FOR DISCUSSION

I. Offer your criticism of the following examples.

2-3-60

1. Jensen Candy Comp.
   121 N. Kellogg St.
   Plainfield 27, New York

   Dear Mr. Kraude;
   ....
   ....

                                    Yours Truly

                                    Fairne Coffee Corp.
                                    t/ T. R. Mellon
                                    s/ T. R. Mellon
   RS/TRM   V. Pres.
   En. 2

2.
                                    5 March 1960
                                    212 So. Carver
                                    City

   A and H Dept. Store
   521 North 6th Street
   City

   My Dear Gentlemen:
   ....
   ....

                                    Respectfully yours,

                                    Mrs. J. M. Cantron

3.   3/5/60

Attn. of Mr. R. Becker
Frame Paving Corporation
2127 South Marfield Bd.
Springfield 3, Mass.

Gentlemen:
....
....

                    Yours truly
                    CONRAD CEMENT CORP.
                 s/ John T. Conrad
                 t/ John T. Conrad
                    President
JTC:rs

4.   August 3, 1960

Canford Metal Corp.
121 South Randolph Street
St. Louis 3, Missouri

Attention of Mr. L. Wein, Treasurer

Gentlemen:
....
....

              Yours for the best in steel products,

              McGowen Steel Corp.
           s/ Max L. Miller
              Comptroller

5. Roberta F. King
   King Style Shoppe
   220 Wilton Boulevard
   Los Angeles, 3, California

   Dear Madame:

   ·
   ·
   Sincerely Yours,

   s/ Mildred Gable

   Mildred Gable
   Sunset Style Mfgrs.

II. Complete the inside address, salutation, complimentary close, and
    signature of the following "scrambled" problems. Indicate the body
    of the letter with two or three horizontal lines.
    1. This letter was sent out by the maxwell chemical company in
       madison wisconsin by its treasurer, louis campbell to the
       grand rapids table company at 120 south fourth avenue in
       grand rapids, michigan. The letter was sent to the attention of
       mr. leo kelly, president, and it was typed by miss millie porne.
    2. Betty jarby typed the letter which was dictated to her by
       harry ralston, sales manager of acme fabric company of
       chicago. The letter was directed to miss e. falle, moderne
       drapery shoppe at 1212 south michigan in ellsworth, cali-
       fornia. The moderne shoppe is located in zone 4 of ellsworth.
       Mr. ralston included an invoice and sales bulletin with his
       letter.
    3. This order letter was sent by mrs. robert long of 220 south
       birch road in gary, new jersey on march 3, 1960 to the per-
       sonal shopping service of the gary department store. This
       store is located in gary, new jersey, at 212 south washington
       drive.
    4. Vice-president robert hayes of the langley lumber company
       dictated this letter to betty roberts. He requested that she en-
       close a check and sales bulletin along with the letter which
       was directed to mr. a. price of price construction company.
       This company is located in the builders' bldg., suite 1412, at
       1219 south bluegrass avenue in new york.
    5. This letter was received by mister bernard castle, assistant
       sales manager of castle coal company of duluth, minn. It was

signed by o. r. taylor of the fairfield paper company of escanaba, michigan. The letter was typed by miss marian wade who is the secretary to vice-president taylor. Castle coal company is located at 5150 west navarro avenue.

III. Revise the following sentences where you feel it is necessary. Pay special attention to tone and clarity.

1. You will find that our prices are not high and that our merchandise is not of poor quality.
2. We know you will not have trouble if you purchase a Brian Heater.
3. We think you will approve our request and not feel that this is an imposition.
4. Now that your television set is repaired, we hope you won't continue to have trouble with it.
5. If you will read the directions, we are sure that you will find it easy to operate our cleaner without difficulty.
6. We received your letter in which you claim we did not send you the No. 212 relay unit.
7. We were surprised to hear that you were dissatisfied with the sweater you recently purchased from us.
8. If you will always present this credit card, our clerks will not make any mistakes when billing your account.
9. You failed to list the colors you desired in the dresses you ordered.
10. I hope you will be happy if you stock our line of merchandise.
11. We believe that you can see, from the policies established in the industry, that your request is completely unreasonable.
12. We hope you will not be dissatisfied with your initial order which we received today.
13. Note how much extra work you have without one of our Quik Kleen Dishwashers.
14. We have now examined the credit form you sent in, and we have investigated the references you listed.
15. We were sorry to hear that the table we shipped arrived with chipped legs, a scratched surface, and a broken drawer.
16. We can't understand your request for credit for the soiled and damaged garment which you returned on August 7.
17. We know that you will not be upset when we tell you that your order will be delayed for ten days.
18. You neglected to send your check with the order.
19. Surely you can see why your claim can't be honored.
20. We find that our profit margin will not be adequate.

IV. Revise the following sentences where you feel it is necessary. Pay special attention to stereotyped expressions, wordiness, and pompous phrasing.

1. Hoping to hear from you in the near future, we remain. . . .
2. We find it a pleasure to tell you that when you find it possible to make your payments of invoices within ten days after we have delivered the merchandise to your place of business, your accounting department may subtract 2 per cent of the total bill prior to making payment for the merchandise sent out.
3. Enclosed please find statement; we are taking the liberty of deducting the sum agreed on.
4. As per your original decision, we hand you herewith our check.
5. Please be advised that merchandise cost prices have been duly noted.
6. After careful investigation, we are pleased to tell you that the merchandise which was to be delivered to your business establishment on September 10 will be delayed a maximum of 12 days, and we are sorry for the inconvenience.
7. According to our records you have not submitted an order in several weeks, and we hope you will now avail yourself of this opportunity.
8. Permit me to say that we hope that this shipment, sent in accordance with your directions, will meet your approval.
9. You may be sure that a repair man will be sent out at the earliest possible moment to handle the situation which you drew to our attention in your basic communication of Auggust 7.
10. Your valued order arrived, and we wish to say that the merchandise requested will be sent out at the earliest possible time.
11. We beg to state that the party listed in your letter of inquiry is no longer employed by this firm.
12. We are pleased to tell you that your request for an adaptation to our No. 231 light fixture which you requested in your letter of October 10 is possible, and that we shall undertake to carry through your request in this particular regard with all favorable dispatch.
13. If you will carefully peruse the indicated instructional forms which are enclosed, you will find that your utilization of the automatic power mower will be expedited under normal conditions.
14. It is our confirmed and frank contention that the merchandise listed on your invoice of April 8 of this year was not received at our establishment in whole or in part, and we there-

fore assume no obligation to compensate you for same.

15. We are unalterably opposed, at least to some degree, to your recommendation that we, at this time, consider that your account be credited for the sum indicated in your basic communication as a credit for loss of so-called good will and miscellaneous factors.

V. Revise the following sentences and *thoroughly discuss the principle* which guided your revision.

1. We find that your small quantity purchases are inconvenient for us and do not permit us to realize a substantial profit.

2. We hope that you will not find this increase in our prices unreasonable, but it is due to present market conditions which have caused a shortage to exist.

3. If you will take the time to read the simply written booklet of directions, you will find the operation of our mixing unit to be extremely easy.

Chapter 20

Inquiry and Reply Letters; Orders and Acknowledgments

In a great many situations in business, industry, and government, the inquiry and the letter of reply are utilized. A dozen times a day questions come up on products, prices, deliveries, and personnel. The answers must be secured, and the best way to get them is to send out letters of inquiry. So, too, firms must reply to the many questions which arrive each day.

Every letter should follow the principles discussed and suggested in the previous chapter, but in addition, a letter should be checked to be sure that it contains the specific attributes recommended for the particular type of missive involved.

THE INQUIRY LETTER

A correspondence supervisor for a large steel corporation recently commented that the inquiry letter could be the most expensive letter in industry. What he was getting at was that it could be the most expensive letter *if not written properly*. Every inquiry letter that is not clear or complete requires that the recipient of it write back to the inquirer and ask for clarification, additional facts, data, or statistics. Then the person who originally sent in the inquiry, must elaborate on the basic letter. Thus letters are mailed out by both inquirer and recipient which would not have been necessary had the first letter of inquiry been clear and complete. With letters costing well over $2.00 each in many firms, such an expense can result in a startling and irresponsible loss of money and goodwill.

To avoid this, the letter writer need only keep a few basic facts in mind.

Inquiry letters are usually classified as either *routine* or *non-routine*. The former usually cover everyday affairs such as, "Do you have a distributor in Montana?" "Can we buy less than a gross?" "What type of lubricating oil should be utilized?" "Does your mower come in any other color besides green?" "Where can I find the Social Security office nearest my home?" "Do you have a specification sheet for your 821A Relay Assembly?"

In almost every instance, the routine letter of inquiry can be replied to by some printed form, price list, specification sheet, or sample package. Because such an inquiry is routine in nature, it is only necessary to remember to be clear, courteous, and specific in asking your question.

Nonroutine Letter of Inquiry

This type of letter usually involves a rather complex problem, a problem which cannot be answered by a printed form but which requires that the recipient sit down and dictate a reply which will give the inquirer the answers to his *nonroutine* questions.

So often the inquirer who receives an unsatisfactory reply has only himself to blame. If *specific* questions are asked, which do not require a great deal of time or money to answer, the reply will usually be acceptable. For example, what can be done with a letter like this:

Dear Sir:
At the present time I am preparing a report on labor and labor relations in your company because of your size and influence in the nation.

With your labor force numbering close to 100,000, I know you can give me valuable information on this subject.

Please let me hear from you soon.

Yours truly,

Surely this inquiry cannot be answered in less that ten volumes. Even if the recipient wished to be helpful, he would not know where to begin. As a result, he might send out a copy of the company annual report with the statement, "We hope you will find the information in the enclosed booklet" or he may request a list of specific questions or he may discard the letter of inquiry completely. In each case, time, money, and good will are lost. However, had the letter been composed along the following lines, the recipient could easily fill the request or decline to do so, but definite action could be taken:

Dear Sir:

I am a senior level student at Harrison College where I am majoring in Industrial Relations.

At the present time I am preparing a report for one of my classes. The subject of the paper is "The Growth and Development of Labor Organizations at International Steel Corporation, 1920-1960." Although I have read and evaluated many of the articles listed in the *Industrial Arts Index, The Business Periodicals Index,* and other sources, I still need the answers to the following questions. Can you assist me?

1. A list of the specific unions at your company which are recognized by your department of industrial relations.
2. A list of strikes, length of time prior to settlement, and the unions involved, 1920-1960.
3. Approximate percentage of your entire work force (exclusive of administrative) which belonged to a union in the following years: 1920, 1930, 1940, 1950, 1960.

The answers to these questions, as well as any other relevant material you would care to send, will be of invaluable aid to me. You may be sure that I shall keep any specific information confidential which you so designate.

Because of semester schedules, I would appreciate hearing from you before November 15. Thank you very much.

Sincerely yours,

Here are two additional nonroutine letters of inquiry. In both cases, action, either favorable or unfavorable, could be taken.

Dear Mr. Patterson:

We have recently purchased a plant in St. Louis formerly utilized by the Grayson Garden Tool Company.

Because the building is about 30 years old, we are renovating it completely. In this process we shall install lighting fixtures which our production lines require because of their precision work.

Your latest catalog lists a recessed fluorescent fixture No. 202 (catalog No. 2713A) which meets our specifications completely provided the following modifications can be made:

1. Four tubes (40 watts each) per unit
2. Instant start feature
3. Maximum depth, 8 inches (because of heating ducts and ceiling joists)
4. Unbreakable translucent cover

All other specifications, such as gauge of metal, color, and wiring of your No. 202 model, are satisfactory.

We shall require 450 of these fixtures delivered to the plant site in St. Louis no later than December 3. Because our purchasing committee would like to select a fixture supplier no later than August 10, a reply from you concerning price per unit and other details, is desired by August 5. All information you give us will, of course, be kept confidential.

Sincerely yours,

Dear Dr. Cannon:

I am the program chairman of the Granville Secondary School PTA. Each year we attempt to present a series made up of well-known educational authorities.

Our series for the approaching year is built around the theme, "Education of the Exceptional Child." Because of your many outstanding contributions in this field, we would be most appreciative if you could tell us about the latest trends in the education of the emotionally disturbed child.

This particular meeting is scheduled for October 12 from 2:00 to 3:00 P.M. We expect approximately 125 to 200 members to attend. If you would like someone to pick you up at the University and bring you to Granville School, that can be arranged easily.

We would be delighted, Dr. Cannon, to receive a favorable reply from you by May 25. Thank you very much.

In all good nonroutine letters of inquiry, there are specific attributes included which will insure that you receive definite action and which will guard against not receiving a reply or receiving a reply which asks for additional information. These attributes follow:

1. A friendly opening
2. A statement identifying the inquirer (may be necessary for the student or individual writing on blank stationery, but hardly seems vital for the treasurer writing on company paper)
3. A statement telling why the request is made and how the information will be used

4. A list of *specific* questions
5. An assurance that the information will be kept in confidence if the request is of such a nature
6. A due date for the reply

In addition, the reply to the letter of inquiry should not require a great deal of effort or expense. The number of questions should be reasonable and they should not be difficult or complex in their make-up. It is also sometimes wise to include a self-addressed, stamped envelope.

Replies to Inquiries

Quite obviously when an individual or a company receives an inquiry, a reply must be sent out. This must always be well written, for a reply can build goodwill, make a sale, or assist the inquirer.

It is somewhat surprising how many firms will spend large sums of money on television, radio, and newspaper advertising—all of which bring in inquiries—and yet have no established procedure for efficiently answering the inquiry letters which come in.

Every inquiry should be answered as quickly as possible regardless of whether the action is affirmative or negative. Here, as in all special types of letters, a recommended series of points should be followed.

LETTER OF REPLY FULFILLING A REQUEST—A GRANT

In a letter granting a request, the following points should be covered:
1. An introductory statement acknowledging the inquiry
2. The grant indicating that the information will be supplied as requested
3. The information or reference to the source where it may be obtained
4. A sales appeal (if the situation calls for it)
5. A friendly close which may contain a constructive suggestion on where further information may be secured

Notice that favorable information—the grant—comes almost immediately in this letter of reply.

Dear Mr. Bankecroft:

Your letter of May 19 requesting information on our methods of evaluating production line workers was received.

When initially hired, all production workers, men and women, are given the Malten Dexterity and Visual Perception Test. This is in addition to the usual physical examination.

All personnel in this category are tested each six months thereafter with either the Malten Form A or Form B Follow-Up Test. For promotion or advancement purposes, the Industrial Human Relations Test, Number 12, is given.

In addition to this, each employee is rated by his immediate superior once every six months on the qualities of efficiency, coöperativeness, industry, and level of morale. We are enclosing a sample of this rating form.

May I also suggest that you see the following two articles if you are not already familiar with them.

A. Greene, "Evaluation of Factory Personnel," *Industrial Monthly Review,* June, 1960, pp. 28-34.

J. Burns, "Testing Production Line Personnel," *Personnel Analysis,* July, 1959, pp. 31-45.

Good luck on your paper, and let us know if we can assist you in any other way.

Dear Mr. Faxtone:

Thank you for your inquiry concerning the fiber gaskets which you will utilize in your new Clipper Lawn Mowers.

Our engineering department has checked the specifications which you sent, and we are happy to tell you that our equipment, and inventory of raw materials, will permit us to give you almost immediate delivery.

We would suggest that on the No. 401 oil seal gasket, you consider a rubber-fiber combination instead of a straight fiber type. Our experience with oil seals recommends it.

We have enclosed six envelopes, each containing three samples of the gaskets you requested. Please examine them carefully and note the quality of the product and the precision of manufacture. Quantity lots can be delivered within 14 days of the receipt of your order. Terms of sales are 2 percent discount when payments are made within 10 days; net, 30 days. Prices per 1000 units are noted on the enclosed specification sheet.

We know that you will be pleased with Star Products; they are guaranteed to give you complete satisfaction. Please wire or call collect if we can supply you with any other information.

In the case where the information requested may be found in an enclosure, the letter may be appreciably shorter.

Dear Miss Crawford:
Thank you for your inquiry concerning the procedure we follow in testing our transistor radios before shipping them to our dealers.
We are happy to send you the information you requested. The answers to all your questions may be found in the enclosed booklet, "Calloway Testing Procedures." I think you will find pages 12-15 especially valuable.
Please let us know if we can assist you in any other way.

LETTER OF REPLY REFUSING A REQUEST

In all cases where the reply is favorable, problems are not usually encountered. It is when one must refuse to give the inquirer what he requested, that we must exercise a full measure of tact and discretion. The following points should be included in a letter of refusal.

1. An introductory statement acknowledging the inquiry
2. An explanation of the situation
3. The refusal which is usually implied but may be stated
4. A constructive suggestion
5. A sales appeal (if the situation calls for it)
6. A friendly close

Notice that in this case, as is true in every refusal situation, an explanation for the refusal is made *before* the actual "turn down." When the explanation is offered first, the refusal will be understood by most reasonable persons. Then, too, when the situation is explained first, it is not usually necessary to say, "Therefore it is impossible," "We regret that we cannot . . ." "We must refuse . . ." In most cases, the reader will be quite willing to accept a phrase such as, "We are sure, therefore, that you can appreciate our position," or "We know that you will agree."
Most people are very reasonable, and if the explanation for the refusal is clear, honest, and tactful, they will usually accept it with no ill feelings.

Dear Mr. Kelly:
We were pleased to receive your request for information on our No. 52 UHF receivers.

As you indicated, these receivers are used by our Air Force and we are that agency's sole supplier. Because of the receivers' highly technical nature and the purpose for which they are used, our Government has classified them as "Top Secret." We know you will understand our position in this case.

We do have another receiver, No. 12 UHF, which we manufacture for use in commercial ships and planes. We are sending you our descriptive brochure on it as well as our general specification list.

We wish you all good luck in your research project at Clinton Technology Center, and we shall be pleased to coöperate in any other way we can.

Notice in the letter above that the writer does not dwell on the refusal. He states the case, explains the situation, and then goes on to a more positive subject. Sometimes, as in the letter below, a sales appeal on a different product may be added after the refusal. Of course this is very positive, and the writer is trying to convey the idea that it has never occurred to him that the reader may *even think* of taking his business elsewhere. A sales appeal must be handled with discretion and consideration of who the customer is. Whether or not a sales appeal should be included depends entirely on the situation, product, customer, and method of presentation.

Dear Mr. Maxwell:

Thank you for your inquiry concerning the 3000 plastic boxes which you would like to have us manufacture for your "Tru Flite Plane Kit."

We have carefully checked the cost of designing and making a die, producing the boxes, and then shipping them to you. The figure which our industrial engineering department has indicated is a great deal in excess of what you suggested. Of course the primary reason for this lies in the fact that you can utilize only a very limited quantity. However, the expense of initial design and set-up remains fixed regardless of the number ordered. If you could utilize a larger quantity, the price would be much less.

We do have an attractive box in stock, however, which we can offer you at a price well below the figure you listed. For a slight additional charge, your product name can be imprinted in two colors on the cover. We are sending you two samples under separate cover together with prices.

Please wire or call us collect and your order will be filled immediately.

In these cases of refusal, notice that the explanation is always given first; the refusal follows.

ORDERS AND ACKNOWLEDGMENTS

Order Letters

The order letter is somewhat of a rarity in business today because most firms and government agencies utilize order forms or purchase order blanks. Nevertheless there are certain basic items of information which should be included in an order letter or on an order form for the most efficient and expeditious handling of the request for merchandise.

1. Shipping information (rail, truck, mail, etc.)
2. Payment information (C.O.D., charge, etc.)
3. Description of merchandise (size, color, model)
4. Catalog number
5. Unit price; total price
6. Destination of shipment
7. Date of delivery desired
8. Quantity desired
9. Miscellaneous data which may be included:
    a. Order number
    b. Salesman's name
    c. Information on substitutions

The example which follows illustrates a simple order letter.

Dear Sir:

The following items are listed in your Spring Catalog. Please ship them out to the address above on a C.O.D. basis. You may send the merchandise via Illinois Central Railway or Midwest Freight Company.

Quantity	Catalog No.	Description	Unit Price	Total Price
1 doz.	323	Leather Watch Bands	$4.50	$ 4.50
2 doz.	681	Summer Earrings (Ass't)	3.00	6.00
½ doz.	981	Bread Trays @	4.00	24.00
¼ doz.	982	Candy Dishes @	2.50	7.50
2 doz.	1083	Silver Polish (8 oz.)	3.00	6.00
			TOTAL	$48.00

I would appreciate receiving this order prior to June 27.

Yours truly,

Phone:
Lincoln 5558

ORDER FORM

M. DANFORD AND COMPANY
Wholesale Office Supplies
220 West Dearborn Avenue
Detroit Michigan

Ship to: _____

_____

Date _____

_____

Please Leave Blank

Bill to: _____

_____

_____

SHIP:		TERMS:	IF OUT OF ITEM SHALL WE SUBSTITUTE?	DATE OF DELIVERY DESIRED
RAIL _____	AIR _____	OPEN ACC'T _____		
MOTOR _____	OTHER _____	C.O.D. _____	YES___ NO ___	
PARCEL POST____		REMITTANCE ENCL. ___		_____
EXPRESS _____				

Quantity	Catalog Number	Unit	Color or Size	Description or Name of Item	Unit Price	Total Price	Leave Blank

Order Form

Order forms are made up according to the needs and demands of the company and the products sold. The one shown on the previous page is rather simple in nature.

Acknowledgment Letters

Unless the orders you place are very routine, such as a weekly request for merchandise which is made on Monday and invariably delivered on Thursday, you will appreciate receiving an acknowledgment.

This tells you that some action is being taken. If, on the other hand, you place an order with Excello for a power saw and you do not hear from them for two weeks, you will probably assume that the order will not be filled and you may then place your order elsewhere.

Acknowledgments of orders are made to avoid such situations as well as for other reasons. An acknowledgment:

1. Tells the buyer that his order has been received and is being processed.
2. Confirms the order as originally entered by listing the merchandise which will be shipped. This permits the buyer to check the list and inform the seller if any conflict exists between what has been ordered and what will be shipped. This can save freight payments which would be made if undesired merchandise were sent out and had to be returned.
3. Is an act of courtesy which tells the buyer his order has been received and is appreciated.

The acknowledgment letter or form should be sent out the same day the order arrives; the buyer will appreciate such quick and courteous action.

It is quite obvious that a dozen different situations arise in every company regarding the orders which come in. Some of these requests for merchandise are from steady customers, new buyers, or delinquent accounts. Sometimes the entire order cannot be filled, only part of it is available, or some restriction does not permit the seller to fill all or a part of the request. It is because of the many situations which may arise that firms have formulated standard letters which need only be copied and personalized with the proper address and salutation before being sent out. Some of the situations which may come up are listed and discussed below.

ORDERS FROM STEADY CUSTOMERS WHICH CAN BE FILLED

In most cases an acknowledgment form, which is a duplicate of the invoice, is sent out. This lists the merchandise so the buyer may check it, and it tells him where, how, and when the goods are being sent as well as how payment is to be made. This is an inexpensive, accurate, and efficient method.

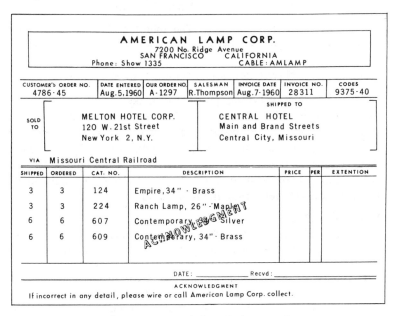

Duplicate Invoice Acknowledgment Form

Some companies send out postal cards to steady customers. Although this acknowledges the order, it usually does not list the merchandise and so the order cannot be confirmed. A third method is the printed form letter which usually states the same thing as a postal card but is somewhat more courteous because it travels in a sealed envelope.

Dear Customer:

Thank you for your order which was placed on _____.
It will be filled and shipped via _____. You
may expect to receive it on or about _____.
Terms of sale are _____.
Thank you very much.

                               Sincerely yours,

                               The Johnston Company

ORDERS FROM NEW CUSTOMERS WHICH CAN BE FILLED

Most firms do everything possible to make a new customer feel welcome. The order is acknowledged, company services are explained, policies are discussed, and appreciation is shown. Of all these points, the customer is primarily concerned with his order; this therefore is commented on first. In some cases, the seller will send a duplicate of the invoice along with a form letter (individually typed of course) welcoming the new account.

Dear Mr. Gaffen:

It was a real pleasure to receive your first order. It has been completely processed and is being shipped just as you requested. It should arrive on August 3.

No doubt Mr. Korbin, our salesman, told you of the many services offered by Star-Brite to its customers. A window trimmer will visit your store each month or oftener if you make a special request. Window posters are mailed to you twice each month and special sales bulletins and store banners are sent out periodically. Of course these services are completely free of charge to Star-Brite's customers.

Terms of sale permit our customers to increase their profit margin by taking a 2 percent discount when payments are made prior to the 10th of the month following sales. All payments are due net within 60 days.

You may be sure, Mr. Gaffen, that we at Star-Brite stand ready to serve you at all times with the highest quality merchandise at the lowest possible prices.

The letter to the new customer which follows is an example where an acknowledgment form is sent along with the personal letter.

Dear Mr. Kelly:

Thank you very much for your first order. It is a pleasure to add your name to the list of Lincoln customers.

We have enclosed a carbon copy of the form which will be used to process your order. You may wish to check it carefully against your own original list.

Here at Lincoln, we constantly strive to assist you and our other customers. In addition to offering you beautifully crafted furniture at low prices, we have other services which will prove advantageous to you.

You may receive 1000 mailers to send out to your customers, and special holiday direct mail pieces and store pennants every 90 days. These are all free of charge and may be secured by calling Mr. Gable, the director of our advertising and customer relations department.

Terms of sales are indicated on the enclosed card which you may wish to pass on to your accountant.

Welcome to Lincoln Furniture, Mr. Kelly. We stand ready to serve you to your complete satisfaction.

You should not think that letters of this type are reserved only for the new customer. One of the wisest moves the businessman can make is to send out, on occasion, courteous, personal letters to steady customers. Let them know that you do not "take them for granted," but that you really appreciate their business.[1]

OTHER ACKNOWLEDGMENT SITUATIONS WHICH ARISE

1. Orders which are incomplete, indefinite, or not clear
2. Orders for merchandise temporarily out of stock
3. Orders for merchandise never handled
4. Orders for merchandise not in stock but for which substitute goods may be offered
5. Orders which must be refused because:
   a. The buyer is a poor credit risk
   b. The buyer is over his credit limit
   c. Filling the order would be unprofitable because of size of order or distance to be shipped
   d. Filling the order would be contrary to franchise or distributorship agreements

---

[1] This topic is discussed in greater detail in Chapter 22 on Sales and Good Will Letters.

Most orders received by large companies may be filled, and these come in from steady customers. But enough of the situations listed above arise so that it is advisable for a firm to make up form letters to handle them. The four letters which follow are examples of acknowledgment situations which may occur.

1. An acknowledgment of an incomplete order:

Dear Mr. Armour:

Your order of March 17 was received and processed. The smoking stands, fluorescent desk lamps, and the coat trees are on their way to you via Martindale Trucking Company. The merchandise should arrive by March 25.

Your order also called for three No. 605 reception room lamps. However you inadvertently did not list the type of trim you desire on these Danish Modern Fixtures. If you will simply check the enclosed card as to whether you prefer the silver, brass, or copper trim, we will fill your request immediately.

I am enclosing a brochure on our new line of Danish Modern office wall clocks. They are a lovely and distinctive addition to every office.

In the above acknowledgment of an incomplete order, the writer has carefully pointed out first what has been done in filling the order and then what yet remains to be carried through. Notice also the tactful statement, " . . . you inadvertently did not list . . ." rather than "you failed or neglected to list."

2. An acknowledgment of an order for merchandise temporarily out of stock:

Dear Mr. Parker:

Thank you for your order for various items of power equipment.

The drill press, jig saw, and planer were shipped via Baltimore and Ohio Railroad and are due to arrive at your Boston warehouse on June 23.

Because of the unusual demand for the 10-inch Durbin Power Saws, we could not ship the one you requested with your order. However, our St. Louis branch shipped three to us yesterday. They are due to arrive in Chicago within this week, and we shall then ship your unit to you immediately.

Will you kindly wire or call us collect as to whether or not you wish us to go ahead and ship the Durbin Saw. We are sure you will have this unit within four or five days after the arrival of your original order. We know the quality and price of this saw will please you.

Here again the buyer is first told what is being sent. Notice also the positive tone concerning the item which is being shipped late.

The writer says ". . . we shall then ship . . . ," not "if satisfactory we shall ship." In the last paragraph the writer does not say "it will be *delayed* four or five days" but he does say, ". . . you will have the unit *within* four or five days."

3. Acknowledgment of an order not in stock and an offer of a substitute:

Dear Mr. Gorton:

Thank you very much for your order for 3000 feet of our No. 303 ½-inch brass tubing.

Early this year we introduced our No. 304 ⅓-inch brass tubing which most of our dealers find completely satisfactory as a replacement item for No. 303. The quality, strength, and composition of the ⅓-inch tube is identical to the ½-inch. However, the price is almost 25 percent less. Unless you have need for the exact ½-inch dimension, we believe you will be more than happy with the No. 304 item. It serves very well in fabrication and furniture trim.

Several samples of the No. 304 tube have been sent to you. Please call us collect, and we will have your request on its way to you immediately.

A letter such as the one above is essentially a sales letter. It tells the buyer what the company does have, and by so doing, points out what is not available in stock.

4. Acknowledgment of an order and refusal to fill (credit problem):

Dear Mr. Kalorie:

Thank you very much for your order of March 25 and the financial statement which you sent along.

We have checked the information and we are delighted with the growth of your firm. In consideration of the fact that you have only been in business for two years and the suburb in which you are located is expanding, your progress has been excellent.

However your liquid position is such that we would strongly recommend that you continue on a cash basis. The advantages of a 2 percent discount, low inventory, and no end-of-month bills are all worth considering.

Your order has been completely processed and will be sent out as soon as we hear whether you would prefer to mail us a check ($412) or have us send the merchandise out C.O.D.

A bulletin describing our April sale for preferred customers is also enclosed.

The letter above has a very strong, yet courteous positive tone. Nowhere does the letter say "No, you can't have. . . ." It tells

Mr. Kalorie what can be done for him and how he will benefit. As a matter of fact, it has apparently never entered the writer's mind that Mr. Kalorie would do anything else but accept the suggestions made.

QUESTIONS FOR DISCUSSION

I. Offer your criticism of the following inquiry and reply letters.

1. Dear Mr. Kelly:

    At the present time I am preparing an article for our college publication, *State Technical Monthly*. The topic of my research concerns the utilization of plastics for wire insulation purposes.

    Because your firm is a leader in the field of wire and cable manufacture, I know that you will be able to assist me in preparing this article.

    I will be most appreciative to receive what information you can send me.

2. Dear Mr. Farnsworth:

    This approaching November we expect to announce our new Metromatic Auto-Washer on the market.

    Because you have supplied us with attractive equipment name plates in the past, we again turn to you as a possible source for this year's product.

    The name plate we would like should have the general appearance of the sketch enclosed and be made of the materials and colored as indicated on the specification sheet. All dimensions are also indicated.

    Our minimum initial purchase will be 10,000 plates. We contemplate that we will require an equal number each month for the six months after November.

    May we have your detailed specification sheet and prices on or before March 15. You may be sure that all quotations you list will be held in confidence.

3. Dear Sir:

    It would be advantageous if the products I manufacture were flame proof.

    From your ad which appeared in the *Builders' Journal*, I gather that your paint has fireproof qualities and retards the spread of flames.

    Will you be good enough to send me details as I may wish to purchase your product.

4. Late next year we shall have an addition to our plant completed. This portion of the plant will contain a conference room which we shall wish to furnish adequately.

It is our understanding that your firm manufactures conference tables, chairs, and related items. May we hear from you as to the possible purchase of a conference table by our company.

5. At the present time we are carrying through research for the purpose of redesigning our 1960 model industrial dishwasher.

As you are probably aware, many of the valves utilize standard solid brass fittings. We have, however, been very much impressed by your plastic No-Leak line. Our experimental tests prove them entirely adequate for our purposes.

We are, therefore, sending you under separate cover eight of our most frequently utilized fittings. We would like to have you examine these and let us know if you can manufacture each of these eight items in your No-Leak quality of plastic. If you find this feasible, we would like the following data:

a. Price per unit
b. Quantity on which quotation is desired:
½-inch Diameter—500 gross
1-inch Diameter—750 gross
c. Delivery requirements: 100 gross of each unit every 30 days beginning 30 days after contract execution
d. Delivery of all merchandise to our Chicago warehouse

We will be happy to supply any other information you may require. Please let us hear from you no later than March 25.

6. We are interested in securing information on your new rust-resistant paint. We have studied your recent advertisement which appeared in *The Industrial Engineer,* and we notice that you claim that when this paint is applied on metal surfaces which are in frequent contact with wet and subzero surfaces, it maintains its original appearance without appreciable damage to the surface for a period of a minimum of five years because of the high quality of its various constituents and the pigments used.

We also notice that you advertise three types of this rust-resistant paint: one which would be in constant contact with liquids, one exposed to frequent changes in climate from subzero to tropical, and one specifically designed for temperate areas.

Your coöperation and answer are requested at your earliest convenience.

7.   Your firm has recently been recommended to us for possible consideration as a supplier of classroom cork bulletin boards.

We are serving as the architect for the New Washington Elementary School in Brighton. The plans call for 65 bulletin boards, 3′ x 5′ each, and framed in a 2-inch aluminum strip.

The cork should be of high quality and have a minimum thickness of ⅜-inch. It should be light green in color.

If you can undertake the manufacture of these items, please send us detailed specifications and the cost per unit.

8. Dear Mr. Ryan:

Thank you for your recent order. We were pleased to receive it.

We regret to tell you, however, that it will be impossible to fulfill your request at this time for item No. 205.

We do have a substitute item to replace No. 205 which we feel is superior. Item No. 205 was declared obsolete approximately six months ago. In its place we are offering No. 305 which is a superior filter that is guaranteed a three-year life.

We know you will be happy if you order our new No. 305. Hoping to hear from you in the near future, we remain,

9. Dear Mr. Maller:

Thank you for your recent inquiry concerning the use of printed circuits in home television sets. It is always a pleasure to learn of the projects that various graduate students are engaged in.

We are sending you a copy of a report which our engineering department recently issued to the board of directors. As you will notice it describes our 1960 experiment which definitely proved that printed circuits were as effective and much less costly than a conventional tube type of arrangement.

May we also suggest you review the excellent article on this subject by Peter T. Downs which appeared in the February, 1960, issue of the *Institute of Radio Engineers*.

Please accept our best wishes for success in your research at the University.

10. Dear Mr. Brunswick:

We were happy to learn that our recent advertisement in *The Industrial Engineer* attracted your interest and prompted your inquiry.

Our research engineers have examined your plans. We are positive that we can design and produce a line of plastic, watertight containers for your chemicals.

A few of the distinct advantages of Atlas Plastic containers are these:

1. Attractive in appearance—designed to increase your sales
2. Inexpensive in quantity purchases—designed to increase your profit margin
3. Dependable in performance—designed to build customer confidence

If you will send us a detailed list of your needs, we shall be pleased to draw up specifications and price quotations. If you would prefer to discuss this in more detail at this time, call or wire collect, and a member of our sales force will be happy to meet with you.

11. Dear Mr. Conklin:

Your request for one of our Deluxe display racks was received today.

The policy of our firm is not to place one of these racks in a customer's store unless the monthly sales of the account average over $1500. As you know your account has not exceeded $500 in any month during the past 18 months.

Nevertheless we have complied with your request (though we think the cardboard unit would be better for you) and a Deluxe rack is being shipped from our warehouse on the 15th. It is a most attractive unit finished in blond oak, and we hope it works out well. Of course the rack remains the property of our firm and should be returned when you have no further use for it.

12. Dear Mr. Gray:

Thank you for your recent inquiry concerning our display racks. It is always a pleasure to cooperate with our customers who are working to increase their sales.

The rack which you inquired about is almost 5 feet in length and has space for a large quantity of merchandise. Because of its size we feel that it would be wiser for you to wait until your purchases reach about $1500 each month. Under your present purchase level, your merchandise would not be displayed to the best advantage in the Deluxe rack.

We do, however, have a smaller laminated cardboard and plastic case which occupies a relatively small counter space. It is most attractive and has been very successful in boosting

our customers' sales. Your salesman, Joe Jerlath, will bring
one out to your store within the next week. He will be happy
to set it up, connect the reflector lights, and give you some
suggestions on its use to add to the ideas you already have.
We are sure it will help increase your sales.

I am also sending you a sample of our new No. 521 high
speed lubricant. It is an excellent item, and we are sure many
of your accounts would be interested in it. I have enclosed a
descriptive folder and price list with the sample.

II. Complete any of the following problems assigned.

1. Mr. Robert T. Finch has applied for a job with your firm. It
   appears that he will be able to fill the position of junior accountant which is open. However, you want to be sure of his
   competence, initiative, and integrity. Write a letter of inquiry
   to Mr. Finch's former employer, Randolph Trucking Company, for confidential information on Finch. The applicant
   worked as a junior accountant for Randolph also.

2. Your company, Kennel Clock Corporation, is seriously considering the purchase of a plant site which is for sale in Lipton,
   Ohio. This factory building, which is now available, would
   serve your present manufacturing needs very well. As personnel director for Kennel, you should write a letter to the
   Lipton Chamber of Commerce inquiring about the availability of labor in Lipton. You are especially interested in
   production, technical, skilled, and clerical workers.

3. For many years you have been manufacturing wooden picture
   frames of various sizes. These are made in walnut, oak, and
   birch. Because the wood must be high grade, well seasoned
   (to prevent warping), and free of knots, the frames are quite
   expensive. You have heard that the Industrial Plastic Corporation makes a variety of products in simulated wood patterns
   at very reasonable prices. Write them a letter of inquiry asking
   about the possibility of having them mold complete picture
   frames for you in wood patterns. If the price is attractive, you
   can probably utilize about 2000 per month in each of the three
   sizes: 4″ x 5″; 6″ x 8″; and 10″ x 12″.

4. Among your other duties as executive assistant to the mayor
   of Fairview, California (pop. 120,000), you are charged with
   preparing the annual report. This is a big job and you haven't
   been very happy with the results. However you have just
   received a copy of the Montgomery, New York, annual report
   which is thorough, attractive, well written, and professional
   in tone and content. Write to the mayor's office in Montgomery and ask about the report. You wonder if it is written

by a management consulting house, a professional writer, or a city employee. If a member of the mayor's staff writes it, you would like to know how much assistance he has, what procedure is followed in gathering data, how and if a budget is established specifically for the report, and how the report is distributed in Montgomery and to what specific groups of citizens.

5. You are contemplating entering the graduate business school of Minneapolis State College. About six years ago you took four graduate commerce courses in the College of Commerce of Kansas University, and you wonder if the credits are transferable to Minneapolis State. Write and ask the registrar at Minneapolis this question. The courses you took are Advanced Economic Theory, Taxation Problems of the Corporation, Industrial Personnel Counseling, and Inter-Personal Relations. A transcript of your work should also be sent. You are also interested in tuition fees, whether formal application for admission must be filed a specific period of time before the term opens, what entrance examinations must be taken, and related items.

6. Assume that you are the registrar of Minneapolis State College. Send a reply to the letter discussed in problem 5 above. Tell him that you can award him 9 hours of graduate credit on three of the courses he listed. However, the course in Inter-Personal Relations is not given graduate credit at your school. Nevertheless, you are sending him a formal application blank, school catalog, and a bulletin of classes for the approaching semester.

7. Reply to Robert T. Baxter, a student at California Institute of Technology. He wanted you to send him information for a paper he is writing on relay components your company manufactures for use in guided missiles. Although you like to assist students, the information he requested has been classified by the United States Department of Defense and cannot be released to unauthorized personnel. Perhaps he might be interested in the specifications and in information on your commercially used relay No. 215.

8. Answer the Atlas Furniture Manufacturing Company's request for information on brass strips which they would like to use as a decorative motif on their new line of contemporary furniture. Your brass strips are available in $\frac{1}{16}$-inch, $\frac{1}{8}$-inch, and $\frac{1}{4}$-inch thicknesses and widths vary from $\frac{1}{8}$-inch to 2-inches in $\frac{1}{8}$-inch intervals. All brass comes in 8-, 12-, and 16-foot lengths and in either polished, satin, or burnished

finishes. You may enclose samples and a price list.

9. Maremont Engineers Association has requested that you address them on November 12. They are interested in the use of various fuels in jet aircraft. Because you are the director of research for Braton Aircraft Corporation, you could do a good job for them; however, you are scheduled to be in Washington on November 12. Perhaps the Association would be interested in hearing you on another date.

10. Assume that you are the administrator for the New Breutville Memorial Hospital. You have just received a request from a third grade teacher, Miss Cannon. She says her class enjoyed several projects in which they raised money for the hospital. Now she would like to bring them in and see the various units of the institution. Unfortunately, the hospital already has patients, and the board of health does not permit visitors who are below 14 years in any city hospital. It may be that the children would like to see the hospital laundry, cafeteria, or supply areas. Or perhaps Miss Cannon would like to borrow your excellent 35-minute color film, *The Center of Life; An American Hospital.*

III. Criticize the following order and acknowledgment letters.

1. Dear Sir:

I saw your ad for men's sweaters in today's issue of the *Washington Star.*

I am enclosing $5.95 for one of the sweaters. Send me either a blue or brown one.

2. Gentlemen:

Enclosed please find my check for $39.50 for the merchandise listed.

All items were selected from your summer catalog.

One No. 20461 Wall Clock, brass	$12.50
Two No. 29613 Floor cigarette stands @ $6.00	12.00
Two No. 28501 Desk lamps @ $7.50	15.00
	$39.50

Please send these items out parcel post within the next week. Thank you very much.

3. Dear Mr. French:

Thank you very much for your recent order. All the merchandise you requested has been packed and shipped. You may expect to receive your order by October 12 via Illinois Central Railroad.

It is always a pleasure to welcome a new customer to Sternes Furniture Distributors. You will find that we are always ready to assist you in any way we can.

In addition to offering you high quality merchandise at low prices, we shall be pleased to send out our window trimmer once each month. If you can utilize store banners announcing sale seasons and special events, we shall be happy to add your name to that list also.

Please let us hear from you whenever we may be of service.

4. Dear Miss Frammen:

Thank you for your recent order for office supplies.

We have shipped out all the merchandise you requested with the exception of the 6 dozen typewriter ribbons. We did not add these to your order because you inadvertently did not indicate the ribbons you prefer.

I have enclosed a tear sheet from our catalog. On it you will find a listing of the various ribbons we carry. Just note, at the bottom of this letter, the catalog number and quantity of ribbons desired, and we shall ship immediately.

5. We were delighted, Mr. Johnson,

To receive your subscription to *American Craftsman Monthly.*

We know that you, like 80,000 other wood craftsmen, will look for your monthly copy eagerly. Once you have opened it, you won't put it down until you've read it from cover to cover. In no time at all, you will find that it has paid for itself through the savings which you make in your workshop.

We have enclosed a bill for your initial subscription; just place your check in the stamped envelope enclosed.

IV. Complete any of the following problems assigned.

1. You have just purchased a new home and will require some garden equipment. You have a catalog from The Garden Shop whose merchandise and prices have been recommended to you.

Enclose a check to cover the cost of a rake at $2.95, a hedge clipper at $3.95, a pruning shears at $2.50, and a garden fork for $3.50. Remember to list the catalog number of each item ordered.

2. Assume you are the purchasing agent for the Myrel Machine Company. Send an order to Prince Paint and Varnish Corporation in Ellentown, Illinois, for the following merchandise:

10 gallons   No. 2134 enamel, white
5 gallons   No. 2175 varnish, spar

10 quarts   No. 303   linseed oil
4 quarts   No. 405   brush cleaner

Have the merchandise sent out C.O.D. You would like to
have it prior to October 10.

3. Acknowledge an order from Mellan Jewelry Store for 6 Time
Right Nautical wall clocks, 2 dozen assorted men's leather
watch bands, 6 Moderne compacts, 1 dozen assorted Empire
cigarette lighters, and 6 Just-Right Toasters. You have all the
items in stock except the Just-Right Toasters which you have
not handled in over a year. You have replaced the Just-Right
line with the Center Toaster which you feel is much more
satisfactory. The Center Toaster has an automatic timer,
heavier heating elements, a one-year guarantee, and is extremely attractive in design. However, it does sell for $140
per dozen whereas the Just-Right sold for $110 per dozen.

You are at a loss to understand how Mellan Jewelry
ordered the Just-Right for it hasn't appeared in your catalog
for the last two years. It is possible that Mr. Mellan used an
old catalog inadvertently, or it may be that he wants an inexpensive toaster. You do feel that the Center Toaster is an
excellent buy. All other merchandise is in stock and ready for
shipment.

4. Acknowledge an order from McGray Manufacturing Company for one Brown and Williams No. 230 punch press. You
have this item in stock and can ship it out immediately; however, the purchase order received from McGray has you
puzzled. It indicates that shipment should be made to their
Cicero, Illinois, plant. As far as you know this plant is merely
used for packaging and storage. You feel that the machine
should go to the McGray plant in St. Louis. Write to their
main office in St. Louis and acknowledge the order and also
check on the destination of shipment. You certainly want to
avoid an unnecessary freight bill if possible.

5. For some months your east coast division salesman has been
trying to get an order from the Garland Department Store.
Their initial order for your line of women's shoes came in
today.

You have all the merchandise in stock and can ship it out
immediately. This may be the beginning of an excellent account. In addition to telling Garland about the order, you
should mention some of your services: 2 percent discount
when payment is made within 10 days, store display service,
shoe return privilege, air freight deliveries in emergencies,
and low prices.

Chapter 21

Claim and Adjustment Letters; Credit and Collection Letters

In day-to-day progress of business, industry, and government, errors occasionally take place. We all know that these incidents do happen, and we accept them as being almost unavoidable in the complexities of daily transactions.

CLAIM LETTERS

A well-written claim letter, sent to the company responsible for the error, will usually result in a satisfactory adjustment.

Claim letters are usually divided into two groups: those which are routine in nature and those which are not and require a good deal of explanation.

The *routine claim letter* may involve a case where the wrong color or size product was sent out or an incorrect quantity was delivered. In each case all that is required is that the letter be clear and specific with a reference to the date and number of the original order, as well as facts on the point under discussion.

Dear Sir:
Your truck delivered our order No. 8134 this morning. All the merchandise arrived as requested except the Dynamic Electric Clocks.
If you will refer to our original purchase order, you will note that we requested 1 dozen No. 604 clocks (brass trim). However we received No. 605 (copper trim).
Please pick up the one dozen No. 605 clocks, and replace with an equal quantity of No. 604.
Thank you.

Nonroutine Claim Letters

This type of claim letter is written where the facts may be subject to question and a clear explanation is required.

The writer of the claim letter has as his primary objective the securing of the adjustment, but at the same time he wants specific action—either approval or disapproval. He certainly does not want delay, procrastination, or postponement of his request. When this takes place, letters which cost time and money must be written back and forth. The claim should strive to achieve a "yes" or "no" answer. If it is the former, it is satisfactory. If it is "no," that is also good because it permits the case to be closed. If the claim writer does not approve, he can take his business elsewhere. If he accepts the decision, then business may be continued. To avoid getting caught in the "we are looking into it; may we suggest you do the same" type of situation, you need only include the following points in your claim letter:

1. An introductory statement referring to the number and date of the original order or transaction
2. A clear statement of the loss or damage incurred
3. A *specific* request for an adjustment
4. A statement which will motivate the recipient to take favorable action
5. A friendly close

TONE OF THE LETTER

This nonroutine claim letter should be thoroughly positive if you are sure your claim is correct, reasonable, and ethical. Any hesitancy in the tone may well be cause for delay and compromise on the adjustor's part.

POOR: We believe the damage took place prior to delivery.
BETTER: We are sure the damage took place while the merchandise was en route to our store.

POOR: We think that the table must have been damaged in your warehouse.
BETTER: When the table was delivered to us, it had already been damaged.

SECTIONS OF THE CLAIM LETTER

Be sure you state exactly what the loss was and exactly what adjustment you desire.

POOR: As you can appreciate, the damage to the car was quite severe.

BETTER: The Acme Auto Service at 103 South Harrison has indicated exactly what the repairs to the car will cost. Their statement is enclosed.

POOR: We believe that it will be quite costly to replace the watch.

BETTER: Madison Jewelers, where the watch was originally purchased, indicated that an exact replacement would cost $85.50.

POOR: We feel that you should make an equitable adjustment.

BETTER: Please credit our account for $45.50.

POOR: Kindly send us a check to cover the cost of purchasing another fixture of similar design.

BETTER: Please send us a check for $29.50 to cover the cost of a Trim line fixture, model No. 305.

In all the revisions above, the tone is positive because there is no doubt in the claimant's mind that he is correct in his request. When you are not sure who is at fault or exactly where the damage took place, then you can only state the facts exactly as they are and request (if you so desire) that the matter be investigated.

In many instances it is helpful to remind the company with whom you are placing the claim, of past business, potential business, practices in the field, or the ethics of the situation. Quite obviously no one is delighted to make an adjustment, especially of a sizable sum. A motivating statement may therefore prove valuable.

In some ten years of close business association, this is the first time we have. . . .

We are now preparing our spring order and as soon as your credit memo for the above claim is received. . . .

We know that throughout the furniture industry a claim such as the above. . . .

We know that you will want to do what is right and we have therefore enclosed the bill. . . .

Sometimes the claimant will want to inject an actual threat, but this is hardly recommended and is not good business practice.

A check for our July invoice will be forwarded immediately after we receive your credit memorandum.

Under usual conditions, a tactful, restrained, and courteous claim will bring the favorable action desired. The example below demonstrates that fact:

Dear Mr. Clayborn:

On May 15 your truck delivered our order No. 72134.

This particular shipment included 24 number 58 fluorescent desk lamps billed at $12.50 each.

We had already sold these 24 units to one of our accounts and as soon as your shipment arrived, we in turn sent the fixtures to our customer. Today we received a call telling us that none of the units contained fluorescent tubes.

Of course we were embarrassed because your model No. 58 unit is described as being sold with the tubes and of course we represented them in this manner to our customer. We immediately sent out 48 General Electric 20 watt tubes to our account.

Undoubtedly someone in your production line forgot to pack the lights with the desk fixtures. Because of our pleasant association during the past five years, we know that you will want to either credit our account for $57.60 ($1.20 per tube) or send us 48 replacement lights.

ADJUSTMENT LETTERS

Just as we expect to send out and receive claim letters, so we also recognize the need for adjustments. Before we can make an adjustment, however, we must determine two important factors:

1. Is the company adjustment policy generous, severe, or moderate?
2. Who is at fault (buyer, seller, third party, not known)?

Company policy on adjustments varies. Some firms will habitually agree to accept almost any reasonable claim regardless of where the fault lies, whereas other organizations will only make adjustments when the fault is theirs.

Buyer at Fault

Buyers may request adjustments when they are not entitled to them. Usually the buyer acts under the belief that his claim is legitimate and fair. It may be that a sweater was washed in an automatic washer when the buyer overlooked the instruction tag which clearly stated, "hand wash in luke-warm water only." Or perhaps, the buyer inadvertently took a 2 percent discount on bills which he paid after the 10-day period normally permitted. Or, it is possible that the buyer's employees did not follow the recommended installation procedure for the motor, and it quickly burned out. We could list another hundred examples of where the buyer is at fault and submits a claim. But we must recognize that most people are honest and when a claim is submitted, the buyer feels that he deserves an adjustment.

In such cases, the recipient of the request may grant, refuse, or make a compromise on the claim. In every instance he should assume that the claim was made in good faith, and therefore the adjustment must be handled with discretion.

The action which is most frequently taken in the case of the buyer at fault is to either grant or refuse the claim. The reason behind granting the claim is to maintain and build good will.

BUYER AT FAULT—GRANTING THE CLAIM

When the claim is granted, the following points should be covered:

1. An introductory statement referring to the specific situation or order
2. A courteous explanation of why the fault is the buyer's (should be done with tact and grace to avoid embarrassing the buyer and to "save face" for him)
3. A statement that makes the grant freely—not grudgingly
4. A sales appeal if the situation warrants it
5. A friendly close

The explanation, in the case above, is made *before* the grant. This is done so that the buyer may understand the situation. To open the letter with the grant when the buyer is at fault may not be wise. Some individuals would not read past the point where they were told they were going to receive what they requested, or even if the explanation is read after the grant, the psychological impact is not as strong.

POOR: Dear Mr. Jay:
  We are happy to tell you that your claim for $85.00 has been granted and a credit to your account has been made.

We would like to point out however, that the installation instructions attached to each pump clearly indicate that the pressure should not exceed the recommended level. This recommendation was not followed and consequently. . . .

BETTER: Dear Mr. Jay:

We received your letter requesting an adjustment on your recently purchased Hamilton pump. We can understand how you felt when it did not function as you expected.

We immediately checked the gauges and found that the pump had been inadvertently subjected to a water pressure much greater than that specifically recommended in the instruction guide packed with each unit. The pressure limits are also noted on the sticker affixed to the face of the pump.

However, we do recognize that these incidents do happen and we have therefore credited your account for $85.00 as you requested.

May we suggest that in the future . . . .

In the letter immediately above, the grant is made but at the same time, the buyer is clearly but courteously made to understand that he is at fault. The possibility of receiving another similar claim from him is slight.

Notice also that the grant is direct. There is no hesitancy or any attempt to make the claimant feel obligated. If you are going to make a grant—make it. The buyer should never be made to feel that he is being given the world with a fence around it.

POOR: Although you are clearly at fault, we have decided to give you the adjustment anyway.

POOR: Through our generosity we are making the adjustment, but we still don't see how you could possibly think you had a leg to stand on with such a claim.

POOR: Of course if you had read the instructions, you would know how unfair your claim is, but we are nevertheless going to approve it.

BETTER: We have approved your claim for we know that the assumptions made by your shipping department foreman were reasonable.

BETTER: From time to time miscalculations such as this happen in every office. We have therefore credited your account as you requested.

Dear Mrs. Backell:

We can certainly appreciate how you feel in regard to your new Fry Rite Electric Pan.

When your pan arrived, we immediately had it checked because we are always desirous of maintaining the excellent reputation of the Fry Rite and at the same time insuring that our customers receive high quality products.

Our technicians found that the *entire* pan had been submerged in water when it was washed. Of course the directions which came with the unit and the caution note pasted on the pan's interior specifically warn against getting the electrical controls (located in the handle) wet.

However, we do recognize your position, and we are sending you a brand new Fry Rite Electric Pan replacement. We know that it will give you much pleasure and satisfaction when used as suggested.

We are also enclosing a booklet describing the new Fry Rite Roaster which is available at all hardware and department stores in your area.

Dear Mr. Gattle:

We received your letter requesting that we replace three No. 45 fans with our model No. 121.

As is printed on all our invoices and sales slips, all returns must be made within 30 days of purchase. This is true throughout the entire heating and ventilation industry. Your purchase of the No. 45 fans was made in April, almost six months ago. However we have carried through your request and shipped out three of the No. 121 units. Because this model cost less than the No. 45, your account has also been credited for $23.00.

We are sure you will be interested in our Excello residential gas-fired replacement units. These have all been reduced 20 percent. A purchase of several will add to your profit margin. May we send some of these out?

Notice in the examples above that a tactful explanation of the situation is made *before* the claim is granted.

Buyer at Fault—Refusing a Claim

When the claim is refused the letter should cover the following points:

1. An introductory statement referring to the specific situation or order
2. A courteous explanation of why the fault is the buyer's (done with tact and grace)
3. The refusal which is usually implied although it may be stated
4. A sales appeal if the situation warrants it
5. A friendly close

When the buyer is at fault the order of points is the same whether the claim is accepted or rejected. Of course it is more difficult to retain the buyer's good will when you must refuse his claim, but most persons are fair minded and will accept a reasonable explanation of a situation which demands a refusal.

Dear Mr. Laurel:

We were certainly disturbed to learn from your letter of May 17 that you were not completely satisfied with your three Pioneer ½-horsepower motors.

Our industrial engineer immediately visited your plant and found that each of the three units powered a No. 62 Durbin Saw. The instruction plate on each saw indicates that either a 1- or 1½-horsepower motor be used. Obviously the load placed on the ½-horsepower units was much too great and caused the motors to burn out. I am sure you will understand our position in not honoring your request in this particular case.

We have asked our shipping department to prepare three Pioneer 1-horsepower units for shipment, on approval, to you. If you will wire your agreement, they will go out to you today. They are listed at just $45.00 each.

In the letter above and in the one which follows, the explanation is made *before* the refusal is indicated.

Dear Mr. Campion:

Thank you for your letter requesting that we credit your account for $21.50.

This sum was listed on your invoice as the total of unearned discounts on the orders of May 27, April 4, and April 15. As you know certain economies are gained when bills are paid within 10 days of receipt of merchandise. This savings we are pleased to pass on to our customers in the form of a 2 percent discount.

This policy of granting a 2 percent discount when payments are made within 10 days is printed on all our statements and invoices and accepted throughout the furniture industry. In your particular case, payments were made long after the period indicated. In fairness to our other customers, as well as ourself, you can appreciate our position in this case.

From August 12 to August 15 we are having a special sale on Maxwell Portable TV's. Normally selling for $110 we are offering them to our dealers at a profit-making $92.00 each. Why not check the quantity you desire on the card enclosed and put it in the mail today.

At times when a claim is made where the buyer is at fault, a compromise may be suggested rather than a complete grant or refusal. In such cases, it is again wise to present an explanation of the situation and then make the compromise offer in a courteous and direct way.

SELLER AT FAULT—GRANTING A CLAIM

The letter that grants the claim when the seller is at fault should include the following:

1. An opening which introduces the situation and makes the grant
2. An explanation of how the incident occurred (may be omitted if explanation of some ridiculous error only magnifies the mistake)
3. An attempt to regain the customer's confidence in the reliability of the company
4. A sales appeal if appropriate
5. A friendly close

Unlike the case when the buyer is at fault, two or three courses of action are not possible. There is only one thing the seller can do with a claim if he is at fault—he must grant it. There should be no "ifs," "ands," or "buts"; the fault should be accepted and the adjustment made.

This is a rather difficult letter to write. The seller must accept responsibility for an error, yet he must do it in such a way that he does not lose the buyer's confidence in the company. The severity of the error and the reasonableness of the buyer will have an affect on whether or not the explanation will be accepted. A delay of one day on a promised delivery may be one thing; a delay of 10 days, quite another.

Dear Mr. Green:

Your account has been credited for the $75.00 which you requested in your letter of February 10.

We can certainly appreciate your situation and we understand completely why you would go out and purchase the Double-Purpose Chairs from a retail source.

Although your order was clearly stamped for February 2 delivery, it was misunderstood, and the shipping ticket was somehow marked for February 12 delivery. In any event, we are happy that all the guests at the Montgomery party were adequately seated.

In our ten years of business relations, nothing like this has happened, and we hope that you will understand our deep desire to handle your future needs with efficiency and economy.

This is the season when picnic aluminum folding tables sell very well. Our 30″ × 72″ Traveler which usually sells for $25.00 is available this week only for $21.00 each or $245. per dozen. Call us today!

In the letter above a brief explanation of the error is given, but sometimes it is better to make the grant and then go on to other matters such as in the following letter.

Dear Mr. Arlon:

You're right—we are sorry.

The two dozen No. 231 men's shirts were sent out to your Elm Street store today just as you requested in your letter of March 12. We certainly regret the inconvenience you had.

We know that your customers will find these Marquette shirts eminently satisfactory as to price and quality.

Under separate cover we are sending you a sample of the new Marquette Summer Pajama line. These men's pajamas are made of the finest cotton batiste, yet they sell for only $4.95 each and give you a full 25 percent profit margin.

Use the enclosed card to order a supply today; we know you will be happy you did.

THIRD PARTY AT FAULT

There are situations where neither the buyer nor seller is at fault, but a third party (such as a railroad or trucking line) is at fault.

In such cases, the seller should explain, as best he can, and then refer the buyer to the third party for an adjustment. When the buyer is a small businessman and perhaps unfamiliar with the process of submitting claims, the seller may do it for him. In no case, however, should the adjustment letter sound like a "buck passing affair." It should be sincere, helpful, and courteous.

Dear Mr. Black:

We were certainly disturbed to learn that two of your Clear Vu Television sets arrived with scratched cabinets.

On March 15 we turned your entire order No. 21653 over to the Interstate Trucking Company. They checked the merchandise and gave us a receipt indicating that all the items were in good condition.

The damage, therefore, must have taken place while Interstate was handling the merchandise.

We have enclosed a standard claim form which you may submit to them. Most of the facts have been filled in and you need only add the amount of the claim, the serial numbers of the items involved, and your signature.

If there is any other way we can assist you in this matter, please do not hesitate to call on us; we shall be happy to serve you.

In addition to these cases, there are others. For example it may be that neither buyer nor seller knows where the fault lies. In such a situation, a delay must be requested while an investigation takes place. Usually the seller may offer to carry through the investigation although it may be necessary (and wiser) for the buyer to do so.

But in *every* adjustment letter, regardless of who is at fault, the tone of the letter should be courteous, sincere, and understanding.

CREDIT LETTERS

So much of American business is carried on on the basis of credit, that it is quite understandable that a large volume of correspondence is necessary to communicate the information contained in the transactions. In addition to letters, credit reports are often necessary. These were discussed in detail in Chapter 10.

The credit manager is the key man in all credit situations. Whether the credit application comes from an individual or a company, the credit man must still go through the same four steps.

1. Gather credit data.
2. Evaluate the data.
3. Make a decision on whether credit should or should not be granted.
4. Write a letter of approval or rejection to the applicant.

In an effort to weigh the usual "C's" of credit (Capital, Capacity of the business, Conditions, and Character) the credit manager will use many sources to secure his information.

CONSUMER APPLICANT

To secure information, the credit department may check the consumer's place of employment, other companies with whom he is doing or has done business, banks (information furnished by banks is very limited), personal references, consumer credit agencies, and the applicant himself.

Once the correspondent has the information, he may evaluate it and make a decision. He then sends a letter to the applicant informing him of the action taken.

WHOLESALE APPLICANT

The routine followed at this level is quite similar, although the sources of credit information may vary slightly. When a company applies for credit, the credit manager usually has the applicant's financial statement available for analysis. In addition, there is information on the applicant's payment record with other companies, data from credit agencies (such as Dun and Bradstreet) and banks, and the credit grantor's own analysis of the applicant's company and character.[1]

Writing the Letter

The letter which grants or refuses credit to the individual is quite similar to the one sent to a company. For that reason, the order of points listed below may be applied to either one. The tone and the amount of detail in the explanation of a refusal may differ somewhat, but basically they are quite similar.

CREDIT LETTER—THE GRANT

The letter granting credit to an individual or company should cover the following topics:

1. An introductory statement thanking the applicant for his interest and request
2. A statement granting credit
3. A statement of company policies and services
4. A friendly close

Granting credit to an individual:

Dear Mrs. Ganter:
Welcome to the Davis Department Store.
Your new charge plate is enclosed, and all you need do is hand it

---

[1] See Chapter 10 for detailed comments on credit agencies.

to any of our courteous, helpful employees with the merchandise you select and say, "Charge it, please." We at Davis shall be pleased to serve all your needs.

You will find that your new charge privilege is very convenient. You may use it at our main store or any one of our three suburban shopping centers.

All bills for merchandise secured in one month are payable by the 10th of the month following. Accounts not cleared by the 10th of the month are designated "Past Due."

Your charge plate will permit you to cash checks with any Davis Store cashier and it will also act as your admission ticket for such events as fashion shows, book review discussions, and home furnishing exhibits.

Make Davis your headquarters for quality merchandise at very attractive prices.

Granting credit to a company:

Dear Mr. Greene:

We are delighted to add your name to the list of Payton's satisfied credit accounts.

For over 50 years Payton's has made every effort to serve the furniture dealers of Cincinnati at the highest possible level. We are sure that within a few months you will also agree that Payton's "takes care" of its dealers by selling quality merchandise at competitive prices.

But that isn't all. We want you to use a host of other privileges: advertising, sales promotion, window trimming and display services, in addition to a generous money making discount.

These and many other plus features are discussed in the enclosed booklet. Read it carefully for it describes the policies and advantages you gain as a Payton dealer.

Welcome to Payton's, Mr. Greene.

Dear Mr. Buckley:

"And his name was inscribed in gold."

We don't know where that quotation came from, Mr. Buckley, but we did inscribe your name on our credit roster. As far as the "gold" is concerned, you will find that in the quality of merchandise, the speed of our service, and the low prices on our merchandise.

Our policies are simple and designed to be of benefit to you. A money saving 2 percent discount is yours when payment is made prior to the 10th of the month following date of purchase. All bills are due net within 60 days. Requests for adjustments must be made in writing.

Monthly flyers, banners, and posters may be secured free of charge from your salesman, Mr. Yarnel.

We shall be pleased to serve you, Mr. Buckley, as we have other New York dealers since 1901. Please call on us often.

In all cases where credit is granted, that news appears immediately because that is what the applicant is most interested in. The details of the business relationship are then discussed in either the letter or an enclosure.

CREDIT LETTERS—THE REFUSAL

This letter, like all refusals, is more difficult to handle than the grant. Here again the explanation precedes the refusal which is often implied or contained directly in the explanation. At times, no explanation is offered; the applicant is merely told what can be done—not what cannot be accomplished. This may be wise when dealing with an individual who may not be as receptive or understanding about an explanation for a "turn-down" as a company controller or accountant would be.

Refusing credit to an individual:

Dear Mrs. Bartoning:

Hamilton's was happy to receive your request for a charge account.

The information which you submitted was examined carefully. We do feel, however, that you would be wiser to remain on a cash basis at the present time and take advantage of the privileges that go along with such an arrangement.

This Friday, June 12, at 1:00 P.M., a special showing of imported women's fashions will be held in our Alexander Room. We have enclosed two admission tickets and we sincerely hope that you and a guest will honor us by attending. If you should need additional tickets, please call me on extension 305.

Dear Mrs. Mablon:

Thank you for requesting a charge account with Bentons.

We have checked the data you submitted, and we find that you already have accounts with five other department stores in Los Angeles. We often find that our customers derive more advantage when they do not have a variety of different accounts to handle.

We therefore feel that you should continue on a cash basis and utilize our fast and. accurate delivery service that speeds quality merchandise to you quickly and efficiently.

We have enclosed our Easter Clothing Booklet which we are sure you will find interesting and worthwhile. Please let us serve you at your pleasure.

Refusing credit to a company:

Dear Mr. Kable:

Thank you for your recent request for credit and the financial statement which we received today. It has been a pleasure serving you on a cash basis during the last two years.

We notice that your financial statement indicates a rather heavy liability position. Rather than add to that situation we feel that you should continue to buy for cash. This will permit you to improve your position by keeping your inventory low and adding to your profit margin through the regular cash discount.

Your store is located in a growing community, and we are sure that within a year, your financial level will be appreciably improved. At such time, we shall be happy to again evaluate your statement.

I have enclosed our "Special Customer" bulletin describing our sale on the contemporary line. We know this merchandise has been one of your best items, and that you will be interested in the 10 percent reduction which you may take from the regular catalog prices on this line. Just call us collect and list the items you desire; they will be shipped out immediately.

It should be noted that each of the refusals either explains the true situation courteously or else says nothing. There are no so-called "white lies," subterfuges, evasive statements, or fictitious reasons given for the refusal. Such deceptions will almost always result in ill feelings when the true situation is made known.

A statement of refusal which accurately states the facts should be made tactfully and discreetly; if it might be too embarrassing, then merely indicate what *can* be done for the applicant. But an untruth is no more acceptable in business correspondence than it is anywhere else. There is no way an intelligent person can rationalize a fabricated statement.

A company that is known for its honesty and integrity enjoys an enviable reputation in the business community.

COLLECTION LETTERS

Although every individual who utilizes credit expects to pay his account as agreed, instances do arise when bills cannot be met.

When that occurs, it calls for action on the part of the collection manager.

The type of action he takes is dependent on many factors: what kind of a risk the debtor is; how long the money has been due; the number of years the business association of the two firms has been carried on; the conditions in the field; and a score of other variables. Because the tone and manner of the entire collection procedure are predicated on so many factors, the collection correspondent has a most "delicate" job.

He must have tact to say what is necessary and not lose good will; he must have vision and courage to go along with a shaky account that has potential; and he must be strict and stern so that he will take severe action in the face of pleas, requests, and excuses. But it is a mistaken notion to assume that the collection manager is interested only in getting the money that is due. His primary aim is to retain good will between the customer and his company and at the same time collect the past due account.

In an attempt to make his subjective job easier and more precise, most credit and collection executives assign their accounts to specific categories:

Good or preferred risk
Fair or acceptable risk
Poor or unstable risk

Classifying accounts in this fashion may really be quite inaccurate if one attempts to place one of these three labels on every account and work from that point. A good risk may be classified that way because of good capital and conditions. However, he may be a slow payer because that is his nature or habit. Or an account may be a poor risk but he bends every effort to make his payments when due so that his credit rating may be improved. Thus a company may be known as a "good risk, slow pay," or "fair risk, prompt pay," or "poor risk, poor pay." The important thing to keep in mind is that behind each account is a person who must be treated as an individual on the basis of his record, history, character, and financial position.

The *tone* of the letters to the good risk will be pleasant, courteous, and understanding. A definite offer to be of assistance is usually made. A similar approach may be used with the fair risk, but in the case of the poor risk, the tone of the collection letters should be stern and direct.

The *time interval* between the letters varies. The number of days between the letters is greater for the good risk than it is for the poor. The latter's funds are probably limited, and there is no point in stretching out the collection procedure. Action and payment are desired as quickly as possible.

The *number of letters* sent before final or court action is taken also changes according to the risk. There is little reason to send a poor risk a series of eight collection letters if he has little capital and many debts. While you are mailing letter number five in a series, he may have closed shop and distributed what assets he had to those who pressed him more severely than you. Obviously the good risk receives more letters before final action is taken than either the fair or poor risk.

The *time before court action* is taken also varies. A man whose character and capital rating have always helped to designate him as a good credit risk may not be taken to court for a year or more, according to the type of business involved and the size of the debt. A poor risk may be hailed into court as quickly as possible.

Miscellaneous Attributes of the Collection Letter

1. Regardless of the type of risk, the collection letter should be courteous. There is never any reason for insults, diatribes, or sarcastic statements.
2. The collection letter should be precise in its listing of dates when specific action will be taken and exactly how much is due.
3. A "you" attitude should be injected in this letter. The debtor should be made to realize that he should pay for *his* benefit. The creditor should not whine, cajole, or beg.

POOR: You should pay us, because if we don't have the money, our bills can't be paid, and we will be hurt.

BETTER: A quick payment of your bill will insure that your excellent credit reputation will be retained.

Steps in the Collection Series

Most credit and collection managers have divided their collection procedure into three steps:

First step—Reminders
Second step—Personal letters
Third step—Final, court or drastic action

Some authorities list a step prior to number one above which they call the invoice stage. This simply involves sending out a duplicate of the invoice which lists the amount owed. However, the bill is not yet past due; therefore it seems unwise to list it as part of the collection series.

THE REMINDER STEP

When payment has become a few days past due, many companies send out a reminder. These may be stickers which are pasted on the face of a duplicate invoice or a rubber stamped message placed in the same place.

PLEASE	HAVE YOU FORGOTTEN?
JUST A REMINDER TO TELL YOU OF YOUR PAST DUE BILL	WE HATE TO HOUND YOU, **BUT THAT BILL · · ·**
Perhaps You Have OVERLOOKED Your Past Due Bill?	*Has Our* **BILL** *Slipped Your Mind?*

Other reminders used are brief form messages on a card or on a sheet of stationery. Sometimes they are made up to appear like greeting cards or pictures.

> Because you have probably been busy, the bill which is due has been overlooked. Will you place your remittance in the mail today— please.

THE PERSONAL LETTERS STEP

The personal letters step is the heart of the collection procedure. Most companies have designed a series for each of the three risk classifications. The series for the good or preferred risk obviously contains more letters than are in the poor risk group; the tone used in each series varies, and the interval between the mailings in the good risk group is longer than in the other two.

Although these letters are often pre-prepared, they are usually individually typed from a model and the name filled in so that a personal touch will be secured.

In this letter writing stage of the collection procedure, the writer must use all the skill he can muster to motivate the recipient to favorable action. His end purpose is to have a check come in in the return mail. To achieve that objective he may persuade, request, threaten, or demand. What may work in one case may not work in another. But he should be prepared to utilize the most effective appeal possible in each case. Some of these are:

1. Appeal to fairness

We did our part by sending you the merchandise you requested when you requested it. Now you should fulfill our request. . . .

2. Appeal to the customer's credit reputation

Through the years you have built up an excellent credit reputation in the furniture industry. It seems ridiculous to tear it down simply because of an unpaid $45.00 bill. We will have to report this delinquency to the Furniture Association if we. . . .

3. Appeal to pride and status

In just three years you have built up an enviable business position in the community. Surely you would not want. . . .

4. Appeal to fear or court action

Although we have sent you several letters, we have not received a response from you. Therefore if a check for $85.00 is not received by April 28 our attorney has been instructed to file legal action against. . . .

These are a few of the reasons which might motivate favorable action. There are others, and one or more of them may be used in the collection letter.

A Typical Collection Series to a Fair Risk:

1. First reminder
2. Second reminder
3. Dear Mr. London:

   Just a brief note to remind you that your balance is now past due. Let's clear this little matter up. A stamped envelope is enclosed. All you need do is slip your check for $95.50 in it and drop it in your "out" basket.

   Thanks so much.

4. Dear Mr. London:

   We sent you a note a week ago regarding your past due account but apparently you overlooked it.

   We have been wondering, however, about your bill. If there is any particular situation which has arisen where we can give you some help, please let us know.

   You have been a customer of ours for many years and we want to assist you in every possible way to maintain your high credit reputation.

   If all is well, just place your check for $95.50 in the enclosed envelope and send it back.

   Our special spring bulletin, just off the press, will be out this week. Check it for outstanding values.

5. Dear Mr. London:

   As the Doctor says when he walks in, "what's the trouble?"

   We have been quite disturbed about your silence in regard to your outstanding account of $95.50. We know how much you value your credit rating in the furniture industry.

   A reputation such as you enjoy was built up slowly and carefully. Certainly one small bill is not worth damaging it. Yet if we do not receive payment or some explanation, we shall be forced to send your name to the United States Furniture Association. Such action on our part would prove detrimental to your reputation throughout the industry.

   We can both avoid a great deal of trouble and unnecessary work if you will send us your check for $95.50 TODAY!

6. Dear Mr. London:

   When I saw your account still in our past due file, I could hardly believe it.

   We have sent you reminders, letters, and more letters. Yet we have had no satisfactory response from you.

   Unfortunately we shall now be forced to take a step which will prove costly to you in both reputation and money.

On March 28, ten days from today, your account will be turned over to Bryant and Bryant, our collection attorneys. You can still avoid the trouble and extra legal expense this will entail if you send us your check for $95.50 immediately. If not, legal action will begin on March 28.

As noted earlier, the number of letters in the series varies. Usually the delinquent account will send in a check after the first or second letter. Of course, the series is then discontinued.

There are various agencies which sell a variety of prepared collection letters for nominal fees. Sometimes large printing shops have these available, and, for a small fee over the cost of the letters, they will add the purchasing company's name and address.

Very often the collection series is written around some theme that may arouse interest. The early letters may talk about going out fishing and coming back with no catch. These continue with references to casting, baiting, and hauling in an empty line. Or the series may begin with references to a ball game; no runs, no hits, but one error and how costly that may prove to the season's record. On the whole, most collection managers agree that a straightforward letter or series seems to work best.

"Different" Letters

It is not too unusual to see collection letters that are "different." They may be humorous, striking, or attention catching. Sometimes they are written like regular letters; other times they are set to verse or typed on a legal form.

Dear Mr. Gray:

Some years ago, when I attended dear old State, I somehow got lost in an archaeology course. How I ever registered for it I'll never know, but I do remember old, old Professor Herman.

Students would bring in ancient Egyptian, Roman, or Greek artifacts. Old Professor Herman would carefully examine the ancient item and tell us the story behind it.

Right now we're in a quandary because we don't know the story behind the nonpayment of your June 2 account for $129.50. Do you think we should send this ancient item off to Professor Herman or can we get the story (and the money) from you?

Yours truly,

P.S. We forgot to tell you. Professor Herman got fed up with mummies and pyramids and changed professions. He is now known as Herman King, Attorney at Law.

Dear Mr. Gray:

You have probably heard about the couple in the Ozarks who put all their bills into an old hat once each month. Then the wife, blindfolded, would pull one out which was paid.

We are sure you don't use a system like that but we are trying to figure out *what* system you do use. Give us a hint; we do need the money and we'd like to get that $85.00 some way without using a magician or a collection attorney.

These "different" letters, like the unusual ones mentioned earlier, have not proved very effective according to collection correspondents. It seems reasonable that if a delinquent account is being pressed by creditors on all sides, he will not give much attention to the cute, clever, or humorous letter. After all if the writer of such a letter thinks the whole affair is funny, perhaps he won't mind waiting a little longer.

Drastic Action Step

Most accounts will respond to a reminder or one of the letters in the collection series. For those few who do not, the creditor must go on to the last step. This involves (1) turning the account over to an attorney for collection, (2) instituting court action, or (3) assigning the account to a collection agency or a credit association.

The Delinquent Consumer Account

Not too much has been said about collection methods for the consumer for two reasons: (1) In most cases the same procedure is used—reminders, letters, court action and (2) most collection situations are between one company and another rather than between a company and an individual.

Perhaps the single area of important difference occurs in the "drastic action step." Quite often when a consumer's debt is not paid after repeated requests his wages may be "assigned" or "garnisheed."

In the case of garnisheement, the creditor secures a court order which directs the employer to deduct a portion of the delinquent's wages and apply it against the debt.

In purchasing "on time" the buyer may sign a form called a wage assignment. If he does not pay as agreed, the creditor can send the assignment form to the delinquent account's employer. That employer *may* (it is not a court order) assign the employee's wages and release only part of it until such time as the creditor sends in a "withdrawal of assignment" form.

This entire area of consumer credit has grown with the tremendous increase in credit buying. With the many types of installment buying, "small down payment" purchases, and "buy now, pay later" appeals, a variety of problems have come up. Because there are always a small number of unscrupulous merchants and buyers who exist, deceptive practices have crept in. A few merchants will charge exorbitant interest rates on credit buying; whereas some buyers will make "time" purchases with the intent to defraud by making one or two payments and then stopping.

In some of our states, laws have been passed which protect the ethical merchant and the honest buyer. More statutes would be wise, for credit buying has many advantages and offers benefits to merchants and consumers when it is properly supervised.

QUESTIONS FOR DISCUSSION

I. Offer your criticism of the following claim and adjustment letters.

1. Dear Sir:

If you will refer to our order No. 214 of February 21 you will note that we purchased a large quantity of cork sheets, your item No. 2434B.

After we cut this merchandise to size and began to punch our products from it, we encountered an unusually large number of unsatisfactory pieces. These frequently exhibited cracks in the cork, and they had to be discarded.

We know that you will want to make an equitable adjustment to take care of this unsatisfactory merchandise.

2. Dear Mr. Gayton:

On January 22 we received an order of brass from you. As you recall, this order was made up of bars and rods of various sizes.

All items were completely satisfactory with the exception of the ¼-inch brass tubing, your catalog No. 21561. If you will check our original order, you will note that our order was entered for this tubing to be delivered in 9-foot lengths. Unfortunately the entire lot of 630 feet was delivered in 7-foot lengths.

We intended to cut this tubing into 3-foot lengths and

further fabricate it for one of our furniture manufacturers. We were also under a "deadline arrangement" which made it necessary for us to process the 7-foot lengths we received without communicating with you further.

You can see, of course, that we have 90 pieces of the brass tubing in 1-foot lengths which have no value to us but which cost $72.00.

Because of the circumstances we feel that you should credit our account for one half the loss incurred: $36.00. We are sure that you will agree that this is a reasonable and equitable request.

Our many years of business association have been very satisfactory, and I am sure you will forward a credit memo at your earliest convenience.

3. Dear Mr. Martin:

As you may recall, your truck delivered an order to us on March 5. Shortly after its arrival we checked it and found that one of the No. 51 contemporary tables was badly scratched on its surface.

We have since had the table refinished by the Nu-Look Refinishing Service. Their bill for $28.00 (which we paid) is enclosed.

Inasmuch as the damage probably took place prior to the arrival of the table at our store, we request that you credit our account for the complete cost of refinishing.

4. Dear Sir:

On March 3 we received a shipment of merchandise from you.

In this delivery were 4000 containers for our No. AB343 head gasket unit. According to our original purchase order No. 33471, dated November 15, the length of this unit was requested to be 26 inches. Through some unexplained oversight on your part these were made up 24 inches in length. Quite obviously our unit cannot be accommodated in this carton.

Will you be good enough to rectify this error as quickly as possible? Our present supply of container No. AB343 is very low and we shall require the 4000 new cartons within two weeks.

You may pick up the unsatisfactory lot immediately or at the time of the replacement delivery.

5. Gentlemen:

Your truck recently delivered an order to our factory. Unfortunately your driver, Mr. Frank Marcuso, backed into our dock No. 3 when the gate was down. Apparently his brakes slipped or he was not aware of his position, for the truck hit the dock door which is always kept closed in the winter.

The damage was sufficiently severe to prevent the gate from being used until it was taken down and the guide rails, handle, and two glass units were repaired or replaced.

Will you kindly send us a check to cover the damages?

6. Gentlemen:

On January 15 we purchased six 50-pound drums of your cleaning and scrubbing compound.

We have just discovered that the contents of one of these drums is caked, soiled, and filled with particles of dirt and cement.

Although we are aware of your 30-day return policy and the fact that this item was purchased three months ago, we are sure you will agree this is an exceptional case. We are sure this faulty container of merchandise was inadvertently shipped to us and that you will want to replace it.

In some 12 years of business association with you, this is the first experience we have had of this nature, and we are sure you will honor our request.

7. Dear Mr. Burns:

We received your request for an $18.50 adjustment of your account on the basis of merchandise which you claim was not up to expected quality.

Inasmuch as all of the items which leave our company are examined by two different inspectors, we wonder if you have not made a mistake or if the damage might have occurred on your premises. Nevertheless we have credited your account, and we hope that this satisfies you.

Please let us hear from you in the future.

8. Dear Mr. Johnson:

We have received your letter of February 17, in which you request that we credit your account for $28.50 for discounts on merchandise which you have purchased.

As is indicated on all our invoices, as well as other literature, this 2 percent discount is granted when payments are made within ten days after receipt of merchandise. As you know, this is a common policy throughout the automotive industry and has been designed to increase the margin of profit of our customers and to assist us in our own accounting procedures.

In your particular case, the amount in question was apparently arrived at on the basis of your order Nos. 321, 4561, and 823. However, your accounting department issued payment for these 28, 26, and 30 days, respectively, after delivery.

We are sure that this fact was overlooked by your auditor and that in all fairness to you and to all our customers, you can appreciate our position in not honoring your request under these circumstances.

We know that you will be interested in a special sale we are having for our preferred customers on our item Nos. 231, 232, and 233. You have used these in quantity lots in the past, and we think you will be interested in the 5 percent discount that is being offered on these until the end of this month. Please wire or call us collect as to your needs, and the merchandise will be dispatched immediately.

9. Dear Miss Adams:

We have received your request of March 12 for a credit of $65.50 to your account. You arrived at this on the basis of your desire to return two cases of our No. 56 high-speed lubricating oil.

As you probably recall from your past business relations with us, all items of this nature are to be utilized within 12 months of packaging. This is clearly indicated on the containers as well as the cartons in which this merchandise is packed. You apparently overlooked this fact in the case of the No. 56 oil, for an examination of your account indicates that it was purchased from us approximately 18 months ago. However, we do recognize that situations like this do occur, and we have credited your account as you requested.

May we suggest that in the future, however, you order only those quantities which will answer your immediate needs. This is a high quality product that is in constant demand, and for that reason we always carry it in stock. We can make shipment to you within 48 hours after receiving your order.

We are sending you our summer catalog, and we know you will find many items that will boost your sales and give you complete satisfaction.

10. Dear Mr. Sherwood:

We received your request for a replacement on our electrical clock No. 253; we have shipped one out to you this morning. There will be no charge for this replacement. In examining the unit which you returned to us, we find that it was made to operate on A.C. current; however, it was inadvertently plugged into a D.C. outlet. Had you requested an A.C.-D.C. unit, we would have been happy to supply it for a very slight additional cost. Your order No. 556 requested our model No. 253, which is described in our catalog as A.C. only.

In the future may we request that you check your orders somewhat more carefully to facilitate sales operations for both you and us.

11. .Dear Mr. Lincoln:

You're right—we're sorry.

We aren't quite sure how in the world your order was sent to Brunswick, Ohio, instead of Brunswick, Illinois. But it did happen, and we can understand that many of your automotive repair jobs were delayed. We can appreciate that this caused you some inconvenience and also required that you purchase replacement head gasket sets from other dealers at a loss to yourself. We have accordingly credited your account for the $27.50 you requested. Needless to say, your original order was sent to you by air freight yesterday. It should arrive on either the 18th or 19th of this month.

In looking over your file I noted that it has been some time since you purchased any of our No. 105 filters. This was always a popular item with you, and it is being offered at a 10 percent discount of the sum listed in our spring catalog. If you wire or call us collect, I can have a quantity sent out immediately. This is an excellent item, and I know you will want to take advantage of this special offer.

12. Dear Mr. Harper:

We received the two sample relay switches which you returned to us.

As you requested, we immediately had the two switches carefully examined by our laboratory. It was determined that these two items were subjected to adverse weather conditions for an extensive period of time, and this caused the corrosion of the delicate contact points.

This particular switch was especially designed for indoor use under humidity and temperature controlled use. This fact is carefully indicated on each carton as well as in the installation directions which are packaged with each switch.

Evidently this was overlooked by your employees. For this reason you can understand our position in this particular case.

If you have a quantity of these No. 531 switches which have become corroded, we can have them reconditioned for you at $0.64 each which is our cost. Or you may wish to have this done by one of your technicians. If you will have him call our engineer, Mr. Makee, the cleaning operation will be explained in detail.

If in the future you require a high-quality relay switch for outdoor use, may we suggest our No. 656. This particular item may be subjected to wide variations in temperature as well as other severe weather factors. It is guaranteed to carry through its basic function for 18 months under all conditions. I am including a sample of the No. 656 with the two reconditioned switches which are being returned to you under separate cover.

II. Complete any of the following problems assigned.

1. Submit a claim to the Baxter Furniture Corporation for two new table model Clear-Tone radios. In the order delivered to your store five days ago, these two radios were among 44 other items. It was just today that you discovered that both Clear-Tone radios received were damaged by water. The containers of each show the water line; the bottoms of the radio cases are warped and unsightly.

   Evidently these two radios were stored so that water could damage them. However, you are positive this could not have happened in your storeroom. Baxter may either deliver two replacements and pick up the damaged items or simply credit your account for $61.00. You have purchased from Baxter for eight years.

2. Four months ago you received six industrial power saws from the Signet Saw Corporation. You in turn sold these saws to manufacturing companies that regularly buy tools and machinery from you. Three of the companies which purchased saws have complained that the motors were not satisfactory and that they "burned out." You investigated and found that the motors were made abroad, they were not very powerful, and they were altogether unsatisfactory. You immediately had one of your men install a 2-horsepower General Electric motor in each of the six power saw units which you sold.

   You have the six old motors which Signet can pick up. The General Electric motors cost $60.00 each and you feel that an adjustment should be made. Decide on what you feel is equitable and write a claim letter to Signet.

3. Six weeks ago you sent a $12.00 personal check to the *Engineers' Monthly Report* for a two-year subscription. Although your bank returned your cancelled check three weeks ago, you still haven't heard from the magazine company. Write to the *Engineers' Monthly* and tell them you wish a copy of the latest issue within a week and your subscription begun, or you want your money refunded.

4. In today's mail you received a bill from the Manhattan Office Furniture Company. An Efficiency Desk was billed at $60.00, and a Deluxe Desk at $85.00. Actually you should be billed for only the Deluxe. On May 12 the Efficiency was delivered, but when you discovered that it did not contain a typewriter drawer and pull-out stand, you had Manhattan pick it up and deliver the Deluxe. Send Manhattan a check for the Deluxe Desk and a request for a credit to your account for the Efficiency.

5. Your adjustment policy is clearly stated on all statements and invoices: "All claims must be entered within 10 days of delivery of merchandise and are subject to inspection if over $10.00."

   This morning's mail brings a request from Mr. Marquette, owner of Marquette's Furniture Store, for a $45.00 credit to his account. He tells you that one of the dining room tables (No. 2134) he received approximately four weeks ago was damaged. He has had the table refinished and has since sold it. However, he has sent you a refinisher's bill for $45.00.

   His record of claims is unusually high; you rather doubt the facts in the case; and, of course, your policy has not been followed. On the other hand, Marquette is a good customer.

   Your decision is to refuse the claim. Write such a letter and try to retain his good will.

6. One of your best customers, Merrimac Metal Corporation, writes in to complain about the quality of the ball-point pens which they recently purchased from you.

   You made up 20,000 of these pens for Merrimac which they, in turn, distribute to their office personnel. The name of the company is stamped on each pen.

   Merrimac wants you to pick up all the pens and credit their account for the original charge of $2,000. The basis for the claim involves the ink in the pens. Merrimac maintains the ink does not flow freely, blots, and is generally unsatisfactory. The 20 pens which they returned with their claim were tested and found to be unsatisfactory.

You are disturbed because Merrimac has always been an excellent customer of office supplies, and you fear this incident may be detrimental to your future association.

Offer to pick up all the pens, insert a new ink cartridge in each, and return them. In addition you may offer a $200 credit to the account to compensate Merrimac for time, effort, and general dissatisfaction.

7. Allison Appliance Store requests that you permit them to return for credit three portable Faxon radios, model No. 230. The request surprises you because you haven't handled Faxon products in two years. However, a check of the Allison file indicates that the radios were purchased 28 months ago.

   These radios are now out of style, and you aren't sure what you can do with them even if you do accept them. Suggest to Allison that he try to sell them at a substantial reduction, and that you will then credit his account for a reasonable sum so that his regular profit will be secured. You may also suggest that if he cannot sell the radios, you will then be prepared to accept them for credit.

8. Mr. Porter returns his Olympic tennis racquet with a request for a refund of $18.00. He says it is obviously "falling apart" after a few weeks of normal use. You examine the racquet and find that the strings are in very poor condition, the top of the frame is badly chipped from striking the ground, and the handle is slightly warped as though it had been permitted to lie in a pool of water for some time.

   Because you feel the request is completely unreasonable, your first inclination is to refuse. However, upon reconsideration you decide to write and offer him a $7.00 credit on any other racquet of his choice.

9. Mrs. Palmer returns a $12.00 knit shirt which she purchased three weeks ago for her husband's birthday. She says she washed it once, and it shrank and lost its "shape."

   You immediately have the shirt sent to your testing laboratory. The report indicates that the shirt was washed in extremely hot water.

   Write Mrs. Palmer and point out that the washing instruction booklet attached to each shirt as well as the collar label, clearly state, "Hand wash only in cool water." This is because of the high quality and delicacy of the imported fabric.

   Of course you assume the hot water washing was inadvertent, but you still feel that in all fairness to yourself and the other customers, you must refuse to honor Mrs. Palmer's request.

III. Offer your criticism of the following credit and collection letters.
   1. Welcome to Bartons—

   And we do mean WELCOME! Your request for credit has been approved and your name entered on a blank ledger page.

   We know that you will want to save money and build business by handling our high quality, low priced merchandise.

   All bills are reduced by 2 percent when payments are made prior to the 10th of the month following date of purchase. Other savings may be secured by following our monthly Red Tag Sales. In addition, of course, every purchase made from our catalog assures you of quality merchandise at the lowest possible price.

   Let us hear from you soon, and again, WELCOME to Bartons.

   2. Dear Mr. Kelly:

   Thank you for your recent request for a credit line with us.

   We have carefully checked the information you submitted. All the businessmen you mentioned spoke very highly of you and your ability. However, an examination of your financial statement indicates a ratio of assets to liabilities which leads us to recommend that you continue making your purchases on a cash basis.

   Your order has been completely processed and will be sent out C.O.D., or you may prefer to send us a check. Wire or call us collect as to which method you prefer.

   3. Dear Mr. Pattel:

   We have just received your first order along with your request that we open a charge account for you.

   As a businessman you should certainly realize that a credit account on a commercial level isn't opened in five minutes. A good deal of investigation is necessary. Therefore we must refuse to charge the order you sent in. If you want the merchandise sent out C.O.D. let us know.

   We will write you about the credit application the first chance we get.

   4. It was a pleasure, Mrs. Solinger,

   To receive your request for a charge account with Mather's. Your interest in civic affairs and charitable organizations in our community is well known and most commendable.

   An account has been opened in your name and a credit identification card is enclosed with this letter. All you need do when making purchases is to hand your card to any Mather clerk and say, "charge it."

We have enclosed a booklet describing our credit service in detail; we know you will be interested in reading through it. May we also remind you of the fashion show and luncheon which is held at noon on the first Monday of each month. This is reserved for our special customers such as you.

Please join us on Monday, March 12, at noon in the Mayfair Room.

5. Dear Mr. Kandel:

Although your bill is now eight weeks past due, and we have sent you three reminders, we still have not heard from you.

Surely you understand that we could not continue in business if many of our accounts followed a course of action such as yours. We would go into bankruptcy in short order.

Now we know that you want to pay your past due account of $85.50 as soon as possible. We have therefore included a stamped envelope, and we would like to have your check by return mail.

6. Can we help, Mr. Brent?

We sincerely want to assist you, for we know something must be wrong. This is the first time in our 10-year business association that your account has become delinquent.

As you know, your balance now due is $255. If some unexpected economic condition has taken place in your community and it is necessary for you to have an extension of time on your account, please let us know. We shall be happy to try to work with you.

Meanwhile, if we can send you any of our high quality merchandise on a C.O.D. basis, please submit your order. We do want to coöperate with you, Mr. Brent.

7. Dear Mr. Cunningham:

About 20 minutes ago my comptroller, Mr. Nevins, walked in looking very puzzled. When I asked him why, he told me that he has not heard from you for four months although he has sent you five letters. Well, I'm puzzled too.

As president of this company, I have always taken a sincere interest in your account as well as the others, but this situation is difficult to understand.

Won't you clarify the issue for Mr. Nevins and me by sending in your check for $125 today. If it is not received within 10 days of the date of this letter, your account will be handed over to Carter and Carter, our collection attorneys. They are never puzzled about what to do.

8. Dear Mrs. Gray:

Fenton's Fine Foods has indicated that you have a delinquent balance of $52.50. This sum is now five months past due.

Although we are reluctant to take drastic action, it will be necessary for us to garnishee your husband's salary if a check is not received on or before October 12.

9. "Make a Fortune"

Is what our credit man told me the other day in reference to your account. What he suggested was that we sell your record to the Antiquarian Society, a group intimately interested in ancient and historical material.

To tell the truth, I was interested in the idea, but I would hate to have our name end up in a rare book room even if you wouldn't mind.

Why not just surprise the dickens out of me and infuriate our credit manager by sending in your check for $95.00 today?

10. Dear Mr. Clayton:

I don't know if you remember our old Mr. Pease. He's been with us for 50 years, and he has more pride in the company than the president.

During the last three weeks, poor old Pease has been mighty nervous. You see, the auditors are due on the first. Everyone has been busy checking files, straightening up bills, balancing accounts, and working on the ledgers. All goes well except that one past due bill of Mr. Clayton's.

Poor old Mr. Pease keeps trying to find a place for it, for he knows the auditors will raise the roof when they see an ancient bill like yours—but there doesn't seem to be a thing he can do.

Why not save old Pease from a nervous breakdown by sending in your check for $85.00 today.

IV. Complete any of the following problems assigned.

1. For some time your salesman has been trying to add Farley Lamp Corporation to your list of customers. Farley finally agrees to send in an initial order, provided you extend a credit line. You have checked his references as well as the credit agency's report, and you find that the company is an excellent risk. His first order just came in. Write the letter granting him a credit account. Remember to review your services.

2. Mrs. Worthington requests that you open a charge account in

your department store in her name. You check and find that her husband is an executive making $18,000 a year; their big suburban home is paid for; and their three children are married and are no longer living with the Worthingtons. The other three department stores in town report that she is a very unsatisfactory customer: often delinquent, a tremendous record of returns, and frequent complaints and claims. Your store records indicate that she has purchased for cash from you.

Write a letter refusing credit but pointing out the advantages of continued cash buying. Remember that she is a busy and influential woman in the community.

3. A relatively new cash customer, Burell Hardware Company, has just submitted a financial statement, references, and other data along with a request for a charge account. He says he would like a $1200 line of credit. Your investigation and evaluation determine he is a good "limited" credit risk. You therefore decide to open an account with a credit limit of $800 for a 12-month period. If all arrangements work out satisfactorily, this limit will go up to $1200 next year. Of course, Burell may supplement its credit purchases with C.O.D. orders.

4. The Blackstone Woolen Corporation has requested that your firm, Capital Bag and Box Company, open an account for them. You ask for a report from Dun & Bradstreet and you secure information from other sources. On the whole, the reports are favorable, but two or three companies report Blackstone as a very slow payer. Other factors in your analysis also make you cautious. Write a letter granting credit to the Blackstone Corporation, but be sure they clearly understand your payment policies.

5. As the collection correspondent for the American Blouse Company, write the first letter in a collection series to Rampon Clothing Store in Waterton, Iowa. Mr. Rampon has been a good customer for five years and has always paid his bills promptly. At the present time he owes $310.50. You have sent him three reminders and there has been no response. You are at a loss to understand the situation although you have heard that the steel company in Waterton is on strike. In addition to trying to secure payment, offer your company's assistance.

6. Kantron's Hardware opened an account with you nine months ago. When you extended credit to him, he was classified as a poor credit risk primarily because of factors in his personal

life. Eight weeks ago he reached his credit limit of $600. This became past due, and when you called him long distance (after several reminders) he said he had just put the check in the mail, and would you release his order for $250 worth of additional merchandise. You do that, but to your dismay his check does not arrive. He now owes $850. Write a severe letter to Mr. Kantron and attempt to collect the total amount due.

7. As the proprietor of the Farm Fresh Food Mart write a collection letter to Mrs. Helen Murphy. Mrs. Murphy has purchased on credit from you for the last four years. In recent months there has been illness in her family and you permitted her bill to run up to $112. However, you have not seen her in three weeks, and she has made no attempt to make any payments on the balance due. You are also aware that Mrs. Murphy is now buying all her household needs for cash from a nearby chain store supermart. Mr. Murphy is employed as a foreman at the Giant Battery Company. Write a collection letter.

8. Assume that you are the credit and collection manager of Wolfe Wholesale Furniture Distributors. Make up a complete collection series for those dealers classified as Fair Risks. Begin with two reminders and then prepare as many letters for the series as you feel are necessary. These letters will be processed and used when needed; the specific names of accounts will be filled in.

Chapter 22

Sales and Good Will Letters

The volume of merchandise being sold by mail today is greater than it has been at any time. Furniture, home appliances, manufacturing tools, books, toys, clothing, foodstuffs, and a thousand and one other items are delivered by the postman to the buyer.

Large and small companies have found that sales letters are the best way to introduce their merchandise to the potential buyer.

Selling through the mail has become such a tremendous industry that hundreds of companies specialize in composing, printing, and mailing out sales letters.

A magazine, *The Reporter of Direct Mail Advertising,* carries the advertisements of dozens of firms which offer products and services in this area. This journal, as well as many others, prints articles describing various methods and techniques of direct mail selling.

It is really no wonder that sales letters have become so popular; they have many advantages over other sales media such as television, radio, and newspaper.

1. The sales letter is direct and personal. The prospect can hold it in his hand and notice that it is addressed to him. This is certainly not true of television, radio, or newspapers.
2. It is selective in that a specific group may be chosen as recipients; nurses, airplane pilots, accountants, etc.
3. It can be used to sell and/or introduce a dollar toy or a $10,000 truck.
4. It can go to wide geographical points quickly and inexpensively.
5. It is simple to check the results.
6. It helps to introduce the product before the salesman calls.

590

7. It does not have the competition of ads of similar products as is the case in one issue of a daily paper or a monthly magazine.
8. Its content can be varied so that it will appeal to different income, social, or cultural levels although the product and price may remain the same.

These are some of the advantages; with a little thought, you will find it easy to double the above list.

MAILING LISTS

Now where are these letters sent? Obviously it must be to potential buyers, regardless of whether they are college students, dentists, or jewelry store proprietors. In every large city there are companies which specialize in the sale of mailing lists.

You may designate almost any group you can imagine, limiting it by vocation, avocation, profession, religion, cultural or recreational interests, location, or "what have you," and a large mailing list company will be able to sell you the names and addresses of just such a roster of persons. It is always wise to secure an up-to-date list that is warranted to be accurate.

SALES LETTER PRINCIPLES

Before the seller may sit down and compose his letter, he should consider the basic principles listed below:

1. The word choice and descriptive details of his writing must be colorful and imaginative. It must reflect sincerity and enthusiasm.

POOR: This white shirt is made of good quality cloth that will give serviceable wear.

BETTER: This fine quality garment is loomed from beautiful long staple Egyptian cotton. Its snow white cloth, ocean pearl buttons, and custom tailoring by real craftsmen provide you with a shirt of incomparable quality and beauty.

2. Knowledge of the potential buyer permits the seller to mold his letter around the former's educational, social, and cultural level. We also know that different groups (such as professors, physicians, high school students, jazz music fans) have specific

desires and needs. Knowing or assuming facts in each case helps us design letters that will be effective with a specific buying group.

3. Knowledge of the product on the part of the seller is also very important. The seller who knows his product intimately can describe it with a level of sincerity and enthusiasm which is almost impossible to achieve by anyone else. Furthermore he can anticipate a buyer's questions and answer them quickly and easily in his sales appeal. In addition, his complete and detailed knowledge of the product will permit him to utilize various facts in the product's background to arouse the buyer's attention and interest.

4. Choosing and applying the central appeal is another basic principle. Specialists in advertising and selling assure us that today's buyer does not have sufficient time or interest in a product to read, analyze, and remember several vital points in its favor. Furthermore, if one point is selected (and perhaps a secondary point) and presented with emphasis, the buyer may more probably retain it in his mind and associate it with the product.

The central appeal is chosen after carefully analyzing the qualities of the product and comparing it with the needs and desires of the prospect. Thus if you were to send out 300,000 letters in the Chicagoland area to sell the Kool-Frost Refrigerator at $299.50, it might be conceivable that four or more different letters should be written.

Although the product and price remain the same, the central appeal would be different. In the upper economic suburban area, the letter might revolve around style and beauty. In a heavily populated low income area, the appeal might be installment buying; in another area, storage capacity; in another segment of the city it might be the new, giant size freezer.

Whatever appeal is chosen, it should receive the most space and attention in the letter. It may be found in the opening, in the body of the letter, and in the close.

The central appeal in the following letter to dealers is increased profits.

Dear Mr. Lampler:

Prince Patio Furniture increases dealers' profit margins again!

Although the Prince Patio line has steadily gained a reputation for high quality and attractive mark-up, we want to break all previous summer sales records for you and our other dealers.

Our offer shoots off on July 4 and will skyrocket until August 4.

During that period of time, your sales will be aided by ads in *American Reader, Homes, News and Views,* and *Today's House and Home.* For the four-week period indicated, ALL prices in our Spring Catalog are reduced a full 15 percent. In addition, we will send you one free Kool-Shade Patio Umbrella and Table Set with each $200 worth of merchandise ordered. As you know, this set is nationally advertised and sold for $35.00.

Now is the time to *save* and *make money.* Look through the special catalog which is enclosed; check your Spring Catalog and send in your money making order *today!* We will fill and ship orders within 24 hours.

ELEMENTS OF THE SALES LETTER

The sales letter may, in some ways, be compared with a traffic situation; the prospect must be made to:

STOP and LOOK
LISTEN
CHECK and TEST
GO AHEAD and BUY

In today's busy world most of us are constantly subjected to the advertisers' claims, suggestions, appeals, or harangues. The businessman receives more than his share of bulletins, salesmen's calls, and letters. Because so many sales announcements are directed to the prospective buyer, we must do something special in our sales letter so that we can gain his attention, motivate him to read, and direct him to buy. The first thing we must do, then, is to make our prospect STOP with our letter; LOOK at it carefully; LISTEN to our description intently; CHECK and TEST the validity of our claims; and then GO AHEAD and BUY.

Stop and Look

How to make the potential buyer stop and look at *your* letter in preference to the others which came in in today's mail is a real feat. Nevertheless it must be done, and there are various ways to do it.

1. Samples of the Product. This is perhaps one of the most effective devices. Who can discard a sample piece of plastic, cloth, metal, a gasket, jar of cream, pad of paper, etc., without first care-

fully examining it. Many companies have actually had their letters printed on a sample piece of metal, wood, or plastic.

2. A Photograph or Picture of the Product.   There are many products and services which are not adaptable to a sample, but a good photograph can often supplement a word-by-word description.

3. A Gadget or Gimmick.   Little plastic figures have often helped make the prospect *stop* and *look*. These may be plastic or cardboard miniature reproductions of the product or any "cute" device. In addition, keys, rings, desk ornaments, and items which "pop up" have also been used to attract attention.

4. Unusual Openings.   Various arrangements of the opening statements can be made to make the prospect *stop* and *look*.

a. Unusual or surprising statement:

> "Would you like to make an extra $5000 this year?"

> "Can you imagine a paint brush 5 feet wide?"

b. Unusual offer:

> "Here is an opportunity to buy Prince Patio Furniture at a 20 percent discount!"

> "Two Swiss Time Watches for the price of one!"

c. Story opening:

> "It began almost 60 years ago in a small province in India when a youngster discovered a most unusual way of weaving cloth. This method, which remained a family secret for almost a generation, was the direct cause of the bloody conflict which. . . ."

d. Important facts about the product:

> When American Steel, National Rubber, and Fairfax Lumber all needed an adhesive that would withstand unusual heat, cold, stress, and strain, they turned to. . . .

e. Inside address beginnings:

> Do You
> Know That You
> Can Save Ten Dollars?

Any of these devices or methods of opening a sales letter will almost invariably arouse enough attention and interest in the prospect to make him *stop* and *look* and go on to the next portion of the letter.

Listen

Once we have the prospect stopped and looking, we can have him *listen* to our description of what the product is and how it will benefit him.

The need for a strong "you" attitude, a positive approach, and a colorful and descriptive choice of words is vital in this section of the sales letter. The prospect must not only visualize the product, but he must also feel that he should buy it because he will benefit from such a purchase.

The Clipper Automatic Lawn Mower is a rugged, efficient unit that is powered by the world famous Martin 2-horsepower motor. The recoil starter insures instant operation, and the Clipper Swedish tempered steel blade provides a razor-like cut of your lawn that would bring envy to a greenkeeper's heart.

In addition, the four recessed wheels permit. . . .

Check and Test

In the highly competitive world in which we live, advertisers sometimes make extravagant claims. Some of these statements we find hard to accept unless they are proved valid. It is for this reason, that the sales letter writer must almost invariably include a statement for the prospect so that he can check and test the reliability of the claims made.

The type of check and test statement made should be chosen in consideration of the reader. Although Betty Burns would be very favorably impressed with a testimonial made by a movie star, Dr. Thomas Down would laugh at it. He would find statistics offered by the University of California's testing laboratory much more acceptable. A list of the different types of check and test statements follows:

1. Testimonials

"For years I have used Tremaine face soap," says beautiful, glamorous movie star Joan Lyons.

2. Product purchasers

United States Metals, Parker Aircraft, and California Rubber are only three of America's major corporations using Ramcraft Switching Controls.

3. Guarantees

Our tires are unconditionally guaranteed to give you complete satisfaction. If you feel they do not give you the performance claimed, return them to your nearest Road-Ride Dealer for a complete refund.

4. Trial period

Use the Turner Toaster for seven full days; if you find it does everything we claim and you expect, send us your check for $17.00. If not, return the toaster and we'll refund your money plus all shipping fees.

5. Samples

Your free sample package of Sta-Brite is enclosed. Use it in your kitchen for a week's time, and you'll agree that you've never before had your dishes and glassware so sparkling clean.

6. Statistics of tests

Laboratory tests carried through by the medical department of Illinois State College proved that three grains of Vito taken daily were significantly effective in reducing the number of colds contracted by the average individual.

7. Demonstrations

One of our technical salesmen will be happy to call, set up the Printomat, and run off your next sales promotion piece—with no obligation to you of course. Then you can see for yourself how expensive printing costs may be eliminated.

Go Ahead—and Buy

The sales letter is neither complete nor effective unless its major purpose is achieved—the sale.

Motivating the prospect to take that final step and *go ahead* and *buy* is not always easy. The words and devices used are dependent once again on the type of prospect. Some individuals will be motivated by an emphatic, insistent approach; others will be swayed by a "low pressure" suggestion to buy.

At times special approaches are used: "limited time" only; special price or free offer; limited supply; free premium; or small down payment.

Using the Four Sections

Although the discussion of the four points in the chapter began with stop and look, went on to listen and check, and concluded with go ahead and buy, they need not always follow in that order. It is possible that a letter might open with a check and test statement that was so startling that it could also serve as a stop and look device. Or a letter may open with an admonition to "Buy now while a supply is available." But every sales letter should contain the four points in some order with a strong and effective central appeal definitely evident throughout.

STOP   [a tiny leather brief case 1″ x 1½″ was clipped to the top of the letter]

LOOK   Dear Professor Hart:
No, we don't expect you to carry your lecture notes, books, and papers in the miniature case above, but we do think you will want to examine the unusual quality of the leather, the beauty of the design, and the appearance of the incomparable top grain cowhide.

LISTEN   This magnificent Collegian Case is so expertly made that we take pride in guaranteeing it for a full five years from date of purchase. Of course the miniature which we have enclosed does not permit you to see the generous interior fully leather lined. The Collegian does not have two or three gussets, but five, and one with a full zipper to hold your very important papers. Documents, notes, books, and pamphlets all fit comfortably and neatly in this Collegian. Its patented accordian pleat construction permits it to expand to a full 4 inches or collapse to 2 inches. The enclosed booklet will also give you some idea of the many other features of this five-year guaranteed Collegian.

LISTEN   The Collegian Brief Case will be the envy of your faculty colleagues for years and years to come. No need to mention either that it doesn't cost thirty or forty dollars. As a matter of fact, anyone finds the price of $17.50 hard to believe.

CHECK   That is its full and complete price together with a five-
and   year guarantee certificate. If in that period of time any
TEST   part of your Collegian needs repair, or if you desire a
      replacement, return the case and we will fill your request.
      No "ands," "ifs," or "buts"; this is an iron clad guarantee
      for your benefit that is underwritten by the American
      Surety Company.

GO AHEAD Either send us your check for $17.50 or circle the
and   C.O.D. box on the enclosed card. We will send the
BUY   Collegian out immediately. If your order arrives before
      April 1, we will be happy to have your name or initials
      stamped on the case in gold.

      Send in your order TODAY and enjoy the Collegian
      next week.

The central appeal in the letter above is the guarantee. It is
mentioned several times in the letter in very specific terms. The
letter itself takes the prospect into consideration and recognizes
his problems, needs, and desires.

OTHER SALES LETTER DEVICES

Sales Letter and Enclosure

Quite frequently in sales letters we find that what we wish to sell
cannot be adequately described in one page or even two. Yet we
also know that a sales letter over a page in length may not be
read by the busy executive. A possible solution is to prepare an
enclosure to accompany the "cover" sales letter.

The enclosure may be a double- or triple-fold booklet affair
which contains a detailed description of the products, as well as
illustrations, diagrams, and pictures.

Such a combination of cover letter and enclosure is especially
valuable for expensive items such as equipment and machinery or
new products which have not yet been introduced to the field.

Sales Letter Campaign

The letter writer often finds that the prospect will react favorably
to a *series* of sales letters all directed to the sale of a specific
product.

Such a series is referred to as a campaign and is carefully planned
to contain three, four, or five letters which are mailed out on predetermined dates. Usually there is a theme running through the

series. This may be preparation for the hot summer by buying a lightweight suit now or begin making purchases now for the busy Christmas season ahead.

GOOD WILL LETTERS

The good will of a business is frequently more valuable than the stock and fixtures—and courts have frequently ruled to that effect.

One of the best ways to keep and build good will is through the inexpensive letter. It is human nature to be flattered by someone's sincerely expressed interest in one's affairs, and there is no better way to do it than through a letter.[1]

An important factor in this type of letter is that it should have good will as its *primary* purpose. The attempt to build good will should not be limited to including paragraphs that will build good will in the body of sales, claim, adjustment, or reply letters. It is important to write a letter that has no other purpose than to build good will!

These letters may be written to the new customer, regular customer, the customer who makes infrequent purchases, and on special occasions such as the Thanksgiving or Christmas season.

Dear Mr. Genton:

In this season many of us sit back and think of all we have to be thankful for in this wonderful country of ours.

All too often we take such magnificent gifts like good health, freedom of speech and worship, and everyday comforts for granted.

Sometimes, too, loyal customers are also taken for granted—but not here at Cable's. We want you to know that we are deeply appreciative of your patronage and courtesy. As always we shall continue to work for your confidence in us by offering you the highest quality merchandise at the lowest possible price, together with careful and efficient service.

A happy and bountiful Thanksgiving Season to you, Mr. Genton.

QUESTIONS FOR DISCUSSION

I. Offer your criticism of the following letters.

1. *Outstanding! Functional! Beautiful!*

These were just a few of the comments that were heard about the new MAYFAIR line at the recent office furniture show

[1] Norman B. Sigband, "What Is Your Most Important Asset," *Credit and Financial Management,* February, 1951.

held in New York. I am sure that if you were there, you would have agreed completely.

The MAYFAIR line of desks, chairs, and related office equipment is as new as a satellite, as functional as a wheel, as comfortable as a rocking chair, and as beautiful as your favorite picture.

Examine the group of eight pictures enclosed, and I am sure you will agree. The MAYFAIR office desk has proved especially popular. Its steel construction guarantees you many years of service and its flowing, contemporary design, its four commodious drawers, and its fully automatic typewriter leaf have won the hearts of secretaries all over America. The American Design Association agreed completely, for its gold medal award for this year went to the MAYFAIR DESK.

Now is the time to give your office that modern, efficient appearance, please the girls, and satisfy yourself. Drop the enclosed card in the mail, and a MAYFAIR salesman will be out to see you on the day you designate. No obligation on your part, of course.

2. (This letter had four swatches of cloth clipped to the top)

Dear Mr. Frank:

"No alternative for quality" is what a famous man once said, and our customers have emphatically agreed for the last 40 years.

If you have privately admired the suits of some of your colleagues, the chance is good that their garments were made at Stylefair. For two score years we have been tailors for a good part of the legal profession here in Boston.

Join these men by coming in and browsing around in our air-conditioned display rooms. You will find thousands of bolts of material from which to make your selection.

Fine, imported silks from Italy, rugged tweeds from Scotland, comfortable worsted wools from England, attractive gabardines from France, carefully woven sharkskins from Spain, and many others plus a complete line of domestic woolens.

As for patterns and colors, Stylefair has them almost without end. Our master tailors will carefully take your measurements and ask you to return for a minimum of two fittings. These artists aren't satisfied with anything less than perfection and once you try a Stylefair suit, you won't be satisfied with anything less either.

Come in today for a suit that will be admired in many tomorrows.

3. Dear Collegian:

Here's a buy that's too good to miss!

If you have some friends at Purdue, Michigan, California, Notre Dame, or in a score of others schools, I am sure they have sent along the good news. And of course hundreds of fraternities, sororities, and college organizations have sent out bulletins. There can be no doubt—it's the hottest item among college students today.

Deans and professors are pleased, and thousands of parents are completely overjoyed. So why delay another minute; buy one today.

Yours for Straight "A's"

P.S. Oops, I forgot to tell you—it's the Collegian Cartridge Pen—only ONE dollar at all college bookstores.

4. (This letter was pasted on the back of a piece of ¼-inch plywood panel)

This "Wood"
Certainly Look
Beautiful in a Den

And any den looks beautiful paneled in one of MARTINDALE'S four prefinished woods. You may choose from warm satin finished walnut, lovely modern blond oak, rich early American cherry, and attractive, rugged knotty pine.

These wood panels are available in 4′ x 8′ sheets that are completely prefinished. No fuss, no muss, no paint, no rub. Just put these panels on your walls and enjoy the compliments of your visitors.

Martindale's panels go up in a jiffy also. You may either nail them directly to your wall studs or paste them on your present plaster finish. The new Martindale Wood Adhesive positively guarantees a completely permanent bond. You will also be pleased to learn that matching wood trim is available for any one of the finishes you select.

U.S. Iron, International Communications, Time Right Clocks, and Madewell Machine Corporation have all chosen Martindale to panel their executive offices. Like you, they also considered the beauty, good taste, and economy of these prefinished woods.

Call Randolph 6-2000, or mail the enclosed card today, to receive additional information on Martindale panels for your home or office.

5. LONELY?
       FRUSTRATED?
           REJECTED?
               INHIBITED?

These were just a few of the piercing words the eminent psychiatrist, Dr. Franz Braun, hurled at Appleby Fontwhistle. Poor Appleby—you see Dr. Braun was his fifth psychiatrist. In his wanderings, Appleby had tossed, turned, squirmed, and slept on some of the best couches in the city. And everywhere he went, the psychiatrist concluded his examination by handing him a bill and saying soothingly "Appleby, there's nothing wrong with you; you just feel 'left out.'" And that was the truth. At every party, at every meeting, at every dinner, Appleby sat quietly and silently.

So Appleby Fontwhistle learned the trouble but not the cure . . . until one day he found a well-read copy of *Current News Weekly*. He read it and enjoyed it thoroughly. He found out about satellites, heart operations, top level world news, recently released movies, and Broadway plays.

That evening at a small, intimate dinner party for 44, he was the center of attention as he answered questions about politics, sports, music, and medicine. He soon became known as "that bright and well-informed young man."

Now, I'm sure you've never had Appleby's problems, but wouldn't you like to have some of his pleasures? You can, too. Just drop the enclosed card in the mail and your subscription to *Current News Weekly* will begin within 10 days.

6. Dear Mr. Farwell:

Today, August 3, may be just another date on your calendar but to me it means something special—and you're involved.

August 3 marks the 40th year Foreman's Fine Furniture has been in business. It's been a period of growth, satisfactions, and advances. What progress we have made has been due to you and other customers, and we want you to know how appreciative we are.

In all those years, we have made every effort to give you quality merchandise at the lowest possible prices. Our artisans have never had any standard less than excellent, and we are sure that is the only level you will accept.

Your courtesy, kindness, and consideration have been inspirations to us, and we want to thank you most sincerely. We hope that in the 40 years to come, we shall continue to enjoy your confidence and loyalty. You may be sure that we shall take every possible step to merit your support.

II. Complete any of the problems assigned.

1. Your mailing list is made up of engineers who have graduated from various colleges in Illinois, Indiana, and Wisconsin. The product you would like to sell them is the Draftsman Pen-and-Pencil Set.

The pen is especially designed for engineers. It has a strong, stainless steel and gold point that writes "fine." The package also includes a medium and a broad point, either of which may be quickly and accurately interchanged in the pen. The pencil has three colors: black, red, and blue. By simply pressing a button the desired lead color becomes available immediately. For a limited time only, you are offering with each pen and pencil set a 6-inch pocket ruler that has its own shirt clip. The set and free gift may be secured within one week by simply returning the card enclosed or sending in a check for $4.95 and thereby saving the cost of handling and postage.

2. Write a sales letter to the neighborhood mothers advertising your "back-to-school" shoe sale. You are especially desirous of moving your Tough-Bilt line which comes in a variety of styles for children from ages 3 to 12. The Tough-Bilt is an all-leather shoe; paper or composition materials are not used. Every shoe has a steel and foam rubber arch support; the tongue is cut full and the points of stress are hand-sewn. Of course you have other shoes in other lines, but you're pushing Tough-Bilt. Prices range from $4.95 to $8.00. In all cases, there is a 15 percent discount from the regular price during this special sale.

3. As a large office equipment dealer you are interested in selling a new line of filing cabinets, The Office Master, which you have just begun to handle. You feel this is an outstanding buy, and you have decided to send all your former customers a sales letter. Your mailing list is made up of various companies which have purchased office equipment at some time during the previous five years.

The Office Master cabinet comes with either regular or legal size drawers. It is all steel, fireproof, with individual locks on each of the four drawers. The drawers have nylon rollers for ease of operation. Rubber moldings cut all noise. Each drawer is equipped with three metal separators which assist in filing. The cabinets are available in four different pastel colors to match office decor: mint green, haze blue, office gray, and goldenrod yellow. The cabinets are being sold for $59.50 each or $325 for six units if shipped to the same address. Freight is prepaid. The American Office Equipment Association has commended it for design and functional utilization.

4. Send a sales letter to each of the prospects on your mailing

list. Your list is made up of college students attending various institutions of higher education in the Illinois, Michigan, Wisconsin, Indiana area.

You manufacture desk lamps and the model you are now producing, "The Collegian," should be especially popular with the group to which you are appealing.

The Collegian is a desk model fluorescent unit that produces a high level of illumination, casts no shadows, is completely silent, and has an instant start feature. The light tilts to various angles. The Collegian is mounted on either a solid walnut, dark mahogany, or limed oak base. The base has a metal insert to accommodate pencils and clips.

The Collegian has been approved by *Collegiate Magazine* testing department and was recently selected for each room of the new dormitories erected at Illinois State College. The price, with all charges prepaid, is $9.95 per unit or a matching pair at $19.00. A picture of the Collegian appears on the stationery.

5. Make up a cover sales letter and an enclosure for the new Arctic Office Fan. These are pedestal-type fans that operate on three speeds and are reversible to either blow or exhaust air. The fans move 5000 C.F.M. on "high." The units have a thermo-control dial which automatically turns the fan off when the room has cooled to a preset temperature level. The height of the fan may be changed from 5 to 7 feet. The head oscillates 90° or remains stationary; it also tilts to direct the air. A.C. or D.C. is available. The fan is equipped with a heavy-duty General Fidelity motor that is guaranteed for five years. It has a chrome stand, grill, and pedestal.

The units are shipped freight and handling prepaid at $89.00 each or three units are shipped to the same address for $250. These fans are especially effective in large offices, stores, institutions, waiting rooms, factory production areas, etc.

In making up the enclosure, complete all copy material, but do not attempt to make the drawings; simply indicate the place for the picture by drawing a square or circle and describing in words what the picture would reflect.

6. Attempt to sell your professor a product or service of your choice. Before writing the letter try to learn those facts which may be helpful not only in choosing a product but also in the central appeal. Such information as marital status, number of children, type of residence (home or apartment), and outside activities may be of value.

7. Write a good will letter to all the furniture dealers who purchase lamps from your lamp manufacturing company. Most of these

dealers are located in small rural towns. The Thanksgiving season is approaching.

8. You are a large men's furnishing store located near a university in Los Angeles. Almost all your major items, such as suits and coats, are purchased by students, staff, or faculty of the school. Write a good will letter to all former customers. The time is early September.

Part III

A Bibliography of Bibliographies and Reference Guide

Chapter 23

A Bibliography of Bibliographies in the Major Fields of Commerce and Engineering

The list of references which appears on the following pages should prove of real value to the researcher who works in the fields of commerce or engineering. By utilizing bibliographies, the investigator can save himself a great deal of time that might otherwise be expended looking through card catalogs, indexes, and various guides.

If, for example, the researcher were interested in the field of cost accounting, he would certainly find the *Classified Cost Accounting Bibliography* of tremendous value. It contains some 28,000 listings in the area of cost accounting, a compilation probably more thorough than the report writer could collect from his own use of reference works.

But this is true in almost every single field. Those persons who utilize bibliographies are well aware of how much work someone else has done for them.

In the listings which follow, no attempt is made to cite textbooks, for it is felt that many texts become obsolete quickly, and what is excellent today, may be dated in a few years. In addition, it is difficult to say which texts are "outstanding" in fields that produce hundreds of books each year. Still another factor which makes such a listing very difficult is space. Several hundred pages would be required to list all the books in the field of accounting alone. Furthermore, why should an attempt be made to catalog them here, when the basic texts, plus pamphlets, magazine articles, bulletins, and other sources are carefully cited in the bibliography of the field?

Bibliographies in eight fields are listed:

Accounting	Foreign Trade
Business Administration	Management
Engineering	Marketing
Finance	Statistics

In each field a three-part division has been made. The first group is made up of general bibliographies. The second section lists handbooks, dictionaries, services, and directories in the field. And the third portion cites periodicals and a selected group of magazines. Annotations are given for many of the bibliographical entries; in other cases, the title sometimes indicates the scope of the work.

Securing some of the works listed may prove a bit of a problem. However, most of them should be available in any large library or through interlibrary loans. As a final resort, a letter to the publisher should produce the desired work.

ACCOUNTING

General Bibliographies

American Accounting Association. *Index to Accounting Review, 1926 Through 1950, and Papers and Proceedings of the American Association of University Instructors in Accounting, 1917 Through 1926.* Urbana, Ill.: The Association, 1951.

American Institute of Accountants. *Accountants' Index.* New York: American Institute Publishing Company, 1921-56.

This is an excellent author and highly detailed subject bibliography of pamphlets, articles, and books in the field of accounting. This work is of invaluable aid to the individual carrying on research in the wide area of accounting.

American Women's Society of Certified Public Accountants. *Bibliography for Use by Speakers.* Chicago: The Society, 1955.

Bentley, Harry C., and Leonard, Ruth S. *Bibliography of Works on Accounting by American Authors, 1796-1934.* Boston: Harry C. Bentley, 1934. 2 vols.

Volume I covers the period 1796 to 1900 and volume II covers the period from 1901 through 1934.

Business Book Bureau. *What to Read on Accounting.* New York: The Kalkhoff Co., 1912.

An impartial review of all the worth-while books until 1912 on accounting theory and practice and on commercial law.

Byers, J. R. B., Dunn, F. A., Mitchell, R. B. (eds.). *Federal Tax Course.* Englewood Cliffs, N.J.: Prentice-Hall, Inc., 1959.
Published each year and brought to date.

Coe, Cecil E. *Bibliography of Accounting and Tax Articles.* Inglewood, Cal.: 1954-1955.

Columbia University Library. *Montgomery Library of Accountancy.* New York: Columbia University Press, 1927-1930. 2 vols.
A check list of books printed before 1850 in the Montgomery Library of Accountancy at Columbia University.

Federal Government Accountants Association. *Bibliography on Federal Accounting, Auditing, Budgeting and Reporting.* Washington, D.C.: The Association, 1952.

Hellman, Florence. *A List of References on Governmental Accounting and Budgeting.* Washington, D.C.: 1940.

Herwood, Herman. *Herwood Library of Accounting.* New York: Herwood and Herwood, 1938.
A catalog of books printed between 1494 and 1900 in the Herwood Library of Accounting.

Institute of Internal Auditors. *Bibliography of Internal Auditing to December 31, 1955.* New York: The Institute, 1956.

Insurance Society of New York, Inc. *Insurance Accounting Bibliography, 1930-1953.* New York: The Society, 1954.

Lipson, Harry A. *A Selected and Annotated Bibliography of Accounting Materials for Retail Concerns.* University of Alabama, Bureau of Business Research, 1951.

Mall, Arthur B. "Bibliography on Estate Accounting." *New York Certified Public Accountant,* XVIII (November, 1947), 736-744.

Maryland Association of Certified Public Accountants. *Catalogue of Books.* Baltimore: Enoch Pratt Free Library, 1954.

Mertens, J., Jr. *The Law of Federal Income Taxation.* Chicago: Callaghan and Company, 1942. 12 vols.

Montgomery, R. H., Wynn, J. O., Blattmacher, H. G. *Federal Taxes, 1949-1954.* New York: The Ronald Press Company, 1954.

Morrison, Thomas L., and Kiely, James J. (comps.). *An Anthology of Selected Readings for the Accountant.* Boston: Bentley School of Accounting and Finance, 1950.
A 94-page guide to critical reading and understanding.

Myer, Joseph C., and Herskowitz, Hermann (comps.). "Third American Checklist of Early Bookkeeping Texts." *Certified Public Account,* April, 1933, pp. 224-231.

National Association of Cost Accountants. *Complete Topical Index, 1920-1946.* New York: The Association, 1946.

A very valuable work which serves as a guide to articles which have appeared in the bulletin of the *National Association of Cost Accountants*. The index is kept up to date by supplements issued quarterly.

National Association of Cost Accountants. *Topical Index Supplement, May, 1946 to August, 1952*. New York: The Association, 1952.

National Committee on Municipal Accounting. *Bibliography of Municipal and State Accounting*. Chicago: The Committee, 1937. Bulletin no. 7.

National Committee on Municipal Accounting. *Government Accounting Bibliography—1945 Supplement*. Chicago: The Committee, 1945. Bulletin no. 13-S.

New York Municipal Reference Library. *Bookkeeping and Accounting: Selected Bibliography for Civil Service Examinations*. New York: The Library, January 14, 1941.

Prentice-Hall Services. Englewood Cliffs, N.J.: Prentice-Hall, Inc.

This publishing house offers services in taxation, banking, and trust, securities, labor, pensions, real estate, and others. One of the most frequently used works is the Federal Tax Service, 5 vols., published yearly. Inserts may be added to any volume to keep the work up to date during the year.

Prickett, A. L. (comp.). *Classified Cost Accounting Bibliography*, Indiana University Business Study no. 29. Ann Arbor, Mich.: Edwards Brothers, Inc., 1946.

This is an extremely detailed, valuable, and highly commendable work containing some 28,000 listings.

Railway Accounting Officers' Association. *American Railway Accounting, a Bibliography, 1926*.

Sibly, Paul O. (comp.). *Index to the Teaching of Bookkeeping and Accounting*. Kirksville, Mo.: Research Press, 1939.

A 10-year bibliography covering the period 1929-1938.

Trueblood, Robert M., and Monteverde, Robert J. "Bibliography on the Application of Statistical Methods to Accounting and Auditing." *Accounting Review*, XXIX (April, 1954), 251-254.

An excellent bibliography prepared in connection with a broad study of the application of statistical techniques to accounting and auditing procedures being carried on at the Graduate School of Industrial Administration, Carnegie Institute of Technology.

U.S. Bureau of the Budget. *Work Measurement and Cost Accounting: Selected References*. Washington, D.C.: Government Printing Office, October, 1945.

U.S. Department of Commerce, Inquiry Reference Service. *Accounting* (Basic information courses). Washington, D. C.: Government Printing Office, August, 1948.

U.S. Library of Congress, Division of Bibliography. *List of Recent References on Governmental Accounting and Budgeting*. Washington, D.C.: Government Printing Office, 1940.

U.S. Library of Congress. "Early Accounting Bibliography." *Certified Public Accountant*, May, 1932, pp. 288-289.

Handbooks and Dictionaries

Backer, Morton (ed.). *Handbook of Modern Accounting Theory*. Englewood Cliffs, N.J.: Prentice-Hall, Inc., 1955.

> The purpose of this book is to familiarize its readers with the major areas of controversy in accounting and to evaluate the relative merit of related proposals which have received or deserve serious consideration.

Beckett, John M., and Fiske, Wyman P. (eds.). *Industrial Accountants' Handbook*. Englewood Cliffs, N.J.: Prentice-Hall, Inc., 1954.

> Primarily for those who use industrial accounting as a means of improving business management.

Bienvenu, Emile. *Accountancy and Business Dictionary*, 2nd ed. New Orleans: Poynton Press Co., 1940.

> An encyclopedia of accounting, financial, and miscellaneous business terms.

Dawson, Sidney S. *Accountants Compendium*. Revised by Arthur Morell and William Cullen. London: Gee and Co., Ltd., 1930.

Grainger, Wilfred H. *Glossary of Accountancy, Commercial and Legal Terms*. London: Gee and Co., Ltd., 1924.

Kane, Robert L., Jr. *C. P. A. Handbook*. New York: The American Institute of Accountants, 1952-1953. 2 vols.

> This is a reference work designed for use by practitioners engaged in the public accounting profession, their staff and office personnel, and students who expect to engage in public accounting.

Kohler, Eric L. *A Dictionary for Accountants*. Englewood Cliffs, N.J.: Prentice-Hall, Inc., 1952.

Lang, Theodore (ed.). *Cost Accountants' Handbook*. New York: The Ronald Press Company, 1949.

> This book develops the fundamental principles of cost accounting and presents the methods and techniques that cost accountants have worked out and found useful.

Lasser, Jacob K. (ed.). *Handbook of Accounting Methods*. New York: D. Van Nostrand Co., Inc., 1954.

Lasser, Jacob K. (ed.). *Handbook of Auditing Methods*. New York: D. Van Nostrand Co., Inc., 1953.

Lasser, Jacob K. (ed.). *Handbook of Cost Accounting Methods*. New York: D. Van Nostrand Co., Inc., 1949.

Lasser, Jacob K. (ed.). *Handbook of Tax Accounting Methods.* New York: D. Van Nostrand Co., Inc., 1951.

> In each volume an effort has been made to get as many experts as possible to tell the story of good practice in their respective fields. Each title has a bibliography for further study.

McKee, Raymond W. *Handbook of Petroleum Accounting.* New York: Harper & Brothers, 1938.

Paton, William A. (ed.). *Accountants' Handbook.* New York: The Ronald Press Company, 1944 (reprint, 1947).

Pixley, Francis W. *Accountants' Dictionary.* New York: Pitman, 1930. 2 vols.

> A comprehensive encyclopedia on all matters connected with the work of an accountant. It has an index to all cases referred to in the text.

Williams, Robert, and Doris, Lillian (eds.). *Encyclopedia of Accounting Systems.* Englewood Cliffs, N.J.: Prentice-Hall, Inc., 1957.

Wixon, Rufus (ed.). *Accountants' Handbook,* 4th ed. New York: The Ronald Press Company, 1956.

> This is a reference work covering the entire field of commercial and financial accounting. It presents in compact form the essential principles, rules, and procedures of accepted accounting practice. The aim of this revision has not been to replace other works but to build on them to meet today's requirements.

Periodicals and Magazines

The Accountants' Digest. Burlington, Vt.: The Accountants' Digest (quarterly).

> A brief digest of articles selected from leading accounting journals. It contains abstracts, book reviews, and an index to periodical accounting literature.

Accountants' Weekly Report. Englewood Cliffs, N.J.: Prentice-Hall, Inc. (weekly).

Accounting Forum. New York: Accounting Society, Bernard M. Baruch School of Business and Public Administration (quarterly).

> A student publication.

The Accounting Review. Menasha, Wisc.: American Accounting Association (quarterly).

> Designed for teachers and students.

California Certified Public Accountant. San Francisco: California Society of Certified Public Accountants (quarterly).

Canadian Journal of Accountancy. Toronto: Canadian Institute of Certified Public Accountants (quarterly).

The Certified Public Accountant. New York: American Institute of
Accountants (monthly).

Controller. Brattleboro, Vt.: Controller Institute of America (monthly).

Illinois Certified Public Accountant. Chicago: Illinois Society of Certified Public Accountants (quarterly).

Journal of Accountancy. New York: American Institute Publishing Co.
(monthly).
> Concerned with practical accounting problems from the viewpoint
> of the C.P.A. It is indexed in the *Engineering Index*, the *Business
> Periodical Index*, the *Index to Legal Periodicals,* and the *Public
> Affairs Information Service.*

Monthly Digest of Tax Articles. Albany, N.Y.: N. A. Newkirk Associates, Inc., Box 4105 (monthly).

National Association of Cost Accountants Bulletin. New York:
National Association of Cost Accountants (monthly).

Taxes, the Tax Magazine. Chicago: Commerce Clearing House, Inc.
(monthly).
> It contains abstracts, book reviews, and illustrations. It is indexed
> in the *Public Affairs Information Service* and the *Index to Legal
> Periodicals.*

BUSINESS ADMINISTRATION

General Bibliographies

Alpha Kappa Psi Fraternity. *Business Books for Serious Reading.*
Denver: Alpha Kappa Psi Fraternity, 1945.
> A carefully selected list of almost 100 books and 8 magazines
> which were chosen for their basic value in the field of business.

Business Executives of America. New York: Institute for Research in
Biography, Inc., 1950.

Business Information Service, Basic Information Sources. Washington,
D.C.: U.S. Department of Commerce.

Business Information Sources. Cleveland, Ohio: Cleveland, Ohio, Public
Library.
> A quarterly bulletin of business information sources which includes an occasional supplement.

Commodity Year Book. New York: Commodity Research Bureau, Inc.,
1955.
> Contains comments and statistics on a large variety of commodities.

Dartmouth College, Amos Tuck School of Administration and Finance.
A Reading List on Business Administration, 6th rev. Hanover, N.H.:
Dartmouth College, 1952.

A list of the leading titles in the various fields of commerce. The listing is by subject and includes magazines and books.

Davenport, D. H., and Scott, Frances V. *An Index to Business Indices.* Chicago: Business Publications, Inc., 1937.

Lists commodity and security indices and other business activities information. A guide to business index numbers.

Davis, Marjorie V. *Guide to American Business Directories.* Washington, D.C.: Public Affairs Press, 1948.

A listing of directories in over 125 commerce fields from "advertising" to "water transportation."

Editorial Directory. New York: Galub Publishing Company, 1952.

Lists close to 1300 trade, business, and professional papers on business trends, industrial developments, research findings, etc.

Egbert, J. C., Holbrook, E. A., Aldrich, M. A. (eds.). *American Business Practice.* New York: The Ronald Press Company, 1933. 12 vols.

The Faxon Librarians' Guide to Periodicals and American Subscription Catalog. Boston: F. W. Faxon Company, 1949.

An alphabetical list of over 2000 American and foreign periodicals. States how often and in what months periodical is issued and indicates in which of the general periodical indices each magazine is included.

Hirshberg, Herbert S., and Melinat, Carl H. *Subject Guide to U.S. Government Publications.* Chicago: American Library Association, 1947.

A selection of those books and pamphlets published by the U.S. government during the past 20 years. The listing is by subject.

Lovett, Robert W. (comp.). *List of Business Manuscripts in the Baker Library.* Cambridge, Mass.: Harvard Graduate School of Business Administration, 1951.

Classified and annotated. Harvard University Graduate School of Business Administration, Baker Library, also has published a list of business biographies and company histories in 1948.

Manley, Marian C. *Business Information, How to Find and Use It.* New York: Harper & Brothers, 1955.

Description of types of information sources and a guide to the sources of information in the different fields of business.

Morley, Linda H., and Knight, Adelaide G. *2400 Business Books and Guide to Business Literature.* New York: H. W. Wilson Co., 1920. Supplement, 1927.

Author, title, subject index to books and chapters in books.

Myren, P. H. (comp.). *Executive Development.* Cambridge, Mass.: Harvard University Graduate School of Business Administration, 1952.

A selected list of books, pamphlets, and articles published since 1935.

Newark, New Jersey, Free Public Library, Business Branch. *Business Books, 1920-1926.* New York: H. W. Wilson Co., 1927.

Newark, New Jersey, Free Public Library, Business Branch. *The Business Bookshelf: A List Based on Use.* (Compiled by Marian C. Manley and Mary E. Hunt.) Newark, N.J.: The Public Library, 1935.

This lists various works which have proved valuable to the businessman. The annotations are very good and the detailed author, subject, and title index is a great aid in locating works.

Newark, New Jersey, Free Public Library, Business Branch. *Business Information and Its Sources.* (Compiled by Marian C. Manley.) Newark, N.J.: The Public Library, 1939.

Publications (books, magazines, and government publications) are grouped under broad subject headings. Suggestions to the businessman on how to use commercial publications are very valuable.

Newark, New Jersey, Free Public Library, Business Branch. *Desk Library of Information Sources.* Newark, N.J.: The Public Library. Vol. XIX, no. 7, 1947.

Annotated list of indexes, lists, and compilations on broadly useful subjects.

Printers' Ink Directory of House Organs. Pleasantville: Printers' Ink Publishing Company, 1954.

Contains an alphabetical list of house publications, an alphabetical list of sponsors of house publications, and a geographical arrangement of the same material.

Public Affairs Information Service. New York: Public Affairs Information Service (weekly and cumulated).

A selective subject list of latest books, pamphlets, government public reports, and articles.

Reading List for Students and Businessmen. Cambridge, Mass: Harvard University Graduate School of Business Administration, 1955.

Reference lists are published by the Baker Library, Harvard University Graduate School of Business Administration. These lists are compiled on various aspects of commerce.

Special Libraries Association. *Business and Trade Dictionaries.* New York: The Association, 1934.

Special Libraries Association. *Guides to Business Facts and Figures.* New York: The Association, 1937.

Indexed and descriptive list emphasizing the less known business reference sources.

Trade and Professional Associations of the United States. Industrial

Effective Report Writing

Series no. 3. Washington, D.C.: U.S. Department of Commerce, 1942.

U.S. Bureau of Foreign and Domestic Commerce. *Commerce Yearbook, 1922-1932.* Washington, D.C.: Government Printing Office. 10 vols.

Review of economic year throughout the world, prepared from the viewpoint of American industry and commerce.

U.S. Bureau of Foreign and Domestic Commerce. *Sources of Regional and Local Business Statistics.* Washington, D.C.: Government Printing Office, 1948.

U.S. Bureau of Foreign and Domestic Commerce. *World Economic Review.* Washington, D.C.: Government Printing Office, 1934. (Part I, U.S.; Part II, Foreign Countries.)

U.S. Department of Commerce. *National Associations of the United States.* Washington, D.C.: Government Printing Office, 1949.

Directory and review of service and accomplishments of organizations which play an important part in American life.

Wasserman, Paul. *Information for Administrators, A Guide to Publications and Services for Management in Business and Government.* Ithaca, N.Y.: Cornell University Press, 1956.

Suggests all types of information sources; comprised not only of many kinds of published material but also of agencies, associations, governmental programs, and other services useful to administrators.

Who's Who in Commerce and Industry. Chicago: A. N. Marquis Company, 1957.

Names of best known men and women the world over in all kinds of useful and reputable commercial and industrial endeavor.

Wilson, Fern L. *Wilson's Index of Publications by University Bureaus of Business Research.* Cleveland: Press of Western Reserve University, 1951.

A compilation of factual business and industrial studies from bureaus of 56 universities. Lists every publication of these bureaus by title, series number, publication date, and out-of-print titles. Index lists publications by subject matter, university, title, all alphabetically.

Handbooks and Dictionaries

Braddy, Nella. *The New Business Encyclopedia.* New York: Garden City Books, 1951.

A revised, up-to-date edition.

Brown, Stanley M., and Doris, Lillian. *Business Executives Handbook.* Englewood Cliffs, N.J.: Prentice-Hall, Inc., 1953.

A volume designed to provide answers to management problems. Tables and forms are included as well as a glossary of abbreviations and a detailed index.

Directors' and Officers' Encyclopedia Manual. Englewood Cliffs, N.J.: Prentice-Hall, Inc., 1955.

A work valuable for its handling of financial and legal aspects of commercial activity. Contains many samples of current business forms.

Donald, W. J. (ed.). *Handbook of Business Administration.* New York: McGraw-Hill Book Company, Inc., 1931.

Fundamentals and procedures of management policy and technique.

Encyclopedic Dictionary of Business. Englewood Cliffs, N.J.: Prentice-Hall, Inc., 1952.

Schwartz, Robert J. (ed.). *Dictionary of Business and Industry.* New York: B. C. Forbes Publishing Company, 1954.

Special Libraries Association. *Handbook of Commercial, Financial and Information Services.* New York: The Association, 1956.

Teall, Edward Nelson. *Modern Business Encyclopedia.* New York: World Publishing Company, 1945.

Provides information on many phases of business procedure including business law, finance and business organizations, and administration in encyclopedic and dictionary form. A miscellany section is planned to provide ready information on many questions that come up every day.

Yocum, James C. *Information Sources for Small Business.* Columbus, Ohio: Bureau of Business Research, College of Commerce and Administration, Ohio State University, 1949.

There are 1300 different entries and sources listed (including cross references), all classified, coded, and annotated.

Periodicals and Magazines

Advanced Management. New York: The Society for Advancement of Management (quarterly).

Book reviews and authoritative articles on specialized phases.

American Business. Chicago (monthly).

General business coverage with special emphasis on office management. Book reviews.

Dun's Review and Modern Industry. New York (monthly).

Aimed primarily at executives. The regular departments include information on new methods, materials, and views of the top management and detailed pictures of current business trends.

The Economist. Chicago (weekly).

Financial, commercial, and real estate news.

Harvard Business Review. Cambridge, Mass.: Harvard Graduate School of Business Administration (bimonthly).

Contains scholarly articles that are carefully written and frequently the result of intensive research. The various fields of commerce are the subjects of the articles.

Journal of Business of University of Chicago. Chicago: University of Chicago (quarterly).

This journal is similar to the *Harvard Business Review* in subject matter although its slant is often toward the commercial problems of the Middle West.

ENGINEERING

General Bibliographies

American Association of Petroleum Geologists. *Comprehensive Index of American Association of Petroleum Geologists, 1917-1936*. Tulsa, Okla.: The Association, 1937.

American Institute of Chemical Engineers. *Minimum List of Recommended Books for a Chemical Engineering Library*. New York: American Institute of Chemical Engineers, 1939.

Arnold, Joseph N. *Engineering Publications, 1918-1953*. Lafayette, Ind.: Purdue University Engineering Bulletins. Vol. XXXVIII, no. 3, 1954.

Barnes, Ralph M., and Englert, Norma A. *Bibliography of Industrial Engineering and Management Literature*. Dubuque, Iowa: William C. Brown Co., 1946.

Butterbaugh, Grant I. *Bibliography of Statistical Quality Control*. Seattle: University of Washington, 1946.

Crane, Evan Jay, Patterson, Austin M., Marr, Eleanor. *A Guide to the Literature of Chemistry*, 2nd ed. New York: John Wiley & Sons, Inc., 1957.

Dalton, Blanche H. *Sources of Engineering Information*. Los Angeles: University of California Press, 1948.

A concise listing of abstract sources, periodicals, reference guides, and bibliographies in the general field of engineering.

The Engineering Index, published by Engineering Index, Inc., 29 W. 39th St., New York 18, New York.

Indexes approximately 1200 engineering and technical publications.

Engineering Societies' Library Bibliography, No. 1. New York: Engineering Societies' Library, 1948.

Engineers' Council for Professional Development. *Selected Bibliography of Engineering Subjects.* New York: The Council, 1937.
Revised by O. W. Eshbach in 1937 with the coöperation of 100 engineers.

Fellows, Roger L. *Enamel Bibliography and Abstracts.* Columbus, Ohio: American Ceramic Society, Inc., 1953.

Halstrom, J. E. *Records and Research in Engineering and Industrial Science,* 2nd ed. London: Chapman and Hall, 1947.
A very useful guide pertaining primarily to English works. First edition of the book was in 1940.

Harvard University Graduate School of Engineering. *List of Contributions from the Graduate School of Engineering, nos. 1 to 250.* Cambridge, Mass.: Harvard University Press, 1939.
Papers published in the journals of scientific and professional societies by members of the staff or student body.

Hawkins, Reginald Robert. *Scientific, Medical, and Technical Books Published in the United States of America,* 2nd ed. (books published to December, 1956).
Prepared under the direction of the National Academy of Sciences, National Research Council's Committee on Bibliography of American Scientific and Technical Books. Washington, 1958. A selected list of titles in print with annotations.

Lachman, Gisella R. *Manufacturing and Mechanical Engineering in the Soviet Union, A Bibliography.* Washington, D.C.: Library of Congress, 1953.

Levens, Alexander (comp.). *List of Publications for Vocational Guidance in Engineering, Architecture and Chemistry.* Minneapolis: 1932, *List of Publications in Engineering.* Chicago: John Crerar Library.

Milek, John T. *Guide to Foreign Sources of Metallurgical Literature.* Pittsburgh: R. Rimbach Associates, 1951.

Parke, Nathan Grier. *Guide to the Literature of Mathematics and Physics, Including Related Works on Engineering Science.* New York: McGraw-Hill Book Company, Inc., 1947.

Roberts, Arthur Denis. *Guide to Technical Literature.* London: Grafton & Co., 1939.
Bibliography on technology and engineering.

Selected Reading for Young Engineers. Engineers' Council for Professional Development, 29 W. 39th St., New York 18, New York.

Shaw, Ralph Robert (comp.). *Engineering Books Avaliable in America Prior to 1830.* New York: The New York Public Library, 1933.
1931 Columbia University thesis (M.S.).

Southeastern Research Institute, Atlanta. *Directory of Engineering Data Sources.* Atlanta: Southeastern Research Institute, 1948.

A 66-page guide to American literature in engineering and related sciences.

U.S. Office of Technical Services. *Bibliography of Scientific and Industrial Reports.* Washington, D.C.: Government Printing Office, 1946.
An index of war research work.

Handbooks and Dictionaries

Brown, Victor Jacob, and Runner, D. G. *Engineering Terminology,* 2nd ed. Chicago: Gilette Publishing Co., 1939.
Definitions of technical words and phrases.

Civil Engineers Encyclopedic Dictionary, 1st ed. Los Angeles: Benson Book Co., Inc., 1930.
A glossary of words, terms, abbreviations, symbols, and lettering pertaining to civil engineering and surveying with illustrations by Robert E. Benson.

Consodine, Douglas Maxwell (ed.). *Process Instruments and Control Handbook.* New York: McGraw-Hill Book Company, Inc., 1957.
Includes bibliographies.

Crispin, F. S. *Dictionary of Technical Terms,* rev. ed. Milwaukee: Bruce Publishing Co., 1948.

Engineers' Year Book of Formulae, Rules, Tables, Data, and Memoranda for 1894-1958. London: Morgan (annual).
Original composition by H. R. Kempe and W. Hanniford Smith; revised by L. St. L. Pendred.

Eshbach, Ovid Wallace. *Handbook of Engineering Fundamentals,* 2nd ed. New York: John Wiley & Sons, Inc., 1952.
Prepared by a staff of specialists.

Faraday, Joseph Escotl (comp.). *Encyclopedia of Hydrocarbon Compounds.* Brooklyn, N.Y.: Chemical Publishing Company, 1946.

Gray, Dwight E. (ed.). *American Institute of Physics Handbook.* New York: McGraw-Hill Book Company, Inc., 1957.
Includes bibliographies.

Heilbron, Sir Ian Morris, and Banbury, H. M. (eds.). *Dictionary of Organic Compounds,* new rev. ed. New York: Oxford University Press, 1953.
Guide to the constitution and physical and chemical properties of the principal carbon compounds and their derivatives, together with the relevant literature references.

Herkimer, Herbert. *Engineers' Illustrated Thesaurus.* New York: Chemical Publishing Co., 1952.

Hetenyi, Miklos Imre. *Handbook of Experimental Stress Analysis.* New York: John Wiley & Sons, Inc., 1950.
A complete and accurate handbook in the plastic field.

Hopkins, Albert Allis (ed.). *The Standard American Encyclopedia of Formulas.* New York: Grosset & Dunlap, 1953.
> Previous editions published under the title: *The Scientific American Cyclopedia of Formulas.*

Hudson, Ralph G. *The Engineers' Manual.* 2nd ed. New York: John Wiley & Sons, Inc. London: Chapman and Hall, Ltd., 1939.
> Includes tables and diagrams.

Jacobson, Carl Alfred (comp. and ed.). *Encyclopedia of Chemical Reactions.* New York: Reinhold Publishing Corporation, 1946.

Jones, F. D. *Engineering Encyclopedia,* 2nd ed. New York: Industrial Press. Brighton, England: Machinery Publishing Company, 1943.
> Definitions of engineering terms and articles in one alphabetical arrangement. First edition in 1941. 4500 subjects.

Kirk, Raymond E., and Othmer, Donald F., *et al.* (eds.). *Encyclopedia of Chemical Technology.* New York: Interscience Encyclopedia, Inc., 1947-1956. 15 vols.
> Supplementary volume issued in 1957.

Mantell, Charles Letnam (ed.). *Engineering Materials Handbook,* 1st ed. New York: McGraw-Hill Book Company, Inc., 1958.

Miner, Douglas F., and Seastone, John B. (eds.). *Handbook of Engineering Materials,* 1st ed. New York: John Wiley & Sons, Inc., 1955.
> Includes bibliographies, diagrams, and tables.

Neward, Maxim. *Illustrated Technical Dictionary.* New York: Philosophical Library, 1944.

O'Rourke, Charles E. (ed.). *General Engineering Handbook,* 2nd ed. New York and London: McGraw-Hill Book Company, Inc., 1940.
> Covers the essentials of all branches of engineering in a survey. It is not designed to take the place of specialized handbooks.

Parker, Harry (ed.). *Kidder-Parker Architects' and Builders' Handbook.* New York: John Wiley & Sons, Inc. London: Chapman and Hall, Ltd., 1931.
> Includes illustrations, tables, and diagrams. Contains data for architects, contractors, and draftsmen.

Sandy, A. H. *Dictionary of Engineering and Machine Shop Terms.* Brooklyn, N.Y.: Chemical Publishing Co., 1944.

Saylor, Henry Hodgman. *Dictionary of Architecture.* New York: John Wiley & Sons, Inc., 1952.

Searle, Alfred Broadhead. *An Encyclopedia of the Ceramic Industries.* London: E. Benn, Ltd., 1929-1930.
> A guide to the materials, methods of manufacture, means of recognition, and testing the articles produced in the clay working and allied industries; arranged in alphabetical order for rapid reference.

Spitz, Armand N., and Gaynor, Frank. *Dictionary of Astronomy and Astronautics.* New York: Philosophical Library, 1959.

Stoutenburgh, John Leeds (ed.). *Dictionary of Arts and Crafts.* New York: Philosophical Library, 1956.

Thurston, Alan Peter (ed.). *Handbook of Engineering Formulae and Data,* 34th ed. London: E. and F. N. Spon, 1951.
> First published in 1862 under the title of *Malesworth's Pocket Book of Engineering.*

Tweney, C. F., and Hughes, L. E. C. *Chamber's Technical Dictionary,* rev. ed. with supplement. New York: The Macmillan Co., 1948.

Tweney, C. F., and Shirshov, I. P. (eds.). *Hutchinson's Technical and Scientific Encyclopedia.* London: Hutchinson. New York: The Macmillan Co., 1935-1936.
> Terms, processes, data in pure and applied science.

Periodicals and Magazines

Bell System Technical Journal. New York: American Telephone and Telegraph Co. (bimonthly).
> Devoted to the scientific and engineering aspects of electrical communication.

Chemical Engineering. New York: McGraw-Hill Publishing Company (weekly).
> A publication dealing with chemical technology.

Civil Engineering. American Society of Civil Engineers (monthly).
> Includes current periodical literature and abstracts of articles on civil engineering subjects from magazines in this country and in foreign lands.

Electrical Engineering. New York: American Institute of Electrical Engineers (monthly).

Engineering. London: Engineering, Ltd.
> An illustrated weekly journal published in London since 1866.

Engineering and Mining Journal. New York: McGraw-Hill Publishing Company (monthly).

Engineering News Record. New York: McGraw-Hill Publishing Company (weekly).

Industrial and Engineering Chemistry. Washington, D.C.: American Chemical Society (monthly).
> Devoted to research, development, design, engineering, and marketing.

Iron and Steel Engineer. Pittsburgh: Association of Iron and Steel Engineers (monthly).

Mechanical Engineering. New York: American Society of Mechanical Engineers (monthly).

The Petroleum Engineer. Dallas: Petroleum Engineer Publishing Co. (monthly).
Primarily designed for operating management.
SAE Journal. New York: Society of Automotive Engineers (monthly).
A journal concerned with the automotive field.

FINANCE

General Bibliographies

American Economists Council for the Study of Branch Banking. *Bibliography on Branch Banking.* 1939.

Commerce Clearing House Federal Banking Law Reports. Chicago: Commerce Clearing House, Inc. 3 vols. (supplements are issued weekly).

Haller, Dorothy. *Consumer Installment Loans, A Bibliography Selected and Annotated.* Washington, D.C.: American Association of Small Loan Companies, 1945.

Kiel, C. *Reference Books for a Bank.* St. Louis: Washington University, 1942.

Masue, Mitsuzo (ed.). *A Bibliography of Finance.* Kobe, Japan: Kobe University of Commerce, 1935.

Moody's Investors Service. *Moody's Manual of Investments, American and Foreign Banks, Insurance Companies, Investment Trusts, Real Estate, Finance and Credit Companies.* New York: Moody's Investors Service, 1928 (annual).

Munn, Glenn G. *Encyclopedia of Banking and Finance.* New York: The Bankers Publishing Company, 1949.
Not only does the author offer careful definitions but many of his bibliographies are very good.

Newcomer, M. *Selected Bibliography on Intergovernmental Fiscal Relations.* Washington, D.C.: Government Printing Office, 1942.

Prentice-Hall Federal Bank Service. Englewood Cliffs, N.J.: Prentice-Hall, Inc. 2 vols. (supplements are issued biweekly).

Rossi, Diana. *International Finance Source Book.* Chicago: Education Department of the Investment Bankers Association of America, 1928.

Special Libraries Association. *The Bank Library, A Selected List of Publications.* Boston: 1937.

U.S. Library of Congress, Division of Bibliography. *The Gold Standard and Bimetallism: A Bibliographical List.* Washington, D.C.: Government Printing Office, October, 1931.

U.S. Library of Congress, Division of Bibliography. *Investment Bank-*

ing: A Selected List of References. Washington, D.C.: Government Printing Office, March 15, 1928.

U.S. Library of Congress, Division of Bibliography. *Money and Banking: A Selected List of References.* Washington, D.C.: Government Printing Office, 1946.

U.S. Library of Congress, Division of Bibliography. *A Selected List of Recent References on the Subject of Money: U. S. and Foreign Countries.* Washington, D.C.: Government Printing Office, 1936.

Westerfield, Roy B. *Selected Bibliography of Money, Credit, Banking and Business Finance,* Boston: Bankers Publishing Company, 1940.
  This is a very useful work in the field listing basic works under subject headings.

Wilder, E. *Consumer Credit Bibliography.* Englewood Cliffs, N.J.: Prentice-Hall, Inc., 1938.

Handbooks and Dictionaries

Bankers' Almanac and Year Book for 1949-50. London: Thomas Skinner and Company, 1956.
  Reference guides to principal banks throughout the world.

Bankers Directory. Chicago. Rand McNally & Co. (semiannual).
  Directory of U.S. and foreign banks.

Bogen, Jules I., *et al.* (eds.). *Financial Handbook.* New York: The Ronald Press Company, 1948.

Montgomery, R. H. *Financial Handbook.* New York: The Ronald Press Company, 1933.

Polk's Bankers Encyclopedia. Detroit: R. L. Polk and Co. (semiannual, monthly supplements).
  A directory of banks in the U.S., Canada, and foreign countries, giving general information, branches, correspondents, etc.

Special Libraries Association. *Handbook of Commercial and Financial Services.* New York: The Association, 1937.

Thomson, William. *Dictionary of Banking.* London: Sir Isaac Pitman and Sons, Ltd., 1922.

Thomson, William. *Dictionary of Banking: Concise Encyclopedia of Banking Laws and Practice,* 10th ed. New York: Philosophical Library, 1952.

Periodicals and Magazines

American Banker. New York: American Banker Inc. (daily).

American Institute of Banking. New York: American Bankers Association (quarterly).

The Analysts' Journal. New York: Society of Security Analysts (quarterly).

Bank and Quotations Records. New York: William B. Dana Company (monthly).

Banking Journal of the American Bankers Association. New York: American Bankers Association (monthly).

Banking Law Journal. Cambridge, Mass.: Bankers Publishing Company (monthly).

Barron's National Business and Financial Weekly. New York: Barron's Publishing Company (weekly).

Federal Reserve Bulletin. Washington D.C.: Board of Governors of the Federal Reserve System (monthly).

> Contains articles on international financial statistics, domestic, financial, and commercial conditions, and on domestic and foreign affairs.

Polk's Bank Information Service. Detroit and New York: P. L. Polk and Company (daily).

Polk's Bankers Information Bulletin. Detroit and New York: P. L. Polk and Company (monthly).

Wall Street Journal. New York, San Francisco, and Los Angeles: Dow-Jones and Company, Inc. (daily).

Weekly Market, Business Review and Forecast. New York: Fitch Publishing Company.

> Analyzes events of the week affecting business, predicts stock market trends, and suggests purchase or sale of specific securities.

Weekly Outlook for the Securities Market. New York: Standard and Poor's Corporation.

> A general market forecast.

FOREIGN TRADE

General Bibliographies

American Economic Association. *Readings in the Theory of International Trade.* Philadelphia: Blakeston Co., 1949.

> Selected by a committee of the American Economic Association. Contains classified bibliography of articles on international economics.

Chamber of Commerce of the United States. *List of Publications of the Chamber of Commerce of the United States.* Washington, D.C.: Government Printing Office (annual).

Chamber of Commerce of the United States, Foreign Commerce Department. *Our 100 Leading Imports.* Washington, D.C.: Government Printing Office, 1945.

Chamber of Commerce of the United States, Foreign Commerce Department. *Our World Trade During the War, 1939-1945.* Washington, D.C.: Government Printing Office, 1946.

Custom House Guide. Custom House. New York: Import Publications, Inc. (annual with supplements each month).

This reference work contains part or all of the relevant tariff acts and trade agreements in addition to lists of freight forwarders, steamship lines, U.S. customs warehouses, brokers, foreign consuls, etc.

Federal Trade Commission. *Post War Imports and Domestic Production of Major Commodities.* Washington, D.C.: Government Printing Office.

The International Trader. New York: International Traders' Manual, Inc. (annual).

An American foreign trade publication.

International Trade Reporter. Washington, D.C.: The Bureau of National Affairs, Inc. (weekly).

A loose-leaf service with bulletins commenting on new trade, tariff and tax regulations in addition to other helpful information.

International Who's Who in World Trade. Washington, D.C.: International Bureau of Trade Extension, 1923.

A commerce reference book giving economic data on merchants, manufacturers, banks, forwarders, steamship lines, etc.

National Foreign Trade Council. *Selected Bibliography of Foreign Trade.* New York: The Council, November, 1928.

Pan-American Associates. *Pan-American Year Book.* New York: The Macmillan Co. (annual).

Lists companies interested in inter-American trade. Thirteen industrial groups are designated.

Reference Book for Exporters. New York: Croner Publications, 1958. Information on export procedure for shipments to all foreign countries.

U.S. Bureau of Agricultural Economics Library. *Periodicals Relating to Shipping.* Economic Library List No. 6. Washington, D.C.: Government Printing Office, October, 1939.

U.S. Bureau of Census. *Catalog of Monthly United States Foreign Trade Statistical Publications.* Washington, D.C.: Government Printing Office.

U.S. Bureau of Census. *Foreign Commerce and Navigation of the United States.* Washington, D.C.: Government Printing Office (annual).

Prior to the issuance of this work, the Bureau of Census published quite a few studies citing statistics in various phases of export-import trade. Printed through 1946; out of print.

U.S. Department of Commerce. *Business Service Check List.* Washington, D.C.: Government Printing Office (weekly).

List of all publications issued currently by the Department, including individual reports in *World Trade in Commodities* and foreign trade statistics.

U.S. Department of Commerce, Bureau of Census. *Monthly Summary of Foreign Commerce of the United States.* Washington, D.C.: Government Printing Office.

U.S. Department of Commerce, Bureau of Foreign Commerce. *Checklist of World Trade Information, Service Reports and Other Current Publications.* Washington, D.C.: Government Printing Office.

U.S. Department of Commerce, Bureau of Foreign and Domestic Commerce. *Foreign Trade* (Basic Information Sources). November, 1944 (out of print).

U.S. Department of Commerce, Bureau of Foreign and Domestic Commerce. Division of Publications. *Summary of Foreign Trade of the U.S.* Washington, D.C.: Government Printing Office (quarterly, cumulated annually).

U.S. Department of Commerce, Office of Information, Inquiry and Reference Section. *Foreign Trade* (Basic Information Sources). Washington, D.C.: Government Printing Office, 1945.

Thorough listing of government and private publications concerned with foreign trade.

U.S. Department of Commerce, Office of International Trade. *Foreign Trade* (Basic Information Sources). Washington, D.C.: Government Printing Office, 1949.

U.S. Department of Commerce, Office of International Trade. *Foreign Trade Practices.* Washington, D.C.: Government Printing Office, 1950.

U.S. Department of Commerce, Office of International Trade. *Guides for New World Traders.* Washington, D.C.: Government Printing Office.

This cites publications designed to give an individual a good background in foreign trade. In addition, it mentions some problems and their solutions in import-export.

U.S. Library of Congress, Division of Bibliography. *A List of Bibliographies of Foreign Commerce.* Washington, D.C.: Government Printing Office, 1934.

U.S. Tariff Commission. *List of Publications of the Tariff Commission.* Washington, D.C.: Government Printing Office (revised annually).

U.S. Tariff Commission. *List of Selected Publications Relating to the United States Tariff and Commercial Policy and the General Agree-*

ment on Tariffs and Trade. Washington, D.C.: Government Printing Office, 1957.

In addition the U.S. Tariff Commission has published the following bibliographies:

Bibliography of Raw Materials, 1939 (supplement, 1940).

Bibliography of Recent Publications Dealing with Post-War Commercial Policy, 1945.

List of Works Containing Standard Discussion of Protection and Free Trade, 1945.

Publications of the U.S. Tariff Commission, 1939, and Accumulative Supplement to List of Publications, 1945.

Reciprocal Trade: A Current Bibliography, 1937. Supplement, 1940.

The Tariff: A Bibliography, 1934.

A select list of references.

Handbooks and Dictionaries

Angel, Juvenal L. (ed.). *International Reference Handbook of Services, Organization and International Marketing Information.* New York: World Trade Academy Press, Inc., 1954.

American Chamber of Commerce in France. *Directory of American Business in France.* Paris, France: 1958.

American Register of Exporters and Importers. New York: American Register of Exporters and Importers, Inc., 1958.

Carmel, John Philip. *International Trader's Manual.* New York: International Traders Manual, Inc., 1946.

A publication for exporters and importers.

Chamber of Commerce of the United States, Foreign Trade Department. *Foreign Commerce Handbook.* Washington, D.C.: Chamber of Commerce of the United States, 1950.

Croner's World Register of Trade Directories. Teddington, England: Croner Publications, 1951.

Directory of American Firms Operating in Foreign Countries. New York: World Trade Academy Press, Inc., 1957-1958.

Covers some 2000 American corporations controlling and operating more than 7500 foreign business enterprises.

Directory of Export Packers. New York: Port Authority of New York.

Exporters' Encyclopedia. New York: Thomas Ashwell & Co., Inc. (annual with current supplements each month).

A comprehensive reference work on numerous phases of export trade, including trade and shipping requirements and miscellaneous data on all countries. Special sections, foreign trade organization, export and shipping practice, reference tables, and general export information. Kept up to date with pamphlets.

Foreign Trade of the United States. International Trade Series no. 7. Washington, D.C.: Superintendent of Documents, 1936-1949.

Handbook of Export Traffic. New York: Duell, Sloan, & Pearce, Inc., 1949.

Hard, Sir Archibald (ed.). *Shipping World Year Book.* London: Shipping World Office (annual).

Henius, Frank. *Dictionary of Foreign Trade,* 2nd ed. Englewood Cliffs, N.J.: Prentice-Hall, Inc., 1947.

Contains a great many trade abbreviations in French, Spanish, German, and English, a guide of procedures to follow in export trade, tables of procedures to follow in export trade, tables of weights and measures, conversion lists, and some 300 documents currently used in import-export trade.

International Chamber of Commerce. *Trade Terms.* Annotated synoptic document no. 16.

Text in French and English.

International Traders' Handbook. Philadelphia: The Commercial Museum, 1936.

Incorporates foreign and domestic weights, measures, and monies.

Kelly's Directory of Merchants, Manufacturers, and Shippers of the World. New York: Cambridge Special Agency, Inc. (annual).

Covers Great Britain, Ireland, Canada, Australia, New Zealand, South Africa, India, and other British colonies and possessions, with a special section on the United States.

Latin American Sales Index. New York: Dun & Bradstreet, Inc.

A guide for the selection of accounts in Latin American markets by areas, lines of business, types of organization, and financial size.

Lloyd's Calendar. London: Lloyd's annual.

Yearbook containing miscellaneous commercial shipping and navigation information, laws affecting commerce, weights and measures of various nations, legal holidays of the world, etc.

Pratt, E. E. *Foreign Trade Handbook,* 2nd ed. Chicago: The Dartnell Corp., 1949.

A guide to exporting.

South American Handbook. New York: H. W. Wilson Co., 1956.

Lists statistics and information on the foreign commerce and transportation facilities of Latin American countries.

Trade Index of U.S. Manufacturers. New York: Dun & Bradstreet, Inc. (annual from 1947).

Index of U.S. manufacturers with direct interest in export and import trade. There are English, Spanish, and Brazilian editions.

United Nations Statistical Office. *Yearbook of International Trade Statistics.* New York: United Nations (annual).

U.S. Department of Commerce. *American Business Directories,* 2nd ed., Industrial Series no. 67. Washington, D.C.: Superintendent of Documents, 1947.

A roster of American directories of assistance in locating sources of supply and prospective customers.

U.S. Department of Commerce, Bureau of Foreign Commerce. *Directory of Foreign Development Organizations for Trade and Investments.* Washington, D.C.: Superintendent of Documents, 1957.

Lists foreign government organizations and private groups of firms and individuals having active programs to encourage trade and investment in countries.

U.S. Department of Commerce, Bureau of Foreign Commerce. *Guides for the Newcomer to World Trade.* Washington, D.C.: Government Printing Office, 1957.

U.S. Department of Commerce, Bureau of Foreign and Domestic Commerce. *Commerce Yearbook.* Washington, D.C.: Government Printing Office, 1922-1932.

Lists detailed information on business conditions in the U.S. and foreign countries, summarizing statistical information originally gathered by government bureaus, trade associations, and trade journals, with reference to source of information.

U.S. Department of Commerce, Bureau of Foreign and Domestic Commerce. *Foreign Directories.* Washington, D.C.: Government Printing Office, 1939.

Excellent list of directories concerned with firms engaged in foreign trade.

U.S. Department of Commerce, Office of International Trade. *Foreign Commerce Yearbook.* Washington, D.C.: Government Printing Office (annual).

U.S. Department of Commerce, Office of International Trade. *Trade Lists.* Washington, D.C.: Government Printing Office.

Listing of foreign firms and individuals covering the usual channels of distribution, sources of foreign supply, and approximately 100 commodity groups.

U.S. Department of Commerce, Office of International Trade. *World Trade Directory Reports.* Washington, D.C.: Government Printing Office.

Reports on individual foreign firms, furnishing pertinent data concerning each firm's method of operation, size, reputation, capital, number of employees, ownership and management, annual business turnover, and representatives in the U.S. and elsewhere.

Van Cleef, Eugene. *Trade Centers and Trade Routes.* New York: Appleton-Century-Crofts, Inc., 1937.

World Markets Directory. New York: Atlas Publishing Company, 1949.
    A listing of more than 60,000 firms engaged in export-import trade in the nations of the world. Reference is made to specific commodities.
Local branches of the U.S. Department of Commerce Library have handbooks and directories for nearly every country in the world, as well as for geographic regions.

Periodicals and Magazines

American Exporter. New York: Johnston Export Publishing Company (monthly).
American Import and Export Bulletin. New York: Import Publications, Inc. (monthly).
    Articles, news, records, etc., on many aspects of importing and exporting. News of government department developments affecting foreign trade.
Biweekly List of Selected United States Government Publications. U.S. Department of Commerce.
Business International. New York (weekly).
    Report to management on international trade and inventories.
Commercial America. Philadelphia: Trade and Convention Center (monthly).
Directory of International Trade. New York: International Documents Service, Columbia University Press (monthly).
The Export Buyer. New York: Commodity Research Bureau (monthly).
    Includes Far East trade directory.
Export and Import Journal of America. New York: Export and Import Journal of America, Inc. (monthly).
    Current events and trends in the U.S. trade with Europe.
Export Trade and Shipper. New York: Thomas Ashwell & Co., Inc. (monthly).
    A journal of general utility to foreign traders, including news, comment, advertising, and directory material covering all phases of foreign trade shipping.
Exporters' Digest and International Trade Review. New York: American and Foreign Credit Underwriters Corp. (monthly).
    Market surveys and conditions, industry abroad, current rulings, transportation, business opportunities, directory material, etc.
Foreign Commerce Weekly. U.S. Department of Commerce, Office of International Trade (weekly).
    Official medium for distribution of data gathered by Foreign Service of U. S., articles, news, listings of countries and com-

modities, trade leads, foreign exchange, announcements of publications, and other departments.

Foreign Trade. Ottawa, Canada: The Queen's Printer (fortnightly).

Foreign Trade Bulletin. Chicago: American National Bank and Trust Company (monthly).

Foreign Trade Letters. U.S. Department of Commerce (weekly).

Foreign Trade Reports. U.S. Department of Commerce, Bureau of Census (monthly and cumulated annually).

Foreign Trade Statistics. U.S. Department of Commerce, Bureau of Census.

Supplements current reports and tabulations.

Import Bulletin. New York: Journal for Commerce of New York (weekly).

Imports listed by products and product groups, by vessel, and by point of origin and port of arrival.

International Financial Statistics. New York: International Monetary Fund (monthly).

International Trade Review. New York: American Foreign Credit Underwriters (monthly).

International trade markets material and financial information on overseas markets.

Monthly Bulletin for Exporters and Importers. New York: Guaranty Trust Company of New York.

Information on foreign exchange restrictions.

New York Forwarder. New York: The New York Forwarder and Foreign Shipper, Inc. (weekly).

A journal of general utility to foreign traders, especially in the forwarding and shipping fields. News, articles, directory material, and advertising on many phases of foreign trading.

Shipping Digest. New York: Shipping Digest, Inc. (weekly).

A magazine for export and transportation executives. Contains news, articles, directory material, and advertising covering all phases of foreign trade shipping. Includes biweekly supplement, *Airshipping.*

World Markets. New York: Atlas Publishing Company (weekly).

MANAGEMENT

General Bibliographies

American Federation of Labor (comp.). *Labor's Library.* Washington D.C.: Worker's Education Bureau, 1952.

American Management Association. *The Management Index.* New York: American Management Association, 1945.

The publications of this association from 1932-1945 are listed.

American Management Association. *Progress in Scientific Management.* New York: American Management Association, 1958.

A complete catalog of A.M.A. publications in eight fields of management.

American Management Association. *Progress in Seven Fields of Management, 1932-1949.* New York: American Management Association, 1949.

This is a catalog of the publications of the American Management Association as well as a list of titles of the association.

Barnes, Ralph M., and Englert, N. A. *Bibliography of Industrial Engineering and Management Literature.* Dubuque, Iowa: William C. Brown Co., 1946.

Over one thousand books and bulletins are listed under carefully selected subject headings. The section on time and motion study is very valuable. To January, 1946.

Berg, Rosa M. (comp.). *Bibliography of Management Literature.* New York: The American Society of Mechanical Engineers, 1931. Supplement, 1937.

This is a very complete listing running from 1902 to 1937.

California Institute of Technology, Industrial Relations Section. *Catalog of Publications on Industrial Relations,* November, 1948.

California Institute of Technology. *A Selected Reading List on Industrial Relations for Supervisors,* October, 1946.

Chamberlain, Neil W. (ed.). *A Decade of Industrial Relations Research, 1946-1956.* New York: Harper & Brothers, 1958.

Chamberlain, Neil W. (ed.). *Sourcebook on Labor.* New York: McGraw-Hill Book Company, Inc., 1958.

Cornell University, New York State School of Industrial and Labor Relations. *Selected Bibliography: Industrial and Labor Relations General Works.* Cornell List no. 4, October, 1948.

Guide for Developing a Public Library Service to Labor Groups. Joint Committee on Library Service to Labor Groups. Adult Service Division, American Library Association, 1958.

Hoebreckx, Omer S. *Management Handbook for Collective Bargaining.* New York: Commerce Clearing House, Inc., 1947.

Hopf, Harry Arthur. *Soundings in the Literature of Management, Fifty Books the Educated Practitioner Should Know.* Hopf Institute of Management, Publication no. 6, Ossining, N.Y.: Hopf Institute of Management, 1945.

A very carefully selected list by an authority in the field.

Management Literature, A Selective List. New York: Special Libraries Association, June 10, 1947.

Moore, Bruce V. *The Personnel Interview; An Annotated Bibliography.* New York: Personnel Research Federation, 1928.

National Office Management Association, Research Committee. *Bibliography for Office Managers.* Philadelphia: The Association, 1945. Books, pamphlets, and magazine articles published between 1938-1944 have been carefully selected and listed under subject classifications.

New York Public Library. *Here Is Labor! A Book List,* 1940.

New York Public Library. *Labor in the World Today, A List of Books and Pamphlets Selected by the Readers' Advisors of the New York Public Library,* 1942.

Princeton University, Industrial Relations Section. *Employment Tests in Industry and Business; A Selected Annotated Bibliography.* Princeton, N.J.: Princeton University Press, 1945.

Princeton University, Industrial Relations Section. *Problems and Policies in Industrial Relations in a War Economy, A Selected Annotated Bibliography.* Report no. 60, May, 1940. Supplements on November 15, 1940; March 1, 1941; August 1, 1941; January 2, 1942; and August 15, 1942.

Schenectady Public Library, Technical Department. *Labor: A Select List of Books on Labor,* 1946.

Special Libraries Association. *A Source List of Selected Labor Statistics.* New York: The Association, 1944.

U.S. Bureau of the Budget. *Management Survey Methods: Selected References.* Washington, D.C.: Government Printing Office, November, 1945.

U.S. Bureau of the Budget. *Property Management: An Annotated Bibliography.* Washington, D.C.: Government Printing Office, September, 1946.

U.S. Bureau of Labor Statistics, Industrial Relations Branch. *A Bibliography on Union-Management Coöperation.* Washington, D.C.: Government Printing Office, November, 1946.

U.S. Bureau of Labor Statistics, Industrial Relations Branch. *A Bibliography on Union-Management Coöperation.* Washington, D.C.: Government Printing Office, May, 1948.

U.S. Civil Service Commission. *Supervision: A Selected List of References.* Washington, D.C.: Government Printing Office, May, 1945.

U.S. Department of Labor, Library. *Seniority in Industrial Relations: A Selected List of References.* Washington, D.C.: Government Printing Office, 1944.

U.S. Library of Congress, Division of Bibliography. *Factory Manage-*

ment: A List of Recent References. Washington, D.C.: Government Printing Office, 1940.

U.S. Library of Congress, Division of Bibliography. *A Selected List of Recent Bibliographies on Employment Management.* Washington, D.C.: Government Printing Office, 1938.

University of Southern California, School of Government. *Office Management, A Selected List of References,* 1939.

University of Texas, College of Business Administration, Bureau of Business Research. *A Selected and Annotated Bibliography of Recent Literature on Personnel Administration and Industrial Relations,* rev., March, 1948.

Vradenburg, Juliet C. *The Guaranteed Annual Wage.* Palo Alto, Cal.: Stanford University Press, 1947.

Listed here are several hundred references on the subject of annual wage.

Handbooks and Dictionaries

Alford, Leon. P., and Bangs, John R. (eds.). *Production Handbook.* New York: The Ronald Press Company, 1945.

Aspley, J. C. (ed.). *The Handbook of Industrial Relations.* Chicago: Dartnell Corp., 1948.

Donald, William J. (ed.). *Handbook of Business Administration.* New York: McGraw-Hill Book Company, Inc., 1931.

Heyel, Carl (ed.). *The Foreman's Handbook,* 3rd ed., New York: McGraw-Hill Book Company, Inc., 1955.

Ireson, William Grant, and Grant, Eugene L. (eds.). *Handbook of Industrial Engineering and Management.* Englewood Cliffs, N.J.: Prentice-Hall, Inc., 1955.

Maze, Coleman L. (ed.). *Office Management—A Handbook.* New York: The Ronald Press Company, 1947.

Mitchell, William Norman. *Production Management.* Chicago: The University of Chicago Press, 1932.

National Industrial Conference Board. *The Management Almanac, 1946.* New York: The Conference Board, 1946.

Where to Find It, Bibliography on Industrial Purchasing. New York: National Association of Purchasing Agents, 1949.

Periodicals and Magazines

Advanced Management. New York: The Society for the Advancement of Management (quarterly).

Factory Management and Maintenance. New York: McGraw-Hill Publishing Company (monthly).

Industrial Relations Magazine. Chicago: Dartnell Corp. (monthly).
The Management Review. New York: American Management Association (monthly).
Modern Industry. New York: Magazines of Industry (monthly).
Modern Management. New York: The Society for the Advancement of Management (monthly).
Monthly Labor Review. U.S. Bureau of Labor Statistics.
Personnel. New York: American Management Association (bi-monthly).
Personnel Administration. Washington, D.C. (monthly).

MARKETING

General Bibliographies

"A Current Reading List for Sales Executives and Salesmen." *Sales Management,* vol. 58, nos. 5, 6, and 7.
Advertising Research Foundation Bibliography. Advertising Research Foundation. New York: 1953.
  A short annotated bibliography of marketing and advertising research.
Allen, Jesse B., *et al.* (eds.). *Committee on the Teaching of Industrial Marketing.* Chicago: American Marketing Association, 1950.
  A list of recent periodical articles on industrial marketing topics.
Books for the Advertising and Marketing Man. New York: The Advertising Federation of America, 1953.
  A general list of books with which those in the field of advertising or marketing would do well to be acquainted.
Books for the Marketing Man. New York: Advertising Federation of America, 1953.
  A classified bibliography on advertising, marketing, selling, and other related subjects.
Bradford, Ernest S. *Survey and Directory, Marketing Research Agencies in the United States.* New York: Bureau of Business Research, City College of New York, 1947.
Bridgeport Public Library. *Books for Advertisers Published 1925-1930.*
Carnegie Institute of Technology. *Books on Advertising and Publishing: A Bibliography of Books Especially Helpful in the Solution of Production and Management Problems in the Graphic Arts,* 1941.
Department of Commerce Publications for Use in Marketing and Distribution. Washington, D.C.: U.S. Government Printing Office, 1955.
  A useful list of U.S. Department of Commerce publications in the

area, containing a number of references of which most researchers are not likely to be aware.

Dun & Bradstreet, Inc., Marketing and Research Service. *Bibliography on Sampling Procedure,* March, 1947.

Falk, Alfred T. *Books for the Advertising Man: A Classified Bibliography on Advertising, Marketing and Related Subjects.* New York: Advertising Federation of America, 1946.

The Industrial (Small Business) Series. U.S. Bureau of Foreign and Domestic Commerce (pamphlets).

Institute of Distribution, Inc. *Reference Sources on Chain Stores.* New York: The Institute, 1947.

An Introductory Bibliography of Motivation Research. New York: Advertising Research Foundation, 1953.

An excellent annotated bibliography citing leading works on such subjects as basic theory, applied psychology, specific research techniques and their applications.

Johnston, E. K. (comp.). *100 Books on Advertising.* Columbia, Mo.: University of Missouri Bulletin, vol. 46, no. 27, 1945.

Jones, Donald H. (comp.). *100 Books on Advertising.* Columbia, Mo: University of Missouri Bulletin, vol. 50, no. 27, September 20, 1949.

Metropolitan Life Insurance Company, Policy Holders' Service Bureau. *Training Salesmen, A Bibliography with Notes.* New York: 1937.

New York (State) Library, *Selected List of References to Material on Billboard Advertising,* March, 1933.

Nystrom, Paul Henry. *Bibliography of Retailing; A Selected List of Books, Pamphlets and Periodicals.* New York: Columbia University Press, 1928.

Outdoor Advertising Association of America, Inc. *Books on Advertising, Poster Art, Outdoor Advertising, Statistics, Law, Sales Booklets.* The Association, n.d.

Parten, M. B. *Surveys, Polls and Samples.* New York: Harper & Brothers, 1950.

This book contains a comprehensive bibliography of 1145 references on surveys and sampling problems organized alphabetically by the author.

Printers' Ink Publications. *Select List of Books on Advertising and Selling.* Pleasantville, N.Y.: 1941.

The Realtor's Bookshelf. Business Management Service Bulletin no. 2. Urbana, Ill.: Business Management Service, College of Commerce and Business Administration, University of Illinois, 1949.

Revzan, David Allen. *A Comprehensive Classified Marketing Bibliography.* Berkeley: University of California Press, 1951. Part I and Part II.

Many of the sections in these two volumes, especially the one on marketing research, contain material that is pertinent to researchers. Part I covers books published through 1949; Part II covers other literature through 1949.

Rhoads, S. H. (ed.). *Guide to Government Information on Retailing.* U.S. Department of Commerce. Government Printing Office, Washington, D.C.

Sales Management Survey of Buying Power. New York: Sales Management, Inc. (annual).

Presents estimated figures of surveys on retail sales, population, and buying power since World War II.

Sessa, Alfred A. *A Retail Book List.* New York: Journal of Retailing, n.d.

A Short Annotated Bibliography of Marketing and Advertising Research. New York: Advertising Research Foundation, 1953.

A listing of some of the main works in this area; most useful to beginning researchers.

Thompson, Ralph B. *A Selected and Annotated Bibliography of Literature on Marketing Research.* Austin, Texas: University of Texas, 1950.

U.S. Bureau of Census, Census of Business: Vol. I, *Retail Trade;* Vol. II, *Wholesale Trade;* Vol. III, *Service Businesses;* Vol. IV, *Construction;* Vol. V, *Distribution of Manufacturer's Trade.* Washington, D.C.: Government Printing Office, 1943.

Excellent detailed study that presents data up to 1939.

U.S. Bureau of Foreign and Domestic Commerce. *Market Research Sources, 1940. A Guide to Information on Domestic Marketing.* (Prepared by Rachel Bretherton, Domestic Commerce Series, published in 1925, 1932, 1936, 1938. Series no. 6, 1925, is titled *Market Research Agencies.*)

Presents good bibliographies of pamphlets, articles and books in advertising, salesmanship and general marketing.

U.S. Bureau of Foreign and Domestic Commerce, Marketing Research Division, Marketing Service Section. *Advertising Fields, Some Sources of Information.* Washington, D.C.: Government Printing Office.

U.S. Bureau of Foreign and Domestic Commerce, Marketing Service Division. *Cooperative Retail Advertising, A Reading List.* Washington, D.C.: Government Printing Office, April, 1931.

U.S. Bureau of Foreign and Domestic Commerce. *Statistics and Maps for National Market Analysis* (Basic Information Sources). Washington, D.C.: Government Printing Office, August, 1936; April, 1937; April, 1940; June, 1944.

U.S. Department of Commerce, Business Information Service. *Chain Stores* (Basic Information Sources). Washington, D. C.: Government Printing Office, July, 1949.

U.S. Department of Commerce, Inquiry Reference Service. *Advertising Economics and Principles* (Basic Information Sources). Washington, D. C.: Government Printing Office, June, 1948.

U.S. Department of Commerce, Inquiry Reference Service. *Direct Mail Advertising* (Basic Information Sources). Washington, D.C.: Government Printing Office, June, 1948.

U.S. Department of Commerce, Inquiry Reference Service. *Marketing Research Procedures* (Basic Information Sources). Washington, D.C.: Government Printing Office, January, 1947.

U.S. Department of Commerce, Inquiry Reference Service. *Retail Store Advertising* (Basic Information Sources). Washington, D.C.: Government Printing Office, June, 1948.

U.S. Department of Commerce. *Retail Credit and Collections*. (Basic Information Sources). Washington, D.C.: Government Printing Office, July, 1948.

University of Illinois, College of Commerce and Business Research. *A Market Research Bibliography*. Urbana, Ill.: University of Illinois, 1931.

University of Texas, College of Business Administration. *A Selected and Annotated Bibliography of Literature on Salesmanship*. Austin, Texas: 1948.

Wales, H. G., and Ferber, R. *Marketing Research: Selected Literature*. Dubuque, Iowa: William C. Brown Co., 1952.
   Contains a number of leading articles in the field that have appeared in various journals, with an extensive bibliography. Covers attitude measurement, consumer and market area research, advertising research, and sales research as well as the survey operation and its use in marketing research.

Wales, H. G., and Ferber, R. *A Basic Bibliography on Marketing Research*. Chicago: American Marketing Association, 1956.
   This bibliography attempts to provide those interested in marketing with a relatively short, up-to-date, and annotated set of references in the area of marketing research.

Westerfield, Ray Bert. *Selected Bibliography of Credit and Business Finance*. Cambridge, Mass.: Bankers Publishing Company, 1940.

Wisconsin University, University Extension Division, Bureau of Business Information. *Retailing: A Select List of Books and Pamphlets*. Madison, Wis.: March, 1934.

Wisconsin University, University Extension Division, *Recent Additions to Selected List of Books on Advertising*. Madison, Wis.

Handbooks and Dictionaries

Aspley, John C. (ed.). *The Sales Manager's Handbook*. Chicago: Dartnell Corp., 1951.

Barton, Roger Avery, *et al. Advertising Handbook*. Englewood Cliffs, N.J.: Prentice-Hall, Inc., 1950.
   Includes a long bibliography listing.

Boone, Julian (ed.). *Industrial Advertising Handbook*. New York: McGraw-Hill Book Company, Inc., 1953.
   This handbook is written by 14 national authorities in the field of mass selling to industry.

Brown, Stanley M., *et al.* (eds.). *Business Executive Handbook*. Englewood Cliffs, N.J.: Prentice-Hall, Inc., 1947.

Davis, Donald W. (ed.) *Advertising Directory*. New York: Advertising Federation of America, 1951.
   A directory from the Bureau of Research and Education on advertising, marketing, public relations, and education in the United States.

Graham, Irwin (ed.). *Encyclopedia of Advertising*. New York: Fairchild Publications, 1952.
   This is an encyclopedia containing more than 1110 entries relating to advertising, marketing, publishing, public relations, publicity, and the graphic arts.

Grohmann, H. Victor. *Advertising Dictionary*. New York: Private Printer, 1952.
   A dictionary of advertising terminology, advertising language, and terms of advertising in common use.

Handbook of Sales Training. National Society of Sales Training Executives. Englewood Cliffs, N.J.: Prentice-Hall, Inc., 1949.

Haynes, Ben P., and Smith, Guerry. *Consumer Market Data Handbook*, Domestic Commerce Series no. 102, U.S. Department of Commerce. Washington, D.C.: Government Printing Office, 1939.

Hayward, Walter Sumner, *et al. The Retail Handbook*. New York: McGraw-Hill Book Company, Inc., 1924.

Nystrom, Paul H. (ed.). *Marketing Handbook*. New York: The Ronald Press Company, 1948.

U.S. Bureau of Foreign and Domestic Commerce. *Consumer Market Data Handbook*. Domestic Commerce Series no. 102. Washington, D.C.: Government Printing Office, 1939.

U.S. Bureau of Foreign and Domestic Commerce. *Industrial Marketing Data Handbook of the United States*. Domestic Commerce Series no. 107, Washington, D.C.: Government Printing Office, 1939.

Periodicals and Magazines

The Advertising Age and Mail Order Journal. Chicago (monthly).

Advertising Age: The National Newspaper of Advertising. Chicago: Advertising Publications, Inc. (weekly).

Advertising and Selling. Philadelphia: Robbins Publishing Company (monthly).

The American Marketing Journal. New York: The American Marketing Society (quarterly).

Chain Store Age. New York: Lebhor-Friedman Publications, Inc. (monthly).

Industrial Marketing. Chicago: Advertising Publications, Inc. (monthly).

The Journal of Marketing. Chicago: The American Marketing Association. (quarterly).

Journal of Retailing. New York: New York University School of Retailing (quarterly).

Printers' Ink. Pleasantville, N.Y.: Printers' Ink Publishing Company (weekly).

Retailing Daily. New York: Fairchild Publications, Inc. (daily).

Sales Management. New York: Sales Management, Inc. (semi-monthly).

Standard Rate and Data Service. Chicago: Standard Rate and Data Service, Inc. (monthly).

Lists the rates and coverage of various advertising media.

Survey of Current Business. U.S. Bureau of Foreign and Domestic Commerce (monthly).

Statistics on advertising and wholesale trades.

Tide. New York: Executive Publications, Inc. (weekly).

STATISTICS

General Bibliographies

Blackett, O. W. *The Literature of Business Statistics, A Bibliography.* University of Michigan Business Studies, vol. VIII, no. 1, Ann Arbor, Mich., 1936.

Buros, O. K. *Statistical Methodology Reviews 1941—1950.* New York: John Wiley & Sons, Inc., 1951.

Butterbaugh, G. I. *A Bibliography of Statistical Quality Control.* Seattle: University of Washington Press, 1946.

A supplement to the above book was published in 1951. Author, title, and publisher are the same as for the original work.

Conover, H. F. (comp.). *A Selected List of Books on Statistical Methods and Their Application.* Washington, D.C.: Library of Congress, 1938 (mimeo).

Conover, H. F. (comp.). U.S. Library of Congress, Division of Bibliography. *List of Recent References on Statistical Methods.* Washington, D.C.: Government Printing Office, 1941 (supplement).

Davenport, D. H., and Scott, F. V. *An Index to Business Indices.* Chicago: Business Publications, Inc., 1937.

Hausdorfer, W. (comp.). *Handbook of Commercial, Financial and Information Services.* New York: Special Libraries Association, 1956.

Houser, P. M., and Leonard, W. R. (eds.). *Government Statistics for Business Use.* New York: John Wiley & Sons, Inc., 1956.

Inter-American Statistical Institute. *Bibliography of Selected Statistical Sources of the American Nations.* Washington, D.C.: Pan-American Union, 1947.

The above work is printed in English, Spanish, Portuguese, and French.

Inter-American Statistical Institute. *International Statistical Standards.* Washington, D.C.: Pan-American Union, 1955.

The above work is an annotated bibliography of the statistical recommendations of international conferences, meetings, and agencies.

Moulton, Elma S. (comp.). U.S. Bureau of Foreign and Domestic Commerce. *Sources of Regional and Local Current Business Statistics.* Domestic Commerce Series no. 115. Washington, D.C.: Government Printing Office, 1940.

New York City University, Graduate School of Business Administration, Bureau of Business Research. *Source-Book of Research Data.* Englewood Cliffs, N.J.: Prentice-Hall, Inc., 1923.

Standard and Poor's Corporation. *Trade and Securities Statistics.* New York: Standard and Poor's Corporation, 1928 to date (annual).

Turner, Jessie (comp.). U.S. Bureau of Foreign and Domestic Commerce. *Sources of Current Trade Statistics.* Market Research Series no. 13. Washington, D.C.: Government Printing Office, 1937.

University of Texas, College of Business Administration. *A Selected and Annotated Bibliography of Literature on Statistical Quality Control.* Austin, Texas: 1949.

Handbooks and Dictionaries

Government Statistics Bureau. *The Handbook of Basic Economic Statistics.* Washington, D.C.: Government Printing Office, 1947.

Kendal, M. G., and Buckland, W. R. *A Dictionary of Statistical Terms.* New York: Hafner, 1957.

Kurtz, A. K., and Edgerton, H. A. *Statistical Dictionary of Terms and Symbols.* New York: John Wiley & Sons, Inc., 1939.

U.S. Bureau of the Census. *Statistical Abstract of the United States.* Washington, D.C.: Government Printing Office, 1878 to date. (annual).

U.S. Bureau of Foreign and Domestic Commerce. *Statistical Supplement to the Survey of Current Business.* Washington, D.C.: Government Printing Office (biennial).

Periodicals and Magazines

American Statistician. Washington, D.C.: American Statistical Association (monthly).

The Annals of Mathematical Statistics. Ann Arbor, Mich.: American Statistical Association (quarterly).

Current Statistics. New York: Standard and Poor's Corporation (monthly).

Dun's Statistical Review. New York: Dun & Bradstreet. (monthly).

The Economist. London (monthly).

Journal of the American Statistical Association. Menasha, Wis.: American Statistical Association (quarterly).

Monthly Bulletin of Statistics. New York: The United Nations (monthly).

The Review of Economics and Statistics. Cambridge, Mass.: Harvard University (quarterly).

Chapter 24

A Reference Guide for Report Writers

In the final composition of the report, the writer is sometimes faced with various questions in the areas of diction, rhetoric, and grammar. He may ask:

Does the question mark go "inside" or "outside" the quotation mark?
Should "who" or "whom" be used in this sentence?
Is the correct word "unorganized" or "disorganized"; is it "continual" or "continuous"?
Is "Far East" capitalized or not in this particular usage?

The information in this chapter is designed to assist the report writer in securing answers to questions similar to these. However, the pages which follow are not meant to be a thorough discussion in the various areas. There are many excellent texts and handbooks on the market which are detailed and thorough in their analysis. For quick reference purposes, however, you are urged to use this section.

CAPITALIZATION

1. The first letter in the opening word should be capitalized in a sentence, a direct quotation, or in a line of verse.

   The young lady was a very competent stenographer.

   "Reports are vital in the progress of industry," said Mr. Smythe.

   Whose woods these are I think I know.
   His house is in the village though;

He will not see me stopping here
To watch his woods fill up with snow.[1]

2. A title that is associated with a name begins with a capital letter.

Senator Douglas
President Jackson
Superintendent Michaelson
Aunt Elizabeth

3. Names of tribes, races, and languages also begin with a capital letter.

Greek
Latvians
Iroquois
Australians

4. Names of holidays, holy days, days of the week, and months of the year begin with a capital letter.

Thursday
December
Memorial Day
Assumption Day
Rosh Hashanah

5. The first letter is capitalized in words which designate the names of treaties, laws, conferences, departments of government, and so on.

The Medieval Period
The Sherman Anti-Trust Act
New York Supreme Court
The Brussels Fair
The Declaration of Independence
Department of Defense

6. The first letter is capitalized in words which refer to names, national or international groups, or documents.

The Senate
Security Council of the United Nations
The North Atlantic Treaty Organization

[1] From "Stopping by Woods on a Snowy Evening" by Robert Frost.

7. When referring to a deity or to the Bible or portions of it or when using other religious references, the first letter in such words is capitalized.

> Bible
> Trinity
> Allah
> Torah
> The Congregation of the Missions
> Those who believe in Him . . .
> God Almighty

8. The first letter of *each* word in titles of magazines, books, essays, movies, plays, and so on, is capitalized. Short prepositions, articles, and adverbs (of, the, as, an) are not capitalized unless they are first words.

> *Journal of Accountancy*
> *Grand Canyon Suite*
> *History of the French Revolution*
> *Midsummer Night's Dream*

9. Capitalize a general term when it is part of a name.

> Rock Island Railroad
> New York City
> Episcopal Church
> College of New England

10. Names of specific geographical areas or directional terms which have reference to parts of the world are capitalized. Words which are derived from directional terms are also capitalized. Words denoting or referring to direction are not capitalized.

> The New East
> The West
> The Orient
> A Northerner
> due southwest of the meadow

USE OF POSSESSIVES

Although a variety of situations arise where the apostrophe should be used to indicate ownership, such usage is primarily based on the following three simple principles:

1. Determine what the basic word in the sentence is.

> Is it *five dollars* or *a dollar?* Is it *father* or *fathers?*
> Is it *Mr. William* or *Mr. Williams?* Is it *the table's legs* or *the
> ten tables' legs?*

After you have determined what the basic word is (as it is used
in the particular sentence), then you need only proceed to Step 2
or Step 3, whichever is applicable.
2. If the basic word does not end in *s* and you wish to make the
word possessive, add an ' and an *s* (*'s*).
3. If the basic word does end in *s* and you wish to make it possessive, add an ' after the last *s* (*s'*).

> The girl's hat blew into the street.
> (The basic word is *girl*, which does not end in *s*; therefore *'s* has
> been added.)

> The men's coats were all colored bright red.
> (The basic word is *men*, which does not end in *s*; therefore *'s*
> has been added.)

> The four desks' tops were damaged by the fire.
> (The basic word in this case is *desks*, because the sentence says
> "four." *Desks* ends in *s*; therefore an ' has been added *after* the
> *s*.)

> His three weeks' salary was certainly adequate for the work he
> performed.
> (The basic word is *weeks* because the sentence says "three." Inas-
> much as *weeks* ends in *s*, the ' has been added *after* the *s*.)

The report writer should attempt to avoid the use of possessives
with inanimate objects, such as *roof's top* or *tables' legs*. Where
convenient, it is probably better to use an "of" phrase, such as:
top of the roof and *legs of the tables*.

Other Uses for the Apostrophe

1. If two or more persons or objects own one item, possession is
indicated on the last named only. If the writer wishes to illustrate individual possession, an apostrophe is used with *each*
name or title.

Brown and Smith's store (They own one store in partnership.)
Brown and Smith's stores (They own two or more stores in partnership.)
Brown's and Smith's stores (They each own one or more stores separately.)

2. In compound words an apostrophe is added to the secondary or last word to indicate possession.

My brother-in-law's home was painted white. (singular possessive)
My brothers-in-law's homes were all painted white. (plural possessive)

3. The possessive should be used with words or phrases that are idiomatic in nature.

Five dollars' worth of materials was used.

A week's salary was lost by his absence.

It required five days' time to process the claim.

4. The apostrophe is used to indicate possession with indefinite pronouns.

One's ideas are not always valid.

Anyone's thoughts are acceptable in this conference.

5. Possession is indicated by the use of the apostrophe in appositives and also in names where a "junior" or "senior" is used.

Tom the plumber's hat blew into the street.

Robert Martin, Jr.'s car failed to start.

6. Pronouns in the possessive case do *not* use the apostrophe to denote ownership. Such words are already possessive.

The book is yours, not hers.

Its side was dented, but it's (this is a contraction for "it is") of no consequence.

This table is ours, not theirs.

7. The apostrophe is used to form the plurals of letters, words, symbols, and numbers.

He made his t's and l's in a similar fashion.

Your typewriter does not strike 3's and 8's distinctly.

His writing is generously sprinkled with *however's* and *consequently's*.

8. When one-syllable words, especially names, end in s, and possession is to be indicated, an *'s* should be added; if the word has more than one syllable, it is usually adequate to add only an apostrophe after the last *s*.

James's dog was lost.

Betty Jones's car was damaged.

Charles' sweater was not in the box.

Mr. Williams' briefcase was not in the office. (If an *'s* had been added in the last two cases, some difficulty in pronunciation would probably have been encountered.)

PUNCTUATION

In reading through these punctuation notes, the student is specifically cautioned against attempting to memorize the rules; he must *understand* every one and ask questions until he does. The explanations given below are, of necessity, brief.

The Comma

1. An adverbial clause which precedes an independent clause is usually set off from the latter one by a comma, especially if the subordinate clause is long.

When I arrived at the factory, I found that both generators were damaged.

2. A comma is used between independent clauses that are joined by a coördinating conjunction such as *and, but, for, or,* or *nor.* If the clauses are very short, the comma may be omitted.

The foreman went to the meeting, and the production line was placed in charge of the new mechanical engineer.

3. Nonrestrictive (or nonessential) clauses are set off by commas.

Mrs. Roberta Thompson, who was one of the women designated

by our chairman, was also very much interested in youth work.

4. Nonrestrictive (or nonessential) phrases are set off by commas.

   Mrs. Peterson, as you know, is a very excellent teacher.

5. The name of a person or place directly addressed is set off by commas.

   I believe, Mr. Underwood, that you would do well to consider the long-range cost of such a program.

6. A mild interjection is set off by a comma.

   Oh, I wasn't sure you would agree.

7. Words or phrases in apposition are set off by commas if they are nonrestrictive.

   Mr. Pike, the well-known president of The Eagles Club, has decided to run for public office.

8. Adjectives in series, modifying the same noun, are separated from one another by commas.

   The painting has splashes of green, blue, yellow, red, and black. (The comma after "red" may be omitted.)

9. Words or short phrases in a series are separated from one another by commas.

   The young lady was attractive and charming, well-groomed and poised, and competent and efficient.

10. A comma may set off a quotation from the rest of the sentence.

    Joan said, "There are several excellent actors among the members of that club."

11. A comma should be employed in a sentence to avoid confusion in interpretation or to prevent the sentence from being read incorrectly.

    The carpenter, the plumber indicated, was dishonest.

12. The omission of a word (usually a verb) is indicated by a comma.

> Gabardine is priced at $3.50; sharkskin, at $4.25; tweed, at $4.50; and flannel, at $3.75.

The Semicolon

1. The semicolon is used between coördinate clauses not joined by a conjunction.

   > Robin set the table; Shelley made the coffee.

2. The semicolon is sometimes used between coördinate clauses which are joined by a conjunction if:
   a. The clauses are long.
   b. The clauses have commas within themselves.

   > When the old man had recovered from his long illness, he was eager to return to his daughter's home; but there were many adjustments to be made.

   c. Obscurity would result were the semicolon not used.

3. The semicolon is used between coördinate clauses which are joined by a formal conjunctive adverb (hence, however, therefore, etc.).

   > The girls had hoped to leave early; however, the festivities did not start until after 9:00 P.M.

4. The semicolon is *not used* before quotations or after the "Dear Sir" in letters.

The Colon

1. The colon is used to formally introduce a list, a statement, a question, a series of statements or questions, a long quotation, and, in unusual cases, a word.

   > In order to paint successfully, an artist requires the following equipment: canvas, oil paints, brushes, solvent, an easel, and cleaning rags.

2. The colon may be used before a concrete illustration of a general statement:

   > The fruit trees bloomed, the grass turned green, the birds returned: it was Spring.

3. The colon should not be used before an informal series or an indirect quotation.

The Dash

1. The dash may be used instead of parentheses especially where informality is desired.

   That house—the one on the corner—is said to be haunted.

2. Insert a dash when a sentence is broken off abruptly.

   Have you heard that—

3. A dash is used near the end of a sentence just before a summarizing statement or an afterthought.

   The evening was perfect; stars, moon, soft breeze, sweet music— romance was in the air.

4. Dashes are used within a sentence where a basic change in the line of thought takes place.

   Tomorrow I must be sure and—now what was I supposed to do tomorrow?

5. To use a dash to end a sentence is a childish device.

The Parenthesis

1. Parentheses are used to enclose matters foreign to the main thought of the sentence.

   Their chain of stores (you know they had nine hosiery shops) was transferred to the NuHose Corporation.

2. When confirmatory symbols or figures are enclosed within parentheses, they should follow the words they confirm.

   The deposit of two dollars ($2.00) was returned to her.

3. Do not use parentheses to cancel a word or passage.

Brackets

1. Brackets are used to insert explanatory matter within a quotation when the quotation comes from another writer.

Dr. Frank in his interesting account of World War II states that the major counter offensive was the Battle of the Ardennes: "Out of the cold, black night of December 18, 1944 [the attack was begun on December 16, 1944] the German offensive through the Ardennes was launched."

Quotation Marks

1. Quotation marks should be used to enclose a direct but not an indirect quotation.

   Bob stated, "I believe that it would be enjoyable if we went to the movies."

2. A quotation of several paragraphs should have quotation marks at the beginning of each paragraph and at the end of the last paragraph.

   "...
   ....
   ....
   "...
   ....
   ....
   "...
   ....
   ...."

3. In narrative, each separate speech, however short, should be enclosed within quotation marks.

   "Yes," said Bob.

   "I disagree," answered John.

   "I'm not sure which is better," said Tom.

4. In formal writing, quotation marks should enclose slang words or expressions.

   He always acted a little "odd."

5. A quotation within a quotation should be enclosed in single quotation marks; a quotation within that, in double marks.

   Commissioner Kelly said, "I agree with Lincoln, 'To sin by silence when they should protest makes cowards of men.' "

6. When a word is followed by both a quotation mark and a question mark or an exclamation point, the question mark or the exclamation point should come first if it applies to the quotation; last, if it applies to the main sentence.

> Did Mary say, "I will not buy a hat"?
>
> Mary said, "Will you buy a hat?"
>
> Did Mary say, "Will you buy a new dress"?
>
> Jack said, "Did you read the article, 'Atomic Energy'?"
>
> Mr. Downs replied, "No, I have not, but I did read, 'War and the World.'"
>
> Peter Town said, "I have studied the article, 'Can We Survive?'"

7. Quotation marks are used to enclose titles of articles, chapters in a book, or any *portion* of a whole unit (such as a book, magazine, opera, etc.) designated.

> The journal *Marketing Analysis* contained an excellent article entitled, "Why Women Buy."

The Apostrophe

1. In contracted words, place the apostrophe where letters have been omitted.

> I don't believe he will attend the meeting.

2. See discussion of possessives for the use of apostrophes in forming possessive singulars and plurals.

The Question Mark

1. Use a question mark after a direct question, not after an indirect question.

> Will Marty bring the skates to school?

2. A question mark used within a quotation should not be followed by a comma, semicolon, or period.

> Betty said, "Do you think the Dean will approve my request?"

3. See section on quotation marks for a discussion of the use of the question mark with quotation marks.

	Singular	Plural
...up One (Subjective or ...ominative case)	I, you, he, she, it	we, you, they
...up Two (Objective case)	me, you, him, her, it	us, you, them

...inative Case

...pronoun in the nominative or subjective case is chosen when ...serves as the subject of a sentence or a clause.

John, Tom, and I (not me) received similar letters from the chairman.

Check yourself: Would you say, "I have received similar letters" or "Me have received similar letters"? Certainly it is the first. Therefore, the sentence must be: "John, Tom, and *I* received similar letters from the chairman."

...pronoun completing the meaning of a connective verb or ...redicate complement (am, is, are, was, were, be, or been) ...ould be in the nominative case.

It was *he* who went to the convention.

Do you feel that this is *she*?

...se the subjective case if the pronoun is the subject of an im-...lied verb.

He is older than *I* (am old).

He is as clever as *they* (are clever).

...ctive Case

...pronoun in the objective case is chosen when it is the object ...verb or preposition or when it serves as an indirect object.

...e sent the packages to John, Robert, and *me* (not I).

...eck yourself: Would you say: "He sent the packages to I" or "He sent the packages to me"? Certainly it is the second; therefore ...the sentence must be: "He sent the packages to John, Robert, and ...me."

The Exclamation

1. The exclamation point is used after words, expressions, or sentences to show strong emotion.

   Close that door!

   Bob exclaimed, "I will not be responsible!"

2. See section on quotation marks for a discussion of the use of the exclamation point with quotation marks.

The Period

1. Place a period after a complete declarative or imperative sentence.

   I believe that emphasis on the study of communication is vital.

2. Place a period after an abbreviation.

   The Martinsville Corp. will not purchase the Excello plant site.

NOTE: In using marks of punctuation with quoted words or statements, remember to place:

   1. Commas and periods *within* quotation marks.
   2. Semicolons and colons *outside* quotation marks.
   3. Question marks, exclamation points, and dashes within the quotation marks when they apply to the quoted matter and outside when they refer to the whole sentence.

PRONOUN REFERENCE

Pronouns, as we know, take the place of nouns. Without pronouns our communication would be dull indeed, for we would have extensive repetition of names, places, and things.

In reviewing pronouns we shall first examine "agreement" and secondly, the correct choice of personal and relative pronouns (I or me? he or him? who or whom?) in specific situations.

Agreement of Pronouns with Their Antecedents

1. The pronoun must agree with its antecedent in person, number, and gender.

Miss Shelley said that she thought her book was placed on her bed by her sister.

The boys said that they wanted to contribute their funds to the Community Chest.

Betty called her parents who said that they were on their way to Aunt Martha's home.

2. Antecedents connected by "or" or "nor" utilize a singular pronoun.

    Neither Shelley nor Robin gave *her* ticket to the gatekeeper. (Note that the sentence says neither *one* nor the other.)

    A truck or tractor will utilize *its* full horsepower on a steep incline.

    John or Bob will be happy to give you *his* book.

In the cases above, the antecedent does not refer to both antecedents of the pronoun but to one *or* the other.

3. Antecedents connected by "and." The pronoun should be plural if it refers to two or more antecedents connected by "and."

    The man and the boy lost their hats when the plane roared down the air strip.

4. When two antecedents are merely different names for the same term or object, the pronoun should be singular.

    The chairman of the board and primary stockholder lost his briefcase just prior to the conference.

It should be noted that "stockholder" is not preceded by "the." When this *is* done, it usually indicates that the items named are different.

    The chairman and the stockholder discussed their mutual problems.

5. When two or more antecedents are intimately associated by usage or practice, a singular pronoun may be used.

    Bread and butter should have its place on everyone's table.

    The porcelain cup and saucer fell from its stand sometime during the night.

---

6. Antecedents or collective nouns which re[f] the impression of "oneness" utilize a sin the sentence indicates plurality, a plur[a] chosen.

    The basketball team finds that its biggest p

    The company received its merchandise o[n]

    The administrative group reviewed their of each month.

7. Common gender antecedents usually uti noun. For preciseness, however, one pr[e] may be used.

    Each student should receive *his* grade to

    Each student should receive *his* or *her*

8. The following words, when utilized as a[n] singular pronouns. Some of these indefin[i] interpreted more and more frequently as

anybody	everybody
neither	someone
either	none
each	everyone
	nobody

Neither of the girls had *her* books availab[le]

Everybody should contribute *his* best effor[t]

None of the men had *his* identification ca[rd]

USE OF PERSONAL PRON[OUNS]

The choice between "I" and "me," "she" [and] "them," etc., is sometimes a difficult one explanation which follows may help you re[cognize] at a previous time. The first step in making a personal pronoun is to be familiar with objective and subjective cases.

He saw Mr. Bryant, Miss Jones, and *me* (not I).

Check yourself: Would you say, "He saw me" or "He saw I"? Certainly it is the first; therefore, the sentence must be: "He saw Mr. Bryant, Miss Jones, and me."

USE OF RELATIVE PRONOUNS

A relative pronoun joins a subordinate clause to its antecedent. *Who, whom, which, what,* and *that* are frequently encountered relative pronouns. *Who* and *whom* are the two that often prove to be troublesome. *Who* is in the subjective case; *whom* is in the objective.

Subjective Case—Who

As in the case of the personal pronouns in the subjective case, *who* is also used as the subject of a sentence or clause.

He is the one *who* (not whom) should be chosen.

Check yourself: Would you say, "He should be chosen" or "Him should be chosen"? Certainly the first is correct and since "he" is in the same case as "who," the sentence must be, "He is the one *who* should be chosen."

Objective Case—Whom

Whom is used under the same conditions as the personal pronouns in the same case: object of the verb or preposition and indirect object.

Whom (not who) did you select?

Check yourself: Would you say, "Did you select him" or "Did you select he"? The first one is correct and since "him" is in the same case as "whom," the sentence must be, "Whom did you select?"

He is the salesman to *whom* (not who) we expect to give the prize.

Check yourself: Would you say, "We expect to give *him* the prize" or "We expect to give *he* the prize"? The first choice is preferable and because "him" and "whom" are in the same case, the sentence must be, "He is the salesman to whom we expect to give the prize."

Whoever and Whomever

These two words follow the same principles discussed earlier. *Whoever* is in the subjective case; *whomever,* in the objective.

> We shall ship the order to *whomever* (not whoever) you choose.
> Check yourself: Would you say, "We shall ship the order to them" or "We shall ship the order to they"? The first choice is better, and since "them" and "whomever" are in the same case, the sentence must be, "We shall ship the order to whomever you choose."

> Tom, Bill, and *whoever* (not whomever) else is chosen will be sent to Florida.
> Check yourself: Would you say, "He is chosen" or "Him is chosen"? The better of the two is the first, and since "he" and "whoever" are in the same case, the sentence must be, "Tom, Bill, and whoever else is chosen will be sent to Florida."

WORD USAGE

Words have precise meanings and should be chosen with care and exactness. *Farther* should not be used for *further; stationery* for *stationary;* or *principal* for *principle.* There is no substitute for the *exact* word. You should always search to find it. The list which follows may aid you in choosing the exact word you need in a particular case. However, the definitions given are very brief and often do not convey the true connotation of the word. In any instance where the slightest doubt exists, do not hesitate to use a good dictionary to secure a more complete definition.

Accent: to stress a specific part of a word ·
Ascent: rising or going up
Assent: to consent or agree to

Accept: to receive
Except: to exclude

Access: to have admittance or admission to
Excess: a surplus or more than necessary

Ad: a short way of writing *advertisement*
Add: to join or unite

Adapt: to accustom oneself to a situation
Adept: proficient or competent in performing a task
Adopt: to take by choice; to put into practice

Advice: counsel
Advise: to recommend a course of action

Affect: to make a change in
Effect: to bring about; a result

Aggravate: to increase; to intensify; to make more severe
Irritate: to exasperate or bother greatly

All ready: completely ready; prepared
Already: previously or beforehand

All right: completely right
Alright: an incorrect usage of *all right*

Allusion: a reference to something familiar
Illusion: a misleading *image* of a real object or a false impression
Delusion: a false belief

Altar: a place to worship or pray
Alter: to change

Altogether: completely or thoroughly
All together: in a group; in unison

Among: refers to more than two
Between: refers to two

Amount: refers to mass or bulk—"A large amount of gravel was delivered."
Number: refers to items which can be counted—"A large number of men came."

Anxious: upset; concerned about a serious occurrence
Eager: very desirous; anticipating a favorable event

Assay: to evaluate
Essay: to try or attempt
Essay: a literary composition

Balance: a financial or accounting term
Remainder: something left over

Bazaar: an establishment that sells merchandise
Bizarre: eccentric in style or mode

Being as, being that: should not be used for *since* or *because*

Beside: next to
Besides: in addition to

Biannually: two times a year
Biennially: every two years

Can: to be able
May: to have permission

Callous: not sympathetic
Callus: hardened area of skin

Canvas: a coarse type of cloth
Canvass: to solicit; survey

Cannon: large gun
Canon: a law, church official

Capital: a seat of government; money invested; a form of a letter
Capitol: a government building

Carat: weight
Caret: mark showing omission
Carrot: vegetable

Cease: to halt or stop
Seize: to grasp or take possession of

Censer: an incense pot
Censor: a critic
Censure: to find fault with or to blame
Criticize: to evaluate; to examine

Cereal: any grain
Serial: arranged in successive order

Choir: organized group of singers
Quire: measure of paper

Cite: to quote from a source
Sight: visual act of seeing
Site: a place, such as a "building site"

Coarse: large particles or unrefined
Course: a direction of progress or a series of studies

Collision: a clashing of objects
Collusion: a conspiracy or fraud

Command: to direct or order
Commend: to praise or laud

The Exclamation

1. The exclamation point is used after words, expressions, or sentences to show strong emotion.

   Close that door!

   Bob exclaimed, "I will not be responsible!"

2. See section on quotation marks for a discussion of the use of the exclamation point with quotation marks.

The Period

1. Place a period after a complete declarative or imperative sentence.

   I believe that emphasis on the study of communication is vital.

2. Place a period after an abbreviation.

   The Martinsville Corp. will not purchase the Excello plant site.

NOTE: In using marks of punctuation with quoted words or statements, remember to place:

   1. Commas and periods *within* quotation marks.
   2. Semicolons and colons *outside* quotation marks.
   3. Question marks, exclamation points, and dashes within the quotation marks when they apply to the quoted matter and outside when they refer to the whole sentence.

PRONOUN REFERENCE

Pronouns, as we know, take the place of nouns. Without pronouns our communication would be dull indeed, for we would have extensive repetition of names, places, and things.

In reviewing pronouns we shall first examine "agreement" and secondly, the correct choice of personal and relative pronouns (I or me? he or him? who or whom?) in specific situations.

Agreement of Pronouns with Their Antecedents

1. The pronoun must agree with its antecedent in person, number, and gender.

Miss Shelley said that she thought her book was placed on her bed by her sister.

The boys said that they wanted to contribute their funds to the Community Chest.

Betty called her parents who said that they were on their way to Aunt Martha's home.

2. Antecedents connected by "or" or "nor" utilize a singular pronoun.

   Neither Shelley nor Robin gave *her* ticket to the gatekeeper. (Note that the sentence says neither *one* nor the other.)

   A truck or tractor will utilize *its* full horsepower on a steep incline.

   John or Bob will be happy to give you *his* book.

   In the cases above, the antecedent does not refer to both antecedents of the pronoun but to one *or* the other.

3. Antecedents connected by "and." The pronoun should be plural if it refers to two or more antecedents connected by "and."

   The man and the boy lost their hats when the plane roared down the air strip.

4. When two antecedents are merely different names for the same term or object, the pronoun should be singular.

   The chairman of the board and primary stockholder lost his briefcase just prior to the conference.

   It should be noted that "stockholder" is not preceded by "the." When this *is* done, it usually indicates that the items named are different.

   The chairman and the stockholder discussed their mutual problems.

5. When two or more antecedents are intimately associated by usage or practice, a singular pronoun may be used.

   Bread and butter should have its place on everyone's table.

   The porcelain cup and saucer fell from its stand sometime during the night.

6. Antecedents or collective nouns which refer to groups or convey the impression of "oneness" utilize a singular pronoun. Where the sentence indicates plurality, a plural pronoun should be chosen.

The basketball team finds that its biggest problem is transportation.

The company received its merchandise on Tuesday.

The administrative group reviewed their suggestions at the end of each month.

7. Common gender antecedents usually utilize a masculine pronoun. For preciseness, however, one pronoun of each gender may be used.

Each student should receive *his* grade tomorrow.

Each student should receive *his* or *her* grade card by Monday.

8. The following words, when utilized as antecedents, should use singular pronouns. Some of these indefinite pronouns are being interpreted more and more frequently as plural, however.

anybody	everybody	somebody
neither	someone	any
either	none	one
each	everyone	another
	nobody	

Neither of the girls had *her* books available.

Everybody should contribute *his* best efforts to the cause.

None of the men had *his* identification card.

USE OF PERSONAL PRONOUNS

The choice between "I" and "me," "she" and "her," "they" and "them," etc., is sometimes a difficult one to make. The brief explanation which follows may help you recall principles learned at a previous time. The first step in making the correct choice of a personal pronoun is to be familiar with the pronouns in the objective and subjective cases.

	Singular	*Plural*
Group One (Subjective or nominative case)	I, you, he, she, it	we, you, they
Group Two (Objective case)	me, you, him, her, it	us, you, them

Nominative Case

1. A pronoun in the nominative or subjective case is chosen when it serves as the subject of a sentence or a clause.

   John, Tom, and I (not me) received similar letters from the chairman.

   Check yourself: Would you say, "I have received similar letters" or "Me have received similar letters"? Certainly it is the first. Therefore, the sentence must be: "John, Tom, and *I* received similar letters from the chairman."

2. A pronoun completing the meaning of a connective verb or predicate complement (am, is, are, was, were, be, or been) should be in the nominative case.

   It was *he* who went to the convention.

   Do you feel that this is *she*?

3. Use the subjective case if the pronoun is the subject of an implied verb.

   He is older than *I* (am old).

   He is as clever as *they* (are clever).

Objective Case

A pronoun in the objective case is chosen when it is the object of a verb or preposition or when it serves as an indirect object.

He sent the packages to John, Robert, and *me* (not I).

Check yourself: Would you say: "He sent the packages to *I*" or "He sent the packages to me"? Certainly it is the second; therefore the sentence must be: "He sent the packages to John, Robert, and me."

He saw Mr. Bryant, Miss Jones, and *me* (not I).
Check yourself: Would you say, "He saw me" or "He saw I"?
Certainly it is the first; therefore, the sentence must be: "He
saw Mr. Bryant, Miss Jones, and me."

USE OF RELATIVE PRONOUNS

A relative pronoun joins a subordinate clause to its antecedent.
Who, whom, which, what, and *that* are frequently encountered
relative pronouns. *Who* and *whom* are the two that often prove to
be troublesome. *Who* is in the subjective case; *whom* is in the
objective.

Subjective Case—Who

As in the case of the personal pronouns in the subjective case,
who is also used as the subject of a sentence or clause.

He is the one *who* (not whom) should be chosen.
Check yourself: Would you say, "He should be chosen" or "Him
should be chosen"? Certainly the first is correct and since "he" is
in the same case as "who," the sentence must be, "He is the one
who should be chosen."

Objective Case—Whom

Whom is used under the same conditions as the personal pronouns in the same case: object of the verb or preposition and
indirect object.

Whom (not who) did you select?
Check yourself: Would you say, "Did you select him" or "Did you
select he"? The first one is correct and since "him" is in the same
case as "whom," the sentence must be, "Whom did you select?"

He is the salesman to *whom* (not who) we expect to give the prize.
Check yourself: Would you say, "We expect to give *him* the prize"
or "We expect to give *he* the prize"? The first choice is preferable
and because "him" and "whom" are in the same case, the sentence
must be, "He is the salesman to whom we expect to give the prize."

Whoever and Whomever

These two words follow the same principles discussed earlier. *Whoever* is in the subjective case; *whomever,* in the objective.

> We shall ship the order to *whomever* (not whoever) you choose.
> Check yourself: Would you say, "We shall ship the order to them" or "We shall ship the order to they"? The first choice is better, and since "them" and "whomever" are in the same case, the sentence must be, "We shall ship the order to whomever you choose."

> Tom, Bill, and *whoever* (not whomever) else is chosen will be sent to Florida.
> Check yourself: Would you say, "He is chosen" or "Him is chosen"? The better of the two is the first, and since "he" and "whoever" are in the same case, the sentence must be, "Tom, Bill, and whoever else is chosen will be sent to Florida."

WORD USAGE

Words have precise meanings and should be chosen with care and exactness. *Farther* should not be used for *further; stationery* for *stationary;* or *principal* for *principle.* There is no substitute for the *exact* word. You should always search to find it. The list which follows may aid you in choosing the exact word you need in a particular case. However, the definitions given are very brief and often do not convey the true connotation of the word. In any instance where the slightest doubt exists, do not hesitate to use a good dictionary to secure a more complete definition.

Accent: to stress a specific part of a word
Ascent: rising or going up
Assent: to consent or agree to

Accept: to receive
Except: to exclude

Access: to have admittance or admission to
Excess: a surplus or more than necessary

Ad: a short way of writing *advertisement*
Add: to join or unite

Adapt: to accustom oneself to a situation
Adept: proficient or competent in performing a task
Adopt: to take by choice; to put into practice

Advice: counsel
Advise: to recommend a course of action

Affect: to make a change in
Effect: to bring about; a result

Aggravate: to increase; to intensify; to make more severe
Irritate: to exasperate or bother greatly

All ready: completely ready; prepared
Already: previously or beforehand

All right: completely right
Alright: an incorrect usage of *all right*

Allusion: a reference to something familiar
Illusion: a misleading *image* of a real object or a false impression
Delusion: a false belief

Altar: a place to worship or pray
Alter: to change

Altogether: completely or thoroughly
All together: in a group; in unison

Among: refers to more than two
Between: refers to two

Amount: refers to mass or bulk—"A large amount of gravel was delivered."
Number: refers to items which can be counted—"A large number of men came."

Anxious: upset; concerned about a serious occurrence
Eager: very desirous; anticipating a favorable event

Assay: to evaluate
Essay: to try or attempt
Essay: a literary composition

Balance: a financial or accounting term
Remainder: something left over

Bazaar: an establishment that sells merchandise
Bizarre: eccentric in style or mode

Being as, being that: should not be used for *since* or *because*

Beside: next to
Besides: in addition to

Biannually: two times a year
Biennially: every two years

Can: to be able
May: to have permission

Callous: not sympathetic
Callus: hardened area of skin

Canvas: a coarse type of cloth
Canvass: to solicit; survey

Cannon: large gun
Canon: a law, church official

Capital: a seat of government; money invested; a form of a letter
Capitol: a government building

Carat: weight
Caret: mark showing omission
Carrot: vegetable

Cease: to halt or stop
Seize: to grasp or take possession of

Censer: an incense pot
Censor: a critic
Censure: to find fault with or to blame
Criticize: to evaluate; to examine

Cereal: any grain
Serial: arranged in successive order

Choir: organized group of singers
Quire: measure of paper

Cite: to quote from a source
Sight: visual act of seeing
Site: a place, such as a "building site"

Coarse: large particles or unrefined
Course: a direction of progress or a series of studies

Collision: a clashing of objects
Collusion: a conspiracy or fraud

Command: to direct or order
Commend: to praise or laud

Complacent: satisfied, smug
Complaisent: obliging

Complement: that which completes or supplements
Compliment: flattery or praise

Confidant: one who may be confided in
Confident: positive or sure

Continual: taking place in close succession; frequently repeated
Continuous: without a break or letup

Core: the center
Corps: a body of troops of soldiers
Corpse: a dead body

Council: an assembly of persons
Counsel: advice; an attorney
Consul: a resident representative of a foreign state

Councilor: a member of a council
Counselor: a lawyer or adviser

Credible: believable or acceptable
Creditable: praiseworthy or meritorious
Credulous: inclined or ready to believe

Critic: one who evaluates
Critique: an analytical examination of work or planned activity
Criticism: an evaluation

Currant: fruit
Current: timely; motion of air or water

Deceased: dead
Diseased: infected

Decent: correct; proper
Descent: a going from high to low
Dissent: disagreement

Decree: a proclamation of law
Degree: difference in grade; an academic award

Defer: to delay or put off
Differ: to disagree

Deference: respect
Difference: unlikeness

Depot: a storehouse for merchandise or goods
Station: a place for passengers; a regular stopping place

Deprecate: to disapprove of
Depreciate: to lessen in value because of use and/or time

Desert: a reward or punishment
Desert: to abandon
Desert: a barren geographical area
Dessert: a course at the end of a meal

Disapprove: not to accept
Disprove: to prove wrong

Disburse: to make payments; to allot
Disperse: to scatter

Discomfit: to frustrate
Discomfort: distress

Discreet: careful
Discrete: single

Disinterested: neutral; not biased
Uninterested: not concerned with; lacking interest

Disorganized: thrown into disorder
Unorganized: not organized or planned

Dual: double or two
Duel: a contest between two antagonists

Dying: expiring
Dyeing: changing color

Elicit: to draw forth, usually a comment
Illicit: unlawful; illegal

Eligible: acceptable; approved
Illegible: impossible to read or decipher

Elusive: difficult to catch
Illusive: deceptive

Emerge: to come out
Immerge: to place in liquid

Emigrate: to travel out of one country to live in another
Immigrate: to come into a country
Migrate: to travel from place to place periodically

Eminent: outstanding; prominent
Imminent: momentarily; very near or threatening

Envelope: container for a communication
Envelop: to surround, cover over or enfold

Erotic: pertaining to love
Erratic: undependable
Exotic: foreign

Exceptional: outstanding; superior
Exceptionable: not acceptable; subject to exclusion

Expansive: capable of extension
Expensive: costly

Extant: living or in existence
Extent: an area or a measure

Extinct: no longer living or existing
Distinct: clear; sharply defined

Facet: a small plane area or surface (a diamond's *facets*)
Faucet: a spigot

Facilitate: to make easier
Felicitate: to greet or congratulate

Faint: to lose consciousness
Feint: to pretend or simulate

Farther: refers to geographical or linear distance
Further: more; in addition to

Fate: destiny
Fete: to honor or celebrate

Fiancé: a man who is betrothed to be married
Fiancée: a woman who is betrothed to be married

Flair: ability
Flare: blaze

Formally: according to convention
Formerly: previously

Freeze: to turn solid because of low temperatures
Frieze: ornamentation on a building wall
Frieze: a type of fabric

Genius: unusual and outstanding mental ability
Genus: a grouping or classification usually on a biological basis

Grisly: ghastly; horrible; very bad
Grizzly: a type of bear; somewhat gray

Guerilla: one who engages in irregular warfare
Gorilla: a large animal of the ape family

Healthful: giving or contributing to health
Healthy: having health

Hoard: to gather; a hidden supply
Horde: a crowd

Holey: having perforations or holes
Holy: sacred from a religious point of view
Wholly: entirely; completely

Human: pertaining to man
Humane: kindly, considerate

Immunity: freedom or exemption from regulations or disease
Impunity: freedom or exemption from punishment

In: indicates "locating within" (She was *in* the car.)
Into: indicates movement to a point within (She stepped *into* the car.)

Incite: to stir up
Insight: keen understanding; intuition

Incredible: difficult to believe
Incredulous: someone who doesn't believe

Indignant: angry
Indigenous: native to an area or country
Indigent: needy; poor

Infer: to arrive at through reasoning
Imply: to suggest or hint

Ingenuous: open; frank
Ingenious: clever; inventive

Its: possessive of *it* (Its form was interesting)
It's: a contraction of the two words *it is* (It's interesting to see)

Later: comparative degree of *late*
Latter: the second of two items

Learn: to acquire knowledge
Teach: to impart knowledge

Less: refers to quantity (*Less* wheat was stored last year)
Fewer: refers to number (*Fewer* men left today than yesterday)

Let: to permit
Leave: physical departure from; to abandon

Lie, lay, lain: to recline
Lay, laid, laid: to place

Likely: probable
Liable: legally responsible
Apt: quick to learn; predisposition

Load: a burden; a pack
Lode: a vein of ore

Loath: reluctant; unwilling
Loathe: to hate; to despise; to detest

Marital: used in reference to marriage
Marshal: an official; to arrange
Martial: pertaining to military affairs

Magnate: a tycoon; important official
Magnet: a device that attracts iron

Maybe: perhaps (adverb)
May be: possibility (verb)

Medal: a badge of honor
Mettle: spirit or temperament
Metal: a mineral substance
Meddle: to interfere

Miner: an underground laborer or worker
Minor: one who has not attained legal age; of little importance

Moral: virtuous; ethical
Morale: spirit

Notable: distinguished
Noted or famous: favorably known
Notorious: unfavorably known

Observance: following or respecting a custom or regulation
Observation: visual act of seeing

Ordinance: a local law
Ordnance: military weapons; munitions

Peak: top of a hill or mountain; topmost point
Peek: a quick look through a small opening

Peal: sound of a bell
Peel: to strip

Percent: should be used after a numeral (20 *percent*)
Percentage: for quantity or where numerals are not used (a larger *percentage*)

Persecute: to subject to harsh or unjust treatment
Prosecute: to bring legal action against

Personal: private; not public or general
Personnel: the staff of an organization

Plaintiff: the complaining party in a lawsuit
Plantive: sorrowful; mournful

Practical: useful, not theoretical
Practicable: capable of being put into practice

Precedence: priority
Precedents: cases that have already occurred

Proceed: to begin; to move; to advance
Precede: to go before

Principal: of primary importance (adjective); head of a school; original sum; chief or official
Principle: a fundamental truth

Provided: on condition
Providing: furnishing (The past tense of *provide*, which is *provided*, also means to furnish or supply.)

Recent: newly created or developed; referring to time relatively near
Resent: to feel indignant

Respectfully: with respect or deference
Respectively: in order named

Rise: to move upward; to ascend (rise, rose, risen)
Raise: to elevate; pick up (raise, raised, raised)

Salvage: material saved from a fire, shipwreck, etc.
Selvage: edge of cloth that will not ravel

Sometime: at one time or another
Sometimes: occasionally

Sit: to be seated (sit, sat, sat)
Set: to cause to be seated or placed in position (set, set, set)

Stationary: not moving; fixed
Stationery: writing paper or writing materials

Straight: direct; uninterrupted; not crooked
Strait: narrow strip connecting two bodies of water; a distressing situation

Statue: a reproduction
Stature: height of a person; reputation
Statute: a law

Their: belonging to them (possessive of *they*)
There: in that place
They're: a contraction of the two words *they are*

Veracity: truthfulness
Voracity: ravenousness; greediness

Vice: wickedness
Vice: a clamp

Waive: to give up; relinquish
Wave: swells of water; a gesture

Who's   a contraction of the two words *who is*
Whose: possessive of *who*

Your: a pronoun
You're: a contraction of the two words *you are*

EXPRESSION OF NUMBERS

The writer may often wonder whether he should use figures or words in referring to numbers which he is using in his reports. At times numbers should be used; in other instances, words are proper. Various rules have been formulated which the careful writer should observe.

General Uses

1. If several numbers are used in one sentence, use figures unless they are all below ten. If the first word is a number, write it out; however, it is wiser to change the sentence.

He sold 112 watches, 65 television sets, and 116 record players.

You will need three books, four colored pencils, and two reference guides.

Twenty-five nurses, 28 physicians, 35 technicians, and 345 patients were in the building.

There were 25 nurses, 28 physicians, 35 technicians, and 345 patients in the building.

2. Use numerals for numbers over ten, but write out in words quantities below ten. Where a sentence lists some above and some below ten, achieve consistency by following one pattern. Round numbers should be written out.

He left 83 quarts of milk, 112 packages of cheese, and 6 strawberry pies.

She requested immediate delivery on three desks, five table lamps, and twenty-five folding chairs.

The folder contained a fifty-page report and a forty-page appendix.

3. When two numbers are used in the same sentence in a different context, one may be written in words and the other, in numerals.

The three men lost a total of $56,550.

4. If one number immediately follows another, the smaller should be expressed in words, the larger in numerals.

He displayed five 95-cent knives.

5. A comma should separate two unrelated numbers if they follow one another.

In 1945, 65 new freighters were constructed.

Dates

1. Always write out the month when expressing a date.

June 27, 1962

12 December 1961

Do not use numerals for the month and the day. Neither of the following is acceptable:

6/27/62

1-3-61

2. Use numerals *before* or *after* the name of a month. Add *d, st,* or *th* if the day of the month precedes the month or is used by itself.

Your order of the *12th* of March was shipped yesterday.

In your report of the *3rd* several facts were not recorded.

Your directive of the *ninth* was posted on the bulletin board.

On *March 15* we will meet.

Addresses

1. Street numbers should always be expressed as figures except number *one* which should be written out.

One East La Salle Street

21 East Dearborn Avenue

212 North Madison Boulevard

2121 South Adams Street

2. Street names from First Street to Tenth Street should be expressed as words. From 11th Street on, figures should be used. You may add *d, st,* or *th* to a number representing a street.

215 East Third Street

2115 West Ninth Avenue

211 North 19th Street

2105 South 63rd Avenue

4005 East 121st Street

3. When a number is used as a street name, separate it from the street number by a dash. If the street direction is used, the dash is not utilized.

3315—15th Street

231—121st Avenue

1515 West 15th Street

275 East 28th Avenue

Amounts of Money

1. All sums of money, whether domestic or foreign, should be presented in figures.

    Smith's bill was $155.50.

    His debt of £50 was transferred to our foreign department.

2. In presenting cents, use the figure followed by the word *cents* or the cent sign or precede the figure by a dollar sign and decimal without the word *cents*.

    It was worth 15 cents.

    He paid $.75 for the notebook.

    It was priced at 65¢.

3. In expressing even sums of money, the decimal and zeros are not used.

    The invoice for $265 was corrected and returned to the Acme Company.

4. In legal statements the numerals should be enclosed by parentheses and the sum written out.

    I hereby agree to the payment of five hundred, five dollars ($505).

    In lieu of immediate compensation, I agree to accept seven hundred dollars ($700) five years from the date of this contract.

Decimals and Fractions

1. When a decimal fraction is not preceded by a whole number, a zero should appear before the decimal unless the fraction itself begins with a zero.

    0.3416

    .04515

2. Simple fractions are usually written out. When whole numbers and fractions make up one unit, a decimal may or may not be used.

25.5

25½

Miscellaneous Quantities, Units, and Measurements

1. Distance. Use numbers unless the amount is less than a mile or meter.

    He walked one-third of a mile.

    It is 12 miles to the station and 250 miles from there to Appleton.

2. Financial Quotations.

    American Zinc and Tin rose to 132⅝.

3. Arithmetical Expressions.

    If you will multiply 562 by 35, you will arrive at the correct answer.

4. Measurements. Figures are used in all instances of measurement.

    He was able to double his production to 120 bushels of wheat per acre.

    He found that 92 ounces were not equal to 3 liters.

5. Specific Numbers. Serial or bulletin numbers are expressed as figures.

    The motor number was 2358132.

    The procedure was described in Bulletin 231.

6. Time. Express time in figures except when the word *o'clock* is used.

    He arrived at 7:30 A.M.

    I will leave at three o'clock.

7. Dimensions. Unit dimensions are expressed in figures. Either *by* or *x* may be used.

    The standard paper size is 8½ x 11 inches.

    The lot was 50 by 125 feet.

8. Age. Use figures to express age except in cases where an approximation is indicated.

> He is 25 years old today.
>
> She is about thirty years of age.
>
> Tommy is now 12 years and 6 months.

9. Governmental Units.

> He was a member of the Eighty-fourth Congress and represented the Fifth District.

10. Book or Magazine References. Major divisions are indicated by Roman numerals; minor units, by Arabic numbers.

> He received Volume XX, Number 31, of the *American Journal*.
>
> You will find Table 4 on page 83 of Part 3.

Index

Set in Times Roman
Format by Cy Axelrad
Manufactured by The Haddon Craftsmen, Inc.
Published by Harper & Brothers, New York